WORLD ENCYCLOPEDIA OF PEACE

(SECOND EDITION)

WORLD ENCYCLOPEDIA OF PEACE

(SECOND EDITION)

VOLUME VII

Honorary Editor-in-Chief

Javier Perez De Cuellar

Editor-in-Chief

Young Seek Choue

OCEANA PUBLICATIONS, INC.®
NEW YORK

•

SEOUL PRESS

World Encyclopedia of Peace (Second Edition)

Published in the United States of America in 1999 and distributed
exclusively throughout the world, except in Korea, by
Oceana Publications Inc.
75 Main Street
Dobbs Ferry, New York 10522
Phone: (914) 693-8100
Fax: (914) 693-0402

ISBN: 0-379-21405-9 (Volume VII)
ISBN: 0-379-21398-2 (Set)

Library of Congress Cataloging-in-Publication Data

World encyclopedia of peace / honorary editor-in-chief, Javier
Perez de Cuellar, editor-in-chief, Young Seek Choue. -- 2nd ed.
    p. cm.
    Includes bibliographical references and indexes.
    ISBN 0-379-21398-2 (clothbound set : alk. paper)
    1. Peace Encyclopedias. I. Perez de Cuellar, Javier, 1920-
II. Young Seek Choue, 1921-
JZ5533 .W67 1999
327.1'03--dc21   99-34811
                                                                CIP

Published simultaneously in the Republic of Korea in 1999 by
Seoul Press
Jin Wang Kim, Publisher
Room 303, Jeodong Bldg., 7-2, Jeodong, Chung-ku
Seoul 100-032, Korea
Phone: (02) 2275-6566
Fax: (02) 2278-2551

ISBN: 89-7225-103-8   94330 (Volume VII)
ISBN: 89-7225-096-1 (Set)

Printed in the Republic of Korea by Seoul Press

CONTENTS

Chronology of the Peace Movement   3

United Nations Secretaries-General   19

Nobel Peace Prize Laureates   35

The Nobel Prizes   275

United Nations Specialized Agencies   299

International Peace Institutes and Organizations   327

CHRONOLOGY OF
THE PEACE MOVEMENT

This section comprises a listing year-by-year of the development of the peace movement. Prominence has been given to the establishment of peace organizations and movements and to the dates of peace congresses and conferences but the most significant publications are also featured.

The chronology is selective and reflects an effort to provide a useful reference. Before an accurate and meaningful inventory can be developed much additional research must be done on both the international peace effort and on the various national and local movements. The study of the history of peace organizations and peace efforts is still somewhat underdeveloped and needs to be expanded. During the nineteenth and twentieth centuries peace organizations blossomed in great multitudes. Just how significant some of these organizations were still needs to be determined. Moreover, a major problem in trying to develop a chronology is that peace organizations were constantly changing their names, combining with other groups to form new bodies, and producing regional and local offshoots which sometimes became more important than the original organization. Some of these changes are indicated here, but it is only a partial accounting.

For a more detailed discussion of developments in the nineteenth century, see the article on *Peace Movements in the Nineteenth Century*. Readers are also advised to refer to the introductory essay: *Peace "Encylopedias" of the Past and Present* and to the article on *Peace Museums*. Some of the organizations and movements displayed in this chronology have individual articles devoted to them; readers are advised to refer to the indices to access these subjects.

This chronology was originally based on the *Biographical Dictionary of Modern Peace Leaders* (edited by Harold Josephson) and is reproduced by the kind permission of the editor and Greenwood Press, Westport, CT, USA. In this second edition, more recent events are included.

Chronology of the Peace Movement

1815	New York Peace Society
	Massachusetts Peace Society
1816	Society for the Promotion of Permanent and Universal Peace (England, later known as Peace Society)
1817	Luddite Movement (England)
1821	Société de la morale chrétienne (France)
1828	American Peace Society
1830	La société de la paix de Genève
1838	New England Non-Resistance Society
	Chartist Movement (England)
1843	Universal Peace Congress (London)
1846	League of Universal Brotherhood (England and the United States)
1848	World Peace Congress (Brussels)
1849	World Peace Congress (Paris)
1850	World Peace Congress (Frankfurt)
1851	World Peace Congress (London)
1858	Ligue de bien public (Belgium)
1863	Gettysburg Address (Pennsylvania)
	Emancipation Proclamation (by Lincoln)
1864	International Committee of the Red Cross (ICRC, Geneva)
1866	Universal Peace Society (United States, later renamed Universal Peace Union)
1867	Ligue internationale et permanente de la paix (Paris, becoming in 1982, Société des amis de la paix, and in 1888, Société français pour l'arbitrage entre nations)
	Ligue internationale de la paix et de la liberté (Geneva)
	Union de la paix (Le Havre)
1868	Association internationale des femmes (Geneva)
1869	Lega della pace e della libertà (Turin)
1871	Algemeen Nederlandsche Vredebond (Dutch Peace Society, after 1901, Vrede door Recht)
	Workmen's Peace Association (England, became International Arbitration League)
1873	Association for the Reform and Codification of the Law of Nations (Brussels, reorganized as International Law Association in 1895)
	Institute of International Law (Ghent)
1877	International Arbitration and Peace Association (England)
1878	Congres international des amis de la paix (France)
	Lega di libertà, fratellanza e pace (Milan)
1879	Women's Local Peace Association (England, became the Wisbech Local Peace Association in 1881)
1880	International Arbitration and Peace Association of Great Britain and Ireland
1882	National Arbitration League (United States)
	Society for Promotion of Danish Neutrality (first Danish peace society, later became

	Danish Peace Society, and still later Danish Peace and League of Nations Society)
1883	Swedish Peace and Arbitration Society
1884	Groupe des amis de la paix du Puy de Dôme (France)
1886	Christian Arbitration and Peace Society (United States)
	Liverpool and Birkenhead Women's Peace and Arbitration Association (England)
	Société de la paix du familistère du guise (France)
	Ligue internationale des femmes pour le désarmement général (Paris, became in 1900 Alliance universelle des femmes pour la paix par l'éducation)
1887-88	Association des jeunes amis de la paix (France, later La Paix par le droit)
	Società per la pace e l'arbitrato internazionale-Unione Lombarda (Milan)
	Associazione per l'arbitrato e per la pace internazionale (Rome)
	Friends Peace Committee (England)
1889	Première Conférence interparlementaire (Paris; later the Interparliamentary Union, annual meetings held until the First World War)
	World Peace Congress (Paris; peace congresses met annually with only five interruptions until the First World War)
	Nihon Heiwa-kai (first Japanese peace society)
	Société suisse de la paix (Switzerland)
	Publication of Bertha von Suttner's *Die Waffen Nieder!*
	Società della pace (Florence)
	Società della pace (Venice)
1889-90	First Pan-American Conference (Washington)
1890	Società della pace (Palermo)
	International Union of American Republics
1891	Österreichische Friedensgesellschaft (Austrian Peace Society)
	International Peace Bureau (Berne)
	Società della pace e l'arbitrato internazionale (Perugia)
1892	Deutsche Friedensgesellschaft (German Peace Society)
	Alliance des savants et des philanthropes (France)
	Deutsche Friendensgesellschaft (DFG, Germany)
1894	Société chrétienne pour la propagande de la paix (Switzerland)
	International Olympic Committee (IOC)
	Alfred Dreyfus Affair (France)
1895	First Lake Mohonk Arbitration Conference (United States)
	Norwegian Peace Association
	Hungarian Peace Society
	Union internationale des femmes pour la paix I (Paris and London)
1896	National Arbitration Conference (Washington)
	Bureau française de la paix
	Ligue des femmes pour la paix et pour le désarmement international (France, later called L'Alliance universelle des femmes pour la paix et pour le désarmement)
1898	Anti-Imperialist League (United States)
	Swedish Women's Peace Association
	Association "Le paix et le désarmement par les femmes" (Paris)
1899	First Hague Peace Conference
	Association des femmes du suède pour la paix (Sweden)
	Société chrétienne des amis de la paix (France)
1900	Peace and Humanity Society (Melbourne, Australia)

	World Peace Foundation (Boston)
	Carnegie Endowment for International Peace Foundation (New York)
1901	First Nobel Peace Prize awarded
	Société de l'éducation pacifique (France and Belgium)
	Société castraise de la paix (France)
	Declaration of African Human Rights (OAU)
1902	Délégation permanente des sociétés françaises de la paix
	League of Peace (Romania)
	International Museum of War and Peace (Lucerne)
1903	Groupe de l'arbitrage international (France)
1904	National Council of Peace Societies (England, became National Peace Council in 1908)
	International Anti-Militarist Union (Netherlands)
	Canadian Peace and Arbitration Society
1905	Zurich Anti-Militarism League
	Rotary Club (Illinois)
1906	Japan Peace Society
	Melbourne Peace Society (Australia)
	Victorian Peace Society (Australia)
	Swaraj Movement (India)
	American Association for International Conciliation
	American Society for International Law
1907	Second Hague Peace Conference
	National Arbitration and Peace Congress (Washington)
	New South Wales Peace Society (Australia)
	Peace Union (Finland)
1908	Creation of Central American International Court of Justice
1909	Ligue des Catholiques français pour la paix (France)
1910	Carnegie Endowment for International Peace (United States)
	World Peace Foundation (United States)
	National Peace Council (New Zealand)
	American Society for the Judicial Settlement of International Disputes
	Publication of Norman Angell's *The Great Illusion*
	Catholic Peace Association (London)
1911	Swedish Peace Association
	Commission on International Justice and Goodwill (United States)
	Ligue internationale des pacifistes Catholiques (France)
1912	African National Congress (South Africa)
1913	Northern Friends Peace Board (England)
1914	Church Peace Union (United States)
	No-Conscription Fellowship (England)
	Australian Peace Alliance
	Dutch Anti-War Council
	World Alliance for International Friendship Through the Churches (Geneva)
	Union of Democratic Control (England)
1915	Woman's Peace Party (United States)
	League to Enforce Peace (United States)
	Fellowship of Reconciliation (England)

	League of Nations Society (England)
	Canadian Women's Peace Party
	Women's Peace Army (Australia)
	Henry Ford's Peace Expedition (1915-16)
	Central Organization for a Durable Peace (The Hague)
	International Congress of Women (The Hague, led in 1919 to formation of Women's International League for Peace and Freedom)
1916	National Conference for Continuous Mediation (Stockholm)
	American Union Against Militarism
	Khilafat Movement (India)
1917	American Friends Service Committee
	People's Council of America for Peace and Freedom
	No-Conscription League (New York)
	Lions Club (United States, Dallas)
1918	League of Nations Union (England)
	Friedensbund Deutscher Katholiken (Germany)
	Woodrow Wilson's Fourteen Points (United States)
	Brest-Litovsk Treaty
1919	Nie Wieder Krieg! (Never Again War!, Germany)
	League of Nations established
	Women's International League for Peace and Freedom (Zurich)
	The Third International Comintern (Moscow)
	International Labour Organization (Geneva)
	International Federation of the Red Cross and Crescent Societies (ICRC)
	Paris Peace Conference (Treaty of Versailles)
1920	Peace Union of Finland
	Peace Organization of Swedish Teachers
	League of Nations Association of Japan
	Gandhi starts first nonviolent civil disobedience campaign
1921	Women's Peace Society (United States)
	No More War Movement (England)
	War Resisters International (originally established as PACO; became WRI in 1923)
	Washington Naval Disarmament Conference (1921-22)
	Women's Peace Society (Japan)
	International Anti-Militarist Bureau (Netherlands)
	National Council for Prevention of War (United States)
	Pen Club (England)
1922	Deutsche Liga für Menschenrechte (Germany)
1923	Announcement of Edward M. Bok's American Peace Award
	League of Nations Non-Partisan Association (United States, changed name to League of Nations Association in 1929)
	Antimilitaristic Union (Finland)
	Woodrow Wilson Foundation (United States)
	War Resisters League (United States)
	Treaty of Mutual Assistance (UN)
	Treaty of Lausanne, Conference of Lausanne (Switzerland)
1924	National Conference on the Cause and Cure of War (United States)

1925	Nordic Teachers' Peace Organization (Denmark)
	Union of Antimilitary Ministers in Switzerland
	Protocol for Prohibition of the Use in War of Asphyxiating, Poisonous or Other Gases, and of Bacteriological Methods of Warfare (Geneva)
	Locarno Pact
1927	Geneva Naval Disarmament Conference
	Catholic Association for International Peace (United States)
1928	National Anti-War League of Japan
	No More War Movement (New Zealand)
	Kellogg-Briand Peace Pact (Pact of Paris)
1929	Anti-War Congress of Intellectuals (Frankfurt)
1930	London Naval Disarmament Conference
	Second all-India nonviolent civil disobedience campaign starts
1931	Emergency Peace Committee (United States)
	Interorganization Council on Disarmament (United States)
	Gandhi Leads Salt March
	Ligue internationale des combattants de la paix (France)
1932	National Peace Conference (United States)
	General Disarmament Conference (Geneva, 1932-34)
	Co-operative Commonwealth Federation (Canada)
1933	Argentine Anti-War Pact
	Catholic Worker Movement (United States)
	American League Against War and Fascism (later, American League for Peace and Democracy)
1934	Peace Ballot (England)
1936	International Mennonite Peace Committee
	Peace Pledge Union (England)
	First World Peace Congress (Brussels)
	Emergency Peace Campaign (United States)
	PAX (England)
1937	No-Foreign-War Crusade (United States)
	Christian Peace Union of Switzerland
	Rassemblement international contre la guerre et le militarisme (Paris)
1938	Keep America Out of War Congress
1939	Commission to Study the Organization of Peace (United States)
1941	Atlantic Charter (United States, New Foundland)
1942	Congress of Racial Equality (United States)
	Publication of Quincy Wright's *A Study of War*
	International League for Human Rights (UN)
1943	Publication of Wendell Wilkie's *One World*
	Cairo Declaration (Egypt)
	Teheran Declaration (Iran)
1944	Pax Christi (France)
1945	French Institute of Polemology (Paris)
	Republication of Emery Reeves' *The Anatomy of Peace*
	United Nations Organization established
	San Francisco Conference
	Arab League

	Food and Agriculture Organization of the United Nations (FAO, Italy)
	Potsdam Declaration (Berlin)
	Yalta Declaration (Yalta)
1946	Swiss Peace Council
	Commission of Human Rights
	Principles governing the general regulation and reduction of armaments, Baruch Plan (UN)
	United Nations Education Scientific and Cultural Organization (UNESCO, Paris)
	International Whaling Commission (IWC, Washington)
1947	United World Federalists (United States)
	Futer-American Treaty of Reciprocal Assistance (Rio Treaty)
	Marshall Plan, European Recovery Program
1948	Canadian Peace Congress
	UN Commission on Human Rights and Universal Declaration of Human Rights (UN)
	International Union for Conservation of Nature
	Convention on the Prevention and Punishment of the Crime of Genocide
	Peace Keeping Forces (UN)
	Bogota Declaration
	World Health Organization (WHO, UN)
	First Apartheid Legistlation in South Africa
	Pax Christi (Germany)
1949	Finnish Peace Committee
	North Atlantic Treaty Organization (Washington)
	Australian Peace Council
	Office of the UN High Commission for Refugees (UN)
	First World Congress of Peace Partisans (Paris, launched World Council of Peace)
	Geneva Convention
	UN Relief and Works Agency for Palestinian Refugees in the Near East (UNRWA)
1950	World Peace Council (Poland)
	"Uniting for Peace" Resolution (UN)
	Atoms for Peace Plan (UN)
	Ohne Mich Bewegung (Germany)
1951	Medical Association for Prevention of War (England)
	Institute of War and Peace Studies (United States)
	United Nations High Commissioner for Refugees (UNHCR, Switzerland)
	Convention relating to the Status of Refugees
	Volksbefragungsbewegung (Germany)
1952	Paulskirchebewegung (Germany)
1953	Korean Armistice Agreement (Korea)
	Balkan Alliance
1954	Convention relating to the Status of Stateless Persons
	South East Asia Treaty Organization (SEATO)
	Five Principles for Peace (between India and China)
	Geneva Conference
	British-French Memorandum (London)
1955	Japan Council Against Atomic Weapons
	Warsaw Treaty Organization (WTO)
	Central Treaty Organization (CTO)

	Russell-Einstein Manifesto
	Afro-Asian States
	Bandung Conference of Non-Aligned Countries (Indonesia)
1956	Hugarian Revolution against Communism
1957	National Committee for a SANE Nuclear Policy (United States)
	Committee for Nonviolent Action (United States)
	(First) Pugwash Conference (on Science and World Affairs) (Pugwash, Canada)
	Journal of Conflict Resolution begins publication (United States)
	International Atomic Energy Agency (IAEA)
	Peace Action (United States)
1958	World without War Council (United States)
	International Institute for Strategic Studies (IISS, London)
	Campaign for Nuclear Disarmament (England)
	European Atomic Energy Community (EURATOM)
	Aktion suhnezeichen (Germany)
1959	Student Peace Union (United States)
	Peace Research Institute (Oslo)
	Center for Research on Conflict Resolution (Ann Arbor, Michigan, United States)
	Das Bad Godesberg Programm (Godesberg, Germany)
	International Peace Research Institute, (PRIO, Norway)
	Antarctic Treaty (Washington)
1960	Voice of Women (Canada)
	Women Strike for Peace (United States)
	Committee of 100 (England)
1961	Turn Toward Peace (United States)
	Canadian Peace Research Institute
	The Peace Corps (United States)
	World Wide Fund for Nature
	Declaration on the Prohibition of the Use of Nuclear and Thermonuclear Weapons
	Ammesty International (AI, London)
	Consideration of Africa as a Denuclearized Zone
1962	Canadian Campaign for Nuclear Disarmament
	Permament Sovereignty over Natural Weath and Resources (UN)
	Committee of 100
1963	Encyclical *Pacem in Terris*
	Treaty Banning Nuclear Weapon Tests in the Atmosphere in Outer Space and Under Water
	Memorandum of Understanding Between the United States and USSR Regarding the Establishment of a Direct Communications Link
	Organization of African Unity (OAU)
1964	*Journal of Peace Research* begins publication (Norway)
	Russel Court
	Group of 77 (Geneva)
	Civil Rights Act (United States)
1965	International Peace Research Association Inaugural Conference (Netherlands)
	Japanese Congress Against A- and H-bombs
	Centre for Conflict Analysis (England)
	National Association for Advancemant of Colored People (United States)

	International Convention on the Elimination of All Forms of Racial Discrimination (UN)
1966	Stockholm International Peace Research Institute (SIPRI, Sweden)
	Interchurch Peace Council (Netherlands)
	International Covenant on Economic, Social and Cultural Rights
	International Covenant on Civil and Political Rights
	Natural Organization of Women (Washington)
	Declaration on Strengthening Peace and Security in Europe (Bucharest Declaration, Hungary)
1967	World Without War Council (United States)
	Pontifical Council for Justice and Peace (Vatican City)
	Peace Research Centre (Australia)
	Treaty of Principles Governing the Activities of States in the Exploration and Use of Outer Space, Including the Moon and Other Celestial Bodies (Washington, Moscow, London)
	Protocol Relating to the Status of Refugees
	Declaration on Violence Against Women
	Treaty for Prohibition of Nuclear Weapons in Latin America (Tlatelolco)
1968	Treaty on the Non-Proliferation of Nuclear Weapons (NPT)
	Club of Rome (Italy)
	Question Relating to Measures to Safeguard Non-Nuclear-Weapon States Parties to the Treaty on the Non-Proliferation of Nuclear Weapons
	First UN Conference on Exploration and Peaceful Uses of Outer Space (Vienna)
	Student Riots in Western Europe
	World Order Models Project (United States)
1970	Comité national d'action pour la paix et le développement (Belgium)
	International Peace Academy (IPA, USA)
	The World Conference on Religion and Peace (WCRP, Mondiale, United States)
	Peace Research Institute Frankfurt (PRIF, Germany)
	Asian Buddhist Conference for Peace (ABCP, Mongolia)
	Peace Studies Program (Cornell Univ., United States)
	International Peace Academy (United States)
	Tampere Peace Research Institute (TAPRI, Finland)
	The Irish Commission for Justice and Peace (Ireland)
	Treaty on the Non-Proliferation of Nuclear Weapons (NPT)
	Statement for Human Environment Quality (UN)
	South Pacific Forum
	Green Peace Movement (Amsterdam)
1971	Declaration of the Indian Ocean as a Zone of Peace
	Treaty on the Prohibition of the Emplacement of Nuclear Weapons and Other Weapons of Mass Destruction on the Seabed and the Ocean Floor and in the Subsoil Thereof Agreement Between on Measures to Improve the USA-USSR Direct Communications Link
	Institute for Peace Research and Security Policy (Hamburg University, Germany)
	Peace Research Centre (India)
	Department of Peace and Conflict Research (Sweden)
1972	Interim Agreement on Certain Measures with Respect to the Limitation of Strategic Offensive Arms (between the United States and USSR)
	Convention on the Prohibition of the Development, Production and Stockpiling of Bacteriological and Toxin Weapons and on Their Destruction (BWC, UN)
	Convention on the Prevention of Marine Pollution by Dumping of Wastes and Other Matter (London)
	Agreement on the Prevention of Incidents on and over the High Seas (between the United States and USSR)

	Treaty on the Limitation of Anti-Ballistic Missile Systems (between the United States and USSR)
	Agreement on the Prevention of Naval Incidents
	United Nations Environment Programme (UNEP, Kenya)
	Strategic Arms Limitation Treaty (SALT I)
	Declaration on the Human Environment (Only one Earth, Stockholm)
1973	International Convention on the Suppression and Punishment of the Crime of Apartheid
	Peace Studies Association of Japan (PSAJ, Japan)
	Alger's Declaration (Algeria)
	The United Nations University (Japan)
	Agreement on the Prevention of Nuclear War (between the United States and USSR)
	The United Nations University (UNU, Japan)
	Department of Peace Studies (Univ. of Bradford, England)
	Mutual Reduction of Forces and Armaments (MRFA, Vienna)
	Paris Peace Treaty on Vietnam War
	Nihon heiwa gakkai (Peace Studies Association of Japan)
1974	Defense and Arms Control Studies Program (Massachusetts Institute of Technology, United States)
	Liaison Committee for Peace and Security (Denmark)
	Latin American and Justice Service (SERPAJ-AL, Ecuador)
	Worldwatch Institute (United States)
	Protocol to the Treaty on the Limitation of Anti-Ballistic Missle Systems (between the United States and USSR)
	Treaty on the Limitation of Underground Nuclear Weapon Tests (between the United States and USSR)
	Samarbejdskomiteen for Fred og Sikkerhed (Liaison Committee for Peace and Security, Denmark)
1975	The Foundation for Peace Studies (New Zealand)
	Agreement for the Application of Safeguards in Connection with the Treaty on the Non-Proliferation of Nuclear Weapons (Between Korea and IAEA)
	Helsinki Final Act
	Institute for Peace Science (Hiroshima Univ., Japan)
	Overleg Centrum voor Vrede (Belgium)
	Council for Security and Cooperation in Europe (CSCE)
	Convention de Lon Entre la CEE et les ACP (Lon,Togo)
	International Baby Food Action Network (IBFAN)
	UN Conference on Woman (Mexico City)
	Groupement de Scienfiques pour l'Information sur l'Energie Nucl aire (GSIEN; France)
1976	Centre for Studies in Peace and Non-Violence (India)
	Hiroshima Peace Culture Foundation (Japan)
	Treaty on Underground Nuclear Explosions for Peaceful Purposes Resolution on Disarmament (between the United States and USSR)
	Institute of Peace and Conflict Studies (IPACS, Canada)
1977	Center for War/Peace Studies (United States)
	Convention on the Prohibition of Military or Any Other Hostile Use of Environmental Modification Techniques
	Treaty on the Limitation of Strategic Offensive Arms (Between United States and USSR)
	Peace Research Institute (IPRI, Italy)
	United Nations Centre for Disarmament Affairs (CDA)
	International Nuclear Fuel Cycle Evaluation (INFCE, United States)

1978	United Nations Centre for Human Settlements (HABITAT, Kenya)
	United Nations Interim Force in Lebanon (UNIFIL, Lebanon)
	Research Institute for Peace and Security (RIPS, Japan)
	Peace Research and Information Group (GRIP, Belgium)
	Program in Arms Control, Disarmament and International Security (ACDIS, Univ. of Illinois, United States)
	Peace Treaty between China and Japan
	Green Party (Germany)
	Christen für die Abrüstung (Germany)
1979	World Disarmament Campaign (England)
	Vlaams Aktic Komitee Tegen Atoomwapeds (Belgium)
	Convention on the Elimination of All Forms of Discrimination against Women (UN)
	Strategic Arms Limitation Talks (SALT II)
	Camp David Agreement
	Health Action International (HAI)
	Arab-Israel Peace Treaty
	Institute of International Peace Studies (Kyung Hee Univ., Korea)
	Women Oppose the Nuclear Threat (WONT, England)
	GCS (Global Common Society) Club International (Kyung Hee Univ., Korea)
	Deutschen Gesellschaft für Friendens und Konfliktforschung (DGFK, Germany)
	Mouvement Pour le Desarmement la Paix et la liberte (MDPL,France)
1980	European Nuclear Disarmament Campaign (England)
	Kvinder for Fred (Women for Peace, Denmark)
	Nej til Tomvaben (No to Nuclear Weapons, Denmark)
	Palme Committee (Sweden)
	International Physicians for the Prevention of Nuclear War (IPPNW, United States)
	University for Peace (Costa Rica)
	United Nations Institute for Disarmament Research (Switzerland)
	Indian Institute for Non-Aligned Studies (India)
	Friends of the Earth (Germany)
	The World Wildlife Fund (Germany)
	Campaign for Nuclear Disarmament (CND; England)
	School of Peace Studies (Bradford University, England)
	Journalists against Nuclear Extermination (JANE, England)
1981	Institute for East-West Studies (United States)
	Charter of the Cooperation Council for the Arab States of the Gulf (UAE)
	The Unified Economic Agreement Between the Countries of the Gulf Cooperation Council
	Multinational Force and Observers
	North-South Summit (Cancun, Mexico)
	European Nuclear Disarmament (England)
	Movement for National Independence, International Peace and Disarmament (Greece)
	Comite pour le Desarmament Nucleaire en Europe (Codene, France)
1982	Comité pour le désarmement nucleaire en France
	Generals for Peace and Disarmament (London)
	International Institutes on Peace Education (United States)
	The Unified Economic Agreement Between the Countries of the Gulf Cooperation Council (Saudi Arabia)
	European Nuclear Disarmament Convention (Brussels)

Center for Peace Research and Strategic Studies (CPRS, Belgium)

Oxford Research Group (England)

Centre Interdisciplinaire de Recherche sur la Paix et D'Etudes Strategiques (France)

National Institute for Dispute Resolution (United States)

UN Second Conference on Exploration and Peaceful Uses of Outer Space (Vienna)

Pess Declaration (Morocco)

Comprehensive Program of Disarmament (UN)

Pesticide Action Network (PAN)

UN Convention on the Law of the Sea (UN)

Strategic Arms Reduction Talks (Geneva)

World Charter for Nature (UN)

World Commission on Environment and Development (WCED, UN)

Korean Assembly for Reunion of Ten Million Separated Families (KARTS, Korea)

1983 Treaty for the Establishment of the Economic Community of Central African States (Libreville)

Second European Nuclear Disarmament Convention (Berlin)

Canadian Centre for Global Security (Canada)

Nederlands Instituut Voor Internationale Betrekkingen "Clingendael" (Netherlands)

Declaracion de Cancun (Mexico)

Contadora Group (Panama)

Peace Canvass 83 (by Campaign for Nuclear Disarmament, England)

1984 Geneva International Peace Research Institute (Switzerland)

Peace Research Centre (Australian National Univ., Australia)

Forum Per I Problemi Delia Pace e Della Guerra (Italy)

The Graduate Institute of Peace Studies (Kyung Hee Univ., Korea)

Memorandum of Understanding on the Direct Communications Link

Convention against Torture and Other Cruel, Inhuman or Degrading Treatment or Punishment (between the United States and USSR)

The Other Economic Summit (TOES, London)

Movement of Small Hands (France)

International Union for Conservation of Nature (IUCN, UNESCO)

Conference of Disarmament in Europe

Declaration on Africa (UN)

International Population Conference (Mexico)

Les Verts (France)

1985 Liv Och Fred Institutet (Sweden)

South Pacific Nuclear Free Zone Treaty (Rarotonga)

Agreement for Cooperation between China and United States Concerning Peaceful Uses of Nuclear Energy (Washington)

African Peace Research Institute (Nigeria)

Centre for FREDS-OG Konfliktforskning (Denmark)

The Chinese People's Association for Peace and Disarmament (CPAPD, China)

International Convention against Apartheid in Sports

International Institute for Strategic Studies (IISS, London)

1986 International Year of Peace Proclaimed by the UN

Agreement on The Prevention of Incidents at Sea beyond the Territorial Sea (between the United States and USSR)

Document of the Stockholm Conference on Confidence and Security Buiding Measures and Disarmament in Europe Madrid Document

Meeting of the Conference on Security and Co-operation in Europe

Vienna Convention on the Law of Treaties between States and International Organization or between International Organization

Forschungsstelle fur Sicherheitspolitik und Konfliktanalyse (Switzerland)

Centro de Estudios y Accion Para la Paz (Peru)

INF Treaty

1987 Gernika Gogoratuz (Spain)

Montreal Protocol on Substances that Deplete the Ozone Layer (Montreal)

Treaty on the Elimination of their Intermediate-Range and Shorter-Range Missiles (between the United States and USSR, Washington)

Agreement Among the United States and Belgium, Germany, Italy, England and Northern Ireland Regarding Inspections Relating to the Treaty between the United States and USSR on the Elimination of their Intermediate-Range and Shorter-Range Missiles, Brussels)

Agreement on the Establishment of Nuclear Risk Reduction Centers (between United States and USSR, Brussels)

Indo-Sri Lanka Agreement to Establish Peace and Normalcy in Sri Lanka (Colombo, Sri Lanka)

Text of Agreements by the Presidents of Central America (Guatemala City)

Treaty on the Elimination of their Intermediate-Range and Shorter-Range Missiles (between the United States and USSR)

Bruntland Report (*Our Common Future*, UN)

1988 Schweizerische Friedensstiftung (Switzerland)

Bilateral Agreement on the Principles of Mutual Relations in Particular on Non-Interference (between Afghanistan and Pakistan, Geneva)

Agreement on Notifications of Launches of Intercontinental Ballistic Missiles and Submarine-Launched Ballistic Missiles (between the United States and USSR, Moscow)

Institut Evropy, Rossiiskaia Akademiia Nauk (Russia)

New Beograd Declaration (Yugoslavia)

Kranoyarsk Declaration (East Siberia)

Glion Declaration (Switzerland)

Swiss Peace Foundation (Switzerland)

1989 Centre for the Study of Violence and Reconciliation (South Africa)

Global Security Programme (Univ. of Cambridge, England)

Agreement on the Prevention of Dangerous Military Activities (between the United States and USSR, Moscow)

Basel Convention on the Control of Transboundary Movement of Hazardous Wastes and Their Disposal

Agreement on Reciprocal Advance Notification of Major Strategic Exercises (between the United States and USSR, Jackson Hole, Wyoming)

Second Optional Protocol to the Internationl Covenant on Civil and Political Rights Aiming at the Abolition of the Death Penalty

International Convention on the Rights of Child

World Wide Fund for Nature

Paris Summit

Montreal Protocol

The Fall of Berlin Wall

1990 Treaty on the Establishment of German Unity ... Unification Treaty (Berlin)

Treaty on Conventional Armed Forces in Europe (Paris)

Agreement on Chemical Weapons and on Measures to Facilitate the Multilateral Convention on Banning Chemical Weapons (between United States and USSR, Washington)

Institut fur Friedens-und Konfliktforschung (Germany)

Instituto de Relaciones Internacionales y de Investigaciones Para la Paz, (Guatemala)

International Convention on the Protection of the Rights of All Migrant Workers and Members of Their Family

World Women Summit Conference

Houston Summit (Texas)

1991 Agreement Establishing the Commonwealth of Independent States (Minsk)

Agreement on Joint Measures with Respect to Nuclear Weapons (Alma Ata)

Agreement on a Comprehensive Political Settlement of the Cambodia Conflict (Paris)

General Assembly Resolution on General and Complete Disarmament

Agreement on Reconciliation, Nonaggression and Exchanges and Cooperation (between South and North Korea)

Strategic Arms Reduction Talks (START)

Guadalajara Declaration (Iberia-America, Mexico)

Global Environment Facility (GEF, Washington)

Cambodia Summit (G7)

1992 Protocol on the Compliance with and Implimentation of Chapter II, Nonaggression, of the Agreement on Reconciliation, Nonaggression and Exchanges and Cooperation between South and North Korea

Agreement to Establish a South-North Korea Joint Military Commission (Winddhoek)

Joint Declaration of the Denuclearization of the Korean Peninsula

Agreement to Establish a South-North Korea Joint Nuclear Control Commission

Treaty of the Southern African Development Community (Winddhoek)

Montreal Protocol on Substances that Deplete the Ozone Layer: Adoption of Adjustment and Amendment by the Fourth Mention of the Parties (Copenhagen)

Central European Free Trade Agreement (Krakow)

Agreement for the Application of Safeguards in Connection with the Treaty on the Non-Proliferation of Nuclear Weapons (between North Korea and IAEA, Vienna)

Treaty of Maastricht (Netherland)

Global Leadership Award (United States)

Petersburg Declaration (Petersburg)

Convention on Biological Diversity (Rio de Janeiro)

Global Forum (Rio de Zaneiro)

Convention on Climate Change (Rio de Janeiro)

UN Conference on Environment and Development (Rio de Janeiro)

Reunification of Germany

1993 Agreement Establishing the Multilateral Trade Organization

UN Peacekeepers Restore Order in Cambodia

Convention on the Prohibition of the Development, Production, Stockpiling and Use of Chemical Weapons and on Their Destruction (UN, Paris)

Treaty on the Further Reduction and Limitation of Strategic Offensive Arms (Between United States and Russia)

World Conference on Human Rights (Vienna)

International Green Cross (ICG, Kyoto)

Peace Treaty between Israel and PLO

1994 Agreed Framework between United States and North Korea (Geneva)

Agreement Establishing the World Trade Organization (WTO) (Morrakesh)

Treaty of Peace between Israel and Jordan (The Araba/Araba Crossing Point)

Agreement on the Gaza Strip and the Jericho Area (Jerusalem, Cairo)

Preliminary Agreement Concerning the Establishment of a Confederation (between Bosnia and Herzegovina and Croatia)

Peace Agreement between Esrael and Palestine (Oslo)

Convention on Nuclear Safety (Paris)

International Conference on Population and Development (Cairo)

Partnership for Peace (Brusells)

Montreal Protocol (Canada)

Green Olympic (Lillehammer, Norway)

Bogor Declaration (Indonesia)

Green Scouts (Seoul)

1995 General Framework Agreement for Peace in Bosnia and Herzegovina (Paris)

Agreement on the Establishment of the Korean Peninsula Energy Development Organization (New York)

Treaty on the Southeast Asia Nuclear Weapon-Free Zone

World Conference on Women (Beijing)

Pelindaba Text of the African Nuclear Weapon-Free-Zone Treaty

World Summit for Social Development (Copenhagen, Denmark)

1996 Comprehensive Test Ban Treaty

Protocol on Prohibitions or Restrictions on the Use of Mines, Booby-Traps and Other Devices as Amended on May 96 (Geneva)

World Food Summit (Rome)

Conference on Human Settlements (Istanbul)

Agreement on Normalization of Relations between Yugoslavia and Croatia (Belgrade)

International Year for the Eradication of Poverty (UN)

1997 Convention on the Prohibition of the Use, Stockpiling, Production and Transfer of Anti-Personnel Mines and on Their Destruction

Hong Kong Reverts to China

1998 International Criminal Court

US and UK Bomb Iraq

1999 European Countries Adopt a Single Currency, the Euro

NATO bombs Serbia

Hague NGO Peace Conference (Hague)

Seoul International Conference of NGOs

UNITED NATIONS SECRETARIES-GENERAL

This section consists of the profiles and peace-related achievements of the former and current UN Secretaries-General, the chief administrative officers of the secretariat of the United Nations. There are 7 separate entries. Articles are arranged chronologically by the period of services, and include biographical sketches as well as major activities of the Secretaries-General. Readers would be able to have an overview, through this section, of the occurrence of major international violent conflicts and the UN peace efforts involved in by each Secretary-General since 1945.

In compiling articles, mainly, the following bibliographies and references were used as the major sources of description: John W. Wright, Andrews and McMeel 1997, *The Universal Almanac*, published by Universal Press Syndicate Company, Kansas; *Encyclopedia Britannica* 1997, published by Encyclopedia Britannica, Chicago; *United Nations Handbook 1996*, published by Minister of Foreign Affairs, Wellington, New Zealand; Ramses Nassit *1988, U Thant in New York, 1961-1974: A Portrait of the UN Secretary-General*, published by St Martins Pr (Short); Richard Sheldon 1987, *Dag Hammarskjold (World Leader, Past and Present)*, published by Chelsea House; Boutros Boutros-Ghali 1996, *Agenda for Peace*, published by United Nations; Boutros Boutros-Ghali 1995, *Visions: Fifty Years of the United Nations*, published by Hearst Books; Boutros Boutros-Ghali 1996, *50th Anniversary Annual Report on the Work of the Organization*, published by United Nations; Boutros Boutros-Ghali 1996, *The United Nations and Human Rights 1945-1955*, published by United Nations; Hooper, Fraklin 1997, *Britannica Book of the Year*, published by Encyclopedia Britannica (1953-1997), Chicago; *The Encyclopedia Americana (1984-1997)*, published by New York Americana Corp; Wilmette, Marguis, *Who's Who in the World (1974-1992)*, Macmillan Directory Division; Irwin Abrams 1989, *The Nobel Peace Prize and the Laureates: An Illustrated Biographical History 1901-1987*, Boston, G. K. Hall; Osmanczyk and Edmund Jan 1990, *Encyclopedia of United Nations and International Agreements*, published by Taylor and Francis in Philadelphia and New York; *Newsmakers 1980-1997*, published by Gale Research Inc., Detroit; *Building Peace and Development*, UN publication in 1994.

United Nations Secretaries-General

Trygve Halvdan Lie

Trygve Halvdan Lie, the first Secretary-General of the United Nations, is a Norwegian who came to his post with wide experience in law, labor relations and foreign affairs. He was Norway's Minister of Foreign Affairs and delegate to the first session of the General Assembly of the United Nations when he was elected Secretary-General on 1 February 1946 for a five-year term.

He first became connected with the United Nations when he was chosen to head the Norwegian Delegation to the United Nations Conference on International Organization at San Francisco in 1945. At this meeting he served as Chairman of the commission which drafted the Charter for the United Nations Security Council. Lie led the Norwegian delegation to the United Nations Conference on international organization in San Francisco, April 1945, and was Chairman of Commission III for drafting the Security Council provisions of the Charter. He was also Chairman of the Norwegian delegation to the United Nations General Assembly in London in January 1946.

On 1 February 1946, Lie was elected the first Secretary-General of the United Nations. He was formally installed by the General Assembly at its 22nd meeting on 2 February 1946. The General Assembly on 1 November 1950 continued Lie in office for a further three years from 1 February 1951. He resigned as Secretary-General of the United Nations in November 1952.

Lie was born on 16 July 1896, in Oslo, Norway, the son of Martin and Hulda Arnesen Lie. He was educated at Oslo University where he obtained a law degree in 1919. On 8 November 1921, he married Hjordis Joergensen. They had three children—Sissel, Guri and Mette.

Lie became a member of the Norwegian Labor Party Youth Organization in 1911. He was an assistant to the secretary of the Labor Party from 1919 to 1922, a legal adviser to the Norwegian Trade Union Federation from 1922 to 1935, and national executive secretary of the Labor Party in 1926. In the Labor Party Government formed by Johan Nygaardsvold, Lie was Minister of Justice for the years 1935 to 1939, then Minister of Trade and Industries from July to September 1939 and, at the time of the outbreak of the Second World War, became Minister of Supply and Shipping. In that capacity he evolved the provisional measures that saved the Norwegian fleet for the Allies, after the German invasion in April 1940. In June that year, he went to England, then the Norwegian Government decided to continue the fight from abroad. He became acting Foreign Minister in December 1940 and was appointed Foreign Minister of Norway in February 1941. Lie was elected a member of the Norwegian Parliament in 1936 and was re-elected in 1945. On 12 June 1945, the Government of which he was a member resigned; Lie was appointed Foreign Minister of the interim coalition cabinet which took over the government at the time, and Foreign Minister in the new Labor Party Government in October 1945.

Lie had the following appointments since leaving the United Nations: Governor of Oslo and Akershus, Chairman of Norway's Board of Energy. By a resolution of the General Assembly in 1958, King Olav of Norway was asked to find a basis on which Ethiopia and Italy could start to settle a border dispute involving the former Italian colony, Somalia. King Olav, in 1959, appointed Lie as Mediator.

Dag Hammarskjold

Dag Hjalmar Agne Carl Hammarskjold was Secretary-General of the United Nations from 10 April 1953 until 18 September 1961 when he met his death in a plane accident while on a peace mission in the Congo. Hammarskjold was unanimously appointed Secretary-General of the United Nations by the General Assembly on 7 April 1953 on the recommendation of the Security Council. He was reelected unanimously for another term of five years in September 1957.

He was born on 29 July 1905 in Jonkoping in south-central Sweden. The fourth son of Hjalmar Hammarskjold, Prime Minister of Sweden during the years of World War I, and his wife Agnes, M.C. (b. Almquist), he was brought up in the university town of Uppsala where his father resided as Governor of the county of Uppland.

At 18, he graduated from college and enrolled in Uppsala University. Majoring in French history of literature, social philosophy and political economy, Hammarskjold received, with honors, his Bachelor of Arts degree two years later. The next three years he studied economics, at the same university, where he received a "filosofic licenciat" degree in economics at the age of 23. He continued his studies for two more years to become a Bachelor of Laws in 1930.

Hammarskjold then moved to Stockholm, where he became a secretary of a governmental committee on unemployment (1930-1934). At the same time he wrote his doctor's thesis in economics, entitled, *"Konjunkturspridningen"* (The Spread of the Business Cycle). In 1933, he received his doctor's degree from the University of Stockholm, where he was made assistant professor in political economy.

At the age of 31 and after having served one year as secretary in the National Bank of Sweden, Hammarskjold was appointed to the post of Permanent Under-Secretary of the Ministry of Finance. He concurrently served as Chairman of the National Bank's Board from 1941 to 1948. Six of the Board's members are appointed by Parliament and the Chairman by the Government. This was the first time that one man had held both posts, the Chairmanship of the Bank's Board and that of Under-Secretary of the Finance Ministry.

Early in 1945, he was appointed an adviser to the Cabinet on financial and economic problems, organizing and coordinating, among other things, different governmental planning for the various economic problems that arose as a result of the war and the postwar period. During these years, Hammarskjold played an important part in shaping Sweden's financial policy. He led a series of trade and financial negotiations with other countries, among them the United States and the United Kingdom.

In 1947, he was appointed to the Foreign Office, where he was responsible for all economic questions with rank of Under-Secretary. In 1949, he was appointed Secretary-General of the Foreign Office

and in 1951, he joined the Cabinet and Minister without portfolio. He became, in effect, Deputy Foreign Minister, dealing especially with economic problems and various plans for close economic cooperation.

He was a delegate to the Paris Conference in 1947, when the Marshall Plan machinery was established. He was his country's chief delegate to the 1948 Paris Conference of the Organization for European Economic Cooperation (OEEC). For some years he served as Vice-Chairman of the OEEC Executive Committee. In 1950, he became Chairman of the Swedish Delegation to UNISCAN, established to promote economic cooperation between the United Kingdom and the Scandinavian countries. He was also a member (1937-1948) of the advisory board of the government-sponsored Economic Research Institute.

He was Vice-Chairman of the Swedish Delegation to the Sixth Regular Session of the United Nations General Assembly in Paris 1951-1952, and acting Chairman of his country's delegation to the Seventh General Assembly in New York in 1952-1953.

Although he served with the Social-Democratic cabinet, Hammarskjold never joined any political party, regarding himself as an independent, politically.

On 20 December 1954, he became a member of the Swedish Academy. He was elected to take the seat in the Academy previously held by his father.

During his terms as Secretary-General, Mr. Hammarskjold carried out many responsibilities for the United Nations in the course of its efforts to prevent war and serve the other aims of the Charter.

In the Middle East these included: continuing diplomatic activity in support of the Armistice Agreements between Israel and the Arab States and to promote progress toward better and more peaceful conditions in the area; organization in 1956 of the United Nations Emergency Force (UNEF) and its administration since then; clearance of the Suez Canal in 1957 and assistance in the peaceful solution of the Suez Canal dispute; organization and administration of the United Nations Observation Group in Lebanon (UNOGIL) and establishment of an office of the special representative of the Secretary-General in Jordan in 1958.

In 1955, following his visit to Peking, 30 December 1954 to 13 January 1955, 15 detained American flier who had served under the United Nations Command in Korea were released by the Chinese People's Republic. Hammarskjold also traveled to many countries of Africa, Asia, Europe, the Americas and the Middle East, either on specific assignments or to further his acquaintance with officials of member governments and the problems of various areas.

On one of these trips, from 18 December 1959 to 31 January 1960, the Secretary-General visited 21 countries and territories in Africa—a trip he described later as "a strictly professional trip for study, for information", in which he said he had gained a "kind of cross-section of every sort of politically responsible opinion in the Africa of today".

Later in 1960, when President Joseph Kasa-Vubu and Prime Minister Patrice Lumumba of the Republic of the Congo sent a cable on 12 July asking "urgent dispatch" of United Nations military assistance to the Congo, the Secretary-General addressed the Security Council at a night meeting on 13 July and asked the Council to act "with utmost speed" on the request. Following Security Council actions the United Nations Force in the Congo was established and the Secretary-General himself made four trips to the Congo in connection with the United Nations operations there. The first two trips to the Congo were made in July and August 1960. Then, in January of that year, the Secretary-General stopped in the Congo while en route to the Union of South Africa on another mission in connection with the racial problems of that country. The fourth trip to the Congo began on 12 September and terminated with the fatal plane accident.

In other fields of work, Hammarskjold was responsible for the organization in 1955 and 1958 of the first and second UN international conference on the peaceful uses of atomic energy in Geneva, and for planning a UN conference on the application of science and technology for the benefit of the less developed areas of the world held in 1962.

He held honorary degrees from Oxford University, England; in the United States from Harvard, Yale, Princeton, Columbia, Pennsylvania, Amherst, John Hopkins, the University of California, Uppsala College, and Ohio University; and in Canada from Carlton College and from McGill University.

U Thant

U Thant, who served as Secretary-General of the United Nations from 1961 to 1971, was chosen to head the world body when Seceretary-General Dag Hammarskjold was killed in an air crash in September 1961.

U Thant was born at Pantanaw, Burma, on 22 January 1909, and was educated at the National High School in Pantanaw and at University College, Rangoon.

Prior to his diplomatic career, U Thant's experience was in education and information work. He served as Senior Master at the National High School, which he had attended in Pantanaw, and in 1931, he became Headmaster after winning first place in the Anglo-Vernacular Secondary Teachership Examination.

He was a member of Burma's Textbook Committee and of the Council of National Education before World War II, and was an Executive Committee member of the Heads of Schools Association. He was also active as a free-lance journalist.

In 1942, U Thant served for a few months as Secretary of Burma's Education Reorganization Committee. In the following year, he returned to the National High School as Headmaster for another four years.

U Thant was appointed Press Director of the Government of Burma in 1947. In 1948, he became Director of Broadcasting, and in the following year, he was appointed Secretary to the Government of Burma in the Ministry of Information. In 1953, U Thant became Secretary for projects in the Office of the Prime Minister, and in 1955, he was assigned additional duties as Executive Secretary of Burma's Economic and Social Board.

At the time of his appointment as Acting Secretary-General of the United Nations, U Thant had been Permanent Representative of Burma to the United Nations, with the rank of Ambassador (1957-61).

During that period, he headed the Burmese delegations to the sessions of the General Assembly, and in 1959, he served as one of the Vice-Presidents of the Assembly's fourteenth session. In 1961, U Thant was Chairman of the United Nations Congo Conciliation Commission and Chairman of the Committe on a United Nations Capital Development Fund.

During his diplomatic career, U Thant served on several occasions as Adviser to Prime Ministers of Burma.

U Thant began serving as Acting-Secretary-General since 3 November 1961, when he was unanimously appointed by the General Assembly, on the recommendation of the Security Council, to fill the unexpired term of the late Secretary-General, Dag Hammarskjold. He was then unanimously appointed Secretary-General by the General Assembly on 30 November 1962 for a term of office ending on 3 November 1966.

U Thant was re-appointed for a second term as Secretary-General of the United Nations by the General Assembly on 2 December 1966 on the unanimous recommendation of the Security Council (resolution 229, 1966). His term of office continued until 31 December 1971.

U Thant received honorary degrees (LL.D) from the following universities: Carleton University, Ottawa, Canada (25 May 1962); Williams College, Williamstown, Massachusetts (10 June 1962); Princeton University, Princeton, New Jersey (12 June 1962); Mount Holyoke College, South Hadley, Massachusetts (2 June 1963); Harvard University, Cambridge, Massachusetts (13 June 1963); Dartmouth College, Hanover, New Hampshire (16 June 1963); University of California at Berkeley, California (2 April 1964); University of Denver, Denver, Colorado (1 April 1964); Swarthmore College, Swarthmore, Pennsylvania (8 June 1964); New York University, New York (10 June 1964); Moscow University, Moscow, Soviet Union (30 July 1964); Queen's University, Kingston, Ontario (22 May 1965); Colby College, Waterville, Maine (6 June 1965); Yale University, New Heaven, Connecticut (14 June 1965); University of Windsor, Windsor, Ontario, Canada (28 May 1966); Hamilton College, Clinton, New York (5 June 1966); Fordham University, Bronx, New York (8 June 1966); Manhat-tan College, New York (14 June 1966); University of Michigan, Ann Arbor, Michigan (30 March 1967); Delhi University, New Delhi, India (13 April 1967); University of Leeds, England (26 May 1967); Louvain University, Brussels, Belgium (10 April 1968); University of Alberta, Edmonton, Canada (13 May 1968); Boston University, Boston, Massachusetts (19 May 1068); Rutgers University, New Brunswick, New Jersey (29 May 1968); University of Dublin (Trinity College), Dublin, Ireland (12 July 1968); Laval University, Quebec, Canada (31 May 1969); Columbia University, New York City (3 June 1969); the University of the Philippines (11 April 1970); and Syracuse University (6 June 1970). He also received the following honorary degrees: Doctor of Divinity, The First Universal Church (11 May 1970); Doctor of International Law, Florida International University, Miami, Florida (25 January 1971); Doctor of Laws, University of Hartford, Hartford, Connecticut (23 March 1971); Doctor of Civil Laws degree, honoris causa, Colgate University, Hamilton, New York, (30 May 1971); Doctor of Humane Letters, Duke University, Durnam, North Carolina (7 June 1971).

U Thant retired at the end of his second term in 1971 and he died on 25 November 1974 after a long illness. He was 65 years old.

Kurt Waldheim

Kurt Waldheim was appointed Secretary-General of the United Nations for a five-year term beginning on 1 January 1972. The Security Council had recommended the appointment on 21 December 1971 and the General Assembly approved it by acclamation on the following day.

The Secretary-General was born at Sankt Andra-Wordern, near Vienna, Austria, on 21 December 1918. He graduated from the University of Vienna as a Doctor of Jurisprudence in 1944. He is also a graduate of the Vienna Consular Academy.

Waldheim joined the Austrian diplomatic service in 1945, and from 1948 to 1951 he served as First Secretary of the Legation in Paris. He was head of the personnel department of the Ministry for Foreign Affairs in Vienna from 1951 to 1955. In 1955 he was appointed Permanent Observer for Austria to the United Nations and later that year became head of the Austrian Mission when Austria was admitted to the Organization.

From 1956 to 1960, Waldheim represented Austria in Canada, first as Minister Plenipotentiary and later as Ambassador. From 1960 to 1962 he was head of the Political Department (West) in the Austrian Ministry for Foreign Affairs, subsequently becoming Director-General for Political Affairs until June 1964.

From January 1968 to April 1970, Waldheim was Federal Minister for Foreign Affairs of Austria. After leaving the Government, he was unanimously elected Chairman of the Safeguards Committee of the International Atomic Energy Agency, and in October 1970 he again became the Austrian Permanent Representative to the United Nations, a post he held until he was elected Secretary-General of the Organization.

In April 1971, he was one of the two candidates for the Federal Presidency of Austria.

During his first three years as Secretary-General, Waldheim made it a practice to visit areas of special concern to the United Nations. In March 1972 he travelled to South Africa and Namibia in pursuance of a mandate given him by the Security Council in order to assist in finding a satisfactory solution for the problem of Namibia.

The Secretary-General paid three visits to Cyprus, in June 1972, August 1973 and August 1974, for discussions with government leaders and to inspect the United Nations Peace-keeping Force in the island. During his visit in August 1974, in the wake of the hostilities, Waldheim arranged for talks to begin between Acting President Glafcos Clerides and Rauf Denktash.

The Secretary-General also made a number of trips to the Middle East in the continuing search for peace in the area. In August 1973, he visited Syria, Lebanon, Israel, Egypt and Jordan; in June 1974 he met with the leaders of Lebanon, Syria, Israel, Jordan and Egypt; and in November 1974 he went to Syria, Israel and Egypt in connection with the extension of the mandate of United Nations Disengagement Observer Force (UNDOF). On these visits, he also inspected the United Nations peace-keeping operations in the area—the United Nations Truce Supervision Organization (UNTSO), the United Nations Emergency Force (UNEF) and UNDOF.

In February 1973, during an official trip to the sub-continent, the Secretary-General discussed with the Governments on India, Pakistan and Bangladesh the problems created by the war between India and Pakistan and ways and means to overcome its consequences. He also inspected the United Nations Relief Operation in Bangladesh, the largest relief operation ever undertaken under the United Nations auspices.

In February and March 1974, the Secretary-General visited a number of countries in the Sudano-Sahelian area of Africa where the United Nations had undertaken a major relief operation to assist the victims of a prolonged drought.

The Secretary-General also opened and addressed a number of major international conferences convened under the United Nations auspices. These include the third session of the United Nations Conference on Trade and Development (Santiago, April 1972), the United Nations Conference on the Human Environment (Stockholm, June 1972), the Third United Nations Conference on the Law of the Sea (Caracas, June 1974), the World Population Conference (Bucharest, August 1974) and the World Food Conference (Rome, November 1974).

The Secretary-General anticipated in Security Council meetings held away from Headquarters, in Africa (Addis Ababa, January 1972) and in Latin America (Panama, March 1973).

He addressed and attended meetings of the Organization of African Unity (OAU) in Rabat (June 1972 on the occasion of the tenth anniversary of the OAU, in Addis Ababa (May 1973) and in Mogadisco (June 1974). He also addressed the Organization of American States (OAS) in Washington (March 1972).

In February 1973, the Secretary-General took part in the Paris International Conference on Vietnam; in December of the same year, he presided over the first phase of the Geneva Peace Conference on the Middle East.

In July 1973, Waldheim addressed the Conference on European Security and Co-operation in Helsinki.

On the invitation of their respective Governments, the Secretary-General paid official visits to a number of countries in Africa, Asia, Latin America, the Middle East and Europe.

Married and the father of three children, Waldheim is the author of a work on Austria's foreign policy, *The Austrian Example*, which has been published in German, English and French.

Javier Perez De Cuellar

Secretary-General Javier Perez de Cuellar assumed office as Secretary-General of the United Nations on 1 January 1982. On 10 October 1986, he was appointed for a second term of office, which began on 1 January 1987.

Perez de Cuellar was born in Lima, Peru, on 19 January 1920. He is a Lawyer and a career diplomat, now retired.

He joined the Peruvian Ministry of Foreign Affairs in 1940 and the diplomatic service in 1944, serving subsequently as Secretary at the Peruvian embassies in France, the United Kingdom, Bolivia and Brazil, and as Counsellor and Minister Counsellor at the embassy in Brazil.

Having returned to Lima in 1961, he was promoted to the rank of Ambassador the following year, successively occupying the posts of Director of the Legal Department, Director of Administration, Director of Protocol and Director of Political Affairs. In 1966, he was appointed Secretary-General (Deputy Minister) for Foreign Affairs. In 1981, he served as Legal Adviser in the Ministry of Foreign Affairs.

Perez de Cuellar has been Ambassador of Peru to Switzerland, the Soviet Union, Poland and Venezuela.

He was a member of the Peruvian delegation to the General Assembly at its first session in 1946 and a member of the delegations to the twenty-fifth to thirtieth sessions of the Assembly. In 1971, he was appointed Permanent Representative of Peru to the United Nations, and he led his country's delegation to all sessions of the Assembly from then until 1975.

In 1973 and 1974, he represented his country in the Security Council, serving as President of the Council at the time of the events in Cyprus in July 1974. On 18 September 1975, he was appointed Special Representative of the Secretary-General in Cyprus, a post he held until December 1977, when he rejoined his Foreign Service.

In July 1974, while Perez de Cuellar was serving as president of the UN Security Council, a rightist military faction overthrew the government of Cyprus, headed by Archbishop Makarios III, in an effort to bring about enosis—the union of Cyprus and Greece. In response, the government of Turkey ordered an invasion of the island to safeguard the rights of the Turkish minority on Cyprus. In a UN effort to ease the tensions, Secretary General Kurt Waldheim, on September 18, 1975, named Perez de Cuellar as his special representative to Cyprus. Although he did not have any special credentials that would qualify him to solve the deep-rooted Cyprus problem, Perez de Cuellar managed to persuade the leaders of the island's Greek and Turkish communities, in 1978, to initiate talks about their mutual differences. Since his efforts had for the time being provided a means of averting further military conflict in an area where ethnic violence was once commonplace, Perez de Cuellar justifiably took pride in his role and regarded his work in Cyprus as his "principal diplomatic achievement."

On 27 February 1979, he was appointed as United Nations Under-Secretary-General for Special Political Affairs. From April 1981, while still holding this post, he acted as the Secretary-General's Personal Representative on the situation relating to Afghanistan. In that capacity, he visited Pakistan and Afghanistan in April and August of that year in order to continue the negotiations initiated by the Secretary-General some months earlier.

In May 1981, he again rejoined his country's Ministry of Foreign Affairs but continued to represent the Secretary-General in the context of the situation relating to Afghanistan until his appointment in December of that year as Secretary-General of the United Nations.

Determined to "give the UN a new sense of self-esteem, of direction, and thus to lend it a new thrust as the protector of civilized behavior in the jungle of international affairs," Perez de Cuellar pledged that he would strive to increase the efficiency of the world body's internal operations and to improve staff morale. On the international scene, he has pledged to work for the alleviation of existing East-West and North-South tensions.

As a UN veteran, Perez de Cuellar was well aware of the problems he would face as Secretary-General. "I didn't seek this job," he said in one of his first public statements, "and it's important that everybody knows I won't seek another term, so that I can be independent enough to win the trust of the members and still speak out in defense of the Charter when I think this will be useful." As quoted in the *Christian Science Monitor* (January 11, 1982), he also asserted: "I am fully aware of the fact that I am not some kind of president of the world and that the UN is at the service of its member states. Some of those who clamor for moral leadership are the first to shout, 'Don't meddle in my affairs' when the UN objects to some of their own misdeeds."

During the early months of his tenure Perez de Cuellar devoted himself mainly to internal matters, in particular the UN's fiscal problems, its bureaucratic cumbersomeness and excessive red tape, and the politization of some of its agencies, such as those charged with assembling statistics on world economic problems. He announced plans to revitalize the civil service, which had become increasingly lethargic and demoralized, largely as a result of the growing conviction of many UN employees that advancement and promotion were dependent on a kind of national patronage system and on personal connections rather than on merit, competence, and dedication.

The confrontation between Great Britain and Argentina in the Falkland Islands, beginning in April 1982, proved to be the first major challenge to face Perez de Cuellar. Initially taking a back seat in order to let United States Secretary of State Alexander M. Haig Jr. serve as mediator, Perez de Cuellar soon became actively involved as an intermediary between the two sides, meeting regularly with their representatives in an effort to work out a solution both could accept. Despite his good offices, however, the dispute soon escalated into a full-scale military conflict and a second mediation effort by Perez de Cuellar, shortly before the British reconquest of the Falklands in June, also was unsuccessful. Nevertheless, the UN Secretary General's efforts to resolve the crisis evoked high praise within the diplomatic community. "While these efforts lasted, everybody gave the Secretary General credit for leaving no stone unturned, for catching the imagination of both parties and the confidence of both." Olara Otunnu of Uganda observed, as quoted in the *New York Times* (July 5,

1982).

"The failure was not the result of his bumbling. He deserves credit for the effort if not the result." United States Ambassador Jeane J. Kirkpatrick told a Security Council meeting: "We can be proud . . . of the Secretary General."

Perez de Cuellar has also won praise for such actions as his appointment of women to key UN posts.

He has served as Professor of International Law at Peru's Academia Diplomatica and Professor of International Relations at Peru's Academia de Guerra Aerea. He is the author of *Manual de Derecho Diplomatico* (Manual of Diplomatic Law (1964))

Perez de Cuellar has received doctorate degrees *honoris causa* from the following universities: the University of Nice; the Jagiellonian University at Cracow; Charles University at Prague; the University of Sofia; the University of San Marcos at Lima; the Free University at Brussels; Carlenton University at Ottawa, Canada; the University of Paris (Sorbonne) ; the University of Visva-Bharati in West Bengal,

India; the University of Michigan; the University of Osnabruck in the Federal Republic of Germany; the Coimbra University at Coimbra, Portugal; the Mongolian State University at Ulan Bator; the Humboldt University of Berlin; the Moscow State University; the University of Malta in Valleta; the Leyden University in the Netherlands; La Salle University in Philadelphia; Tufts University in Medford, Massachussetts; the Johns Hopkins University in Baltimore, Maryland; and Cambridge University in the United Kingdom.

In the course of his career, Perez de Cuellar has been decorated by some 25 countries.

In October 1987, he was awarded the Prince of Asturias Prize for the promotion of Ibero-American co-operation. In January 1989, he was awarded the Olof Palme Prize for International Understanding and Common Security by the Olof Palme Memorial Fund. In February 1989, he was awarded the Jawaharlal Nehru Award for International Understanding.

Perez de Cuellar is married to the late Marcela Temple. He has two children.

Boutros Boutros-Ghali

Boutros Boutros-Ghali became the sixth Secretary-General of the United Nations on 1 January 1992, when he began a five-year term. At the time of his appointment by the General Assembly on 3 December 1991, Boutros-Ghali had been Deputy Prime Minister for Foreign Affairs of Egypt since May 1991 and had served as Minister of State for Foreign Affairs from October 1977 until 1991.

The Secretary-General's priority has been to strengthen the United Nations Organization, to enable it to seize the opportunities offered by the post-Cold War era, and to realize the goals of the Charter and the objectives of peace, development and democracy.

On 31 January 1992, the Secretary-General, at the first Security Council meeting ever held at the level of heads of State and government, was invited to prepare an analysis and recommendations on ways to strengthen the capacity of the United Nations for preventive diplomacy, peacemaking and peace-keeping. The Secretary-General added to these dimensions of peace a further concept, that of post-conflict peace-building. His report, entitled *An Agenda for Peace*, was published on 17 June 1992.

An Agenda for Peace defines the role and functions of the United Nations in a new era which has seen the establishment of numerous peace-keeping

operations and observer missions under the authority of the Security Council and the command of the Secretary-General. The report, which was translated into at least 29 languages, had been the focus of wide-ranging discussions.

On 3 January 1995, the Secretary-General issued a supplement to *An Agenda for Peace* as a position paper. This paper highlights certain areas where unforeseen difficulties have arisen with regard to United Nations peace-keeping operations. The supplement reviews the lessons learned and offers guidelines for improving future operations.

Since the Cold War ended, the United Nations has mounted more peace-keeping operations than in its previous 40 years, involving the deployment of some 70,000 troops, military observers and civilian police, in addition to civilian personnel. These operations include notably the United Nations Angola Verification Mission III, the United Nations Observer Mission in El Salvador, the United Nations Operation in Mozambique, the United Nations Operation in Somalia, the United Nations Protection Force in the republics of the former Yugoslavia, and the United Nations Transitional Authority in Cambodia.

The Secretary-General also appointed a number of Special Envoys and Representatives to advise him on the creation of conditions for ending hostilities, defusing tensions or consolidating peace in various areas of the world.

Peace-building activities, to provide the foundations for lasting peace, include measures to enhance confidence, to reform and strengthen democratic institutions, to integrate former combatants into civilian society, and to restore the fabric of war-torn societies so as to prevent a recurrence of conflict.

Since his first year in office, the Secretary-General has worked towards a reinvigorated and expanded vision of development. A series of landmark conferences has been held, including the Summit on the Economic Advancement of Rural Women, held at Geneva in February 1992, the United Nations Conference on Environment and Development, held at Rio de Janeiro in 1992, and the World Conference on Human Rights, held at Vienna in 1993.

In May 1994, the World Conference on Natural Disaster Reduction was held in Yokohama. In September 1994, the International Conference on Population and Development was held in Cairo, and the World Summit for Social Development was held in Copenhagen in March 1995. In September 1995, the Fourth World Conference on Women was held in Beijing. The Second Conference on Human Settlements, "The City Summit", has taken place in Istanbul in 1996. The Secretary-General sees this series of conferences as a continuum, offering unique opportunities to raise levels of awareness and to set norms and standards. In these conferences and summits, Member States and non-governmental organizations, as well as concerned individuals, work together to create a global commitment to all aspects of development.

The Secretary-General's own vision of development was set out in May 1994 in a report to the General Assembly entitled *An Agenda for Development*. In his report, the Secretary-General addressed peace, the economy, the environment, society and democracy as the five foundations of development. The Secretary-General also examined the multiplicity of actors engaged in development work and outlined his vision of the role of the United Nations in development in an increasingly complex world. Universal respect for and protection of human rights is an integral part of development, he declared. Human rights, including group rights such as those of indigenous peoples, women, children and the disabled, are a focus of the Secretary-General's attention. In November 1994, in response to the request of the General Assembly, the Secretary-General issued his recommendations for the implementation of *An Agenda for Development*.

The two agendas, peace and development, are inextricably linked. In February 1995, the Secretary-General published in companion volumes, as parallel texts, the revised *An Agenda for Peace* and *An Agenda for Development*.

The Secretary-General advocated a strong supporting role for the United Nations in the democratic transformation which has characterized the post-cold-war period. The United Nations has responded to the calls of some 40 nations for assistance in the organization and supervision of democratic elections. The presence of more than 2,100 observers in the South African elections in April 1994 made it the largest United Nations electoral assistance operation ever mounted. Recognizing that democracy is far more than the holding of free and fair elections, the United Nations has also developed various programmes to cooperate in the development of democratic institutions, rule of law and popular participation. In addition, the best support for democracy must lie in the democratization of international life, which the Secretary-General pursued throughout his term.

The financial crisis, suffered by the Organization because assessed contributions for the regular budget and for peace-keeping are not paid on time and in full, threatens the effective operations of the Organization. The Secretary-General has commissioned a number of studies aimed at ensuring that the United Nations is an organization capable of meeting the challenges of the next 50 years.

The Secretary-General undertook a programme of restructuring and reform designed to reduce the number of high-level posts in the Secretariat, to decentralize decision-making and to reduce costs and managerial inefficiencies.

However, the capacity of the United Nations to deal with vastly expanded operations was a particular source of concern to the Secretary-General.

Boutros-Ghali travelled to more than 50 countries to represent the United Nations and to offer his good offices to further the cause of peace. In December 1993, he was the first non-Korean to cross the DMZ from Seoul to Pyongyang.

The Secretary-General's role in advancing the goals of peace, development and democracy has been recognized by many awards and honorary degrees.

He was awarded a doctorate of law honoris causa from the Institute of State and Law of the Russian Academy of Sciences, Moscow (September 1992); a doctorate honoris causa from l'Institut d'Etudes politiques de Paris (January 1993); the Christian A. Herter Memorial Award from the World Affairs Council,

Boston (March 1993); a doctorate honoris causa from The Catholic University of Louvain, Belgium (April 1993); the "Man of Peace" award, sponsored by the Italian-based Together for Peace Foundation (July 1993); an honorary doctorate degree from the University of Laval, Quebec (August 1993); and the Arthur A. Houghton Jr. Star Crystal Award for Excellence from the African-American Institute, New York (November 1993).

Boutros-Ghali received a PH.D. in international law from Paris University in 1949. His thesis was on the study of regional organizations. Boutros-Ghali also holds a Bachelor of Laws degree, received from Cairo University in 1946, as well as separate diplomas in political science, economics and public law from Paris University.

Between 1949 and 1977, Boutros-Ghali was Professor of International Law and International Relations at Cairo University. From 1974 to 1977, he was a member of the Central Committee and Political Bureau of the Arab Socialist Union.

In addition, he was given the Grand Prize for World Peace from the Oughtopian Foundation in Korea (1996).

Boutros-Ghali was born in Cairo on 14 November 1922. He is married to Leia Maria Boutros-Ghali.

Kofi Annan

Kofi Annan was recommended by the Security Council for appointment by the General Assembly as Secretary-General of the United Nations for a term of office from 1 January 1997 to 31 December 2001.

A national of Ghana, Annan returned to the post of United Nations Under-Secretary-General for Peace-Keeping Operations in March 1996, after having served as the Special Representative of the Secretary-General to the former Yugoslavia and the Special Envoy to the North Atlantic Treaty Organization (NATO) throughout the transition period which followed the signing of the Dayton Peace Agreement. He was originally appointed Under-Secretary-General for Peace-keeping Operations on 1 March 1993, a year after his appointment as Assistant Secretary-General in the same department.

Prior to those posts, Annan was employed by the United Nations in a number of other senior capacities. In all, he has devoted more than 30 years to the United Nations, serving in places as diverse as Addis Ababa, Cairo, Geneva, Ismailia (Egypt) and New York.

Among those positions, Annan served as Assistant Secretaty-General for Programme Planning, Budget and Finance and Controller of the United Nations. Following the invasion of Kuwait by Iraq in 1990, Annan was sent by the Secretaty-General to Iraq to help see what could be done to improve the situation on the ground and to facilitate the repatriation of over 900 international staff. While there, Annan became engaged in negotiations for the release of Western hostages and in bringing attention to the plight of over 500,000 Asians stranded in Kuwait and Iraq. Subsequently, he led the United Nations team negotiations with Iraq on the possible sale of oil for purchases of humanitarian aid.

Earlier, Annan had held concurrently the positions of Assistant Secretary-General in the Office of Human Resources Management and Security Coordinator for the United Nations system, following appointments as Director of the Budget and as Deputy Director of Administration and Head of Personnel in the Office of the United Nations High Commissioner for Refugees.

Annan returned to his home country during the period from 1974 to 1976 as the Managing Director of the Ghana Tourist Development Company, serving concurrently on its Board and on the Ghana Tourist Control Board.

Apart from his official duties, Annan has long been involved in the areas of education and development and the welfare and protection of international staff. He is currently on the Boards of Trustees of Macalester College in St. Paul, Minnesota, and the Institute for the Future in Menlo Park, California. He was, for many years, Chairman of the Board of Trustees of the United Nations International School in New York, and he served as a Governor of the International School in Geneva from 1981 to 1983. Within the United Nations, Annan has contributed to the work of the Appointment and Promotion Board and the Senior Review Group (both of which he chaired), to the Administrative, Management and Financial Board, to the Secretary-General's Task Force for Peacekeeping, and to the United Nations Joint Staff Pension Fund.

Kofi Annan, who speaks English, French and several African languages, studied at the University of Science and Technology at Kumasi and completed his undergraduate work in economics at Macalester College, which awarded him its Trustee Distinguished Service Award in 1994, in honour of his more than 30 years of service to the international community. He undertook graduate studies in economics at the Institut universitaire de hautes etudes internationales in Geneva. As a 1971-72 Sloan Fellow at the Massachusetts Institute of Technology, he received a Master of Science degree in Manage-

ment. In June 1996, Cedar Crest College in Allentown, Pennsylvania, awarded him the honorary degree of Doctor of Public Service.

Annan was born in 1938. He and his wife, Nane, live in New York. They have three children.

NOBEL PEACE PRIZE LAUREATES

This section comprises articles on all recipients of the Nobel Peace Prize from 1901 to 1998. There are 97 separate entries. Articles appear in chronological order by date of prize. In cases where an organization has received a prize more than once, the entry appears at the date of the first award; a cross-reference has been inserted at the appropriate date of the second or third award.

Each award has been divided into two sections: the main section relates the work of the individual or organization which led to the award of the Nobel Peace Prize; the minor section provides biographical details, placing the peace activities of the Laureate concerned in a wider context.

An attempt has been made in each article to reflect the thinking of the Nobel Committee in awarding the prize. The aim has therefore been less to provide a retrospective assessment than to examine each Laureate in the light of the contemporary preoccupations and enthusiasms of the Committee and of the peace movement itself. Readers are advised to refer to the article in Volume III on Nobel Peace Prizes for a perspective upon all the awards and upon the shifts in thinking which have influenced the decisions of the Nobel Committee.

There are a number of standard reference works for the Nobel Peace Prizes. The most important source is Frederick W. Haberman (ed.) 1972 *The Nobel Lectures, Peace*, published in three volumes by Elsevier, Amsterdam. Readers may also find the following sources useful: the work of A. Schou in the Nobel Foundation and W. Odelberg (eds.) 1972 *Nobel: The Man and His Prizes*, 3rd rev. edn. published by Elsevier, New York; M. Lipsky 1966 *The Quest for Peace*, published by Barnes and Company, South Bruswick; T. Gray 1976 *Champions of Peace*, published by Paddington Press, New York. Younger readers might be interested in the work of E. Meyer 1978 *In Search of Peace*, published by Abingdon Press, Nashville, Tennessee. For entries on Laureates during the period 1986 to 1998, the Internet was used extensively for gathering information.

Quotations from the Nobel award ceremonies have been taken from *Les Prix Nobel*, published annually by the Imprimerie Royale, Stockholm. We are grateful to the Nobel Foundation for permission to reproduce these quotations.

CONTENTS

NOBEL PEACE PRIZE LAUREATES

Henri Dunant (1901) and the Red Cross (1917, 1944, 1963)	35
Frédéric Passy (1901)	38
Elie Ducommun (1902)	40
Charles-Albert Gobat (1903)	41
Sir William Randal Cremer (1903)	43
Institute of International Law (1904)	45
Baroness Bertha Sophie Felicita von Suttner (1905)	47
Theodore Roosevelt (1906)	50
Ernesto Teodoro Moneta (1907)	52
Louis Renault (1907)	54
Klaus Pontus Arnoldson (1908)	57
Fredrik Bajer (1908)	58
Auguste Marie Francois Beernaert (1909)	60
Paul Henri Benjamin Balluet, Baron d'Estournelles de Constant de Rebecque (1909)	61
International Peace Bureau (IPB) (1910)	63
Tobias Michael Carel Asser (1911)	65
Alfred Hermann Fried (1911)	67
Elihu Root (1912)	69
Henri La Fontaine (1913)	71
Thomas Woodrow Wilson (1919)	74
Leon Bourgeois (1920)	76
Karl Hjalmer Branting (1921)	78
Christian Lous Lange (1921)	80
Fridtjof Nansen (1922) and the Nansen Office (1938)	82
Sir Austen Chamberlain (1925)	86
Charles Gates Dawes (1925)	88
Aristide Briand (1926)	90
Gustav Stresemann (1926)	93
Ferdinand Buisson (1927)	95

Ludwig Quidde (1927) 97

Frank Billings Kellogg (1929) 99

Lars Olof Nathan Söederblom (1930) 100

Jane Addams (1931) 103

Nicholas Murray Butler (1931) 106

Sir Norman Angell (1933) 108

Arthur Henderson (1934) 111

Carl von Ossietzky (1935) 114

Carlos Saavedra Lamas (1936) 116

Lord Edgar Algernon Robert Gascoyne Cecil (1937) 119

Cordell Hull (1945) 122

Emily Greene Balch (1946) 125

John Raleigh Mott (1946) 127

The Quakers (1947) 130

Lord John Boyd Orr Of Brechin (1949) 132

Ralph Bunche (1950) 135

Leon Jouhaux (1951) 138

Albert Schweitzer (1952) 141

George Catlett Marshall (1953) 144

United Nations High Commissioner for Refugees (UNHCR) (1954, 1981) 147

Lester Bowles Pearson (1957) 149

Dominique Pire (1958) 151

Philip J. Noel-Baker (1959) 154

Albert John Lutuli (1960) 156

Dag Hjalmar Agne Carl Hammarskjöeld (1961) 159

Linus Carl Pauling (1962) 162

Martin Luther King, Jr (1964) 166

United Nations Children's Fund (UNICEF) (1965) 168

René Cassin (1968) 171

International Labour Organization (ILO) (1969) 173

Norman Borlaug (1970) 175

Willy Brandt (1971) 177

Henry A. Kissinger (1973) 180

Le Duc Tho (1973) 182

Sean MacBride (1974) 182

Eisaku Sato (1974) 185

Andrei Sakharov (1975) 186

Mairead Corrigan and Betty Williams (1976) 188

Amnesty International (1977) 190

Menachem Begin (1978) 192

Anwar al-Sadat (1978) 195

Mother Teresa (1979) 197

Adolfo Pérez Esquivel (1980) 199

Alfonso Garcia Robles (1982) 201

Alva Myrdal (1982) 203

Lech Walesa (1983) 204

Desmond Tutu (1984) 207

International Physicians for Prevention of Nuclear War (IPPNW) (1985) 209

Elie Wiesel (1986) 211

Oscar Arias Sanchez (1987) 213

United Nations Peacekeeping Forces (1988) 217

Dalai Lama (1989) 223

Mikhail Gorbachev (1990) 228

Aung San Suu Kyi (1991) 231

Rigoberta Menchu Tum (1992) 234

Nelson Mandela (1993) 236

Fredrik Willem de Klerk (1993) 240

Shimon Peres (1994) 243

Yitzhak Rabin (1994) 247

Yasser Arafat (1994) 251

Pugwash Conferences on Science and World Affairs (ICBL) (1995) 254

Joseph Rotblat (1995) 257

Jose Ramos-Horta (1996) 259

Carlos Felipe Ximenes Belo (1996) 262

Jody Williams (1997) 263

International Campaign to Ban Landmines (1997) 265

David Trimble (1998) 269

John Hume (1998) 270

Nobel Peace Prize Laureates

Jean Henri Dunant and the Red Cross
(1901)   (1917, 1944, 1963)

Henri Dunant, founder of the Red Cross, shared the first Nobel Prize for Peace with Frédéric Passy in 1901.

The choice of Henri Dunant for the Peace Prize was greeted with heated controversy. Was it the intent of Alfred Nobel to award the mitigation of war's horrors? Nobel's personal friend of many years, Baroness von Suttner, voiced her opinion in vivid prose: "St. George rode forth to kill the dragon, not to trim its claws," she said. Von Suttner thought that allowing the monster war to develop its hideous nature freely would assure its eventual destruction from excess of evil, and she greeted this first award of the Peace Prize with scorn: "I observe that the division of the prize corresponds neither to the letter of the will nor to the testator's intention, which I know well." She did, however, applaud the choice of Frédéric Passy, founder of the Ligue International et Permanente de la Paix (International and Permanent Peace League), who had been vigorously promoting peace conferences for 50 years. "Only the whole amount should have gone to him," she declared.

But the 1917, 1944, and 1963 awards to the Red Cross were destined to overrule von Suttner's objections. In its long history of assisting the victims of war, the Red Cross rescues "in the dark storm of war the idea of human solidarity and respect for the dignity of every human being, precisely at a time when the real or alleged necessities of war push moral values into the background" (Max Huber acceptance speech 1944).

The Red Cross was conceived in just such circumstances—on the plains of Northern Italy where the Battle of Solferino raged, one of the bloodiest conflicts of the nineteenth century. It was not a participant who was so fatefully moved by that awful scene, but a sensitive young Swiss businessman who had come looking for Emperor Napoleon III to discuss water rights in Algeria. All day Henri Dunant had watched from a hill through his binoculars as the battle became a massacre, with 40,000 men lying wounded or dead by nightfall.

It was not unheard of in 1859 to leave the wounded where they fell, this being accepted as their fate. But Henri Dunant was of no such mind. Commandeering men and women of the neighborhood, he worked feverishly with the few doctors there to give the wounded, from all sides, what help was possible. Without equipment, or even enough water, their aid was tragically insufficient. But the scene seered itself into his mind: Dunant's life had been changed.

Later, when he did meet with Napoleon III about the water rights, the Emperor's lack of interest and even knowledge of a drought in Algeria failed to matter to Dunant (although his indifference was not shared by his friends and associates whom he had persuaded to invest in this Algerian venture). Dunant was haunted by the battle scene, and after this nightmare had obsessed him. Over the next months, he wrote and privately published a small book, *A Memory of Solferino (Un Souvenir de Solferino)* in which he proposed a plan to prevent such unnecessary suffering in the future. "Would it not be possible in time of peace and quiet," Dunant asked, "to form relief societies for the purpose of having care given to the wounded in wartime by zealous, devoted, and thoroughly qualified volunteers?" In his plan he provided that friend and foe alike, wounded and volunteers, all should have the protection of a neutral status.

Dunant had touched a universal chord of humanitarianism and people responded in such numbers that the book was twice reprinted. In Dunant's native city of Geneva a society for public service (La Société Genevoise d'Utilité Publique) appointed a committee of five, including Dunant, which arranged a conference at Geneva in October 1863 in which 16 countries participated. Here the Red Cross was born, taking its name from the reversed Swiss flag adopted as its emblem in honor of Dunant.

The Red Cross was to grow steadily in scope and

stature. But such a fate was not met with by its founder. Dunant continued to invest his own resources and all of his time and energy in preparation for the next conference, traveling from country to country to extract promises of representatives. And indeed, in the next year a second Geneva conference yielded the rules of conduct regarding war-wounded and prisoners-of-war to which 12 countries became signatories. But Dunant had neglected his business and exhausted his own fortune. Suddenly he found himself facing bankruptcy, a status which carried great disgrace in his country. Shunned by friends, and even by family, he fled to Paris. There he sank into poverty and a self-imposed oblivion which he himself lifted only during the Franco-Prussian War when he once again, acting as a neutral Swiss citizen, became active on the battlefields, risking his life daily to effect the exchange of prisoners.

During this time he met with progressive Frenchmen, among them Frédéric Passy, with whom he would one day share the Nobel Prize, and he discussed with them ideas such as the rehabilitation of prisoners-of-war and training programs for soldiers for peacetime trades. They considered ways of preventing war through international arbitration courts. But though Dunant served briefly as secretary of Passy's peace society, he seemed a broken and humiliated man. At last he retired to a hospice in his native Switzerland where he lived for the rest of his life. Attempts to draw him back into active participation in the Red Cross brought limited results: he organized a Red Cross chapter in the area of his retirement; he wrote an article for Baroness von Suttner's peace paper upon her invitation. But when the news of his Nobel Prize came he sent Dr. Hans Daae to accept the award for him and directed that his share of the prize money be banked. There it stayed until his death nine years later, when, in compliance with his will, it was divided between charities in Norway and Switzerland.

A monument over his grave bears the figure of a man kneeling to offer water to a dying soldier, and a simple inscription reads: JEAN HENRI DUNANT, BORN 1828, DIED 1910. FOUNDER OF THE RED CROSS.

The Red Cross has evolved far beyond the scope of the symbol on Dunant's grave. In 1963, the year marking the centennial of the Red Cross, the Nobel Prize for Peace was divided between two sister organizations of the Red Cross: the International Committee of the Red Cross and the League of Red Cross Societies. On two previous occasions the Red Cross received the Peace Prize, both in connection with its

services during military conflicts: in 1917, during the First World War and in 1944, during the closing years of the Second World War. From its celebrated beginning with Dunant's efforts to mitigate the suffering strewn in the wake of warfare, it has become an international movement concerned with the prevention and alleviation of human suffering, whether from man-made causes or natural catastrophes. It has remained independent of any government and draws much of its effectiveness through its zealously guarded neutrality.

It functions through three organizations: the International Committee of the Red Cross, the League of Red Cross Societies (which coordinates a worldwide network of national societies), and the International Conference of the Red Cross. Most countries still use the symbol of the reversed Swiss flag, a red cross on a white background, but Moslem countries use the red crescent, and Iran uses a red lion and sun.

Its highest authority rests with the International Conference of the Red Cross, a deliberative body, which calls together at four-year intervals a conference of delegates from the International Committee of the Red Cross, from the League of Red Cross Societies, and from the national Red Cross Societies (numbering 102 active societies with approximately 170,000,000 members at the time of the 1963 award), and also representatives from the governments which have signed the Geneva convention. Each delegate has one vote, and the decisions of the Conference bind the worldwide national Red Cross Societies by moral authority. A permanent International Red Cross Commission of nine members exists to discuss problems arising between conferences, and to decide when and where the next conference will be held.

The activities of the League of the Red Cross Societies and the International Committee of the Red Cross are frequently intertwined, except where the strict neutrality of the Committee separates its tasks from those of the Societies. When awarded the Nobel Prize for Peace jointly with the Committee in 1963, the League was commended for its coordinating role with the 102 active National Societies, and the resulting cooperation between people of different countries, races, creeds, and color was cited as a major contribution to international understanding and peace.

The International Committee, composed of 25 Swiss citizens, acts as intermediary between belligerents during war, and as arbitrator of disputes in times of peace. Its neutrality is of extreme importance in order that it may act free of political influences. Its members never carry weapons—they go about their tasks armed only with moral authority. The International Committee fulfills three functions which could not be performed by any other group: the protection of war victims, collecting and supplying information on missing persons, and providing relief in countries for those under duress through war.

In offering protection to war victims, Swiss delegates are sent to prisoners-of-war camps to ensure humane treatment for the captives, including adequate diet, living and detention quarters, medical care, and working conditions. They interview prisoners without the presence of witnesses. If problems are spotted, the delegates submit immediate requests for improvement. If necessary the International Committee itself will take difficulties to the higher authorities, using the principle of reciprocity as a lever. During the Second World War, the International Committee's delegates carried out 11,000 camp visits. This service is now extended to civilians who are interned in wartime concentration camps where it is possible to gain admittance.

In their second function, the International Committee provides a vast network of information about prisoners-of-war and missing persons through its Central Tracing Agency. During the Second World War, with the help of thousands of volunteers, it assembled 40 million information cards in order to communicate with families anxious for news of their kin, and it communicated with as many as 6,000 families a day. Its Tracing Service at Arolsen, Germany, took on the huge and tragic task of gathering information on persons missing from concentration camps.

The Committee's third task is to supply and distribute material relief—food, clothing, medical supplies, and books. During the Second World War it organized a fleet of 14 ships which sailed under the Red Cross flag. During peacetime the Committee continues its work, gathering and distributing aid in the wake of natural disasters—earthquakes, floods, and fires—and in the aftermath of man-made catastrophes, uprisings, and myriad forms of violence.

The Committee has continued its efforts toward the development of international humanitarian law through the first Geneva Convention, written during the second Geneva conference and signed by 12 nations. Revisions of this Convention include protection during naval warfare in 1906, and for prisoners-of-war in 1929, as well as a Convention drawn up in 1949 offering protection to civilians equal to that, at least, which is extended to prisoners-of-war. It gives certain guarantees to combatants in civil wars; it prohibits executions without fair trial; it lays down

humane conditions of internment and the right to protection by the International Committee. These Conventions carry only the implementation of moral authority, and sometimes the Committee faces the insurmountable difficulty of national sovereignty denying it access to a problem.

With the coming of the twentieth-century technology of nuclear physics, all Conventions are mocked until war shall yield to international law. Yet the International Committee has played a part even at the level of nuclear confrontation. During the Cuban Missile Crisis of 1962, when the United States, the Soviet Union, and Cuba engaged in a harrowing game of "brinkmanship," the Committee was asked to set up a system of 30 inspectors to ensure that no long-range atomic weapons were being delivered to Cuba. The International Committee succeeded in gaining the necessary consent to search from all three concerned powers as well as from all maritime powers whose ships called at Cuba. The crisis was resolved before the Committee was required to act, but it had proven equal to a peace-maintenance task which perhaps it alone could have performed.

Mr. Boissier, President of the International Committee, spoke of this evolution of war with the threat to all humanity posed by the hydrogen bomb. The International Committee has attempted to concentrate not on any particular weapon, he said, but on a principle which it took to the governments of the world via a draft of a proposed regulation made through the last International Red Cross Conference: "Whatever weapons are employed, the civilian population must not be harmed or at least not exposed to risks out of all proportion to the military objectives," it read. "But alas, the answer was silence," Boissier reported.

He offered hope through developing an active sense of community among people which would promote a sense of mutual responsibility for the good of humankind. "When war creates its tragic gap between nations, the Red Cross remains the last link," he said. "Its struggle against suffering is a vivid reproach to those who inflict it. It intervenes in the midst of violence, but does not have recourse thereto. The Red Cross, therefore, makes a powerful appeal, to all men, in favour of peace."

Biography of Henri Dunant

In June of 1859 Henri Dunant, a young Swiss businessman, followed Napoleon III to Italy with the intent of discussing with him water rights in Algeria. By this unlikely circumstance, Dunant happened upon the scene of the Battle of Solferino. The massacre he witnessed there turned his business trip into a personal commitment to work for a permanent, neutral, international society of volunteers, devoted to the aid of the sick and wounded during wartime.

His book, *A Memory of Solferino* [*Un Souvenir de Solferino*], recounting the affair and presenting his plan of action, galvanized society, and within a year Dunant and four members of a Geneva Committee had engineered a successful conference in Geneva with delegates attending from 16 countries. Here the Red Cross was established, choosing as its emblem the inverted flag of Dunant's native Switzerland.

Dunant set about arranging a second conference for the next year, which proved successful for the Red Cross, but financially disastrous for Dunant who had neglected his business in his feverish pursuit of his humanitarian project. From this point on, Henri Dunant suffered separation from the prospering Red Cross as he went into bankruptcy in 1867 and withdrew into a self-imposed exile which he lifted only to work on the battlefields of the Franco-Prussian War, and to work briefly with the French pacifist movement under Frédéric Passy. He returned to a hospice in Switzerland, impoverished, largely forgotten, refusing all attempts of encouragement toward rejoining society.

In 1901 he was awarded the first Nobel Prize for Peace jointly with Frédéric Passy. He did not go to receive the award, nor did he spend any of the prize money. He died nine years later, leaving a will directing the award money to charities in Norway and Switzerland.

History of the Red Cross

The Red Cross is an international movement engaged in alleviating human suffering from both natural catastrophes—floods, fires, earthquakes, famine—and man-made disasters, war and myriad violent conflicts that leave helpless victims in their wake. Its broadest aim is to improve the quality of human life throughout the world, and it accomplishes its task largely through the use of volunteers.

It was founded by a Swiss, Henri Dunant, in 1863, beginning as a neutral society with volunteers devoted to mitigating the suffering of the wounded and prisoners in wartime. It has evolved into an international organization represented by nearly all of the countries of the world and operating on a broad humanitarian basis through three organizations:

The International Conference, its highest deliberative body, holds conferences every four years with representatives from the other two Red Cross organizations and from governments signatory to the Geneva Conventions. It is here that policies and recommendations are made, and a skeletal committee of nine is maintained to function between conferences.

The International Committee of the Red Cross is composed of 25 citizens of Switzerland whose strict observance of neutrality enables them to cross international borders, during war or peace, and observe prisoner-of-war camps, run a vast network of information regarding missing persons, prisoners-of-war, and, when permitted, inmates of detention camps. Whenever possible, they assist in setting up communication between these people and their concerned families. During the Second World War, with the assistance of 4,000-5,000 volunteers, one million incoming and 900,000 outgoing messages were handled each month.

The Red Cross League facilitates cooperation between the worldwide network of 102 National Red Cross Societies, their membership numbering over 170,000,000. This is the source from which the Committee draws volunteers. Therefore the work of the Red Cross League and the International Committee often mesh. In peacetime they join together to extend disaster relief, help evacuate and resettle refugees, reunite families, and distribute relief supplies.

At the second Geneva conference in 1864 the provisions of the first Geneva Convention were signed by 12 nations, providing for relief of suffering for the wounded on battle-fields. Since that time the expansion of Red Cross activities has been effected through successive similar "Conventions," the last notable revision covering civilians throughout the world under both war and peacetime circumstances. Nearly every country of the world is now a party to these four Geneva Conventions and has a National Society. Over most of the world the emblem of the Red Cross has remained the reversed Swiss flag, a red cross on a white background, honoring its Swiss founder. Exceptions are the Moslem countries, which use the red crescent, and Iran, which uses a red lion and sun.

RUTH C. REYNOLDS

Frédéric Passy
(1901)

The first Nobel Prize for Peace was awarded to Frédéric Passy and Henri Dunant in 1901. Frédéric Passy was known as "The Apostle of Peace"—a title he richly earned. For 65 years he trod lecture platforms, put pen to paper, pouring out a prolific output from pamphlets to books, and with scholarly acumen used his training in law and economic theory in efforts to track down and destroy the causes of war.

Passy was moved by the Crimean War and the Loire flood to question why humanity could be callous to suffering in war yet feel sympathy to that caused by natural disasters. For him it was not an idle question, but rather the catalyst which thrust a generally liberal humanitarian into a lifelong commitment to a "war against war." Into this fight Passy carried two overriding weapons: a belief in free trade and a faith in arbitration. He thought that hostilities found nourishment in the acrid brew of competition, and he ardently supported the cause of free trade through which, he thought, competitors would be turned into partners in common enterprise, with the resulting environment dissolving away the cause of war.

Passy was a persuasive man. He wrote eloquent pleas in the journal *Le Temps* for peace between France and Prussia in their contest over Luxembourg in 1867, and he was widely credited for helping to avert a threatened war. In the same year he founded the Ligue Internationale de la Paix, later known as the Société Française pour l'Arbitrage entre les Nations. In 1871, following the Franco-German war, he published *Revanche ou Relévement* (Revenge or Retreat), a famous appeal for a solid peace between France and Germany on the basis of voluntary arbitration, with Alsace-Lorraine as an independent neutral area.

His greatest tool for arbitration was an organization he co-founded with William Cremer (Nobel Peace Prize winner for 1903) designed to further communication, collaboration, and understanding—all tools of arbitration—between the legislators of the nations of the world. Called the Interparliamentary Union, it created regularly spaced occasions for the members of parliamentary bodies of as many nations as could be so persuaded to meet and discuss issues, to explore ways of improving collaboration between nations through their parliaments, and above all, to iron out conflicts before they could grow into "causes" in the arena of international hostilities. "It is an important assembly," Passy said, "not only on account of the number, but also the character of the members, among whom are the presidents or vice-presidents of several legislative assemblies of Europe."

Like many of Passy's projects, the Interparliamentary Union prospered. Passy recalled that the first meeting was held in a hotel parlor. Since then, he said, "they have been convened in the capital of Rome, and presided over by the president of the Chamber of Deputies, and at Bern in the Federal Palace . . . at The Hague, and at Brussels in the Senate Chamber." The Union functioned through the influence and character of its members, and its only means of enforcement was through moral authority.

Passy was twice elected to the French Chamber of Deputies, and while he was there he successfully urged arbitration in a dispute between France and the Netherlands over French Guiana. He also supported legislation favorable to labor, opposed the colonial policy of the government, drafted a proposal for disarmament, and presented a resolution calling for arbitration of international disputes.

Passy was capable of an unvarnished assessment of the perennial state of Europe. When he looked beyond the earnest endeavors carried on within the walls of peace conferences, beyond the work of others laboring in the field of peace, and out upon the cold reality of world events, he could speak with biting realism. In a lecture he delivered in 1891 he said, "I need hardly describe the present state of Europe to you. The entire able-bodied population is preparing to massacre one another; though no one, it is true, wants to attack and everybody protests his love of peace and determination to maintain it, yet the whole world feels that it only requires some unforeseen incident, some unpreventable accident, for the spark to fall in a flash . . . ."

But when he was immersed in the most absorbing work of his life, writing of the peace congresses, the parliamentary approach to arbitration, then another side of Passy, that aspect of the man that enabled him to never yield to discouragement, emerged. In 1896, he wrote in a stunning article published in the *American Journal of Sociology* a summary of the many successes of the peace movements. He closed this article saying, "As for myself, I have labored unceasingly in this cause for thirty years, and in spite of temporary defeats and mortifications, I have never despaired of ultimate success . . . the horizon is brightening; deeds have spoken louder than words; the public mind is awakening to the necessity of arbitration. Nothing now remains for those who have fought in its behalf but a little more perseverance and hope . . . it is time to say openly . . . that the reign of violence is over and the universal conscience demands the rule of justice."

Biography

Frédéric Passy was born in 1822 in Paris, where he lived all his life. Educated as a lawyer, he left the French civil service to continue his education in the field of economics. As a theoretical economist he wrote *Mélanges économiques*, a collection of essays relating to his research. He established his scholarly reputation with his lecturing at the University of Montpellier. He belonged to the liberal tradition of the British economists Richard Cobden and John Bright, and was an ardent advocate of free trade.

He was also a firm believer in arbitration, and he worked vigorously for replacing war with arbitration as an instrument of conducting international relations. His eloquent plea for peace in *Le Temps* helped avert war between France and Prussia over Luxembourg. Following the Franco-German war he proposed arbitration between the two countries and independence for Alsace-Lorraine. As a member of the French Chamber of Deputies for terms beginning in 1881 and 1885, he successfully urged arbitration of a dispute between the Netherlands and France concerning the French Guiana-Surinam boundary. With William Cremer he founded the Interparliamentary Union, a vehicle for communication, collaboration, and, in case of difficulties, arbitration between members of the parliaments of all the countries who could be persuaded to participate, including countries in the New World.

His *Pour la Paix*, written when he was 87 years old, is an account of his work for international peace, including the founding of the Ligue Internationale de la Paix and the Interparliamentary Union, the development of peace congresses, and the value of the Hague Conferences.

He died in Paris on June 12, 1912.

Bibliography

Passy F 1896 Peace movement in Europe. *Am. J. Sociol.* 2(1)

RUTH C. REYNOLDS

Elie Ducommun
(1902)

The Chairman of the Nobel Peace Committee, Jorgen Gunnarson Lovland, in toasting Elie Ducommun and Charles-Albert Gobat, who shared the 1902 Peace Prize, commented on their Swiss nationality, saying that it was quite natural that three of the first four Nobel Prize winners should be Swiss because Switzerland had long been a haven for the persecuted, offering sympathy and support for peace, humanity, justice, and brotherhood among nations. Lovland thanked Ducommun for his work toward peace, done during the long, difficult years when it was received with a shaking of heads and a shrugging of shoulders, with apathy, if not with contempt.

By the close of the century, however, the peace movement had escalated beyond apathy and contempt to an increasing worldwide acceptance which Frédéric Passy, co-winner of the first Nobel Prize for Peace, described in the *American Journal of Sociology* (July 1896): "A few years ago it would have been an easy task to give an account of the peace movement in Europe, at least so far as its outward manifestations were concerned. Although there had been peace congresses held at more or less frequent intervals in Brussels, London, Frankfurt, Paris or Geneva . . . they seemed to have little influence. Times have changed."

"In the first place a most striking and significant fact is the ever-increasing rapidity with which these societies for the promotion of peace have sprung up." In the United Kingdom, the Peace Society was the only important one of its kind for a long time. "Today it has the satisfaction of seeing numerous societies which have sprung up . . . ." The story was repeated in France, and he wrote that Italy, "oppressed as it is by its military system, is a perfect hotbed for anti-military societies." Especially noteworthy progress had been accomplished in all of central Europe, in Prussia, and in Austria-Hungary. Not more than two or three years previously there had been only one peace society in Germany; "today there are at least thirty . . . . Belgium and Holland have their own societies which are daily increasing in numbers and influence." All of these societies were putting out publications of their own, more or less widely circulated, newspapers, pamphlets, reviews, tracts, and programs. Books and periodicals were proliferating.

Such was the burgeoning nature of the international peace movement which found its first civil servant in Elie Ducommun. But the movement "was not an organic, living body," Passy said. It was only with the establishment of an authorized and permanent central information bureau for all peace work that the peace societies were united in an organic whole. Called the Bureau Internationale Permanente de la Paix (Permanent International Bureau of Peace), it was located in Bern, Switzerland, and Ducommun became its indefatigable general-secretary. Serving without pay, he organized the bureau into an institution Passy described as "the heart and brain of the whole movement, in both the old world and the new."

Passy wrote, "it has accomplished for international peace and justice that which has been done in other departments by international postal and telegraph bureaus, and by international copyright laws. By this means all the different publications on this subject are collected, news is recorded, information obtained, doubtful or obscure questions explained, propositions forwarded and opinions received. Thus it is coming to be, under the efficient direction ... of M. Elie Ducommun, the living soul of the great body of peacemakers all over the world" (Passy 1896).

It was a monumental undertaking, both administratively and in its sheer clerical scope, and Ducommun achieved it alone, including issuing a bimonthly news-sheet, *Correspondence Bimensuelle*. Despite this burden, he still found the time to edit and write numerous articles and pamphlets. In one of the most famous of these, he refuted the popular idea that war, when it came, though fearful, would necessarily be of very short duration. He argued that, on the contrary, a system of trenches and fortresses could lead to a long-drawn-out war of attrition with alternating advances and retreats. He foretold, with awful accuracy, the shape of things to come in the First World War.

In addition, with the help of a council of 19 members, Ducommun planned the International Peace Congresses and implemented their decisions. All of this formidable peace work was accomplished in the free time he had after other considerable pursuits. He was, for example, a member of the Grand Council in Bern for ten years. For 30 years, beginning in 1875, he was secretary-general of the Jura-Bern-Lucerne railroad, later called the Jura-Simplon line, a position that required, according to Frédéric Passy, "the rarest qualities of exactitude, order, activity, and firmness." These qualities Ducommun also devoted to directing the International Bureau of Peace, as witnessed by its progress. This organization was run single handedly by Ducommun and the work was continued by Charles-Albert Gobat with whom he shared the Peace Prize.

In his Nobel lecture Ducommun commented on one question often asked of pacifists: "Granted that war is evil, what can you find to put in its place when an amicable solution becomes impossible? The treaties of arbitration concluded in the past few years provide an answer," he said. "The Convention for the Pacific Settlement of International Disputes signed at The Hague in 1899 by twenty-six nations offers a solution to international conflicts by a method unknown in the ancient world, in the Middle Ages, or even in modern history—a method of settling quarrels between nations without bloodshed."

Biography

Elie Ducommun was born on February 19, 1833, son of a clockmaker from Neuchâtel, Switzerland. After completing his early studies in Geneva at the age of 17, he tutored in a wealthy family in Saxony for three years and perfected his German. Upon his return to Geneva, he taught in public schools for two years. He then began a career in journalism which would prove to be a distinguished one, editing first a political journal, the *Revue de Genéve*, and upon moving to Bern, founding a radical journal, *Der Fortschrift* (*Progress*), which was also published in French under the title *Progrés*. He took an active part in the movement for European union, editing the news-sheet *Les États-Unis d'Europe*, published by the Ligue Internationale de la Paix et de la Liberté (International League for Peace and Freedom) founded in 1867. In 1871 he edited *Helvétie*. He also published poetry.

Ducommun held political posts of local consequence: in Geneva, prior to his leaving in 1865, he was a member of the Grand Council for nine years, becoming vice-chancellor in 1857 and chancellor of the state of Geneva in 1862. In Bern he was a member of the Grand Council for 10 years. For 30 years, beginning in 1875, he was secretary-general of the Jura-Simplon railroad line.

In 1889 Ducommun participated in the first of the regular International Peace Congresses. Two years later he became general-secretary of the newly founded International Peace Bureau, to which he devoted much time and for which he published *Correspondance Bimensuelle*. He wrote a number of articles and pamphlets for the peace movement and lectured.

Elie Ducommun died in Bern on December 7, 1906.

Bibliography ─────────────────────────

Passy F 1896 Peace movement in Europe. *Am. J. Sociol.* 2(1)

RUTH C. REYNOLDS

Charles-Albert Gobat
(1902)

The peace societies, which the Nobel Committee Chairman, Jorgen Gunnarsson Lovland, called "the popular peace movement," were doubly honored by the award of the 1902 Peace Prize to two of their strongest advocates, Charles-Albert Gobat and Elie Ducommun. Chairman Lovland congratulated Dr. Gobat as a practitioner of a new type of diplomacy—parliamentary diplomacy. "Far from finding himself in opposition," Lovland said, "he has already demonstrated that these two kinds of diplomatic service can and do exist in cordial cooperation."

Charles-Albert Gobat was a gifted lawyer, legislator, educator, and advocate for peace. He simultaneously practiced law and taught at Bern University. He became interested in education and rose to a top administrative position as superintendent of public instruction for the Canton of Bern. He demonstrated his liberal bent by his progressive reforms in primary training, by lowering the pupil-teacher ratio, by introducing studies in living languages, and by providing vocational and professional training as alternatives to strict classical education. He demonstrated his capability as administrator by getting the budgetary means for supporting his program.

Concurrent with this activity, Gobat applied himself with customary vigor and effect to a political career. In 1882 he was elected to the Grand Council of Bern, and he was president of the cantonal government from 1886 to 1887. From 1884 to 1890 he was a member of the Council of States of Switzerland, and from 1890 until his death a member of the National Council.

Gobat was attracted to the Interparliamentary Union from its inception by two recipients of the Nobel Peace Prize, William Cremer (1903) and Frédéric Passy (1901). It was a vehicle admirably suited to embrace his advocacy of peace through arbitration. The Union offered opportunities for members of parliaments from all countries to discuss international issues with each other, and thereby to enhance collaboration among nations through the means of parliamentary and democratic institutions. Transcending national boundaries without limiting the independence of any nation, or setting itself above the parliaments to which its members belonged, it was, in the words of Frédéric Passy (1896), "indeed a higher parliament, but one which possesses its influence through the weight and character of its members themselves, and which exerts a moral authority." Its most vital objective was to achieve international arbitration. In the intervals between the sessions of the Interparliamentary Union it was represented by a delegation of 15 members over whom Gobat presided. This delegation was charged with monitoring the political scene in the name of the Union.

Gobat ardently promoted arbitration. As a legisla-

tor he sponsored its application to Swiss commercial treaties wherein all treaties contained a clause which required the submission of any conflicts between the signing parties to the Permanent Court of Arbitration at The Hague.

When Gobat was presiding at the Union's fourth conference in 1892 at Bern, it established the Interparliamentary Bureau, choosing Bern as its locale. Gobat directed this Bureau for the next 17 years. Like the Permanent International Bureau of Peace, the Interparliamentary Bureau was a permanent information and administrative office. Gobat supervised the myriad details involved in listing parliamentary groups of various countries, initiating formation of groups where none existed, acting as a link between national groups, keeping track of activities in the peace movement and in the field of arbitration, attending to the administration of conferences, their agendas, and publications of proceedings, and presiding over a monthly publication for which he frequently wrote contributions. This he did almost unaided, and without remuneration.

It was decided in 1904 at the twelfth Interparliamentary Conference to call for a second Hague Peace Conference. Gobat, acting as the Union's spokesman, asked the US President, Theodore Roosevelt, to appeal to all nations to participate. Roosevelt consented, and shortly thereafter had the US Secretary of State issue a circular to the other nations.

In his Nobel lecture, Gobat described the important potentialities he visualized coming from future Hague Conferences: "Civilization and morality have not yet influenced nations to consider inviolable a promise or agreement, solemnly signed and sealed, when it becomes part of international law. Ordinary citizens are obliged and, if need be, compelled by force to meet their commitments. But let higher obligations of an international order be involved, and governments repudiate them, more often than not with a disdainful shrug of the shoulders."

This dilemma he saw amenable to a system of conciliation and mediation wherein with every possible conflict there would be an already established group of nations from which at least one could offer its good offices. "Good offices" would mean intercession between the belligerents in an effort to effect conciliation. A further step would be mediation. Whereas good offices would be limited to assuring preliminary conciliation, the mediator could go so far as to propose terms of settlement.

Gobat cited an instance in which such a procedure had actually worked. President Theodore Roosevelt (Nobel Peace Prize winner for 1906) persisted in offering his good offices to the warring Russians and Japanese. Exhausted by a terrible war, both accepted and peace was concluded. Thus President Roosevelt was the first head of state to apply the rules of the Hague Convention concerning the preservation of general peace.

Upon the death of Elie Ducommun in 1906, Gobat succeeded him as director of the International Peace Bureau, itself subsequently a Nobel Peace Prize winner in 1910.

Gobat had the privilege of living to the last moment of his life doing that in which he most believed. On March 16, 1914, while attending a meeting of the peace conference at Bern, he arose as if to speak and collapsed. He died shortly after.

Biography

Charles-Albert Gobat was born in Tramelan, Switzerland, son of a Protestant pastor. A gifted scholar, he studied at the Universities of Basel, Heidelberg, Bern and Paris, and took his law degree *summa cum laude* from Heidelberg in 1867. His legal career included both the practice of law and teaching at Bern University. He opened an office in Delemont in the Canton of Bern which became a leading legal firm.

After 15 years Gobat became interested in education and was appointed superintendent of public instruction for the Canton of Bern. During his 30 years in this position he introduced such progressive measures as lowered pupil-teacher ratio, studies in living languages, and vocational and professional training as an alternative to strict classical education.

In the 1880s he became active in cantonal and national politics, and in 1882 he was elected to the Grand Council of Bern. He was elected president of the cantonal government for the 1886-1887 term. From 1884 to 1890 he was a member of the Council of States of Switzerland, and from 1890 a lifelong member of the National Council.

From its inception in 1888, Gobat worked with the Interparliamentary Union, an organization in which members of parliaments from all nations could meet, discuss, and it was hoped, arbitrate in disputes before they became insurmountable problems.

When the Interparliamentary Bureau was founded as an action of the fourth Union Conference, its locale placed in Bern, Gobat became its general-secretary, keeping available information about peace movements, international conciliation, and communication among national parliamentary bodies. This he did with devotion and without remuneration.

Upon the death of Elie Ducommun, who headed the Permanent International Bureau of Peace, Gobat stepped into this role.

Best known among his books on international affairs is *Le Couchemar de l'Europe* (The Nightmare of Europe), which he wrote in 1911.

Charles-Albert Gobat died on March 16, 1914, while in attendance at a peace conference.

Bibliography —————————————————

Passy F 1896 Peace movement in Europe. *Am. J. Sociol.* 2(1)

RUTH C. REYNOLDS

Sir William Randal Cremer
(1903)

The 1903 Nobel Prize for Peace was awarded to William Cremer in recognition of the 34 years of effective work he devoted to the cause of peace, most notably through the initiation and organization of the Interparliamentary Union. "It has been the great object of my life to build up and endow a great peace organization which should be powerful enough to combat the forces which make for war," Cremer declared in his Nobel lecture.

That was an impressive goal to be realized by a child of an impoverished family of the working class. Cremer was born in Fareham, England, in 1828 to a coach painter and his wife. Cremer's indomitable mother raised her three Children alone when the father deserted his family during Cremer's infancy.

Through sacrifice and determination she sent her son to a Methodist church school, but when he was 15 his formal education ended as he entered the building trade as an apprentice carpenter.

Cremer supplemented his meager education by attending lectures, and one night he heard a lecture which powerfully affected the course of his life. The speaker suggested that international disputes could be settled by arbitration. It was an idea that found fertile soil in Cremer's mind, and he was destined for a powerful role in bringing it to successful fruition.

The young carpenter proved to be a gifted administrator. In 1858, at the age of 30, he was elected to a labor council campaigning for a nine-hour day; later that year he was one of seven who directed labor during a lock-out of 70,000 workers. He helped form a union for his trade, the Amalgamated Society of Carpenters and Joiners. In 1870 he formed a workers' committee to promote the United Kingdom's neutrality during the Franco-Prussian conflict. This committee developed into the International Arbitration League. "We were laughed to scorn as mere theorists and utopians," he said. "The scoffers declaring that no two countries in the world would ever agree to take part in the establishment of such a court."

By then a recognized leader, Cremer went to Parliament in 1885 and remained there for the rest of his lifetime, except for the period 1895-1900 when he suffered his single defeat in the hustings. Cremer used his power as a Member of Parliament to advance his sustained work for peace.

The Hague Tribunal became a reality, with the initiating efforts of Cremer's workers' committee having played a vital role in its creation. The wealthy US industrialist Andrew Carnegie supplied funds for the construction of its home in the Palace of Peace at The Hague. In his Nobel lecture, Cremer recalled some of its successes: in 1904 a Russian fleet fired on English fishing trawlers at Dogger Bank, sinking a vessel and damaging five others, in the process killing two and wounding six. Despite the "frantic efforts of some British journals to provoke a conflict," the two governments agreed to resort to the offices of the Hague Tribunal. The affair ended with Russia paying an indemnity of £65,000.

With its peacekeeping machinery at the ready, the Hague Tribunal accomplished many friendly mediations and arbitrations. By far the most important was the dispute between the United States and the United Kingdom when the *Alabama*, a ship constructed at British shipyards for the Confederacy during the Civil War, manned by a Southern captain with a partially British crew, wreaked havoc with Northern shipping. The Hague ruled in favor of the United States, and the British accepted the decision (see Articles: *Arbitration, International*).

In 1887 Cremer felt the League came into its "proven phase" when the governments of the United Kingdom and the United States entered into a treaty which bound them to settle their differences by arbitration. It set a precedent, and within 12 months 13 similar treaties were concluded between various nations: Great Britain and France; France and Italy; Great Britain and Italy; Denmark and Holland; Great Britain and Spain; France and Spain; France and Holland; Spain and Portugal: Germany and Great Britain; Great Britain, Norway, and Sweden; Great Britain and Portugal; Switzerland and Great Britain;

Sweden, Norway, and Belgium. Seven other treaties had been drafted between the United States and European countries at the time of Cremer's accounting during the Nobel award lecture.

Cremer answered skeptics about the actual use of the treaties once drawn up with the example of France and Great Britain. "All of the differences between the two countries, some of which had lasted for centuries, have been equitably adjusted," he said in a review of the first 12 months of the treaty. He was confident that under the treaties disputing nations would have time, during arbitration, to cool their tempers and the chances of war would be greatly diminished.

This "people's victory," fruit of the efforts of the British and French workers who inaugurated the first Treaty of Arbitration, excited the interest of Frédéric Passy and other French deputies, and together they expanded Cremer's efforts into a new force, called the Interparliamentary Union. The Union provided opportunities for members of parliaments from every cooperating country to meet together, discuss issues, and if any disputes were imminent, to prevent them from becoming "causes" and fanned into military conflicts.

Passy, co-winner of the first Nobel Peace Prize, described the participants of the Interparliamentary Union in an article published by the *American Journal of Sociology* (July 1896): "It is an important assembly, not only on account of the number, but also the character of the members, among whom are the presidents or vice-presidents of several legislative assemblies of Europe . . . it is indeed a higher parliament, but one which possesses its influence through the weight and character of its members themselves and which exerts a moral authority . . . ."

In his Nobel lecture Cremer pointed out that the Union had not only reduced frictions between European countries, but had also brought together the United States and European countries, with resulting increased understanding between nations of the Old World and the New. "There is still a great work before us," Cremer declared in closing his lecture. "The advocates of peace are, however, no longer regarded as idle dreamers . . . our cause has, especially of late, made wonderful progress and we are nearing the goal of our hopes."

Cremer gave the money from his Nobel prize to the International Arbitration League. Thus he realized his lifelong dream of endowing a great peace organization which would combat the forces that generate war.

Biography

William Randal Cremer was born in Fareham, England, on March 18, 1828. He was the son of a coach painter who deserted his family of two daughters and the infant Cremer, and of an indomitable mother who saw that he got some education before he entered the workforce as an apprentice in the building trade. He became a leader among the workers, helping to found a union, the Amalgamated Society of Carpenters and Joiners. He realized the first step in his life-long dream of contributing to a peaceful world by forming a workers' committee to advocate British neutrality during the Franco-Prussian War (1870-1871). This group developed into the Workmen's Peace Association, which in turn contributed to the creation of the International Arbitration League, of which Cremer became Secretary. It ultimately developed into the Hague Tribunal.

Cremer was elected to the House of Commons in 1885;

with the exception of five years, from 1895 to 1900, he remained there until his death. He attracted the notice of Frédéric Passy, and in 1888 the two founded the Interparliamentary Union, a mechanism for the free communication between Members of Parliaments internationally, and for arbitration in international affairs through ongoing communication and understanding between Members of Parliaments.

Cremer married twice, his first wife dying in 1876, his second in 1884. He was knighted in 1907. He died in London in 1908.

Bibliography

Passy F 1896 Peace movement in Europe. *Am. J. Sociol.* 2(1)

RUTH C. REYNOLDS

Institute of International Law
(1904)

In 1904 the Nobel Peace Prize was awarded to the Institute of International Law (Institute de Droit International). Under its banner of *Justica et Pace* (justice and peace), this Institute of a totally private nature seeks to provide the general principles of international jurisprudence needed to underlie effective work for peace. "We cannot hope to achieve peace until law and justice regulate international as well as national relations," its president, Georg Hagerup, said in receiving the 1904 award. "*Justica et Pace* means eliminating, as far as possible, the sources of international friction which result from uncertainties and differences of opinion in the interpretation of the law. It means constructing by unremitting and patient work, block by block, the foundation that will support the rule of law over nations and peoples."

Presently located in Geneva, as of 1986 the Institute has a total of 60 members and 72 associates. It continues to promote the progress of international law wherein its range of activity covers the codification of international law, both public and private. In private international law, it strives to minimize or eliminate difficulties from differences existing in laws of different countries. In public law, it works to develop peaceful ties between nations. The organization may be credited for many previously unwritten and inexact laws now codified, legislated, and placed on statute books.

Founded in 1873 by G. Rolin-Jaquemyns, a Bel-

gian jurist, and editor of the *Revue de droit international et de législation comparée*, with 10 distinguished jurists from as many countries, this private association of scholars from all nations who come together for the study, codification, and promotion of international law draws its members from candidates who have made a scholarly contribution in either the area of theory or of practice in international law, and who are free from political pressures. The Institute strives for a reasonably balanced representation from the nations of the world.

In his Nobel lecture, Hagerup warned against too easy an interpretation of arbitration, pointing out that careful preparatory work is required. It is in this area that the Institute of International Law has supplied invaluable services. The Institute was charged with most of the burden of preparing for the First International Arbitration Conferences at the Hague in 1899 and 1907, and these conferences utilized the Institute's studies on the laws of war, expecially those on the codification of land war prepared at its 1880 session in Oxford called *Handbook of the Rules and Observances of Warfare*. Recognizing the "considerable place war occupies in the pages of history," the Institute sought in this handbook to reduce the destruction of war. During the Russo-Turkish War, it facilitated the neutralization of the Suez Canal in the event of war, under the principle of neutralizing all areas vital to international communication. Similarly, under the influence of the Institute, submarine cables were given international protection in a treaty signed by 27 states in Paris on March 14, 1884. Also, the Interparliamentary Union, founded in 1888 for the purpose of establishing and maintaining permanent lines of communication and conferences between members of parliaments from various countries over the world, acknowledged dependence upon the Institute for assistance based upon international public law.

Between 1873 and 1969, 15 directly applicable resolutions and many other indirectly applicable resolutions coming from the Institute were used in settlements of international disputes. Its range in time and subject covers from the above international treaties of the 1880s on the Suez Canal and on the submarine cable to recent discussions by the Institute on pollution of international waters providing direction for research on that pressing, contemporary problem.

The Institute has worked out general rules in the area of private international law. It formulated codifications of extradition rules, of uniform treatment of marriage, divorce and trusteeship, of rights of citizenship, of treatment of private property during wartime.

The Institute of International Law does not itself participate in the settlement of international controversies. (There is a historical exception to this rule in its adoption of a resolution in 1877 pertaining to the application of international law in the war between Russia and Turkey.)

Hagerup's closing remarks on the Institute of International Law in his 1904 Nobel lecture have proven prophetic: "If our work has had some success, it is undoubtedly because of our efforts to 'calculate the limits of the possible,' as one great statesman put it; because of our patience in refusing to advocate premature solutions; and because of our belief in the necessity of developing *gradually* and *progressively* as our statutes bid us."

He said the Institute's independence of any authority or political faction constitutes its strength. The continuing study devoted to the nature of law, to the conditions of its development, and its place in the progress of human civilization in general, gave members the necessary perspective with which to judge factors holding the most promise to encourage support of international law and justice.

"All attempts to further human progress should have far-reaching aims," Hagerup said, "and those who wish to take an active part in the effort should not lose patience if the progress sometimes appears

to be very slow, or even to sustain interruptions and setbacks ... but let us take heart in the discerning word spoken by Mirabeau a century ago: 'Law will one day become the sovereign of the world.'"

History

The Institute of International Law (Institute de Droit International) was founded by a group of international jurists in 1873 in recognition of the need to promote international law, in both private and public fields. Their guiding spirit and initiator was Gustave Rolin-Jaquemyns, a Belgian jurist and editor of the *Revue de droit international et de législation comparée*, who following the Franco-Prussian War of 1870-71, began a correspondence with jurists over the world to seek ways of establishing collective action toward creating a body of international law.

At his invitation 10 eminent jurists assembled for meetings in the town Hall of Ghent in September, 1873: Tobias Asser of the Netherlands (Nobel Peace Prize Winner in 1911), Wladimir Besobrasoff of Russia, J.K. Bluntschli of Germany, Carlos Calvo of Argentina, David Dudly Field of the United States, Emile de Laveleye of Belgium, James Lorimer of Great Britain, P.S. Mancini of Italy, Gustave Moynier of Switzerland, and Augusto Pierantoni of Italy. This group established the Institute, electing Mancini President. They held their first session in Geneva in 1874 at which time they established the general principles for international judicial proceedings; the next year the Institute formulated rules for the competency of the tribunals. The actual forms of procedure were dealt with in 1877 and the following year the rules were drawn up for the execution of judgments.

The participants are confined to jurists with a demonstrated record of scholarly attainment, either practical or theoretical, and who are free of political pressures. Maintaining a balanced representation from the nations of the world further influences choice of membership. The participants fall into three categories. The associates are kept at 72 in number. This group forms the source from which the members, 60 in number, are drawn. Members deal with administrative matters such as finances, regulations, and election of members and honorary members. They choose the third category of participants, honorary members, from persons distinguished in the field of law.

The president is usually selected from the country scheduled to host the next session of the Institute, and, along with the first vice-president, is elected at the end of a given session. These two officers remain in office until the close of the following session. The second and third vice-presidents are elected at the opening of each session and remain in office until the start of the next session. The secretary-general and the treasurer are elected for three sessions and may succeed themselves. These six officers form the body of the Bureau of the Institute, which holds and exercises the executive power of the Institute.

Following the Nobel Prize, and with additional grants from the Carnegie Endowment for International Peace, plus lesser gifts, the Institute has accrued the financial footing with which to reimburse members for travel expenses, to underwrite the expenses of the sessions, and to pay for publications.

The Institute conducts a continuous study of existing international law, but it does not intervene in actual international disputes. It does, however, formulate and endorse specific proposals serving the goal of creating an international community respecting law and justice.

See also: *Articles: Arbitration, International; International Law*

Bibliography ————————————————

Abrams I 1957 The emergence of the International Law Societies. *Review of Politics* 19

RUTH C. REYNOLDS

Baroness Bertha Sophie Felicita von Suttner
(1905)

The 1905 Nobel Peace Prize went to the Austrian Baroness Bertha von Suttner. Of all the peace leaders of the quarter century before 1914, she enjoyed the greatest international reputation. To her contemporaries this handsome woman of dignified presence seemed to personify the cause she served. Her fellow peace workers called her their "general-in-chief"; her detractors scoffed at "Peace-Bertha" and delighted in the cartoons that satirized the peace movement in her womanly form. Whether drawing applause, brickbats, or simply public attention, she was certainly one of the best-known women of her day.

The Peace Prize was the supreme recognition of the Baroness's many contributions to the peace cause. She was the author of the most widely read antiwar novel of the time, *Die Waffen nieder!*, (see Articles: *Die Waffen nieder!*), a tireless propagandist for peace by pen and in lectures throughout the Germanic countries and as far afield as the United States, a major figure at world peace congresses, an organizer and inspirer of peace societies in Germany and Austria-Hungary. More quietly, she carried the peace message in personal meetings with statesmen and diplomats.

These may seem unusual attainments for the former Countess Bertha Kinsky, a descendant of army officers, born in 1843 in the Austro-Hungarian empire, but the Countess did not remain on the conventional paths marked out for a highborn Austrian lady. After acquiring foreign languages and social graces, she very early asserted her independence. When her family fortunes were depleted, she took a job to earn her own living as governess to the daughters of the Baron von Suttner. She and the son of the family fell in love and eloped to the Caucasus. There they read widely in science, philosophy, and history and became published writers themselves. Finally forgiven by the von Suttner family, the couple returned to Austria to take their place among the liberal intelligentsia of that center of intellectual and cultural fermentation.

As a firm believer in Immanuel Kant's ethical idealism (see Articles: *Kant, Immanuel*) and in evolution and progress, it was not unusual that Bertha von Suttner chose to write a novel on the evils of war which seemed so out of keeping with the future she envisaged. What was not to be expected was that her research on the wars of the mid-century would make her such a committed pacifist, nor that the novel would meet with such stunning success and involve her "with all my being" in the newly developing peace movement.

The novel was published in 1889, just when the modern peace movement was organizing internationally. While peace-minded deputies from national legislatures were establishing the Interparliamentary Union, representatives from peace societies emerging on the Continent were meeting with their Anglo-Saxon counterparts to take up again the world peace congresses that had not been held for many years. The Baroness soon became one of the leaders of the movement, vice-president of the Commission of the International Peace Bureau when it was established in 1892 to provide some coordination for the unofficial peace efforts in the different countries. She inspired and organized peace societies and interparliamentary groups in Central Europe and served as an important force for moderation and conciliation when political and religious differences arose.

In reading through her abundant correspondence which she carried on in three languages—letters selected for her *Memoirs*, and those unpublished but fortunately preserved in the Library of the United Nations in Geneva—one is impressed by the high regard in which she was held by her co-workers, and one marvels at the extent and variety of her exchanges with so many influential personages from all over Europe—politicians, diplomats, writers, professors, and others.

Among her friends was Alfred Nobel, the dynamite magnate, whom she had known before she became a pacifist and who had written to congratulate her after reading *Die Waffen nieder!* The letters they exchanged tell of how the Baroness cultivated his interest in the peace movement, first enlisting his financial support for her own peace efforts and eventually contributing to his decision to endow the movement through his Peace Prize. It is clear from their correspondence and other evidence that Nobel never expected that the Baroness would have to wait until the fifth year of these awards to receive her own prize.

Suttner poured her creative energies so completely into her work for peace that after *Die Waffen nieder!* she never wrote another successful novel, but in her writing on international events for the peace periodicals she displayed skills as a most perceptive and adept political commentator, the first woman political journalist in the German language.

In conjunction with the meeting of the First Hague Peace Conference (1899), Suttner held a salon for the delegates that was the first effective international peace lobby on record. Through their discussions with the diplomats the Baroness and the other peace advocates succeeded in persuading the conferees of the importance of establishing machinery to resolve international conflicts rather than concerning themselves exclusively with the less hopeful matter of reduction of armaments, which the Czar's original call for the conference had emphasized. It turned out that the Hague Conference produced negligible results for disarmament, but at least a first step was taken in the direction of peacekeeping machinery through the agreement to establish the Permanent Court of Arbitration at The Hague.

Although the Baroness talked of the need for a federation of Europe, it was the institutionalization of arbitration that was the more immediate objective of the Baroness and her friends. They wanted to be looked upon as practical reformers, not just visionaries, and they did not urge a fundamental change in the international order. As established members of the upper and middle classes, even further from their minds was the contention of the socialists that the

only way to end war was to change the social order. The two groups agreed only on their criticisms of war and war policies. The German Social Democrats did run *Die Waffen nieder!* in their newspaper, but the Baroness had not written it to arouse the masses to political action.

Such was the basis of the most biting criticism of Bertha von Suttner, written by a German pacifist 10 years after her death. Carl von Ossietzky, no socialist but a staunch antimilitarist journalist (and 1935 Peace Prize laureate), blamed her for starting off the German peace movement on the wrong track with her "tearful novel." He paid her honor for her "extraordinary and honest efforts" but said that "she fought with holy water against cannon, she adored with touching childishness treaties and institutions—a priestess of sentiment, she appealed to the consciences of kings and statesmen . . . ."

It is unfortunate that Bertha von Suttner is remembered by so many only for her portrayal of human suffering in her novel. Through the years, in her day-to-day activities as pacifist and lecturer, she appealed for the exercise of reason and good sense in the conduct of foreign policy. Her commentaries on world affairs pointed again and again to the fateful consequences of ill-conceived policies. Her Nobel lecture was no sentimental denunciation of war but a reasoned appeal for peace, based upon an abiding faith in the moral evolution of humanity and a conviction that she was serving "the greatest of all causes."

This faith sustained her in the face of the abuse of the militarists and jingoists and the much more serious obstacle of general apathy. At the end of the century there had been no major war for a generation and public opinion was complacent, concerned at most with the burdens of the armed peace rather than with the fear of war. Even the measure of success that the peace leaders gained at the First Hague Conference evoked little general response. "Cold, cold are all the hearts," the Baroness lamented, noting that there was far more interest in current sports events.

It was particularly difficult to raise the flag of peace in the empires of Germany and Austria-Hungary, where military institutions were deeply rooted. Yet her activities there helped the peace forces in other countries to maintain that the movement was indeed international.

Bertha von Suttner set a precedent for the leadership that women would one day be taking in the international peace movement. The Baroness was "general-in-chief," at a time when a woman was neither expected nor encouraged to play a role as a public figure. It would take another 25 years, in fact, before the Norwegian Nobel Committee would bestow their next Peace Prize on a woman, Jane Addams.

Fate spared Bertha von Suttner from having to witness the catastrophe she had labored to prevent. She died in 1914 in Vienna, shortly before the outbreak of the First World War which brought the cancellation of the World Peace Congress which was to have met there in her honor, with the first showing of the Danish film of *Die Waffen nieder!*

The Baroness has since been honored in several countries through place names, postage stamps, and even an Austrian banknote. There is still a peace society in Vienna that keeps her memory alive. In 1989 the 100th anniversary of the publication of *Die Waffen nieder!* was commemorated in a number of events that took place in European countries, and in 1993 the 150th birthday of Bertha von Suttner was celebrated at a special exhibit at the Library of the United Nations in Geneva. The baroness has continued to be the subject of publications. The best biography, published in Germany in 1986 went through a number of editions and in 1997 appeared in English translation.

But who reads *Die Waffen nieder!* any more? The horrors of nineteenth-century warfare which it depicted so vividly were already outpaced in the war that began the year of her death. All the same, Suttner was the first to sound the alert so convincingly in a popular medium, and she was not unheard. The coming of the war in 1914 did not invalidate what the Baroness and her friends had been saying; it confirmed their warnings. She said in her Nobel lecture in 1906 that "this question of whether violence or law shall prevail between states is the most vital of the problems of our eventful era . . . . Inconceivable . . . would be the consequences of the threatening world war which many misguided people are prepared to precipitate."

The mediocre statesmen who stumbled into war in the summer of 1914 do not compare very favorably with the high-minded humanitarians who had tried so hard to prevent it. If we judge such humanitarians, working for a distant aim, rather by the quality of their effort than by their success or failure in bringing the new world into being, then Bertha von Suttner must receive the very highest marks.

Biography

Baroness Bertha von Suttner was born Bertha Felicie Sophie von Kinsky, in 1843 daughter of impoverished Austrian nobility. Her father, Count Franz Josef Kinsky, an Austrian field marshal, died shortly after her birth. On her mother's side she was descended from the family of the German poet, Theodor Körner. From 1873 to 1876 she was governess in the wealthy von Suttner family. In this position she met the family scion, Baron Gundaccar Arthur von Suttner, seven years her junior, and they fell in love with one another. The family opposing the match, Bertha von Kinksy answered an advertisement written by Alfred Nobel, a wealthy inventor, for a secretary. After an exchange of correspondence, she was invited for an interview and was accepted for the position. However, she stayed only five days, and then eloped with Baron von Suttner. The couple lived in the Caucasus, earning a meager living writing, supplemented by occasional other work, until they were received again in the von Suttner family, at which point they returned to Vienna.

Although her acquaintance with Nobel had been brief, it had lasting import, for they carried on a correspondence for the remainder of Nobel's life regarding their mutual interest in peace. It was through this correspondence that she exerted considerable influence toward his establishing the Nobel Peace Prize (see Articles: *Nobel Peace Prizes*). They met again in 1887 when the von Suttners were staying in Paris, and then in 1892 in Berne where the Baroness was attending a peace conference.

In 1888 Baroness von Suttner wrote *Das Maschinenzeitalter* (The Machine Age), and in 1889 the novel which was to catapult her to fame, *Die Waffen nieder!* (Lay Down Your Arms!). Tolstoy compared her novel to Uncle Tom's Cabin, an American novel which greatly promoted antislavery sentiment in the United States. It is generally considered that *Lay Down Your Arms!* was one of the most influential novels of the nineteenth century.

The Baroness founded the Austrian Peace Society (*Osterreichische Friedensgesellschaft*) in 1891, and the same year took a leading role in the International Peace Congress in Rome. She helped found the International Peace Bureau and became vice president of its governing Commission. In 1892 Alfred Fried, founder of the German Peace Society (and 1911 Peace Prize co-winner), started a periodical which he named after Baroness von Suttner's famous novel, and persuaded her to become its editor-in-chief. She remained in this position until 1899. She also attended many conferences and lectured extensively.

Baroness von Suttner's pacifism had a scientific and free-thinking basis, reflecting the thought of Herbert Spencer and Charles Darwin; it was intended to convince the upper and middle classes.

A prolific writer, she wrote not only on peace and social issues, but also tales of romances. Among her titles are: *Hanna* (1894), *Krieg und Frieden* (1986), *La Traviata* (1898), *Schach der Qual* (1898), *Die Haager Friedenskonferenz* (1900), and *Marthas Kinder* (1902). This last was a continuation of *Die Waffen nieder!*.

Baroness von Suttner died in Vienna in 1914, shortly before the outbreak of the First World War.

Bibliography ────────────────

Abrams I 1962 Bertha von Suttner and the Nobel Peace Prize. *Central European Affairs* XXII

Abrams I 1991 Bertha von Suttner (1843-1914). Bibliographical Notes. *Peace & Change. A Journal of Peace Research* 16

Braker R 1995 *Weapons of Women Writers. Bertha von Suttner's "Die Waffen nieder!" as Political Literature in the Tradition of Harriet Beecher Stowe's "Uncle Tom's Cabin."* New York

Chickering R 1975 *Imperial Germany and a World Without War: The Peace Movement and German Society, 1892-1914.* Princeton, New Jersey

Cooper S 1991 *Patriotic Pacifism. Waging War on War in Europe, 1815-1914.* New York, Oxford

Grossi V 1994 *Le Pacifisme Européen 1889-1914.* Brussels

Hamann B 1986 *Bertha von Suttner: Ein Leben für den Frieden.* Munich; tr. 1997 *Bertha von Suttner, A Life for Peace*, with introduction by I. Abrams. Syracuse, New York

Kempf B 1972 *Woman for Peace: The Life of Bertha von Suttner.* London

Lengyel E 1975 *And All Her Paths Were Peace: The Life of Bertha von Suttner.* Nashville

Pauli H 1957 *Cry of the Heart: The Story of Bertha von Suttner.* New York

Playne C E 1936 *Bertha von Suttner and the Struggle to Avert the World War.* London

Suttner B von 1972 The evolution of the peace movement, In: Haberman F W (ed.) 1972 *Nobel Lectures, Peace*, Vol. 1. Elsevier, Amsterdam

Suttner B von 1909 *Memoren.* Stuttgart (reissued as *Lebenserinnerungen*, ed. by Fritz Böttger East Berlin 1969; English transl. 1910. *Memoirs of Bertha von Suttner: The Records of an Eventful Life*, 2 vols. Boston, Massachusetts; reissued 1972, New York with introduction by Irwin Abrams)

Suttner B von 1889 *Die Waffen nieder! Eine Lebensgeschichte.* Dresden (English transl. 1892 *"Ground Arms!" The Story of a Life.* Chicago, Illinois; authorized transl. 1894; "revised by the authoress, 2nd edn. London; reissued 1972 as *Lay Down Your Arms! The Autobiography of Martha von Tilling.* New York, with introduction by Irwin Abrams)

IRWIN ABRAMS

Theodore Roosevelt
(1906)

The 1906 Nobel Peace Prize was awarded to Theodore Roosevelt in recognition of his successful mediation between Japan and Russia resulting in the Portsmouth Treaty in 1905. Roosevelt's award represented three new departures from previous choices: Roosevelt was the first American to receive the prize; he was the first statesman to be honored not for a lifetime of effort toward peace, but for one specific action; and his was the first award to arouse a storm of protest from peace societies on the charge of an attitude of belligerence and support of militarism.

Roosevelt was indeed on record as having eulogized war "as a necessary means of settling great national and international differences and problems." He proclaimed before the Naval War College in 1897 that "No triumph of peace is quite so great as the supreme triumphs of war . . . ." He feared that his fellow Americans were growing soft and would become "an easy prey for any people which still retained those most valuable of all qualities, the soldierly virtues" (quoted in Lipsky 1966 pp. 67-69).

But some of his actions were hallmarks in arbitration practiced by a head of state: Roosevelt was among the first to submit a dispute to arbitration at The Hague when he brought an old quarrel between the United States and Mexico before the International Court; he negotiated treaties with France, Germany, Portugal, and Switzerland, and thus directed world opinion toward arbitration and influenced other nations to use the court.

However, it was not his encouragement of arbitration but his success as mediator in ending the Russo-Japanese war which the Nobel Committee cited when it announced his award. Japan, having first attempted to use arbitration over the issue of Russia's eastward expansion in search of an ice-free Pacific port, resorted to war and defeated the Russian forces repeatedly but never decisively. The American Peace Society originally asked President Roosevelt to offer his services as mediator, but this he refused to do except by request of one of the belligerents. Japan then secretly encouraged Roosevelt to mediate. This he agreed to do, although he wrote privately to a friend, "I have not an idea whether I can or cannot get peace .... I have done my best. I have led the horses to water, but Heaven only knows whether they will drink or start kicking one another beside the trough." At the opening meeting of the adversaries he proposed a toast to the speedy achievement of a just and lasting peace. But such was not to be, and for three weeks two sets of envoys negotiated. Roosevelt proved himself a skillful mediator, soothing injured pride on all sides, and when the Treaty of Portsmouth was finally signed both the Czar and the Japanese emperor sent messages of appreciation, as did nearly every peace society.

Roosevelt was open about his low opinion of professional peace advocates, saying that "There is no more utterly useless and often mischievous citizen than the peace-at-any-price, universal arbitration type of being who is always complaining either about war or else about the cost of armaments which act as insurance against war." He said they were demanding mutually incompatible things when they proposed peace at any price and at the same time justice and righteousness.

The pacifists viewed Roosevelt with equal scorn. Christian Lange, Nobel Laureate for 1921 and an early secretary of the Nobel Committee, observed that if one lifted the veil of Theodore Roosevelt's pan-Americanism one would find American imperialism.

Gunnar Knudsen, member of the Nobel Committee, who presided at Roosevelt's presentation ceremony, offered the award with comments which offer insight into the Committee's view on both sides of the controversy: "Twelve or fifteen years ago, Gentlemen, the cause of peace presented a very different aspect from the one it presents today. The cause was then regarded as a utopian idea and its advocates as well-meaning but overly enthusiastic idealists who had no place in practical politics, being out of touch with the realities of life. The situation has altered radically since then, for in recent years leading statesmen, even heads of state, have espoused the cause .... The United States of America was among the first to infuse the ideal of peace into practical politics. Peace and arbitration treaties have now been concluded between the United States and the governments of several countries. But what has especially directed the attention of the friends of peace and the whole of the civilized world to the United States is President Roosevelt's happy role in bringing to an end the bloody war recently waged between two of the world's Great Powers, Japan and Russia."

In his Nobel lecture Roosevelt offered some comments on peace "as a practical man," and explained that he was recommending only what he had actually tried to do during the period of his presidency. He advocated arbitration, and encouraged further development of the Hague Tribunal and of the conferences and courts at The Hague. History has borne him out in his prediction that the weakness inherent in efforts made by The Hague would be the absence of any police power to enforce the decrees of the court.

Roosevelt deplored the cost of the growth of armaments and said the Great Powers of the world should be able to reach an agreement which would put an end to such extravagance of expenditures. While he acknowledged that there was no adequate safeguard against deliberate violation of peace treaties, he still encouraged nations to conduct effective arbitration among themselves, with explicit agreement that each contracting party would respect the other's territory and their mutual sovereignties. "The establishment of a sufficient number of these treaties would go a long way toward creating a world opinion which would finally find expression in the provision of methods to forbid or punish any violations," Roosevelt said.

When Roosevelt left the presidency in 1908 he stated truthfully that during his seven-year administration "we were at absolute peace, and there was no nation in the world with whom a war cloud threatened, no nation in the world whom we had wronged or from whom we had anything to fear."

The picture of Roosevelt is, then, full of paradoxes. One writer on the Nobel Peace Laureates commented, "The point is, that when the road to peace happens to coincide momentarily with the maneuvers and gyrations of the politician, such a coincidence is strictly accidental. The tactics could just as easily have coincided with war. The exigencies of the moment control." (*Lipsky* 1966 p. 71)

Biography

Theodore Roosevelt was born in New York City on October 27, 1858, the second of four children of Theodore Roosevelt and Martha Bulloch Roosevelt. Theodore was a spindly child owing to asthma. He adored his father, of whom he wrote, "I realize more and more every day that I am as much inferior to Father morally and mentally as physically," and he set out on a self-taught regime of riding, boxing, and shooting to conquer his ill health. Handicapped also with poor vision, Roosevelt was tutored until he entered Harvard at age 18, apparently to good effect. He won membership in Phi Beta Kappa, he excelled in sports, and he began a scholarly work, *The Naval War of 1812*, which was published two years after his graduation in 1880.

That same year, he married Alice Hathaway Lee, a marriage of obvious great happiness which ended tragically four years later with Alice's death following the birth of a daughter. (The baby Alice survived and was destined to become a famous Washington observer as Alice Roosevelt Longworth.)

During the marriage Roosevelt had served in the New York State Assembly and established a sound reputation as a reformer, which he maintained during his entire political career. Following his wife's death, he invested part of his family heritage in a Wyoming ranch which he ran with great success and vigor, restoring again his own failing health and regaining his emotional equilibrium.

Roosevelt subsequently married Edith Kermit Carow, and they had four sons and a daughter. For two and a half years he continued writing and vigorously pursuing sport, until a political opportunity came with an appointment to the US civil service. There he served six years, much of the time as its head, and he again attacked corruption with a concrete program of reforms. He then left Washington for two turbulent years as president of the New York City Police Commission. Although corruption returned after he left, he accomplished some permanent reforms.

In 1897, President McKinley named Roosevelt assistant secretary of the Navy. The next year brought a war with Cuba which Roosevelt supported under his advocacy of "superior" nations exercising the right and the duty to dominate "inferior" nations in the interests of civilization; he resigned his secretaryship, accepted a colonel's rank in the 1st US Volunteer Cavalry and proceeded to ride to fame as leader of his "Rough Riders."

Upon his return to New York, Roosevelt successfully ran for governor of New York state, and he became such a success that even fiercely opposing Democrats acknowledged his sweeping and successful reforms. Indeed, some of his own party with personal interests in the corruption Roosevelt was cleaning out induced him to run on the national Republican ticket as Vice-President.

He was Vice-President for less than a year when upon the assassination of President McKinley he became President on November 14, 1901. He was re-elected in his own right in 1904 for his second term.

Roosevelt was far more prudent in his conduct of foreign policy than his previous stream of pronouncements regarding the virtues of war as an instrument in international relationships had led the peace societies to expect. He was the first national leader to call upon the power of the International Court of Arbitration at The Hague, where he asked for mediation on an old problem between Mexico and the United States.

His most controversial action centered on Panama, where he overrode the Colombian senate's rejection of his offer to buy out a French company's rights to construct a canal through Panama in 1903. He tacitly encouraged a revolution in Panama, and out of this maneuver the new Republic of Panama granted the United States full sovereignty over a ten-mile (16 km) strip through which the Panama Canal was later built.

Roosevelt's domestic program was accurately described as a "Square Deal," and he attacked a number of internal problems courageously, including racial discrimination against the black and oriental races.

In June 1905, Roosevelt accepted Japan's request to mediate a stalemated war between Russia and Japan. They met in Portsmouth, New Hampshire, and with a show of considerable skill on Roosevelt's part reached a peace treaty in September.

Theodore Roosevelt died in 1919.

Bibliography —————————————————————

Harbaugh W 1983 Theodore Roosevelt. In: *Encyclopedia Americana*, International edn. Danburg, Connecticut

Lipsky M 1966 *The Quest for Peace*. Barnes and Co., South Brunswick

Meyer E 1978 Theodore Roosevelt. *In Search of Peace*. Abingdon, Nashville, Tennessee

RUTH C. REYNOLDS

Ernesto Teodoro Moneta
(1907)

Teodoro Gaetano Moneta, known since childhood as Ernesto Teodoro, is remembered, above all, as being the only Italian to have won the Nobel Peace Prize. It was awarded jointly to Moneta and the French jurist Louis Renault in 1907.

Moneta was born on September 20, 1833, son of Giuseppina Muzio and Carlo Aurelio Moneta, a tradesman who lived in a Milan still under Austrian domination and rife with patriotic and humanitarian sentiments. He was little more than a child when, taking after his father, he was infused with a strong feeling of love for his country. This is shown by his behavior during the Milan insurrection of 1848: without even leaving his own home, he joined in the fighting on the side of the insurgents by dropping stones and bricks onto the Austrian patrols. In January 1849, he left Milan for the Kingdom of Sardinia and Piedmont with the intention of enlisting to fight in the first Italian War of Independence against Austria, but was rejected because he was too young.

Following the defeat of Piedmont in 1849, he returned to Milan, where, a short while later, he and his 13 brothers and sisters had to face considerable economic problems after the death of their parents. As soon as these problems had been solved, Moneta renewed his activity on behalf of the patriotic cause. Although he had adopted his father's republican principles, he nevertheless supported the plan of the Societa Nazionale Italiana to unify the entire peninsula under a monarchy, headed by Vittorio Emanuele of Savoy.

Moneta began a military career in 1859 by enlisting in the Garibaldian company, Cacciatori delle Alpi, and fighting together with several of his brothers in the second Italian War of Independence. The following year, 1860, witnessed Garibaldi's expedition to Southern Italy, in which Moneta also took part. In 1866, he reenlisted in the regular army in order to participate in the third Italian War of Independence. This event is given particular attention by Moneta in the most interesting part of his most wide ranging work, *Le Guerre, le Insurrezioni e la Pace nel Secolo XIX*, written in his later years when he had come to direct all his efforts to propagandizing pacifist convictions.

Moneta first became involved in journalism through his collaboration with *Unità Nazionale* and, more frequently, *Il Piccolo Corriere d'Italia*, the two organs of the patriots who wanted a united Italy. In 1867, following his abandonment of his military career, the year before, he was appointed editor of *Il Secolo*, where he stayed for almost 30 years. This innovatory, independent, and democratic newspaper would become one of the most important Italian publications of the following decades, due in large part to the efforts of Moneta. When he took up his post, the slaughter he had witnessed fighting in the battle of Custoza in 1866 was still fresh in his mind, and his conception of pacifism was already taking shape. It would subsequently find expression in his writings and, above all, in his numerous speeches. In this context, importance should be attached to his antiwar position with regard to the tension between Italy and France, resulting from the latter's occupation of Tunis (1881), and his swift condemnation of Italian colonial expansion into Eritrea.

Moneta increasingly dedicated more time to the spreading of his pacifist ideas. He began to play an active role in the international pacifist movement, especially after founding in Milan, in 1887, the Unione Lombarda per la Pace e l'Arbitrato Internazionale. In 1898, he founded *La Vita Internazionale*, of which he himself was editor. This was the official publication of the Union Lombarda per la Pace, later entitled the Societa per la Pace. It appeared twice a month and included prestigious names amongst its contributors. In the reactionary and militarist climate of Italy at the end of the century, it was confiscated and charged with publishing an antimilitarist article by Leo Tolstoy (see Articles: *Tolstoy, Leo*). Feeling that he was also at risk, Moneta was forced to take refuge for a while in Switzerland.

The first decade of the new century still saw him undertaking long journeys, despite his age and advancing blindness, to where the International Peace Congresses were held. (These were frequently organized after the one which took place in Paris in 1889). In 1907, amid general consensus, he was awarded the Peace Prize. The high point in the life of this old pacifist from Lombardy was the Nobel lecture he gave in Oslo, in 1909, on the subject "Peace and Law in the Italian Tradition."

The year 1911 marked the beginning of years which were to pose painful moral questions. Moneta's years of participation in the international peace movement had not led to the abandonment of his own patriotic values, which had been assimilated during his youth. This gave rise to agonizing contradictions, such as his justification of Italy's decision to undertake, in 1911, the war against Turkey for the conquest of Libya and, later on, his stand in favor of Italian intervention in the First World War against the Central Powers. For many years Moneta had been in favor of Italy remaining in the "Triple Alliance" with Germany and Austria, and a strong critic of the extremist positions of anti-Austrian patriotism. He considered the former as leading to stability and the latter as fomenting unrest. Nevertheless, in 1915, he adopted a position of "democratic interventionism," supporting France and the United Kingdom against Germany and Austria in the First World War. The action led to very severe attacks on him by most exponents of the international peace movement. But in the very last days of his life he expressed his support for the program of justice and humanity in relations between peoples put forward in 1918 by US President Woodrow Wilson.

Despite its eclectic nature, the pacifism of Ernesto Teodoro Moneta had a theoretical and ethical depth of its own, and was largely based on his faith in scientific progress, which he felt would lead to greater tolerance and solidarity among nations. Unlike the typical Quaker conception of pacifism, Moneta was not opposed to the use of arms against aggression and in the case of a country losing its freedom as the result of arbitrary outside intervention. As a consequence, on the one hand a nation should be educated in the creed of universal brotherhood and also, on the other, all citizens should receive military training from the moment they attend school, so as to be ready to defend their country's freedom and independence. This is the essential element in the idea of "peace of the strong and free," which for Moneta was connected to the necessity of the "nation under arms." In a world of nations prepared only to fight defensive wars, Moneta believed that war would never actually break out because of the lack of aggressors.

Biography

Ernesto Teodoro Moneta was born on September 20, 1833, in Milan, Italy, son of aristocratic, but impoverished, parents. At 15 he fought next to his father in the Milanese insurrection of 1848 against Austrian rule. He witnessed the shooting and agonizing death of three Austrian soldiers, and their suffering planted the seeds of revulsion against war in his mind, although he continued to participate in Italy's battle for independence, fighting with Garibaldi in 1859 and 1860 later under General Sirtori. In 1861 he joined the regular Italian army and fought in the battle of Custoza in 1866.

In 1867, he became editor of *Il Secolo*, and in the succeeding 29 years within its pages supported Italy's unification and social progress, side by side with his growing sense of pacifism. In 1887 he founded the Società Internazionale per la Pace: Unione Lombarda (International Society for Peace: Lombard League) and through it campaigned for disarmament, a league of nations, and the use of arbitration for settling international disputes. In 1890 he began an annual almanac called *L'Amico della Pace*, and in

1898 founded *La Vita Internazionale* (International Life), a successful pacifist fortnightly review.

Now an international activist, he increased his activities on behalf of pacifism. In addition to writing, he lectured and attended peace conferences. He became the Italian representative on the Commission of the International Peace Bureau in 1895. In 1906 he presided at the International Peace Conference in Milan, which led to his award of the Nobel Peace Prize in 1907.

Moneta was, however, prepared to sanction the use of military force under certain circumstances; in national self-defense, for example, and where he saw Italy's freedom at risk. Thus he supported Italy's war against Turkey on the grounds of an Italian civilizing mission in Libya, and in 1915, he advocated Italian entry into the First World War to combat the imperialist designs of the Central Powers.

Ernesto Moneta died in Milan on February 10, 1918.

Bibliography

Bauer R 1980 *Ricordo di Ernesto Teodoro Moneta, Premio Nobel per la Pace 1907* Società per la Pace e la Giustizia Internationale Milan (Text of the commemorative speech given by Riccardo Bauer)

Colombo A 1983 L'anniversario del primo (e unico) Premio Nobel italiano nel campo politico-sociale: Ernesto Teodoro Moneta. *Corriere della Sera* September 17, 1983

Combi M 1968 *Ernesto Teodoro Moneta, Premio Nobel per la Pace 1907*. Mursia, Milan

Moneta E T 1904, 1905, 1906, 1907 *Le Guerre, le Insurrezioni e la Pace nel Secolo XIX*, 4 vols. Società Internazionale per la Pace, Milan

Moneta E T 1909 *La Pace e il Diritto nella Tradizione Italiana. Conferenza Tenuta a Cristiania il giorno 25 Agosto 1909 nel Salone dell'Istituto Nobel per la Pace*. La Compositrice, Milan

Moneta E T 1910 *L'Opera delle Società della Pace dalla loro origine ad oggi. Relazione tenuta a Como il 18 Settembre 1910 al Congresso Nazionale Pacifista*. Società Internazionale per la Pace, Milan (Extract from *La Vita Internazionale* September 20 and October 5, 1910)

ETTORE A. ALBERTONI

Louis Renault
(1907)

Louis Renault, co-winner of the 1907 Nobel Peace Prize, was a foremost professor of law. Nobel Committee Chairman Lovland called him "the guiding

genius in the teaching of international law in France." He was counselor to the French Ministry of Foreign Affairs, and France's representative at all the international legal conferences to which the French government was party, and was, together with Tobias Asser (Nobel Laureate in 1911), very largely responsible for the positive results achieved at the Conferences of Private International Law at The Hague. With scholarly skill and perseverance, he fought for the concepts of law, both in his teaching and in his practice.

In the late nineteenth and early twentieth centuries many jurists met at stipulated intervals, seeking to create a system of international law which would implement improved international relationships, and eventually replace war as an ongoing mechanism for resolving conflicts. With the jurist's capacity for precise and economical summation, Renault defined their task as "the juridical organization of international life."

Few men could match Renault's preparation for this role. He had taught Roman, commercial, and international law at the Universities of Dijon and Paris and at the Sorbonne. He was among the early members of the Institute de Droit International [International Institute of Law], and one of the first judges of the Permanent Court of Arbitration at The Hague. Renault was appointed jurist consultant to the French Foreign Ministry in 1890, and for the next 20 years, as the leading French authority on international law, he acted as its key representative at international conferences covering international private law, international transport, military aviation, submarine cables, naval affairs, the abolition of white slavery, and the revision of the Red Cross Convention of 1864. He became the single most valued authority on international law upon whom the republic relied.

Renault saw a commonality across the side range of conferences he attended: they all sought to substitute law for the arbitrary. To resolve the difficulties that arose, he said that each country had to learn to relinquish stubborn adherence to its own ideas and to concede whatever it could without actually injuring its own essential interests.

Renault strove to produce positive results and to prevent discussions on generalities and technical formulations from protracting proceedings. He used resilience and intelligence above legal inflexibilities. For instance, he did not adhere to a fixed international democracy. He observed that while the quality of nations is juridically incontrovertible, equality, pushed to its last limits of literalness, could become absurd. For example, the United Kingdom and Luxembourg are equal states before the law. "Would it not be ridiculous if the voice of Luxembourg carried as much weight on a maritime issue as that of Great Britain?" he asked. On the other hand, he attributed a unique and vital role to small nations in these conferences: "they are most frequently the true representatives of justice precisely because they do not have the strength to impose injustice," he said.

His insight on the strengths and weaknesses of demanding unanimity foresaw some of the difficulties which would in later years plague the League of Nations and the United Nations: while, on the one hand, unanimity may lead to stalemate, on the other, it is an indispensable safeguard against hasty decisions and against coalitions of interests. He perceived that unanimity does allow compromise in the sense that a resolution can represent the will of the conference as a whole, in spite of some disagreements. "It is a matter of tact and prudence," Renault declared. "Such delicate problems are not resolved mathematically."

No nation, he felt, should be forced into anything against its will. Instead of laying down hard and fast rules, nations should limit themselves to recommendations, he said. This would not constitute a legal obligation, but rather a moral duty. Renault lay his finger upon the true source of hope over the long span of years: "It is no small matter that a moral duty be recognized by the majority of nations," he said. "By force of circumstance, it eventually becomes a part of custom and compels as much acknowledgment as if it had constituted a strict obligation in the first place."

Renault was *rapporteur* at the conferences; he drafted reports and recommendations and consequently exercised a decisive influence upon the agreements and the form they took.

When the Hague Tribunal was opened to conduct cases of international arbitration, he was named one of its 28 arbiters. During the first 14 years of its existence, Renault was chosen to be involved with six of the court's 13 cases—more than any other arbiter. His reputation for impartiality was so firmly established that during the so-called Savarkar Case between the United Kingdom and France in 1910 both parties to the dispute requested the services of Renault as a judge.

In the first Hague Peace Conference in 1899, Renault, as the reporter of the Second Commission, was concerned with naval warfare. In his Nobel lecture he pointed out some of the many difficulties presented by naval warfare, since war at sea involves the relations between the belligerents themselves and also those between belligerents and neutrals. The interests are therefore divergent, Renault said that negotiations of any sort at the Conference were an achievement, since the great seafaring nations had previously refused to be drawn into discussion on this subject. But on this occasion great effort was made. Understanding was reached on several points, and a basis for future discussion and agreement was established.

In the second Hague Conference of 1907 his role was even more vital. He was spokesman on four problems. Renault's report in his Nobel lecture on these problems and their treatment at the Conference offers rare insight into the conferences of this period. It is interesting to note that these problems he reviewed were considered and resolved, at least in part, in 1907, just seven years before the outbreak of the First World War in 1914. They are an eloquent commentary on the hope that was basic to the international peace movement prior to that war.

Renault spoke on the following four problems:

(a) *The opening of hostilities.* For a long time people had posed the question of whether a government on the verge of war had an obligation to warn its adversary before opening hostilities. The Conference agreed unanimously that there must be a warning in the form of a reasoned declaration of war, or an ultimatum with conditional declaration of war.

(b) *Application of Geneva Convention to naval warfare.* The issue of laying automatic submarine contact mines, acknowledged to be a threat to peaceable shipping long after the end of hostilities, was discussed, but not satisfactorily resolved at this conference.

(c) *Obligations and rights of neutral countries in the case of naval warfare.* The importance of this problem lay in reducing the danger of any extension of hostilities resulting from conflicts between belligerents and neutrals. Renault reported that the Convention appeared on the whole to provide a fair settlement of the matter.

(d) *International Prize Court of Appeal.* The right to seize private property in the course of war at sea had long been a point for argument. Renault reported with surprised satisfaction that a group of great seafaring nations took the initiative in resolving this matter. A compromise was reached and a comprehensive, carefully drafted proposal was submitted to the Conference in the name of four great powers, Germany, the United States, France and Great Britain.

Renault warned against attempting to move too fast, in the belief that minds cannot be reshaped quickly. "There are some forms of resistance and even of hesitation that only time, allied with education, can overcome," he said.

"Anything that contributes to extending the domain of law in international relations contributes to peace," this distinguished jurist told his Nobel award audience. "Since the possibility of future war cannot be ignored, it is a *farsighted* policy that takes into account the difficulties created by war in the relations between belligerents and neutrals; and it is a *humanitarian* policy that strives to reduce the evils of war in the relations between the belligerents themselves and to safeguard as far as possible the interests of noncombatants and of the sick and the wounded. Whatever may be said by those who scoff at the work undertaken in this field by the Peace Conferences, wars will not become rarer by becoming more barbarous."

Biography

Louis Renault was born on May 21, 1843, at Autun. His father was a Burgundian bookseller and bibliophile. A gifted student, Renault took prizes in philosophy, mathematics, and literature before taking three law degrees in Paris, all with extraordinary honors. He taught Roman and commercial law at Dijon, criminal and international law at the University of Paris. In the latter discipline he so distinguished himself by his teaching and publications in the field, including *Introduction a l'étude du droit international*, that he was offered the chair of international law within seven years. His scholarly output of reports, notes, and articles published in law and political science journals, his books, including notably a nine-volume work of collaboration with Charles Lyon-Caen, *Traite de droit commercial*, his countless lectures, and his continued career as a foremost teacher in his field all brought him recognition as France's leading authority on international law. He was appointed a legal consultant to the Foreign Office, and became the one authority in international law upon whom France relied.

He was a key delegate to many important international meetings between 1893 and 1907, where he was responsible for the drafting of reports and recommendations. In recognition of his service he was given the titular title of Minister Plenipotentiary and Envoy Extraordinary.

Renault served on the panel of 28 arbiters for the Hague Tribunal, where he was chosen to serve in more cases than any other arbiter.

He was named to the Legion of Honor and to the Academy of Moral and Political Sciences in France, and was awarded decorations from 19 foreign nations. He received honorary doctorates from several universities, and was chosen to be president of the Academy of International Law created at The Hague in 1914.

Renault died on February 6, 1918, while still active in his career.

RUTH C. REYNOLDS

Klas Pontus Arnoldson
(1908)

It is interesting to look at the choice of the two Scandinavian award winners of the 1908 Nobel Peace Prize, Klas Pontus Arnoldson and Fredrik Bajer, in terms of the context of its time. A wave of peace movements was awash over the world. In the words of a co-winner of the first Nobel Peace Prize, Frédéric Passy, "the labors of the champions of international arbitration are not only treated with politeness and respect, but are even seriously discussed in the columns of newspapers."

The peace movements proliferated to the point of requiring a clearing house for information and a unifying organization to coordinate their efforts. This came about in an agency called the International Peace Bureau, and the international arbitration movement required and received the same service from the Interparliamentary Bureau.

The wars of 1864 and 1870-1871 kindled Klas Arnoldson's passion for the peace movement and he was instrumental in the founding of the Swedish Peace and Arbitration Association in 1883. He became its secretary and also the editor of *Tiden* [The Times], a medium for peace information and free debate. He resigned from *Tiden* in 1885 and became editor of *Fredsvannen* [The Friend of Peace] from 1885 to 1888 and the *Nordsvenska Dagbladet* [North Sweden Daily] from 1892 to 1894. A great part of his energies went into writing and lecturing on behalf of arbitration.

As a member of the Swedish parliament from 1882 to 1887 he put into practice his ideals in liberal political philosophy. He introduced legislation to extend the franchise and supported the extension of religious freedom. He also followed his pacifist convictions, pursuing an antimilitaristic policy and drafting a controversial resolution asking the government to investigate the possibility of guaranteed neutrality for Sweden. In 1888 he mounted a campaign for a popular petition addressed to the king favoring arbitration agreements with foreign nations. When he extended this campaign to Norway he contributed some of the impetus for the Norwegian parliament's passage of a resolution on arbitration.

In the final constitutional crisis which resulted in the dissolution of the union between Norway and Sweden in 1895, Arnoldson tended to favor Norway's claims. His attitude met with outrage in Sweden, and his award of the Peace Prize was regarded by many as an affront to the nation. "A disgrace to every Swedish man who takes pride in his national honor" with a prize paid for in Swedish money! In response the Nobel Committee pointed out that Arnoldson's candidacy had been proposed by the unanimous vote of the Swedish Group of the Interparliamentary Union.

In his Nobel lecture Arnoldson proposed the idea of a world referendum on peace in which an appeal would be issued for every adult man and woman to sign the following declaration: "If other nations will abolish their armed forces and be content with a joint police force for the whole world, then I, the undersigned, wish my own nation to do the same." To this cause, and to other causes of peace, Arnoldson contributed his Nobel Prize money. "It enables me to serve the cause of peace in yet other ways and with even stronger perseverance. So will I try to carry my burden of gratitude, and to discharge the mission to which I have been called," he pledged.

Biography

Klas Pontus Arnoldson was born in Gäteborg, Sweden, the son of a caretaker. Because of the family's financial straits he was forced to leave school after his father's death when he was 16. Although he worked thereafter for a railway, Arnoldson did not cease his education but carried on, self-taught, through prolific reading and writing. It was during this period that he developed liberal ideas on religion and politics and became interested in peace.

He served in parliament from 1882 to 1887, during which time he introduced legislation to extend the franchise, favored the extension of religious freedom, and pursued an antimilitaristic policy. In 1883 he worked toward the establishment of the Swedish Peace and Arbitration Association, becoming its secretary. He edited *Tiden* [The Times], a publication on peace information and free debate. From 1885 to 1888, he edited *Fredsvannen* [The Friend of Peace], and from 1892 to 1894 the *Nordsvenska Dagbladet*

[North Sweden Daily]. An ardent supporter of arbitration, in 1888, he campaigned for a petition to the king in favor of arbitration agreements with foreign countries, and in 1890, he took his cause to receptive audiences in Norway, contributing to the Norwegian parliament's passage of an arbitration resolution to the king.

Along with a lifetime of journalistic pieces, Arnoldson published a historical essay on international law, *Ar varlds-* *fred mojlig?* [Is World Peace Possible?], *Religionen i forskningens ljus* [Religion in the Light of Research], and a history of the pacifist idea, *Seklernas hopp* [The Hope of the Centuries].

Klas Pontus Arnoldson died in Stockholm in 1916.

RUTH C. REYNOLDS

Fredrik Bajer
(1908)

For over 40 years Fredrik Bajer, journalist and member of the Danish parliament, lent his prolific pen, his politics, and his presence to the cause of peace and it was in recognition of this work that he was awarded the Nobel Peace Prize in 1908 alongside Klas Pontus Arnoldson.

The son of a clergyman, Bajer began his career as an army officer, serving as lieutenant in the Dragoons. Before his military career ended at the close of the 1864 war with Prussia, he had been drawn to the peace movement, and was in touch with Frédéric Passy, founder of the French peace society (and co-winner of the first Peace Prize in 1901). During the next few years he laid an important foundation for his later international activities by studying languages, mastering French, Norwegian, and Swedish. In 1872 he was elected to the Danish House of Representatives, and his efforts in the peace movement shared his attention with work toward the emancipation of women—he was among the founders of the Dansk Kvindesamfund [Danish Women's Society]—and with his dedication to the cause of Scandinavian unity. For two years he edited the journal of the Nordisk Fristats Samfund [Society of Nordic Free States].

In 1882 Bajer founded the first Danish peace society, and its title, Foreningen til Danmarks Neutralisering [Society for the Promotion of Danish Neutrality; later called the Danish Peace Association] defined his initial emphasis in working for peace. In time, however, he became increasingly interested in international peace efforts. He took an active part in the European peace movement, participating in the International Congress in Bern in 1884. He was a prominent delegate to the first Scandinavian peace conference in 1885, and in 1889 he attended the Interparliamentary Conference held in Paris. He regularly represented the Danish Peace Association at the congresses until 1914. He founded the Danish Interparliamentary Group in 1891, acting as its secretary for 25 years, and he helped in the creation of the Scandinavian Interparliamentary Union in 1908.

Bajer's confidence and interest in arbitration grew, and he served as a member of the council controlling the Interparliamentary Union. He put his convictions into practice by guiding through the Danish parliament a proposal to establish arbitration agreements between Sweden and Norway.

In his Nobel lecture Bajer defined the range of international peace efforts by using a military metaphor: "There are three columns marching forth, the *international*, the *interparliamentary*, and the *intergovernmental*," he said. "These three columns must maintain contact with one another. In battle, it is useless to attack alone, however courageous one may be; one has to maintain contact to the left and to the right; otherwise nothing of great moment can be achieved. This contact . . . is of the utmost importance if results are to be achieved in the peace movement." It is appropriate that among Bajer's most enduring recommendations for the peace movement was its major point of "contact," the International Peace Bureau at Bern. It was at his suggestion that it was established in 1891.

The International Peace Bureau became a permanent agency for the collection and dissemination of information coming from all the peace organizations of the world. It did for those scattered efforts what satellites and computers do for information-dependent agencies today. Its first and second secretary-generals, Elie Ducommun and Charles-Albert Gobat, were both earlier Nobel Laureates (in 1903), and both worked with dedication and without pay. Bajer was president of its Board of Administration until 1907, when he declined re-election and was named honorary president.

The outbreak of the First World War in 1914 brought the International Union of Peace Societies to an abrupt end, and it diminished the role of the International Peace Bureau. However, the Bureau has continued on, and, now headquartered in Geneva, it still acts as a clearinghouse for communications between different national and international peace organizations, and between those organizations and national governments. In the place of arranging the once-proliferating peace congresses, it is more likely today to be organizing seminars on specific projects such as UN peacekeeping operations.

Bajer pinpointed another dilemma constantly present in the dissemination of information for *any* cause. Peace literature was being read mainly by the already convinced. "Up to now, we have had too much. . . preaching to the converted. We should direct special efforts toward those who remain unconverted," he said in his Nobel lecture. His solution, at least for that moment, was to offer a prize in money for the best article on the subject of peace to appear in a national newspaper. His solution was innovative, if temporary, but his observation on that dilemma has stood the test of time.

Bajer also noted in his lecture that we have long possessed the science of war, and it has been "marvelously developed." Whenever a new idea comes along, warfare immediately takes possession. On the other hand, the "waging of peace" is in its infancy. He ventured the prophecy that there would one day be ministers of peace in the cabinet, seated beside the ministers of war.

Bajer himself made many personal contributions in "waging peace." An example was his suggestion for the answer to the Nordic countries' vulnerability during wartime due to the strategic importance of the water routes around their coastlines. Bajer advocated that Nordic neutrality in the same vein as Switzerland's traditional neutrality be internationally recognized. His proposal was adopted by several international organizations, but later he became convinced that Denmark should pursue neutrality independently without relying on other states to guarantee it.

Bajer was a gifted and prolific writer. His legacy of observations from a life spent in the cause of preventing war is well-represented by this closing paragraph of his Nobel lecture:

> [Waging peace] is civilization's battle between rule by law and rule by power. In this context, pacifists should stress more and more that it is the rule of law for which they are fighting . . . .

What contributes largely to the confusion of ideas is the accepted division of the world into major powers and small states. We understand a "power" to be a state which has a large population and well-developed armed forces, army and navy, and so on. This is comparable to believing that a great man is a very tall and big man. By a great man, however, we mean a man who, because of his spiritual gifts, his character, and other qualities, deserves to be called great and who as a result earns the power to influence others. By the same token it must follow that the state we now call a small state is in reality a power if it plays such a role in the development of civilization that it marches in the front ranks and wins victories in the fight for law which surpass those of the so-called great powers.

Biography

Fredrik Bajer was born on April 21, 1837, son of Alfred Beyer, in Vester Egede, near Naestved, Denmark. (Bajer adopted the altered spelling of his name in 1865.) Bajer served in the army as a lieutenant in the Dragoons, commanding troops in Northern Jutland during the war against Prussia and Austria in 1864. Discharged during the general reduction of troops following the end of the war, he studied languages, mastering French, Norwegian, and Swedish, and became a teacher and translator. He was dedicated to education, serving in the Pedagogical Society and participating in the first Scandinavian conference of teachers held in Göteborg in 1870.

In 1872, he was elected to the *Folketing*, the Danish House of Representatives, where he served for the next 23 years. A leading spokesman for women's rights, he supported legislation in their behalf and helped found the Danish Women's Society. Bajer promoted Nordic unity and cooperation, starting the Society of Nordic Free States, and Scandinavian unity, which he associated with neutrality and peace. He founded the first Danish peace society, the Society for the Promotion of Danish Neutrality, later called the Danish Peace Association. He attended many peace conferences, including the International Congress at Bern, where he suggested the International Peace Bureau be established. A clearinghouse for information exchange between peace organizations over the world, it was a unifying force in the peace movement and Bajer was a president of its Board of Administration from its inception in 1891 until 1907. He was a delegate to the first Scandinavian peace conference in 1885 and he founded the Danish Interparliamentary Group in 1891; he helped in the creation of the Scandinavian Interparliamentary Union in 1908. A firm supporter of arbitration, he served as a member of the council controlling the Interparliamentary Union.

Fredrik Bajer died in Copenhagen in 1922.

RUTH C. REYNOLDS

Auguste Marie Francois Beernaert
(1909)

The 1909 Nobel Peace Prize was shared by Auguste Beernaert, whose name the Nobel Committee called renowned in the international peace conferences. He represented Belgium at the two Hague Peace Conferences, was a member of the Permanent Court of Arbitration, and honorary president of the Société de Droit International [International Law Association]. The Nobel Committee declared that Beernaert's prominent position in the international movement for peace and arbitration made his award fully in keeping with the spirit of Alfred Nobel's intentions for the prize.

Auguste Beernaert was born on July 26, 1829, son of a government functionary and a mother who herself undertook the early education of her son and daughter. The outstanding competence of both teacher and pupil is reflected in Beernaert's scholastic record at the University of Louvain (Leuven) where he took his doctorate in law in 1851 with highest distinction. He spent two years at the Universities of Paris, Heidelberg, and Berlin on a traveling fellowship, studying the status of legal education in France and Germany, and submitting his report to the Minister of the Interior.

After his admission to the bar in 1853 he first clerked for a former president of the Chamber of Representatives, after which he set up an independent practice, specializing in fiscal law. In the next 20 years he earned a reputation as a scholar for his published works in legal journals, and a comfortable income from his law practice.

In 1873, he startled legal circles by sacrificing his lucrative practice to become Minister of Public Works. Over the next five years Beernaert proved himself an able administrator and an ambitious reformer. He succeeded in improving Belgium's road, rail, and canal systems, and established new port facilities at Ostend and Anvers. He attempted, but did not succeed, to end child labor in the mines. The year 1884 saw his rise to the leadership of his government. First named Minister of the Department of Agriculture, Industry, and Public Works, four months later, following several resignations from the cabinet, King Leopold II named him Prime Minister and Minister of Finance, positions that he held for 10 years.

Under Beernaert's administration the state of the Congo was created in 1885 with Leopold as sovereign. The Congo was later to present problems to Beernaert.

In his last year of office he was instrumental in enacting constitutional reforms, including universal suffrage, the right of voting being granted to 10 times the number of citizens who had formerly enjoyed it. In 1894, on the constitutional question of proportional representation, Beernaert's cabinet fell. Although he returned to law practice, he continued to serve the government, accepting the advisory post of Minister of State. From 1895 to 1900 his colleagues elected him the president of the Chamber of Representatives. During this period he actively worked in international attempts to abolish slavery, and he solidified into active opposition the dismay he felt at the exploitation of the Congo.

Beernaert was a strong internationalist, and following his resignation as Prime Minister he became an active member of the Interparliamentary Union. He presided over several of its conferences, he served as president of its Council, and as president of the Executive Committee when it was formed in 1908.

As Belgium's first representative at the two Hague Conferences in 1899 and 1907 Beernaert had an opportunity to observe for himself the negative nature of the debates dealing with the question of disarmament. He expressed his grave misgivings about the de facto recognition of the principle of military occupation which came out of the two conferences.

Beernaert spearheaded proposals to unify international maritime law. While the conventions of 1885 and 1888 which met at his initiative failed to be adopted by several nations, the conventions dealing with collision and assistance at sea drawn up in 1910 under his chairmanship were signed by many nations.

At the second Hague Conference he found himself, as advocate of the principle of compulsory arbitration, placed in a dilemma over the Congo question. King Leopold was not inclined to apply this principle to the Congo dispute and Beernaert was obliged to softpedal the issue. This event cancelled some of Beernaert's effectiveness in the international field. But his contribution in establishing the positive influence which smaller nations could have on international relationships was very real.

Biography

Auguste Marie Francois Beernaert was born on July 26,

1829, in Ostend, Belgium. Educated in the first instance by his mother, a woman of outstanding intelligence, he took his doctorate in law at the University of Louvain (Leuven) in 1851 with highest honors. Following two years of study on the status of legal education in France and Germany he returned to Belgium, where he practiced law from 1853 to 1873, specializing in fiscal law, and earned a reputation as a scholar through his articles appearing in legal journals. In 1873 he became Minister of Public Works. An able administrator, he improved his country's rail, canal, and road systems, and established new port facilities. He attempted, but failed, to abolish child labor in mines.

In 1884 Beernaert became Prime Minister, having served the previous four months as Minister of the Department of Agriculture, Industry, and Public Works before resignations in the cabinet brought about his rise to leadership. During the 10 years of his administration his accomplishments were many: he balanced the budget; many domestic reforms affecting the welfare of workers were enacted; suffrage was extended to 10 times the number of citizens previously voting. The Congo, which had been developed largely under the responsibility of King Leopold II, became an independent state placed under Leopold's sovereignty.

Beernaert's cabinet fell in 1894 on the constitutional question of proportional representation, and Beernaert returned to law practice, although retaining some service in the government. He accepted the advisory post of Minister of State and served as the president of the Chamber of Representatives. He headed the Commission of Museums and Arts.

He joined in an international opposition to slavery, including the exploitation of the Congo. A leading pacifist, he became active in the Interparliamentary Union, presiding over several conferences and serving as president of its Council after 1899 and president of its Executive Committee in 1908. He represented Belgium at the two Peace Conferences at The Hague in 1899 and 1907. He was a member of the Permanent Court of Arbitration, and frequently acted as arbiter of international disputes.

On his way home from the 1912 Geneva conference of the Interparliamentary Union he contracted pneumonia and died in a Lucerne hospital on October 6, 1912.

RUTH C. REYNOLDS

Paul Henri Benjamin Balluet, Baron d'Estournelles de Constant de Rebecque (1909)

"Paul Henri Benjamin d'Estournelles de Constant has become thoroughly dedicated to the movement for peace and arbitration," Chairman Lovland of the Nobel Committee declared in presenting the 1909 Peace Prize to the French co-winner with Auguste Beernaert. "D'Estournelles' work for peace has not been performed blindly," Lovland said. "As a diplomat he learned to understand international policy and has planned his efforts accordingly." Among the group of international jurists who won the Peace Prize prior to 1914, d'Estournelles was the one who turned to a political career to render his international activity more effective.

Born on November 22, 1852, at La Fleche in the Sarthe district, Paul Henri Benjamin Balluet, Baron d'Estournelles de Constant de Rebecque, was the son of a family that could trace its ancestry back to the Crusades. He was educated in law at the Lycée Louis le Grand in Paris, and in preparation for a career in the diplomatic service he studied and received a diploma there in oriental languages. He traveled widely in the Orient.

He entered the diplomatic corps in 1876 as an attaché in the consular department of the Ministry of Foreign Affairs, representing France in the next six years in Montenegro, Turkey, the Netherlands, Britain, and Tunis. Recalled to Paris in 1882, he assumed the assistant directorship of the Near Eastern Bureau of the Ministry of Foreign Affairs. He returned to London in 1890 as counselor to the Embassy, with the title of minister plenipotentiary. As chargé d'affaires he was involved in averting a threatened war between France and Britain during a French-Siamese border dispute when the British objected to a blockade imposed by the French.

The five years he spent as counselor to the Embassy convinced d'Estournelles of the general impotence of members in the diplomatic service. In 1895 he resolved to abandon the "gilded existence of the diplomatist in order to undertake the real struggle . . . against ignorance" by obtaining an elective seat in the legislature and attempting to remedy the situation in which "the silent majority allow themselves to be persuaded that they know nothing of 'Foreign Affairs'" (*International Peace* pp. 5-6).

And so, on May 19, 1895, he began his political career as deputy from Sarthe, the same constituency that had years earlier elected his famous great-uncle, the author Benjamin Constant de Rebecque. Elected senator from the same region in 1904, he held that seat as an active Radical Socialist until his death.

D'Estournelles participated at both Hague Peace Conferences, in 1899 and 1907, in the French delegation. At the first conference he led the successful struggle to strengthen the language dealing with arbitration and the court in Article 27 of Convention I, thereby securing agreement on compulsory arbitration that was recognized as being more vitally important than most countries had originally been willing to concede. The obligation was, however, still only a moral one, and during the first few years the tribunal was systematically sabotaged by the Great Powers.

D'Estournelles countered with increased efforts to encourage the use of arbitration. One notable success was persuading Theodore Roosevelt (Nobel Peace Prize winner in 1906) to refer a US-Mexican dispute to the Hague Tribunal. He influenced Andrew Carnegie to underwrite a large amount of the cost of building a Peace Palace in The Hague, a monument eulogizing not the heroes of past wars, but the ideal of peace.

D'Estournelles sought a political solution to Europe's problems. He believed that foreign policy should ultimately be controlled by parliaments, and that consequently parliamentary arbitration groups should be developed and strengthened. In 1903 he founded a parliamentary group composed of members of the French Chamber and Senate without regard to party. Their purpose was to advance international arbitration, chiefly through the exchange of visits with foreign parliamentarians.

D'Estournelles' ultimate goal was the formation of a European Union. His immediate goal was a Franco-German *rapprochement*. However, he faced not only vengeful feelings directed against Germany, but also a violent anti-British mood which was whipped up over the Fashoda incident in 1898. He therefore worked also for a Franco-British *rapprochement*, and in 1903 he visited the British parliament at the head of the French parliamentary group for voluntary arbitration. The British paid a return visit to Paris shortly after a treaty of arbitration had been signed between the two countries. These event helped make possible the Franco-British entente in 1904, but d'Estournelles insisted that this agreement, like the Franco-Russian alliance of 1894, must not be used against Germany. The balance which these two agreements created contributed to a lessening of tensions.

In 1903 d'Estournelles also founded a Franco-German association in Munich. He agreed that past events could not be forgotten, but urged that both

countries recognize that peace was an absolute imperative. "War," he declared, "drives the republics into dictatorship, the monarchies into the grip of revolution." In 1905 he founded the Association for International Conciliation in Paris, with branches abroad.

D'Estournelles observed that the rivalry between the European countries resulted in steadily increasing military expenditures, and that this weakened Europe's position in the world economy. He pointed out the advantage that would come with a European Union which would hold no threat to any important non-European power, such as the United States. D'Estournelles thought that many influential Americans were eager to see a greater measure of European cooperation. "The Americans are businessmen, and they prefer well-organized and stable conditions to the armed peace which presents a constant menace to world peace" he declared.

While he worked toward his long-range goal of the formation of an European Union, d'Estournelles also continued to pursue activities of a diplomatic and juridical nature, such as working within the Interparliamentary Union, as a member of the Permanent Court of Arbitration, and as president of the European Center of the Carnegie Endowment for International Peace.

During the First World War d'Estournelles supported his country's effort, turning his home into a hospital for the wounded. But following the war he continued his campaign for international understanding. He joined Leon Bourgeois, Nobel Peace Prize winner for 1920, in presenting a plan for the League of Nations to Clemenceau in 1918. He never ceased trying to bring together parliamentarians of various nations, especially those of France and Germany.

Biography

Paul Henri Benjamin Balluet, Baron d'Estournelles de Constant de Rebecque, was born on November 22, 1852, at La Fleche, in the Sarthe district of the Loire Valley. The son of an aristocratic family, he traced his ancestry back to the Crusades.

He was educated at the Lycée Louis le Grand in Paris, with a degree in law and a diploma from the School of Oriental Languages. As an attaché in the consular department of the Ministry of Foreign Affairs he represented France from 1876 to 1882 in Montenegro, Turkey, the Netherlands, Britain, and Tunis. In 1882 he assumed assistant directorship of the Near Eastern Bureau of the Ministry of Foreign Affairs.

In 1890 d'Estournelles became chargé d'affaires in London, and in 1893 he helped avert a war between France and Britain over a blockade during the French-Siamese border disputes. This incident sealed his conviction of the impotence within the diplomatic service, and he decided to pursue a political career in which he thought he might act with more effect. He sought and won a seat in the legislature as deputy for Sarthe in 1895. A radical Socialist, he was elected senator from the same region, and he held that seat for the remainder of his life.

In 1899, he served on the French delegation to the first Hague Peace Conference, seeking to strengthen arbitration. While on a lecture tour in the United States, he persuaded President Theodore Roosevelt to submit a longstanding dispute between the United States and Mexico to the Hague Tribunal.

Mutual goodwill missions under his chairmanship between London and Paris helped pave the way for the Franco-British Entente Cordiale of 1904; a visit to Munich resulted in the Franco-German Association in 1903. In 1905 he founded the Association for International Conciliation at Paris, with branches abroad.

He was an active member in the Interparliamentary Union, a delegate to the second Hague Peace Conference of 1907, a member of the Permanent Court of Arbitration and president of the European Center of the Carnegie Endowment for International Peace.

Although he supported the French effort during the First World War, following its close he continued his work toward international understanding, presenting with Leon Bourgeois a plan for the League of Nations to Clemenceau in 1918. He never ceased trying to bring together parliamentarians of various nations, particularly those of France and Germany.

D'Estournelles had tremendous energy and eclectic interests. He published translations from the classical Greek, wrote on Greek culture, won the French Academy's Prix Therouanne in 1891 with a book on French politics in Tunisia, and wrote a play based on the Pygmalion myth. His outpour of speeches and pamphlets covered topics ranging from French politics to feminism, from arbitration to aviation. Married to an American, Daisy Sedgwick-Berend, his command of English was excellent, and he became a leading French authority on the United States. He found time to engage in fencing, yachting, and painting, and when the automobile and the airplane came on the scene he pursued a keen interest in both.

D'Estournelles died in Paris on May 15, 1924 at the age of 72.

Bibliography —————————————————————————

International Peace 1906 Baron d'Estournelles de Constant and others. Edinburgh Peace and Arbitration Society, Edinburgh

RUTH C. REYNOLDS

International Peace Bureau (IPB)
(1910)

The Nobel Peace Prize for 1910 was awarded to the International Peace Bureau (IPB) to assist it in its established work of strengthening the peace movement through disseminating information between peace societies and peace congresses spread throughout the Old and New Worlds.

In the last two decades of the nineteenth century, peace societies had multiplied rapidly in a variety of countries (see Articles: *Peace Movements of the Nineteenth Century*). Frédéric Passy, co-winner of the first Nobel Peace Prize, and a foremost peace advocate, described the peace movement in Europe in the *American Journal of Sociology* in 1896. In the United Kingdom where the Peace Society had long been the only organization of its kind, he said, it had been joined by the International Arbitration and Peace Association, the International Arbitration League, and the Women's Peace Association, to name only a few. In France the Société Francaise pour l'Arbitrage included many well-known public figures; and in its wake a variety of local Christian organizations and women's societies took up the work for peace. Italy Passy called a "perfect hotbed for anti-military societies." The story was correspondingly heartening in many other countries: Portugal, Greece, Romania, all of Central Europe—Prussia, Austria, and Hungary.

A mass of literature poured out from these organizations and Passy also observed coverage in the regular press which would have been unthinkable a few years previously. It logically followed that the number of peace congresses increased proportionately, and, from 1889 on, an international peace congress was held annually in a different city—Paris, London, Rome, Berne, Budapest, Chicago, Boston, Milan all hosted them.

Inevitably, communication between the different societies and national groups was imperfect and often slow; which caused problems when circumstances required an immediate, concerted response. Thus there was an urgent need to coordinate this burgeoning activity. Fredrik Bajer, journalist, Danish parliamentarian, and ardent pacifist (and 1908 Peace Prize co-winner), brought to the third Peace Congress in Rome held in 1891 the concept of a central office and executive organ for this purpose. The following year the Bureau Internationale et Permanente de la Paix (Permanent International Peace Bureau) was founded with its headquarters at Berne. Passy described the far-reaching results. The peace movement in spite of its occasional grand demonstrations, had not been an organic, living body. It was only after the establishment of a legally incorporated International Bureau in Switzerland that the different peace societies became united into an organic whole, and this bureau, being a center of information and activity, became the heart and brain of the whole movement in both the Old World and the New. It accomplished for international peace and justice that which had been done in other spheres by international postal and telegraph bureaus, and by international copyright laws. Different publications were collected, news was recorded, information obtained, doubtful or obscure questions explained, propositions forwarded, and opinions received—all through the auspices of the Bureau. Passy called it "the living soul of the great body of peacemakers all over the world."

Also, the Bureau handled arbitration procedures and bilateral peace treaties. Along with arranging communication between the various individuals and organizations, it published *Correspondence bimensuelle* and a yearbook, *Annuaire du mouvement pacifiste.*

All this was accomplished through the dedication and skillful services of Elie Ducommun for the first 15 years of the organization, and, following his death in 1908, by Charles-Albert Gobat—both working without recompense. These men were co-winners of the second Nobel Peace Prize in 1902, Gobat having at that time been directing a similar organization which serviced the members of the Interparliamentary Bureau.

Owing to the high quality of their administrative and clerical skills, in a happy partnership with deep and sustained dedication, Ducommun and Gobat had each run this complex, vital service on a budget of from 8,000 to 9,000 francs (US$ 4000 to US$ 4500 current rate). The Peace Prize money gave the Bureau much needed financial stabilization.

Despite this success, the First World War dealt the Bureau a near lethal blow when the International Union of Peace Societies came to an end. Following the war an international governmental body, the League of Nations came into being. Although tentative, defective, and weak, the League existed to support the ideas of arbitration and mediation which had kept the prewar peace organizations occupied and purposeful. It would seem, then, that the *raison d'être* of the IPB disappeared when a central, unifying nongovernmental organization no longer seemed necessary. But the Bureau continued on, concentrating its efforts on communication of ideas and proposals of the peace movement from outside governmental organizations to agencies within governments. It became diversified in the organizations it worked with. Now serving multiple purposes as they arose, the IPB no longer functioned as a unifying agency.

The IPB changed it locale. In order to facilitate the reconstructed activity of peace movements and to work in closer contact with the new League of Nations, the Bureau moved in 1924 to Geneva, which is still the site of its headquarters. It continued to organize annual conferences, to build up and maintain a library, and to publish a periodical.

During the Second World War the work of the Bureau again came to a halt. In 1946, the year following the close of that war, it was reestablished as a new international organization called the International Liaison Committee of Organizations for Peace (ILCOP). After several years of negotiations, the Swiss Federal Council, which had been holding the frozen assets of the Permanent International Peace Bureau, recognized the ILCOP as the legal successor to the Bureau, and released the funds in its holding. The library went to the United Nations. Shortly after, the ILCOP readopted the name International Peace Bureau.

The Bureau still continues with much the same objectives. Its aim remains to "serve the cause of peace by the promotion of international cooperation and nonviolent solution of international conflicts." It works to facilitate communication between different national and international peace organizations, and between these organizations and governmental and intergovernmental bodies. Its established principle is one of nonalignment with such bodies. It no longer acts as a unifying agent, decision maker or mouthpiece for the peace movement as a whole. It does make the organization of international conferences the center of its activities, but such conferences are now more seminars than congresses, concentrating on different aspects of one given subject or project.

The preparation for such a project may be in considerable depth, taking two to four years for completion. The Bureau will handle a maximum of two such major projects at a time. The procedural steps are these: preparation of available documentation in a "working paper" and the conference itself, often preceded by a smaller preparatory seminar whose participants are recruited to secure attendance from three categories: (a) representatives of governments and governmental bodies, (b) peace research workers and other experts in the specific field, and (c) representatives of peace organizations and other national and international organizations concerned with the specific subject of the conference. It handles also the editing, publication, and distribution of the Conference Report, completed with any further documentation collected; and the final follow-up on the Conference findings and decisions, which in many cases involves transmitting proposals to certain governments or certain intergovernmental bodies (Herz 1969 p.4).

Today membership is open to: (a) international organizations working primarily for peace and international cooperation; (b) national peace councils or other federations coordinating the peace movement of their respective countries; (c) international organizations having the promotion of peace and international cooperation as one of their aims; (d) national and local organizations working directly for peace and international cooperation, or having the work for peace as one of their aims. Associate membership without voting rights is open to organizations and individuals who support the aim of the International Peace Bureau (Herz 1969 p.10).

History

The International Peace Bureau (IPB) was founded in Berne in 1891 with Fredrik Bajer (1908 Peace Prize co-winner) as its first president, and Elie Ducommun (1902 Peace Prize winner) its secretary-general. Its purpose was to coordinate information and answer questions. It did the planning for peace congresses, assisted with programs, implemented their decisions, and disseminated information following the congresses. It collected and issued information through a fortnightly publication, *Correspondance bimensuelle*, and a yearbook, *Annuaire du mouvement pacifiste*.

All this activity was taken care of first by Ducommun, and then, following his death in 1906, by Charles-Albert Gobat (1903 Peace Prize co-winner), who succeeded him as secretary-general. Both men worked with dedication and without pay.

The First World War had a great effect on the IPB. Following its close in 1918, and with the coming of the League of Nations, which was visualized as an organization assuming many of the functions which volunteer peace organizations had performed before the war, the Bureau changed its emphasis. It moved to Geneva to be near the League, and concentrated its efforts on gathering broad outlines of opinion within nongovernmental organizations and communicating these to governmental agencies. It continued to organize annual conferences, built up a library, and issued a periodical.

The Second World War, however, brought the IPB to a halt. Its assets were placed under the supervision of the Swiss Federal Council. Following the war the Bureau reorganized under the name of the International Liaison Committee of Organizations for Peace, (ILCOP) and after several years was recognized officially by the Swiss Federal Council as the legal successor to the International Peace Bureau, its funds being restored. The library went to the United Nations. The original name, the International Peace Bureau, was readopted soon after. Its program remains to "serve the cause of peace by the promotion of international cooperation and nonviolent solution of international conflicts." To this end it still acts as a clearinghouse for ideas, and still coordinates the activities of different peace organizations, but it no longer acts as an agent, a decision maker, or a mouthpiece for the peace movement as a whole. It cooperates with the United Nations as well as with nongovernmental bodies.

Bibliography

Herz U 1969 *The International Peace Bureau: History, Aims, Activities*. International Peace Bureau, Geneva
Passy F 1896 Peace movement in Europe. *Am. J. Sociol.* 1

RUTH C. REYNOLDS

Tobias Michael Carel Asser
(1911)

Tobias Asser was co-winner with Alfred Fried of the Nobel Peace Prize in 1911. An ardent and intelligent advocate of arbitration, he made his major contribution to peace in the field of international private law.

The Nobel award honored his role in the foundation of the Permanent Court of Arbitration of the first Hague Peace Conference in 1899.

Asser was an authority on international private law, and was convinced that arbitration could be accommodated by international conferences. Under his influence the Dutch government summoned four conferences at The Hague, in 1893, 1894, 1900, and 1904, for the Unification of International Private Law. Asser presided over all four. They attained the goal he had in mind, preparing the foundation for conventions which would establish uniformity in international private law, leading to greater public security and justice in future international relations. From the findings of these conventions, the responsibility then passed to participating countries to codify their national legislation accordingly.

Most of the countries of Europe sent representatives to the first two conferences, and they drew up a treaty establishing uniform international procedures for conducting civil trials. The conferences of 1900 and 1904 accomplished treaties covering family law, such as marriage, divorce, legal separation, guardianship of minors, and bills of exchange.

In collaboration with Dr. Rolin-Jaquemyns and John Westlake, Asser started the *Révue de droit international et de legislation comparée* (Journal of International Law and Comparative Legislation) in 1869. Four years later he was one of the founders of the Institute of International Law at Ghent, and later became its head.

On the practical side of international affairs, Asser accepted a position as legal adviser to the Netherlands Ministry of Foreign Affairs in 1875. In 1893 he resigned his professorship and retired from the bar to become a member of the Dutch Council of State, the government's highest administrative body. Beginning in 1898 he served as president of the State Commission for International Law. He was The Netherland's delegate to the Hague Peace Conferences of 1899 and 1907, where he made the practical and vital plea that the principle of compulsory arbitration be introduced into the economic area.

By now highly renowned as a negotiator, and equipped with fluent command of German, French, and English, Asser participated in virtually every treaty concluded by the Dutch government from 1875 to 1913. In the field of international law, he made a highly significant contribution to the international scene with his negotiations resulting in the neutralization of the Suez Canal. He succeeded in getting Spain and the Netherlands elected to the Suez Canal Commission as representatives of the smaller nations, along with the Great Powers.

Asser had the satisfaction of sitting as a member of the Permanent Court of Arbitration at The Hague when it heard its first case in 1902. The dispute was the United States and the Bishops of the Catholic Church versus Mexico, and the contention was over a fund set up in the eighteenth century to finance the Catholic Church in California. Following the war between the United States and Mexico in 1845 to 1848, after which the defeated Mexico ceded Upper California to the United States, Mexico refused to pay the Californian bishops monies due to them from the fund. The award was to the United States and the Bishops.

Again in 1902 Asser arbitrated a dispute, this time between the United States and Russia, over the seizure of five sealing vessels on the Bering Straits. Although the case was not taken to the Hague Tribunal, it was settled according to the code of that court.

"Asser has above all been a practical legal statesman," Jorgen Gunnarsson Lovland, Chairman of the Nobel Committee, said, and continued, "He holds a position in the sphere of international private law similar to that enjoyed by the famous French jurist Louis Renault in international public law. Indeed, his public activity has overshadowed his scholarly writing, which is of great importance in its own right. As a pioneer in the field of international legal relations, he has earned a reputation as one of the leaders in modern jurisprudence. It is therefore only natural that his countrymen should see him as successor to, or reviver of, The Netherlands' pioneer work in international law of the seventeenth century."

Biography

Tobias Michael Carel Asser was born in Amsterdam on April 28, 1838. His life was greatly influenced by his father and grandfather who were well-established lawyers and by his uncle who was a Dutch minister of justice. Asser was a brilliant student and in 1857 he won a competition with his thesis *"On the Economic Conception of Value."* He turned away from his business studies and took up law at the Amsterdam Athenaeum where he earned his doctorate in 1860. Later that year he was appointed a member of an international commission to abolish tolls on the Rhine River.

In 1862, he accepted a teaching appointment as professor of private law at the Athenaeum. He continued as a professor of international and commercial law when the institution was elevated to university status.

He persuaded the Dutch government to call several conferences of the European powers to design codifications of international private law. He was appointed as the presiding official for the 1893 and 1894 Hague Conferences. These conferences established uniform international procedures for conducting civil trials. The treaty took effect in May 1899. He also presided over the 1900 and 1904 conferences which produced treaties governing international family law. He was soon appointed legal counselor to the Dutch Foreign Office and in 1904 he became minister of state.

He was arbitrator in the dispute between the United States and Russia on the Bering Straits, and between the United States and Mexico on the Pious Fund of the Californias. The 1902 United States and Mexico dispute was the first dispute ever to reach The Hague Arbitration Court.

Asser was co-founder of the international law journal *Revue de droit international et de législation comparée* in 1869. He took part in the Ghent Conference which established the Institute of International Law, an organization he later headed.

He was legal adviser to the Netherlands Ministry of Foreign Affairs in 1875, became a member of the Council of State in 1893, served as president of the State Commission for International Law beginning in 1898 and was a delegate to the 1899 and 1907 Hague Peace Conferences.

Asser enriched the literature of the law. His more important works are *Schets van het internationaal Privaatrecht*, written in 1877, and *Schets van het Nederlandsche Handelsrecht*, written in 1904. For his juridical scholarship with its many forms of contributions to and clarifications of international law he was awarded honorary degrees by the Universities of Edinburgh, Cambridge, Bologna, and Berlin. A library of international law which Asser gathered with the help of contributions from 20 countries is housed in the Peace Palace at The Hague; it is appropriately and simply named "The Asser Collection."

Tobias Asser died on July 29, 1913.

See also: Articles: *Arbitration, International; International Law*

RUTH C. REYNOLDS

Alfred Hermann Fried
(1911)

When Alfred Fried was honored as co-winner with Tobias Asser of the 1911 Nobel Prize for Peace the Nobel Committee called him "the most industrious literary pacifist in the past twenty years." It was high praise indeed for a self-educated man who left school at 15 to work as a bookseller and who applied himself to the literary arts with such diligence that he mastered scholarly writing and created what the Nobel Committee called "the best journal in the peace movement."

Fried founded the Deutsche Friedensgesellschaft (German Peace Society) and edited its major publication, *Monatliche Friedenskorrespondenz* (Monthly Peace Correspondence), between 1894 and 1899. A disciple of Bertha von Suttner (1905 Nobel laureate), he and the Baroness worked closely together on peace promotion projects and, like her, Fried became a popular lecturer throughout Germany and Austria. He named a pacifist journal he was starting after her famous book, *Die Waffen nieder!* (Lay Down Your Arms!). Furthermore, he persuaded von Suttner to edit it. Eight years later, in 1899, it became *Die Friedenswarte* (The Peace Watch). Norman Angell, Peace Prize Laureate of 1933 and author of the highly successful *The Great Illusion*, called it "The most efficient periodical of the Pacifist movement in the world."

Fried edited *Die Friedenswarte* until his death, keeping its appeal toward intellectuals whose support he felt was vital to the cause of peace. He made an important contribution in influencing German views on the problems of international law, which previously had been heavily influenced by the Prussian ideology of might. The journal continues on, and is now published in Berlin. Its editorial policy under both Fried and later editors, beginning with Professor Hans Wehberg, has observed absolute objectivity in its treatment of the peace question.

Fried's goal was to go beyond questions of disarmament, which he considered only palliative, to address the causes lying behind warfare. He believed that international tension leading to wars would be alleviated by increased international understanding followed by appropriate legislation. With healthy international relations, based on legal and political orderliness replacing the existing armed peace, which Fried regarded as international anarchy, "symptoms" like military build-ups and wars would disappear automatically.

Fried contributed to the creation of the Verband für internationale Verstandigung (Society for International Understanding) in 1911. His theory of internationalism did not preclude nationalism, and he visualised a "Pan-European Bureau" modeled on the Pan-American pattern which would unite the countries of Europe while still respecting the sovereignty of each. He conceived of internationalism as based on international understanding, nourished by a central source of information on cultural, economic, and political issues. He established an annual review to promote interest in international cooperation. Called *Annuaire de la vie internationale*, it presented the example of Pan-America and also the Hague Conferences as existing steps taken in this direction.

Fried practiced truth in his journalism, and he scorned those who violated this principle for any reason. He called writers hired to beat the drums of war "priests of Philistinism," with the "pleasant task of mocking and making ridiculous the work of the Hague Conference according to the spirit of their mandates." To counter such bias in the press, he helped found the Union International de la Presse pour la Paix. Nor did he possess the usual tolerance for propaganda which inevitably accompanies war. During the First World War, although deploring and dissociating himself from the German official war policy, he openly refuted the untruths he saw about Germany in the French, British, and American press.

Fried was in Vienna in 1914 when the war broke out. Since his writing there would be subject to censorship, he availed himself of the neutrality of Switzerland and there continued publishing *Die Friedenswarte*. He also edited a periodical whose ambitious title reflected its remarkable aims in the midst of war-torn Europe: *Blätter für internationale Verstandigung und Zwischenstaatliche Organisation* (Papers for International Understanding and Interstate Organization). During his exile in Switzerland he kept a diary which was published following the war under the title *Mein Kriegstagebuch* (My War Journal). It was a monumental work in which he recorded his sentiments and activities, along with those of his colleagues, their histories, and coverage of organizations within the peace movement. In 1917 he published a collection of Baroness von Suttner's shorter writings to keep alive the cause of peace.

Prodigious though his literary output was, it far from constituted all of Fried's contribution in the peace movement. He had an impressive capacity as an organizer, and he was secretary-general of the Union Internationale de la Presse pour la Paix, a member of the Berne Peace Bureau, and secretary of the International Conciliation for Central Europe.

Fried was dismayed by the Versailles Treaty and organized a journalistic campaign protesting it; he tirelessly pressed the point that the war had proven the validity of the pacifists' analysis of world politics.

He wrote a less scholarly, but pungent evaluation of one of the graver problems challenging the peace movement, a comment which retains a ring of truth even to contemporary times: "The events of an international bicycle race are described in great detail and are eagerly swallowed up by the readers, just as the least significant comedian on the local stage is better known to the public than the people who make world history or the great events of historical importance."

The collapse of Austria-Hungary swept away the personal resources of Fried, and he died in poverty in Vienna on May 5, 1921, at the age of 57.

Biography

Alfred Hermann Fried was born in Vienna on November 11, 1864. Leaving school at 15, he first worked as a book seller. He moved to Berlin at 24, where, self-educated, he became a distinguished and successful journalist. A disciple of Baroness Bertha von Suttner (1925 Peace Prize winner), he founded the German Peace Society (*Deutsche Friedensgesellschaft*) and edited its major publication, *Monthly Peace Correspondence* (Monatlich Friedenskorrespondenz) from 1894 to 1899. He started a peace journal with von Suttner as editor called *Lay Down Your Arms!* (Die Waffen nieder!) after the title of the Baroness's famous novel. Eventually this became *The Peace Watch* (Die Friedenswarte) a periodical addressed to intellectuals, which has continued to the present day and is now published in Berlin. In 1905 Fried launched an annual review, *Annuaire de la vie internationale*, reflecting his interest in international cooperation.

Fried was a member of the Bern Peace Bureau, secretary of the International Conciliation for Central Europe, and secretary-general of the Union Internationale de la Presse pour la Paix. A founding member of the Society for International Understanding (Verband für internationale Verstandigung), he believed in economic cooperation and political organization among nations, with full respect of the sovereignty of each one, as the way to prevent wars rather than through disarmament.

During the First World War, which he deplored, he lived in Switzerland and continued with publication of *The Peace Watch*. He also wrote a major work on the peace movement called *My War Journal* (Mein Kriegstagebuch) which recorded not only his sentiments, but those of his colleagues, their history and that of the organizations of the peace movement.

Following the war Fried organized a journalistic campaign protesting against the Versailles Treaty. He lost his personal resources in the collapse of Austria-Hungary and died in poverty in Vienna on May 5, 1921.

See also: Articles: *Die Waffen nieder!*

RUTH C. REYNOLDS

Elihu Root
(1912)

The 1912 Nobel Prize for Peace was awarded to an American stateman, Elihu Root. We have the opinion of 1931 laureate Nicholas Murray Butler, adviser to seven presidents, that "No American in the last half-century has equalled him in the field of constructive statesmanship or in intellectual grasp and power of exposition." The editors of the *New York World* agreed that Root was "one of the few living statesmen of the first intellectual rank."

Yet this Peace Prize laureate first served in the government as Secretary of War from 1899 to 1901 in the cabinets of William McKinley and Theodore Roosevelt. A case might be made that in this post, Root's work was diametrically opposed to Nobel's desire for a "reduction of standing armies and outlawing of war." With a reading of Root's outstanding Nobel lecture, however, questions about the qualifications of the man are laid to rest. It is an unflinching examination of the problems existing between humankind and permanent peace, and an eloquent statement about the philosophy behind his statesmanship which addressed these problems.

Root opened his lecture with the assertion that the humanitarian purpose behind the Peace Prize was more than a reward; it should also stimulate thought upon the means and methods best adapted, under the changing conditions of future years, to approach and ultimately attain the end Nobel so much desired. He warned that the simplicity of the subject is misleading: "The recognition of the horrors of war and the blessings of peace, the mere assemblage of peaceloving people to interchange convincing reasons for their common faith are not enough to reach or modify the causes of war . . . . And the mere repetition of the obvious by good people . . . is subject to the drawback that the unregenerate world grows weary of iteration and reacts in the wrong direction."

He said that the limitation of this mode of promoting peace lies in the fact that war is the natural reaction of human nature in the savage state, while peace is the result of acquired characteristics, a matter primarily of development of character and the shifting of standards of conduct—a long, slow process. Root's work, both within his several government posts and his activities following his government service, was a steady effort to shift the standards of conduct wherever he might.

Root realized more clearly than most people the necessity of gaining the confidence of the Latin American states. He made a great effort as Secretary of State to overcome the considerable suspicion with which the United States was viewed by its neighbors to the south. He proposed that the Pan-American Conference of 1906 should take place deep in their territory, and his suggestion of Rio de Janeiro was well-received. Even more important was his extensive goodwill tour, visiting Uruguay, Argentina, Chile, Peru, Panama, and Colombia. He made countless addresses stressing the desire of the United States to cooperate on an equal basis. Then, the following year, he took the initiative in convoking a Central American Peace Conference at Washington and he persuaded Latin American states to participate in the Second Hague Peace Conference.

His accomplishments in Latin America continued. A complicated relationship with Colombia was settled after two years of negotiations. He was able to regularize the relationship with San Domingo, and, in cooperation with Mexico, assisted in ironing out points of difference between the Central American republics. All this patient work resulted in the establishment of a permanent court of arbitration for Central American states at Carthage, Costa Rica, and the creation of the Pan-American Bureau in Washington, DC.

In the matter of arbitration with European countries, the United States had a history of presidents interested in achieving arbitration treaties from the time of President Cleveland (1885-89 and 1893-97), and the Senate had an equally long record in setting up insurmountable obstacles. Secretary Root himself was an ardent advocate of arbitration, and spoke of it in his Nobel lecture. "There have been occasional international arbitrations from the very early times, but arbitration as a system, a recognized and customary method of diplomatic procedure rather than an exceptional expedient, had its origin in the Hague Conference of 1899," he said, ". . . these declarations, although enforced by no binding stipulation, nevertheless have become principles of action in international affairs because, through the progress of civilization, and the influence of many generations of devoted spirits in the cause of humanity, the world had become ready. . . ."

"Plainly, the next advance to be urged . . . is to pass on from an arbitral tribunal, the members of which are specifically selected . . . for each case, and whose service is but an incident in the career of a diplomatist, to a permanent court composed of judges who devote their entire time to the performance of judicial duties . . . ."

Deeply convinced that the time was ripe to advance arbitration, Root succeeded in persuading the Senate to forgo their objections to treaties of arbitration with European countries, and in 1908-1909 he managed to achieve some 40 reciprocal treaties of arbitration with various Latin American and European countries as well as with Japan.

Root believed there was no international controversy so serious that it could not be settled if both parties wished to settle it. Conversely, there were few controversies so trifling that they could not be made the occasion for war if the parties really wished to fight. Root pinpointed disposing causes which create an atmosphere of belligerency, among which were race and local prejudice breeding dislike and hatred between the peoples of different countries. He had opportunity to combat an instance of just such an attitude. A wave of Japanese immigration had swept over the Pacific Coast, and racial discrimination had run rampant. Japanese children were being refused admission to California schools. Root, however, persuaded California authorities to withdraw all objections to Japanese children in the schools. He negotiated a "Gentleman's Agreement" with the Japanese government by which Japan would control immigration to the United States, thereby avoiding passage of exclusionary immigration laws.

Root became a senator in 1909, serving in the Senate until 1915. As chief US Counsel before the Hague Court in 1910, he settled the US-British controversy over the North Atlantic coastal fisheries. Along with Lord Bryce, he resolved current US-Canadian problems of the time and created the Permanent American-Canadian Joint High Commission for the settlement of any future difficulties. Also while he was a senator, he had an opportunity to display an interest in justice obtained over and above nationalistic partiality by reversing the US Panama Act, a bill passed in 1912 which exempted US shipping from paying tolls to use the Panama Canal while levying charges against other nations' shipping. Under his guidance this was repealed in 1914.

He was the leading Republican supporter of the League of Nations. Despite the failure of the United States to join the League, he was granted the opportunity to contribute to his long-time dream of a permanent court furthering the role of arbitration between the community of nations. At the request of the Council of the League he served on the League's commission of jurists which framed the Statute for the Permanent Court of International Justice which was set up in 1921.

However, in 1929 after intermittent discussion between the League and the United States concerning certain reservations the Senate had insisted upon in its 1926 ratification of the Protocol of US participation in the court, Root convinced the delegates from 55 nations to accept a revised Protocol. But when he appeared before the US Senate Foreign Relations Committee to urge ratification he met an obstinate Senate which failed to act at that time and ultimately declined to ratify at all.

Root was also the first president of the Carnegie Endowment for International Peace, serving from 1910 to 1925. He helped to found its European counterpart, and worked on its programs for the advancement of pure science.

These opportunities to act upon his dedication to the cause of international arbitration did not alter Root's realism toward the long and arduous road ahead before the threat of war would yield to a major acceptance of arbitration. Nor did the reversals he encountered destroy his faith in an ultimate resolution. "The attractive idea that we can now have a parliament of men with authority to control the conduct of nations by legislation or an international police force with power to enforce national conformity to rules of right conduct is a counsel of perfection," he said. "The world is not ready for any such thing . . . . Human nature must come much nearer perfection than it is now, or will be in many generations, to exclude from such control prejudice, selfishness, ambition and injustice . . . ."

Yet it was in the inherent traits of human nature that Root placed his confidence for the ultimate permanent prevalence of peace. "There is so much good in human nature that men grow to like each other upon better acquaintance, and this points to another way in which we may strive to promote the peace of the world," he said. He recommended international conciliation through personal acquaintance between peoples, with little courtesies and kindly considerations; by the exchange of professors between universities, by exchange of students between countries, by expressions of praise and honor rather than the reverse. In sum, "by constant pressure in the right direction in a multitude of ways . . . ."

"Each separate act will seem of no effect," he said, "but all together they will establish and maintain a tendency towards the goal of international knowledge and broad human sympathy . . . ."

"Not by invoking an immediate millenium, but by the accumulated effects of a multitude of efforts, each insignificant in itself, but steadily and persistently continued, we must win our way along the road to better knowledge and kindliness among the peoples of the earth which the will of Alfred Nobel describes as 'the fraternity of nations.'"

Biography

Elihu Root was born on February 15, 1845, in Clinton, New York, son of Oren Root, a mathematics professor at Hamilton College. From this same college Root graduated at the age of 19, first in his class. After teaching at Rome (New York) for one year, he entered the Law School of New York University and received his law degree in 1867. He became a highly successful corporate lawyer. From 1883 to 1885 he was US district attorney for the southern district of New York. He served as legal adviser to Theodore Roosevelt during much of the latter's political career in New York.

A member of the reform element in the Republican Party, in 1899 Root accepted the post of Secretary of War in the McKinley cabinet. During the next five years he worked out arrangements for the former Spanish areas which came under US control following the Spanish-American War, devising a plan for returning Cuba to the Cubans; he eliminated tariffs on Puerto Rican goods and provided for civil government in Puerto Rico, and established US authority in the Philippines. He reorganized the administrative system of the War Department, reorganized the Army, establishing new procedures for promotion, and founded the Army War College.

In 1905, he became Secretary of State under President Theodore Roosevelt, and during his four years in this post he mended deteriorating US-South and Central American relations with a diplomatic tour, and persuaded the Latin American states to attend the second Hague Peace Conference. He brought the consular service under the Civil Service. He negotiated a "Gentleman's Agreement" with Japan in which that country agreed to limit immigration, and he influenced the West Coast to cease practices of racial discrimination against Japanese children by barring them from schools. He concluded an unprecedented number of treaties of arbitration with many Latin American and European nations as well as with Japan.

Root sponsored the Central American Peace Conference in Washington which resulted in the creation of the Central American Court of Justice, and along with Lord Bryce resolved US-Canadian problems then outstanding and created the Permanent American-Canadian Joint High Commission for settlement of future disputes. He served in the US Senate from 1909 to 1915, during which time he reversed a bill exempting US shipping from paying tolls to use the Panama Canal while other nations had to pay charges. As chief counsel for the United States before the Hague Tribunal he settled the controversy between the United States and the United Kingdom over North Atlantic coastal fisheries.

He was the leading Republican supporter of the League of Nations, recommending acceptance of the Versailles Treaty with minor reservations. He served on the League's commission of jurists which framed the statute for the Permanent Court of International Justice. Between 1910 and 1925 he was the first president of the Carnegie Endowment for International Peace, advancing pure science and peace programs, and helped to found its European counterpart.

He received many honors from many countries, including the LL.D. degree from Hamilton, Harvard, Yale, Columbia, New York University, Williams, Princeton, the University of Buenos Aires, the University of San Marcos, and the University of Lima. He won the Woodrow Wilson Foundation Medal in 1926.

Elihu Root died in New York City on February 7, 1937.

See also: Articles: *Arbitration, International; Pan-Americanism*

RUTH C. REYNOLDS

Henri La Fontaine
(1913)

The 1913 Nobel Prize for Peace was awarded to Henri Marie La Fontaine, whom the Nobel Committee called "the true leader of the popular peace movement in Europe." Henri La Fontaine was an internationalist whose fervent devotion to his ideals was matched by the extraordinary talents he brought to their actualization. Highly educated, he was one of Belgium's leading jurists, a zealous reformer, a pro-fessor of law, for 36 years a senator in the Belgian legislature (and the senate's vice-president for 14 of those years), a dedicated educator, and a prolific writer.

In addition, he had an immense talent and proclivity for organization. He inaugurated an ambitious bibliographical scheme wherein he established the Institute International de Bibliographic. This "House of

Documentation" was a vast information retrieval scheme in which he filed, indexed, and provided information for retrieval on anything of note published anywhere in the world. With the help of a subsidy from the Belgian government, and through collaboration with Paul Otlet, he brought some of his plan to realization by developing a universal classification system and by producing reference works, particularly bibliographies of social sciences and peace. This developed into the Union of International Associations, located in Brussels. It was granted consultative status with the Economic and Social Council of the United Nations in 1951 and with UNESCO in 1952. It remains the only center in the world devoted to documentation, research, and promotion of international organizations, particularly the voluntary variety.

The peace movement before the First World War was so widespread, both in the Old World and the New, that it required a global network to unite the efforts of peace societies and the proliferating peace congresses and conferences. An organization was created to act as a clearinghouse for an ongoing exchange of information. Called the International Peace Bureau (Nobel Peace Prize winner of 1910), it was first organized and directed by the 1902 Nobel Peace Prize winner Elie Ducommun. Following his death, the co-winner of the 1902 prize, Charles-Albert Gobat, took up the leadership. La Fontaine accepted the directorship following Fredrik Bajer, co-winner of the 1908 prize.

La Fontaine also actively participated in the peace conferences. In 1889 he became secretary-general of the Société Belge de l'Arbitrage et de la Paix, and thereafter attended virtually all of the peace congresses held in the following 25 years. He was a member of the Belgian delegation to the Paris Peace Conference in 1919 and to the First Assembly of the League of Nations in 1920 and 1921. To these deliberations La Fontaine brought his uncompromising internationalism backed by his judicial expertise. He also gave his legislative support to the League of Nations, the establishment of an economic union with Luxembourg, the Locarno Pacts, the Kellogg-Briand Pact, disarmament, and the legal means of settling international disputes.

Another organization of paramount importance to La Fontaine was the Interparliamentary Union. Created in 1888 by two Nobel Prize winners, Frédéric Passy (1901) and William Cremer (1903), its purpose was to encourage and accommodate members of parliaments from nations all over the world to meet at specified intervals for discussions on matters of

mutual interest. Of particular importance was the solving of problems before they became so entangled with special interests and so charged with emotion that they became difficult or impossible to arbitrate. To La Fontaine, the Union was an embryo world parliament, a supreme vehicle for arbitration, the precursor of a world government. He poured his energy and his professional acumen as a leading international jurist into making it work. He was chairman of its Juridical Committee prior to the First World War and a member of two of its important commissions, one on preparation of a model world parliament and the second on drafting a model treaty of arbitration.

Although La Fontaine's ultimate dream was of a world state, he was realistic enough to recognize that it was not coming soon, and during the First World War he wrote his best-known work, *The Great Solution: Magnissma Charta*, to sketch a "constitution" which would be appropriate for the many intervening years to come, but which would eventually be incorporated in the world state, and which in the meantime would prevent future wars. He proposed a plan for an international intellectual union, accompanied by the creation of international agencies that logically follow from the acceptance of the international idea, such as a world school and university, library, language, parliament, court, bank, and clearinghouses for labor, trade, immigration, and statistical information. In later years some of these ideas are thought to have influenced affiliated bodies of the League of Nations, such as the Institute of Intellectual Cooperation.

Also during the war he wrote *International Judicature*, outlining the essentials for a supreme court of the world, but he allowed himself little hope at the time. He wrote in a letter, "The peoples are not awake ... [There are dangers] which will render a world organization impossible. I foresee the renewal of ... the secret bargaining behind closed doors. Peoples will be as before, the sheep sent to the slaughterhouses or to the meadows as it pleases the shepherds. International institutions ought to be, as the national ones in democratic countries, established by the peoples and for the peoples" (letter to David Starr Jordan, President of Stanford University, dated December 29, 1916).

Henri La Fontaine's letter proved prophetic within his lifetime. He lived to see his native Belgium invaded once again.

Biography

Henri Marie La Fontaine was born on April 22, 1854, in Brussels, Belgium. Besides serving in the Belgian senate for

36 years, for 14 of which he was its vice-president, this gifted scholar was also a distinguished international jurist, educator, vigorous reformer, and prolific writer. An internationalist, his overriding interest was peace through arbitration.

La Fontaine studied law at Brussels University, and was admitted to the bar in 1877. In 1893 he became professor of international law at the Université Nouvelle in Brussels.

La Fontaine supported and eventually directed the International Peace Bureau, through which he played a substantive role in arranging the Hague Peace Conferences of 1899 and 1907. He also worked vigorously in the Interparliamentary Union when he became eligible for that organization through becoming a member of the Belgian senate. He was a member of the Belgian delegation to the Paris Peace Conference in 1919 and to the League of Nations Assembly in 1920, both organizations benefiting from the influence of La Fontaine's lifetime of work toward international organizations.

He founded the Centre Intellectuel Mondial which later merged into the League of Nations Institute for Intellectual Cooperation. He proposed the organization of a world school and university, a world parliament, and an international court of justice.

La Fontaine organized a vast information retrieval scheme in which he proposed to file, index, and provide information for retrieval on anything of note published anywhere. He produced a universal classification system out of this project, and some bibliographies in the fields of social sciences and peace. It ultimately led to the Union of International Associations, and became a resource center for the Economic and Social Council of the United Nations in 1951 and UNESCO in 1952.

La Fontaine was involved with education all his life; he occupied the chair of international law from 1893 to 1940, first at the Université Nouvelle when it was a branch of the Free University of Brussels, and then at the Institut des Hautes after the branch merged with the University. He offered courses of lectures on disarmament, the League of Nations, international misunderstanding, world federation, and the law in relation to political and moral crises in the world.

From his prodigious writing, these titles are outstanding works on internationalism: *Manuel des lois de la paix: Code de l'arbitrage* (A Manual on the Laws of Peace: Code of Arbitration), *Pasicrisie internationale: Histoire documentaire des arbitrages internationaux* (Documentary History of International Arbitrations), a source book of 368 documents on arbitration between 1794 and 1900, printed in whole or in part in their original languages, and *Bibliographic de la paix et de l'arbitrage internationale*, a reference work of 2,222 entries. One of his most famous titles, *"The Great Solution,"* offers a set of principles for organized international relations.

He was a leading spokesman for women's rights, taking an advanced position on the place of women in the legal profession, and he was president of the Association for the Professional Education of Women.

La Fontaine enjoyed mountain climbing, and organizer that he was, he compiled an international bibliography of *Alpinism*.

Henri Marie La Fontaine died in Belgium in 1943.

RUTH C. REYNOLDS

Prize Not Awarded
(1914-16)

Red Cross
(1917)
see Henri Dunant and the Red Cross
(1901)   (1917, 1944, 1963)

Prize Not Awarded
(1918)

Thomas Woodrow Wilson
(1919)

The Nobel Peace Prize for 1919 was awarded to the President of the United States, Woodrow Wilson, in recognition of his introducing "a design for a fundamental law of humanity into present-day international politics." The president of the Norwegian parliament, Anders Buen, further declared that "the basic concept of justice on which it is founded will never die, but will steadily grow in strength . . . ."

In his response, President Wilson expressed his "very poignant humility before the vastness of the work still called for by this cause," adding that "if there were but one such prize, or if this were to be the last, I could not, of course, accept it. For mankind has not yet been rid of the unspeakable horror of war. I am convinced that our generation has, despite its wounds, made notable progress. But it is the better part of our wisdom to consider our work as only begun. It will be a continuing labor . . . ."

Wilson entered politics in 1910, becoming Governor of New Jersey, a state that had long been dominated by corporate interests. He brought firmness and purpose to his new role, pushing through the legislature laws designed to clear up corruption and protect the public from exploitation by the big trusts. His success catapulted him into the national arena, where he won the Democratic nomination for the Presidency. Largely because Theodore Roosevelt had split the Republican vote, Wilson became President of the United States within two years of leaving Princeton.

Wilson's political philosophy was simple. He was a liberal individualist, insistent upon the right of unprivileged persons. These principles as applied to tariff and currency reform, labor legislation, and the doctrine he would later seek of self-determination for oppressed nationalities would all spring from this same source.

During his first two years he dominated Congress and achieved reforms of long-term historical significance, revising tariffs downward, creating a banking system under governmental control, and establishing a commission which checked overwhelming concentration of power in industry.

But with the coming of the First World War in 1914, Wilson's attention was chiefly directed to protecting the United States' neutrality. The British increasingly restricted US commerce, but this affected only trade. Far more serious was Germany's submarine warfare which threatened human life. By careful and patient negotiation Wilson avoided an open breach with the Germans for almost three years, even after the sinking of the liner *Lusitania* with the loss of a thousand lives, 128 of them American. Through negotiation, Wilson succeeded in persuading Germany to abandon its U-boat warfare.

In 1916 Wilson was re-elected, largely on the electorate's approval of his keeping the United States out of the war. Wilson made repeated efforts to bring the belligerents together, but his hopes were dashed when Germany declared unlimited warfare on the seas.

Wilson did not take lightly the immense responsibility of leading the American people into war. "It is a fearful thing to lead this great, peaceful people into war, into the most terrible and disastrous of all wars, civilization itself seeming to be in the balance," he told Congress as he asked for a declaration of war on April 2, 1916.

During that same month Wilson started to formulate the terms of peace when war should end. During his speech to Congress he had spoken of the reasons powerful enough to justify entering the war: "for democracy, for the right of those who submit to authority to have a voice in their own governments, for the rights and liberties of small nations, for a universal dominion of right by such a concert of free people as shall bring peace and safety to all nations and make the world itself at last free."

These were the principles he continued to visualize as basic to a lasting peace resting on a foundation of justice for all. In January, 1918, he gave his speech of the Fourteen Points. Eight of his points referred to specific national settlements; the others recommended open diplomacy, freedom of the seas, free trade, reduction of armaments, readjustment of colonial claims, and establishment of the League of Nations to enforce the peace terms and prevent future wars. As a historical scholar, he could understand Baroness von Suttner's warning, "Every war, whatever the results may be, contains within itself the seed of future wars." Wilson was determined to break the historical pattern of repeating injustices, and he saw the League of Nations as the means to that end.

It has been suggested that President Wilson unwisely assumed personal direction of the United States' part in the negotiations at the Paris Peace Conference. Certainly both party leaders in the United States opposed this. The months in Paris would put Wilson dangerously out of touch with the outlook of his own people. But Wilson felt a personal responsibility, a duty he could not delegate, to help bring about an enduring peace.

However, a first mistake was certainly his failure to include any Republicans in the group he took with him to the conference. In the congressional elections of 1918 the Republicans had won the ascendancy in Congress, and this would have been the strategic, as well as the fair, thing for President Wilson to have done. He was at the zenith of his power during this time, and he went to Paris as the herald of a new age, an universally acclaimed champion of international justice. It may have been difficult to think in terms of home politics under such circumstance, but in failing to do so Wilson unwittingly contributed to the ultimate defeat of his cherished plans for the League.

Furthermore, he soon found himself outmaneuvered by seasoned career politicians. As the deliberations progressed, old ambitions, suspicions, and prejudices surfaced, and Wilson discovered that the world's ablest diplomats were striving to advance not the cause of international justice which he had come to serve, but their separate interests and aspirations in behalf of their respective governments. He saw his Fourteen Points broken and compromised by a network of secret treaties and understandings previously unknown to him.

Wilson returned home with the first draft of the Treaty of Versailles in order to be in Washington DC when Congress adjourned. Thirty-seven Republican senators declared their opposition to the League covenant and protested its inclusion in the treaty. When Wilson returned to Paris he found that in his absence the allied premiers had passed a resolution that would have resulted in the separation of the League covenant from the treaty. In exchange for keeping the League in the treaty, the wily European diplomats succeeded in bartering away Wilson's Fourteen Points. Wilson was forced into accepting a seriously flawed treaty, imposed by the will of the victors upon the vanquished, dividing the globe into indefensible little chunks, and most seriously, crippling Germany with a plan that it should pay for the war through savage reparation demands.

Wilson lost the faith of the European peoples who had pinned upon him their hopes for a new and revolutionary kind of peace. Lloyd George wrote after Wilson's death, "I believe I may say that never have I seen such vicious, cruel vituperation as was heaped upon him at home and in Paris ... such abuse never was leveled at any man in like position in history and it hurt him terribly."

At home, Wilson carried the Treaty of Versailles back to secure ratification by two-thirds of the Republican-controlled Senate. In this he failed by 15 votes. However, it is the opinion of many historians that Wilson could have had his treaty had he been willing to accept relatively minor changes relating to certain reservations on the collective security provisions which membership in the League would entail. His initial failure to take a high-ranking Republican with him to Paris, his loss of contact with the American public during the many months spent in Paris, his inability to countenance changes in the treaty when the Senate offered compromise, and a serious deterioration in his health following a stroke which rendered impossible his further efforts to persuade either the public or the Senate all added up to Wilson's fatal choice of taking the issue of unconditional ratification into the 1920 presidential campaign. It was his hope that the American public would vote a mandate for the treaty by electing a new Democratic president. But with the resounding defeat of the Democrats, all hopes for the treaty died.

Despite Wilson's failure to secure a just peace and the United States' entrance into the League, he must still be credited with introducing before the world a concept of international justice and morality which had lasting significance. He bequeathed his generation, and following generations, with a faith that such an order might be possible, and in the United Nations, much of Wilson's work and idealism came to fruition.

Biography

Thomas Woodrow Wilson was born in Stauton, Virginia, on December 28, 1856, son of a Presbyterian minister and a devout mother whose own father was also a Presbyterian minister. He was raised in a pious, loving, and rigidly authoritarian home.

While in college Wilson evinced an early and deep interest in government and political science. During his senior year at Princeton he wrote a paper comparing the British and US systems of government which was published in the *International Review*; at Johns Hopkins University his Ph.D. dissertation was a scholarly study of US congressional government.

In 1885 he began 25 years of teaching, first at Bryn Mawr College for two years, then at Wesleyan for two years, and finally at Princeton, where he remained until 1910. He became the president at Princeton, and brought reforms in the social and academic systems which raised Princeton to distinguished new heights among US universities.

In 1910 he entered politics, and as a reforming governor of New Jersey cleared corruption and put through legislation protecting the public from exploitation by big trusts. In

1912, as a Democratic candidate for the Presidency, he won chiefly owing to a split in the Republican party. Though plagued by a near civil war in Mexico he managed reform legislation of historical significance, but his greatest achievement was maintaining US neutrality during the First World War. This took tact and determination in the face of British and German warfare at sea, the former intrusive upon US trade and the latter, with the use of submarines, endangering American lives. Wilson repeatedly attempted mediation between the belligerent nations, but to no avail. The most severe test of his diplomacy was the German sinking of the *Lusitania* with the loss of 128 American lives among the thousand victims of that tragedy. Wilson sent a stiff note to the German government, and with persistent negotiations extracted a promise from the Germans to discontinue their U-boat warfare.

In 1916 he was re-elected, chiefly on his keeping the United States out of the war, but soon after his re-election Germany declared unlimited warfare on the seas. As a result, on April 2 the United States entered the war. Wilson proved a skillful wartime executive, but he also began a carefully constructed plan for the treaty which would come at the war's end. He wished for a peace so just that it would contain no seeds for a future war. His peace plan was the "Fourteen Points," eight of which involved more or less specific territorial and political problem solving, and six concerned with general principles of international relations: open covenants, freedom of navigation, removal of economic barriers, reduction of armaments, readjustment of colonial claims, and establishment of a League of Nations.

Wilson went to Paris to represent the United States in the negotiating of the Treaty of Versailles. There he was outmaneuvered by the seasoned diplomats Lloyd George of the United Kingdom and Clemenceau of France, whose negotiations were based upon their own national interests, upon their belief in military might, and upon their determination to crush Germany under massive reparation assessments. A vindictive document, the Treaty of Versailles retained only the League of Nations from Wilson's Fourteen Points for a peace based on justice.

Wilson's defeat was completed when he took the treaty home for congressional ratification. The Senate refused to pass an unmodified treaty; Wilson refused to compromise. Now seriously broken in health following a stroke, he unwisely carried the deadlocked issue into the 1920 presidential election. With his subsequent defeat the treaty with its vital provision for the United States' entrance into the League of Nations was never ratified.

Although he failed to get either a just peace or the United States' entrance into the League of Nations, Wilson must still be credited with a campaign for world order which had a lasting significance. He gave his generation, and following generations, the faith that such an order might be possible, and the Charter of the United Nations reflects his aspirations.

Wilson was married in 1885 to Ellen Louise Axson. They had three daughters, Margaret Woodrow, Jessie Woodrow and Eleanor Randolph Wilson. Mrs Wilson died in the White House shortly after the outbreak of the First World War. In 1916 he married Edith Bolling Galt, who survived him by many years.

Woodrow Wilson died in Washington, DC, on February 3, 1924.

Bibliography ———————————

Current History 1924 The death of Woodrow Wilson. 19(6)

RUTH C. REYNOLDS

Leon Victor Auguste Bourgeois
(1920)

The 1920 Nobel Peace Prize was awarded at the first ceremony to be held following the most devastating military conflict the world had seen—a "war to end all wars." The choice of France's Leon Bourgeois for the 1920 Prize, and retroactively of Woodrow Wilson of the United States for the 1919 Prize, represented the great hope vested in the League of Nations as an instrument for fulfilling this promise of lasting peace. Bourgeois was the embodiment of the continuity of this ideal, from the time of the Hague Peace Conferences of 1899 and 1907 when he laid the groundwork for the League to the gathering of its first Assembly in 1920.

Bourgeois believed that international cooperation could be achieved on the basis of the principles of arbitration and international justice that had been evolved at the Hague Conferences. The League he saw as a juridical military organization whose function would be to preserve peace, if necessary by sanctions. It would be called upon only when needed. This was the basis on which he built the case for the League when, as a necessary adjunct to arbitration, he announced somewhat prematurely in 1908 that "the League of Nations is created. It is very much alive."

The President of the Norwegian Parliament,

Anders Buen, saluted Bourgeois as representative of the will for peace "through good days and bad." His praise summarized the position of countless other members of the peace movement whose activities had been in full flower at the onset of the First World War. These activists within peace and arbitration organizations over the world rallied in support of their countries through years of the very violence they had sought to prevent. But even as the war raged through 1914 to nearly the close of 1918, many were formulating a peace designed to prevent future wars.

A realist, Bourgeois viewed the position of his country as precarious without an international organization. In 1916 he had written, "We must see things as they are .... Now the balance of power, however skillful diplomats may be, results in the triumph of the greatest number and the most brutal, and not in the triumph of the noblest, the proudest, the worthiest. It is another policy, therefore, the policy of justice, which alone can give peace and security to France and the nations which do not seek to establish themselves by violence. There will be no policy of justice if the League of Nations is not set up."

A commission was established in 1917 to study the mechanisms through which the Société des Nations might work. Bourgeois was a leading contributor to the work of this commission, and it was he who submitted its conclusions to the Paris Peace Conference in January 1919.

The hope for a peace treaty based upon justice dispensed without regard to victor and vanquished was destroyed at the Paris Peace Conference with the creation of the Treaty of Versailles. The one beacon of hope now rested with the League of Nations. The Assembly of the League met for the first time on November 15, 1920, and Bourgeois was France's principal representative.

In a communication to the Nobel Committee in 1922, Bourgeois wrote of the new international law whose doctrine was uncontested by any civilized nation. He posed the question, "Have we arrived at a stage in the development of universal morality and of civilization that will allow us to regard a League of Nations as viable? What characteristics and what limitations should it have in order to adapt itself to the actual state of affairs in the world?"

Bourgeois expressed encouragement. He pointed to the immense progress already made in the political, social, and moral organization of nations: public education had spread to nearly every corner of the globe; democratic institutions were evident everywhere, with a weakening of the class prejudice so obstructive to social progress; an increasing number

of social institutions now offered support to the rights of the individual, and Bourgeois believed that this would lead ultimately to the concept of the individual's responsibility for his or her conduct being in no way at odds with society itself.

He saw all these factors as preparation for the intellectual revolution that would lead people to understand the absolute necessity of having an international organization which would recognize and accommodate these principles. A fundamental necessity would be the guarantee that nothing essential could be violated by any of the contracting parties. This would require a "sovereign standard" by which each settlement could be measured and checked as needed, an absolutely impartial international law. Such a law came into being at the Hague Peace Conferences, Bourgeois maintained, and if this law was all too obviously violated in 1914 and during the war years, the Allied victory had righted the wrong done. It had been fought and won in the name of ending all wars.

As a realist, Bourgeois acknowledged the need for a means of enforcement beyond that of moral force. But he stipulated that no nation could find itself suddenly involved against its will in a military operation without the explicit consent of its government. He said that in connection with the difficult problem of limitation of armaments neither the Council nor the Assembly of the League had ever believed it possible to enact relevant statutes without the express support of every nation. He proposed that each nation would remain free to give or withhold its consent to any concerted military action. This left but one possible punishment open to the recalcitrant nation: the loss of the benefits of membership in the League.

In 1921, the Assembly of the League had adopted a resolution presented by Bourgeois concerning the establishment of the Commission on Intellectual Cooperation. Bourgeois defined intellectual cooperation as the pooling of all intellectual resources for mutual and equitable exchange. "All living organisms must have a driving force, a moving spirit," he wrote. "From all these diverse forces arising from nations and races, is it not possible to give birth to a communal soul, to a common science for a communal life, associating but not absorbing the traditions and hopes of every country in a concerted thrust for justice?"

Bourgeois concluded his message to the Nobel Committee with the acknowledgment that many years of trial must yet elapse and many retrogressions yet occur before an organization like the League of Nations could realize its potential and achieve its purpose. But he dared to hope that the "potent benefits of peace and of human solidarity will triumph . . . ."

Biography

Léon Victor Auguste Bourgeois was born on May 21, 1851, in Paris, where he lived most of his life. A diligent student, he studied at the Massin Institution and the Lycée Charlemagne. Enthusiastic and with eclectic interests, his curriculum included studies in Hinduism and Sanskrit, as well as the fine arts, including music and sculpture. Following a degree from the Law School of the University of Paris he practiced law for several years. In 1876 he entered government service, in which he was destined ultimately to serve in virtually every major post in the French government. Between 1876 and 1887 he served as deputy head of the Claims Department of the Ministry of Public Works, as secretary-general of the Prefecture of the Marne, under prefect of Reims, prefect for Tarn, secretary-general of the Seine, prefect of Haute-Garonne, director of personnel in the Ministry of the Interior, director of Departmental and Communal Affairs, and chief-commissioner of the Paris Police Department.

In 1888 Bourgeois was elected deputy from the Marne. He attended Radical Socialist Congresses and became their outstanding orator. That same year he became Undersecretary of State, in 1889 the elected deputy from Reims, and in 1890 Minister of the Interior.

As Minister of Public Instruction his radical reforms encompassed primary and secondary education systems as well as universities; he regrouped university faculties and expanded the availability of postgraduate education. In 1892 he gave up his second Public Instruction portfolio to accept the Ministry of Justice portfolio. He formed his own government in 1895 and attempted to implement a general income tax, a retirement plan for workers, and plans to separate church and state, but in six months his government fell in a constitutional fight over finances.

In 1899 as chairman of the French delegation he presided over the Third Commission of the Hague Peace Conference dealing with international arbitration. Working with the British and US delegations he was party to a proposal to establish a Permanent Court of Arbitration, to which he became a member in 1903.

In 1902 he became president of the Chamber of Deputies, but resigned in 1904 for reasons of health. In 1905 he sought and won election as the senator from Marne, a position he held for the rest of his life. In 1906, he became Minister of Foreign Affairs.

As chairman of the First Commission on Arbitration at the second Hague Peace Conference in 1907, he laid the groundwork for the League of Nations, earning the accolade of being its spiritual father. In 1912 he served as Minister of Public Works, in 1914 as Minister of Foreign Affairs. He was Minister of State during the First World War and Minister of Public Works again in 1917.

Bourgeois headed a commission of inquiry on the creation of the League of Nations in 1918 and prepared a draft of the findings. As president of the French Association for the League he attended the 1919 Congress of organizations interested in its establishment. That year he also represented France in a League of Nations Commission chaired by President Woodrow Wilson of the United States.

The year 1920 saw him at the apex of his career as he became president of the French Senate and the first elected president of the Council of the League of Nations. But both health and sight were failing him, and in 1923 he retired. He died in 1925 at Chateau d'Oger, France. In recognition of his distinguished political career and statesmanship France honored Leon Bourgeois with a public funeral.

His publications include *Solidarité de la prevoyance sociate, Le Pacte de 1919 et la société des nations,* and *L'Oeuvre de la société des nations.*

See also: Articles: *League of Nations*

RUTH C. REYNOLDS

Karl Hjalmer Branting
(1921)

The faith once held by members of the Nobel Committee in the peace congresses and international arbitration of pre-First World War days was transferred after the war to the League of Nations. In 1921, they chose to honor the two men primarily responsible for the admission of Sweden and Norway to the League, Karl Branting and Christian Lange. Sweden and Norway had recently accomplished a peaceful settlement

of their own, and this was a microcosmic achievement of what was expected of the League of Nations. Calling Branting and Lange "worthy recipients of the Peace Prize," the Committee declared it "an honor and a pleasure for us that they should be representatives of two kindred neighboring nations determined to live at peace with each other."

Branting, Prime Minister in Sweden's first Social

Democratic government in 1920, and again in 1921-1923 and 1924-1925, was Sweden's first delegate to the League, and he attended the Assembly sessions of 1920 and 1921. He soon led the cause of making the League the instrument of democracy and international understanding which it was intended to be, and he worked especially diligently in planning for an effective disarmament. This was in diametric opposition to the opinion of the Peace Laureate of the previous year, Leon Bourgeois, and by a bitter irony of fate, Bourgeois's first public speech after he had received the Prize turned out to be an attack on the limitation of armaments. Lord Robert Cecil of Britain, who would receive the Nobel Prize for Peace in 1937, was the only representative of a major power who supported Branting. It proved impossible to get even slight concessions in the limitation of armaments.

As far as national defense was concerned, while Branting was strongly opposed to unnecessarily large appropriations at the expense of social services, this did not mean that he supported "defense nihilism." It *did* mean an ordering of priorities wherein the defense of freedom should be organized in such a way as to equalize political rights and economic benefits. Otherwise, Branting believed, even the most liberal military grants would be wasted. "Should disaster befall us, and if in the hour of danger we could only muster an army the bulk of which nourished a doubt as to *what* they really had to defend in this native land, in which all they can hope for is work and toil in days of good health and the poorhouse in their old age, then our fate would be sealed," Branting once said in a speech regarding military expenditures (Schou 1972 p. 531). Therefore, in Branting's opinion, far-reaching social reforms implied not only the best domestic policy, but also the best possible defense policy. While Branting was in public office he supported liberation of the working classes with universal suffrage, national insurance, and increased democratization. He advocated the peaceful settlement of the question of separation of Norway from Sweden's crown.

No other Nobel Laureate gave a Nobel lecture so eloquently defining the renewed hope of that postwar period for peaceful conflict resolution, this time through the League of Nations. He remarked on the similarity between Alfred Nobel's fundamental ideas and the Covenant of the League, and declared that the League was succeeding, after unparalleled devastation by the war, in opening perspectives of a durable peace and of justice between the free and independent nations of the world, both large and small. He called that devastation the birthpangs of a

"new Europe" in which disputes between members would be solved by legal methods and not by military superiority.

He saw a further realization of Alfred Nobel's testament in the reduction of armaments called for by the League, and in the annual meetings of the League's Assembly, which he regarded as in effect the official peace congresses which Nobel had suggested. And this time they would bind the participating states to an extent that political leaders at the turn of the century would have regarded as "utopian." He recalled that Bertha von Suttner once quoted from a private communication addressed to her by Nobel saying that "It could and should soon come to pass that all states pledge themselves collectively to attack an aggressor. That would make war impossible . . . ." Branting urged that the League of Nations become universal, so that it could truly fulfill such a task.

He visualized the League as an equalizer between the large powerful states and the small nations. With a fully functioning League, the power to command attention would be available to the small nations, even those who were so isolated and powerless that individually they could exert little influence on the great powers in world politics.

Branting concluded with the acknowledgment that to create an organization which would be in a position to thus protect peace in the world of conflicting interests and egotistic wills would be a frighteningly difficult task. But we must meet the obstacles whatever they may be, he said, for they pose far less than the dangers that will continue to menace civilization if present conditions persist.

Branting was a staunch supporter of state sovereignty, defending the right of a nation to shape its own destiny, free from external pressure. True internationalism he visualized as "sovereign nations in a free union." The only road to follow, he said, is that of the imperishable ideal of fraternity among free nations.

Biography

Karl Hjalmar Branting was born on November 23, 1860, in Stockholm, Sweden, son of Lars Branting. Educated at Beskow School, with a distinguished record in mathematics and Latin, he studied mathematics and astronomy at the University of Uppsala, and accepted a position in 1882 as assistant to the director of the Stockholm Observatory. In 1883, after coming under the influence of the French socialist Paul Lafargue and the German socialist Eduard Bernstein, Branting abandoned his scientific career and joined the staff of the Stockholm paper *Tiden* [The Times] as foreign editor, becoming its editor-in-chief the next year. Upon that paper's financial demise in 1886 he became editor-in-chief of another socialist newspaper *Socialdemokraten*. This paper became a potent force in Swedish politics during his 31 years of association with it. Branting believed in socialism based upon democracy, with the active involvement of the workers a necessity. To this end he formed workers' clubs, helped organize unions, and became one of Sweden's most forceful speakers. Known as the "father of socialism in Sweden," he was a prominent founder of the Social Democratic Labor Party in 1889, and served as its president from 1907 to his death in 1925.

Branting mobilized the working classes in support of the demand for adult, equal, and direct suffrage, but at the same time cooperated with the Liberals, resulting in a Liberal-Socialist coalition government in 1917, with Branting as Minister of Finance. This government brought about a constitutional reform of 1919 giving the right to vote to all males. However, the coalition dissolved when the Liberals refused to support the Social Democrats' demand for tax reform, unemployment insurance, and nationalization. He

returned to the Prime Minister in October 1921 at which time the franchise was extended to women. He resigned in April 1923 under the impact of a combination of Liberals and Conservatives. In 1924 he once again became Prime Minister, but resigned the following year because of ill health.

Branting held a lifelong interest in international affairs. He supported the Allied position during the First World War, though maintaining Swedish neutrality. He served as Sweden's representative to the Paris Peace Conference in 1919, and led Sweden into the League of Nations, where he served as the Swedish delegate and was named to the Council of the League in 1923. Branting was chairman of the Assembly's Committee on Disarmament in 1920-1921, and a member of the Council's Committee on Disarmament in 1924. He helped with the drafting of the Geneva Protocol, a proposed international security system requiring arbitration between hostile nations.

Karl Branting died on February 24, 1925, in Stockholm.

RUTH C. REYNOLDS

Christian Lous Lange
(1921)

Christian Lange, co-winner with Karl Branting of the 1921 Nobel Peace Prize, is unique among the Peace Prize laureates for his lifetime association with the Nobel organization, beginning with the year of its inception. In 1900 Lange was appointed first-secretary to the Norwegian Parliament's Nobel Committee and to the Norwegian Nobel Institute then in its formative stage. He assisted in planning the Institute's building, and the library of the Institute stands as a legacy to Lange's service during this period. He looked upon the Institute as a "peace laboratory, a breeding place of ideas and plans for the improvement and development of international relations."

During 1907, when the Second Hague Peace Conference convened, the Norwegian government sent Lange as one of its technical delegates. After his intense organizational activity during the formation of the Nobel Institute, he resigned his position in 1909, but continued to function as an adviser to the Institute until 1933. He then joined the Committee itself, where he remained until his death in 1938.

Lange was one of the world's foremost exponents of the theory and practice of internationalism. He worked with the Interparliamentary Union, an organization offering opportunity for the annual assembly of the members of parliaments from all over the

world, often including the presidents or vice-presidents of legislative assemblies, to meet and discuss current affairs. Its primary hope was to handle any incipient problems, resolving conflicts before these could become entangled beyond solution. In the intervals between the sessions a skeletal committee of 15 members watched over the political horizon for the Union. The goal of the Union was to function as a higher parliament which, without limiting the basic independence of any nation, could function to exert a moral authority.

The Interparliamentary Union furnished Lange with his first official connection with internationalism when, in 1899, he was appointed secretary of the committee on arrangements for the Conference to be held that year in Oslo. It was his capacity for organization noted by members of the nascent Nobel organization on that occasion which brought about his appointment in their Institute and on their committee and his resulting lifelong association with the organization. Ten years later, following his resignation as first-secretary of the Nobel Institute in 1909, he returned to the Interparliamentary Union, becoming its secretary-general following Charles-Albert Gobat (1903 Peace Prize co-winner). In this position he administered the affairs of the Interparliamentary

Bureau, the organizational arm of the Union through which information from over the world was collected and disseminated; he met with parliamentary groups in various countries and helped prepare the agenda for annual meetings. He edited the Union's publication and lectured and wrote on the Union.

He supervised the move of the Bureau from Berne to Brussels, and tightened its organization. However, the outbreak of the First World War in 1914 threatened its very existence as Germany overran Belgium. Lange fled to Oslo, and from his home there continued to keep international contacts alive in any way possible. The Interparliamentary Union owes its continued existence largely to Lange's efforts with the assistance of Lord Weardale, its president.

During this period Lange also taught history at the Norwegian Nobel Institute, and he started a history of the development of internationalism from its earliest days, titled *l'Histoire de l'internationalisme* (see *Peace "Encyclopedias" of the Past and Present: An Introductory Essay*). Auguste Schou, director of the Norwegian Nobel Institute, remarked that Lange's work accorded with the principles basic to the League of Nations, and that Lange had made an important contribution by participating in the work of ideological preparation for the League.

At Interparliamentary Union meetings held during the war Lange contributed greatly to the formation of plans for the revival of international cooperation at the war's end. When the war was over he convened the Council of the Union in 1919. He moved the administrative and editorial headquarters to Geneva to be close to the League of Nations, and it was there that the first conference following the war took place in 1921.

Lange was active in other organizations also. From 1916 to 1929 he was a special correspondent for the Carnegie Endowment for International Peace. He prepared a report on conditions in the warring countries, especially the Soviet Union, which was published by the *New York Times*. He also worked with a Dutch group called the "Central Organization for a Lasting Peace."

Lange spoke eloquently of internationalism in his Nobel lecture. He said he preferred the term internationalism to the term pacifism because internationalism was more positive, giving a "definite conception of how society should be organized." Internationalism in Lange's view embraced a social and political theory tackling concrete problems of how nations should organize their mutual relationships on a sound basis in economics and technology. "Today we stand on a bridge leading from the territorial state to the world community," he said. "Politically, we are still governed by the concept of the territorial state, economically and technically, we live under the auspices of worldwide communications and worldwide markets." The resulting mutual dependence between the world's peoples is the feature most to be reckoned with in present-day economics. Communications made possible simultaneous reactions to an event all over the world, creating "a common mental pulse beat for the whole of civilized mankind."

The task of politics, Lange said, is to find external organizational accommodations for what has been developed in economic, technical, and intellectual fields. The great and dominating political task of our time is to find patterns of organization which will adapt to world unity and cooperation between nations. Lange joined the internationalists of his day in looking to the League of Nations for this purpose.

From the opening of the League until his death, Lange was active in the League as a Norwegian delegate, his background in international relationships, both in theory and in practice, giving him the role which his biographer, Oscar Falnes, described as "a sort of standing adviser." A partial list of his duties in the League attests to Lange's interest in disarmament: in 1920 he provided a general orientation for the Assembly's Committee VI on Disarmament, in 1936 he chaired the Assembly's Committee VI on Arms Reduction, and in 1938 he served on the Assembly's committee on armament problems.

Lange maintained that militarism goes hand in hand with nationalist economic isolationism to maintain the sovereign state against the forward march of internationalism. No state is free from it; there are merely differences of degree. "Militarism is basically a way of thinking," he said. And it is against this concept of the sovereign state that the League of Nations must now do battle, Lange argued, because through technical developments the sovereign state has become "a lethal danger to human civilization."

Lange was emphatic in his assurance that both diversity in national intellectual development and individual characteristics in local governments were wholly compatible with internationalism. "It is the political authority over common interests that internationalism wants to transfer to a common management," he said. "Thus, a world federation, in which individual nations linked in groups can participate as members, is the political ideal of internationalism." Before the war a first groping step was taken in this direction with the work at The Hague. Lange called the League of Nations the "first serious and conscious attempt to approach that goal."

Biography

Christian Lous Lange was born on September 17, 1869, in Stavanger, Norway. He studied history, French, and English, graduating from the University of Oslo in 1893. In 1919 he received a doctorate in the history of internationalism. He served as first-secretary to the Nobel Committee in Oslo, helping the Nobel Institute in its formative stages and establishing a distinguished research library there from 1899 to 1909, and remained as an adviser or on the Committee for the rest of his life. In 1907 he was a delegate from Norway to the Second Peace Conference at the Hague. In 1909 he became secretary-general of the Interparliamentary Union, an international organization of parliamentarians who met on a regular basis for discussions, and which had a Bureau where information between members and their legislative assemblies could be exchanged. It was largely owing to Lange's persistent dedication to keeping the Union contacts alive during the First World War that the Union survived during that period.

Lange also worked with a Dutch group, the Central Organization for a Lasting Peace and was active in the League of Nations, where he strongly supported disarmament. He was a special correspondent for the Carnegie Endowment for International Peace from 1916 to 1929.

In 1932 he received the Grotius Medal of the Netherlands. Christian Lange died in Oslo on December 11, 1938.

RUTH C. REYNOLDS

Fridtjof Nansen and the Nansen Office
(1922)   (1938)

The 1922 Nobel Peace Prize was awarded to Fridtjof Nansen, a man beloved in his native Norway, whose Arctic explorations held the drama of a Norse saga and opened new vistas upon the Arctic and in oceanography. He was revered as few others have been for his monumental efforts to alleviate the cruel after-effects of war upon frightened refugees beyond count, upon victims of famines, and upon prisoners of war. "The Nobel Peace Prize has in the course of the years been given to all sorts of men," a Danish journalist observed. "It has surely never been awarded to anyone who in such a short time has carried out such far-reaching *practical* peace work as Nansen" (Jens Marinus Jenson, *I Folkeforbundets: Tjeneste*, Kobenhavn, 1931, p. 101).

The Nobel Peace Prize for 1938 was awarded to the Nansen Office, the organization which continued Nansen's work. Nobel Committee Chairman Stang, who presented the awards on both occasions, said the Nansen Office had continued to carry a message not only to thousands of refugees all over the world who have waited helpless and wretched, or have roamed from country to country without respite, but also a message to each of us. He admonished those fortunate enough to be secure within their respective countries not to forget that the world is much greater than their little corners of it, and to remember that humankind's children, wherever they may be and whatever they believe, are joined together by a common destiny and by an indissoluble and inflexible solidarity.

Fridtjof Nansen was born in 1861, the son of a prosperous lawyer in Christiania (Oslo). As a young man, he went on a sealing ship for a voyage into Greenland waters. When he saw the Greenland ice cap he determined that he would one day cross it. Six years later, in May 1888, he set out to do so, and his approach to planning the expedition clearly spoke of the philosophy Nansen used for surmounting obstacles. He proposed a way of no return. His party would travel from the uninhabited east to the inhabited west; thus once his party was put ashore there could be no retreat. The six men climbed to 9,000 feet above sea level, and met with storms and intense cold which forced their wintering in an Eskimo settlement. They returned in May 1889, triumphant, the first explorers to bring back information about the region's interior.

During this expedition Nansen became intrigued by the strange patterns in ocean currents. He observed that a current would carry a piece of driftwood from the Siberian coast to the Arctic Ocean, and he knew of the ill-fated ship, the *Jeanette*, caught in the pack ice off the Bering Strait, which drifted in a northwesterly direction for nearly a year before sinking. Nansen reasoned that this same drift of ice would serve as means of exploring the polar regions. If a ship were designed to ride up on the ice when the pressure enveloped its hull, the ship could likewise drift with the currents from Siberia across the Arctic Ocean toward the Greenland Sea. It would be a voyage, he thought, which would answer questions as to whether there was another continent or only an open polar sea. Nansen turned his conjecture into a wellplanned expedition, building a ship appropriately named the *Fram*, which translates as "forward," and which once again described the manner in which he worked. For when it became apparent that the *Fram* would not drift right over the Pole, but would bypass it, Nansen set out with a companion, two sleds, two kayaks and 28 dogs to make a dash across the ice floes for the Pole. Although they did not reach this goal, they did reach the highest latitude anyone had ever gone. Again Nansen was forced to winter on an expedition, this time with his companion in a stone hut with polar bear and walrus meat they hunted furnishing food, and with blubber supplying fuel. In the spring the two men made their way south and rejoined their shipmates on the *Fram*. They all returned to Norway and a heroes' welcome.

Nansen then accepted a chair of oceanography at the university in Christiania (Oslo), taking part in a number of sea voyages. This might well have accounted for the rest of his life, for it suited him admirably, but as he grew older he became drawn to the problem of relations between nations. He interrupted his research in 1905 to take part in negotiations with Sweden for Norway's independence. After the desired dissolution of the Union, when Norway invited the Danish Prince Carl to become its king, Nansen was one of those chosen to escort him to his new kingdom. Nansen also served as his country's minister to the United Kingdom until May 1908. In the next few years he again led several oceanographic expeditions into polar regions, but the outbreak of the First World War in 1914 changed his life. Nansen looked on the war with horror. "The people of Europe, the 'torchbearers of civilization' are devouring one another," he said, "trampling civilization under foot, laying Europe in ruins and who will be the gainer? For what are they fighting? Power—only power."

Because the war made it impossible for Norway to import grain from the Eastern European countries, it turned to the United States. However, the United States was at war and was reluctant to sell to a neutral Norway. Nansen headed a commission appointed to persuade the United States to sell the grain. For almost a year between 1917 and 1918 negotiations dragged on, and Norway's eventual success was owing chiefly to Nansen's patience and diplomatic skill.

During the war years Nansen promoted the concept of an organization at the war's end which could bring about a secure and lasting peace. He ardently supported the League of Nations, spending the early part of 1919 in Paris as president of the Norwegian Union

for the League, trying to bring influence to bear on the statesmen at the Peace Conference. He urged Norway's early entry, saying the League could be "a protection for the weak and oppressed, a judge in the disputes of its members, a force for peace and justice." From 1920 until his death he was a delegate to the League from Norway. He advocated the admission of Germany, and to this end he brought about personal contact between the Foreign Ministers of France and Germany, Aristide Briand and Gustav Stresemann (co-winners of the 1926 Peace Prize).

It was the League of Nations which cast Nansen into his role as rescuer of the war's bereft. Frederik Stang, Chairman of the Nobel Committee, described well the difficulty of comprehending Nansen's task: "The human mind cannot visualize this enormous activity any more than it can grasp astronomical figures. One starving person, one human being lying like forgotten wreckage on a street corner, wasting away bit by bit—this we understand; here our feeling is so strong it becomes compassion. One refugee, even a crowd of refugees, pushing their children and their possessions in wheelbarrows in front of them— this we understand. But millions of these, hunted like game from country to country, behind them the fires of their burning homes, before them the emptiness of a future over which they have no control—here our minds stop dead; instead of producing images, they merely playback the statistics presented to them . . . a program whose aim is to rescue a continent's millions from misery and death, this presents proportions so immense and involves such a myriad of jumbled details that we give up and allow our minds to rest."

Nansen put it simply. He said that when one has beheld the great beseeching eyes in the starved faces of children, the eyes of agonized mothers, the ghostlike men, then one's mind can be opened to the full extent of the tragedy.

His first humanitarian task came in April 1920 when the League appointed him High Commissioner responsible for the repatriation from the Soviet Union of about 450,000 German and Austro-Hungarian prisoners of war. With minimum funds, with skill and ingenuity, Nansen approached the Soviet and German governments and concluded agreements for the delivery of the prisoners. Homeless, starved, tortured, unwanted, the prisoners had been waiting for four, five, and even six years. In September 1921, Nansen was able to report to the League of Nations that 350,000 prisoners were repatriated via the Baltic, 12,000 via Vladivostok, and 5,000 via the Black Sea.

But before he had even finished this task, Nansen

was given the still more difficult task of resettling Russian refugees from all over Europe. In June 1921 the Council of the League, pressured by the International Red Cross and other organizations, appointed Nansen High Commissioner for Refugees under the auspices of the League of Nations. His assignment was to promote mutual cooperation between nations so that needy prisoners and Russian refugees could be transferred to countries where work was available. Some nations responded favorably, but others refused to cooperate. Nansen asked, "Why were there some who did not want to help?" and he conjectured, "In all probability their motives were political. They epitomize . . . the lack of will to understand people who think differently. They call us romantics, weak, stupid, sentimental idealists, perhaps because we have some faith in the good which exists even in our opponents, and because we believe that kindness achieves more than cruelly . . . ."

A large number of refugees originally from countries separated from Russia after the war were taken back home. For those stripped even of a country to call their own, Nansen invented the "Nansen Passport," a document of identification for displaced persons. It first helped the vast numbers of White Russians who had emigrated at the time of the Revolution. Nansen took on the task of resettling them in new countries where they could earn a decent living. The "Nansen Passport" came to be recognized by 52 governments, and eventually gave identity to countless thousands.

In August 1921 the Red Cross asked Nansen to undertake yet a third rescue mission. Millions of Russians were dying in the famine of 1921-22 and Nansen was asked to direct the famine relief work. While the Russians starved, there were huge quantities of grain in other countries—in the United States the wheat lay rotting for lack of buyers, and in Argentina the maize was used as fuel for railway engines. Adequate transportation was available but political differences led to arguments concerning support for the Soviet regime. Nansen answered these objections: "I do not believe that we are supporting the Soviet simply because we are showing the Russian people that there is compassion in Europe. But suppose that such aid *would* support the Soviet—is there any man who dares come forward and say: It is better to allow twenty million people to die of starvation than to support the Soviet government?" At the League assembly in September he made an urgent appeal: "We are running a race against the Russian winter," he said. "Make haste to act before it is too late to repent."

Nansen's appeal to the League was turned down, but he then repeated it to the world at large. With the help, in particular, of the American War Relief Bureau directed by Herbert Hoover, at least ten million lives were saved. Some double that estimate. But Nansen expressed deep regret at the League's failure to participate. He believed that had the League, with its great authority, lent its support the situation in the Soviet Union would have been saved, and the conditions in both the former Soviet Union and Europe would have been totally different and greatly improved. Nansen warned that the future must not be built on distrust and hatred. The first prerequisite, he said, is understanding of the trends that mark our times and what is happening among the mass of the population.

In 1922 Nansen, as High Commissioner for Refugees, directed the work of aiding the victims of the Greco-Turkish War. Presented with the problem of the Greek refugees who poured into their native land from their homes in Asia Minor after the Greek army had been defeated by the Turks, Nansen arranged an exchange of about 1,250,000 Greeks living on Turkish soil for about 500,000 Turks living in Greece. He saw to their appropriate identifications and to the provisions necessary for a new start in life.

Basic to all of Nansen's success was his skill in breaking down myriad barriers which stood between the victims of misfortune and their rescuers. The Nobel Committee Chairman ventured a reason why this man could see Europe's misery at first hand, accept a sense of responsibility for alleviating it, and call forth the necessary energy, initiative, self-sacrifice, and patience to arrive at solutions. He recalled a mature man who, on the basis of his scientific knowledge, developed the theory that a current flows from east to west across the Polar Sea. Then once he had come to this conviction, he allowed his ship to be frozen into the eastern ice to be carried over the Pole. The current was there and carried him forward to his goal. "And is it not the same thing that we have now witnessed?" Chairman Stang asked. "An undercurrent has again carried Nansen forward: the deep current of human feeling which lies beneath the layer of ice in which nations and individuals encase themselves during the daily struggles and trials of life. He believed in this current, and because he did, his work has triumphed."

Fridtjof Nansen died in Oslo on May 13, 1930. His biographer, Jon Sorensen (1932), wrote, "Seldom or never has the sorrow of a nation been so much a sorrow of love. And it was more than a nation which grieved. A whole world mourned."

Fridtjof Nansen exemplified before the world a moral and universal responsibility toward those caught in the wake of the inhumane practice of war. During the early years there were times when his work advanced rapidly, not just as a result of a common compassion towards refugees, eloquent as Nansen had been in nurturing this latent virtue, but because of a shortage of labor in many countries. Refugees with sound health and skills were needed. But during the worldwide economic depression which began in 1929 jobs became critically scarce. Countries closed their doors, placing restrictions on importation of foreign-made goods and imposing immigration barriers. Not only were refugees not allowed in; some of them were deprived of their existing work, and once again they faced the cold fate of the unwanted. Michael Hansson, president of the Nansen Office, said that refugees who had been living an uncertain existence for 20 years should have acquired a moral right to live in peace and security. The main task of the Nansen Office for some years had been to help refugees, those no longer able to work, and those dismissed from jobs in favor of the local unemployed. Somehow they must be allowed assimilation in the country of their residence. Their constant fear of being driven away once again from whatever humble homes they had created, their loss of country, of possession, even of identity except as objects of charity represented an unfinished task begun by Nansen and taken over by the Nansen Office.

The accomplishments of the Nansen Office included construction of whole villages in Syria and Lebanon to house the Armenian refugees who were occupying Nansen's energies and concern during the last part of his life. By the end of 1935 it had settled approximately 10,000 in Erivan and 40,000 in Turkey. With minimal support from the League of Nations, always short on funds, so that some staff energies always had to be spent in seeking support, the Nansen Office had managed financial, legal, and material aid to almost a million refugees.

The rise of the Nazis to power in Germany brought critical new problems. Four thousand inhabitants of the Saar had to leave their homes when the district once more became part of the German Reich, and through the Nansen Office new homes were created for them in Paraguay. By 1935 a High Commission for Refugees from Germany had already been in existence for two years. The Norwegian government, acting out of concern for the swelling hordes of refugees coming out of Germany, suggested that this organization be merged with the Nansen Office

under the authority of the League of Nations, with its seat in London. At the time this arrangement was to become operative, January 1, 1939, with Sir Herbert William Emerson the new High Commissioner, three million Jews were slowly dying of starvation in Poland, an unknown number remained in Germany, and animosity toward the Jews was spreading over southern and eastern Europe, in Hansson's words, "like a plague." He estimated that five million Jews in Europe needed the means and a place to seek a new life. In addition, he said, Europe had thousands of other political refugees.

The Nansen Office pointed out some basic, universal implications involved in its work. As well as the moral responsibility of humanitarianism, countries should recall what Nansen taught: that if intelligent human beings are abandoned and abused, bereft of work within their capabilities, their sheer desperation may be channeled into activities which could ultimately cost society sums many times the amount needed for the initial modest assistance which would have enabled them to integrate into their adopted communities. It is not only a moral step; it is also a wise one. The Nansen Office continued Fridtjof Nansen's commitment toward peace from which there is no turning back.

Hopeless as the work for refugees can seem, Hansson insisted "the one thing we must not do *is to give it up*. I feel sure that the new High Commissioner will continue this work in accordance with the traditions of the Nansen Office and in the spirit of Fridtjof Nansen." It is indicative of the ominous nature of the times in which the Nansen Office had been working that its Peace Prize award was the last made before the outbreak of the Second World War.

History

The Nansen International Office for Refugees continued the rescue work started by Fridtjof Nansen, who operated through the League of Nations as its High Commissioner for Refugees. Nansen, Norwegian scientist and explorer, had abandoned a world-renowned career in Arctic exploration and oceanography to help the refugees created by the First World War. In the early 1920s, as High Commissioner, he worked with Russians—prisoners of war, those who left Russia in the wake of the revolution there, and those living there when a major Volga crop failure brought about a devastating famine. In 1923 his mandate was extended to include Armenian refugees. Between 1924 and 1929 the International Labour Organization gave material assistance, but at all other times the High Commission, under Nansen's direction, fulfilled all functions itself. The refugee problem expanded, and the Commission's mandate correspondingly broadened to include Assyrians, Assyro-Chaldeans, and Turkish refugees.

Following Nansen's death in 1930, and the later abolition of the office of the High Commission for Refugees, the League Secretariat assumed responsibility for the refugees, while the actual assistance to them was provided by the Nansen International Office for Refugees, an autonomous body under the authority of the League.

On a diminishing scale the League provided administrative expenses for the Nansen Office, while the stream of refugees who required their assistance grew. The Office increasingly depended upon private revenues and upon fees charged for the "Nansen Certificate," an international passport devised originally by Nansen who recognized the need for identification on the part of thousands of refugees who had lost their identification with their own countries. Also stamps were sold as a fund-raising device in France and Norway.

With the coming of the worldwide depression, the refugee problems were exacerbated by the scarcity of jobs. The Nazis in Germany, the civil war in Spain, the growing wave of anti-Semitism in Southern and Eastern Europe, and the tendency to toss helpless refugees from countries where they attempted to settle, and then prevent action on their behalf when attempted by the League of Nations—all contributed to a growing avalanche of refugees. Even so, the Nansen Office gave material, legal, and financial help to almost a million refugees. It kept the cause of the refugees alive, and achieved the adoption by 14 countries of the Refugee Convention of 1933, a modest charter of human rights. It arranged the settlement in Paraguay of 4,000 Germans required to leave Germany with the rise of the Nazis to power after 1933, and continued with the problem of Armenians in Syria and Lebanon with Nansen had struggled, constructing villages in Turkey which housed nearly 40,000 Armenians, and resettling another 10,000 in Erivan.

With the rise of the Nazi government in Germany, the problem of refugees became so acute that the League established a High Commission for Refugees from Germany, This Commission, which also took responsibility for both Austrian and Sudetenland refugees, worked with the Nansen Office. Both were scheduled to be dissolved on December 31, 1938, to be replaced with a new agency of the League of Nations, the Office of the High Commissioner for Refugees, with headquarters in London.

Bibliography

Adams W 1939 Extent and nature of the world refugee problems. *Annals of the American Academy of Political and Social Science* 203 (May)

Sorenson J 1932 *The Saga of Fridtjof Nansen*. Norton, New York

RUTH C. REYNOLDS

Prize Not Awarded
(1923-24)

Sir Austen Chamberlain
(1925)

The 1925 Nobel Peace Prize was awarded jointly to Austen Chamberlain of the United Kingdom and Charles Dawes of the United States after an absence of awards for two years. The announcement was delayed for still a third year and made with that of the 1926 awards. Perhaps it was the giant shadow cast by the laureate of 1922, Norway's famous explorer and humanitarian, Fridtjof Nansen, beneath which candidates for 1923 and 1924 seemed to pale. Possibly Christain Lange's advice to the Nobel Committee about waiting for a truly worthy recipient reinforced its reluctance. No explanations were given by the Nobel Committee; indeed their customary presentation speech was omitted. And none of the four laureates from the two years' awards were present or sent speeches although Gustav Stresemann delivered a delayed speech on June 29, 1927, at Olso University which was broadcast throughout Norway, Sweden, and Denmark. But the ceremony fell upon the thirtieth anniversary of Nobel's death, and Fridtjof Nansen gave a speech which paid eloquent tribute to the Committee's choice. The four laureates, Charles Dawes of the US and Austen Chamberlain of Great Britain for 1925, Aristide Briand of France and Gustav Stresemann of Germany for 1926, created two international pacts: the Dawes Plan, which bears its chief architect's name, and the Treaty of Locarno drawn up by the other three. Nansen said the Dawes plan was the first dawning of the day after a long darkness, marking the beginning of the policy of reconciliation which led to the Locarno agreements. And the Locarno agreements, he said, introduced a radical and complete change in European politics, transforming the relations between the former antagonists in the war and infusing them with an entirely new spirit—one deriving from the almost unprecedented attempt to base politics on the principle of mutual friendship and trust.

Nansen said it was neither idealism nor altruism but a sense of necessity which prompted these men to their accomplishments, and he further noted that none of them were "idealistic pacifists" but realistic politicians and responsible statesmen who recognized that the only chance of creating a future for humankind was to unite in a desire to work together.

The award to Chamberlain had indeed aroused its share of objections. He was called "a national politician thrust upon the world scene." A review of the circumstances surrounding the events leading to the Locarno agreements, however, might occasion gratitude that that was indeed the case. It was Chamberlain who first heeded Germany's proposals for such a pact, and he played the decisive part in achieving its fruition. At the end of 1922 the German Chancellor, Wilhelm Cuno, had proposed that the powers with interests along the Rhine should agree not to make war on one another for a period of 30 years unless such action was decided upon by plebiscite, but this was rejected by the French. In the next year the Germans came up with another proposal, this time based on a treaty of arbitration, but again without success. In February 1925 the German government, with Stresemann as Foreign Minister, tried again, this third time suggesting a pact expressly guaranteeing the Rhine frontiers by means of a collective and individual pledge. Yet again France's response was cool, but Chamberlain, as UK Secretary of State for Foreign Affairs, expressed enthusiastic interest. When France's government changed and Briand became its Foreign Minister, the longed-for meeting was arranged to follow the close of the sixth assembly of the League of Nations in September 1925.

It was agreed later that at the conference Chamberlain supplied the main motivating spirit. The atmosphere was kept friendly, as attested to by Chamberlain's brief message when accepting the Nobel Prize in which he acknowledged his colleagues as "statesmen both remarkable for the magnanimity of their spirit, for the independence of their judgment, and for their love of peace," and said, "Without their help, I would have been able to do nothing."

Throughout the conference, where representatives of seven powers—the United Kingdom, Germany, France, Belgium, Italy, Poland, and Czechoslovakia—met at Locarno in southern Switzerland, words like "allies" and "enemies" were never used, and the old hostilities associated with such words dropped away. Major powers surrendered their absolute right to make war—an event without historical precedent. And this was localized around the Rhine. "For the first time since Louis XIV, King of France between 1643 and 1715, the Rhine had ceased to be a cause of dissension in European politics. So closes a chapter in history," Nansen exulted in his Nobel ceremony speech.

Under the Treaty Germany, Belgium, France, the United Kingdom, and Italy mutually guaranteed the peace in Western Europe, and Germany undertook to arbitrate in disputes with France, Belgium, Poland, and Czechoslovakia. The United Kingdom and Italy committed themselves to declare war on Germany if Germany attacked France, and to declare war on France if France attacked Germany. The German-Belgian and the German-French frontiers were guaranteed inviolable as established by the Versailles Treaty through a Security Pact.

An important part of Germany's acceptance back into the community of nations was its admission to the League of Nations. This Stresemann had requested in 1919, but only to be rejected. The Treaty of Locarno approved the admission of Germany to the League, and this was to provide a place for continued friendly and valuable interchange between the statesmen who created the Locarno agreements.

Circumstances provided a final and appropriate tribute to the statesman who had led the way in accepting Germany's proposal for attempting these negotiations: it was on Chamberlain's birthday, October 16, in 1925 that the Foreign Ministers initialed the documents known as the Treaty of Locarno

With the advantage of hindsight it can be seen that the agreements came too late to provide a lasting solution to complex problems, many of them deeply rooted in history, others the direct heritage of the Versailles Treaty. Within 10 years Germany, Italy, and Japan had withdrawn from the League of Nations, and Germany had formally and unilaterally repudiated the Treaty of Versailles and had violated the Treaty of Locarno by reoccupying the Rhineland. Nevertheless, the four statesmen had presented to the world an enlightened attempt to base international relations on the principles of friendship and mutual trust.

Biography

Joseph Austen Chamberlain was born in Birmingham on October 16, 1863, the eldest son of Joseph Chamberlain, the British statesman known as the "Empire-builder." His half-brother, Neville Chamberlain, was Prime Minister from 1937 to 1940. Austen Chamberlain's schooling included Rugby and Cambridge, plus nine months at the Ecole des Sciences Politiques in Paris and twelve months in Berlin. Upon his return to Birmingham he became his father's private secretary, a further preparation for a political career which began in 1887 when he took a seat in the House of Commons, representing East Worcestershire. His maiden speech there drew praise from William Gladstone. When his father died in 1914, Chamberlain succeeded him in the seat for West Birmingham, and remained there for the rest of his life.

His 45 years in the House of Commons fall into two periods: the first, from 1892 to 1922, dealing primarily with domestic questions, the second, from 1922 to his death in 1937, with international questions. He held a series of responsible posts from 1895 to 1906: Civil Lord of the Admiralty, financial secretary to the Treasury, Postmaster-General, and Chancellor of the Exchequer.

Under Asquith's coalition government Chamberlain served for two years as Secretary of State for India, resigning in 1917. The next year Lloyd George made him his Chancellor of the Exchequer. From 1919 to 1921 Chamberlain saw to it that the enormous debts accumulated during the war were paid, and maintained a stable currency and strengthened the national credit.

Chamberlain succeeded Bonar Law as leader of the Conservative Party in 1921, staying its head for 18 months until the withdrawal of the Conservatives from Lloyd George's coalition, at which time he chose to stand by the Prime Minister.

In the Baldwin government of 1924 to 1929, Chamberlain was a Secretary of State for Foreign Affairs. Here he reflected his father's training, combining a realistic philosophy with a moral fearlessness, and bringing patience, determination, and resourcefulness to his task. His first impor-

tant act as Foreign Secretary was to reject the proposed Geneva Protocol, not because of its requirement for compulsory arbitration of international disputes, but because it was the Council of the League of Nations which was deciding what action member states should take to enforce the authority of the League in time of crisis. This was a contested procedure in some diplomatic circles, and Chamberlain offered the tempering suggestion that the best way in theory to deal with situations as they arose was to "supplement the Covenant by making special arrangements in order to meet special needs."

The apogee of his career as Foreign Secretary was the Treaty of Locarno. Composed of eight agreements, it included the Rhine Guarantee Pact with Germany, Belgium, France, the United Kingdom, and Italy as signatories; individual treaties of arbitration between Germany and former enemy nations; guarantee treaties involving France, Poland, and Czechoslovakia; and a collective note on the entry of Germany into the League of Nations.

When he returned to London, Chamberlain received a triumphant welcome, and was knighted.

During his later years in the Foreign Office Chamberlain dealt with problems with China and Egypt. He attempted in vain to defend British interests against the encroachments of the Chinese Nationalists, but lacked the necessary support from the United States and Japan. He prepared the way for a treaty on Anglo-Egyptian relations which was signed in the mid-1930s.

Chamberlain saw early the dangerous threat posed by Adolf Hitler. He favored both the imposition of sanctions against Italy during the Abysinnian crisis and their removal when they failed to prevent an Italian victory.

He wrote *Down the Years*, a reminiscence with character studies and essays, and *Politics from Inside*, consisting chiefly of letters he wrote from 1906 to 1914 to keep his ailing father informed of governmental and diplomatic events.

Sir Austen Chamberlain died on March 17, 1937.

RUTH C. REYNOLDS

Charles Gates Dawes
(1925)

Charles G. Dawes, American financier and Vice-President of the United States was co-winner (with Austen Chamberlain of the United Kingdom) of the 1925 Nobel Peace Prize for his leadership in preparing a plan which stabilized a wildly inflationary German economy and led to the acceptance of Germany

into the European community as a nation in good standing. Nobel Laureate Fridtjof Nansen, called the Dawes Plan the first light shed in the darkness of postwar Europe.

The circumstance of the awarding of the 1925 Prize was notably irregular. The Prize was the first to be awarded since that of Fridtjof Nansen in 1922. Its announcement was delayed a year, and took place at the same time as that of the 1926 awards. No presentation speech was made for the 1925-26 awards by a member of the Nobel Committee, although a distinguished audience at the ceremony, which marked the thirtieth anniversary of Alfred Nobel's death, were fortunate in hearing a stirring address by Fridtjof Nansen. None of the four co-winners were present at the ceremony, nor did they send a written speech as was often done in the event of absence. (Germany's Gustav Stresemann did deliver a Nobel lecture, but not until June 1927.) Most unusual of all, however, was the fact that none of the co-winners were known for their work in peace. But they had participated in the creation of two international pacts, the Dawes Plan and the Locarno Treaty, which brought partial restoration to a critically ill world economy and a consequent hope for international harmony in an extremely tense world. It may be said that these two important pacts were the objects of honor in both years' prizes. It may also be noted that they affected the careers of their statesmen-architects, directing their policies thereafter toward internationalism. In his lecture at the 1926 Prize ceremony Nansen called the Dawes Plan important both economically and politically for Europe and the United States. But its great significance, he said, lay in its indication of a psychological change in European mentality. The Plan's peaceful policy of reconciliation opened the way to the Locarno agreements.

The Treaty of Versailles following the First World War placed a moral responsibility upon Germany for all damage done to the populations of the Allied countries, but it did not deal directly with the financial aspects of the reparations. It provided for a Reparations Commission to translate the Treaty's provisions into actual figures through assessments of damage, and to establish the method and schedule of payment by May 1921. Such a Commission did attempt to comply, but it provided only a computation of legal liability and a suggested schedule of payment, and made no attempt to assess German's capacity to meet such payments. Germany could not begin to meet the amounts and schedule indicated, and defaulted on its payments altogether in 1923. Thereupon Belgium and France occupied the Ruhr, Germany's major coal mining and industrial center. The population of the Ruhr responded with passive resistance, and the German government suspended deliveries. These events destabilized European industrial production, and ignited a wild inflation of the Reichsmark threatening the total disintegration of Germany's economy and endangering Germany's whole constitutional fabric.

The Allied Reparations Commission was ready for the assistance of experts. The United States was affected by Germany's economic difficulties, whose effects were now being felt beyond Europe; and US Secretary of State Hughes suggested that Germany's capacity to pay reparations should be investigated. A competent committee for his purpose was formed in late 1923. The United States sent General Charles G. Dawes and Owen D. Young. The United Kingdom, France, Italy, and Belgium also sent personnel for the committee. It began its meetings in Paris on January 14, 1924, and made its report—the Dawes Plan—on April 9, 1924. It was recognized in the first place that as long as the occupation of the Ruhr continued, Germany was not a complete fiscal unit and that there could be no guarantee of it having a balanced budget. Second, the reparation liabilities under the Versailles Treaty figured among the budgetary expenses, and if they were in excess of budgetary possibilities it became impossible to guarantee that steps taken for the stability of the currency would be permanent. The Committee adopted a business attitude and considered political factors only insofar as they affected the practicability of the Plan. It sought the recovery of the debt, not the imposition of penalties, and it insisted that success in stabilizing Germany's economy and balancing its budget depended upon the return of the Ruhr to Germany. The country's finances were to be reorganized with the assistance of loans from European and US investors with repayments guaranteed by mortgages on the German railways and on German industries.

The Plan salvaged Europe's economy, although it was not a permanent solution. Most importantly, it halted, at least temporarily, the endless conflicts about Germany's reparations which had contributed to the anxiety and insecurity among Europe's nations during their first five years of peace. The last of the Belgian and French troops departed from the Ruhr on July 31, 1925.

Charles Dawes was well-qualified for this mission he accomplished so successfully. Trained in law, he had turned his hand rather to business ventures, administrating 28 gas and electric plants with his brothers, and moved successfully into banking. He had entered government service as a comptroller of the currency under President William McKinley. He had integrated the system of supply procurement and distribution for the entire US Expeditionary Force, and later performed the same service for the Allies by devising a central purchasing board, as well as a unified distribution authority. He had opposed many members of his Republican Party by strongly urging Congress to accept the Treaty of Versailles and the League of Nations. He had instigated a stringent and highly successful reform within each department and unified purchasing.

He donated the Nobel Peace Prize award money to the endowment of the newly established Walter Hines Page School of International Relations at Johns Hopkins University.

Biography

Charles Gates Dawes was born on August 27, 1865, into a family with a history of distinguished service to its country which ranged over seven generations, from his father's service as a brevet brigadier-general in the Civil War to General William Dawes, who rode with Paul Revere in 1775 to warn fellow colonists of the British advance at the opening of the American Revolution, and then to the first William Dawes, who in 1628 had been among the Puritans who came to America. Charles Dawes himself was Vice-President of the United States at the time of his Nobel Peace Prize award in 1925, a prize he shared with Austen Chamberlain.

Educated at Marietta College, Dawes also studied for two years at the Law School of the University of Cincinnati. He did not practice law, although he may well have applied it to his advantage in his many highly profitable business ventures: he controlled a city block of business offices in Lincoln, Nebraska, and a meat-packing company; he invested in land and in bank stocks and directed a bank in Nebraska. He amassed his large personal fortune when he purchased control of a plant manufacturing artificial gas in Wisconsin, and another north of Chicago, thus beginning

a gas and electric plant empire of 28 plants between himself and his brothers. He founded and became president of the Central Trust Company of Illinois.

Dawes turned this talent into service for his government, beginning with the comptrollership of the currency under President McKinley. During the First World War, while on General Pershing's staff, he integrated the system of supply procurement and distribution for the entire US Expeditionary Force, and later repeated a like service for the Allies by creating a central purchasing board and a unified distribution authority; rising eventually to the rank of General. Appointed to the newly inaugurated position of Director of the Budget following the war in 1920, he reformed budgetary procedures throughout the federal government.

In 1923, the League of Nations invited Dawes to chair a committee to analyze and recommend appropriate action on the problem of German reparations. The outcome of the work of this committee was the Dawes Plan.

From 1924 to 1932, Dawes devoted his entire attention to public service: as Vice-President from 1925 to 1929, as adviser to the Dominican Republic on financial operations in 1929, as ambassador to the United Kingdom from 1929 to 1932, as delegate to the London Naval Conference in 1930. During the Depression he chaired the Reconstruction Finance Corporation, a governmental agency empowered to lend money to banks, railroads, and other businesses to prevent economic collapse.

A gifted as well as a disciplined man, he wrote books, played the flute and piano, and established grand opera in Chicago while devoting time to both family life and civic duties. His published works include *A Journal of the Great War, Notes as Vice President*, and *A Journal of Reparations*.

Charles Dawes died at his home in Evanston, Illinois, on April 23, 1951.

RUTH C. REYNOLDS

Aristide Briand
(1926)

The 1926 Nobel Peace Prize was shared by Aristide Briand of France and Gustav Stresemann of Germany. Co-architects with the United Kingdom's Austen Chamberlain of the Locarno Treaty, they created an international pact which broke the deadlock of confusion and hostilities in postwar Europe.

The ruinous First World War brought devastation unparalleled in history to the peoples of Europe, and its cruelty infected the peace which followed. Despite the efforts of some enlightened statesmen who fought for a treaty designed to secure a peaceful

future, the bitterly contested Versailles Treaty degenerated into an instrument of vengeance. Reparations were demanded of Germany beyond its capacity to pay. Endless conflicts about the reparations produced tensions and insecurity among the nations of Europe for four years following the war and Germany's efforts to meet payments plunged that country into a runaway inflation, paralyzing its economy and endangering its constitutional government. When Germany defaulted altogether in 1923, France and Belgium sent troops into the Ruhr, Germany's coal mining and industrial center, and to the districts between the bridgeheads on the right bank of the Rhine. German officials and leading citizens were expelled from the region. The repercussions of this occupation sent shock waves through Germany; the population engaged in passive resistance, and their supportive government suspended deliveries. Germany's remaining financial resources were completely drained and production lagged all over Europe, threatening its precarious political equilibrium. At this critical juncture a committee was sent to review the reparations in relation to Germany's capacity to pay. Known as the Dawes Plan, the findings of this committee, headed by Charles Dawes, American financier and co-winner of the 1925 Nobel Prize, introduced some sanity into the situation with a nonpolitical, soundly based review of Germany's financial situation, and assistance devised accordingly. It secured a breathing space for Germany, but a temporarily averted crisis could not offer permanent solutions to myriad and complex problems still outstanding, and Germany made a series of overtures for further arbitration.

The last proposal, centering on vexed questions about the Rhineland, was presented by Gustav Stresemann, then Chancellor. Following the war, French policy aimed at detaching the left bank of the Rhine including Alsace, cutting away from Germany 8 percent of its territory, 11 percent of its population, 12 percent of its coal supply, and 80 percent of its iron ores.

Stresemann was eager for diplomatic dialogue on the problem. This was the situation into which Aristide Briand stepped as an incoming Foreign Minister. Briand saw a hope that with the principal grievances removed a new democratic Germany might emerge. Briand's open reception to Stresemann's overture for negotiation marked a reversal of tenacious hostilities and opened the way to the Locarno agreements. The Treaty of Locarno, negotiated throughout 1925, was finally signed on December 1. It was a pact of nonaggression between France, Germany, and Belgium, guaranteed by the two supposedly impartial powers, Great Britain and Italy. The Treaty brought about a radical change in European politics. The hostile and protracted stalemate in relations between European nations yielded to an unprecedented attempt to base politics on the principles of mutual recognition of the common need for security.

Briand, Stresemann, Chamberlain, and Dawes were not the pacifists customarily associated with the Peace Prize. They were practical, high-level politicians with strong nationalistic outlooks. But they were realists. Briand aptly remarked, "The war has taught us one thing, namely, that a common fate binds us together. If we go under, we go under together. If we wish to recover, we cannot do so in conflict with each other, but only by working together." Whatever doubts existed about their personal qualifications as Peace Prize laureates—and many were expressed—there was no hesitation in welcoming the Dawes Plan and the Locarno Pact as, in Fridtjof Nansen's words, "the first dawning of the day after long darkness." Arthur Balfour called Locarno, "The symbol and cause of a great amelioration in the public feeling of Europe." The two initiatives may well be construed as the true recipients of the 1925 and 1926 Peace Prizes. It is certainly notable that all four of the statesmen responsible for these diplomatic instruments were awarded their prizes simultaneously, the 1925 Prize being given retroactively.

Briand, Stresemann, and Chamberlain made careful preparations for the conference in Locarno scheduled to take place following the closing of the Assembly of the League of Nations in September 1925. They came from diverse backgrounds, but they were bound by the common goal of seeking a general security wherein political and economic stability could be achieved. They shed the vocabulary of a decade—the words "allies" and "enemies" were never used throughout the conference—and tensions and hostilities gave way to a spirit of sober negotiation and arbitration. For the first time in history, major powers surrendered their absolute right to make war. Furthermore, the surrender was localized to that historical storm center, the Rhine. After the evacuation of the Ruhr, Germany suggested a pact between the powers interested in the Rhine which would give a mutual guarantee for the existing frontiers. In the Locarno Pact this mutual guarantee was given with Germany's promise not to try to recover Alsace—Lorraine.

The Locarno Treaty was a series of diplomatic agreements for peace and arbitration. Germany, Belgium, France, the United Kingdom and Italy together guaranteed the peace in Western Europe, and Germany undertook to arbitrate about disputes with France, Belgium, Poland, and Czechoslovakia. The United Kingdom and Italy were committed to declare war on Germany if Germany attacked France, and to declare war on France if France attacked Germany.

Germany's entry into the League of Nations was a condition for putting the Locarno agreements into effect. This carried the enormous import of restoring Germany into the European community as a nation in good standing, and it was a privilege which had been previously denied it when Stresemann had made application for Germany's membership in the League in 1919.

Germany's admission was welcome in a speech by Briand. Among other things, he said: "No more war! . . . From now on it will be for the judge to decide what is right. Just as individual citizens settle their disagreements before a judge, so shall we also resolve ours by peaceful means. Away with rifles, machine guns, cannons. Make way for conciliation, arbitration, peace!"

Briand continued for the next five years to direct foreign policy on the basis of law replacing discord and an increasing belief in the international approach. Possessed all his life of a sharp eye for reality and political acumen—some would say political opportunism—it reflected his increasing belief in internationalism that he proposed a sweeping concept of an European Union at the League of Nations in May 1930. But the one-time Gallic nationalist politician had moved ahead of his peer statesmen, and his proposal was rejected.

Far more tragic was the fate of the Treaty of Locarno. In his acceptance message for the Nobel Peace Prize Briand had declared, "My ambition is that ten years hence the people will say that we deserved this award." Ten years later, however, Germany, Italy, and Japan had withdrawn from the League of Nations and Germany had violated the Pact by reoccupying the Rhineland.

It is the opinion of certain international observers that the history of that decade would have been better served if Briand and Stresemann had lived longer. For instance, in the year that brought the Second World War, Nicholas Murray Butler, Peace Prize cowinner in 1931, ventured his opinion: "It will always remain my firm conviction that had Stresemann and Briand been spared for another decade to maintain and to strengthen their mutual confidence and their commanding leadership in their respective countries, conditions in Europe and the world would be very different today from what they unhappily are."

Biography

Aristide Briand was born in Nantes on March 28, 1862. As a law student he became interested in politics and wrote for *Le Peuple* and *La Petite République*. He was a cofounder of L'Humanité. A member of the Unified Socialist party, in 1902 he was elected to the Chamber of Deputies as deputy for Loire. He served as *rapporteur* on a committee charged with writing a law on the separation of church and state,

and served on the portfolio of public instruction and worship under the Sarrien ministry in 1906. His acceptance of this post in a bourgeois ministry led to his expulsion from the Unified Socialist Party. Briand also served in this post under Clemenceau.

He formed his first cabinet, the first of his spells as Premier, in July 1909, taking the portfolio of the interior and worship himself. In October 1910 he responded to a threatened strike on the railways by mobilizing all railroad workers who were still subject to military service and dismissed those who disobeyed, and he had the members of the strike committee arrested. Following the fall of his government in 1911, he became Minister of Justice in Poincaré's cabinet in January 1912. When Poincaré was elected President of the Republic in January 1913, Briand succeeded him as Premier. This government was quickly brought down over questions of electoral reform.

In August 1914, during the First World War, Viviani offered Briand the portfolio of justice. Then, when Viviani's cabinet fell in October 1915, Briand formed a government in which he held the portfolio of foreign affairs. He made its character one of a national coalition by including as ministers without portfolio the Socialist Guesde, the Catholic Conservative Cochin, and the three former ministers de Freycinet, Combes, and Bourgeois (the latter the Peace Prize winner for 1920). By the summer of 1916 he was accused of lack of vigor in prosecution of the war, and he formed a new cabinet. This government fell in 1917 over a difference of opinion between the Chamber of Deputies and the Minister of War, Lyautey.

For three years Briand took little part in government affairs. In September 1917 he was approached by von der Loucken, civil commissioner of Germany in Brussels, with a proposal for a meeting to discuss peace. Briand was favorably inclined to accept but was dissuaded by the Minister of Foreign Affairs.

In 1921 he again formed a government and took charge of foreign affairs. His special concern was application of the Treaty of Versailles, especially regarding Germany's war reparations. In the autumn of that year he went to Washington as the French representative to a conference on naval disarmament.

In 1922 Briand discussed with Lloyd George in London the question of an Anglo-French defensive pact. Upon his return to Paris he found he had lost support for the pact and resigned as Premier in January 1922.

In 1925 he took the portfolio of foreign affairs in Painlevé's cabinet and began the most successful years of his career with his participation in bringing about the Locarno agreements in 1925. On November 22 he became the new head of government, but the following March his ministry fell over an issue of a financial measure the Chamber refused to support. He accepted the office again, but with the depreciation of the franc the situation deteriorated and the government fell in June. Once more Briand reconstructed a ministry, bringing in Caillaux as Minister of Finance, but a month later it too was defeated. In the succeeding coalition Briand again became Minister of Foreign Affairs. He directed the government of France on the basis of European consolidation and reconstruction.

In 1927 Briand offered the US Secretary of State, Frank Kellogg, a proposal for a treaty renouncing war as an instrument of national policy. He visualised it as a precedent for other nations from the beginning and this was done. Known as the Kellogg-Briand Pact, it gathered 63 signatories, including all the nations.

Briand's last proposal was a concept put forth at the United Nations for an European Union. But when he failed to get the post of Foreign Minister with the next government, the proposal languished.

Briand occupied the French Foreign Office longer than any other diplomat since Talleyrand. He was Premier more often than any other politician in France. He was a member of 25 different minorities, and was in office for 16 years and 5 months. Politically he moved from his original leftist position to the right, but at the same time from his original nationalistic views to internationalist.

His published works include *La Séparation des églises et de l'état* and *Paroles de paix*. Aristide Briand died on March 6, 1932.

RUTH C. REYNOLDS

Gustav Stresemann
(1926)

The Nobel Committee looked upon the Treaty of Locarno as a longed-for release from postwar hostilities and the entrance into a fresh diplomacy of arbitration and peace. Of central importance was its establishment of a new and better relationship between France and Germany. Therefore the 1926 Peace Prize honored the German and French statesmen-architects of the Locarno agreements, Gustav Stresemann and Aristide Briand.

The First World War, unparalleled in history for suffering wreaked upon whole populations, had ended in the bitterly contested Versailles Treaty which had heaped upon the defeated Germans a crushing load of reparations for damages inflicted upon the Allied populations. But it assigned no monetary assessment to these reparations, instead providing for a Reparation Commission to translate these reparations into Reichsmarks by 1921. The commission did so, but without regard to Germany's capacity to meet the recommended cost of the expiation demanded of it. As a consequence, though Germany made efforts, it fell short; by 1923 it was apparent the wild inflation of the Reichsmark made the assessment impossible to meet and Germany defaulted altogether. This brought on the French-Belgian occupation of the Ruhr, Germany's vital coal mining and industrial center. The expulsion of German officials touched a keen nerve center in Germany, and the German government suspended deliveries and supported the area's population in a policy of passive resistance. Only the Dawes Plan of 1924, drawn up by one of the United States' leading financiers,

Charles Dawes (1925 Peace Prize co-winner) in cooperation with representatives from the United Kingdom, France, and Belgium, saved Germany from economic and political disaster, and prevented corresponding havoc spreading throughout the world's economy. The Plan adjusted the reparations to meet Germany's capacity to pay. Germany received an international loan, its finances were stabilized with the reorganization of the Reichsbank under Allied supervision, and recognition was made of the economic necessity to return the Ruhr. This constituted a progression from hostility to cooperation between Germany and the other nations of the European community. Gustav Stresemann had been present each step of the way.

A glance at Stresemann's biography might raise questions about his suitability as a Peace Prize candidate. He was an ardent German patriot, supporting prewar German policy, and fiercely loyal to the Kaiser. He approved unrestricted submarine warfare, having argued as early as 1907 in favor of a creation of a strong navy. It may be said to his credit, however, that in 1917 when he became the leader of the National Liberal Party, although supporting the war, he also urged that Germany should be prepared for peace if acceptable peace terms were offered. He believed in force, in authority, in discipline.

Stresemann's great value was his realism. He began to see that Imperial Germany had believed in force without possessing adequate force to back up its policies. A month after the armistice of November 11, 1918, Stresemann formed the German People's

Party as successor to the National Liberal Party. This party was at first monarchist, but gradually changed to republicanism, as did Stresemann himself. He was elected to the national assembly at Weimar to frame a new constitution in 1919, gained a seat in the new Reichstag in 1920, and was a member of the opposition until 1923, when he became Chancellor of a coalition government. It was a chaotic time: inflation had taken the Reichsmark from 4.2 to the dollar to 4,200,000,000,000 to the dollar. Stresemann's administration was short—just two months, during which time he dealt firmly with an insurrection in Saxony, restored order after Hitler's attempted *Putsch* failed, ended the passive resistance of Germans in the Ruhr to the French occupying forces, and turned to stabilizing the German currency. After resigning his Chancellor's portfolio, Stresemann became Secretary of Foreign Affairs in the following administration, and held this position with distinction under four governments. Against this background, Stresemann welcomed the Dawes Plan.

Stresemann worked well with Briand of France and Austen Chamberlain of the United Kingdom (1925 Nobel laureate), and they made careful preparations for the conference which was to meet at Locarno, Switzerland, to draw up mutual security pacts. These statesmen came from different backgrounds, but they arrived with a common goal: to provide general security so that political and economic stability could be achieved. In the words of Fridtjof Nansen (1922 Nobel laureate), the men who met at Locarno were not idealistic pacifists; they were realistic politicians and responsible statesmen who, having originally pursued directly conflicting policies, had come to the realization that the only chance of creating a real future for humankind was to stand united in a sincere desire to work together.

The words "allies" and "enemies" were never uttered by any delegate throughout the conferences. Under these circumstances old hostilities lost their hold and, for the first time in history, major powers surrendered their absolute right to make war. The surrender localized around one particular storm center, the Rhine. The Treaty of Locarno, which was signed on December 1, 1925, was a pact of nonaggression between France, Germany, and Belgium, guaranteed by two supposedly impartial powers, Great Britain and Italy.

By the Pact, the United Kingdom and Italy were committed to declare war on Germany if Germany attacked France, and to declare war on France if France attacked Germany. A treaty of mutual guarantee, or security pact, guaranteed the inviolability of the German-Belgian and the German-French frontiers as established by the Versailles Treaty. Stresemann can be credited here as working side by side with Chamberlain and Briand on integrating Germany into a new, peaceful European League.

Entry into the League of Nations was a condition for putting the Locarno Pact into effect. This was a triumph for Stresemann, who had tried to secure entrance into the League for Germany in 1919 but had been rejected.

Stresemann appealed in a national broadcast for support of the Treaty saying, "Locarno may be interpreted as signifying that the States of Europe at last realize that they cannot go on making war upon each other without being involved in common ruin."

Stresemann's comments upon the Locarno Pact in his Nobel lecture express a spirit commensurate with the qualities of a man of peace. He offered a rare and honest insight into the soul of a vanquished people: "Germany had to assume superhuman reparations which the people would never have borne had there not existed an ageless legacy of service to the state . . . . I am speaking of the middle classes who saw the fruits of a lifetime of work vanish and who had to start from scratch to earn a bare livelihood . . . . Theirs was an economic uprooting. But there was a mental and political uprooting, as well . . . [they] were now without a solid foundation for their thinking and emotions."

Stresemann told them that the Locarno agreements represented a policy for the future: "Germany faces this future with a stable nation which has been based upon hard work, upon an economy which will give increasing millions income and security . . . and upon a vital spirit which strives for peace . . . ," he said.

Stresemann looked beyond his nation, and for him the Treaty of Locarno transcended old boundaries, both spiritual and geographic: "I do not think of Locarno only in terms of its consequences for Germany," he said. "Locarno means much more to me. It is the achievement of lasting peace on the Rhine, guaranteed by the formal renunciation of force by the two great neighboring nations and also by the commitment of other states . . . . It can and it ought to be the basis for a general cooperative effort among these nations to spread peace wherever their material power and moral influence reach . . . . *Treuga Dei*, the peace of God, shall reign where for centuries bloody wars have raged." More prosaically, his comments were echoed by Arthur Balfour who called Locarno "The symbol and cause of a great amelioration in the public feeling of Europe."

Stresemann's hope did not pass the test of history.

Within 10 years Germany, Italy, and Japan had withdrawn from the League of Nations, and Germany had formally and unilaterally repudiated the Treaty of Versailles and had violated the Locarno agreements by reoccupying the Rhineland. It is, however, the opinion of certain international observers that the history of that decade would have been different if Stresemann and Briand had lived longer. For instance, in 1939, the year which brought the opening of the Second World War, Nicholas Murray Butler (1931 Peace Prize co-winner) voiced this opinion: "It will always remain my firm conviction that had Stresemann and Briand been spared for another decade to maintain and to strengthen their mutual confidence and their commanding leadership in their respective countries, conditions in Europe and the world would be very different today from what they unhappily are."

Biography

Gustav Stresemann was born in Berlin on May 10, 1878, son of Ernst Stresemann, a prosperous tavern keeper. He was educated at the Andreas Real Gymnasium in Berlin, and at the Universities of Berlin and Leipzig. His doctoral dissertation was an economic investigation of the bottled beer trade in Berlin, combining the practical and the theoretical by assessing the pressures of big business capitalism on the independent middle class of Berlin.

In 1901, he entered commerce as a clerk in the Association of German Chocolate Manufacturers, and a year later took over the management of a local branch of the Manufacturers Alliance. Through his organizational ability and persuasiveness, he increased membership in the Alliance from 180 in 1902 to 5,000 in 1912—a clear demonstration of the executive ability he had to carry into his political career. Other talents which would carry him to the highest level of government posts were early visible—his leadership and his eloquent persuasiveness were evident in his school years.

From 1906 to 1912, he held a seat on the town council of Dresden, in 1907 he won election to the Reichstag, and in 1917 he was elected leader of the National Liberal Party. He supported German prewar policy, and during the war

supported unrestricted submarine warfare, but he urged Germany to accept a peace if a reasonable offer was made. He helped defeat the Bethmann-Hollweg government.

After the Armistice in November 1918, Stresemann formed the German People's Party as successor to the National Liberal Party. His newly formed party was monarchistic in the beginning but grew progressively more republican, as did Stresemann himself. He was Chancellor briefly of a coalition government, August 13 to November 23, 1923. During this period inflation was out of control, Hitler attempted his notorious *Putsch* in Bavaria, and there was an insurrection in Saxony. Stresemann dealt firmly with all these crises, but was forced to resign as Chancellor when his vigorous measures against the communists in Saxony caused him to forfeit the support of the Social Democrats. Thereafter he held a post of Secretary of Foreign Affairs through four governments, with a record of distinction.

He participated in administrating the Dawes Plan, which restructured reparations on the basis of Germany's ability to pay, and negotiated successfully with the Western Allies over the question of maintaining national boundaries established at Versailles. Stresemann was a major architect along with the United Kingdom's Austen Chamberlain (1925 Nobel laureate) and France's Aristide Briand of the several international agreements called the Treaty of Locarno. The Treaty was the first international agreement of major nations in which they surrendered the right to make war as they wished, substituting instead a series of pacts which they thought would offer mutual security and secure the peace.

Stresemann signed a rapprochement with the Soviet Union, the Treaty of Berlin, in 1926. That same year he saw Germany at last accepted into the League of Nations, and he served as delegate there from 1926 to 1929. As German delegate, he was one of the first to declare his readiness to sign the Kellogg-Briand Pact, renouncing war as an instrument of national policy.

In 1929 at The Hague, Stresemann accepted the Young Plan for the evacuation of the Ruhr; but he did not live to see it implemented.

Gustav Stresemann died in Berlin on October 3, 1929.

RUTH C. REYNOLDS

Ferdinand Buisson
(1927)

Ferdinand Buisson was 87 at the time he received the 1927 Nobel Prize for Peace as co-winner with Ludwig Quidde. For many decades Buisson had undertaken the task of reorienting public opinion away

from war and to the higher ideal of peaceful cooperation among nations and the award was made for a lifetime of work devoted to this ideal. Sixty years previously he had helped Frédéric Passy, co-winner of the first Peace Prize(1901), form the Bureau Internationale et Permanente de la Paix (Permanent International Bureau of Peace). The same year, 1867, he had attended the First International Peace Conference at Geneva, where he advocated a United States of Europe. Known as "the world's most persistent pacifist," Buisson wrote literally thousands of articles and stood before countless lecterns speaking for the cause of peace.

Though fundamentally opposed to war, Buisson firmly believed that France was rightfully defending itself in the First World War. He believed that the defeat of Germany was necessary to ensure peace and justice in Europe. But he was bitterly disappointed with the Treaty of Versailles, and together with many other advocates of peace believed that hope now rested with the League of Nations. He was convinced that it was necessary to counteract the dangerous element of vengeance in the peace treaty by establishing friendship and understanding between France and Germany.

Buisson was born in Paris and was educated at the Lycée Bonaparte. He left school at 16 to help support his family upon the death of his father. His first job in his long career in education began at that time as a tutor in Paris. He later completed his education at the University of Paris, successfully passing the state teachers' examination in philosophy. However, Buisson's sharp sense of political justice kept him from taking the necessary oath of allegiance to Napoleon III in order to teach in his own country. He went into political exile in Switzerland, and there he held the chair of philosophy at the Academy of Neufchatel from 1866 to 1870.

He attended the First Geneva Congress of Peace and joined the Ligue Internationale de la Paix et de la Liberté (International League of Peace and Liberty) founded by Charles Lemonnier in 1867. He wrote articles denouncing militarism and began his lifelong campaign for the intensive education of the masses as the way to put an end to war.

With the establishment of the Third Republic in France Buisson was free to return there in the latter part of 1870. He was appointed inspector of elementary education, but the new government which soon came to power looked askance at his advocacy of secularization of schools, and he lost this post. With the coming of a more liberal ministry, however, Buisson came back into service as inspector-general of elementary education. He held this post from 1878 to 1896, and made many reforms in the French primary system of education. In 1896 he was appointed to the faculty at the Sorbonne as professor of the science of education. Buisson turned his prolific pen to pedagogy, and among many books wrote his major four-volume work, *Dictionnaire de pédagogie et d'instruction primaire*. He was also editor-in-chief of a leading educational journal, *Manuel général d'instruction primaire*.

The Dreyfus case outraged his sense of justice and Buisson campaigned to reverse the Dreyfus decision and helped found the Ligule des Droits des Hommes (League of the Rights of Man), serving as its president for 13 years beginning in 1898, and after his retirement from active work remaining its honorary president for life.

In 1902 he was elected to the Chamber of Deputies as a Radical Socialist. There he presided over the commission for the separation of church and state. He worked tirelessly for the League of Nations. He protested the French Ruhr policy and supported reconciliation with the Germans. He sat in the Chamber until 1914 and reentered it in 1919.

At the time of the Ruhr dispute following the Franco-Belgian occupation Buisson went on speaking tours across France protesting the French policy and advocating Franco-German reconciliation. At the age of 84 he engaged in a speaking tour of Germany, and during one address said, "A force exists which is far greater than France, far greater than Germany, far greater than any nation, and that is mankind. But above mankind itself stands justice, which finds its most perfect expression in brotherhood."

Biography

Ferdinand Edouard Buisson was born in Paris on December 20, 1841, the son of a Protestant judge of the St Etienne Tribunal. Educated at the Collége d'Argentan and the Lycée Etienne, he left school at 16 in order to support his family. He subsequently completed his secondary education at the Lycée Condorcet and took a degree at the University of Paris. At the age of 51 he received his doctorate in literature.

In 1866 he took his first teaching post, at Switzerland's Academic de Neufchatel. He participated in the Geneva Peace Congress which founded the Ligue Internationale de la Paix et de la Liberté, and during this period he began writing. He was instrumental in the founding of the journal *Les états-Unis d'Europe*, which first appeared in 1867; and his contributions included the influential *L'Abolition de la guerre par l'instruction* (Abolishing war through education).

With the establishment of the Third Republic, Buisson returned to France and became inspector of primary education, from which position he resigned over the outcry regarding his stance in favor of secular education. Later he became secretary of the Statistical Commission on Primary Education, and in 1878 inspector-general of primary education in France. In the following year he became director of primary education, and during the 18 years he held this position he established free, compulsory, secular primary education and participated in its implementation.

A scholar as well as an administrator, from 1896 to 1902 he was professor of education at the Sorbonne. He authored a four-volume work, *Dictionnaire de pédagogie et d'instruction primaire*, and became editor-in-chief of *Manual général d'instruction primaire*, a journal of education.

He wrote and spoke supporting the reversal of the Dreyfus decision, in connection with which he helped found the League of the Rights of Man in 1898, serving as its president for 13 years, and remaining honorary president for life.

From 1902 to 1914 Buisson sat in the Chamber of Deputies as a Radical Socialist, supporting compulsory, secular schooling, chaired a commission on the issue of separation of church and state, and served as vice-chairman of a commission on proposals for social welfare legislation. He sat on the Commission for Universal Suffrage and supported the principle of proportional representation.

He returned to the Chamber in 1919 and served until 1924. He donated the proceeds of the Nobel Peace Prize to pacifist programs.

Ferdinand Buisson died at his home in Thieuloy-Saint-Antoine on February 16, 1932.

RUTH C. REYNOLDS

Ludwig Quidde
(1927)

The 1927 Nobel Peace Prize went to Ludwig Quidde, co-winner with Ferdinand Buisson. Quidde was a distinguished historian whose scholarly gifts infused all that he did in a long career as a pacifist.

From a country so resolutely war-oriented as Germany, Quidde's antimilitaristic stand made him the more remarkable among the peace advocates honored by the Nobel Prize. Fredrik Stang, Chairman of the Nobel Committee, said that Quidde's interest in the peace movement grew out of a combination of his historical studies, his ethical ideals, his distrust of the military, and the urging of his wife, Margarethe, whom he married in 1882. Stang called Quidde's political ideology "a direct heritage from the Enlightenment," and said that Quidde strove to imbue the German people with a sense of justice which would of itself generate social reform.

Certainly Quidde had the courage of his convictions. He delivered a political speech in 1896 for which he was accused of lese-majesty; he was tried, convicted, and sentenced to three months in the Munich prison Stadelheim. This was following an experience of publishing anonymously an attack on German militarism, and, in quick succession, his famous *Caligula*, ostensibly a historical study and this time published openly under his own name. Done with scholarly care for detail, it was in truth a thinly disguised and scathing attack on Kaiser Wilhelm II and the Byzantine nature of the Prussian society over which he reigned. The ruthless use of power, his vanity as an actor, his conceit as an orator—all these attributes of the Emperor were satirized. Was the Emperor first-century Roman or twentieth-century German? Quidde denied an intended analogy, thus leaving the proof of intended similarity to the prosecution, a project too embarrassing to pursue. By his own cleverness Quidde had outwitted his prosecutors, and he thus escaped conviction on the charge of lese-majesty.

Quidde threw himself into political activity, much of it centered around peace. The oldest son of a wealthy Bremen merchant, he was of independent means and could therefore give his undivided time and energy where he wished. He filled a position on the council of the International Peace Bureau in Berne where Elie Ducommun, Nobel laureate in the second year of the awards (1902), served as secretary-general. Quidde rose to a position of leadership in the World Peace Congress in Glasgow in 1901, and in 1905 he joined Frédéric Passy, co-winner of the first Nobel award (1901), at the Lucerne Congress held to achieve a rapprochement between Germany and France. In 1907 he supervised the organization of the World Peace Congress and in 1914 became president of the German Peace Society, remaining in that position for 15 years.

With the outbreak of the First World War Quidde fled to The Hague. He tried to maintain contact with the English and French peace associations but his attempts were fruitless and won him only an accusation of treason when he returned to Germany. The charges were dropped, but he was under close observation for months and endured censorship of his mail and confiscation of his pamphlets.

Despite this mistrust, in 1919 Quidde was elected to the Weimar National Assembly. There he argued against Germany's accepting the Treaty of Versailles. He approved and supported the League of Nations, and favored Germany's entry into it.

Quidde tried to revive the German peace movement and headed the German Peace Cartel. In 1924 he was arrested for writing an article protesting against secret military training and was imprisoned in Munich under the emergency regulations then in force in Bavaria.

Quidde did not believe that disarmament was the answer to securing peace. Armaments are necessary, he said in his Nobel lecture, only because of the real or imagined danger of war. He subscribed to the theory that disarmament will be the result of secure peace rather than the means of obtaining it. The security he spoke of is that attained by the development of international law through an international organization based on the principles of law and justice. But psychology is more powerful in life than logic, he said. When distrust exists between governments, when there is a danger of war, the governments would not be willing to disarm even when logic indicates that disarmament would not affect military security at all. Hence the observation that without a secure peace, even if all countries disarmed proportionately, military security would not be served. But the limitation of armaments is worthwhile quite apart from reasons of security, in that armaments place an enormous burden on the economic, social, and intellectual resources of a nation.

Quidde also pointed out that every success in limiting armaments is a sign that the will to achieve mutual understanding exists, and every such success supports the fight for international law and order. One important step to international justice comes through mediation, he said. "We pacifists can boast of having been among the first to recognize the necessity of setting up a system for mediation alongside that for arbitration. The Lucerne Congress of 1905 passed the Fried-Quidde motion calling attention to the importance of an organized means of mediation .... Arbitration courts can be used for those cases which are suitable for litigation. But the most serious and dangerous disputes arise over conflicts of interest which are not subject to the rules of legal process. In such cases, mediation is needed to decide what is equitable and fair .... International mediation needs to be organized just as much as does arbitration."

Quidde warned that we must learn that we have a choice only between total devastation that will result from a future war and a peace secured by rule of law.

He turned to Immanuel Kant's *Zum ewigen Frieden*, (Perpetual Peace) a discussion about how it might be possible to ensure peace. "He did not present the point of view of the moral philosopher who bases his hopes on an improvement in mankind," Quidde said. "Oh, no! Kant found the only assurance for peace in the idea that war would become so terrible and unbearable that human beings, even though they remain as morally weak as they now are, would be forced to work together for peace" (see Articles: *Perpetual Peace*).

Quidde followed with an observation on a higher ethical level: "The same technology which has made war so terrible has given us the means to bring the whole world within one international organization. The moral basis of such an organization must not be merely the fear of war. It must be the conviction that it is a moral duty to do away with war and to secure peace. Only on this basis can we hope to reach complete disarmament and a peace secured by treaties."

Biography

Ludwig Quidde was born in Bremen in 1858. A distinguished historian educated at Strasbourg and Gottingen, he specialized in German history in the Middle Ages. In 1889 he founded the *Deutsche Zeitschrift für Geschichtswissenschaft* (German Review of Historical Science), and edited it until 1896. He spent 1890-92 as a staff member of the Prussian Historical Institute in Rome. He later taught history at the University of Munich.

A dissenter who opposed Germany's militarism, Quidde served three months in a Munich prison for a political speech in 1896. Undaunted, he wrote a satire on Caligula, a thinly disguised attack on Kaiser Wilhelm II. Though tried for lese-majesty, he was not convicted and the work enjoyed tremendous success.

An ardent pacifist, he worked with the International Peace Bureau in Bern, led the World Peace Congress in Glasgow in 1901, and joined Frédéric Passy (1901 Peace Prize co-winner) at the 1905 Lucerne Congress in an effort to achieve Franco-German rapprochement. He supervised the organization of the Second World Peace Congress at Geneva in 1907 and was president of the German Peace Society for 15 years.

Quidde spent the First World War in The Hague. Upon his return to Germany he was elected to the Weimar National Assembly. There he argued against Germany accepting the Treaty of Versailles and supported the League of Nations and Germany's entrance into it. He tried to revive the German peace movement and headed the German Peace Cartel.

Quidde did not believe disarmament would secure peace.

He believed in the development of international law through an international organization based on the principles of law and justice.

With the coming of Hitler to power in 1933 he again went into exile, this time in Geneva. He wrote and attended Peace Congresses and founded the Comité de Secours aux Pacifistes Exiles to care for fellow political exiles from Germany.

Ludwig Quidde died in March 1941 in his eighth year of exile.

See also: Articles: *Arbitration, International; Mediation*

RUTH C. REYNOLDS

Prize Not Awarded
(1928)

Frank Billings Kellogg
(1929)

The 1929 Nobel Peace Prize was awarded to Frank Kellogg, US Secretary of State, for his part in drawing up the Kellogg-Briand Pact (1928) condemning recourse to war as a solution to international discord. The pact was signed by 63 countries, including all the major nations, and the Nobel Committee pronounced it not only a noteworthy example of the efforts of the United States, but also a sound and conscientious collaboration on the part of the international front for the advancement of peace.

The actual idea of abolishing war as a juridical institution by means of treaties was indeed an American one, originating in 1923 with a Chicago lawyer, S. O. Levinson, who had begun an "Outlawry of War" movement in the United States, likening the abolition of war to that of dueling and slavery. Nicholas Murray Butler (Peace Prize co-winner in 1931) had taken an interest in the movement as part of his crusade to create a truly "international mind." He mentioned to the French Foreign Minister, Aristide Briand (Peace Prize co-winner in 1926), in a meeting in June 1926 that he thought the time had now come for nations to renounce war through a voluntary agreement. Briand chose a memorable date for Americans on which to respond with a declaration of his interest in the movement. On the tenth anniversary of the entry of the United States into the First World War, a devastating conflict which was still generating intense efforts to find a path to lasting peace, he wrote in an open letter to the press on April 6, 1927, "If there were any need between these two great democracies to testify more convincingly in favor of peace and to present to the peoples a more solemn example, France would be ready publicly to subscribe, with the United States, to any mutual engagement in Paris a draft of a treaty of perpetual friendship between the two countries, proposing that the two parties would solemnly declare that they condemned war and renounced it as an instrument of their national policies."

At first, Secretary Kellogg fought shy of the proposal, partly fearful of a two-nation entanglement. But Nicholas Murray Butler did not share his hesitation. In a letter to the *New York Times* he initiated a campaign arousing public opinion in its favor. With the idea of elevating the French bilateral proposal to a multilateral pact which would draw in the nations of the world, Kellogg became persuaded. He replied in a note to Briand on December 28 that the government of the United States was prepared to consult with the government of France with a view to the conclusion of a treaty among the principal powers of the world, open to signature by all nations, to condemn war and renounce it as an instrument of national policy in favor of peaceful settlement of international disputes. From this day forward Kellogg gave it his every attention. It entailed a considerable amount of work and diplomatic skill to coordinate the various views, but the pact was signed in Paris on August 27, 1928. The signatory powers were the United States, Great Britain, France, Italy, Japan, Germany, Belgium, Poland, and Czechoslovakia; but it was later endorsed by 63 nations, among them all the major powers.

Frank Kellogg would seem to have been an unlikely candidate for a Peace Prize laureate. He had never made any claim to being a peace lover or an internationalist—indeed he was an isolationist—but, in his favor, it may be noted that he *had* voted as a senator against the ratification of the short-sighted Treaty of Versailles.

Kellogg was appointed Secretary of State in 1925, in which position he served until 1929. During his secretaryship he improved US relations with Mexico, tranquilized an impending conflict between Chile and Peru, and achieved conciliatory treaties with all the Latin American nations except Argentina, and with 15 other powers. All in all he signed 80 treaties of various kinds, but none was so important to him as the Pact of Paris, commonly called the Kellogg-Briand Pact.

Kellogg had shown diplomatic skill in resolving the conflict between the initial view of the French that the treaty should first be bilateral, with the United States and France working out a pattern for other nations to follow, and the view of the United States that the pact should include as many nations as possible. He never lost faith in the underlying concept, the renunciation of war as an instrument of national policy; but the failure to make provision for enforcement was an obvious shortcoming. In his Nobel lecture Kellogg said he knew there were those who believed that peace would not be attained until some supertribunal was established to punish the violators of such treaties, "but I believe," he said, "that in the end the abolition of war, the maintenance of world peace, the adjustment of international questions by pacific means will come through the force of public opinion, which controls nations and peoples—that public opinion which shapes our destinies and guides the progress of human affairs."

Biography

Frank Billings Kellogg was born in Potsdam, New York, on December 22, 1858, son of Asa Kellogg and Abigail Billings Kellogg. When he was nine years old his family moved to a farm in Olmstead, Minnesota. With only five more years of schooling before he was taken out to help his father on the farm, he nonetheless continued via self-education with borrowed textbooks, and with a two-year apprenticeship in a law office he passed to the Bar in 1877.

In the next 20 years Kellogg became highly successful, counting among his clients railroads, iron-mining companies and steel-manufacturing firms and counting among his friends Andrew Carnegie, John D. Rockefeller, and James J. Hill. Despite these associations, however, he first attained national fame as a "trustbuster" lawyer, carrying out the enthusiastic antitrust policy of President Theodore Roosevelt. He was named president of the American Bar Association in 1912 and 1913. He was a member of the National Committee of the Republican Party from 1904 to 1912, and three times a delegate to its national conventions. In 1916 he was elected to the US Senate, serving until 1922. In March 1923 he went as a delegate to the fifth Pan-American Conference in Chile, and later that year President Coolidge named him ambassador to the United Kingdom. While on the assignment he worked on reparation questions and the acceptance of the Dawes Committee report. Between 1925 and 1929 he was Secretary of State in Coolidge's cabinet, during which time he saw critical problems with Mexico on oil and land expropriation solved by legal rather than military means, and his Caribbean and South American nations policies received mixed review, with liberals calling them too aggressive, but the middle opinion finding them a "retreat from imperialism." Toward China, with whom relations were troubled by attacks against foreigners in Shanghai and Nanking, and by problems of tariff autonomy and abolition of extraterritoriality, his policy was recognized as carried out "in goodwill."

During his secretaryship, he signed 80 treaties of various kinds, a record set for that time. In pursuance of his belief in the efficacy of the legal arbitration of disputes, 19 of them were bilateral treaties with foreign nations. No treaty was so important to Kellogg as the Pact of Paris, commonly known as the Kellogg-Briand Pact.

He was, toward Europe, basically an isolationist, although following his bringing the Kellogg-Briand Pact to a successful conclusion with 63 signatories he served as judge of the Permanent Court of International Justice at The Hague from 1930 to 1935.

Kellogg received many honors, among them the French Legion of Honor and honorary degrees from Carleton College, Lawrence University, Harvard, the University of Minnesota, Princeton, Trinity College, and Oxford University.

He married Clara M. Cook of Rochester, Minnesota, in 1896.

Frank Kellogg died at St Paul, Minnesota on December 21, 1937.

RUTH C. REYNOLDS

Lars Olof Nathan Söederblom
(1930)

The Nobel Peace Prize of 1930 was awarded to Sweden's Archbishop Nathan Söderblom. He was a primate in the cause of world peace as he was a primate in his own church in Sweden. The Nobel Committee stated, in presenting the award, that Söderblom understood the enormous importance of the church in the fight for peace, and the powerful influence which the church could bring with it. "The Christian church has sinned grievously and often against the teaching of Him whose first commandment to men was that they should love one another. This church surely has a unique opportunity now of creating that new attitude of mind which is necessary if peace between nations is to become reality," Committee member Mowinckel said.

Söderblom came superbly qualified for this task by training and through personal dedication. During his undergraduate studies at Uppsala University he began a formidable mastery of languages with honors in Greek and competency in Hebrew, Arabic, and Latin. For the next six years he studied theology and probed into the history of religions, learning whatever languages necessary to do so. His Doctor of Theology degree at the Protestant Faculty of the Sorbonne stands as an eloquent testament to his in-depth studies continued while a pastor at the Swedish Church in Paris, for his was the first such degree ever granted to a foreigner.

While attending a Christian student conference in New England, Söderblom heard a lecture which prompted an entry into his diary prophetically descriptive of his destined dedication: "Lord, give me humility and wisdom to serve the great cause of the free unity of thy church." This was to become his great contribution to the search for peace. Even before the war, he had made a beginning in his work of uniting the church communities of the world, and thus promoting international understanding.

It was a long road from the spiritual wreckage left in the wake of the First World War to an Ecumenical Council which Söderblom called "as magnificent an achievement as the League of Nations." He shared that experience of many years in his Nobel lecture, offering a moving and descriptive history of the ecumenical movement. The account given below closely follows that lecture, distilled to include only the major stations along the road.

During the war Christians were filled with anguish; they asked themselves whether the church, which had been called the "Prince of Peace," had fulfilled its duty. Many of the clergy, of different countries and different creeds, in both the Old World and the New, increasingly felt the need for a Christendom which was united in at least the essential principle of living according to the commandment of love. Thus

united, they would constitute a more powerful crusade for peace. During the war, in the summer of 1917, a congress was called of those churches whose nations would grant passports for travel with the purpose of declaring Christian unity, and to express before the world the belief that the values of Christendom transcended those of individual nations.

Agreeing not to discuss the war, or purely political measures for achieving peace, they examined what the different churches could accomplish in the struggle against war, and how they could bring about the proper state of mind needed for better international understanding. Reckless nationalism had to be replaced by Christian brotherhood that would transcend national boundaries. The outcome of the congress, called the Conference of Churches in Neutral Countries, was a threefold set of statements designed for consideration by the body of churches, and as a guide for its work: (a) the unity of Christians; (b) Christians and the life of society; and (c) Christians and the law. The supranational character of the Conference had immense effect as a harbinger and implement of peace—embodying a spiritual entity that addressed people as human beings and not as speakers of given languages and members of given races and nationalities.

The Evangelical Church, war weakened and discordant though it was, became the first community of people in the world who brought together responsible men and women from both camps after the Great War. It met at the International Committee of the World Alliance at Oud Wassenaar in October 1919. There Söderblom proposed the international ecumenical conference which was eventually held at Stockholm in 1925.

The breakthrough occurred in 1925 at Stockholm. The Ecumenical Council which came into being represented, officially or semiofficially, the larger part of Christendom. By meeting to discuss precisely those matters about which they differed, doctrinal differences were diminished; and in the process there emerged a sense of the essential spiritual and religious unity throughout the whole Evangelical Church.

However, Söderblom said, Christians should not wait for full agreement before they start practicing the duty of love imposed by the Master. While discussions concerning doctrinal matters and the church ordinances may be long-ranged, Christians must follow immediately the divine command to love one another. No result of the Stockholm meeting has been more obvious and noteworthy, he said, than the realization that, according to the Gospel, God must be first in people's hearts and must thus also rule over the people, over groups in society, and over nations themselves.

The ecumenical revival does not belong just to the circle of priests and laymen, he said. It must force its way outward and become the property of society, a concern of all churches and of all people.

Three essential tasks toward the cause of peace emerged from these ecumenical meetings: (a) To instill the spirit of fraternity and truth into the heart of humankind. (b) The church itself must realize and impress upon others the absolute nature of God's commandments which extend justice beyond the boundaries of nations, thereby substituting cooperation for self-assertion. (c) It follows from the point just made that the armed forces must be stripped of their previous role, which has been fostered by fear, by lust for power, and by serving Mammon. Söderblom said we must instead make them the safeguard of security, peace, and liberty, just as the police force is the safeguard within the state.

If efforts toward peace are to get anywhere, he said, they must be more realistic than in the past. The question is not whether one is orthodox in conforming to some peace formula or other, but whether one does something to promote peace. We must not allow ourselves to be lulled into any simplistic peace dream. We must struggle to win peace, struggle against schism, against hatred and injustice. This fight must be directed primarily toward the primitive human within us. Impatient minds may perhaps find such a concept hopeless, pessimistic, and old fashioned but, Söderblom insisted, we must face reality. The noble and practical measures for world peace will be realized only to the extent to which the supremacy of God conquers the heart of humankind.

At the Ecumenical Council held at Eisenach in 1928 four points were evolved in the "Eisenach Resolution":

(a) A wholehearted welcome extended to the solemn declaration made by the leading statesmen of the world in the names of their nations that they condemn war as a means of settling international disputes and denounce it as a tool of international power politics.

(b) The belief that the settlement of international disputes by war is irreconcilable with the spirit of Christ, and therefore irreconcilable with the spirit and conduct of His church.

(c) The conviction that the time must come when existing treaties have to be revised in the interest of peace, but maintaining that all international disputes and conflicts which cannot be solved through diplomacy or mediation must be settled through arbitration by the International Court of Justice or some other court of law acknowledged by all parties involved.

(d) The legal system being the work of God, the duty of the church is to stress its sanctity and to work for its extension beyond national boundaries. The church must uphold the binding nature of any contract obliging nations to settle disputes through arbitration or legal channels. Thus, if the government of a church's own country disregards this obligation to submit a dispute to such a procedure, that church must condemn any war developing from this situation, and must disclaim, in both word and action, any connection with it.

What we are recommending, Söderblom said, is not a breach of loyalty; on the contrary, it is obedience to a higher obligation. A supranational judicial system is being built. Binding treaties between nations who are committed to conciliation or arbitration when disputes arise rather than to war represent the foundations of a larger edifice of the rule of law. What we do advocate is obedience to the rule of Christ and His apostles instructing us to respect civic law. All people and all nations must participate in the construction of a supranational legal system, which, according to Christian doctrine, is a continuation of God's creation.

In due course, the Life and Work Movement of which Söderblom was the inspiration came to join forces with the other great wing of the ecumenical movement, the predominately Anglican Faith and Order Movement. Their fusion led in 1948 to the formulation of the World Council of Churches. This organization with its headquarters in Geneva is active worldwide in its continuing efforts to unify the world's churches in the struggle for universal peace (see Articles: *World Council of Churches* (wcc)).

Apart from the ethical values of Christianity, Söderblom believed that the Christian way of life was in itself of great value to the cause of peace. In a sermon in 1917 he emphasized two factors: first the Christian belief in the impossible and the fact that faith "took the long view," and the other, the ability of the Christian way of life to strengthen confidence in the community based on law.

Biography

Nathan Söderblom (named Lars Olof Jonathan) was born in Trono, in the Swedish province of Halsingland, son of Jonas Söderblom, a pietistic pastor, and Sophia Blume Söderblom. He took his bachelor's degree at the School of Theology in Uppsala in 1886, after which he continued his studies there and (from 1888 to 1893) edited the *Student Missionary Association review* (*Meddelanden*). In 1893 he was ordained a priest, taking first a position as a chaplain in a mental hospital in Uppsala, following which he accepted a call to the Swedish Church in Paris in 1894, where he stayed until 1901. He continued his studies, mastering ten languages to pursue the origins and history of Asiatic religions including translations from Sanskrit, Persian, and Chinese. The Sorbonne made him a Doctor of Theology, the first foreigner ever to receive that honor. From 1901 to 1914 Söderblom occupied a chair in the School of Theology at Uppsala University, and concurrently from 1912 to 1914 was professor of comparative theology at the University of Leipzig. In 1914 he was elected as Archbishop of Uppsala, by virtue of which he also became primate of the Church of Sweden. He was elected a member of the Swedish Academy in 1921.

In 1923 he visited the United States under the auspices of the World Alliance for Promoting International Friendship, delivering a series of lectures at Harvard, Yale, and other universities and being received at the White House by President Coolidge.

Internationally Söderblom was known as one of the architects of the ecumenical movement of the twentieth century. As early as 1909 he was working toward intercommunion between the Swedish Church and the Church of England. The culmination of his efforts took place at the Stockholm Conference held in 1925 between Anglican, Protestant, and Orthodox Christians.

In 1927 he was a member of the World Conference on Faith and Order at Lausanne. This conference culminated in a final report which established common ground on a number of key doctrinal questions.

His theological writings include studies of the origins of religions, religious history, the character of the Church of Sweden, and Indian modes of worship.

He was married to Anna Forsell and they had 13 children.

He was in the midst of a famous lectureship, the Gifford Lectures in Edinburgh in 1931, at the time of his death on July 12.

RUTH C. REYNOLDS

Jane Addams
(1931)

The Nobel Prize for Peace in 1931 was awarded to Jane Addams and Nicholas Butler for their assiduous work of many years toward reviving the ideal of peace in their own nation and the whole of humanity. "In honoring Jane Addams," the Nobel Committee said, "we also pay tribute to the work which women can do for peace and fraternity among nations . . . . Jane Addams combines all the best feminine qualities which will help us to develop peace on earth."

Jane Addams was a powerful moving force from the laissez-faire of unrestricted capitalism to a consideration of responsibilities toward the individuals within capitalist society. She asked for a "social ethic" to take the place of an "individualistic ethic." And people listened to her because for 40 years she translated her social ideals into action through Hull House.

Much has been written about Addams as "the Angel of Hull House." She is pictured as a feminine version of St. Francis, sacrificing comfort, security, and all the amenities of life which her well-to-do family had offered her, in order to lose herself in the poverty of a Chicago tenement district. But this is a poor exchange for the reality: a capable administrator, a complex, intelligent woman of immense persuasive ability who participated in almost every major reform of her era. Addams had no desire to descend to the poverty level. Her interests were to lift the level all about her out of poverty.

She learned her basics in sociology from what she found about her. She learned from young working girls in factories and sweatshops. She learned from garbage, from suicide, from dirt. She learned from children things she had not known in her own childhood. She read voraciously. Then, from what she learned, she developed a program centered upon the question: how could the quality of life be raised? Under her hand, Hull House was always a place where beauty was cultivated, and it was home to a multicultural spread of interests and activities.

She was intensely practical when that best served the purpose, insisting that the fullest possible good be required from existing public and social agencies, and demanding new agencies when the old had been proven inadequate. She went through the streets of Chicago's tenement district as the duly commissioned inspector of streets and alleys, determined to make the agencies of government act to the benefit of the dwellers in those underprivileged areas. Her great administrative genius was to deal with people on the level of their highest potential.

Year after year Addams saw nearly all the migrant races of the world pass by her doorstep. Living among them, she entered their psychology, learned their point of view, and appreciated their racial contribution to the national culture. She developed many ways of promoting justice through understanding. She used hospitality to bring together guests who might exchange differing points of view. Hull House was a living demonstration that neighborliness between men and women of different classes was possible. She endowed it with her own brand of caring. "It was that word 'with' from Jane Addams," said a working-woman, "that took the bitterness out of my life. For if she wanted to work with me and I could work with her, it gave my life new meaning and hope."

Hull House grew into a center of several buildings accommodating cultural enrichment of the people of that impoverished area. It helped them learn to look after their interests. It became a friendly center for organizing against sweatshop working conditions, and this culminated in legislation passed against exploitative work practices.

Finding ways of giving stability to the immigrant family was the earliest and one of the most lasting Hull House goals. The Immigrants Protective League had its inception there. The nursery and kindergarten, and the clubs for boys and girls which were established there freed mothers who had to work outside the home. Hull House arts and crafts gave the immigrants a sense of tradition, of recognition of their various skills, a feeling of social stability and personal value.

Hull House stood first of all for social democracy. Addams' experiences there persuaded her of the necessity for progressive social legislation to bring democracy into areas where it had not been practiced before. Hull House participated in establishing juvenile courts, creating public baths in the tenements, instituting medical inspection in the schools. It served to awaken the nation's conscience to the desperate plight of the underprivileged in us cities.

Addams became intent upon improving the social system beyond her Chicago neighborhood. Her public career expanded to state and national legislation,

seeking to improve working conditions of women and children everywhere, guaranteeing compensation for injuries to the heads of families. Increasingly she participated in mediation, particularly in the field of labor disputes. In a strike of the Amalgamated Clothing Workers of America she helped bring about an agreement in 1910 which laid a foundation for industrial peace in an industry nationally known for its "sweatshop practices." She influenced the settlement of the great Pullman strike of 1894 through arbitration, out of which grew a public demand for the State Board of Arbitration and Conciliation.

During the 40 years she lived at Hull House she sought, above all else, a moral change which would create peace and contentment where there had previously been only divisive exploitation. Addams fell far short of this goal, but she created shifting us attitudes toward poverty and reform, and toward a social order responsive to the needs of far more of its people.

She carried her passionate concern for understanding between peoples to the international scene. It was a natural series of steps from municipal ordinances, state and national legislation to the means for establishing a peaceful world order.

Addams was a pacifist. In her view the worst thing about war was its total prevention of the mutual understanding of peoples. Living in Hull House among representatives of a score of nations had convinced her that in each human being there are universal emotions which transcend national and cultural boundaries. She sought the means to express these universal emotions. She had repeatedly witnessed her immigrant neighbors modifying their provincialism and taming the ferocity of their nationalism. Entries in her notebooks show that she hoped this "internationalism" would be the forerunner to developing a similar instrument in the cause of world peace. As late as 1913 she spoke at a meeting in Carnegie Hall of a "rising in the cosmopolitan centers of America of a sturdy and unprecedented international understanding which in time would be too profound to lend itself to war." The applause of the audience was overwhelming. But one year later the First World War came, and Addams witnessed the revitalization of old antagonisms between the very neighbors who had inspired her dream.

Addams never supported the United States' entry into the war, despite abuses and insults. She accepted an invitation to become president of the International Congress of Women meeting at The Hague in 1915. It was typical of her active pacifism that she would join in planning for a wise peace to have in readiness for the war's end. In reading the resolutions which came out of this conference, it is striking how they anticipated the 14 points introduced by President Wilson of the United States. Afterwards Addams, with other delegates, visited both the warring and neutral countries to promote the idea of a conference of neutrals which would offer continuous mediation to the belligerents. She supported the League of Nations, the World Court, disarmament and education for peace.

The Congress of Women met in 1919 in Zurich and founded the Women's International League for Peace and Freedom. This is a permanent federation of women with organized sections in 25 countries and a worldwide membership. It operates to promote new methods in international relations for removing animosities and righting wrongs without resort to war. Addams served as its president until 1929, and as honorary president for the remainder of her life.

Addams' long career in pacifism is beautifully summarized by one of her biographers, James Linn: "It was a struggle long-continued and brave. It involved, and finally concentrated, the help of thousands of other women in many countries, finally in almost all countries. It engaged the attention, admiration, and in the end, the genuine conviction of many statesmen. It led her through first the patronizing commendation of millions, then through their obloquy and insult. It culminated, three weeks before she died, in a celebration personally triumphant, in which were joined not only some of the best known men and women of her own country, but the ambassadors of England, France, Russia and Japan, praising her as no American woman had ever before been internationally praised. But it was a struggle based not on emotion, and not on economic principles, but on understanding" (Linn 1935 p. 285).

Biography

(Laura) Jane Addams was born in Cedarville, Illinois, on September 6, 1860, daughter of John H. and Sarah (Weber) Addams. Her father was a successful businessman and served as a state senator for 16 years. She graduated from the Rockford Female Seminary in 1881 as valedictorian and was granted a bachelor's degree. She entered the Women's Medical College of Philadelphia, but frail health owing to a congenital spinal curvature forced her withdrawal. She spent the next two years in Europe studying the poor districts in European cities, and her visit to Toynbee Hall, a settlement house in London, inspired her to plan a similar house for the underprivileged in Chicago. In 1889 she and her friend, Ellen G. Starr, leased the former mansion of Charles Hull and established a center providing for

a higher civic and social life and improved conditions in the industrial districts of Chicago. These included juvenile courts, public baths, industrial education, and medical inspection in schools. Addams undertook to supervise the cleaning of streets in the Hull House neighborhood and was appointed garbage inspector for this purpose by the mayor.

Addams and Starr put great effort into soliciting financial aid as well as interest and participation in furthering the cause of social welfare. By its second year Hull House was host to 2,000 people every week. Addams' reputation grew and she went into larger fields of civic responsibility. She was one of the founders of the NAACP (National Association for the Advancement of Colored People), and was vice-president of the Woman Suffrage Association. In 1905 she was appointed to Chicago's Board of Education and thereafter chaired the School Management Committee. She participated in the founding of the Chicago School of Civics and Philanthropy in 1908, and during the ensuing year became the first woman president of the National Conference of Charities and Corrections.

A feminist, Addams believed that women must participate fully in society and exercise the right of suffrage. She worked tirelessly towards preventing war, and in 1906 she gave a series of lectures at the University of Wisconsin which were published under the title *Newer Ideals of Peace*. She spoke at a ceremony commemorating the building of the Peace Palace at The Hague in 1913. During the next two years, as a lecturer sponsored by the Carnegie Foundation, she spoke against the United States' participation in the First World War.

In 1915 she became chairwoman of the Women's Peace Party and president of the International Congress of Women convened at The Hague, and in 1919 at Zurich, where the congress founded the Women's International League for Peace and Freedom. Addams served as its president until 1929, when she assumed honorary presidency until her death in 1935.

Her publications are: *Democracy and Social Ethics* (1904), *Newer Ideals of Peace* (1907), *The Spirit of Youth in the Streets* (1909), *Twenty Years at Hull House* (1910), *A New Conscience and an Ancient Evil* (1912), *The Long Road of Woman's Memory* (1916), and *Peace and Bread in the Time of War* (1922). She held the honorary degrees of LL.D. from eight universities, among them the University of Wisconsin (1904) and Smith College (1910), and the M.A. of Yale (1910).

Bibliography

Christian Century 1935 Jane Addams. 52 (June 5)

Davis A 1973 *American Heroine*, Oxford University Press, New York

Farrel J 1967 *Beloved Lady*, John Hopkins Press, Baltimore,

Maryland

Kellogg P 1935 Jane Addams, 1860-1935. *The Survey* 71 (June)

Levine D 1971 *Jane Addams and the Liberal Tradition.* State Historical Society of Wisconsin, Madison, Wisconsin

Linn J 1935 *Jane Addams*, Appleton-Century, New York

Lovett R 1930 Jane Addams at Hull House. *The New Republic* 62 (May 14)

Taylor G 1935 Jane Addams, the great neighbor. *Survey Graphic* 24 (July)

RUTH C. REYNOLDS

Nicholas Murray Butler

(1931)

In naming Nicholas Murray Butler a co-winner of the 1931 Nobel Peace Prize, the Nobel Committee honored his efforts of a lifetime spent in promoting peace through heightened international understanding between people and nations. President of Columbia University, Dr. Butler worked as an educator and as an adviser to seven presidents. As a friend of statesmen of foreign nations and as an advocate of internationalism, he was the living embodiment of his own concept, the "international mind." Butler chaired the Lake Mohonk Conferences on International Arbitration which met periodically between 1907 and 1912, was president of the US branch of Conciliation Internationale, and headed the section on international education and communication in the Carnegie Endowment for International Peace.

The Nobel Committee praised Butler as an educator who stimulated popular thought and then translated public will into positive action. His every specific idea implanted in the popular will brought us another step along the road to a new society, the Committee said.

Butler was drawn from his preoccupation as an educator and highly successful president of Columbia University to embrace a second role as internationalist peace worker by Baron d'Estournelles de Constant (Paul Henri Benjamin Balluet), winner of the 1907 Peace Prize. Baron d'Estournelles interested Butler in Conciliation Internationale. Committee member Koht described this organization at the award ceremony: "In my opinion it would be difficult to name another peace organization which has persisted in such effective, tenacious, and steady work for the cause of peace as has this American group under the presidency of Butler." Butler was a fine administrator, and a persuasive man. It was Butler's influence which prompted Andrew Carnegie, the American philanthropist, to donate US $10 million in 1910 to establish the Carnegie Endowment for International Peace. This organization financed visits of professors, economists, and outstanding authorities to make "peoples hitherto strange and remote" more familiar with each other through personal contact with representatives from each of their cultures.

Carnegie chose Butler to develop the Endowment's division for education and publicity. Butler set up lecture courses, international relations clubs, conferences, and study programs in an effort to create an enlightened and sympathetic public opinion toward international affairs. It was a striking example of the combination of his skill as an educator and the responsible use of politics to achieve world peace through expanding horizons of international understanding and cooperation.

To such a staunch internationalist as Butler the First World War came as a great shock, as it did to many who were working within the peace movements of that period. But following the war, Butler renewed his efforts through the organization to addressing the problems that might imperil international peace in the future. He sent experts to examine potential causes of war in the Balkans, the Far East, and Mexico, and compiled reports on points of potential political danger. International relations clubs were organized in Britain, Australia, Canada, South Africa, India, China, Japan, the Philippines, and various South American countries. After the war the ravaged libraries of Rheims, Belgrade, and the University of Louvain were rebuilt.

The Carnegie Endowment also financed the reconstruction of the commune of Fargniers in Aisne, which had been designated by the French government as the village which had suffered most during the war. It also underwrote the administrative costs of several international conferences, notably the Balkan Conferences of 1930 to 1934. It sponsored studies of international law, the history of the First World War, of the Saar conflict, and of international relations generally. The Endowment maintained a large library and compiled treaty texts and diplomatic documents; it also issued a periodical, *International Conciliation*. Butler later succeeded to the presidency of the Endowment.

Butler's goal was to create what he called an "international mind." Taken from the title of a book of Butler's addresses made at the Lake Mohonk Conferences, it was defined by its author as the habit of thinking of the nations of the civilized world as friendly and cooperative equals. Thus he attempted to educate Americans out of their isolationism and to convince them to take their overseas responsibilities more seriously. He believed that no civilized nation could live in isolation. "When private citizens and public officials look upon international obligations and international relations as the upright man looks upon his personal promises and personal relationships, the peace of the world will be secure," he said.

His persuasion of the American people to overcome their isolationism resulted in the Kellogg-Briand Pact (1928), an agreement between France and the United States to outlaw war. Ratification of the United States and France was followed by practically all the world powers. Unfortunately, the pact lacked the authority of enforcement, and left the door open to so-called "wars of defense." The ink was hardly dry on the pact before Butler was lamenting: "No sooner had it been ratified by sixty-three governments than at least one-half of them began arming for war under the pretense of arming for defense, at a rate that had never been equalled in all history."

But it did make one more contribution toward the development of a public concept about the responsibilities inherent in the maintenance of peace. "Those who set their sights on awakening and education public opinion cannot expect swift victories of the kind that win popular acclaim," the Nobel Committee said. Butler's patient groundwork in developing a desire and will for peace on the part of many people is necessary before concrete accomplishments can come into being. "Nothing in society ever moves forward of its own momentum; progress must always be sustained by the human thought, human will, and human action to transmute the need into a living social form." The Committee declared that it was for just such effort over the course of a long career that it was paying tribute to Butler.

For another 10 years after receiving the award, Butler continued to work actively, encouraging international understanding between nations and peoples. Only the onset of blindness slowed his vast correspondences, his lectures, and his use of the political forum to promote the "international mind."

Biography

Nicholas Murray Butler was born in Elizabeth, New Jersey,

son of Henry L. Butler, a manufacturer, and Mary Murray Butler. In 1882 he received his bachelor's degree in philosophy from Columbia College, in 1883 a master's degree, and in 1884 a doctorate, also from Columbia College (later to become Columbia University). In 1884-1885 he studied in Paris and Berlin, and in the fall of 1885 he joined the faculty of Columbia in the department of philosophy. He remained at Columbia for 60 years; there he established the Teachers College and founded the *Educational Review*, which he edited for 30 years.

A distinguished educator, he served on the New Jersey Board of Education from 1887 to 1895, and participated in creating the College Entrance Examination Board in 1893. He became acting president of Columbia in 1901 and president in 1902, a position he maintained until his retirement in 1945. He was president of Bernard College and Teachers College from 1901 to 1945. Under his presidency Columbia University became a major educational institution.

Butler served in politics with equal distinction, both at home and abroad. He was a delegate to the Republican convention, for the first time in 1888 and the last time in 1936. With Elihu Root, whom he met when studying abroad in Paris and Berlin following his doctoral degree in 1884, and William Howard Taft and Theodore Roosevelt, Butler constituted a fourth in a powerful political quartet in the early part of the twentieth century. It was the split of this group in 1912, with Roosevelt running for the Presidency as candidate of the Progressive Party, and Taft for the Republican Party with Butler as Vice-President, which resulted in the victory of the Democratic candidate, Woodrow Wilson.

Butler worked as an educator in a lifetime effort to bring about world peace through international cooperation and the education of the body politic through an enlightened electorate. He chaired the Lake Mohonk Conferences on International Arbitration from 1907 to 1912, where he coined the concept of "international mindedness" wherein all nations are conceived as working together as friendly and cooperative equals.

He was appointed president of the US branch of Conciliation Internationale, founded by Baron d'Estournelles, himself a Nobel Peace Prize winner in 1909. He persuaded Andrew Carnegie to endow US $10 million toward the Carnegie Endowment for International Peace, which he finally linked to the US branch of Conciliation Internationale. Butler served first on the Endowment's section for international education and communication, then founded the European branch of the Endowment, with headquarters in Paris. Later, in 1925, he became president of the Endowment, a post he held until 1945.

Butler held honorary degrees from 37 colleges and universities, including Yale, Harvard, Princeton, Johns Hopkins, Chicago, St. Andrews, Manchester, Oxford, Cambridge, and California. He was the recipient of decorations from 15 foreign governments and a member of more than 50 learned societies and 20 clubs.

He wrote *The Meaning of Education* (1898, revised edition 1915), *True and False Democracy* (1907), *The American as He Is* (1908), *Education in the United States* (1910), *The International Mind* (1913), *A World in Ferment* (1918), *The Faith of a Liberal* (1924), *The Path to Peace* (1930), *Between Two Worlds* (1934), an autobiography entitled *Across the Busy Years* (1939), *Why War?* (1940), *Liberty, Equality, Fraternity* (1942), and *The World Today* (1946).

Butler married Susanna Edwards Schuyler in 1887. They had one daughter, Sarah Schuyler. Susanna Butler died in 1903. In 1907 Butler married Kate La Montagne.

He died on December 7, 1947.

RUTH C. REYNOLDS

Prize Not Awarded
(1932)

Sir Norman Angell
(1933)

The 1933 Nobel Prize for Peace was awarded to Norman Angell, journalist and author, whom the Nobel Committee called "the great educator of public opinion," and said that, as a writer, he had done as much as anyone in our time to "remove the wrong conception that war benefits anyone."

"Norman Angell speaks to the intellect," said Committee Chairman Christian Lange (1921 Peace Prize co-winner). "He is cool and clear. He has a profound belief in reason and in rationalism. He is convinced that at long last reason will prevail when we succeed in sweeping away the mists of illusion and intellectual error."

Norman Angell spent a lifetime of continuous and concentrated attack upon the misconceptions that make war possible—misconceptions held by the populace and leaders alike. He asked people to ponder why nations have so often followed policies with peaceful intent, only to have war as the outcome. He asked them as individual citizens to probe their role in this process.

Angell was catapulted to international fame through an early book, *The Great Illusion*, published in 1910. It sold over two million copies and was translated into 25 languages. From that time forward he reached an audience of millions through his books, which numbered 41 in all, through years as a journalist in Europe and the United Kingdom, and at lecture halls in the Old World and the New. He thought of those millions in terms of the individuals represented, and it was to the individual that he made his appeal.

This was his approach to *all* groups of peoples. During the two world wars he supported his country in the war effort. He took exception to pacifists, who,

he said, perhaps did not see very clearly that the refusal to endow law with power did not diminish the total amount of force in the world, but left it in the hands of the lawless, the most violent. But his participation in the wars against Germany did not lead him into stereotyped images of the enemy. He was revolted by those who saw the German not as a person at all, but as an abstraction. To Angell Germany was "an entity which included underfed children, old women and ignorant peasants as well as besotted high-collared officers."

Therefore his overwhelming question of all peoples was why, and in what manner, had the public mind been at fault, and in what ways, through each individual unit, might it create a change. He was convinced that the large measure of public support given to policies making for international conflict came not from a lack of specialist or technical knowledge on the part of the public, but from misapplication of the knowledge they had. He illustrated this common occurrence through the attitudes often held about the League of Nations. "We who urge the League of Nations are told so often that we forget human nature, that we overlook the fact that men are naturally quarrelsome. The fact that men are naturally quarrelsome is presumed to be an argument against such institutions as the League. But it is precisely the fact of the natural pugnacity of man that makes such institutions necessary. If men were naturally and easily capable of being their own judges, always able to see the other's case, never got into panics, never lost their heads, never lost their tempers and called it patriotism—why then we should not want a League. But neither should we want most of our national apparatus of government either—parliaments, congresses, courts, police, ten commandments. These are all means by which we deal with the unruly element in human nature . . . ."

"You cannot change human nature" is an illusion that destroys clear thinking. Angell pointed out that what we call "human nature" is in fact not a constant factor, but alters with changes in cultures. The field of peace itself holds concrete examples of changed behavior: wars based on religious motives are a thing of the past, as are violent conflicts such as dueling or blood feuds.

Angell told his audiences that humankind's deep tragedy is that it so rarely sees reality. We see what we desire to see. We have before our eyes mists, stereotypes inherited from our parents, from our grandparents, and they from theirs. Intellectually we are wearing the cast-off clothes of our ancestors, and we do not see that they no longer fit us. Political leaders frequently labor under the same misconceptions.

Angell had intimate knowledge of public opinion in three of the big powers of the world. He began his life as Ralph Norman Angell Lane in a well-to-do but unpretentious Victorian household in Holbeach in Lincolnshire, England, one of six children of Thomas Angell Lane and Mary Brittain Lane. A precocious boy, he was reading Herbert Spencer, T. H. Huxley, Voltaire, Darwin, and John Stuart Mill by the time he was sent, at the age of 12, to the Lycée de St. Omer in France by his father, who believed in international education. Angell recalled Mill's essay *On Liberty* as his prime source of intellectual excitement during those years. After attending a business school in London he went to Geneva, where he studied at the University and edited a biweekly English paper. A year later, however, he set off for the United States, convinced that Europe was hopelessly enmeshed in insoluble problems. He settled in the western part of the United States, and for seven years worked at varying jobs: as a vine planter, an irrigation ditch digger, a cowboy, and a prospector, ending up as a journalist, reporting for the *St. Louis Globe-Democrat* and later the *San Francisco Chronicle*.

"My first prompting to the importance of the international problem came from my experience out West," Angell once told an interviewer. "The folklore of the West and Mid-West was deeply anti-British . . . the Redcoat was the villain and all that. Riding over the range with other cowboys, I learned that I was a cruel, imperialist oppressor, that the British were blood-suckers. Well, I knew that England was I multiplied 40 million times and that it simply wasn't so. I said to myself, 'this is the danger to mankind—not just Anglophobia, but the ease with which fantasies, fables and myths can possess a whole people.'"

He returned to France, where over the years he worked for the *Daily Messenger* (an English-language paper), *Éclair* and the Paris edition of the British *Daily Mail*. In 1912, after receiving public acclaim through *The Great Illusion*, he resigned his newspaper work to dedicate himself to writing and lecturing on the futility of war and on internationalism.

Having returned to England, Angell was briefly involved in politics, serving as a Labour Member of Parliament for one term from 1929 to 1931. But he preferred to work for internationalism outside the parliamentary arena, and did not pursue his political career. He worked with groups promoting internationalism: the Council of the Royal Institute of International Affairs, and the League of Nations Union. He was knighted for public service in 1931.

Angell devoted his life to stripping away cultural and emotional myths destructive to clear thinking. He passionately believed that common sense and rational thought on the part of the populace were the *sine qua non* of attaining permanent peace. "A decision has to be taken," he said. "It has to be taken, academic specialists, but by the voting millions of over-driven professional men, coal heavers, dentists, tea-shop waitresses, parsons, charwomen, artists, country squires, chorus girls who make and unmake governments, who do not hesitate, as we have seen, again and again, to override the specialist or expert and impose their opinion upon him. With them rests the final verdict."

He vigorously attacked the illusion of the profitability of war in the modern world of interdependent nations. The truth, illustrated by history observable by all, is that even the so-called winners have become losers, not only in terms of human life, but in terms of economic and general well-being. Angell pointed out that if "victorious" wars were economically advantageous, then citizens of those big powers which have built their world empires through wars would be economically better off than the citizens of small peaceful nations. But, he said, a review of capital and revenues in these two categories of nations furnished proof that this was not so. In 1933 Dutch, Swedish, Swiss and Norwegian stocks stood higher on the world's exchanges than did those of the United Kingdom, of France, and of Germany.

Angell warned that to shut our eyes to the role that the individual plays in the perpetuation of policies that lead to war is to perpetuate victimization. A few score officials, or capitalists, cannot by their physical power compel hundreds of millions of individuals year after year to go on paying taxes, to take vast risks with their own welfare, and to jeopardize their society if those millions are persuaded that the taxes, the risks, and the sacrifices are quite unnecessary and, indeed, harmful. The only means by which the individual can be liberated from the potential power of exploitive groups is through insight into the nature of those impulses and motives to which the exploiters so successfully appeal.

He pointed out that the Nazis began as a party of ten persons. Ten persons had no force against the power of the German nation. The latent strength of that party of ten persons rested in its potential power to reach the public mind. Without that popular appeal it could never have come into being. Similarly, war would be impossible without the acquiescence of large sections of the public.

Nationalism can assume forms that are demonstrably dangerous to the community of nations precisely because it strikes responsive chords deep in human impulses and instincts. Thus, "Until we are taught to recognize—what our history books do not teach—that the fault is usually ours as much as some other nation's, we have not taken the first step to that wisdom which alone can save us," Angell said. In the same way that we have come to see that it is irrelevant and unworthy to fight about religion, so we must come to see that it is irrelevant and self-defeating to fight about our nationalisms. Angell pleaded for a "world philosophy" and a "world conscience" through which nationalisms would give way to a "community of nations." He assured his audiences, "We can still make a cosmos out of this chaos by taking thought."

Angell traveled widely in the United States, giving lectures. He worked with President Woodrow Wilson in the development of Wilson's plan for the League of Nations founded upon the principles of collective security. Angell held collective security to be a cornerstone in internationalism. In a statement of principles he wrote in 1918 he said that under any system in which adequate defense rests upon the individual nation's preponderance of power, the security of that one nation must involve the insecurity of other less powerful nations.

He declared that if we will not defend other nations in their right to life, then inevitably the time will come when it will be impossible to defend the right to life for our own nation. If each is to be his or her own and sole defender, then any minority which can make itself stronger than any single nation can place not one but all at its mercy. A little gang of ruthless men could overcome 20 nations because when one

was attacked the others remained indifferent.

Angell's words proved prophetic. This was the story of the fall of the League of Nations.

After the two atomic bombs fell upon Japanese cities in the violent end to a war and in the opening of a new—and irreversible—era Angell wrote that a new alternative had been established: "We prevent war, or we perish."

In summing up his life in his autobiography, Angell wrote: "The end I chose—elimination of war—I would without any hesitation whatsoever choose again. No other single task would be more worth the efforts of a lifetime."

Biography

Ralph Norman Angell Lane was born on December 26, 1872, one of six children of Thomas Angell Lane and Mary Brittain Lane. Raised in Holbeach in Lincolnshire, England, he attended British elementary schools, the Lycée de St. Omer in France, and a business school in London, before spending one year at the University of Geneva. At this point his education took another tack as he left Europe, which he found hopelessly entangled in social problems, and went to the westernmost part of the United States. There he pursued many trades—ranch-hand, cowboy, prospector among them—finally becoming a reporter, first for the *St. Louis Globe-Democrat* and later the *San Francisco Chronicle*.

In 1898 Angell went to Paris, where he was subeditor of the English-language *Daily Messenger*, then staff contributor to *Éclair*. He covered the Dreyfus case for American papers. In 1905 he became editor of the Paris edition of Lord Northcliffe's *Daily Mail*. In 1912 he resigned to devote himself completely to writing and lecturing on the theme of the futility of war, and to educate public opinion about the need to replace competitive nationalism with "a community of nations."

In 1910 *The Great Illusion* was published under the name Norman Angell, which he later legalized. It sold over two million copies and was translated into 25 languages. In 1933 he updated the book, applying the thesis of 1909 to 1933 and stated the case for cooperation as the basis for civilization; in 1938 he again updated it under the title *The Great Illusion—Now*, in which he documented his theses with events of the previous five years.

Angell was not a rigid pacifist; he supported his country in both world wars. His quarrel was with armed aggression and the illusion that war could ever be profitable.

From 1929 to 1931 he was a Labour member of the House of Commons, representing Bradford North. He chose to leave politics to take his case for internationalism directly to the people without hindrance from party ties.

He wrote regularly for newspapers and journals and edited *Foreign Affairs* from 1928 to 1931. He was knighted for public service in 1931 upon the recommendation of Ramsey MacDonald.

In 1932, *The Unseen Assassins* was published. It attracted wide attention for its discussions of imperialism, nationalism, and effective education of the common man.

He was a member of the Council of the Royal Institute of International Affairs, and executive of the Comité mondial contre la guerre et le fascisme (World Committee against War and Fascism), an active member of the Executive Committee of the League of Nations Union, and president of the Abyssinia Association.

He traveled the lecture circuit almost every year, and at the age of 90 went on a two-month lecture tour of the United States.

Sir Norman Angell died on October 7, 1967, at the age of 94.

Bibliography

Christian Century 1934 Nobel Peace Prize for Angell and Henderson. 51 (December 19)
Miller D B 1986 *Norman Angell and the Futility of War: Peace and the Public Mind*. Macmillan, London
New York Times 1967 Sir Norman Angell dies at 94; Won Nobel Peace Prize in '33. (October 9)

RUTH C. REYNOLDS

Arthur Henderson
(1934)

The 1934 Nobel Peace Prize went to Arthur Henderson, British parliamentarian, Foreign Secretary in MacDonald's cabinet, delegate to the Assembly of the League of Nations, and president of the World Disarmament Conference at Geneva. As he received this honor, the Conference was tottering on the edge of disaster. Equally at risk stood the League of Nations, that bulwark from which a lasting peace was to be launched, and the Nobel Committee called Arthur Henderson "among the bravest and most faithful on this bulwark."

The Committee presented the award with a tribute to Henderson's endeavors in behalf of that Conference: "Not many would have been able to hold out so long; not many would even have been strong enough, and still fewer would have possessed the necessary authority. If the Conference is still alive and if there is still a thin thread of hope, it is primarily because of Mr. Arthur Henderson."

Lloyd George once said, "Disarmament would be regarded as the real test of whether the League of Nations was a farce or whether business was meant." Henderson became the embodiment of the League's disarmament effort. He had been in Parliament almost continuously after 1903, and until the First World War his efforts had been almost exclusively in behalf of labor. But, as that war drew to a close, Henderson's thinking took on an international dimension. In 1917 he went to Russia as an official observer for the British government. In 1918 he initiated a conference at Bern, with delegates from the defeated and neutral countries joining the victorious ones, to produce recommendations to send to Versailles where the Allies were drawing up the terms of the peace. In 1924, while Home Secretary in MacDonald's cabinet, Henderson spent most of his time on two international problems: the implementation of the Dawes Plan to introduce some reason into the reparations demanded of the Germans, and the drafting of the Geneva Protocol on the ultimate settlement of international disputes by arbitration.

Henderson had some concrete successes. During his two years as Foreign Secretary in MacDonald's government from 1929 to 1931 he brought about the United Kingdom's resumption of diplomatic relations with the Soviet Union which had been severed since 1917, he maneuvered acceptance of the Young Plan for German reparations by the creditor nations and Germany, he arranged with France's Foreign Minister, Briand (1926 Peace Prize co-winner), for the evacuation of French troops from the Rhineland prior to the date stipulated in the Treaty of Versailles, and he furthered the cause of Egyptian independence, which was achieved in 1936. Henderson also attended the entire sessions of the Tenth and Eleventh Assemblies of the League of Nations. Lord Cecil (1937 Peace Prize winner) called him "the most successful foreign minister we have had since 1918, with no brilliant and shiny qualities, but with that faculty for being right which Englishmen possess. His political courage was great—almost the rarest and the most valuable quality for a statesman." It was a virtue Henderson was in need of frequently.

Following the First World War, many statesmen as

well as peace advocates understood the vital need for solving the cyclic nature of arms build-up and wars. Woodrow Wilson's Point Four wanted adequate guarantees given and taken that national armaments would be reduced to the lowest point consistent with domestic safety. Germany's greatest misgiving about the Treaty of Versailles concerned its required unilateral disarmament, and the German government wrote to the Paris Peace Conference: "Germany is prepared to agree to her proposed disarmament provided this is a beginning of a general reduction of armaments." France's Clemenceau replied: "The Allied and Associated Powers wish to make it clear that requirements in regard to German armaments were not made solely with the object of rendering it impossible for her to resume her policy of aggression. They are also the first step toward that general reduction and limitation of armaments which they seek to bring about as one of the most fruitful preventatives of war and which it will be one of the first duties of the League of Nations to promote."

The connection made between the fate of humankind and successful disarmament was not confined to statesmen and diplomats. Twelve million signatures were presented to the Disarmament Conference by The Women's Societies on a document declaring that the delegates must choose between "world disarmament or world disaster." A questionnaire by Lord Cecil, which he called the "Peace Ballot" and which was sent out unofficially, received a return of eleven and a half million replies, out of which the massive majority of eleven million were in favor of arms reduction by international agreement.

But the commission charged with the formulation of a definite plan for disarmament by the League of Nations was doomed to failure from the beginning. The commission provoked the opposition of the various national bureaucracies because commission members were appointed by the League and were not official representatives of the various governments. Called the "Temporary Mixed Commission," it worked for five years making studies, condemning private manufacture of munitions, and pressing for control of the traffic in arms, before it came to an end in 1925 when the United Kingdom refused to have anything further to do with it.

The League created a new Preparatory Commission to work toward an international conference. It worked without noticeable effect for five years. Meanwhile the familiar pattern of arms build-up described by Lord Grey, British foreign minister, grew apace: "The increase of armaments that is intended in each nation to produce consciousness of

strength and a sense of security does not produce these effects. On the contrary, it produces a consciousness of the strength of other nations and a sense of fear. Fear begets suspicion and distrust and evil imaginings of all sorts till each government feels it would be criminal not to take every precaution; while every government regards every precaution of every other government as evidence of hostile intent."

It was Henderson's efforts which were largely responsible for the creation of the Disarmament Conference in 1932. In recognition of this he presided over its opening sessions despite the fall of the government in which he, as British Foreign Secretary, had first scheduled the Conference. He interpreted his election to the office of president as a mark of trust in him personally; but this circumstance had the unfortunate consequence of the British delegation working quite independently of Henderson. Sir John Simon, now the British Foreign Secretary in Mac-Donald's National Coalition Government, looked askance at the idea of real collective security and disarmament under international control, and the negative and arbitrary policy of the British delegation must bear some of the responsibility for the collapse of the Conference.

At the opening of the Conference Japan was committed to an act of war, and Hitler withdrew Germany from it in 1933. It was only Henderson's patience and his deep conviction that there could be no real disarmament except on the basis of the collective security system within the League of Nations that kept the Conference going through 1934. He believed the Conference to be a focal point of a struggle between anarchy and world order, between those who would think in terms of inevitable armed conflict and those who sought to build a durable peace.

Henderson's Nobel lecture did not carry the tone of one whose task is well on its appointed way. "Men and women everywhere are once more asking the old question: is it peace?," he began. "They are asking it with anxiety and fear; for, on the one hand, there has never been such a longing for peace and dread of war as there is today. On the other hand, there have never been such awful means of spreading destruction and death as those that are now being prepared in well nigh every country."

He told his Nobel audience that a policy of international cooperation which would effectively guarantee world peace would require a political commitment wherein each nation would cease judging its own rights for itself, and participate in a system of world law and order. Nations must subordinate in some measure national sovereignty in favor of worldwide institutions and obligations: "The establishment of a world commonwealth is, in the long run, the only alternative to a relapse into a world war. The psychological obstacles are formidable but not insurmountable," he said. ". . . It will be no light and simple task . . . it is, on the contrary, perhaps the greatest and most difficult enterprise ever imagined by the audacious mind of man. But it is a task which has become a necessity."

The failure of the Disarmament Conference foreshadowed the Second World War, but Henderson's biographer, Mary A. Hamilton (1938), states, "If any man is clear of responsibility, it is Arthur Henderson."

Biography

Arthur Henderson was born on September 13, 1863, in Glasgow, Scotland, son of David Henderson, a manual worker, who died nine years later, leaving the family in poverty. Arthur left school to help earn himself and his family a living. Upon his mother's remarriage he returned to school, but for three years only. His education continued, however, in sprightly conversations during the lunch hour of the General Foundry works where he worked as an apprentice, and through reading newspapers. He held membership in the Ironfounders' Union all his life. In 1896 he was chosen district delegate of his union, a salaried full-time position.

Skill in speaking learned in a debating society and in work as a lay preacher in the Salvation Army and later in the Methodist Church helped launch him into a political career begun as town councillor in 1892. In 1896 he moved to Darlington, and there he was elected to the Durham Country Council. In 1903 he became the first Labour mayor of Darlington.

All his life Henderson supported Labour. He won election to Parliament in 1903 under the sponsorship of the Labour Representation Committee, he chaired the conference in 1906 which formed the Labour Party, and he was its secretary from 1911 to 1934.

Henderson served almost continuously in Parliament after 1903, sometimes through general elections and other times by regaining a seat through by-elections. He was chairman of the Parliamentary Labour Party, chief whip three times, president of the Board of Education 1915-16, Paymaster-General in Asquith's government in 1916, and a minister without portfolio, acting primarily as an adviser on labor questions, in Lloyd George's government.

Following the First World War Henderson's activities took on an international bent. In 1917 he went to Russia as an official observer for the United Kingdom, and in 1918 he initiated the call for a conference at Bern to formulate recommendations for the delegates then drawing up the Peace Treaty at Versailles.

In 1923 he was chairman of the Labor and Socialist International at Hamburg. The next year he was Home Secretary in MacDonald's cabinet, during which time he worked on the implementation of the Dawes Plan for German reparations and on the drafting of the Geneva Protocol on the ultimate settlement of international disputes by arbitration.

He became a Foreign Secretary in the MacDonald government in 1929. During his two years in office he brought about resumption of diplomatic relations with the Soviet Union, severed since 1917, he maneuvered acceptance of the Young Plan for German reparations by Germany and creditor nations, and arranged for the early evacuation of French troops from the Rhineland. He furthered the cause of Egyptian independence, which took place in 1936. He attended the entire sessions of the Tenth and Eleventh Assemblies of the League of Nations. A dedicated supporter of the League's disarmament effort, he served as president of the ill-fated Disarmament Conference in Geneva beginning in February 1932 and ending in 1935.

Henderson married Eleanor Watson in 1888. They had a daughter and three sons. The sons all served in the armed forces in the First World War, and the eldest was killed in action. The other two became Henderson's colleagues in the House of Commons in the last part of his life.

He was awarded the Wateler Peace Prize of the Carnegie Foundation in 1933 for the "energy, persistence, ability and impartiality" with which he had presided over the Disarmament Conference.

Arthur Henderson died on October 20, 1935.

Bibliography

Hamilton M 1938 *Arthur Henderson: A Biography*. Heinemann, London

New York Times 1934 Henderson to get Nobel Peace Prize. December 9

New York Times 1934 Many shifts made in London policies: Henderson Prize ignored. Peace award to one outside government wins but scant mention and less praise. December 16

The Times 1935 Eulogy in House of Commons. October 23

RUTH C. REYNOLDS

Carl von Ossietzky
(1935)

The award of the 1935 Nobel Peace Prize to Carl von Ossietzky brought a storm of protest upon the heads of the Nobel Committee, but also intense support. During the period of von Ossietzky's candidacy a great many people felt that Alfred Nobel's injunction that the Prize go to "the person who shall have done the most or the best work for fraternity between peoples" could hardly apply to an imprisoned and defeated member of a powerless peace society in a dictatorship seemingly bent on war, and they regarded him as at most a symbol in the struggle for peace rather than a champion. More vehement voices joined this chorus with the objection that such a choice would antagonize Germany to no good purpose. Finally, from Germany itself came the warning not to provoke the German people by "rewarding this traitor to our country."

But peace advocates struggling in the midst of ever-increasing international tensions looked upon this martyred journalist as a supreme fighter for "fraternity among peoples." In a worldwide campaign they urged the favorable consideration of his candidacy for the award. Six previous recipients of the Peace Prize joined them. One of them wrote, "All of us have in some way or other tried to do something for peace, but we say that he has done more than any of us."

As petitions in behalf of von Ossietsky continued to pour in, the Nobel Committee arrived at a solution. The two Committee members who had, either presently or in the past, held government positions, resigned and were replaced by substitutes. Thereupon the Committee was a separate entity from the government, and it announced the award to Carl von Ossietzky. When the German minister to Norway protested, he was told, "The Norwegian government is in no way concerned. Kindly address yourself to the Nobel Committee."

In bestowing the award on von Ossietzky *in absentia*, the Chairman of the Nobel Committee addressed the question regarding von Ossietzky's status as only a symbol in the struggle for peace. "In my opinion this is not so," he said. "Carl von Ossietzky is not just a symbol. He is something quite different and something more. He is a deed and he is a man. It is on these grounds that Ossietzky has been awarded the Nobel Peace Prize, and on these grounds alone . . . . The wish of the Nobel Committee has always been to fulfill its task and its obligation, namely to

reward work for peace. That and nothing else . . . . In awarding the Nobel Peace Prize to Carl von Ossietzky we are therefore recognizing his valuable contribution to the cause of peace—nothing more, and certainly nothing less.

Carl von Ossietzky's fight for peace was waged with a honed and talented pen. He was an outstanding stylist—trenchant, witty, and elegant. He carried on his fight for democratic principles in a Europe already consorting with dictatorial doctrines as a cure for the harsh harvest of the vengeful Treaty of Versailles, and he correctly divined that the suppression of free opinion and a free press was closely connected with Germany's distress during the postwar period.

Von Ossietzky had been an ardent pacifist even before his experiences as a front-line soldier in the First World War. As a young journalist he drew charges of "insult to the common good" from the Prussian War Ministry for his article criticizing a promilitary court decision in *Das Freie Volk* (The Free People). When called to make a court appearance, his fine was secretly paid by his young English wife, Maud Wood, whom he had married on May 22, 1914.

In 1916 he fought in the Bavarian Pioneer Regiment. The effect of this experience was to crystallize his lifelong pacifism into a personal commitment from which there was no turning back. He would instill into his fellow Germans a "peace mentality." While secretary of the German Peace Society he helped found the *Nie Wieder Krieg* (No More War) movement. But he had little taste for clerical work and organization. The well-chosen phrase was the weapon of his choice. He edited and wrote for liberal papers urging the German people to create a progressive nation under civilian, not military, leadership.

A fellow journalist, Hubert Herring (1936), described him and the events which led to his imprisonment: "I knew Carl von Ossietzky well in 1923. He and his wife and daughter lived in a dingy tenement in an unfashionable street in Berlin . . . . He was a man of wrath uncorrupted by bitterness. He denounced with fury the willful sinfulness of the Allies who in their blindness had seared Germany with the brand of unforgettable guilt, and who, by the branding, had persuaded Germany that her only road of salvation lay in the creation of a Germany which could meet might with might . . . ."

"With even more vigor, he turned his fury upon

those who were working corruption within the German republic. Ossietzky was a devout republican, but he saw the German republic eaten away by the disease which was the inheritance of Versailles. He threw his fragile strength against the insolence without and the poison within. The French were in the Ruhr that summer, and the Allies were busily devising ways for collecting the uncollectable debt incurred under the terms of the fictitious peace. Ossietzky was as harsh in his judgment upon the Allies as any other German, but his deeper sorrow sprang from the recognition of the lack of moral grandeur in the men who were leading Germany from disaster to disaster .... Ossietzky knew that German arms and armaments would never bring redress, that the redemption of Germany must come by the plotting of new ways of national living."

"In 1931, shortly before Hitler came to power, the republic jailed him as a traitor for his attacks upon the development of the German military air force. He was released, and after Hitler's accession his friends urged him to escape. He refused indignantly. "'A man,' he said, 'speaks with a hollow voice across a national border. As a prisoner for the cause of freedom I would serve the struggle for peace better than as a free man outside of Germany.'"

Von Ossietzky spoke his mind about Hitler. Unlike many around him, he never underestimated Hitler and his movement. He realized the strong appeal which the movement had for the German middle classes that had always held aloof from real liberalism. On February 26, 1933, he gave a lecture in which he discussed the possibilities of a united front against Nazism. On February 27 the Reichstag fire took place, and the same night he was arrested and began his long and tortured years in various concentration camps. Never robust, the misery and the cruelty of those Nazi camps broke what little he had left of health.

Nothing official was told about von Ossietzky's fate, although a Vienna paper quoted a co-prisoner who said von Ossietzky had been badly treated by storm-troopers and that his teeth had been knocked out with a revolver butt.

He was transferred from Sonnenburg concentration camp to the camp of Esterwegen-Papenburg, and it was there, due to the persistence of Wickham Steed and Romain Rolland, that they, with a few other international journalists, were allowed to visit. They found him broken in health and spirit and he declined to speak freely.

After the German minister in Norway had been informed of the award, the Nazis moved von Ossietzky from the camp to a Berlin hospital. There the tubercular, 47-year-old pacifist received the news of his $39,303 award. He sent a message that said, in part, "I am surprised and glad .... The time has come when nations will agree to sit around a green table and put a halt to [the rearmament] insanity."

Journalists requested authorization to interview the laureate. German officials were present during the interview granted them, in which von Ossietzky said, "I count myself as belonging to a party of sensible Europeans who regard the armaments race as insanity. If the German government will permit, I will be only too pleased to go to Norway to receive the Prize and in my acceptance speech I will not dig up the past or say anything which might result in discord between Germany and Norway."

This wish was not fulfilled. Despite the declaration of the German Propaganda Ministry that von Ossietzky was free to go, documents of the secret police have since revealed that he was refused a passport. Although in a civilian hospital, von Ossietzky was kept under surveillance until his death.

His award had tremendous repercussions in the press. Radicals and socialists rejoiced, but the news was received by Germany with rage that percolated from Hitler down. Calling it a "brazen challenge and insult to the New Germany," it demanded that von Ossietzky refuse the prize. This he would not do. Hitler then decreed that no German thereafter should accept a Nobel Prize.

For some time the whereabouts of the prize money was a mystery. Norway at first could not get in touch with von Ossietzky. When they eventually received a message from him that he was free to receive the prize money, they placed the funds at his disposal in a bank. Since von Ossietzky was not permitted to leave the hospital, the power of attorney was given to his lawyer, who delivered still another blow to von Ossietzky by embezzling the money. Von Ossietzky's last public appearance was at a court hearing where the lawyer was sentenced to two years' hard labor. Only 16,500 Reichsmarks were left, and this the German government took for his "board and room" of the last four years. His wife received nothing. In 1954 the government of the Federal Republic of Germany awarded their daughter 5 Deutschmarks ($1.92).

Herbert Herring (1936) called him "an inconspicuous man with a weak voice, a delicate body and a flaming eye, but history and Adolf Hitler have made that voice overtop the pounding of studded boots on the pavements of Unter den Linden."

Biography

Carl von Ossietzky was born in Hamburg on October 3, 1889, son of a civil servant who died when he was two. His mother married Gustav Walter, a Social Democrat, when Carl was nine. His stepfather proved influential in shaping von Ossietzky's later political attitudes.

As a young journalist von Ossietzky first worked for *Das Freie Volk* (The Free People), the weekly organ of the Democratic Union. In 1913 an article criticizing a promilitary court decision drew charges of "insult to the common good" from the Prussian War Ministry.

In the First World War von Ossietzky fought in the Bavarian Pioneer Regiment. His pacifism intensified by the war, he returned to Hamburg determined to educate people to a "peace mentality." He held a position as secretary of the German Peace Society, creating the monthly *Mitteilungsblatt* (Information Sheet), and became a regular contributor to *Monisten Monatsheften* (Monists' Monthly). He helped to found the *Nie Wieder Krieg* (No More War) organization in 1922. He was also foreign editor on the *Berliner Volkzeitung* (Berlin People's Paper).

In 1926 the founder and editor of *Die Weltbuhne* (The World Stage), Siegfried Jacobsohn, offered him a position on the editorial staff. Following the death of Jacobsohn, von Ossietzky continued his former editor's efforts to publicize the secret rearmament of Germany. He was tried for libel, found guilty, and sentenced to one month in prison.

In March 1929 he published an article by Walter Kreiser further exposing Germany's rearming. Accused of treason, he was sentenced in November 1931 to 18 months in prison, but was amnestied in December 1932.

He refused to leave Germany despite the growing danger posed by the Nazis, saying a man speaks with a hollow voice across a border. On February 27, the evening following the Reichstag fire, he was arrested and thrown into prison, and then into concentration camps at Sonnenburg and at Esterwegen-Papenburg, where cruel treatment broke his health.

He was awarded the Nobel Prize for Peace in 1935, but he was not granted a passport to attend the presentation ceremony. Germany interpreted the award as an insult to the "New Germany," and a decree was passed in January 1937 forbidding Germans to accept any Nobel Prize.

Ridden with tuberculosis, von Ossietzky was kept in a civilian hospital following the award, but under constant surveillance. His lawyer embezzled the prize money.

Carl von Ossietzky died, at the age of 48, of meningitis, on May 4, 1938. He left a widow, Maud Wood, whom he had married on May 22, 1914, and a daughter, Rosalinde Ossietzky-Palm.

Bibliography

Herring H 1936 Both win the Nobel Prize! *Christian Century* 53 (December 16)

New York Times 1936 Germany enraged by Ossietzky Prize. November 25

New York Times 1938 Von Ossietzky dies in Berlin hospital. May 5

Newsweek 1936 Germany: Inventor of dynamite posthumously rewards 'traitor.' December 5

Time 1936 International—Nobel Prize prisoner. 28 (December 7)

RUTH C. REYNOLDS

Carlos Saavedra Lamas
(1936)

The 1936 Nobel Prize for Peace was awarded to the Argentinian Carlos Saavedra Lamas. International lawyer, practical statesman, skilled mediator, educator, and academician, Dr Carlos Saavedra Lamas was an architect of treaties who put the keystone into place for every South American diplomatic triumph devised in the mid-1930s. Urbane, son of a family rich in the tradition of public service, he had acquired a thorough grounding in academic training. He put these attributes to the delicate tasks of mediation, arbitration, and other creative means for settling international conflicts.

Saavedra Lamas entered politics early. It was as a young man that he first displayed his flair for diplomacy by saving Argentina's floundering arbitration treaty with Italy in 1908-09. As a member of the Argentine Chamber of Deputies, long before he was to take the post as Foreign Minister he became the unofficial adviser to both the legislature and the Foreign Office on the analysis and implications of proposed treaties. His first government post of importance, held before he was 30, was as national Minister of Justice and Public Education in 1915. He proved himself a progressive educator.

Saavedra Lamas was an aristocrat, a descendant of Don Corucho Saavedra, the first President of Argentina. He was a distinguished student, receiving his Doctor of Laws degree *summa cum laude*, and continuing his studies in Paris. He was widely traveled. He began an academic career destined to span 40 years by accepting a professorship of law and constitutional history at the University of La Plata. Later he inaugurated a course in sociology at the University of Buenos Aires; he taught political economy and constitutional law at the Law School of the University and eventually became its president.

He led as an Argentinian academician in the field of labor legislation. He was the first university professor to lecture in Argentina in that field. He wrote treatises on the existing system and the need for a universally recognized doctrine on the treatment of labor. Notable particularly were his *Centro de legislacion social y del trabajo* (Center of Social and Labor Legislation) in 1927 and the three-volume *Codigo nacional del trabajo* (National Code of Labor Law) in 1933.

On the international labor scene, Saavedra Lamas supported the founding of the International Labour Organization in 1919 and was unanimously elected president of its 1928 Geneva conference. On a local and practical level, he drafted labor legislation in Argentina. In his Nobel lecture he said that social peace must be erected on the basis of greater social justice. "Unemployment is a great tragedy," he said. "The man who goes about hopelessly seeking work in order to earn bread for his children is a living reproach to civilization."

International law also captured his interest, and his scholarly output in this field included *La Crise de la codification et de la doctrine argentine de droit internationale* (The Crisis of Codification and the Argentine Doctrine of International Law) in 1931. Saavedra Lamas authored legislation on many subjects with international ramifications, including asylum, colonization, immigration, arbitration, and international peace.

In 1932 General Agustin P. Justo, the incoming President of Argentina, chose Saavedra Lamas as his Foreign Minister. One of Saavedra Lamas' early accomplishments in this position was persuading Argentina to rejoin the League of Nations after an absence of 13 years. He was an ardent supporter of the League, and he represented Argentina at every important international meeting during this period. He initiated the 1932 declaration in which the American republics agreed not to recognize any change of territory in the Americas resulting from a force of arms. The Pan-American Society of New York in 1933 awarded him its medal in recognition of his international work.

In his first year as Foreign Minister he began work

on his Antiwar Pact, which would contain some of the merits of the Kellogg-Briand Pact, an international statement outlawing war except as a defensive measure against aggression. Saavedra Lamas visualized his pact coordinated with the existing Pan-American Union and the US-Latin American relationship. Upon the latter relationship Saavedra Lamas had previously made major diplomatic impact by influencing the United States to rethink its interpretation of the Monroe Doctrine (see Articles: *Monroe Doctrine*). This doctrine, originally written by President Monroe in 1823 to discourage future colonization by European powers in the Americas, and to forbid European intervention in American affairs, had unfortunately come to be seen as an accommodation for American imperialism by securing the interests of the North American business community in its South American financial ventures. Saavedra Lamas launched vigorous opposition to such imperialistic intervention, and he had the satisfaction of seeing a policy change come about, particularly under US Secretary of State Cordell Hull (1945 Peace Prize laureate) and President Franklin D. Roosevelt.

In his Antiwar Pact Saavedra Lamas hoped to coordinate these three factors: the Pan-American Union, the League of Nations, and a noninterventionist United States. The particular feature of his pact was that, unlike the Kellogg-Briand Pact, which called for the outlawry of war on a moral basis, his pact would provide sanctions which could be used against an aggressor. Another feature unique to this pact was a provision for procedures *during* a conflict. It provided for the reestablishment of peace, while at the same time maintaining the principle of neutrality. This was to be accomplished through carefully formulated and guaranteed international cooperation among the neutral nations.

The conclusion of Saavedra Lamas' Antiwar Pact was doubly successful: it was signed by Argentina, Brazil, Mexico, Chile, Uruguay, and Paraguay in October 1933 and eight months later by 14 Spanish American States, the United States, and Italy. Within a year, the treaty was actually put to the test. One of the signatory powers, Paraguay, was the victim of an aggression on the part of Bolivia. The subject of the dispute was the northern portion of the Gran Chaco country where frontiers had not been properly fixed since the end of Spanish rule. A military deadlock had set in which the League of Nations had been unable to break. In May 1935 Saavedra Lamas took the course of action outlined in his Antiwar Pact, approaching the Brazilian, Chilean, and Peruvian diplomatic representatives in Buenos Aires about setting up a mediatory operation. A commission was created using these nations along with the United States and Uruguay. Saavedra Lamas served as chairman. The two belligerents accepted a proffered settlement, and on June 12, 1935, the armistice protocol was signed. Saavedra Lamas' Antiwar Pact had operated successfully on a South American controversy, under his leadership. At the peace negotiations which were initiated shortly afterwards Saavedra Lamas also played a leading role. He presented his Antiwar Pact to the League of Nations, where it was well-received and signed by 11 countries. In 1936 he was elected president of the Assembly of the League.

At this Assembly, when Saavedra Lamas alluded to the six American states whose work of conciliation had succeeded in ending the war in South America, he gave careful emphasis to the fact that two of the six, the United States and Brazil, were not members of the League. From this he made the hopeful extrapolation that the possibility therefore existed in future mediation cases of winning the cooperation of nations *outside* the League. "I see this as a significant signpost for the diplomacy of peace," he said. "We must regard it not as an isolated or exceptional occurrence, but as one which will become the rule."

Saavedra Lamas retired as Foreign Minister in 1938 and returned to academic life. Between 1941 and 1943 he accepted the presidency of the University of Buenos Aires, and, following that, completed his academic career as a professor for an additional three years.

He was awarded the Grand Cross of the Legion of Honor of France and similar honors from Brazil, Chile, Bolivia, Colombia, Portugal, Spain, Poland, Bulgaria, Belgium, and Yugoslavia. He accepted, in 1935, the Star of the German Red Cross. This was from the same country whose government raged against the award of the 1935 Nobel Peace Prize to its imprisoned journalist, Carl von Ossietzky, whose crime was to protest publicly against the remilitarization of Germany. Von Ossietzky's award, given a year late, was presented at the same ceremony with Saavedra Lamas. The two recipients could scarcely have made more contrasting contributions to peace. But they had one thing in common: neither one attended the ceremony—Saavedra Lamas because he was presiding at the Inter-American Conference for the Maintenance of Peace meeting in Buenos Aires, and Ossietzky because as a prisoner for life in the Nazi prison system he was denied the privilege of attending the ceremony.

In a radio address given in response to the award, Saavedra Lamas said: "We are living in the aftermath

of a great war. The fabric which civilization has been weaving in its efforts of centuries, once broken, is difficult to reconstruct. Under its broken web there appears to be a native barbarism ... War of aggression, war which does not imply defense of one's country, is a collective crime. In its consequences on the mass of the poor and humble, it does not possess even that blaze of valor, or of heroism, that leads to mutual national interest; it means the undermining and even the end of culture. It is the useless sacrifice of courage erroneously applied, opposed to that other silent courage that signifies the effort to aid others to improve existence by raising all in this fleeting moment of ours to higher levels of existence."

Biography

Carlos Saavedra Lamas was born in Buenos Aires on November 1, 1878, into an aristocratic Argentine family descended from Argentina's first President, Don Corucho Saavedra. He was educated at Lacordaire College and the University of Buenos Aires, where he received the Doctor of Laws degree *summa cum laude*, subsequently continuing his studies in Paris. Educator as well as statesman and lawyer, during an academic career which spanned 40 years, Saavedra Lamas taught law and constitutional history at the University of La Plata, sociology at the University of Buenos Aires, and constitutional law and political economy at the Law School of the University, as well as serving as its president in 1941-43.

He was a leading academician in labor legislation and international law. In the former capacity he was the first Argentinian professor to lecture in that field, and his publications included *Centro de legislacion social y del trabajo*, (1927), *Trites internationaux de type sociale* (1924), and *Codigo nacional del trabajo*, a three-volume work (1933). In the field of international law he published *La Crise de la codification et de la doctrine argentine de droit internationale*. He also drafted legislation in many areas of international application: asylum, colonization, immigration, arbitration, and peace.

He held the following governmental posts: director of Public Credit, 1906, secretary-general for the municipality of Buenos Aires, 1907. In 1908 he served two successive terms in parliament; in 1915 he was Minister of Justice and Education and in 1932 became Foreign Minister.

He was responsible for most of the South American diplomatic successes of the 1930s, including achieving improved South American relations with North America by working, most notably with US Secretary of State Cordell Hull (1945 Peace Prize laureate) and President Franklin D. Roosevelt, toward less imperialism from North America. He initiated in Washington, DC, the Declaration of August

3, 1933 which put the American states on record as refusing to recognize any territorial change in the hemisphere brought about by force. He drew up the Treaty of Nonaggression and Conciliation which was signed by six South American countries in October 1933, and by all of the American countries at the Seventh Pan-American Conference at Montevideo two months later. He wrote the Antiwar Pact and guided its successful application to ending the stalemated conflict between Paraguay and Bolivia. He presented the Antiwar Pact to the League of Nations, where it was signed by 11 countries in 1936. That year he was elected president of the Assembly of the League.

The Pan-American Society of New York awarded him its medal in recognition of his international work in 1933. He was awarded the Grand Cross of the Legion of Honor of France and similar honors from Brazil, Chile, Bolivia, Colombia, Portugal, Spain, Poland, Bulgaria, Belgium, and

Yugoslavia. He received the Star of the German Red Cross for his work for world peace in 1935, and won the Nobel Prize for Peace in 1936.

Carlos Saavedra Lamas died on May 5, 1959, in Buenos Aires. He left a wife, Rosa Saenz Pena de Saavedra Lamas, and a son, Carlos Roque.

Bibliography

Herring H 1936 Both win the Nobel Prize! *Christian Century* 53 (December 16)
New York Times 1936 Saavedra Lamas wrote Peace Pact. November 25
New York Times 1959 Dr. Saavedra Lamas dies at 80; Won Nobel Peace Prize in 1936. May 6

RUTH C. REYNOLDS

Lord Edgar Algernon Robert Gascoyne Cecil
(1937)

The 1937 Nobel Prize for Peace went to Viscount Cecil of Chelwood, British parliamentarian and cabinet minister, one of the architects of the League of Nations and its faithful defender. From the inception of the League until 1946 when it ceased to function, he devoted almost his entire public life to this international instrument for maintaining peace. Three British Prime Ministers, Ramsay MacDonald, Stanley Baldwin, and David Lloyd George, representing the three major parties in the United Kingdom, paid him a rare tribute: "The formation and maintenance of the League of Nations are due to the labours of many distinguished men of many nationalities, but it has fallen to Lord Cecil to devote himself single-mindedly to strengthening the League and promoting an intelligent understanding of its work among all classes of his fellow citizens."

Edgar Algernon Robert Gascoyne Cecil was born in 1864 into one of England's most distinguished families among the landed aristocracy. He was the third son of the Marquess of Salisbury, leader of the Conservative party and three times Prime Minister between 1885 and 1902. The education which Cecil received at home until he was 13 was far more interesting, he wrote in his autobiography, than his subsequent four years at Eton. It was an upbringing remote from pacifism as his father accepted the legacy of Disraeli and continued the United Kingdom's imperialist policy.

Cecil read law at Oxford and was called to the Bar

in 1887. He became an accomplished advocate and, in due time, a Queen's Counsel. In 1906 he was elected to parliament and sat on the Conservative benches.

With the outbreak of the First World War in 1914 he joined the Red Cross and went to Paris to organize the Department of Wounded and Missing. The experience left him with an abhorrence of war. In 1915, in Asquith's coalition government, he became Undersecretary for Foreign Affairs under Sir Edward Grey, and the following year, in Lloyd George's government, he became Minister of Blockade, serving in this position from 1916 to 1918. In the course of these posts Cecil was introduced to concepts of pacifism through collaboration with leading Liberals such as Asquith and Grey. In 1915 the League of Nations Society was founded, probably the first organization to use that name. Cecil joined in this work in 1916, and it became the predominant influence in his life. The conversion from his youthful unawareness of the problems of peace to a conviction which dominated his life had begun.

In 1918 Cecil initiated through Lord Grey, then the Foreign Secretary, a commission to draw up the first British draft of a Covenant for the proposed League of Nations. Cecil was its driving force, and together with his long-time friend, General Jan Smuts, composed much of the draft. It was Cecil who originated the plan of having the League handle social, economic, and humanitarian functions, while Smuts suggested the Secretariat and the concept of mandates. This became the working draft of the Covenant, and Cecil and Smuts, together with Woodrow Wilson, are considered the authors of the Covenant in its final form.

On November 12, 1918, the day following the Armistice, Cecil spoke at the University of Birmingham about plans for the League of Nations. He said the victors had a moral obligation to construct a lasting peace through an instrument designed for international cooperation and arbitration. As early as June 1919 he called for the admission of Germany and the Soviet Union into the League. That same year he became president of the League of Nations Union. He also became president of the International Federation of the League of Nations Societies. Both of these organizations were means for educating people about the League, one national, the other international.

The dynamic force upon which the League should rest, Cecil urged, was that of vigilant and informed public opinion. He said that publicity was the very lifeblood of the League of Nations. When the inevitable conflicts arise, and a peaceful solution by legal judgment or arbitration and mediation is sought, public opinion should be given a voice. Cecil insisted that the Assembly should meet annually, and that the meetings should be open to the public. A unique attribute which Cecil added, new to international politics, was opening the Assembly's sessions each year with a general debate. The Assembly thus became a free tribune.

Cecil seemed tireless in his work on behalf of the League. At the Paris Peace Conference he was the British representative in charge of negotiations for a League of Nations. At the first three assemblies he served as delegate for the Union of South Africa by choice of General Smuts. In 1923 he made a five-week tour of the United States explaining the League to American audiences. From 1923 to 1927 he was the minister responsible, under the jurisdiction of the Foreign Secretary, for British activities in League affairs.

Cecil pleaded for the fundamental moral principles necessary for the effective work of the League. "Do not let us be afraid of our power," he said. "Let us go on from strength to strength. It is not by doing too much that the League is in any danger. The one danger that threatens the League is that it may gradually sink down into a position of respectable mediocrity and useless complication with the diplomatic machinery of the world . . . . We must be ready to take a bold line in the great work of reconciliation and pacification that lies before us."

The very hesitancy that he spoke against seemed to

Cecil increasingly to be the policy of the Conservative Party. In 1927 at great personal cost he severed the official ties which bound him to the Party. He wrote, "As time went on I became increasingly conscious that that view was not really accepted by most Conservative politicians and was indeed hotly and violently rejected by large numbers of the right wing of the Party. Not only indeed did they reject in their hearts the League of Nations, but they did not propose to take any step for getting rid of war. Clearly, they and I could not honestly belong to the same party."

The very weakness that he feared drove its first shaft into the heart of the League in 1931-32 when the League failed to take action against Japan upon that member country's armed intervention in Manchuria. Sanctions which were urged in many quarters were not used because the Great Powers on whom the burden of enforcement would rest refused to run the risk of war with Japan to compel it to observe its Covenant obligations.

Cecil delivered a dynamic speech on the relevance of disarmament to what had happened. Disarmament, he said, was the touchstone for the will to peace. If disarmament were once carried through, the international atmosphere would suddenly be transformed. The nations would have cast their ultimate vote for peace. If, on the other hand, they rejected disarmament, the world would sink back into dependence upon military might as Japan had just done.

Another contributing factor to the failure to face up to the potential strength of the League through concerted action on the part of its members lay with the old traditional diplomats. They believed that foreign affairs are a matter which only those who have had special training can handle. Debate carried on openly, with little regard for the technical phraseology of diplomacy, would offend their every instinct.

Cecil launched two major attempts to mobilize UK public opinion behind the strong League, decisive in action. The first was a national voluntary referendum in the form of a questionnaire called the "Peace Ballot." The respondent was asked to comment upon the desirability of the League of Nations, on disarmament, on economic sanctions against aggressors, and on military sanctions. The optimists had hoped to receive four to five million replies. In fact eleven and a half million replies poured in, out of which an overwhelming majority, eleven million, were in favor of the League of Nations, ten and a half million for disarmament, ten million for the use of economic sanctions against an aggressor, and 6,780,000 for military sanctions. It happened during the time of a general election, and the Baldwin government proclaimed its firm support for the Peace Ballot findings.

Meanwhile, the Ethiopian crisis loomed, with Italy, a member country, committing an act of overt military aggression on Ethiopia. Once the election was over, the Baldwin government retreated from its stated position and chose to abandon the sanctions, embarking instead upon the largest rearmament program in British history. So Cecil again went to the people. This time, together with the French politician Pierre Cot, he planned the *Rassemblement universel pour la paix* (International Peace Campaign). Founded in March, 1936, its object was to unite peace efforts into an international common front in order to promote concentrated action against violence. It, too, received heartening response from the populace. But Cecil later was to look back and perceive that they had attached too much hope to the conception that no nation would be so rash or so arrogant as to set itself against the public opinions of the world.

In his Nobel address Cecil conjectured that the failure to check Italy had its roots in the League's initial failure to check Japan. Aggressive nations throughout the world were able to observe that, in spite of the League and its Covenant, the old military policies could be successfully reinstated. The consequences were rapid and fatal to the League. Germany forcibly reoccupied Rhineland provinces in 1936. In the civil war in Spain which started in the same year, outside nations intervened—Italy and Germany sent troops and military supplies to support the nationalist rebels and the Soviet Union provided assistance to the Republican forces. Austria was absorbed by Germany on April 10, 1938. Japan, now out of the League, intensified its campaign against China in 1937.

It was evident that the League was faltering. Germany, Japan, and Italy had withdrawn and the Soviet Union had been expelled. Only 46 of the 63 member states remained. Cecil contended that the League itself had been valid in concept; it was the governments which had failed. Anthony Eden agreed: The Council of the League was "as serviceable a piece of diplomatic machinery as I have ever known," he said. Perhaps the most tragic comment of all came from Winston Churchill: during the Second World War he told Cecil, "This war could easily have been prevented if the League of Nations had been used with courage and loyalty by the associated nations."

Cecil concluded that the great question posed by the League's failure was whether the revival of the old ideas was going to make its way amongst the nations of the world. "Do not let us underrate the danger," he said. "It threatens everything we care for

. . . Let me say that in my view it is quite certain that we can prevent it. I have myself no doubt on that point at all. The vast majority of the peoples of the world are against war and against aggression. If they make their wishes known and effective war can be stopped. It all depends upon whether they are willing to make the effort necessary for the purpose."

Cecil was created first Viscount of Chelwood in 1923. His work for world peace was commemorated on his coat of arms. The two supporting lions have olive branches on their shoulders.

Biography

Viscount Cecil of Chelwood was born Edgar Algernon Robert Gascoyne Cecil in London in 1864, son of the Marquess of Salisbury, leader of the Conservative Party and three times Prime Minister between 1885 and 1902. He was educated at Eton and at University College, Oxford, where he studied law. He was called to the Bar in 1887. He was a Conservative Member of Parliament for Marylebone East from 1906 to 1910, and for the Hitchin Division of Hertfordshire from 1911 to 1923.

Cecil served with the Red Cross during the First World War, was Undersecretary for Foreign Affairs, 1915-1916, and Minister of Blockade from 1916 to 1918. He became Assistant Secretary of State for Foreign Affairs in 1918.

Cecil's public life was devoted to the League of Nations. With General Jan Smuts he wrote the British draft of the Covenant of the League, which proved to be the working draft from which the final Covenant was written with the co-authorship of US President Woodrow Wilson. At the Paris Peace Conference he was the British representative in charge of negotiations for the League of Nations. From 1920 to 1922 he represented the Dominion of South Africa in the League Assembly. He was Lord Privy Seal, 1923-24, and Chancellor of the Duchy of Lancaster, 1924-27, during which two posts he was the minister responsible, under the jurisdiction of the Foreign Secretary, for British activities in League affairs.

In 1927, he left the Conservative Party owing to differences regarding the League about which he found many Conservative politicians were distinctly unenthusiastic; and thereafter worked independently to promote public opinion in support of the League. He was president of the British League of Nations Union from 1923 to 1945, and joint founder with Pierre Cot, French politician, of the International Peace Campaign (*Rassemblement universel pour la paix*) in 1936.

Cecil was awarded many honors. He was created first Viscount of Chelwood in 1923 and made a Companion of Honor in 1956. He was elected the chancellor of Birmingham University, 1918-44, and rector of the University of

Aberdeen, 1924-27. He won the Peace Award of the Woodrow Wilson Foundation in 1924. He was presented with honorary degrees by the Universities of Edinburgh, Oxford, Cambridge, Manchester, Liverpool, St. Andrews, Aberdeen, Princeton, Columbia, and Athens.

His publications include: *Principles of Commercial Law, Our National Church, The Way of Peace, A Great Experi-* *ment, A Real Peace*, and *All the Way.*

He married Lady Eleanor Lambton, daughter of the Second Earl of Durham, in 1889.

Viscount Cecil of Chelwood died on November 24, 1958, at the age of 94.

RUTH C. REYNOLDS

Nansen Office
(1938)
see Fridtjof Nansen and the Nansen Office
(1922)   (1938)

Prize Not Awarded
(1939-43)

Red Cross
(1944)
see Henri Dunant and the Red Cross
(1901)   (1917, 1944, 1963)

Cordell Hull
(1945)

The 1945 Nobel Prize for Peace was awarded to Cordell Hull for his long and indefatigable work toward promoting understanding between nations. During his nearly half-century of service to his government, Hull's single most pressing goal was the stabilization of international relations based on a fair economic interchange between nations. This he believed to be fundamental to the cause of world peace. It was "the driving spirit behind his fight against isolationism at home, his efforts to create a peace bloc of states on the American continents, and his work for the United Nations Organization," the Nobel Committee said.

Born in a log cabin in the mountains of Tennessee in 1871, Hull is associated with both the real and the mythological values of the American frontier. It is a tradition that marked his long career, and it offers insight into the character of the man. Benjamin Stolberg, in the *American Mercury* (April 1940) offered an illuminating profile: "Hull comes from the land of the great frontier border leaders—Andrew Jackson, Henry Clay, Lincoln, Andrew Johnson . . . its families represented the only social phenomenon which is distinctly American—the rise of the Common Man and his folk democracy. It is this tradition which gives Hull the characteristic folk outlook of the frontier, and above all, the personal traits which it developed . . . always principled . . . suspicious of the human animal, without moral indignation and without cynicism . . . and when necessary, fearless."

After graduating from Mount Vale Academy in Celina, Tennessee, Hull attended the National Normal University in Ohio for a winter, and from there he went to Cumberland University Law School, known for its "short order" law curriculum. By 19 years of age he was admitted to the bar. Following his brief schooling, Hull's education continued on, self-taught. With his native intelligence and tireless industry, he acquired expertise in his chosen field of economics, and in time he became a leading authority on taxation and tariff.

In 1893, when he was 21, Hull was elected to the Tennessee state legislature, where he served until the Spanish-American war in 1897. The following year he returned to Celina and resumed the practice of law until 1907, when, at the age of 30, he was appointed Judge of the Fifth Tennessee Circuit. The vigorous young judge turned out to be "so tough on the sinful that crime lost much of its allure and nearly all of its profits."

Four years later Hull returned to the call of politics, and after a campaign in which he "stunned the mountaineers with tax talk," he went to Congress from the Fourth Tennessee District on a margin of 17 votes. It was the beginning of a long and sustained career in public service during which Hull put into practice the principles of fairness and steadfastness of purpose he had absorbed in his frontiersman youth.

Hull renewed interest in the income tax law originally introduced by his mentor, Congressman McMillin, and subsequently killed by the Supreme Court. Hull wrote a modern draft which became the First Federal Income Tax Act in 1913, in which Hull was convinced that the direct taxation of wealth, rather than indirect taxation of the consumer, would shift the heaviest burden to the rich and away from those less able to bear it. This same drive for fairness was to guide Hull's approach to international relations, and determine his foreign policy. At the time of his Peace Prize award, the Committee said, "We see him as representative of all that is best in liberalism, a liberalism with a strong social implication."

On all levels, individual, national, and international, Hull acted on his belief that the practice of mutual cooperation would resolve tensions. He held that high tariffs were barriers obstructing fairness in trade, and therefore posed a threat to lasting international peace. In a speech Hull made before Congress on September 10, 1918, he explained these views: "Believing as I have that the best antidote against war is the removal of its causes rather than its prevention after the causes once arise, and finding that

trade retaliation and discrimination in its more vicious forms have been productive of bitter economic wars which in many cases have developed into wars of force, I introduced the resolution in the House of Representatives congress [providing for] the organization of an international trade-agreement to eliminate by mutual agreement all possible methods of retaliation and discrimination in international trade" (Hinton 1942 p. 112).

The League of Nations took up the task of reducing trade restrictions, and its efforts culminated at the World Monetary and Economic Conference held in London in 1933 which Hull attended as Secretary of State. Faithful to his conviction that economic imbalance was the root of most wars, Hull headed the United States delegation to the Conference only to see the stability he sought blasted by President Roosevelt, who rejected Hull's plan for currency stabilization on the grounds that a nation's prosperity depended more upon healthy internal economic structure than upon the price of its currency in relation to the price of currencies of other nations. Hull did not believe in this move toward economic nationalism. In a speech given two months later he declared, "The world is still engaged in wild competition, in economic armaments which constantly menace both peace and commerce."

Hull carried his campaign for free and reciprocal trade to the Pan-American Conference in Montevideo. There, with his homespun simplicity, he overcame initial suspiciousness and won the Latin Americans' confidence by abandoning traditional diplomatic protocol and approaching each statesman on an individual and personal level. An agreement was successfully drafted which defined the rights and obligations of each nation. By the time of the subsequent Buenos Aires and Lima Conferences, in 1936 and 1938, the outlook in Europe had become more ominous. One major stumbling block before which Hull was helpless was that the South American countries were members of the League of Nations and the United States was not. But the success that was achieved by the Good Neighbor Policy in Latin America initiated by Roosevelt was built upon the groundwork of Hull's skillful replacement of the "dollar diplomacy" with an establishment of trust within the Latin American countries.

Despite the setback of the London Conference of 1933, Hull was able the next year to secure the Trade Agreements Act which empowered the President to lower tariffs by 50 percent and to reduce import restrictions for countries who would reciprocate. On the basis of this bill Hull concluded 27 trade agreements. This marked a radical change in the economic policy of the United States, one that Hull saw as an important step toward improved international relations.

As Secretary of State, Hull had to face the Axis powers just as a wave of isolationism swept the United States. While the isolationists regarded peace primarily as peace for the United States, Hull thought in terms of a flexible form of neutrality which would permit the United States to cooperate with other countries in maintaining peace. The United States cannot unilaterally proclaim peace for herself alone, Hull said.

With the coming of the Second World War, Hull devoted himself to the cause of defeating the aggressive Axis powers, but he also looked ahead to problems which would arrive with peace. He drafted six clauses governing the future policy of the four allied powers which were adopted at the Moscow Conference of 1943.

His greatest contribution to world peace, to which he devoted his final efforts in the face of failing health, was setting up the United Nations. He visualized a postwar organization within which international cooperation might at last dominate the world scene. President Roosevelt called Hull the "Father of the United Nations." When he received Hull's resignation by reason of illness, the President expressed the hope that Hull might preside over the UN's first session "as the one person in all the world who has done the most to make this great plan for peace an effective fact." The President continued his message with words which serve well as a summary of Cordell Hull's long and distinguished career: "In so many different ways you have contributed to friendly relations among nations that even though you may not remain in a position of executive administration, you will continue to help the world with your moral guidance."

Biography

Cordell Hull was born in 1871 in a log cabin built by his father in the mountains of Tennessee, one of five sons of William Hull and Elizabeth Riley Hull. Raised in the backwoods, Hull absorbed the democracy practiced by the frontiersmen who gathered at the local schoolhouse to learn about government affairs and to discuss politics. At 16 he went to Mount Vale Academy at Celina, Tennessee, where he was greatly influenced by Congressman Benton McMillin, brother of the headmaster. Following graduation from Mount Vale Academy, a whirlwind education of one winter at National Normal University in Ohio, and a course in law at Cumberland University, Hull was admitted to the

bar at 19. He continued his education on his own and acquired expertise in taxation and tariff.

In 1893 at the age of 21, Hull was elected to the Tennessee State Legislature, but his career was interrupted by the Spanish-American War in which he served briefly as a captain in the Fourth Tennessee Regiment. Upon his return to Celina, he resumed practicing law until appointed a judge of the Fifth Tennessee District, where he earned a reputation for fairness and common sense.

Four years later he yielded to the call of politics and successfully ran for a seat in the House of Representatives, where he served until 1931 (with a two-year hiatus, 1920-22, during which he was pressed into service as Chairman of the National Executive Committee of the Democratic Party). In Congress he became known for his taxation programs, the former designed to encourage worldwide economic health, and the latter to distribute the burden of revenue costs in terms of the citizens' ability to pay. To this end he authored the federal income tax system of 1913, and its revision of 1916.

In 1931 he was elected to the Senate, and when Franklin Roosevelt became President two years later, Hull became his Secretary of State, a position he held for a record 12 years. During this time he implemented Roosevelt's Good Neighbor Policy in the Latin American countries, resulting in an agreement that "no state has the right to intervene in the internal or external affairs of another."

Although Hull's design for international economic stability which he carried as head of the US delegation to the Monetary and Economic Conference in London in 1933 was overruled by Roosevelt's decision in favor of economic nationalism, by the next year Hull had sufficiently gained the confidence of the President to allow passage of the Trade Agreements Act, providing the President with authority to lower existing tariff rates by as much as 50 percent to those countries willing to make reciprocal concessions. This was a great triumph for Hull's dream of an international commerce so healthy and so unhampered by barriers of nationalism that the root cause of war could thereby be addressed.

As an internationalist, Secretary of State Hull had a difficult role with regard to the growing isolationism within his own country and the aggressiveness of the Axis powers without. He correctly read the increased need for military defense, and recognized the possibility of a future surprise attack by the Japanese whom he condemned for their moves in Indochina. He played a prominent part in the Pan-American Conference in Havana in 1940 in which an arrangement was devised to ready the Americas to meet unitedly any threat from abroad.

During the Second World War, Hull gave forward-looking attention to the problems that would come with peace. To this end he drafted six clauses governing the future policy of the United States, the Soviet Union, the United Kingdom, and China, which were adopted at the Moscow Conference of 1943.

His crowning achievement was his preparation of a blueprint for the United Nations, which Hull saw as a major step toward the creation of a "world order under law." For this great service to which Hull gave his strenuous and final efforts as Secretary of State, President Roosevelt called him the "Father of the United Nations."

Illness forced his resignation from public service, but Hull was able to attend the first session of the United Nations in San Francisco in 1945 as a senior advisor to and member of the United States delegation. He was awarded the Theodore Roosevelt Distinguished Service Medal in 1945.

Cordell Hull's *Memoirs* was published in 1950. He was married to Rose Francis Whitney in 1917. He died on July 23, 1955.

Bibliography

Basso H 1940 "Jedge" Hull of Tennessee. *The New Republic* 102 (May 27)
Hinton H 1942 *Cordell Hull: A Biography*. Hurst and Blackett, London
Newsweek 1940 Tug of war pressure on US increasing, but Secretary Hull holds firm. 16 (October 14)
Stolberg B 1940 Cordell Hull: The vanishing American. *American Mercury* 49 (April)

RUTH C. REYNOLDS

Emily Greene Balch

(1946)

The Nobel Peace Prize for 1946 was awarded to John Mott and Emily Greence Balch. Balch shared the prize in recognition of her lifelong, indefatigable contributions to the cause of justice and peace, and for the rich sense of ethics she introduced to this work. "International unity is not in itself a solution," she declared. "Unless it has a moral quality, accepts the discipline of moral standards, and possesses the quality of humanity, it will not be the unity we are interested in."

Emily Balch, daughter of a successful lawyer, was raised in an intellectual home; the influence was reflected throughout her life. A member of the first graduating class at Bryn Mawr in 1889, she furthered her education in Paris, studying economics on a Bryn Mawr fellowship in 1890-91, out of which she wrote *The Poor in France*. She completed her studies with courses taken at Harvard and the University of Chicago, and with an additional year spent studying economics in Berlin, from 1895 to 1896.

Later in 1896 she joined the faculty at Wellesley, and by 1913 she headed the department of economics and sociology. She believed in personal research and application of what was learned. This made her an outstanding teacher, and she encouraged students to investigate social conditions on their own to augment their reading. She herself acted on the same principle. As a student she had become familiar with the poverty and slums existing in the same city as her own comfortable home. She worked in a social center, the Denison House, in the South Cove District of Boston during its first winter.

Balch was the first college professor to introduce the problems of America's immigrants into college courses. Her work on the Slavic immigrants was outstanding. The Nobel Committee Chairman, Gunnar Jahn, called it "a landmark in the scientific analysis of immigration problems" and one which illustrated her practice of thorough preparation. She visited Slav centers in the United States and she did a year's research in the regions of Austria-Hungary from where many Slavic immigrant came.

Balch pioneered in trade unionism and was a founder of the Women's Trade Union. She chaired the Massachusetts Minimum Wage Commission and was a guiding spirit in drafting the United States' first minimum wage law. She became a disciple of Jane Addams (Nobel Peace Prize winner for 1931), and like her, Balch persisted in a lifetime allegiance to her vision of justice.

In 1915, early in the First World War, she went as a delegate to the International Congress of Women at The Hague. There she took a fateful step: she helped to found the Women's International Committee for Permanent Peace, which became the Women's International League for Peace and Freedom (WILPF), and in so doing, she participated in creating the organization in which she was to work for the rest of her life. It was symbolic of her dedication to WILPF that she gave her Nobel Peace Prize money to it.

At The Hague, the women in the new organization prepared peace proposals to take to officials of the

---

Nobel Peace Prize Laureates — 126

nations at war, neutral and belligerent alike. (Such a procedure was possible, Chairman Jahn explained, because "the monstrous beast of war had not yet fully bared his fangs.") Balch went to Russia and the Scandinavian countries. When she returned home she talked with President Wilson and Secretary Lansing. Balch later wrote of these conferences, "For one brief . . . moment in my life I consorted with men in the seats of power."

The soundness and practicality of these proposals was attested by President Woodrow Wilson of the United States: "Without any doubt the best which have so far been proposed," he said of them. Parts of these proposals were later incorporated in the League of Nations Covenant. Balch had made a principal contribution to this proposal out of her wealth of knowledge and her innate sense of practicality.

Her opposition to the war cost Balch her teaching post at Wellesley in 1918 when the faculty declined to renew her contract. She wrote of that ordeal, "It is a hard thing to stand against the surge of war-feeling, against the endless reiteration of every printed word, of the carefully edited news, of posters, parades, songs, speeches, sermons . . . where is the line," she asked herself introspectively, "dividing inner integrity from fanatical self-will?"

The dismissal left Balch at 52 with her professional life cut short and no particular prospects. But she was not destined to be idle. The *Nation* magazine offered her a position on its editorial staff, and she also wrote *Approaches to the Great Settlement* during this period. During the years between the two world wars, she participated in most of the nine congresses WILPF held. They ranged over a wide area of concerns: drug control, minority problems, and, as always, work toward disarmament.

The Second World War plunged Balch into a long and painful struggle as she sought to reconcile her pacifist convictions with the terrifying excesses of the Nazi regime. Her decision to support the war brought her into disagreement with organization which she had long supported: the Quakers, the Fellowship of Reconciliation, and the War Resisters' League. Characteristically, much of her work took the form of looking ahead to the problems which would follow the war: she studied and wrote proposals for internationalization of defense bases, of the polar regions and of all important waterways; in 1944 she drafted a set of peace terms based upon constructive international settlements, and this was publicized by the United States WILPF. Sensitive as always to the face of injustice, she also sought aid for the victims of the Fascist regimes, and for the American Japanese

who were forced into relocation camps and stripped of their basic rights as American citizens.

The WILPF scheduled its second conference in Zurich immediately following the war while the Allies were discussing the peace treaty in Paris. The women studied the emerging treaty and offered resolutions of which the Nobel Committee Chairman, Gunnar Jahn, said it would have been judicious to have heeded.

After the Zurich conference, Balch stayed on in Geneva as the secretary-general of the International Women's League until 1922. She returned in 1934 for a year and a half, donating her services as acting international secretary to the financially hard-pressed WILPF.

Balch gave years of relentless effort to WILPF. "She never embarked on a campaign until she was sure of the facts," Chairman Jahn remarked. He cited an example which proved successful. In 1926 the American branch of the League endeavored to secure the withdrawal of US troops from Haiti after 11 years of occupation. As a representative of the American branch of WILPF, Balch first traveled to Haiti with a delegation and studied the situation. With Balch as principal author, they drew up a report, *Occupied Haiti*, which Jahn pronounced "conclusive proof of her ability to get to the root of the problem and of her consummate skill in devising a practical and democratic solution that would greatly benefit the people." Balch implemented the study with a campaign for the cessation of American intervention in the island's affairs. When the American government did indeed withdraw the troops, it used many suggestions from the study.

William E. Hocking, historian, offers a summary of the unique quality of Emily Balch: "No other life known to me has been so consistently and almost exclusively devoted to the cause of peace and with such pervasive good judgment and effect . . . Her own thought was recognized as responsible . . . and won its way to the minds of those who were making decisions. It will be long before the sum of her labors can be gathered, but when it is done, its achievements will be recognized as the more remarkable because its methods have been so much the quiet ways of friendly reason" (quoted in Lipsky 1966 p. 151).

Biography

Emily Greene Balch was born on January 8, 1867, in Jamaica Plain, Massachusetts, daughter of Francis V. Balch and Ellen Noyes Balch. She graduated in the first class of Bryn Mawr College in 1889 and continued her studies in economics and social sciences in Paris, at Harvard and the University of Chicago, and in Berlin. She taught economics and sociology at Wellesley College from 1896 until 1915, at which time she headed the department of economics and sociology.

In 1915, with the First World War then in its first year, she attended a convention of the International Congress of Women at The Hague, where she participated in the founding of the Women's International Committee for Permanent Peace, later named the Women's International League for Peace and Freedom (WILPF), in which she was to devote most of her efforts toward peace and justice throughout her life.

From the womens' conference at The Hague, two delegations visited neutral and belligerent countries, one of them headed by Balch, where they were accorded polite, but inconclusive, interviews with statesmen. She also participated in a Neutral Conference for Continuous Mediation sponsored by Henry Ford, joined the Collegiate Anti-Militarism League, and sat on the council of the Fellowship of Reconciliation. These anti-war activities cost Balch her teaching position at Wellesley and she joined the staff of *Nation*, a weekly magazine sympathetic to the twin causes of peace and justice. In this same period she wrote *Approaches to the Great Settlement*.

Balch attended the WILPF conference in Zurich following the war's end in 1919, where the women delegates studied the peace proposals and made recommendations. She became secretary-general of the international section of WILPF, a post she held until 1922 and again in 1934-35.

Balch continued her work for peace and justice chiefly through WILPF, but also through service to other international organizations and commissions, including the League of Nations. Her investigations into the US occupation of Haiti

exemplify a successful venture in which the League succeeded, again under the leadership of Balch, in getting the US troops withdrawn.

Balch reluctantly supported the Second World War out of horror at the excesses of the Nazi regime. She wrote proposals for a constructive peace treaty, she vigorously supported the United Nations, and she worked to assist the victims of the Nazi regime and in behalf of the American Japanese who were interned and stripped of their rights as citizens during the war.

Balch always espoused the concept that practical solutions, no matter how technically refined, count for nothing unless they have an ethical foundation. Throughout her life she served the causes of humanitarianism, justice, and peace in myriad ways: through service on immigration boards and on industrial education boards; she fought for regulation of child labor; she participated in the struggle for women's suffrage; she combated racial discrimination; she worked in the United Nations, the Society of Friends, and the Fellowship of Reconciliation. Through application of her expertise in economics and social science she made valuable studies: *Public Assistance of the Poor in France, Outline of Economics, A Study of Conditions of City Life, Our Slavic Fellow Citizens, Approaches to the Great Settlement, Occupied Haiti, Refugees as Assets, The Miracle of Living* (poems), and *Vignettes in Prose*.

Emily Greene Balch died on January 9, 1961.

Bibliography —————————————————

Lipsky M 1966 *The Quest for Peace*. Barnes and Co., South Brunswick

RUTH C. REYNOLDS

John Raleigh Mott
(1946)

The 1946 Nobel Peace Prize was given to John Raleigh Mott and Emily Greene Balch. Mott received the award in recognition of his creation of worldwide organizations uniting millions of young people in work for ideals of peace and tolerance among nations. "Mott's work has been devoted to the most fundamental issue of all . . . he has prepared the soil in which the hope of the world will grow," the Nobel Committee said.

The son of an Iowa timber merchant, Mott grew up surrounded by books; his family and church exerted a strong religious influence, and his mother imparted to him an early love of European history. His first

year in college was spent at a Methodist preparatory school, but he transferred to Cornell University to take advantage of its wider curriculum. Though he belonged to the Cornell Young Men's Christian Association (YMCA), Mott was not intensely interested in religion during his first year. But during his second year he came into an auditorium just as a guest lecturer thundered, "Seekest thou great things for thyself? Seek them not. Seek ye first the Kingdom of God." It was a fateful moment for Mott. "On those few words," he wrote later, "hinged my life-investment decision." Mott entered upon a period of intense Bible study which he characteristically translated into action by doing religious work in the county jail. Caught up in foreign missionary enthusiasm among the student body, he was chosen to be their representative at the first interdenominational Christian Student Conference of 251 young men from 89 United States and Canadian colleges. He was elected president of the Cornell YMCA, and, displaying a gift for inspiring and organizing, he developed within Cornell one of the largest and best organized student religious societies in the world.

Mott graduated Phi Beta Kappa, with a degree in history and political science. Now certain of his commitment to Christian missionary work, he accepted a traveling secretary's position with the national YMCA. This began a lifetime career in which he became, in the words of the Nobel Committee, a "living force, opening young minds to the light which . . . can lead the world to peace and bring men together in understanding and goodwill."

It is not a simple matter to trace all of the organizations served by this zealous and capable man. Certainly the YMCA was central in his career. He held the student secretaryship and the foreign secretaryship of the international committee of the YMCA before assuming its general-secretaryship and finally its presidency. His name, more than that of any other, became associated with the YMCA movement. But Mott could serve as an executive officer of more than one major and international organization at once because he had the genius of the executive who can select competent assistants and skillfully delegate administrative details to them. During the 27 years that he traveled among colleges over the world for the YMCA, collaborating with the student leaders in planning complete programs of activity, he also worked as chairman of the faltering Student Volunteer Movement for Foreign Missions. Working with the YMCA, Young Women's Christian Association (YWCA), and Interseminary Missionary Alliance, he revitalized student groups, and under his directorship over 10,000 student volunteers were sent abroad.

Mott's success can better be understood in terms of his preparation for any task undertaken. When he was to visit a country he first studied its culture, its customs, and its religious and political background. He was able to talk with those he would meet as a friend who knew the country, the people, and their way of life. He met new situations with an open mind, receptive to other ways of thinking.

Mott defined the purpose of all his work as weaving together Christian forces all over the world. In 1893 he organized the Foreign Missions Conference of North America, uniting the missionary units of the

entire North American continent. In 1895, with Karl Fries, he founded the World's Student Christian Federation with delegates from five student units representing ten countries present at its first meeting. Mott toured in its behalf for the next two years and doubled its membership. He was able to organize national student movements in India, China, Japan, Australia, New Zealand, and parts of Europe and the Near East as well as to establish 70 local Christian units. By 1920 the World's Student Christian Federation was estimated as having a membership of 300,000 young men and women in more than 3,000 educational institutions in 27 countries.

In 1910 Mott was chosen to be the presiding officer of the World Missionary Conference. He toured the Far East holding regional missionary conferences in India, China, Japan, and Korea. He used his time to a creative maximum, spending his days organizing this work and his evenings speaking to huge audiences of native students. Over the years the conferences attracted more and more delegates, and Mott took an active part in the leadership of all the gatherings. The students who flocked to Mott's organization were not only Protestants—they came from the Roman Catholic and Orthodox churches, from the Thomist Christians in India, from the Nestorian, Syrian, and Coptic churches. Mott's aim was to give the Christian world new leaders whose love and tolerance would transcend the old frontiers which had previously separated people.

During the First World War the YMCA undertook wide relief activities, both material and spiritual, for the Allied armies in the field, and for prisoners of war on both sides. Nobel Committee Chairman Ingebretsen described this humanitarian work as a "gathering of the resources of his organizations in a mighty effort to span the abyss of hatred of those days . . . Mott himself was always on the move, traveling from country to country and visiting the fronts, entering into negotiations with statesmen in belligerent as well as in neutral state, recruiting suitable helpers for this vast project, for which he collected no less than two hundred and fifty million dollars." Mott's YMCA, with 25,000 volunteers, worked to render captivity for the prisoners mentally and physically bearable, so they might be better prepared to return to normal life after the war.

After the armistice, Mott turned his attention to rehabilitation programs with a success that brought about an invitation to Mott and his assistants to bring their program to Poland, Czechoslovakia, Greece, Bulgaria, Rumania, Estonia, Latvia, and Lithuania. President Taft of the United States called it "one of the greatest works of peace ever carried out in the entire history of war," adding that it was chiefly due to Mott's organizing genius and inspiring leadership. Mott received the Distinguished Service Medal for this work.

In 1913 President Wilson had offered Mott the ambassadorship to China. "I do not know when I have been so disappointed," the President had remarked upon receiving Mott's refusal. However, in 1916, when a serious conflict arose between the United States and Mexico, Mott served on a delegation sent to Mexico to resolve difficulties. And he joined an American diplomatic mission to Russia in 1917.

During the Second World War the YMCA once again worked in prisoner-of-war camps. And at the war's end, the 80-year-old Mott set out on worldwide travels to reestablish international links which the war had broken. He arranged the first world conference of the YMCA, held in Geneva that summer.

Mott combated racial prejudice wherever he found it the world over. The Nobel Committee called his work to subdue racial antagonism "a link in the chain of peace which he tried to forge around the world." This included Mott's own country, where racial prejudice blighted the lives of thousands of American citizens. Mott formed associations in the southern states composed of members of whites and blacks together. In 1914 the first congress ever held for black and white Christians from northern and southern states was organized under Mott's chairmanship. "This is the principle that has governed all of Mott's work among the different churches and missions, among races and nations," Committee Chairman Ingebretsen said. "The three great world organizations which have flourished under his leadership for a generation, the Student Federation, the YMCA, and the International Missionary Council have in his hands been instruments for creating that spirit of Christian tolerance and love which can give peace to the world."

The *Christian Century* (February 1955) summarized Mott's long and distinguished career. Declaring that Mott stood alone, unmatched by any of his contemporaries, and editorial read, "He saw with prophetic clarity the first signs of a new world being born, and he set into motion the ecumenical forces by which Christian churches East and West marshaled their forces to face the changing order . . . he was an embodiment of a whole cycle of Christian history."

Biography

John Raleigh Mott was born in Livingston Manor, New York, on May 25, 1865, son of John S. Mott and Elmira Dodge Mott. His family moved to Postville, Iowa, where his father, a timber merchant, was elected the first mayor of the town. Mott's childhood was influenced by affectionate, cultured, and religious parents, and the Methodist Church. He started college at a Methodist preparatory school and then transferred to Cornell University. There three sentences he heard from a visiting Cambridge lecturer, J. Kynaston Studd, set the course of his life: "Seekest thou great things for thyself? Seek them not. Seek ye first the Kingdom of God."

Mott became vice-president of the Cornell YMCA, and in the summer of 1886 he represented Cornell at the first Christian Student Conference, where 251 young men from 89 American and Canadian colleges met. This sealed Mott's determination to enter a career as a Christian missionary. He showed outstanding aptitude during the following year when he was elected president of the YMCA, and after his graduation from Cornell in 1888 with a degree in history and political science, he became secretary of the International Committee of the YMCA. He continued in this career, traveling to institutions of education throughout the world and influencing millions of young people toward work for Christian ideals of tolerance, understanding, and goodwill between individuals and between nations.

At the same time, Mott accepted an administrative post at the faltering Student Volunteer Movement for Foreign Missions, uniting the intercollegiate YMCA, YWCA and Interseminary Missionary Alliance, and under his directorship it became strong, disciplined, and dependable, recruiting over 10,000 United States and Canadian student volunteers.

In 1885 he turned his remarkable talents of inspiring and organizing to the Foreign Missions Conference of North America, uniting missionary units over the North American continent. In 1895, with Karl Fries of Sweden, Mott organized the World's Student Christian Federation with delegates representing 10 countries present at its first meeting. Following Mott's tour of promotion over the next two years, it doubled that number. He organized 70 local units and student movements in India, China, Japan, Australia, New Zealand, and parts of Europe and the Near East. By 1925 the World's Student Christian Federation had a membership of 300,000 students in more than 3,000 schools in 27 countries.

Mott worked on many projects simultaneously. After he was chosen presiding officer of the World Missionary Conference, he toured the Far East, holding missionary conferences in India, China, Japan, and Korea during the days and speaking to huge audiences of students in the evenings. By delegation of authority to skillfully chosen assistants, and by maximum use of his own time, he was able to hold the student secretaryship and the foreign secretaryship of the International Committee of the YMCA until 1915, its general-secretaryship until 1928, and its presidency from 1926 to 1937, while over the years simultaneously providing leadership to other organizations.

During the First World War the YMCA carried relief and spiritual guidance to the Allied armies and to prisoners-of-war on both sides under Mott's direction as General-Secretary of the National War Work Council and leader of the United War Work Campaign. In the Second World War the 80-year-old Mott showed his characteristic zeal in administering similar programs.

In 1947 Mott resigned from the World's Alliance of Young Men's Christian Associations.

Mott married Leila Ada White in 1891; they had two sons and two daughters. He died in 1955 at his home in Orlando, Florida, at the age of 89.

Bibliography

Christian Century 1928 John R. Mott. November 8
Christian Century 1955 John R. Mott. 72(February)
Time 1946 A for effort. November 25

RUTH C. REYNOLDS

The Quakers
(1947)

The Nobel Peace Prize for 1947 was awarded to the Quakers, represented by their two relief organizations, the Friends Service Council (FSC) in London and the American Friends Service Committee (AFSC) in Philadelphia. The Chairman of the Award Committee, Gunnar Jahn, said, "The Quakers have shown us that it is possible to translate into action what lies deep in the hearts of many: compassion for others and the desire to help them—that rich expression of the sympathy between all men, regardless of nationality or race, which, transformed into deeds, must form the basis for lasting peace. For this reason alone the Quakers deserve to receive the Nobel Prize today."

The Quakers' full name is "The Religious Society of Friends," and they were conceived during the English Revolution in the seventeenth century. Religious organizations have often fought heroically for their freedom, but less often have they been willing to defend the freedom of others once they have won their own struggle. The principle fought for is thus reduced from the high level of freedom to the lesser level of a given system of beliefs defended. The Quakers extend total tolerance toward other religions, they have never considered dogmas and fixed forms as important to them, and they have remained as they began—a religious community acting upon the belief that there is a measure of the divine in human beings, and this fundamental goodness, universal to all, they seek to translate into action.

Quaker pacifism is not passive nor negative, Henry J. Cadbury, AFSC Chairman, told the Nobel award audience. "It is part of a positive policy. The prevention of war is an essential part of that policy." Dr. Cadbury, American theologian, one of the founders

of the AFSC, as well as its chairman from 1928 to 1934 and from 1944 to 1960, said that the Friends believe they must work for the prevention of war by all means in their power: by influencing public opinion in peacetime, by interceding with governments. by encouraging international organization, and by setting an example.

Their work began in prisons, and they have worked for social justice throughout the world, alleviating suffering wherever they found it. This includes the AFSC's work with the American deprived—the black, the American Indian, the Mexican-American, the migrant worker, the Virginia miner—augmenting their 300-year history of aid worldwide. Perhaps, though, the Quakers are associated most with their work of relief and rehabilitation for the victims of war. They were to be found on the scene during many armed conflicts since their inception, administering aid without regard for political creed—in the Napoleonic Wars, the Crimean War, the Boer War, and during the period of American slavery.

In the First World War, young Quaker men and women worked in France caring for children, providing refugees with the necessities for beginning over again, and rebuilding homes. Following that war, Quaker teams crossed previous barriers of nationalities, politics, and creeds to fight the awesome suffering left in its wake: homelessness, famine, and disease, in the Soviet Union, Poland, Serbia, Germany. In a few short years they were aiding refugees escaping Hitler's Germany, Spain's helpless children in the Civil War, Japanese in concentration camps in the United States, the British during the London blitz. Following the Second World War the Quakers engaged in such wide and vast programs—covering

Arab refugees on the Gaza Strip, relief programs in India, China, and Japan as well as the countries of Europe—that the very magnitude of their accomplishment testifies to the outside help this relatively small group of about 200,000 members attracts. Through their inspiring example, the Quakers have long brought out the latent humanitarianism in others.

But this international service goes beyond humanitarianism; it is more than merely mopping up, cleaning up the world after war, Cadbury explained. It is the Quakers' witnessing for peace. "It is aimed at creating peace by setting an example of a different way of international service," he said. The Quakers' relief programs are designed to lead people on the self-help, and from there to paths they can take toward creating a peaceful world.

In their service to others, the members of the Friends reach for empathy with those whom they would help. Margaret A. Backhouse, Chairman of the Friends Service Council, as well as Vice-Chairman of the Friends Relief Service, talked about training oneself "to enter into the condition of others." Not satisfied to be administrators of assistance from a distance, the Friends seek personal contact with those whom they help. They desire to share knowledge, and out of this flow of increased mutual understanding they hope to draw from those with whom they are working the will first to strive for their own betterment, and then to give of themselves to helping others. "Self-interest can reestablish a man's self-esteem, but it is only the first step toward the realization of the brotherhood," she said, ". . . By sharing his goods and, better still, sacrificing his time and energy, he can break down barriers and enter into the lives of others, developing the good within himself."

". . . This appeal to the good in people can cut across deep-rooted prejudices and break down political, national, and credal enmities," Backhouse declared, ". . . men must learn to live in the life and power which takes away the occasion of all wars."

In the spirit of appealing to the reasonableness in humankind, the Friends have inaugurated a series of Quaker International Centers. Known as "Quaker Embassies," and staffed by people from at least three or more countries, they invite men and women to come and discuss conflicting views on neutral grounds and in friendship. Besides offering the Quaker message, these centers provide a training ground for Quaker ambassadors of peace, and a base from which these people can operate during crises. The Quakers also hold conferences for diplomats, and maintain international affairs representatives in key cities all over the world and at the United Nations.

"Today the Quakers are engaged in work that will continue for many years to come," Chairman Jahn said in closing his presentation address, "but . . . it is not in the extent of their work or in its practical form that the Quakers have given most to the people they have met. It is in the spirit in which this work is performed . . . they have shown us the strength to be derived from faith in the victory of the spirit over force. And this brings to mind a verse from one of Arnulf Overland's poems . . . . I know of no better salute:

> The unarmed only
> can draw on sources eternal
> The spirit alone gives victory.

History

The Religious Society of Friends (Quakers) was founded in 1647 by George Fox in England in the midst of the English Revolution. In 1660 the Society sent a manifesto to Cromwell: "We utterly deny all outward wars and strife, and fightings with outward weapons, for any end, or under any pretense whatever; this is our testimony to the world . . . and we certainly know and testify to the world that the Spirit of Christ, which leads us into all truth, will never move us to fight and war against any man with outward weapons, either for the kingdom of Christ, or for the kingdom of this world. Therefore, we cannot learn war anymore." These words have continued to define the Quakers' attitude toward war. They believe in the goodness present in every human being, and seek to translate this "inner light" into good works performed selflessly and across all barriers of nationality, religion, or creed. As vehicles for such action, the Service Council of the British Society of Friends (FSC) was founded in 1850, and the American Friends Service Committee (AFSC) was founded in 1917. Initially the AFSC served to provide young American Friends with a means to serve as conscientious objectors during the First World War in ways commensurate with their love of humankind and their abhorrence of war. All too soon they were similarly engaged in like services in the Second World War. Between the two wars and following them, they acted as the American arm of a religious community serving the Quaker tenet of "God in every man," and acting upon the faith taught by their founder that the power of love can take away the occasion for all wars.

Most widely known for its work in relieving the suffering and ravages of war and the cruel period which inevitably follows, the AFSC has had a tragically ample demand for such endeavors: communal rioting upon the partition of India, relief for Arab refugees on the Gaza

Strip, the Korean War, the Hungarian Revolution, the Algerian War, the war in Vietnam, the Nigerian-Biafran War. Whenever possible, the Friends work with people caught in conflict on both sides, without regard for defining friend and foe.

These activities have been accompanied by programs designed to ease the tensions which lead to wars. Since poverty existing side by side with opulence provides cause for such tensions, with nations as with individuals, the Friends have increased their aid to include social and technical assistance in developing nations, among them Pakistan, India, Zambia, Peru, Mexico, and Algeria. Family planning is included in many of these projects.

Since the early 1950s, the AFSC has brought mid-career diplomats to off-the-record conferences where they may make informal exchanges released from the strictures of protocol. The program has been expanded geographically to include Africa and parts of Asia, and expanded in personnel to include young people outside of diplomacy who might be in a position to help prevent situations of tension from developing between their countries; they provide training in spreading goodwill and understanding.

With similar purpose in dispelling tension, the AFSC has attacked both injustice and poverty in their own country: among Indian, Mexican-Americans, migrant workers, prisoners, blacks, and the poor.

The AFSC works continually on creating an informed public opinion on issues of war and peace. Through speaking tours, publications of peace literature, vigils, and participation in demonstrations and protests of like-minded groups, by a campaign to end the draft, the Committee works to arouse fellow Americans about the growth of the military-industrial complex in the United States.

"A good end cannot sanctify evil means; nor must we ever do evil, that good may come of it," wrote William Penn, the Quaker who founded Pennsylvania; "let us then try what love can do." When the AFSC celebrated its fiftieth anniversary in 1967, "To See What Love Can Do" became its motto.

See also: Articles: *Penn, William; Quakerism*

RUTH C. REYNOLDS

Prize Not Awarded
(1948)

Lord John Boyd Orr Of Brechin
(1949)

The Nobel Peace Prize for 1949 was awarded to Lord Boyd Orr of Brechin, farmer, scientist, physician, and humanitarian, who applied his combined skills to a lifetime dream of removing hunger from the face of the Earth. Early in life he began research on the relationship between nutrition and metabolism. He saw a connection between this nutritional research and hunger. Pointing out that the Chinese word for peace is "ho-ping," which means food for all, Boyd Orr believed that cooperation by the nations is a common war against want would be the key to ultimate collaboration on international political issue. For Boyd Orr, the application of his research was always in behalf of his vision of a world without hunger, a world which would thereby have taken a vast step toward permanent peace.

The son of a Scottish farmer, John Boyd Orr earned his way through the University of Glasgow and taught long enough to accumulate funds for fur-

ther education. He demonstrated an interest in a wide area of subjects, and unusual capability. He graduated with a background in theology, a doctorate in science, and an M.D. degree. After a brief career in the military in the First World War, in which he did research in military dietetics, he returned to Aberdeen where he had just begun establishing the Rowett Institute. During his 25 years as its director he founded and directed the Imperial Bureau of Animal Nutrition, he served as editor-in-chief of the journal he created there, *Nutritional Abstracts and Reviews*, and Rowett became world famous as a British Empire clearinghouse of information.

Boyd Orr's years at the Rowett Institute were devoted to both animal and human nutrition. A flourishing 1,000-acre stock farm demonstrated the success of ongoing animal research, and during that time he did a series of studies on the diet of the people of Britain. One of them, titled *Food, Health and*

Income, revealed an "appalling amount of malnutrition" among the people of England regardless of economic status.

In 1935 he was knighted for his services to agriculture. He was a member of the British Nutrition Committee, served on the Colonial Agriculture and Animal Health Council, and was Chairman of the Scottish Scientific Advisory Committee advising the government on the health of the people of Scotland.

In the Second World War the application of nutritional ideas Boyd Orr had pioneered resulted in a diet in wartime England which, though under the strictures of rationing, produced a level of health beyond all expectations.

Boyd Orr's nutritional concern encompassed hungry people everywhere. "Hunger and want in the midst of plenty are a fatal flaw," he said, "constituting one of the fundamental causes of war." He observed that the opulence of the few can no longer be hidden in a world which science had shrunk to a point where, "measured in time of transport and communication, the whole round globe is now smaller than a small European country of a hundred years ago."

Boyd Orr was convinced that the United Nations offered the world the necessary vehicle through which nations could cooperate to apply science to developing the food supply, and to creating the World Bank necessary to solving the economic complexities of food distribution. In 1945, now retired from Rowett, although serving as a rector of Glasgow University and occupying a seat in the House of Commons, he still took time to give vital assistance in the planning of the Food and Agriculture Organization (FAO). This specialized agency within the UN held the promise for Boyd Orr of carrying out much of his lifelong work, and he became its first Director-General.

"The world would be a much safer place for our children if there were fewer soldiers thinking of armaments for the next war and more statesmen thinking of food for the next generation," he said, and he worked zealously for a cooperation between nations in a common war against want. "It is difficult to get nations to cooperate on a political level," he said, "The world is torn by political strife. But through the FAO the nations are cooperating. Here at the council table representatives of governments are not talking about war ... they are planning for the greatest movement that will make for peace—increased food production, the strengthening of agriculture and food for the people of the world." But he was often frustrated by the lack of authority and funds needed to implement the FAO's planning.

The most important function of the FAO was to assist in agricultural production throughout the world, and under Boyd Orr's direction it became the most efficient organization in this field, addressing a series of technical and economic problems which had to be solved before any real progress in the development of agriculture could be made. Besides the vast undertaking of teaching farmers modern methods, particularly in the developing countries where primitive methods were still being practices, Orr saw the need to plan for worldwide food distribution. He proposed the creation of a World Food Board which would stabilize food prices, create reserves of food to meet shortages, raise capital to finance the sale of surpluses to the countries in the greatest need, and finally, establish a World Bank to provide credit for the development of world agriculture. He traveled extensively to generate support for his comprehensive food plan.

To Boyd Orr's bitter disappointment, neither the United Kingdom nor the United States would support the World Food Board, and an advisory body with no executive authority, the World Food Council, was established instead. Boyd Orr declared in his Nobel lecture, "If the sixty governments which adhere to these specialized agencies and have given them a great deal of cooperation and lip service would agree to devote to them one unit of their currency for every one hundred they are devoting to preparation for war, and allow them freedom of action, I venture to predict that within a few years the political issues which divide nations would become meaningless and the obstacles to peace would disappear."

In April 1948 he resigned from his directorship and gave his full attention to leadership in other areas of peace activities: he served as President of the British Peace Council, of the World Federalist Association, and of the World Peace Association.

Boyd Orr said that any change in science brings about changes in the structure of society, and these changes involve conflict and confusion. "The most important question today," he asserted in his autobiography, *As I Recall*, "is whether man has attained the wisdom to adjust the old systems to suit the new powers of science and to realize that we are now one world in which all nations will ultimately share the same fate."

Boyd Orr spent his long life defining the problems and solutions created by a science to which he himself made valuable contributions, and he simultaneously gave of his creative energies to search for means to "adjust old systems" to meet the challenge of that science.

Biography

John Boyd Orr, farmer, educator, scientist specializing in nutrition, medical doctor, and humanitarian, was born on September 23, 1880, in Kilmaurs, Ayrshire, Scotland, one of seven children of R.C. Orr, a farmer. His family was poor, therefore Boyd Orr had not only to earn his own education, but to help pay for the schooling of brothers and sisters. After graduating from the University of Glasgow, which he attended on a scholarship following schooling in his village, Boyd Orr taught long enough to accumulate funds for his own further education. He demonstrated an eclectic appetite for education, matriculating first in theology, then entering into the sciences out of interest in Darwin's revolutionary theories which Boyd Orr wished to judge for himself. When he graduated from Glasgow he had both an M.D. degree and a doctorate degree in science, having earned a Bellahouston Gold Medal and a Barbour research scholarship. During his lifetime Boyd Orr was to put all these academic disciplines to distinguished use.

He began his career with a position he called "humble and poorly paid" at Aberdeen University working in a basement laboratory as Director of Animal Nutrition Research. Out of this experience he was later to become the director of the Rowett Institute of Research, and in 25 years he brought it from the initial planning stage on paper to world fame as a British Empire clearinghouse of information.

Boyd Orr's primary interest was in nutrition, and he conducted first animal studies, the success of which was reflected in a flourishing 1,000-acre stock farm connected with the Rowett Institute. His study on early pioneering work at the Institute in mineral metabolism, *Minerals in Pastures and their Relation to Animal Nutrition*, became a classic.

By the mid-1920s, Boyd Orr was a member of the Colonial Advisory Council of Agriculture and Animal Health, and did research in pastural problems in Australia. For the British Empire Marketing Board research committee he did a study on two African tribes, one meat-eaters and blood drinkers, the other consuming milk and cereals.

From this point on, Boyd Orr turned his attention to human nutrition. He made a pioneering and permanent imprint in this field. In 1935 he was knighted for his services to agriculture, and that same year he was appointed to the League of Nations Committee to investigate world nutrition. He was Chairman of the Scottish Scientific Advisory Committee which advised the government on matters affecting the health and welfare of the people of Scotland.

His study on the diet of the people of Britain, *Food, Health and Income*, revealing an appalling level of malnutrition among the British, served as the basis for the British policy on food in the Second World War and resulted in a healthy diet even under the strictures of wartime rationing.

In 1945, while he was serving as rector at Glasgow University, and as one of three elected representatives of Scottish universities seated in the British Parliament, he was unanimously elected Director-General of the Food and Agriculture Organization (FAO), a specialized agency within the UN. The FAO was the embodiment of much of Boyd Orr's lifetime work, and he left Parliament after a year and a half to give it his full energy.

His devotion to the FAO was based on his conviction that an adequate worldwide food supply, delivering people from want, would be a basis for peaceful cooperation between classes, nations, and races. To this end he worked for the FAO on a comprehensive plan which would cover all contingencies of food production and distribution. It began with a program to train farmers, particularly in developing countries, a formidable task designed to assist them in the leap from primitive farming to twentieth-century techniques. The plan included establishing a World Food Board which would stabilize food prices and create reserves to meet shortages—Boyd Orr saw no place for restrictive farming in a world containing hungry people. The plan also included the establishment of a World Bank which would help finance all aspects of world food production and distribution. To his bitter disappointment, neither the United Kingdom nor the United States would support the World Food Board, and a World Food Council, an advisory body without means of implementing any program advised, was established.

In April 1948, Boyd Orr resigned from his directorship and gave his attention to his other posts in peace activities: President of the British Peace Council, of the World Federalist Association, and of the World Peace Association.

Lord Boyd Orr received many honors and awards. He was a Fellow of the Royal Society, elected for his fundamental research in physiology; he was an Honorary Graduate LL.D. of St. Andrews and Edinburgh Universities, Scotland, and of Princeton University, United States.

He and his wife, the former Elizabeth Pearson, had one son and two daughters.

He died at his home in Scotland in June 1971 at the age of 90.

RUTH C. REYNOLDS

Ralph Bunche
(1950)

A distinguished US official in the United Nations who succeeded in achieving an armistice between the Arabs and the Israelis won the Nobel Prize for Peace in 1950. Ralph Bunche, one of the youngest laureates honored with the Peace Prize, was first a distinguished scholar in the subject of international relations, then an educator, and finally an official in the US government and in the United Nations.

Ralph Johnson Bunche was born on August 7, 1904, in Detroit, Michigan, one of three children of Fred Bunche, a barber, and Olive Johnson Bunche, an amateur musician. Bunche was raised in a closely knit family kept strong and supportive by his grandmother, Lucy Johnson. She was raised in slavery and Bunche recalls her as "the strongest woman I ever knew." "Nana" Johnson was the dominant influence in his growing years.

At an early age Bunche began to contribute to the family's support, starting as an errand boy when he was seven. Bunche's mother and father both died in his tenth year, and Nana took the family to live in Los Angeles. By the age of 12 he was working long hours in a bakery, often until 11 or 12 o'clock at night. "Life was no idyll," recalled Bunche. "I was learning what it meant to be a Negro . . . . But I wasn't embittered by such experience, for Nana had taught me to fight without rancor. She taught all of us to stand up for our rights, to suffer no indignity, but to harbor no bitterness toward anyone, as this would only warp our personalities . . . she instilled in us a sense of personal pride strong enough to sustain all external shocks, but she also taught us understanding and tolerance . . . ." Her words formed the foundation upon which Bunche was to build a distinguished career in interracial and international relationships.

Although always obliged to combine work with school, Bunche showed early his formidable intellectual gifts. He won a prize in history and another in English in his elementary school years; in high school he was a skilled debater and all-round athlete. He graduated valedictorian of his class in Jefferson High School in Los Angeles. At the University of California at Los Angeles he paid his way through college by working as janitor, part-time carpet layer, petty-officer's messman, and teaching assistant in political science. He showed an unusual blend of talents. He performed with academic distinction, developing an interest in the field of race relations while majoring in international relations. He was a star guard on three championship varsity basketball teams, played football and baseball, he was sports editor of the college yearbook, and took part in oratorical and debating contests. A member of Phi Beta Kappa, he graduated *summa cum laude* in 1927, with a scholarship to Harvard in hand. His community expressed its pride in this talented young man in a concrete fashion, sending him to Harvard with a gift of a thousand dollars to augment his scholarship.

Bunche completed a Master's degree in political science at Harvard during 1928, after which he taught at Howard University for four years. In 1932, he returned to Harvard for his doctorate, alternating study with continued teaching. For his doctoral thesis he decided on comparing the rule of a mandated area, French Togoland, with a colony, Dahomey in French West Africa. Funded for the necessary travels through two fellowships, the Ozias Goodwin and the Rosenwald Field, he set off in Africa with a native truck, determined to conduct his own investigations, and disdaining customary practices of reliance on official reports. The resulting thesis won Bunche the Toppan Prize as the best thesis in the social sciences.

After two more years at Howard University, Bunche was awarded a two-year postdoctoral fellowship in anthropology and colonial policy from the Social Science Research Council. He studied at Northwestern University in 1936 and the London School of Economics in 1937. Then he applied to South Africa's Capetown University. Once he had convinced the authorities that his purpose was not to incite the natives to revolt, he was admitted and began a study on African tribes in the Kenya highlands. This time traveling in a second-hand Ford, he lived for three months among the Kikuyus as an honorary tribal citizen. Native drums would announce his arrival before each stop and he would be greeted with ceremony and feasting.

Out of his researches Bunche wrote *A World View of Race*, exposing myths about races which, in the hands of ignorant or unscrupulous politicians, were exploited to further their own ends. He analyzed British and French colonial policies, which, though different, each committed the grievous policy of denying the natives an opportunity to develop their potential.

Bunche regarded racial problems as a part of the larger problem of the haves and the have-nots, expanding internationally to intricate difficulties between the prosperous established countries and the underdeveloped countries. Bunche did not see the problem as lying with the individuals within a nation or a group. "Most of us, I believe, would be quite tractable if the pressures exerted by groups or by society would give us the chance," he once wrote. "But relations between people are never governed by individuals ... for the individual is subordinated to the group in all important questions."

In 1936 Bunche served as a codirector of the Institute of Race Relations at Swarthmore College, and from 1938 to 1940 as a staff member of the Carnegie Corporation of New York. In the latter capacity he served as chief aid to the Swedish sociologist (and Nobel Prize winner) Gunnar Myrdal in conducting a survey on the conditions of the Negro in America (see Articles: *Myrdal, Gunnar*). While collecting their data the two were "run out" of Southern towns three times.

With the coming of the Second World War, Bunche, in 1941, began working for the government as Senior Social Science Analyst in Africa and the Far East, in the Office of the Coordinator of Information. The next year found him Principal Research Analyst for Africa and the Far East for the same branch of the government, now called the Office of Strategic Services(OSS), and the following year Chief of the Africa Section of the Research and Analysis Branch of OSS. From there he transferred to the State Department, where his rise was equally rapid. On February 1, 1945, he became Acting Associate Chief of the Division of Dependent Area Affairs, "which means," the *Christian Science Monitor* commented, "that he knows about all there is to know on this subject." He was the first black man to break through the racial barriers and hold the post of Acting Chief in the State Department Office.

By this time Bunche had attended nine international conferences, serving as adviser or delegate, within four years. He had helped draw up the nonself-governing territories and trusteeship sections of the United Nations Charter and worked on plans for the disposal of the Italian colonies.

Bunche officially entered the United Nations "on loan" from the State Department in May 1946 when he joined the UN Secretariat as Director of the Trusteeship Division which he had helped organize. "He is as well qualified as is humanly possible for the post," the New York *Herald Tribune* declared. "Americans must regard [him] with pride and humility." It was the opening to the most important assignment of his career. From June to September 1947 he was in Palestine as special assistant to the representative of the Secretary-General of the UN Special Committee on Palestine. Bunche was credited with contributing a large part in the drafting of the Committee's historic report.

On December 3, 1947, Bunche was appointed the Principal Secretary of the United Nations Palestine Commission. The *New York Times* commented that his "experience, understanding, and character should be of inestimable value to the new commission as it takes up its complicated and critical task." The Committee had recommended dividing the country into Jewish and Arab states. In early 1948, while fierce fighting persisted between the Jews and Arabs, the Commission, directed by Bunche, reached an informal agreement to ask the UN Security Council for an international armed force to effect the partition of the Holy Land. The UN appointed Count Folke Bernadotte as mediator and Ralph Bunche as his chief aide, their first task being to secure a truce. They succeeded in obtaining a truce lasting from June 11 to July 9. But on July 10 hostilities broke out once more.

The Chairman of the Nobel Committee, Gunnar Jahn, described the incident, which contributed so vitally to the Peace Prize award, in his presentation speech.

> The two men who met in 1948 to undertake this common task could hardly have been more unlike . . . . On the one hand, Folke Bernadotte, grandson of King Oscar II of Sweden and nephew of Sweden's reigning monarch, steeped in all the traditions of a royal family; on the other, Bunche, whose grandmother had been born in slavery, who had been brought up in poverty, who was entirely a self-made man.
>
> Folke Bernadotte was scantily informed on the Palestine conflict . . . Bunche, Head of the Trusteeship Department of the United Nations, had back of him an education and training directed precisely at recognizing and understanding the problems raised by international disputes.
>
> Yet the two men had one thing in common: they both believed in their mission.

Bernadotte was assassinated on September 17, 1948, and Bunche became his successor as the acting mediator. He immediately endorsed the Bernadotte plan for settling the Palestine dispute by awarding Galilee to the Jews, the Negev desert area to the Arabs, and the city of Jerusalem to the United Nations, and he appealed to the UN Security Council to order a ceasefire to allow both parties to try to reach an agreement on an armistice as a preliminary to a final settlement. His proposal was approved by the Security Council on November 16.

It was a daring proposal, Chairman Jahn explained, for an armistice is more than a ceasefire; it is in effect a preliminary to peace. It turned out that Bunche had judged the situation correctly. Negotiations between the Arab states and Palestine dragged on for 11 months, and required the greatest demands on the mediator, for the Arabs did not want to sit at the same table with the Jews. Bunche was compelled to negotiate separately with each side, constantly having to clear away the mutual distrust. This was not mediation between two parties, but between Palestine on the one hand, and seven Arab states on the other, and agreements had to be concluded separately with each of the seven. By exercising infinite patience, Bunche succeeded in persuading all parties to accept an armistice. When asked how he managed it, Bunche replied,

> Like every Negro in America, I've been buffeted about a great deal. I've suffered many disillusioning experiences. Inevitably, I've become allergic to prejudice. On the other hand, from my earliest years I was taught the virtues of tolerance; militancy in the fight for rights, but not bitterness. And as a social scientist I've always cultivated a coolness of temper, an attitude of objectivity when dealing with human sensitivities and irrationalities, which has always proved invaluable—never more so than in the Palestine negotiations. Success there was dependent upon maintaining complete objectivity.
>
> Throughout the endless weeks of negotiations I was bolstered by an unfailing sense of optimism. Somehow, I knew we had to succeed . . . . (*American Magazine*, February 1950 p. 125)

Bunche's reply, Chairman Jahn said, described the man: his childhood heritage from his grandmother, the knowledge, education, and experience he gained in a life dedicated to service. It was the sum of all these factors which created the skilled mediator who succeeded in getting these hostile parties to lay down their arms. "The outcome was a victory for the ideas of the United Nations . . . but it was one individual's efforts that made the victory possible," Jahn said.

Chairman Jahn acknowledged that there remained "even greater challenges than before." Bunche continued to meet that challenge. "The objective of any who sincerely believe in peace clearly must be to exhaust every honorable recourse in the effort to save the peace," he observed. Bunche served as Under Secretary-General for Special Political Affairs from 1955 to 1967, and as Under Secretary-General of the UN from 1968 to 1971.

Biography

Ralph Johnson Bunche was born in Detroit, Michigan, on August 7, 1904, one of three children of Fred and Olive Johnson Bunche. After his parent's death when he was a young child, he was raised by his grandmother, Lucy Johnson, an indomitable woman, raised in slavery, who influenced young Ralph with a lasting sense of self-worth, integrity and the capacity for hard work, intelligently directed. His intellectual gifts surfaced early, and while working to help augment the family income from elementary school on he distinguished himself with continuous awards. He graduated valedictorian of his class at Jefferson High School in Los Angeles. A member of Phi Beta Kappa, he graduated *summa cum laude* from the University of California at Los Angeles in 1927. With a series of scholarships and fellowships he earned his Master's degree in political science at Harvard, in 1928, and after four years on the faculty of Howard University he returned to Harvard to earn his Ph.D. in 1934, writing a dissertation on "French Administration in Togoland and Dahomey" for which he won the Toppan Prize for the best dissertation in the social sciences. He did postdoctoral work at Northwestern University in anthropology in 1936, at the London School of Economics studying anthropology and colonial policy in 1937, and the same year at the University of Capetown, South Africa, where he did several months of field work among the Kikuyus in the Kenya highlands. The fellowships which helped finance his education were: University Scholarship, Harvard, 1927-28; Ozias Goodwin Memorial Fellowship, Harvard, 1929-30; Rosenwald Fellowship, 1932-33; Toppan Prize, Harvard, 1934; Social Science Research Council Fellowship, 1936-38.

Throughout his career Bunche maintained strong ties with education. He chaired the Department of Political Science at Howard University from 1928 until 1950; he served as codirector of the Institute of Race Relations, Swarthmore College, in 1936; he taught at Harvard University from 1950 to 1952; he served on the New York City Board of Education, 1958-64; on the Board of Overseers of Harvard University, 1960-65; on the Board of the Institute of International Education; and as a trustee of Oberlin College, Lincoln University, and New Lincoln School.

Bunche was active in the Civil Rights Movement in America. He participated in the Carnegie Corporation's survey of the Negro in America with Gunnar Myrdal; he was a member of the "Black Cabinet" consulted on minority problems by the Roosevelt Administration; he declined President Truman's offer of the position of assistant secretary of state because of the segregated housing in Washington, DC; he helped to lead the civil rights march organized by Martin Luther King Jr. in Alabama in 1965; he supported the action programs of the National Association for the

Advancement of Colored People (NAACP) and of the Urban League.

After the start of the Second World War he entered government service and held the following posts: Senior Social Science Analyst, Africa and the Far East; Office of the Coordinator of Information [later known as the Office of Strategic Services (OSS)], 1941-42; Principal Research Analyst, Africa and the Far East, OSS, 1942-43; Chief, Africa Section, Research and Analysis Branch, OSS, June 1943-January 1944; Divisional Assistant, Colonial Problems, Division of Political Studies, Department of State, January-July 1944; Area Specialist, Expert on Africa and Dependent Areas, Division of Territorial Studies, Department of State, July 1944-February 1945.

In the Division of Dependent Area Affairs, Office of Special Political Affairs, Department of State, he was Acting Associate Chief, February-April 1945, and Associate Chief, April 1945-March 1947, interlapping with his post as Acting Chief, July-October 1945 and November 1945-January 1946.

Bunche was appointed by President Truman as US Commissioner, Anglo-American Caribbean Commission, September 1945-June 1947. At the request of Secretary-General Trygve Lie he began service in the United Nations as Director, Division of Trusteeship, in 1946. In June 1947, the confrontation between the Arabs and the jews in Palestine brought him to the most important assignments of his career. He was the first appointed assistant to the UN Special Committee on Palestine, then Principal Secretary of the UN Palestine Commission. This commission was charged with seeing to the activation of the partition approved by the UN General Assembly. In early 1948 the fighting between the Arabs and the Israelis became severe and Count Bernadotte was appointed as mediator with Bunche as his chief aide. Four months later Bernadotte was assassinated and Bunch was named acting mediator. After 11 months of nearly continuous negotiating, Bunch secured the necessary signatures for armistice agreements between the State of Israel and the Arab states.

He served as delegate or adviser at many conferences: twice in the US delegation at the Institute of Pacific Relations—once in Mont Tremblant, Canada, in 1942 and in Hot Springs, Virginia, in 1945. He was a member of the Secretariat, Pacific Council meeting, Atlantic City, 1944;

Assistant Secretary to the US delegation at the Dumbarton Oaks Conference in 1944, and adviser to two International Labour Organization Conferences, in Philadelphia, 1944, and in Paris, 1945. At the First Session, General Assembly, UN, in London, 1946, he was Technical Adviser, Trusteeship, in the US Delegation. He served as Technical Expert, Trusteeship, to the US Delegation, UNCIO, San Francisco in 1945.

Bunche was Special Assistant to the Representative of the Secretary-General, UN Special Committee on Palestine, June-September 1947, and Principal Secretary, UN Palestine Commission, December 1947-May 1948. He was Principal Secretary and Personal Representative of the Secretary-General with the UN Mediator on Palestine, September 1948-August 1949. He directed peacekeeping efforts in Suez in 1956, in the Congo, 1964, and Cyprus, 1964.

He wrote *A World View of Race* in 1937, and numerous articles on colonial policy, trusteeship, race relations, and minority problems.

He was awarded the Spingarn Prize by the NAACP in 1949; Four Freedoms Award, 1951; Peace Award of Third Order of St. Francis, 1954; Golden Key Award, 1962; and US Presidential Freedom award, 1963. During the three years following his return from Palestine he was given over 30 honorary degrees.

He married Ruth Ethel Harris in 1930; they had one son and two daughters. He continued his career in the UN: from 1955 to 1967 he served as Under-Secretary for Special Political Affairs, and from 1968 to 1971 as Under-Secretary-General. He died on December 9, 1971.

See also; Articles: *Arab-Israeli Conflict: Peace Plans and Proposals*

Bibliography ———————————————————————————

Bunche R 1968 *A World View of Peace*. Kennikat Press, Port Washington, New York

Hamilton T A 1930 Peacemaker extraordinary. *Americas* 2(November)

Ross I 1950 Dr. Bunche of the UN *American Mercury* 70 (April)

RUTH C. REYNOLDS

Leon Jouhaux

(1951)

The 1951 Nobel Prize for Peace was awarded to Leon Jouhaux, a long-time leader in the French labor movement, as the person "who has worked most or

best for promoting brotherhood among the peoples of the world, and for abolition or reduction of standing armies, and for the establishment and spread of peace congresses." The only labor leader ever to be award-ed the Peace Prize, this was a recognition of Jouhaux's lifetime of unceasing work toward the accomplishment of all of Alfred Nobel's stipulations for the award of the Prize. He based his life's work on the premise that the removal of social and eco-nomic inequalities, both within nations and between nations, was the most important means of combating war. Jouhaux worked for 45 years through the International Federation of Trade Unions, the International Labour Organization, the League of Nations, the United Nations, and the European Movement to bring about a social environment capa-ble of sustaining a society in which war would no longer be possible. Jouhaux called the award a recog-nition of the "importance and steadfastness of the pacifist efforts of trade unionists."

Jouhaux participated in his first strike in 1900. The occasion must have been poignant for the 20-year-old, for the cause was protesting the use of white phosphorus, a substance which had disabled his father after years of working in a match factory. The month-long strike led to the abolition of the use of the toxic material, and to Jouhaux's dismissal for his part in the strike as recording secretary. His union later secured his reinstatement.

Already he showed attributes of a leader, with impressive industriousness, organizing ability, a strong personality, and the ability to speak persua-sively. He became interested in pursuing a possible relationship between labor unions and peace. His labor union, Confédération Générale du Travail [General Confederation of Labor], known as CGT, held biannual congresses. As early as 1898 it had gone beyond questions of organization and corporate claims and had taken its stand in favor of general dis-armament. Jouhaux was impressed by its tenets call-ing war a calamity and armed peace ruinous to the people who must shoulder the burden of its support with money that would be better spent on serving humanity.

In 1906 Jouhaux was appointed representative of his union at the congress of that year. There the dele-gates considered replying to declarations of war with a declaration of a revolutionary general strike. Nor did the trade unions confine themselves to passing motions at congresses. They established international liaisons and supported every policy furthering the cause of justice and understanding between nations.

In 1909 Jouhaux became secretary-general of the CGT, a position he held until 1949. "The trade-union movement was emerging from its infancy," Jouhaux said, "with an aim to protect and extend the rights and interests of the wage earners, and," he empha-sized, "*to achieve international fraternity and soli-darity.*" The CGT pitted its full strength against the war it saw impending, joining with laborers from other nations, including Germany, in declaring that war offered no solution to the problems facing them.

Jouhaux recalled that the First World War did not end their quest; rather, it intensified their passion for pacifism. They began to lay plans for participation in the peace which would come. Jouhaux was editor of *La Bataille Syndicaliste* [The Syndicalist Battle], the principal organ of the CGT, and he encouraged the CGT to call for arms limitation, international arbitra-tion, and an end to secret treaties.

In 1916 at the Leeds Conference he presented a report which laid the foundation for the International Labour Organization (ILO). The ILO was subsequently established as part of the Treaty of Versailles follow-ing the war in recognition of the goal of peace between classes as well as peace between nations. Its masterstroke was its policy of "tripartism" which gave representation alike to workers, employers, and governments, providing a unique opportunity for greater understanding between the three groups through the invaluable context of working together. Through the ILO the work of Jouhaux and the labor unions had materialized into the only worldwide organization in existence in which international cooperation is the business of workers and their employers as well as governments. Jouhaux became a perennial labor delegate to this specialized agency whose goal was to create an infrastructure of peace.

In 1919 the trade unions organized the Fédération Syndicale Internationale [International Federation of Trade Unions] better known as FSI (succeeded by the World Federation of Trade Unions in 1945) with Jouhaux becoming its first vice-president. It acquired a membership of over 20 million. Its activities included offering concrete help to workers through-out the world: the Austrian workers escaped famine as a result of the many trainloads of supplies sent by various trade unions; and the FSI intervened on behalf of the Russian workers, sending three representatives to live in Russia supervising the distribution of food and medicines sent by the Federation.

Nor did the Federation limit itself to mitigating the cruel consequences of war. Its program emphasized worldwide economic and social stability. Jouhaux declared that "it is not distorting history to say that it was largely through the efforts and propaganda of our International Federation that the government of the USSR was recognized by the majority of the great powers." He pointed to the proposals ultimately put before the League of Nations; the majority had their inception in congresses of this international labor organization. Between 1925 and 1928 he was a French delegate to the League of Nations.

In the 1930s he and the CGT were a linchpin in the Socialist Front Populaire, fighting Franco, Laval, and Hitler, and in a reversal of his usual policy, he worked alongside the communists.

Jouhaux wrote four books in his field. Of particular distinction was his treatise on disarmament, *Le Désarmament*. But the opposing forces were gathering, and in the fall of 1939 Europe again became enveloped in war. After the fall of France in 1940, Jouhaux joined the Resistance movement (for which he received the Medal of the French Resistance after the war), but in 1941 he was captured by the Germans and interned first at Evaux-les-bains (Creuse) until December of that year and then deported to a German concentration camp. From there he was rescued in 1945.

Upon liberation he immediately resumed peace work; he was a French delegate to the United Nations, and vice-chairman, and then chairman, of the French Economic Council, a governmental official advisory board on economic matters. Through these offices he was able to keep alive before the French government and before the world his basic tenet that no peace can be established and maintained in the absence of a sound economic foundation.

From the time of the 1906 congress of the CGT, Jouhaux had worked on the principle of union independence from political parties. When he returned he found that the CGT had become infiltrated by communists who practiced a strong political involvement. Jouhaux sought to preserve the integrity and independence of the CGT, but when forced to share the secretaryship with the communist Benoit Frachon he found himself in intense friction with the communist determination to sabotage the Marshall Plan through French labor. Jouhaux led the noncommunist members out of the CGT, their numbers estimated at over a million, and formed the anticommunist Force Ouvriére [Workers' Force] in December 1947.

"The free trade-union movement is called on to play an essential part in the fight against international crisis and for the advent of true peace," Jouhaux said. For the worker, Jouhaux stood for the safeguarding of civil liberties, specifically the right of all citizens to hold their own opinions on the great questions of moral, philosophical, political, and economic import and to express them freely. He said this must not be merely theoretical, but that democracy must offer every individual effective opportunities, pointing out

that "One who must be constantly preoccupied with his own subsistence cannot be an alert citizen."

For the welfare of the international community he would have the organized working class take an active part in the construction of Europe. "We want to make Europe simply a peninsula of the vast Eurasian Continent, where for thousands of years war has been the only way to resolve conflicts between peoples. We want Europe to be a peaceable community, united, despite and within its diversity, in a constant and ardent struggle against human misery."

Jouhaux called on the labor movement to play an essential part in the fight against international crisis and for the advent of peace. "The scope of the task is enormous, matched only by its urgency," he said.

Biography

Leon Jouhaux was born in Paris on July 1, 1879. His father, a veteran of the Commune of Paris, was an activist for the workers' welfare at the match factory where he was employed. Jouhaux was forced at 11 to leave his elementary school and augment the family income. Efforts to return for interrupted intervals were abandoned by his fourteenth year because of the family's impoverishment. Throughout his life Jouhaux worked at his education and ended on a university level.

Jouhaux participated in his first strike at the age of 21. Based on protest over the dangerous use of white phosphorus in a match factory, the strike was successful in bringing about its ban. Fired for his participation as recording secretary in the strike, and forced to find employment where he could, Jouhaux was reinstated through the efforts of his union, the Confédération Générale du Travail, known as CGT, and in 1906 he was appointed as the CGT's representative at its biannual congress. In 1909 he was elected its secretary-general, a post he held until 1947.

An ardent internationalist, and convinced that war brought intense misery and no solutions, Jouhaux fought all his life to bring the workers of the world into participation both in efforts to prevent war and in the peace treaties which followed the two world wars. He called for arms limitations, worker participation through peace congresses, international arbitration, as well as the more usual trade union functions of defending the civil and economic rights of the workers. To this end he edited *La Bataille Syndicaliste*, the newspaper of the CGT; participated at the Leeds Conference in 1916 where he played a principal role in laying the foundation for the International Labour Organization (ILO); was influential in getting the ILO incorporated in the Treaty of Versailles, and served as perennial French delegate to that organization; and served as perennial French delegate to that organization; and served as a member of the French delegation to the League of Nations from 1925 to 1928. He was the first vice-president of the International Federation of Trade Unions.

After the fall of France in the Second World War, he joined the Resistance movement, subsequently being captured and interned by the Germans until the end of the war in 1945. He received the Medal of the French Resistance in 1946. Upon his return to the CGT he found differing philosophies between himself and the communist members regarding the union's political independence an impossible barrier to surmount, and left the central organization of the CGT along with other leaders to form the Force Ouvriére [Workers' Force]. Jouhaux also served as a member of the

French delegation to the United Nations. He was elected president of the International Council of the European Movement in 1949. His published works include: *Organisation Internationale du Travail, Le Désarmement, La fabrication privée des armes*, and *Le mouvement syndical en France*. He died on April 28, 1951.

Bibliography ───────────────────────

American Federationist 1954 Leon Jouhaux. 61(6)
Time 1951 Nobel Prizewinner. 58 (November 19)

RUTH C. REYNOLDS

Albert Schweitzer
(1952)

In presenting the 1952 Nobel Peace Prize to Albert Schweitzer, Gunnar Jahn, chairing the Nobel Committee, said that Schweitzer "will never belong to any one nation. His whole life and all his work are a message addressed to all men, regardless of nationality or race . . . . Mankind yet searches for something which will allow people to believe that one day they will enjoy the reign of peace and goodwill."

Albert Schweitzer remarked upon this quest in his Nobel lecture: "The idea that the reign of peace must come one day has been given expression by a number of peoples . . . . The originality I claim is . . . the intellectual certainty that the human spirit is capable of creating in our time a new mentality, an ethical mentality. Inspired by this certainty, I too proclaim this truth in the hope that my testimony may help to prevent its rejection as an admirable sentiment but a practical impossibility. Many a truth has lain unnoticed for a long time, ignored simply because no one perceived its potential for becoming reality."

Albert Schweitzer's life is an embodiment of truths revealed to him, as he put it, by "growing into" the ideals that were a part of his childhood and youth. The son of a Lutheran pastor, Schweitzer grew up in the presbytery of a small village in Alsace with a brother and three sisters in a warm and harmonious family. His happy childhood is attested to by his return to that village on every occasion possible when returning to Europe on fund-raising visits from Africa.

Schweitzer began the study of the piano when he was five, the organ at eight. By the time he was nine he was able to substitute for the parish organist at church services. It was an auspicious start to the

career of a brilliant musician who would one day study under the legendary Charles Marie Widor, with fee waived because of unique promise, and who was destined to become an organist of distinction.

Qualities that were discernible in the child became the basic foundation of his later life despite all the experience and extensive education which followed. Chairman Jahn recounted an experience in Schweitzer's childhood which illustrates the ethical personality that was developing within the boy. An elderly Jew who occasionally passed through the village became a target for ridicule from the boys. The old man responded to their goading with only a gentle smile. That smile overpowered Albert Schweitzer, and he took great care thereafter to greet the old man with respect.

This quality in the child flowered into a deep compassion for every living thing, Jahn said. It became a voice within the young Schweitzer which gave him no peace: did he who had enjoyed such a happy childhood and youth have the right to accept all this happiness as a matter of course? The natural right to happiness and all the suffering prevailing in the world merged in his mind and brought forth a decisive direction to his future work. It became steadily clearer to Schweitzer that those who enjoy many of the good things of life should in return repay to others no less than they have received. We should all share the burden of life's suffering.

Meantime, as these principles were maturing in Schweitzer's mind, he started his studies at Strasbourg in the theological college of St. Thomas. In 1896, at the age of 21, while still a student, Schweitzer arrived at a lifetime decision: he would allow himself the following nine years in which to study philosophy and theology and to pursue his music, and thereafter he would pledge his life to easing the suffering of humanity.

In those nine years he completed his licentiate (a degree higher than the doctorate in German universities) with a thesis on Immanuel Kant's views on religion; he studied the organ, again with Widor in Paris; he became first a *Privatdozent* in theology at the University of Strasbourg in 1900, and in 1903 he was appointed the principal of the theology faculty there. He wrote *The Mystery of the Kingdom of God* and *Quest of the Historical Jesus*. At the same time he was writing a major biography of Bach and becoming a world-renowned interpreter of Bach's music. His work on the building of organs written during this period remains a classic in that field.

Distinguished careers in music, theology, philosophy, and education were open to him when, in his twenty-ninth year, he read an appeal from the French Protestant Missionary Society in Paris asking for help for the Negroes in French Equatorial Africa. For Schweitzer, the appeal was his long-awaited answer to the place of fulfillment of his pledge.

The missionaries were asking for a doctor, however, as well as a missionary. To qualify for the post, Schweitzer spent the next seven years studying medicine. His new profession held a unique attraction for Schweitzer: "For years I had used the word. My new occupation would be not to talk about the gospel of love, but to put it into practice," he said.

While pursuing his medical studies he served as curate at the church of St. Nicholas in Strasbourg, he gave concerts on the organ, conducted a heavy correspondence, and examined the teaching of St. Paul, especially that of dying and being born again "in Jesus Christ." It resulted in a book, *Paul and His Interpreters*, published in 1912. That same year he resigned his position as curate and married Helene Bresslau; the daughter of a scholar, and a scholar herself, she trained as a nurse in order to share her husband's life in Africa.

By now the Paris Missionary Society had become wary of Schweitzer's unorthodox views and barred him from preaching at the stations. But they accepted him as a medical doctor. The site for the hospital was at Lambarene, on the Ogooue River. A few miles from the Equator, it is in the jungle, its climate among the world's worst, with days of merciless heat and clammy nights and seasonal torrential rains. The two Schweitzers were to meet with leprosy, dysentery, elephantiasis, sleeping sickness, malaria, yellow fever, plus the more usual diseases, and with only a broken-down chicken-coop for their first hospital. The natives flocked by foot, by improvised stretcher, and by dugout canoe for medical attention.

Schweitzer had just begun to clear the jungle for building a hospital when the First World War broke out. As German citizens the Schweitzers were interned as prisoners of war, but during the nine months before their internment they had treated 2,000 native patients.

Internment gave Schweitzer the opportunity to start writing the two-volume *The Philosophy of Civilization*, his masterwork in ethics. Schweitzer's ethical system is boundless in its domain. He summarized it once by saying, "A man is ethical only when life, as such, is sacred to him, that of plants and animals as that of his fellow men, and when he devotes himself helpfully to all life that is in need of help." Crystallized within the phrase "reverence for life," its applications are far reaching. The concept "does not allow the scholar to live for science alone, even if he is very useful to the community in so doing," Schweitzer explained. "It does not permit the artist to exist only for his art, even if it gives inspiration to many . . . it demands from all that they should sacrifice a portion of their own lives for others."

When Schweitzer was released from internment in 1918 he was gravely ill, and it was not until 1924 that he was able to return to Africa. From that date on he lived the rest of his life in Africa, with sporadic visits to Europe to raise funds for the hospital at Lambarene.

The *New York Times*, in a long and respectful obituary of Schweitzer, voiced a criticism of this period too often heard not to require an answer:

> . . . there was undisputed grandeur in his view that a man is ethical only when life is sacred to him. Such idealism underlay Schweitzer's hospital at Lambarene. His desire to bring Western medicine and healing to the jungle was grand, even heroic, in 1913. Less admirable were his treatment of Africans as children, his autocracy and his refusal to keep step with medical gains. His hospital was rickety, dirty and way out of date; yet it was invariably crowded, whereas a sleek and gleaming one nearby had bedspace to spare.
>
> The Gabonese preferred Schweitzer because he seemed part of the landscape, because he was a pioneer, because he cared when few white men did. These facts, not his faults, are his true measure.

Schweitzer did not leave Africa to accept his Peace Prize. But he regarded the award as a mandate to address the issues of peace, and he honored this obligation with a stirring written message:

Let us dare to face the situation. Man has become superman. He is a superman because he not only has at his disposal innate physical forces, but he also commands, thanks to scientific and technological advance, the latent forces of nature . . . however, the superman suffers from a fatal flaw. He has failed to rise to the level of superhuman reason which should match that of his superhuman strength. He requires such reason to put this vast power to solely reasonable and useful ends, and not to destructive and murderous ones. Because he lacks it, the conquests of science and technology become a mortal danger to him rather than a blessing.

Schweitzer deplored that we are becoming inhuman to the extent that we become "supermen." We have learned to tolerate that people are killed en masse, and in that resignation we are guilty of inhumanity. He said the horror of this should shake us out of our lethargy so that we can direct our hopes and our intentions to the coming of an era in which war will have no place. This we can accomplish, he declared, only through a change in spirit. He said the League of Nations and the United Nations were both doomed to fail in a world in which there was no prevailing spirit directed toward peace. Only when an ideal of peace is born in the minds of the peoples of the world will the institutions set up to maintain this peace effectively fill that function.

We may well ask if the spirit is capable of achieving the changes that must be made. Schweitzer answered that we must not underestimate its power, the evidence of which can be seen throughout the history of humankind. The humanitarianism which is the origin of all progress toward some form of higher exercise is the child of this spirit. He said, "All that we have ever possessed of true civilization, and indeed all that we still possess, can be traced to a manifestation of this spirit . . . . But the situation today is such that it must become reality in one way or another; otherwise mankind will perish."

Biography

Albert Schweitzer was born on January 14, 1875, in Kayserburg, Alsace, one of five children of Louis Schweitzer and Adele Schillinger Schweitzer. Raised in a presbytery in Gunsbach by loving and liberal parents, he developed early a sensitivity to those around him which transcended empathy and embraced a profound sense of personal responsibility. Highly gifted in music, he started learning the piano at five, the organ at eight, and by nine could substitute for the parish organist when needed. He studied under the eminent organist, Charles Marie Widor, and became an organist of note, particularly as an interpreter of Bach.

Schweitzer studied theology at the University of Strasbourg on a Goll Scholarship, taking his licentiate (a degree slightly higher than that of the doctorate in German universities) in 1900 and continuing on at Strasbourg as acting principal of the theological college. In 1902 he received the post of *Privatdozent*, and in 1903 he was appointed to the office of principal of the theological college. From 1903 to 1905 he worked on his *Quest of the Historical Jesus* and began a biography of Bach. He also wrote an influential treatise on the art of organ building.

When he was 21, he entered into a pledge that he would spend the next nine years in the study and writing of theology and philosophy, and in his pursuit of music; thereafter he would give the remainder of his life to the direct service of humanity.

In response to an appeal for a medical missionary, Schweitzer, in his thirtieth year, began to fulfill his pledge by entering the study of medicine, which he financed through giving lectures and organ concerts. In 1912 he married Helene Bresslau, who left her own scholarly pursuits to train as a nurse. With money raised from Alsatian churches and concerts, the Schweitzers left for the tropical community of Lambarene. During the nine months they served there before they were interned as alien citizens upon the outbreak of the First World War they treated 2,000 native patients.

During his internment, Schweitzer became severely ill, but recovered and continued to orient his activities around the day he might return to Africa. He wrote *On the Edge of the Primeval Forest*; he gave concerts, he traveled and gave lectures. During 1922 and 1923 he wrote the two volumes of his great philosophical work, *The Decay and Restoration of Civilization* and *Civilization and Ethics*. He took advanced courses in obstetrics and dentistry, and attended lectures at the Institute for tropical hygiene in Hamburg. In 1924 he returned to Lambarene, and began construction of a new building two miles upstream in 1925. Except for trips to provide funding for the hospital, Lambarene became Schweitzer's permanent home, and by the early 1960s he had expanded the medical facilities to over 70 buildings. It became his habit to spend parts of his nights writing, and thus he continued to increase the legacy of theological and ethical thought he left to the world.

Schweitzer believed that the abdication of thought has been a decisive factor in the decay of civilization. In his own life he continued in his quest for the ultimate ethical values, and suddenly the phrase "reverence for life" came to him, crystallizing his search of many years. Schweitzer said, "A man is ethical only when life, as such, is sacred to him, and when he devotes himself helpfully to all life that is in need of help."

Honorary degrees were conferred upon Schweitzer from

Prague, Oxford, St. Andrews, Edinburgh, and Zurich.

Albert Schweitzer died in his Lambarene hospital on September 5, 1965. In a posthumous tribute, US President Johnson wrote: "The world has lost a truly universal figure. His message and his example, which have lightened the darkest years of this century, will continue to strengthen all those who strive to create a world living in peace and brotherhood."

Bibliography

Christian Century 1965 Albert Schweitzer. 82(37)

RUTH C. REYNOLDS

George Catlett Marshall
(1953)

In 1953, for the first time in the history of the Nobel Peace Prize, the award went to a professional soldier. The choice of thus honoring General George Catlett Marshall was met with intense criticism. Many felt that his position as Chief of Staff of the United States Army during the time of the development and use of the atomic bombs eliminated him forever from the roll call of peacemakers. George Marshall acknowledged this position with neither surprise nor rancor, saying that his experiences with the tragedies of war had left him deeply moved to find some means or method of avoiding another calamity of war.

The Peace Prize was not given to Marshall for what he accomplished during the war, the Nobel Committee said, explaining, "Nevertheless, what he has done after the war for peace is a corollary to this achievement, and it is this great work for the establishment of peace which the Nobel Committee has wanted to honor."

The wisdom General Marshall learned in his military career was a clear and passionate conviction that the overriding lesson of the last world war must be to recognize that another such war is now impossible. And when in 1947 Marshall accepted President Truman's appointment as Secretary of State, it was because he believed that he had come to understand some of the causes of war, and he intended to remove those causes insofar as it would fall within his power to do so.

Within his military experience Marshall developed two traits: one the insatiable desire to learn, to know, to understand, and the second his keen and wide-awake interest in the welfare of the individuals for whom he was responsible, be they soldier or civilian. Both of these traits nurtured the spiritual and social evolution of his mind. He displayed this eagerness to find out about his fellow human beings under his care early in his career when, at the age of 21, he was made commanding officer of some of the small and utterly lonely outposts in the Philippines. While there he made a study of the language, customs, and mentality of the Filipinos.

During the period between the wars Marshall was stationed in Tientsin for three years. And just as in the Philippines, where he had become an authority on their history and culture, so he applied himself to the language, both spoken and written, of the Chinese people and studied their history and culture. He was the only US officer who could examine Chinese witnesses who appeared before him without the use of an interpreter.

During the Depression when soldiers' pay was so low that it rendered a hardship on soldiers with families, Marshall taught his troops to raise chickens and hogs and tutored them in vegetable gardening. He instituted a lunch-pail system whereby each member of a soldier's family could have a meal-in-a-pail for 15 cents. Marshall and his wife ate the same fare so there would be no note of condescension. It was a true Marshall Plan in microcosm.

Marshall's military career might well be encapsulated by recounting an event fairly early in his army life, and one near its close. The first occurred in 1916 when a camp where he had been in charge of the training program closed. The commanding officer was required to make an efficiency report on his officers. When asked the routine question, "Would you desire to have Marshall under your immediate command in peace and in war?" Lt. Colonel Johnson Hagood said, "Yes, but I would prefer to serve *under his command* . . . . In my judgement there are not five officers in the army so well qualified as he to command a division in the field." The second event followed the Allied victory in the Second World War. Henry Stimson, US Secretary of War, said to Marshall in the presence of 14 generals and high officials, "I have seen a great many soldiers in my lifetime, and you, Sir, are the finest soldier I have ever known."

General Marshall was the first career soldier

appointed US Secretary of State. He came with a wealth of background. As Chief of Staff he had taken part in the conference at sea between President Roosevelt and Winston Churchill which resulted in the Atlantic Charter. He assisted Roosevelt, Churchill, and the Combined Chiefs of Staff at a meeting which set up principles of unity of command in the Far East. Other conferences, some attended by Stalin and Chiang Kai-shek, have historical significance—at Casablanca, Quebec, and Yalta. He was with President Truman on a special mission to China, then in the throes of civil war. The following year, on February 12, 1947, he became Secretary of State.

In some of his early actions as Secretary of State he recommended aid to European displaced persons, continuance of relief abroad after termination of the United Nations Relief and Rehabilitation Administration (UNRRA), and recommendations to Congress for proposals to permit the United States to join the UN International Refugees Organization. He supported the Stratton bill to admit 400,000 European displaced persons into the United States.

On June 5, 1947, at Harvard University commencement exercises, the new Secretary of State revealed his "Marshall Plan," later officially named the European Recovery Program (ERP). Dean Acheson (1961), a later Secretary of State, recalled the formation of the Marshall Plan. He said Marshall was determined that European recovery should come from and be devised by the Europeans themselves. There were many critics, Acheson recalled, but he said the plan would never have succeeded without the decision Marshall made.

Acheson recalled that Marshall also insisted that the offer should be made to all of Europe and not merely to Western Europe. To the storm of protests that "The Russians, if included, would sabotage the plan," and that "Congress would never appropriate the money," Marshall remained adamant in his stand. If Europe was to be divided more deeply and more lastingly than it was already, Moscow had to do it, not Washington.

Upon Marshall's invitation, Bevin, Molotov, and Bidault met in Paris to discuss Marshall's suggestions. In July, 16 European nations, including the United Kingdom and France, met at the Paris Economic Conference on the ERP. The Soviet Union and its satellite nations boycotted the meetings, but Marshall held fast to his original plan described in his Harvard speech: "Our policy is directed not against any country or doctrine, but against hunger, poverty, desperation and chaos . . . . Any government that is willing to assist in the task of recovery, will find full

cooperation." Marshall thought it logical that the United States should do whatever it could to assist in the return of normal economic health over the world, without which, he was convinced, there could be no political stability and no assured peace. He insisted that political passion and prejudice should play no part.

"Your work stands," Chairman Jahn said to Marshall at the award ceremony. "Your intention was to create in the economic field a cooperation between the nations, embracing the whole of Europe, because you meant that unless people are free from fear, poverty and distress, there will be no sound foundation for a lasting peace. You did not know that some countries should not be willing to accept the help offered to them . . . . It is the greatest example the world has seen of help given from one people to others and a true expression of brotherhood between nations."

In his Nobel lecture Marshall warned that millions who live under subnormal conditions are coming to a realization that they may aspire to a fair share of the God-given rights of human beings: "If we act with both wisdom and magnanimity, we can guide these yearnings of the poor to a richer and better life through democracy . . . but we must understand that these democratic principles do not flourish on empty stomachs."

Marshall deplored that in the past "we have walked blindly, ignoring the lessons of the past, with the tragic consequences of two world wars and the Korean struggle as a result." He urged that schools accept the responsibility for educating toward peaceful security, both in terms of its development and of its disruption. They must be taught as far as possible without national prejudices. They must learn to seek out the factors which favor peace. Marshall declared, "I am certain that a solution of the general problem of peace must rest on broad and basic understanding on the part of free peoples . . . and on a spiritual regeneration which would reestablish a feeling of good faith among men."

Biography

George Catlett Marshall was born on December 31, 1880, in Uniontown, Pennsylvania, son of George Catlett Marshall, a prosperous businessman, and Laura Bradford Marshall. He graduated in 1901 from the Virginia Military Institute as Senior First Captain of the Corps of Cadets, voted to the highest cadet rank at the institute by his classmates. He was commissioned a second lieutenant in the US Army and attached to the Thirtieth Infantry stationed in the

Philippine Islands, where he remained for 22 months. After several years' duty in the West and on the West Coast he was selected to attend the Infantry-Cavalry School at Fort Leavenworth, Kansas, of which he was a senior honor graduate in 1907. He was next assigned to study at the Army Staff College, where he headed his class and to which he returned as instructor for two years following his graduation. Beginning in 1913 he again saw duty in the Philippines.

When the United States entered the First World War, Marshall accompanied the first convoy of the First Divison to France, where he proved himself to be an outstanding tactician, and ended as Chief of Staff of the Eighth Army Corps. His rise in the army continued in meteoric fashion: by the opening of the Second World War, at the recommendation of General Pershing, President Roosevelt bypassed 20 major and 14 brigadier generals to make Marshall General of the Army, with five-star rank.

From 1941 General Marshall was one of the members of the policy committee guiding the atomic studies of US and British scientists. A member also of the Combined Chiefs of Staff of the United States and the United Kingdom, maintaining liaison with the Soviet Union through an Allied Military Mission to Moscow, and with China by the Allied Military Council at Chungking, Marshall exercised an important influence on the United Nations strategy.

Many of his tasks were diplomatic: he was present at the conference at sea leading to the Atlantic Charter, and at conferences at Casablanca, Quebec, Cairo-Teheran, Yalta and Potsdam.

At his own request Marshall secured his release from duty as Chief of Staff and was appointed "Special representative of the President to China, with the personal rank of Ambassador." As a means of preventing famine, creating employment, and helping to institute a democratic government, Marshall recommended a loan to China. He was called back to the United States to assume the cabinet position of Secretary of State under President Truman in 1947. At his first press conference, in February 1947, he declared that the international control of atomic energy and the general issues involved in preserving the peace must be solved before any discussions on worldwide disarmament would be valid.

In other early actions he recommended aid to European displaced persons and continuance of relief abroad after termination of the United Nations Relief and Rehabilitation Administration (UNRRA). With Dean Acheson, Eisenhower, and others, Marshall formulated the "Truman Doctrine" (see Articles: *Truman Doctrine*), a "simple, declarative statement of the New United States policy" to prevent the imposition of totalitarian regimes on European nations.

On June 5, 1947, he unveiled his Marshall Plan, official-ly named the European Recovery Program (ERP) before a Harvard University commencement audience. He described the plan as "not directed against any country or doctrine, but against hunger, poverty, desperation, and chaos. Its purpose would be the revival of a working economy in the world so as to permit the emergence of political and social conditions in which free institutions can exist." He required the European countries to design their own plans for using the monetary aid so that this would be a European plan. He insisted that all countries be included, and the Soviet Union's boycott of the 16-country meeting in Paris to implement ERP, was its own choice.

At the United Nations, Secretary Marshall proposed that the veto not be used in peaceful settlement of disputes and in the admission of new members in order to prevent its abuse. He also proposed the establishment of a continuous-session, all-nation interim committee on peace security which would "consider disputes at the request of the Security Council or individual states, recommend special General Assembly sessions it deemed necessary, and determine whether this little assembly should be made permanent." The plan for the "Little Assembly" was accepted later by General Assembly delegates with some modifications. Marshall also supported the Stratton bill to admit 400,000 European displaced persons into the United States.

For one year during the Korean War, he served as Secretary of Defense, from which position he resigned in September 1951.

Marshall received the Distinguished Service Medal for his service in the First World War, its Oak Leaf Cluster for Second World War duty, and many other medals, both from his own country and from France, the United Kingdom, the Soviet Union, Italy, Morocco, and various Latin American countries. He also received numerous honorary degrees.

Marshall married Elizabeth Carter Coles in 1902. Three years after her death in 1927, he married Katherine Boyce Tupper Brown. Although Marshall wrote no diaries or personal records, Katherine Tupper Marshall's *Together; Annals of an Army Wife*, written in 1946, presents an informal biography of General Marshall and herself.

General George C. Marshall died on October 16, 1959.

Bibliography

Acheson D 1961 General of the Army George Catlett Marshall *Sketches from Life of Men I Have Known*. Harper, New York

Marshall K 1946 *Together: Annals of an Army Wife*. Tupper and Love, New York

RUTH C. REYNOLDS

United Nations High Commissioner for Refugees (UNHCR)
(1954, 1981)

Through the ages the giving of sanctuary has become one of the noblest of human traditions. The 1954 and 1981 Nobel Peace Prizes were awarded to the Office of the United Nations High Commissioner for Refugees (UNHCR) in recognition of its sustained work toward ensuring the rights of refugees—people without political power, existing on the sufferance of strangers, who by 1981 numbered over 10 million individuals.

In presenting the 1954 award, the Nobel Committee said, "This is work for peace, if to heal the wounds of war is to work for peace, if to promote brotherhood among men is to work for peace. For this work shows us that the unfortunate foreigner is one of us; it teaches us to understand that sympathy with other human beings, even if they are separated from us by national frontiers, is the foundation upon which a lasting peace must be built."

The two awards honored a tradition long familiar to Norwegians through the work of their countryman, Fridtjof Nansen. An explorer, scientist and statesman, he devoted his life after the First World War to administering humanitarian aid to refugees. In 1921 the League of Nations appointed him High Commissioner for Refugees, and for the leadership, vigor, and spirit he brought to the office he received the Peace Prize in 1922. After his death the momentum of his work continued through what was known simply as "the Nansen Office." In 1938 the Nansen Office joined the select group of Nobel Prize winners, creating a chain of tradition which leads to the UNHCR.

The Nansen award barely preceded the Second World War, which created unprecedented numbers of uprooted men, women, and children. At the war's end 44 nations joined to create the United Nations Relief and Rehabilitation Administration (UNRRA). Its task was to help with the voluntary repatriation of over 7 million persons during the following two years. For the many other refugees who could not, or did not wish to return to their countries, another temporary body, the International Refugee Organization, was created, and it organized the resettlement of more than 1.5 million refugees.

These were the forerunners of the UNHCR, organizations which met specific problems created by the devastating world wars of the twentieth century. But it had become clear that not all the problems of refugees could be solved with their services, and the General Assembly of the United Nations decided to establish the Office of the United Nations High Commissioner for Refugees. With ill-fated optimism it was created for only three years, after which time its need would be subject to review. UNHCR, 31 years old when it received its second award of the Peace Prize, was still not officially a permanent body. But its services remained essential as violations of human rights and armed conflicts continued to afflict the world.

High Commissioner Hartling called UNHCR's expanding tasks "keeping pace with history in the making," as more than 100 new countries gained independence, sometimes in violent circumstances. Increasing international conflicts motivated the Commission to develop intermediary skills in order to act in behalf of refugees caught in the cross currents between powers.

As a means of establishing minimum standards for the treatment of refugees, a universally binding instrument was created at the 1951 Geneva Convention, followed by a supplementary protocol in 1967. The UNHCR was assigned the task of verifying that the 90 acceding countries each passed national legislation fully complying with these instruments, and further verifying that such legislation had been effectively implemented.

Hartling listed a portion of the Commission's accomplishments; its most gratifying service for the great majority of refugees has been assisting them to return to their homes. In 1954 Dr. Van Heuven Goedhart gave a haunting definition of "home." "Home is more than just a roof over the refugee's head," he said. "It is the all-embracing term for a series of elements which together constitute an individual's independence, and therefore his freedom and dignity."

This basic concept is costly to execute; it requires much organization. It can involve wide-ranging operations when refugees without funds or employment return to empty, or even destroyed, homes.

The first large-scale repatriation operation took place in 1962 with the return of 250,000 Algerians who had fled to Morocco and Tunisia during strife in their own country. In 1972, 10 million refugees returned to their homes in their newly independent state, Bangladesh, after months spent in relief camps in India. That same year UNHCR helped bring back over 150,000 Sudanese refugees. In 1973, UNHCR assisted in one of history's largest airlift population exchanges when it organized a two-way movement of large numbers of people between Bangladesh and Pakistan.

In Africa, with the independence in 1974 of territories formerly under Portuguese administration, hundreds of thousands of refugees were assisted in returning to their homes in Guinea-Bissau, Mozambique, and Angola. Similar efforts on behalf of other refugees in Africa returning to their countries following independence intensified in 1975. By 1981 the numbers of people from Southeast Asia, Afghanistan, and the Horn of Africa who had received assistance from the Commission had swollen to proportions defying easy counting; estimates ranged from three to five million.

Countries accepting refugees without the means to care for them became a problem. The very presence of refugees can become threatening for the host countries, causing suspicion and political unrest; food supplies and economic resources can be severely strained. The refugees, deprived of support, having nothing, are helpless. "This is where concerned national and international efforts can bring stability to a situation fraught with danger," Hartling said. The UNHCR can encourage a decisive display of international cooperation in which programs of considerable magnitude can be planned, financed, and implemented to provide for refugees and ultimately lead to their self-sufficiency." Hartling cited Tanzania as an excellent example of such a program. "When refugees came from Rwanda and Burundi," he said, "we cleared up the bush, put up a refugee camp, gave them seeds and tools and they lived there. After some time, they took care of themselves. Today, thirty-six thousand of them have their own village—not a camp. They are no longer refugees. They are naturalized Tanzanians."

The Nobel Committee of 1981 singled out for praise UNHCR's work with the "boat people" from Vietnam, who, together with refugees from Laos and Cambodia, had been fleeing to other countries throughout Southeast Asia since 1975. Since 1977, UNHCR had assisted in the resettlement of more than 700,000 Asian refugees at the time of its 1981 Peace Prize award.

Serious political problems began to challenge the ingenuity of UNHCR as the chief host country, the United States, questioned whether the continuing migration was truly based on political necessity. The US government suggested it could result from the lure of better economic possibilities for refugees in the United States. For UNHCR, balancing the demands of major contributors, of communist opponents and of

countries like Thailand that have not signed the UN Covenant on Refugees is a difficult task.

During its first 30 years UNHCR had helped some 25 million people, but Commissioner Hartling estimated that at the time of the second award there were still about 10 million refugees throughout the world. With the later population upheavals a new cooperation was observed as both private enterprises and governments joined with UNHCR to carry out some of the largest population movements in history.

In dealing with the countries which the refugees are leaving, as well as the host countries receiving them, UNHCR has used diplomatic channels, offering its good offices as arbitrator between governments with differing interests to safeguard. The consideration of the refugees themselves has been UNHCR's guiding principle. Nobel Committee Chairman Sanness summarized this well: "The Office of the United Nations High Commissioner for Refugees is a bridge linking the world community conceived as a community of states, and the world community conceived as a community of men and women."

As they made the awards, the Committees on each occasion expressed their appreciation for all UNHCR had done for these "painful legacies of war." Looking toward a future still fraught with problems, they asked it to continue "to carry the flaming torch that Fridtjof Nansen once lit."

History

In 1948 the UN General Assembly established the International Refugee Organization to provide legal and political protection for refugees. At that time the greatest number of refugees were Europeans displaced by the Second World War. Three years later the agency was renamed the Office of the United Nations High Commissioner for Refugees (UNHCR). Minimum standards for refugees laid down by the 1951 Geneva Convention and supplemented by a 1967 protocol form the legal basis for UNHCR. It is UNHCR's role to assist in their implementation. For its vigorous and successful program, UNHCR won its first Nobel Peace Prize in 1954.

The growth of UNHCR's task reflects the upheavals and increasing violence following the Second World War. At UNHCR's inception in 1951 there were 51 countries in the world; at the time of its second award in 1981 there were 154. The High Commissioner for Refugees protects people who cross international borders without a passport. The UN has decreed that such people have protection, and the High Commissioner for Refugees becomes their ambassador. To this end, UNHCR has offices in 90 countries. Secondly, the UNHCR supplies relief. But its long-range purpose is to assist toward establishing self-sufficiency, either through refugees returning home or establishing them in a host country.

UNHCR is strictly nonpolitical: its doctrine is humanitarian. Its funding comes mainly from 20 countries. By 1981 it had assisted over 25 million refugees, but it estimated there remained 10 million in need of help at that time.

High Commissioners who have served in the past are: C. J. Van Heuven Goedhart (1951-56), Auguste R. Lindt (1956-60), Felix Schnyder (1961-65), and Prince Sadruddin Aga Kahn (1965-76). Poul Hartling, a former Prime Minister of Denmark, was named High Commissioner in 1977.

Bibliography

Hartling P 1981 An inside look at agency that won Nobel Peace Prize (Interview). *U.S. News and World Report* 91(October 26)

Shawcross W 1981 The fourth world: Who's minding the refugees? *The Nation* 233 (November 28)

Time 1981 Timely honor. 118(October 26)

RUTH C. REYNOLDS

Prize Not Awarded
(1955-56)

Lester Bowles Pearson
(1957)

Lester Bowles Pearson, the first Canadian to be awarded the Nobel Peace Prize, won the honor in 1957 because of the "powerful initiative, strength and perseverance he has displayed in attempting to prevent or limit war operations and to restore peace," the Nobel Committee said. Called "the diplomat of the atomic age," Pearson was an internationalist. "The scientific and technological discoveries that have made war so infinitely more terrible for us are part of the same process that has knit us all so much more closely together," he said. "Today, less than ever, can we defend ourselves by force, for there is no effective defense against the all-destroying effect of nuclear missile weapons . . . . Peace must surely be more than this trembling rejection of universal suicide . . . ."

"The best defense is not power," Pearson maintained, "but the removal of the causes of war and international agreements which will put peace on a stronger foundation than terror of destruction." Pearson's visionary diplomacy rested on the solid foundation of his study of history, first at the University of Toronto and then at Oxford. He taught history for four years at Toronto.

His first years served in the government in the Department of External Affairs also enhanced his preparation for his later role as diplomat as he gathered wide experience and broadened his outlook. During this time he attended numerous international conferences, among them the Hague Conference on International Law, the Geneva World Disarmament Conference, and meetings of the League of Nations.

From 1935 to 1941 he served in the Office of the High Commissioner for Canada, which placed him in London and extended his sphere of experience to include Europe. He returned to Canada to accept the post of Assistant Undersecretary of State for External Affairs. The following year he went to Washington as Canadian minister.

During the early years of the Second World War he joined those who were starting to build a structure of peace long before the end of the war. In 1943, he made a strong contribution to a conference in Hot Springs held to plan for the distribution of the world's food, and from which came the constitution for the Food and Agriculture Organization (FAO). He was reported as responsive and intelligent, with a flair for working out effective compromises between opposing viewpoints.

Pearson spoke at the close of that conference: "We at this Conference know, and we have shown, what science could do if harnessed to the chariot of construction. Man's fears have, however, harnessed it also to another chariot, that of atomic obliteration. On that chariot race, with science driven by both contestants, all our hopes and fears . . . are concentrated."

It was abundantly clear which chariot Pearson was driving. He took part in organizing the United

Nations Relief and Rehabilitation Administration (UNRRA) to reestablish the economies of war-ravaged countries, and to take care of displaced persons inevitably following in the wake of war. Pearson undertook this task because he believed in a better world for humankind. "UNRRA must not merely do its job well," he said, "it must do it so well that it will give heart and courage to the governments who, slowly but steadily, are building up the international structure of peace . . . ."

Pearson became Secretary of State for External Affairs in 1948, and during the nine years he held this position his chief contributions to international affairs were accomplished through the United Nations. He negotiated, and guided through the General Assembly, the plan that established the State of Israel (thereby earning Israel's Medallion of Valor).

He drafted the speech used by his Prime Minister, Louis St. Laurent, proposing the establishment of the North Atlantic Treaty Organization (NATO). Pearson headed the Canadian delegation to NATO in 1951-52. He would have liked to have seen it expanded beyond a defensive alliance to include cooperation among NATO countries covering political, economic, and cultural fields. "No person, no nation, no group of nations can view with comfort the prospects for a world where peace rests primarily on the deterrent effect of collective military strength and regional political unity . . . . Even adequate collective force for defense is no final solution," he said.

When the bitter Arab-Israeli conflict over Palestine came to the UN he participated in the resolution of the UN committee that the United Kingdom should give up its mandate over Palestine, and that the country should be divided into an Arab and a Jewish state. Also as Secretary of State for External Affairs, he played a major part in the Korean truce of 1953.

Pearson's skill as a diplomat reached its zenith when Nasser nationalized the Suez Canal and the ensuing conflict was brought before the Security Council of the UN. Before a solution could be resolved, Israel marched into Egypt, and the next day the United Kingdom and France bombed Egyptian airfields. The action split the Western Alliance, brought on a crisis in the Commonwealth, and posed a threat of a new world war. The Security Council could do nothing in the face of the British and French vetos. Pearson began working on a plan of compromise. He also drafted and submitted a resolution for a neutral international UN peacekeeping force to supervise the cessation of hostilities. The favorable outcome of his work marked the UN's first successful peace move. "It may well be said that the Suez crisis was a victory for the United Nations and for the man who contributed more than anyone else to save the world at that time. That man was Lester Pearson," Nobel Chairman Jahn declared.

A colleague once described Pearson's talents as a negotiator: "He sits down with a person from another country without ingrained hostility or prejudice or superiority." Although the Soviet Union twice blocked his nomination for Secretary-General of the UN, a Russian paid him a rare compliment. "I always listen with great attention to the Canadian delegate," Andrei Y. Vishinsky said, "because he often says what others may think but are afraid to say."

In his Nobel lecture, Pearson alone of all the Laureates brought up the powerful psychological attraction war holds for humankind. He quoted a Canadian psychiatrist, Dr. G. H. Stevenson:

> People are so easily led into quarrelsome attitudes by some national leaders. A fight of any kind has a hypnotic influence on most men. We men like war. We like the excitement of it, its thrill and glamor, its freedom from restraint. We like its opportunities for socially approved violence. We like its economic security and its relief from the monotony of civilian toil. We like its reward for bravery, its opportunities for travel, its companionship of men in a man's world, its intoxicating novelty. And we like taking chances with death. This psychological weakness is a constant menace to peaceful behavior. We need to be protected against this weakness and against the leaders who capitalize on this weakness.

Pearson's answer was twofold: people should face the fact that the consequences of nuclear war would hold none of war's previous attractions; and the peoples of the world should learn to know each other. He especially addressed the two Superpowers, pointing out that Western fears of the Soviet Union have been partly based on a lack of understanding and information about the people of that country. Similarly, the Soviet people, whom Pearson believed wished for peace, were in fear of the West. "How can there be peace without people understanding each other, and how can this be possible if they don't know each other?" he asked, adding that while contact can mean friction as well as friendship, more contact and freer communication would overcome this. "I can find nothing to say for keeping one people malevolently misinformed about others," he said. Quite to the contrary, Pearson urged that countries encourage contact between their citizens and those of other countries. To at least permit this he regarded as "an acid test for the sincerity of protestations for better relations between peoples."

"We are now emerging into an age," he said, "when different civilizations will have to learn to live side by side in peaceful interchange, learning from each other, studying each other's history and ideals, art and culture, mutually enriching each other's lives. The only alternative in this overcrowded little world is misunderstanding, tension, clash and—catastrophe."

Pearson found hope in humanity's history; "The fact is," he said, "that to every challenge given by the threat of death and destruction, there has always been the response from free men: 'It shall not be' . . . . May it be so again . . . as we face the awful and the glorious possibilities of the nuclear age."

Biography

Lester Bowles Pearson was born in Toronto, Canada, on April 23, 1897, the son of the Reverend Edwin Arthur Pearson and Annie Sarah Bowles Pearson. He attended schools in Toronto, Peterborough, and Hamilton, and graduated from the University of Toronto with a history degree. During the First World War he enrolled in the ambulance corps overseas, and then in the Royal Flying Corps, from which he was invalided home in 1918. He returned to England and earned a master's degree in history at Oxford. He then joined the faculty at the University of Toronto.

In 1928 Pearson joined the government service in the new Department of External Affairs. He was an adviser or delegate at the following: the London Naval Conference and the Conference on the Codification of International Law at The Hague, The Royal Commission on Wheat Futures, the Imperial Conference on Economic Cooperation, the Geneva Disarmament Conference, the League of Nations, and the International Commission on Commodity Prices.

In 1935 Prime Minister William Lyon McKenzie King appointed him to the Canadian High Commissioner's Office in London, first as a secretary, then as a counselor. In 1941, he returned to Ottawa as Assistant Undersecretary of State at the Department of External Affairs. He went to Washington as Canadian minister-counselor the following year and became the Canadian Ambassador three years later.

Pearson believed that the United Nations represented the world's best chance for peace, and he contributed to its planning stage with the Food and Agriculture Organization (FAO) and the United Nations Relief and Rehabilitation Administration (UNRRA). He was senior adviser to the Canadian delegation at San Francisco in 1945 when the UN was launched. During the next 11 General Assemblies Pearson was a potent force in balancing the influence exerted by the United States and the United Kingdom through his participation in the UN's most important committee handling political and security questions. He was elected president of the General Assembly in 1952, also the year he presided over the North Atlantic Treaty Organization Council in Lisbon.

While Secretary of State for External Affairs, Pearson shared responsibility for the partition of Palestine in 1947. He played a major part in the Korean truce of 1953.

On April 22, 1963, Pearson was sworn in as the fourteenth Prime Minister of Canada. The *New York Times* described his five-year administration as "impressive," even though his Liberal Party was a few seats short of a majority. He brought in a national pension plan and a family assistance program. He broadened old-age security benefits, laid the foundations for the present national Free Medical Service, and inaugurated a massive study of French-English bilingualism and biculturism.

Pearson accumulated many awards and honors during his long service to his country and to the world. He was made an officer of the Order of the British Empire in 1935, and was admitted to the Privy Council of Canada in 1948. The government of Israel awarded him its Medallion of Valor. He held more than 20 honorary LL.D degrees, from universities in Canada, the United States, the United Kingdom and other countries. Pearson wrote two books, *Democracy in World Politics* (1955) and *Diplomacy in the Nuclear Age* (1959).

On August 22, 1925, he married Maryon Elspeth Moody. They had a son, Geoffrey Arthur Holland and a daughter, Patricia Lillian Hannah.

Lester Bowles Pearson died on December 27, 1972, in his home near Ottawa, Canada.

Bibliography

New York Times Biographical Edition 1972 Lester Pearson dies at 72. 3 (July-December)
Time 1963 A new leader. 81 (April 19)

RUTH C. REYNOLDS

Dominique Pire
(1958)

The Nobel Committee awarded the Peace Prize for 1958 to Father Dominique Pire for his tireless efforts to help refugees to leave their camps and return to a life of freedom and dignity. "Father Pire's work is known to all of us in Western Europe," the Committee said. "We have read of this man who, on his own initiative, has set himself the task of rescuing the handicapped refugees, the 'Hard Core,' the residue. These are the old and infirm who remained in the camps, doomed to stay there without hope of a brighter future, men for whom our hard, ruthless world . . . has had no further use."

Father Pire was guided by the principle that "each refugee is a being of infinite worth, who deserves all our attention, all our love, whatever his nationality, his religion, his learning, his moral misery." He was imbued "with the certainty of the deep unity of the human race. Newton said, 'Men build too many walls and not enough bridges.'" Pire claimed to be nothing more than "a man looking at his brothers and trying hard to get men to look at *their* brothers."

Pire had an early acquaintance with the inhumanity of war. During the First World War, he saw his grandfather shot by the Germans, and the four-and-a-half year old boy fled with his family to France. They returned four years later to find their home in ruins.

When Pire was 18 he entered the Dominican monastery of LaSarte in Huy, a small town in Belgium. There he began studies which would take him to the Dominican University in Rome. He gained a Doctorate of Sacred Theology eight years later. He returned to the monastery in Huy to teach, and there he remained all his life. He also served as curé to the impoverished agricultural laborers of LaSarte.

After the Second World War, in addition to these duties, Father Pire began setting up camps for Belgian and French refugee children. On one fateful day in 1949 he heard a US United Nations Relief and Rehabilitation Administration (UNRRA) official describing the plight of Europe's displaced refugees. "It was such a heartbreak," recalled Pire, "that it suddenly seemed to me that there was nothing I could do—except do everything I could to remedy all that." He began to act that evening, writing to the 47 names the UN official had given him when Pire asked what he might do. He visited displaced persons (DPS) camps. He learned that of the eight million DPS stranded by the war there remained 150,000 refugees whom no country would have. He witnessed their squalid, unhygienic surroundings and lack of privacy. He saw men who no longer hoped for work, women who had lost their dream of a home. "They were people who had been sitting for twelve years on their suitcases in a railway station, waiting for a train that would never come." Pire said.

Father Pire tried to obtain information about the refugees which would lead him to their former friends. He hoped to assist in reestablishing contact with them and to help the refugees to find new friends willing to start a sustained relationship, usually through letters. From this came a "sponsoring" movement which in nine years, by the time of Pire's Nobel award, had grown to 18,000 persons, each "sponsoring" families of refugees with Pire's simple formula of a little time, some packages and money, and much love.

He began a bimonthly newspaper, named "*Hard Core,*" in poignant salute to the refugees' plight. He delivered hundreds of lectures, in person, on radio, and on television, to raise funding. With the money he began to help refugees leave the camps. First, he attended to the problem of the old people. In four years he founded four homes for elderly refugees. There they were encouraged to call on forgotten skills like sewing and embroidering, to earn the sweet taste of independence through the sale of the fruits of their labor. Once forgotten and helpless, now they could look forward to care for the rest of their waning lifetimes. One woman wrote to Father Pire, "I feel that spiritual values are the most important things in our earthly lives, and that without them life itself is so full of sadness that it is scarcely worth living . . . . Thank you for comforting me and for having made the last years of my life the best. I face the end . . . with serenity."

Father Pire found that the displaced "suffer from a 'rusting of the soul,' from a total uprooting, not only from their own countries, but from the society of men." Material help alone offered no cure for their malady. Pire's answer was to build "European villages," groups of about 20 houses near a city. Not in the city, where they could turn into ghettos, but "a neighborhood glued onto a city." The first of these villages was constructed in 1956 at Aachen (Aix-la-Chapelle) in the Federal Republic of Germany. There its 200 residents, rescued from their encampments, could set up housekeeping in family units. Father Pire believed that people must again know the pride of a clean home with curtains at the window, and be able again to look with hope toward earning their livelihood, before the "weight of the odor and noise" of the DP camps would fall away.

The year after receiving the Nobel Prize, Father Pire widened his crusade with an association called "Open Heart to the World." It included a University of Peace established at Huy where people of all opinions and conceptions could join together to engage in dialogue. Its sessions throughout the year, ranging from two days to two weeks, welcomed anyone interested in pursuing the subject of peace.

In 1960 Father Pire began a project of an "Island of Peace" in East Pakistan, where, in Moslem terrain, a team trained in tropical medicine and agronomy began a program designed eventually to establish a self-sufficient community. Forty thousand inhabitants developed an agricultural settlement there, based on the plan that with the end of the training project the entire program would be turned over to the initiative of the local inhabitants. A second peace island was opened in Kalakaddu, Madras, India, in the early 1960s.

Father Pire's work became formalized into a master organization, known as "Aid to Displaced Persons and European Villages." It has self-governing national sections in the Federal Republic of Germany, Austria, Belgium, France, Luxembourg, and Switzerland. There are national secretariats in Denmark, Italy, and the Netherlands. Because the work is supported by private contributions "from the hearts of men," the movement became popularly called "Europe of the Heart."

As Pire expanded his work to an international scope the programs remained rooted in his initial projects. World Friendships is an agency that encourages fraternal dialogue carried on through correspondence by people of different heritages; in 1958 it had about 6,500 participants. World Sponsorships administrates material help from people on a person-to-family basis, emphasizing education of children; it has about 400 enrolled "godparents." More and more displaced persons were rescued from their lives in the camps as the village project progressed; over a thousand refugees began renewed lives in seven villages throughout Europe.

In his Nobel address Pire shared the experiences of many of the refugees who had corresponded with him. Like Anne Frank, whose portrait hung in his office to keep before him an example of courage, Father Pire practiced sharing the riches of the heart. He told his audience that Aid to Displaced Persons is a means for the individual to act toward peace. While the common citizen feels he has little say in the great political questions, "he has every say and every opportunity to put words into practice on the Displaced Persons problem." And this can start a potent path toward peace. What one man cannot do alone, the love of many may achieve. Father Pire believed that no surer road to peace exists than the one that starts from little islands and oases of genuine kindness, constantly growing in number and being continually joined together "until one day they will ring the world."

When he accepted the Nobel Peace Prize Father Pire had made a pledge: "I should like to use the moral credit of the Nobel Peace Prize in such a way that when I die this credit will return to you, not only whole and intact, but increased, augmented by the way in which I have used it, so that later on, your successors will be able to offer in the Nobel Peace Prize even greater moral credit, because your 1958 laureate has borne it well." His pledge is fulfilled; his words now stand as a memorial.

Biography

Dominique Georges Henri Pire was born in Dinant, Belgium, on February 10, 1910. He was the son of a civic official, Georges Pire. At the age of 18 he entered the Dominican monastery of LaSarte in Huy, Belgium, and took the name Henri Dominique. He took his final vows on September 23, 1932. He continued his studies in the Dominican University in Rome, was ordained in 1934, and received his doctorate in theology in 1936. After studying the social sciences for a year at the University of Louvain (Leuven), Belgium, he returned to the Huy monastery to teach sociology and moral philosophy.

In 1938 he began his long service to the unfortunate by founding the Mutual Family Aid Service and the Open Air Camps for children. During and after the Second World War the stations were more than just camps, they were missions feeding thousands of Belgian and French children. During the war the Reverend Father Pire was a chaplain to the resistance movement, an agent for the intelligence service, and a participant in the underground escape system for downed Allied flyers. For his efforts he was awarded the Military Cross with Palms, the Resistance Medal with Crossed Swords, the War Medal, and the National Recognition Medal.

In addition to his duties as curé of LaSarte, Father Pire decided early in 1949 to study the refugee problem. He visited refugees in Austria, wrote *Du Rhin au Danube avec 60,000 D.P.*, and founded the Aid to Displaced Persons organization. Pire approached his work with refugees on three different levels. He found 18,000 Europeans to sponsor refugee families by sending them letters of encouragement and parcels with needed supplies. He established four homes for aged refugees. Recognizing that the younger refugees needed to have a home, the opportunity to gain economic independence, and circumstances amenable to achieving psychological wholeness, he conceived the idea of building small villages for refugees on the outskirts of cities. He constructed seven of these villages through private donations.

In 1957 the Aid to Displaced Persons organization became the Aid to Displaced Persons and European Villages, an international charitable association, with self-governing bodies in 10 European states.

After receiving the Nobel Peace Prize in 1958, Father Pire established The Heart Open to the World. This organization now sponsors the University of Peace at Huy, World Friendships, World Sponsorships, and Islands of Peace.

Throughout his 32 years of service promoting the dignity and brotherhood of humanity, Father Pire lived simply in the Huy monastery. He died at the age of 58 in the Louvain (Leuven) Roman Catholic Hospital on January 30, 1969.

Bibliography ————————

America 1958 Nobel Prize winner. 100 (November 22)
America 1963 Pere Pire's peace corps. 109 (October 5)
New York Times 1969 Dominique Pire is dead at 58; Priest won Nobel Peace Prize, January 31
Time 1958 Belgium "open on the world." 72 (November 24)

RUTH C. REYNOLDS

Philip J. Noel-Baker
(1959)

The 1959 Nobel Prize for Peace was awarded to Philip John Noel-Baker for a lifetime of support to the League of Nations and the United Nations, and in recognition of his sustained and tireless efforts dedicated to disarmament. "I do not think it an exaggeration to say that he has had some share in practically all the work that has been carried out to promote international understanding in its widest sense," the chairman of the Nobel award committee, Gunnar Jahn, said. "The dark years of this century in Europe started in 1914 and they are still with us. Throughout this span of time, for forty-five years, Philip John Noel-Baker has dedicated his efforts to the service of suffering humanity, whether in time of war or in the intervals between wars. But above all else, his efforts to prevent war breaking out have been tireless and ceaseless."

Noel-Baker was born in 1889 into a family of a long line of Quakers, and he grew up under the influence of parents who worked selflessly in behalf of London's poor. His father, Joseph Allen Baker, was a Member of Parliament between 1900 and 1918, and worked indefatigably to forge links between peace efforts throughout the world. Noel-Baker honored the example set by his father and his Quaker heritage through a lifetime devoted to study, teaching, writing, legislating, and organizing for peace.

His schooling began at a Quaker school in York, continuing at Haverford College in Pennsylvania, and from 1908 to 1912 at Cambridge University. There he took honors in history and in economics at King's College in 1910 and 1912 respectively. In 1911 and 1913 he was named the Whewell Scholar in International Law. Following his completion of a degree in international law, he continued his studies at the Sorbonne and in Munich during the year preceding the First World War. He mastered six languages—German, Greek, French, Italian, Norwegian, and Spanish.

It was Chairman Jahn's opinion that Noel-Baker's academic discipline can be observed throughout his lifetime's work: "In all he has said and written, he has never succumbed to the temptation of making a statement that was not well-founded on meticulous documentation."

In 1914 Noel-Baker accepted the post of vice-principal of Ruskin College at Oxford, but when the First World War broke out, as a Quaker he served in the ambulance corps on the Belgian, French, and Italian fronts, receiving several decorations. At the close of the war he immediately turned his efforts to the cause of peace, serving as principal assistant to Lord Robert Cecil (Peace Prize Winner of 1937) on the committee which drafted the League of Nations Covenant at the Peace Conference in Paris. In 1920, he began his work as adviser to Fridtjof Nansen in Nansen's tremendous humanitarian work throughout the world in the wake of the First World War, and later in the League of Nations. But his principal efforts in the early 1920s were as a member of the Secretariat of the League and principal assistant to the League. From 1922 to 1924 he was private secretary to the British representative on the League's Council and Assembly, after which returned to England to become first Cassell Professor of International Relations at the University of London.

He entered politics in 1929 and was elected as Labour Member of Parliament for Coventry. He was a member of Britain's delegation to the 1929-30 sessions of the League of Nations Assembly, and served from 1929 to 1931 as parliamentary private secretary to Foreign Secretary Arthur Henderson (Peace Prize winner of 1934) who chaired the Disarmament Conference.

Subsequently, representing Derby and Derby South, Noel-Baker was elected to the National Executive Committee of the Labour Party in 1937. In 1942 he accepted a post in Churchill's wartime government, and in 1945, when Attlee came to power, served in a number of ministerial posts. But his work as a member of the British government covered a great deal more: it was Noel-Baker who directed negotiations with India, Ireland, and Newfoundland, and Chairman Jahn credited him with a large role in the successful issue of negotiations with India on the question of independence.

He was in charge of British preparatory work for the United Nations. Bringing his wealth of experience from the League of Nations, he exerted considerable influence, laying groundwork for various sections of the United Nations such as the Food and Agriculture Organization (FAO) and the International Refugee Organization (IRO). He supported the regulation of traffic in arms, atomic control, economic aid for refugees, and the reintroduction of the Nansen "passport." Noel-Baker participated actively in the work of the United Nations Relief and Rehabilitation Administration (UNRRA), and represented the United Kingdom in the World Health Organization (WHO) and the UN Economic and Social Council.

He was a prolific writer. Chairman Jahn praised Noel-Baker's books for their timeless value: "All that Noel-Baker has written reflects his tremendous depth of knowledge, and the soundness, shrewdness, and eminent common sense of his views give his books a value far beyond the age in which they were written."

Jahn called Philip Noel-Baker "the man who possesses the greatest store of knowledge on the subject of disarmament and who best knows the difficulties involved." His book *The Arms Race—A Programme for World Disarmament* summarized a lifetime of research and experience. All the attempts made to reach agreement on disarmament since the First World War were traced, and Noel-Baker described the repeated efforts to find an acceptable system of control. He believed that up to 1955, the Soviet attitude was responsible for the lack of success in this area, but he was particularly critical about what he calls the "Western volte face" of May 10, 1955, when the Western powers, under the leadership of US Secretary of State Harold Stassen, backed away from agreement after the Soviet Union had fully accepted the Western disarmament proposals, including inspection. What Noel-Baker calls "a moment of hope" slipped away, never to be regained.

In his Nobel lecture Noel-Baker pleaded for disarmament as the supreme issue standing before the international community. He ruled out "limited war" as now obsolete. "Some people honestly believe that small steps will be easier to take than large ones," he said. "I prefer the words of John Stuart Mill: 'Against a great evil, a small remedy does not produce a small result; it produces no result at all.'"

Noel-Baker thought the greatest danger facing humanity to be the incredibly fatalistic apathy of people. He asserted that governments, general staffs, and peoples simply have not grasped what modern armaments mean—the very employment of the word "defense" to describe modern military preparations is an extreme example of a language which no longer serves reality. "For every nation disarmament is the safest and most practicable system of defense," he declared.

In his definitive *The Arms Race*, Noel-Baker wrote, "No one who has closely followed disarmament negotiations since 1919 is likely to be guilty of facile optimism about the prospect of peace. But no one who understands the present arms race should be guilty of facile pessimism, which is by far the graver fault. Defeatism about the feasibility of plans for disarmament and ordered peace has been the most calamitous of all the errors made by democratic governments in modern times."

Biography

Noel-Baker was born Philip John Baker in England on November 1, 1889, son of Joseph Allan Baker and Elizabeth Moscrip, descendants from a long line of Quakers. (Noel-Baker took his wife's surname, Noel, in combination with his own.) His father, a humanitarian and pacifist, held a seat on the London County Council from 1895 to 1907 and in the House of Commons from 1905 to 1918. Noel-Baker followed in the Quaker tradition, striving to help his fellows without regard to race or creed, and labored to build a world without violence or war.

He began his college studies at Haverford College in Pennsylvania, and continued at Cambridge from 1908 to 1912. There he took honors in history and economics tripos in 1910 and 1912 respectively. In 1911 and 1913 he was named the Whewell Scholar in International Law. Following his completion of a degree in international law at Cambridge, he studied at the Sorbonne and in Munich.

At the outbreak of the First World War, Noel-Baker was vice-principal of Ruskin College, Oxford, but he subsequently served in the ambulance corps on the Western Front.

Noel-Baker not only excelled in his academic studies, but also starred as an athlete, becoming president of the athletic club at Cambridge and running in the 1912 Stockholm Olympics. This was an interest he followed intermittently for many years; he won the silver medal in the 1500 meter run in the 1920 games at Antwerp and captained the British track team that year and in the 1924 games at Paris.

From 1920 to 1922 he was a member of the League of Nations Secretariat. In 1920 he also began assisting Fridtjof Nansen as an adviser, first in Nansen's humanitarian work in alleviating the suffering following in the wake of war, and later when Nansen represented Norway in the League. From 1922 to 1924 he served as private secretary to the British representative on the League's Council and assembly. From 1924 to 1929 he was the Cassell Professor of International Relations at London University. From 1929 to 1931, he was a member of the British delegation to the League's Assembly. He worked with Arthur Henderson, Chairman of the Disarmament Commission, from 1931 to 1933. He recalled his League experience and wrote of further research in *The Geneva Protocol for the Pacific Settlement of International Disputes; The League of Nations at Work; Disarmament; and Disarmament and the Coolidge Conference.*

From 1936 to 1942, Noel-Baker was a member of the Opposition in the House of Commons, but accepted the office of Joint Parliamentary Secretary to the Minister of War Transport offered by Winston Churchill in 1942. In the Attlee government in 1945 he began serving successively as Minister of State in the Foreign Office, Secretary of State for Air, Secretary of State for Commonwealth Relations, and Minister of Fuel and Power. When the Labour Party lost power he joined the shadow cabinet, becoming vice-president of the foreign affairs group in 1961 and chairman in 1964.

At the close of the Second World War Noel-Baker helped with preparatory work for the United Nations much as he had with the League of Nations. As a delegate to the Food and Agriculture Conference in Canada he helped make the FAO a viable service organization in the UN. He helped draft the UN Charter in San Francisco in 1945, and sat as a member of the British delegation in 1946. In the General Assembly he supported the International Refugee Organization (IRO) and sought regulation in arms traffic and atomic control. He helped with the reintroduction of the Nansen passport so vital to refugees without a country, and he supported financial aid for refugees.

In the 1950s Noel-Baker returned to academic life. In 1958 he published *The Arms Race: A Programme for World Disarmament*, summarizing the results of extensive research and personal experiences. It won the Albert Schweitzer Book Prize in 1961.

Noel-Baker was made a life peer in 1977 as Baron Noel-Baker of Derby, the city he represented in the Commons for many years.

Philip John Noel-Baker died on October 8, 1982.

Bibliography

Christian Century 1959 Disarmament advocate wins Peace Prize. 76(46)
Russell E 1960 Philip Noel-Baker. *Int. Relations* 2(1)

RUTH C. REYNOLDS

Albert John Lutuli
(1960)

Albert John Lutuli,[1] Zulu Chief and African patriot, the 1960 recipient of the Nobel Peace Prize, declared that the award had, for him, a threefold significance:

> On the one hand, it is a tribute to my humble contribution to efforts by democrats on both sides of the color line to find a peaceful solution to the race problem .... On the other hand, the award is a democratic declaration of solidarity with those who fight to widen the area of liberty in my part of the world .... From yet another angle, it is welcome recognition of the role played by the African people during the last fifty years to establish, peacefully, a society in which merit and not race would fix the position of the individual in the life of the nation.

Lutuli was born into a heritage of tribal leadership.

His grandfather was a chief of the Zulu tribe in Groutville; the title was passed to one of his sons. Lutuli was born around 1898 in Rhodesia. His father died when Lutuli was a young child, and Lutuli was raised in Groutville, where his devoted mother, Mtonya Gumede, saw to her young son's education, beginning at the local Congregationalist mission (primary) school. From there Lutuli progressed to a boarding school, the Ohlange Institute, and then to a teachers' training program at a Methodist institution in Edendale in 1917. After teaching there for two years he went on to complete a teachers' training course at Adams College on a scholarship. It was there that he accepted a teaching post as one of two Africans to join the staff.

Lutuli's Christian background remained a powerful force in his life, and he merged his inheritance of

Zulu culture with the ethics of European Christianity to achieve a patient, persistent stance in his struggle for the dignity of his people. A fellow Christian remarked, "To him, nonviolence is a thing of the spirit, not one simply of organized protests and demonstrations" (Blaxall 1961). A leader of immense dignity, Lutuli earned a respect which transcended political and geographic boundaries; he personified before the world the black South African's struggle to end oppression and to participate in Africa's social revolution and its entrance into the family of nations in the role of peacemaker.

For 15 years Lutuli found fulfillment as an educator, and among his subjects was the history of the Zulu people. In 1935 he was invited by the members of the Zulu community to assume the functions of Chief of the Abasemakholweni tribe. It was with some hesitation that he left the security and the tranquility of an educator's life. The salary of the Chief is paid by the state, a fact that was later to have great significance for Lutuli because this gave the state the power of dismissal. When he took over as tribal chief, Lutuli devoted much time to working with his 5,000-strong tribe, performing the judicial function of a magistrate, the mediating function of an official acting as representative of his people, and at the same time as representative of the central government. He worked toward the betterment of his people's economic status—he taught them how to improve their sugar-cane fields, for instance—and he endeavored to help them blend their Zulu culture with Christian teaching. During those years he and his wife raised and educated their seven children.

But the forces of oppression in South Africa were accelerating. "There is nothing new in South Africa's apartheid ideas," Lutuli explained, "but South Africa is unique in this: the ideas not only survive in our modern age, but are stubbornly defended, extended, and bolstered up by legislation at the time when, in the major part of the world, they are now largely historical and are either shamefacedly hidden behind concealing formulations, or are being scrapped." And the South African government participates in the oppression. "The brotherhood of man is an illegal doctrine, outlawed, banned, censured, proscribed and prohibited; . . . to work, talk or campaign for the realization in fact and deed of the brotherhood of man is hazardous, punished with banishment, or confinement without trial, or imprisonment." With white minority power resting on a heavily armed military, Lutuli said an effective democratic channel to peaceful settlement of the race problem had never, during a 300-year-relationship, existed.

In 1944, Lutuli sought such a channel through the African National Congress (ANC), an organization founded in 1912 by nonwhite Africans who had obtained a higher education. Their purpose was to use their talents toward democratic political development. Lutuli brought his customary zeal and strong leadership to the organization, and after holding lesser offices, in 1952 he was elected its president, an office he held until the Congress was banned in 1960.

At first, the ANC tried to influence political development by means of petitions and deputations to the authorities, but when their attempts were met with ever more restrictive laws, the organization took stronger action based on boycotts, defiance campaigns, and strikes. It was here that Lutuli asserted his powerful influence toward nonviolent resolution, balancing the more defiant fringe who wanted a South Africa that was an entirely nonwhite state.

"How easy it would have been in South Africa for the natural feelings of resentment at white domination to have been turned into feelings of hatred and a desire for revenge . . . ," he remarked. A black racism could have developed equal to that of their oppressors to counter the white arrogance. Lutuli asserted that it was no accident that this had not happened.

"It is because, deliberately and advisedly, we discarded the chance of an easy and expedient emotional appeal. Our vision has always been that of a nonracial, democratic South Africa which upholds the rights of all who live in our country to remain there as *full* citizens, with equal rights and responsibilities," he said.

The government ordered Lutuli to either withdraw from the Congress or give up his position as tribal chief. Lutuli refused to comply with either request, declaring to the Native Affairs Department in Pretoria that a chief, by Zulu tradition, was first of all a leader of his people and only secondarily a functionary of the government. "I only pray to the Almighty to strengthen my resolve," he said, "for the sake of the good name of our beloved country, the Union of South Africa, to make it a true democracy and a true union in form and spirit . . ." The government ordered him deposed and forbade his visiting any of the major towns or cities of the Union of South Africa for 12 months. But as a gesture of confidence in Lutuli, the ANC nonetheless elected him president-general a month later, and this position he held until the organization was outlawed in 1960.

The Nobel Committee Chairman, Gunnar Jahn, commented on this period. "It was first and foremost for the work he carried on during these years, from the 1940's to the present, that we honor him today .... If the nonwhite people of South Africa ever lift themselves from their humiliation without resorting to violence and terror, then it will be above all because of the work of Lutuli ...."

Lutuli was cruelly harassed for his activities. Repeated travel bans were imposed; in 1956, he was charged with treason and held in custody for nearly a year until the charges were dropped. Since his home exile started in 1959, visitors were reportedly barred to him, including the Nobel Prize investigators and the British Prime Minister Harold Macmillan (*Life* 1961). His travel ban was lifted for a brief 10-day period to allow him to attend the Nobel Prize award ceremony.

Lutuli was killed in an accident in July 1967 at the age of 69. He left a legacy of pioneering work toward an Africa now still visionary: "In a strife-torn world, tottering on the brink of complete destruction by man-made nuclear weapons, a free and independent Africa is in the making," Lutuli told his award audience. "Acting in concert with other nations, she is man's last hope for a mediator between the East and West, and is qualified to demand of the great powers to turn the swords into ploughshares," he declared.

"Africa's qualification for this noble task is incontestable, for her own fight has never been and is not now a fight for conquest of land, for accumulation of wealth or domination of peoples, but for the recognition and preservation of the rights of man and the establishment of a truly free world for a free people."

Biography

Albert John Lutuli (1898?-1967) was heir to a tradition of Zulu tribal leadership. His grandfather was chief of a small tribe at Groutville in the Umvoti Mission Reserve near Stanger, Natal. His father became a Christian missionary and spent most of his later years in the Matabele missions of Rhodesia. His father died when Lutuli was a small child.

His devoted mother, Mtonya Gumede, supported his education and he completed his teachers' training course in 1917. After spending two years as principal of an intermediate school he completed a Higher Teachers' Training course at Adams College, attending on a scholarship. Upon graduating he became one of two African faculty members at the college. He spent the next 15 years in education, his political activity confined to a deep interest in bettering the education available to black children. In 1927 he married a fellow teacher, Nokukhanya Bhengu. They had seven children.

After considering the call of his tribe for two years, Lutuli assumed the position of tribal chief, a position salaried by the state. He continued to display his tremendous zeal and patience as he worked for the progress and welfare of the 5,000 people in his tribe.

But the restrictions imposed by the Union of South Africa on its nonwhite population became increasingly severe. Lutuli's concern for the tribe expanded to encompass all black South Africans. In 1944 he joined the African National Congress (ANC), an organization founded in 1912 to obtain legal enfranchisement and human rights for all South Africans, inviting members of other racial groups who also believed in human brotherhood to join them in this work. In 1945 he was elected to the Committee of the Natal Province Division of the ANC, and in 1951 he became president of the division.

In 1952 he joined with other ANC leaders in organizing nonviolent activities to protest discriminatory laws. He was ordered by the South African government either to withdraw from the Congress or to relinquish his position as tribal chief. Lutuli refused to do either and was dismissed from his post as tribal chief. One month later he was elected president-general of the ANC, a position he held until the government banned the organization in 1960.

The government sought to limit his effectiveness by restricting his movement with repeated travel bans throughout his term of office. He was charged with high treason in 1956 but the charges were dropped in 1957. He was arrested in 1960 for publicly burning his travel pass after demonstrators against the Pass Law were massacred in Sharpeville. Although Lutuli had been outspoken in his stand against violence, and had advocated the peaceful enfranchisement of black South Africans, the ANC was banned after the Sharpeville incident.

The ban confining him to a radius of 15 miles from his home was lifted one final time for a 10-day period so that he and his wife might attend the Nobel Peace Prize ceremonies in Oslo.

Though the ban on Lutuli also included prohibiting his publishing any work, the continued respect accorded him throughout the world was reflected by a number of honors: the South African Colored People's Congress nominated him for president, the National Union of South African Students made him its honorary president, the students of Glasgow University voted him their rector, and the New York City Protestant Council conferred an award on him.

In July 1967, at the age of 69, Lutuli died in an accident near his home.

Notes ———————————————

1. Lutuli preferred the spelling of his name used here, although "Luthuli," a commonly used spelling, may be a closer phonetic rendering.

Bibliography ———————————

Blaxall A 1961 Honor deserved. *Christian Century* 78 (November 22)

Life 1961 A prize for a Zulu Chief. 51 (November 17)

RUTH C. REYNOLDS

Dag Hjalmar Agne Carl Hammarskjöeld
(1961)

The Nobel Committee awarded the Peace Prize for 1961 posthumously to Dag Hammarskjöld. As Secretary-General, with finesse and patience, this gifted diplomat molded the United Nations into a dynamic instrument for the realization of an organized international community. He challenged those countries which he observed clinging to outdated concepts of national sovereignty, and opened before them vistas of cooperative interchange which would transcend coexistence by balance of power and establish a lasting basis for peace.

In his final report which he wrote to the General Assembly on August 17, 1961, he deplored the philosophy of member states which advocated sovereignty with armed competition, a philosophy at total variance with the needs of a world of ever-increasing interdependence; and he outlined ways through the United Nations in which they could develop international cooperation. A month later he was killed in the line of duty. His report now stands as his last testament.

Dag Hammarskjöld worked with the same quiet strength he observed in his father: "A man of firm convictions does not ask, and does not receive, understanding from those with whom he comes into conflict. A mature man is his own judge. In the end, his only firm support is being faithful to his own convictions," Hammarskjöld said, in speaking of his father before the Swedish Academy as he took the seat left vacant there by his father's death.

Dag Hammarskjöld was the youngest of four sons born to Agnes Almquist Hammarskjöld and Hjalmar Hammarskjöld, Prime Minister of Sweden, member of the Hague Tribunal, governor of Uppland, and chairman of the Board of the Nobel Foundation. Hammarskjöld described the influence of his parents: "From generations of soldiers and government officials on my father's side I inherited a belief that no life was more satisfactory than one of selfless service to your country—or humanity. This service requires a sacrifice of all personal interests, . . . the courage to stand up unflinchingly for your convictions. From scholars and clergymen on my mother's side I inherited a belief that, in the very radical sense of the

Gospels, all men were equals as children of God."

Both at school and at the Uppsala University his career was one protracted academic triumph, C. P. Snow tells us in his *Variety of Men* (1967 p. 209): "A whole class above the rest; in fact, a whole class above anyone for years past; he was not only as clever as a man can reasonably be, but fanatically hard-working (as he stayed all his life)." During that time Hammarskjöld began the mastery of German, French, and English which reached such fluency that in later years a baffled diplomat, after listening to Hammarskjöld practicing the diplomat's art of tactful obfuscation, pronounced him "the only man alive who can be totally incomprehensible with complete fluency in four languages." He was equally capable in discoursing on poetry, from the German Hermann Hesse to the American Emily Dickinson, and on music and painting, and in later years, in indulging in sophisticated dialogue on Christian theology. He was also a competent athlete and enjoyed skiing and gymnastics.

His degrees were in economics and law, as were his early professional posts, and he devoted 31 years to Swedish financial affairs, Swedish foreign relations, and global international affairs. He served as secretary of the Bank of Sweden in 1935, and as undersecretary of the Department of Finance of the Swedish government from 1936 to 1945. From 1941 to 1948, overlapping the undersecretaryship for four years, he was placed at the head of the Bank of Sweden.

Hammarskjöld worked in the Ministry of Social Welfare with his eldest brother Bo, and gained a reputation as an international financial negotiator for his part with the United Kingdom in the postwar economic reconstruction of Europe, for his reshaping of the United States—Swedish trade agreement, for his participation in the Marshall Plan, and through his leadership on the Executive Committee of the Organization for European Economic Cooperation. It is entirely logical that his introduction to the Swedish Ministry of Foreign Affairs was by way of becoming its financial adviser. From there he became the deputy foreign minister, with cabinet rank. In foreign affairs he followed a policy of international economic cooperation.

Hammarskjöld's initial role in the United Nations was as Sweden's delegate in 1949 and again from 1951 to 1953. Following more than two years of disagreement over a successor for Trygve Lie, Hammarskjöld was elected Secretary-General in 1953, receiving 57 votes out of 60. "Ironically," the *New York Times* (1961) observed, "the big powers had selected Mr. Hammarskjöld . . . because they believed he would be content to be the efficient administrator and avoid a politically controversial role." But as he accepted the position, Hammarskjöld said he was not advocating a "passive role" for the Secretary-General, but an active one—"active as an instrument, a catalyst, an inspirer" (the *New York Times*, April 2, 1953). In Snow's words, "He was a symbol of a longing for reason in world politics—a longing felt by masses of people in small countries, and by many in great ones" (Snow 1967 p. 216).

His first major triumph came in 1955 when he made a dramatic flight to Beijing and succeeded in negotiations for the release of 15 US airmen from the People's Republic of China. But he also suffered defeats. In 1956 the United Nations did not succeed in getting representatives into Budapest after Soviet tanks crushed the Hungarian revolt. It was not for lack of typical Hammarskjöldian drive. He would work all day and into the night on occasions of stress. But after 10 UN resolutions and numerous personal efforts on Hammarskjöld's part, it became one of his disappointments that, in his own words, fell "in between the honesty of striving and the nullity of result."

During the next six years he was involved in struggles on three of the world's continents. He approached them through what he called "preventive diplomacy," and in doing so established more independence and effectiveness within the post of Secretary-General itself. In the Suez Canal crisis of 1956 he exercised his own personal brand of diplomacy with the nations involved, as well as working with many others in the UN. Hammarskjöld surprised many people by the force of his attack on Israel, the United Kingdom, and France for their invasion of Egypt following the seizure of the canal by Egypt's President Nasser. Under pressure from the United Nations and from the United States, they withdrew their forces. This was the first occasion of the use of the UN Emergency Force (UNEF)—indeed, the first international force mobilized by any international organization.

When Hammarskjöld accepted a second term he underscored his determination to maintain his office as an independent force and to act without political dictation from any state. Rolf Edberg, the Swedish Ambassador to Norway, who accepted the posthumous award to Dag Hammarskjöld, said of his compatriot, "[He] was much concerned with the awakening and fermenting continent which was to become his destiny. He once said that the next decade must belong to Africa or to the atom bomb. He firmly believed that the new countries have an important mission to fulfill in the community of nations . . . Africa was to be the great test for the philosophy he wished to see brought to life through the United Nations."

In 1959 Hammarskjöld toured 21 African lands and came away impressed by the political maturity of many of the leaders he had met. He also came away convinced that financial and economic aid on a huge scale had to be found for those countries. It was on the occasion of the UN intervention in the Congo that he incurred the full force of Soviet attacks upon his leadership. With the decision of the Security Council, for the first time the UN used armed force to intervene actively in the solution of a problem involving the termination of colonial rule. Belgium was ordered to withdraw its troops from Congo territory, and the Secretary-General was authorized in consultation with the Congo government to provide whatever military aid might prove necessary until the country's own forces were in a position to carry out their functions. The UN force was to function as a noncombatant peace force; there was to be no intervention in disputes involving internal policy. This, however, did not meet the expectations of the Congo, which had visualized the UN forces expelling the Belgian troops. The UN assumption was that Belgium would comply with the order of the Security Council and withdraw her troops from the Congo. But this Belgium failed to do. While Hammarskjöld sought to attain Belgium's peaceful compliance with its promise to leave, the Congo leader, Patrice Lumumba, appealed to Khrushchev for Soviet aid. The Soviet campaign against Hammarskjöld peaked with the angry speech of Premier Khrushchev in the Assembly. He upbraided the Secretary-General for not having used military force in support of Lumumba, and demanded that Hammarskjöld be replaced by a three-member executive representing the Western, Soviet, and neutral camps. The Congo crisis had become entangled in the East-West conflict.

The Nobel Committee's Gunnar Jahn said of this occasion, "All that occurred cannot be given here; but an examination of the available documents covering this period will establish that it was the United Nations alone that worked to realize the establishment of the Republic of the Congo as an independent nation, and that the man who above all others deserves the credit for this is Dag Hammarskjöld."

Hammarskjöld himself answered Khrushchev's demand with the calm reply that he would remain in his job as long as "they wished"—referring to the small states and middle-ranking powers. And he added: "It is not Soviet Russia or any of the Great Powers that need the vigilance and protection of the UN; it is all the others." But he was not destined to live long enough to see the crisis brought to a conclusion. On September 18, 1961, he died in an airplane accident on the way to a meeting which he hoped would bring an end to the fighting in the Congo between the Katanga troops and the UN forces.

In his diary Hammarskjöld wrote, after he had been Secretary-General for a couple of years, "In our era, the road to holiness necessarily passes through the world of action." C. P. Snow (1967 p. 214) secularized Hammarskjöld's religious idiom: "The statement has a deep meaning for many twentieth century men. In our world, can a man feel even remotely reconciled to himself unless he has tried to do what little he can in action? That is a question which has required an answer of many of us; it is a part of the condition of modern men . . . Hammarskjöld was speaking for our time: he knew it better than most."

Biography

Dag Hjalmar Agne Carl Hammarskjöld was born on July 29, 1905, in Jonkoping, Sweden, the youngest of four sons of Hjalmar L. and Agnes Almquist Hammarskjöld. He was descended from a family of statesmen and military men dating back to the Swedish knight, Peder Hammarskjöld, who was titled by Charles IX in 1610. His father was a famous jurist, a university professor, and during the First World War, Sweden's Prime Minister.

Hammarskjöld earned the Swedish equivalent of a B.A. and M.A. and a law degree from Uppsala University between 1925 and 1930. He held the post of secretary of the Swedish Government Committee on Unemployment 1930-34, for one year, 1933, concurrently with an associate professorship of political economics at the University of Stockholm, and the following year he received his degree of doctor of philosophy with a major in political economy from Uppsala. His thesis was titled *Konjunkturspridnisigen: en teoretisk och historisk undersokning* (A Theoretical and Historical Survey of Market Trends).

He served as undersecretary of the Department of Finance of the Swedish Government between 1936 and

1945. Concurrently, beginning in 1937, he joined the advisory board of the Swedish government as its counselor on the economic status and affairs of the country, holding this position until 1948. He was simultaneously chairman of the board of governors of the Bank of Sweden and member of the Board of Foreign Exchange from 1941 to 1948, having joined the latter in 1940.

Hammarskjöld was a delegate for the Swedish government in negotiations with the United States and the United Kingdom on the postwar economic reconstruction of Europe, the discussions lasting between 1944 and 1948. He entered the diplomatic service in 1946 as specialist in finance for the Swedish Foreign Office, during which time he explained the Swedish import bans to protesting US State Department officials. His ultimate base of argument was on favoring "a postwar necessity" and a "farsighted means of restoring the European economy."

Hammarskjöld participated in the organization meeting for the Marshall Plan in 1947, and served as his country's chief delegate to the Organization for European Economic Cooperation (OEEC) in 1948 and as vice-chairman of its executive committee in 1948-49. He became Assistant Foreign Minister in 1949 and predicted in January 1950 that Sweden would surmount its postwar economic deficit "in two years" and become sufficiently solvent to aid neighboring countries. He became Deputy Foreign Minister and a member of the Swedish Cabinet in 1951, and chairman of an organization comprising Scandinavian countries and the United Kingdom with the purpose of promoting economic cooperation between these countries (UNISCAN) in 1950.

Hammarskjöld began his distinguished service in the UN as Sweden's delegate in 1949 and 1951-53. He became vice-chairman of the Swedish delegation to the UN General Assembly in 1953, and the next year he headed the delegation. In April 1953 he was elected Secretary-General of the UN by a vote of 57 of the 60 member states of the General Assembly. He stated that he was not advocating a "passive role" for the Secretary-General, but an active one "as an instrument, a catalyst, and an inspirer." He was as good as his word, personally negotiating the release of US soldiers captured by the Chinese in the Korean War, and actively seeking resolution to problems of the Middle East throughout his stay in office, including the Suez Canal crisis of 1956 during which the UN's Emergency Force (UNEF) was first commissioned and used.

With his second term, which began in 1958, he expressed keen interest in Africa, touring 21 African lands in 1959. With the eruption of the crisis in the Congo, an open break between the East and West seemed imminent as the Soviet Union castigated Hammarskjöld for failing to use the United Nations Emergency Force to expel Belgian troops, while Hammarskjöld sought to attain Belgium's peaceful compliance with its promise to leave. The Soviet

Union demanded his resignation in favor of a tripartite leadership divided between East, West, and a neutral country. Hammarskjöld replied that it was not the Soviet Union, nor any of the Great Powers, which stood in need of the protection of the UN, but the smaller nations, and he would stay in his job as long as the small states and middle-ranking powers wished.

On September 17, 1961, Dag Hammarskjöld was killed in an airplane accident on the way to a meeting between the Katanga troops and the UN forces which he hoped would bring an end to the fighting in the Congo. Among his collected papers of autobiographical and introspective comments there were many references to death. In one of these he said, "The only value of a life is its content—*for others*

.... Therefore, how incredibly great is what I have been given, and how meaningless what I have to 'sacrifice.'"

Bibliography ———————————————

Hammarskjöld D 1964 *Markings*. Faber and Faber, London/Knopf, New York

New York Times 1961 Hammarskjöld greatly extended UN's scope through leadership and personal initiatives. September 19

Snow C P 1967 Dag Hammarskjöld. *Variety of Men*. Charles Scribner's Sons, New York

RUTH C. REYNOLDS

Linus Carl Pauling
(1962)

The award of the 1962 Nobel Peace Prize to Linus Pauling was in recognition that, with the opening of the atomic age, scientists had become a vital force in humankind's struggle to achieve a peaceful existence. "It is Linus Pauling's highly ethical attitude to life—the deepest driving force within him—that drew him into the fight against nuclear weapons," the Nobel Committee said, and continued, "Through his campaigning he has manifested the ethical responsibility that science, in his opinion, bears for the fate of mankind, today and in the future . . . ."

Born in 1901, the young Linus showed early signs of his intellectual gifts. It sent his father inquiring about some appropriate titles for a nine-year-old boy. "He has read all the books in sight," the bewildered parent wrote to the editor of the *Portland Oregonian*. "All the books in sight" included his father's *United States Pharacopeia* and the *Dispensatory of the United States of America*.

The following year Pauling's father died. A retired neighbor befriended the young boy and acted as a guiding spirit to a young mind bursting beyond the ordinary boundaries of boyhood. Under his neighbor's warm and watchful interest, Pauling learned Greek to supplement his Latin, and also to speak German fairly well. He delighted in independent pursuits like learning chess from the *Encyclopedia Britannica*. But his greatest joy centered on the makeshift laboratory his elderly friend provided out of discarded equipment from a nearby dental college. There Pauling indulged an early love for science.

As he grew into adolescence, Pauling's mind never fitted into conventional molds. Taking all the math-ematics and science he could in his first three-and-a-half years of high school, he left without a diploma owing to a misunderstanding regarding graduation requirements, and the following fall, at 16, he entered Oregon State College. There his education continued, individualistic in style, formidable in scope. The possibility of understanding chemical activity as a sub-molecular process excited Pauling. Years later he looked back upon that period and wrote, "I was simply enthralled by chemical phenomena, by the reactions in which substances disappear, and other substances, often with strikingly different properties, appear, and I hoped to learn more and more about this aspect of the world. It has turned out, in fact, that I have worked on this problem year after year, throughout my life."

Oregon State College gave up any thought of guiding the explosions of his mind, allowing him to take whatever courses he wished when he chose to. He was given the run of the laboratories for experiments he devised to test the validity of what he read.

The First World War had created a shortage of teachers, and in his senior year Pauling was assigned to teach the freshman chemistry class to women undergraduates. The event proved fateful for Pauling, not principally for its demonstration of his extraordinary ability, but because of his ablest student, Ava Helen Miller. Beautiful and bright, she entered his life, and soon his heart, and in just six weeks after their first meeting they were engaged. During his first year at graduate school she became his wife and thereafter his cherished partner until her death in 1981.

Following Pauling's Ph.D. *summa cum laude* at the California Institute of Technology (CIT) he studied on a Guggenheim Fellowship in Europe, where he extended his knowledge in the field of physics, fascinated with the new theory of quantum mechanics. At 26, Pauling became the youngest member on the CIT faculty. He discovered a great joy in teaching young students eager to learn. In later years, as he became a world-renowned professor, Pauling never lost this delight and continued always to teach a course in freshman chemistry.

During these early years of research his first interest was in physical chemistry. The perception and insight that would result in his classic essay *The Nature of the Chemical Bond* came to Pauling in one of those extraordinary intellectual leaps characteristic of his style. "I worked at my desk nearly all that night," Pauling recalled, "I was so full of excitement I could hardly write." In 1954 he earned the Nobel Prize in Chemistry for his "research into the nature of the chemical bond and its application to the elucidation of the structure of complex substances."

Pauling's formal studies had been centered on inorganic chemistry, but true to his individualistic style, when organic chemistry and biology came into his area of interest he set about mastering them. He acquired an encyclopedic breadth of information on proteins. With insatiable curiosity he investigated amino acids present in hemoglobin. This led him to blood cell abnormalities and his discovery that sickle-cell anemia is a hemoglobinopathy. He pioneered in the relationship between molecular abnormality and heredity, the chemical basis of mental retardation, and the mechanism of anesthesia. With their critical implications to medicine, this research brought Pauling honors from a new field: the Thomas Addis medal from the American Nephrosis Society, the John Phillips Medal for Contributions to Internal Medicine, the Rudolf Virchow Medal for Medical Research, and the Modern Medicine Award for 1963.

Pauling became a scientist of world renown. William Stuckey called Pauling an "almost extra-terrestrially brilliant scientific prophet . . . who gave the 20th century its ruling theory on how elements bond themselves into molecules, paved the way for the discovery of the form and function of DNA, . . . revealed the distortion in hemoglobin that gives sickle-cell anemia its name." Professor Jonathon Singer, a member of the National Academy of Sciences, and creator of the most accurate chemical picture of a cell membrane, remarked, "He was the most brilliant man I ever met . . . . The forty years of Paulings contribu-

tions to chemistry and medicine make up perhaps the single most profound and enlightening body of research an American, perhaps *anyone*, ever put together." The British journal *New Scientist* in 1978 ranked him with Newton, Madame Curie, and Einstein in a list of the 20 most important scientists of all time. His honors include more than 40 national and international awards and medals, and 40 honorary degrees, including the prestigious MA from Oxford.

But as the Second World War raged through its tragic five years, it was bringing Pauling ever closer to the event that would draw him from his beloved world of molecules, atoms, and subatomic particles. During that war Pauling worked on rocket fuels for the navy and developed a powder that could shoot a rocket off at high speed. Learning of an urgent need for an oxygen meter in submarines and airplanes, in one week he designed, constructed, and delivered an instrument that would warn crews when the oxygen content was dropping to the danger level. (This is still being used by doctors to measure the oxygen content of the blood during anesthesia.) With his associate, Daniel Campbell, Pauling made a synthetic plasma to replace blood. These services brought him the Presidential Medal for Merit.

With the dropping of the two atomic bombs at the war's end, suddenly science and politics formed a totally different kind of bond for Pauling to ponder. It was to change his life forever. Catalysts to his reaction were Albert Einstein and Ava Helen Pauling. Einstein said, "The atomic bomb has altered profoundly the nature of the world as we know it, and the human race consequently finds itself in a new habitat to which it must adopt its thinking . . . . There is no defense in science against the weapon which can destroy civilization. Our defense is in law and order . . . ." Ava Helen Pauling put it more succinctly: "What good will science do if the world is destroyed, Linus?" she asked.

Pauling determined to fit himself for the role of a responsible scientist—citizen. As he had once independently studied the fields of biology and medicine, he now turned his attention to international affairs. "I estimate that my independent studies in the field of international affairs are equivalent to several years of full time work," he once replied to a reporter who asked why he presumed to opinions in that field when Secretary of State Rusk did not attempt comments in biochemistry or nuclear physics.

In 1946, at Einstein's request, Pauling joined six other scientists in the Emergency Committee of Atomic Scientists. Their purpose was to inform the public of what they, as scientists, knew about the new atomic age and the unprecedented dangers it posed for humankind.

In company with Ava Helen, Pauling went on hundreds of lecture tours. "Nobel had wanted to invent a substance or a machine with such terrible power of mass destruction that war would thereby be made impossible forever," Pauling told his audiences. Nobel's wish now appeared as prophecy fulfilled. "The energy released in the explosion of this bomb was greater than that of all the explosives used in all of the wars that have taken place during the entire history of the world, including the First and Second World Wars," he said.

Now that war had seemingly been rendered impossible, Pauling was working toward a world he described as "in metamorphosis from its primitive period of history, when disputes between nations were settled by war, to its period of maturity, in which war will be abolished and world law will take its place." But the hope humankind had cherished of an age of peace that would follow the war gave way to a "balance of terror" in which an escalating armaments race became the guardian of peace.

Pauling threw all his energies against the development of more terrible weapons. His aim was above all to prevent the hydrogen bomb, and he sought to do this by educating his fellow citizens about its capacity for catastrophe. "This bomb," he declared, "may have a destructive effect, a hundred, a thousand, nay ten thousand times greater than that of the bombs dropped on Hiroshima and Nagasaki." He made this warning as early as 1947, and subsequent tests with the hydrogen bomb proved the validity of his predictions.

"It is not necessary," he said, "that the social and economic systems in Russia be identical with that in the United States in order that these two great nations can be at peace with one another." The only essential requirements are mutual respect and mutual recognition that "war has finally ruled itself out as arbiter of the destiny of humanity." He wrote to both the US and the Soviet governments, throwing his prestigious weight against development of the hydrogen bomb. But the arms race had created an atmosphere that deafened the ears of the public and the centers of political power alike. It began to threaten freedom of speech, and Pauling's passport was revoked.

Both the United States and the Soviet Union created and tested hydrogen bombs, the United States in 1952, and the Soviet Union in 1953. "There does not seem to be any theoretical limit to the size of these weapons," Pauling observed, and he and Mrs. Pauling continued with their tireless crusade of education.

In July 1955, Pauling was one of the 10 signatories to the Russell-Einstein Manifesto. The Mainau Declaration, also of July 1955, included 52 Nobel Prize winners among its signatories, most of whom were scientists. Presenting themselves as scientists of different countries, different creeds, and different political persuasions, they said it was with horror that they watched science giving humankind the means to destroy itself. Acknowledging that on a temporary basis the balance of mutual fear was now acting as a deterrent, they dismissed as a dangerous delusion any hope for a permanent sense of safety within such a system. "All nations must come to the decision to renounce force as a final resort of policy. If they are not prepared to do this, they will cease to exist," the declaration read.

Pauling's knowledge of genetics provided authenticity to his estimates of the frightening toll of leukemia and bone cancer among the living children, and of the malformations possible in children yet unborn, with each atmospheric bomb test carried out.

Albert Schweitzer issued a Declaration of Conscience in Oslo on April 24, 1957. The following month Pauling wrote the Scientists Bomb-Test Appeal, which within a few months was signed by 11,021 scientists from 49 countries. The Paulings presented the Appeal to Dag Hammarskjöld, Secretary-General of the United Nations, declaring that it represented the feelings of the great majority of the scientists of the world. But the paranoia gripping the country seemed to block reception of unwelcome information. The Senate Internal Security Committee appeared able only to fear the hand of communists behind his estimated statistics. Under the threat of contempt of Congress they demanded to know who helped gather the signatures. Pauling, perceiving the vilification he himself was receiving, feared a like danger to those who had helped him and refused to answer. He openly and willingly answered all other questions. He reiterated what anyone who had known him had long ago observed: Pauling was not a man to be bound by doctrinaires and counterdoctrinaires. "Nobody tells me what to think," he said, and freely denied having ever been a communist. Senators Dodd and McCarthy had on this occasion overstepped even the bounds granted them by the paranoic fears gripping the country, and the Senate Committee dropped the proceedings.

October 10, 1963, the day of Pauling's 1962 Nobel award deferred from the previous year—an award he declared Ava Helen Pauling shared—was a time of double celebration. With a stroke of timing exquisitely tinged with justice, the Limited Test Ban Treaty became effective on the same day. It presented a powerful rebuttal to the strange reception Pauling's own country rendered the award. For the first time ever the US ambassador did not attend the December ceremony of a US Nobel Prize winner. The press stood divided: "A Weird Insult from Norway," headlined *Life* magazine, while the prestigious *Bulletin of Atomic Scientists* editorialized to its small but informed readership its pleasure, "as fellow Americans, that the Norwegian Parliament has now given this special recognition to his role as scientist-citizen." Pauling gave a calm reception to criticism. "New views have always been greeted as heretic," he once reminded a reporter.

Characteristically, Pauling recommends seeking information. "We must have research for peace," he contends in his book *No More War!*, "It would embrace the outstanding problems of morality. The time has come for man's intellect, his scientific method, to win over the immoral brutality and irrationality of war and militarism .... Now we are forced to eliminate from the world forever this vestige of prehistoric barbarism, this curse to the human race."

Pauling still divides his time between his scientific pursuits and peace. Much of his research is in maximizing human health. But in his work for peace he battles the greatest health hazard of all.

At his Nobel award ceremony the Committee Chairman paid tribute to Pauling's legacy to human kind: "Should he, through his tireless efforts, have contributed—if only a little—to restoring to science its ideals, then Linus Pauling's campaign will in itself have been of such value that we living today cannot even appreciate the full extent of the debt we owe him."

Biography

Linus Carl Pauling was born in 1901 in Portland, Oregon, son of Herman William Pauling, a pharmacist, and Lucy Isabelle Darling Pauling. After primary and secondary schools in Condon and Portland, he attended Oregon Agriculture College (now Oregon State University). Receiving a BS in chemical engineering in 1922, he then went to California Institute of Technology (CIT), where he studied chemistry, physics, and mathematics, taking a PH.D. *summa cum laude* in 1925. He married Ava Helen Miller in 1923. Following his doctorate he went to Europe on a Guggenheim Fellowship to study quantum physics. In 1927, he returned to CIT, where he became the youngest member on the faculty. During the 1930s and 1940s his development leading to his classic work, *The Nature of the Chemical*

Bond, was responsible for the valence-bond theory's dominance of chemistry.

Pauling's interest in, and mastery of, biological sciences led to study of the hemoglobin molecule, and from there to an encyclopedic knowledge of proteins. His interest was attracted to serology through Karl Landsteiner, the discoverer of blood types. First he worked on problems of immunology, but shifted his attention during the Second World War to practical applications, which resulted in his finding an artificial substitute for blood serum. He went on to invent an oxygen detector, first used for military application, but eventually a permanent tool for anesthesiologists. He also developed a powder that could shoot a rocket off at high speed, and for these services he was awarded the Presidential Medal of Merit.

After the war, Pauling became interested in sickle cell anemia, and he discovered that hemoglobinopathy was caused by a single amino-acid anomaly in one of the polypeptide chains. While at Oxford as a guest professor in 1948, he discovered the alpha helix.

In 1954 he received the Nobel Prize for Chemistry for his research into the nature of the chemical bond and its applications to the elucidation of the structure of complex substances.

With the coming of the atomic age, and the resulting arms race, Pauling became increasingly disturbed about the fallout resulting from nuclear bomb testing. In 1958 Ava Helen and Linus Pauling organized an anti-bomb-test petition signed by over 11,000 scientists around the world, and they presented this to Dag Hammarskjöld, Secretary-General of the United Nations. Pauling was then called before the Senate Internal Security Commission to account for the signatures collected. He willingly answered all questions regarding himself, but refused to divulge the names of others involved.

Also in 1958, the first edition of his book *No More War!* was published. He and his wife gave hundreds of lectures, wrote papers and letters, and attended conferences to strengthen the peace movement over the world. For this activity Pauling was awarded the deferred 1962 Nobel Peace Prize on October 10, 1963, the same day as the Limited Test Ban Treaty between the United States and the Soviet Union entered into force.

Pauling left CIT to go to the Center for Study of Democratic Institutions, where he continued his double activities in science and peace. In the former discipline his close-packed spheron theory provided an explanation of nuclear properties, including asymmetric fission.

In 1967 Pauling became research professor of chemistry at the University of California in San Diego, where he researched the molecular basis of memory and published a paper on orthomolecular psychiatry. He spent the early 1970s at Stanford University, and in 1973 founded the

Linus Pauling Institute in Palo Alto. Pauling's interest has since centered on nutrition, and particularly vitamin C. In 1970 he published the controversial *Vitamin C and the Common Cold*, and with Ewan Cameron, *Cancer and Vitamin C*. He has published over 500 scientific papers on molecules, hemoglobin, protein, immunology, anesthesiology, sickle cell anemia, and human nutrition.

His honors included more than 40 national and international awards and medals, and 40 honorary degrees (including a diploma from his high school and an M.A. from Oxford).

Dr. and Mrs. Pauling's four children are Linus, Jr., a psychiatrist practicing in Hawaii, Peter, a chemist at the University of London, Linda, a graduate of Reed College, who is married to Barclay Kamb, professor of geophysics at the California Institute of Technology, and Crelin, a biochemist and geneticist at the University of California at Riverside.

Linus Pauling died in 1994.

Acknowledgment: The author thanks Dr. Robert Paradowski, of the Rochester Institute of Technology, from whose biography of Dr. Pauling appearing in *No More War!* much material was drawn.

Bibliography ───────────────

Bendiner E 1983 The passions and perils of Pauling. *Hospital Practice* 18(4)
Bulletin of Atomic Scientists 1963 The Pauling Prize: A welcome honor from Norway. 19 (December)
Life 1963 A weird insult from Norway. 55 (October 25)
Pauling L 1963 Pauling's position [letter]. *Harpers* 227 (October)
Pauling L 1983 *No More War!* Dodd, Mead, New York
Stuckey W 1976 Plain Harold and Linus superstar. *Science Digest* August
Wasowicz L 1985 Linus Pauling: America's brilliant scientific maverick still fighting the establishment. *Ames Daily Tribune Weekender Edition* January 19

RUTH C. REYNOLDS

Red Cross
(1963)
see Henri Dunant and the Red Cross
(1901)   (1917, 1944, 1963)

Martin Luther King, Jr.
(1964)

In 1964 the Nobel Peace Prize was awarded to the American civil rights leader, the Reverend Martin Luther King, Jr. King called the award "a recognition of nonviolence as the answer to the crucial political and moral question of our time—the need for man to overcome oppression and violence without resorting to violence and oppression." He asked to share it with "those devotees of nonviolence who have moved so courageously against the ramparts of racial injustice . . . the real heroes of the freedom struggle, they are the noble people for whom I accept the Nobel Peace Prize."

King had read correctly the Nobel Committee's thinking. "It was not because he led a racial minority in their struggle for equality that Martin Luther King achieved fame," Chairman Jahn said in presenting the award . . . "King's name will endure for the way in which he has waged his struggle." Jahn observed that "Martin Luther King is the first person in the Western world to have shown us that a struggle can be waged without violence."

Martin Luther King, Jr. spent his youth in the Southern United States, the son of a Baptist minister. His father's efforts to shield his children from the humiliations of racial discrimination could not fully protect them from the community's relentless lessons in inequality. They left an indelible mark on the young Martin King.

King studied for the ministry in the North, where discrimination still existed in social practices but was not sanctioned by law, nor as pervasive as in the South. While studying at Boston he met and married Coretta Scott, a talented young music student from Alabama. After he took his doctorate degree in divinity at Boston University in 1955, the young couple returned to Montgomery, where King served as minister at the Dexter Avenue Baptist Church. They found their black community in sharp division over the issue of human rights: some cloaked their feelings in apathy; some were fearful of the personal consequences of speaking out. Even the clergy was divided, as some ministers felt their pastoral duties lay outside secular movements. In 1955, after the failure of an attempt to unite the blacks, King said, "The tragic division in the Negro community could be cured only by some divine miracle."

Later that year, "the divine miracle" began with Rosa Parks, an exhausted black woman who refused to give up her seat to a white male on an Alabama bus. Her subsequent arrest sparked the unifying protest that had been lacking. A bus boycott was started. King was elected chairman of the organization which was forming to conduct the boycott. He recalls in his book, *Stride for Freedom*, his reluctance to accept. He was beginning to question the moral rectitude of conducting a boycott when he recalled a line in Thoreau's essay *Civil Disobedience*: "We can no longer lend our cooperation to an evil system." Thoreau's words answered King's inner doubts.

King also entertained a practical doubt that the people would unite behind a boycott. The next morning when he looked out of his window and saw buses absolutely empty of Negro passengers, this doubt, too, was answered. This was the beginning of a civil rights movement that was to sweep the South. The young King (he was 26 at the time) led a boycott lasting 382 days when no blacks used the buses in Montgomery. They carpooled or walked, some as many as 12 miles a day. One black woman summarized why such a grueling regime could be followed by so many for so long: "My feet are tired," she said, "but my soul is rested" (quoted in Lipsky 1966 p. 199).

The boycott brought the first victory in civil rights for the black community. But King knew that freedom was something they would have to earn over and over again. His own life was changed: he became not only minister to the Baptist church in Alabama, but a moral leader whose pulpit expanded over the Western world. Between 1957 and 1968, King traveled over six million miles and gave over 2,500 lectures and speeches; during this time he wrote five books and numerous articles. He led the massive protest in Birmingham, Alabama, as the world gazed on through television screens or read accounts in graphically illustrated papers. The result King called "a coalition of conscience" and he wrote

his inspiring manifesto *Letter from a Birmingham Jail*. He planned drives for voter registrations and directed the nonviolent march to Washington, DC, where he delivered a masterful address, *I Have a Dream*. He talked with President Kennedy and campaigned for President Johnson. He was awarded honorary degrees, and named Man of the Year by *Time* magazine in 1963.

All this was accomplished in the midst of 20 arrests, at least four assaults, uncounted insults and threats to his life, and the personal grief he felt with the suffering of his people. It is a measure of the man that he did not dwell on this brutality and humiliation in his Nobel lecture; he spoke of it only in illustrating the practice of nonviolence, commending his people for "taking suffering upon themselves instead of inflicting it on others."

Instead, he addressed in his lecture the larger problems facing humankind worldwide; problems rooted, he said, in our "poverty of spirit which stands in glaring contrast to our scientific abundance." On this occasion King proved himself a leader not just of a section of humankind in the United States, but of humankind everywhere.

"This problem of spiritual and moral lag, which constitutes modern man's chief dilemma, expresses itself in three larger problems which grow out of man's ethical infantilism," King said. "Each of these problems, while appearing to be separate and isolated, is inextricably bound to the other. I refer to racial injustice, poverty and war."

American racial injustice he saw as only one manifestation of a wider, global problem. We are leaving colonialism behind, he said. Likewise the specter of poverty must be abolished: ". . . if man is to redeem his spiritual and moral lag, he must go all out to bridge the social and economic gulf between the haves and the have-nots of the world . . . . There is nothing new about poverty. What is new is that we have the resources to get rid of it."

King said that man's proneness to war is still a fact. "Wisdom born of experience should tell us that war is obsolete . . . but we shall not have the will, the courage and the insight to deal with such matters . . . unless we are prepared to undergo a mental and spiritual reevaluation . . . ," he warned.

Martin Luther King was assassinated in his thirty-ninth year as he was preparing to lead a peaceful protest march in sympathy with the garbage workers in Memphis, Tennessee. He left behind a legacy which merges with that of Gandhi. "Gandhi," he once said, "was probably the first person in history to lift the love of Jesus above mere interaction between individuals to a powerful and effective social force."

Biography

Martin Luther King, Jr. was born in Atlanta, Georgia, on January 15, 1929, the son of a Baptist minister. His primary and secondary schooling took place in Atlanta, where he learned bitter lessons about inequality as did all black children.

He studied for the ministry at Crozer Theological Seminary, where he won the Plafker Award as the outstanding student and the J. Lewis Crozer Fellowship for graduate studies. One of six Negroes in a class of 100, King was elected president of the class. He took his B.D. in 1951 and continued his studies at Harvard in 1952-53 and at Boston University where he took a PH.D. in the field of systematic theology in 1955. During his studies King became deeply influenced by India's Gandhi. He once said that from his Christian background he gained his ideals, and from Gandhi his operational techniques.

During this time, he met and married Coretta Scott, a music student studying in Boston. In 1954 they returned to Montgomery where he took a post as pastor while finishing his doctoral dissertation. King observed with regret that the black community seemed hopelessly divided on issues of human rights, many seemingly ground to an apparent helplessness by continual and brutal oppression.

All this changed when a tired black woman, Rosa Parks, refused to relinquish her seat to a white man on a Montgomery bus. Her arrest ignited a vital spark in the black community, and united, they arose to the occasion with a 382-day boycott of Montgomery buses. King accepted leadership of the Montgomery Improvement Association, the organization administering the boycott.

King's deep Gandhian convictions on the efficacy of nonviolence met and passed severe tests as his home was bombed and he and the community were harassed. Out of the victory of the boycott there grew a resistance movement throughout the South which coalesced in the Southern Christian Leadership Conference in 1957. King became its president. His pastorate was expanded over the entire South, and his voice heard over the world as he traveled nearly 800,000 miles and made 208 speeches that year.

King inspired nonviolent civil disobedience, and he led protest marches before the eyes of the world via television and wide media coverage as the marchers were set upon by dogs, water hoses, and arresting police. From his own arrest and incarceration following the Birmingham March came King's classic statement on the struggle for civil rights, *Letter from a Birmingham Jail.*

The march on Washington in behalf of the civil rights bill pending in the US Congress was followed by a partial victory in Congress of a bill King described as going far toward solving problems, but "not far enough." This march will be forever commemorated by King's famous "I Have a Dream" speech.

By 1964 when King's endorsement supported the election of President Johnson, many honors had come to him: He had received honorary doctorate degrees from Chicago Theological Seminary, Morgan State College, Central State College, Boston University, Howard University, Lincoln University, University of Bridgeport, Bard College, Keuka College, Springfield College, Wesleyan University, Yale University, and the Jewish Theological Seminary. He had been honored by Willy Brandt, by Lutheran Bishop Dibelius, and by an audience with Pope Paul VI.

King led a massive voter registration effort, and he continued to lead protest marches. His assassination on April 4, 1968, was on the eve of just such a march scheduled to take place in Memphis, Tennessee.

Martin Luther King, Jr. left four children, a grieving widow, and a world deprived of a vitally needed leader.

See also: *Articles: Nonviolence*

Bibliography

King M Jr. 1965 Toward brighter tomorrows. *Ebony* 20 (March)

Lipsky M 1966 *The Quest for Peace.* Barnes and Co., South Brunswick

RUTH C. REYNOLDS

United Nations Children's Fund (UNICEF) (1965)

The Nobel Peace Prize for 1965 was awarded to the United Nations Children's Fund (UNICEF) in recognition of its promotion of community among nations. UNICEF's Zena Harman, chairwoman of its executive board, said she thought Alfred Nobel would have approved of the choice of this award. She asserted that today's children are a central factor in the strategy for peace and survival.

The accomplishments of UNICEF over the two decades preceding its award earned it a worldwide acceptance of the Nobel Committee's decision. But its initial acceptance was far from unquestioned.

Originally UNICEF was envisaged as purely a temporary measure to solve the postwar crises facing Europe's many helpless children. Nobel Committee Chairwoman Lionaes recalled her experiences as a Norwegian delegate to the UN where many delegates maintained that the UN, as a political forum, was not justified in dealing with such a "minor" peripheral problem as aid to children. "It was a blessing for UNICEF and the millions of children it took to its heart from that very first day of its existence that it had a leader like Mr. Maurice Pate," she said. Pate served from its founding in 1946 until his death in 1965. "He was UNICEF's never slumbering conscience," Lionaes recalled, ". . . he never allowed formalities to impede him in his work . . . he recruited his fellow-workers from among those who were prepared uncompromisingly to pursue the policy of compassion."

When UNICEF tackled its first assignment of aiding the children of war-torn Europe it found children in that bitter winter of 1947 undernourished, ill, many homeless, and clothed only in rags. UNICEF calculated the number of such children at 20 million and mounted an unprecedented relief campaign, furnishing six million children and mothers with a meal a day.

As the economic reconstruction of Europe proceeded, within four or five years its countries were able to resume care of their own children. But it quickly became apparent that there were millions of children in the newly developing countries of Asia, Africa, and Latin America who were sick, starving, and dying. Harman described their plight: "abandoned in the backwash of history, left behind in the surge of time." By 1950 these helpless victims had forced the UN General Assembly to the recognition that UNICEF could no longer be considered an emergency measure; it would be a permanent necessity for many decades.

The task facing UNICEF was overwhelming. Priorities had to be established. Malnutrition reigned over much of these countries; in its wake diseases such as malaria, trachoma, tuberculosis, and yaws carried off the weakened children. Ignorance threatened to lock future generations of children in the same tragic cycle unless an educated generation were created to free them. Although need has always been in sad excess over the means to meet it, with the help of the World Health Organization (WHO), the Food and Agriculture Organization (FAO) and the United Nations Educational, Scientific, and Cultural Organization (UNESCO), UNICEF began a patient, ongoing, dedicated inroad into these problems. But even these combined UN organizations could never have done this work on their own, nor would it have been

appropriate for them to try to do so. They worked in countries whose governments solicited their aid, making contributions not less than that of UNICEF itself. While the aid given usually consisted of technical assistance, goods, and equipment which had to be purchased with foreign currency, the receiving country made its contribution in the form of its own products, local personnel, transport services, or however it could. The interest generated by UNICEF's program for children became so great that the contribution of governments comprised two and one-half dollars for every UNICEF dollar. Thus the very aid itself acted as a successful spur to self-help.

Long-range projects were launched for encouraging the production of foodstuffs rich in protein by creating dairies, and building factories to produce dried milk, by building industries to process fish-meal, all in preparation for the time when regions could take over the balanced feeding of their own children.

Indonesia exemplifies UNICEF's successful eradication of a painful and widely spread disease. Yaws attacked an estimated ten million throughout that land when it gained independence in 1950. Together with the World Health Organization, UNICEF succeeded in liberating whole villages from this scourge; and Harman stated with confidence that in a few years time the eradication of yaws would be complete in Indonesia.

Harman related an example in Mexico where UNICEF together with other organization in the UN helped the people to help themselves; they called on 2,800 men who, on foot, on horseback, and in motorboats, traversed the length and breadth of the country disinfecting three million houses with DDT in the course of 1960 alone. Not a single death due to malaria was reported that year. Agricultural production also rose.

In 1961 an important shift in policy occurred. It became apparent that despite all the assistance UNICEF and other UN organizations had provided, the statistical need kept apace, indeed leapt ahead. For due to the resulting rise in population growth, without solutions made at the base root of problems, real achievement would continue to elude them.

A growing interest in developing countries for intelligent planning in their economies reflected their grasp of the problem. "And yet," Harman reflected in her Nobel lecture, "maybe these words of Nehru contain a dangerous truth: 'In one way or another in all our thinking on development plans for factory plant and machinery, we lose sight of the fact that, in the last resort, development depends on the human factor.' It is this fundamental viewpoint that prompts UNICEF's efforts to ensure that the interests of the children are safeguarded in the development plans now being drawn up." These plans included both the education of the children themselves and the education of the adults in local training programs.

"UNICEF aid comes marvelously alive in the field," Executive Director H. Labouisse said, "when you see a whole pilot region raising its standards simultaneously in education, nutrition, sanitation and health, with everyone lending a hand, from the local teachers and doctors to the poorest families of the jungle villages." Labouisse outlined the broad plans for use of the Nobel Prize. UNICEF would establish a fund for the training of personnel in fields serving children in the developing countries. It hoped to train specialists, leaders for the future.

The statistics representing the first 25 years of UNICEF activity are impressive: 71 million children were examined for trachoma and 43 million were treated; 425 million were examined for yaws and 23 million were treated; 400 million were vaccinated against tuberculosis; countless millions were protected from malaria, and 415,000 were discharged as cured of leprosy. Supplementary materials and articles of clothing have been dispensed in billions— quite apart from emergency aid to hundreds of thousands of victims of floods, earthquakes, and other natural disasters.

In the training program, 12,000 health centers and several thousand maternity wards have been established in 85 countries; help has been given for providing equipment for 25,000 teacher-training schools, 56,000 primary and secondary schools, 965 vocational schools, 31 schools for training vocational instructors, 600 schools for training dietary personnel; equipment has been supplied for 4,000 nutrition centers and community gardens, and for 9,000 school gardens and canteens.

Nobel Chairwoman Lionaes told the award audience that in the long-term view no economic development is possible unless the growth of a healthy and enlightened generation of children is given priority in the plans for development. "Today the people of the developing countries are fully alive to their own misery; and they are determined to leave it behind," she said. "They contemplate the riches of the West—our surplus food, our fantastic technology, the health . . . all our material well-being—they compare this with

the misery of their own children." This contrast creates a dangerous tension-factor, which threatens the peace of the world.

"The aim of UNICEF is to spread a table, decked with all the good things that Nature provides, for all the children of the world. For this reason the organization is a peace-factor of great importance."

History

UNICEF was established by the United Nations General Assembly on December 11, 1946, as an emergency measure for rendering aid to postwar children following the Second World War, and it originally used the phrase "Emergency Funds" in its title. Its first aid went principally to war-torn Europe, providing food, clothing, and health care for children. It clothed five million children, vaccinated eight million against tuberculosis, rebuilt food facilities, and fed millions of children.

In 1951 UNICEF was recognized as a permanent organization and dropped the "Emergency" from both name and plans for the future, dedicating itself to long-range projects eradicating disease, educating and assisting local peoples to achieve as much of this as possible. It equipped for, and educated in, the agricultural techniques for production of high protein foods.

By 1961 a firm connection had been established between the welfare of a nation, the chances for diminished tensions between nations, and the care given to children. The necessity was recognized for a generation of well-fed, well-educated children before historical bondage to the past could be broken and replaced with planning for a successful future. UNICEF accordingly increased its education and training programs.

Although the achievements of UNICEF, cooperating with other UN agencies, were impressive up to 1965, with disease diminished, malnutrition reduced, and education programs begun, the needs of millions of children continued to far outpace the means for addressing them. This was especially painful in the face of unlimited sums spent on weaponry worldwide.

Bibliography

Life 1965 Nobel Peace Prize for the Love of Children
The New Yorker 1965 The Peace Prize. November 6

RUTH C. REYNOLDS

Prize Not Awarded
(1966-67)

René Cassin
(1968)

The 1968 Nobel Peace Prize was awarded to the distinguished French jurist, René Cassin, principal author of the UN *Declaration of the Rights of Man*, in recognition of his "respect for human worth, irrespective of nationality, race, religion, sex or social position . . . for his contribution to the protection of the rights of man, as set forth in the Universal Declaration of Human Rights."

After receiving a doctorate degree in juridical, economic, and political sciences, Cassin had just begun a career as counsel in Paris when with the outbreak of the First World War he was mobilized into the infantry. This proved a turning point in his life. He sustained an abdominal wound which hampered him for the rest of his life, and which deepened his horror of war. "That war put its indelible and unmistakable stamp on me," he said in his Nobel lecture. It was not the battlefield experience, nor the suffering that followed, which so marked him. "It was the agonized perception of the lasting and wasteful consequences of war," he said.

It was characteristic of the innate fairness of this eminent jurist that he not only insisted upon compensatory aid to those wounded in the war, but that he also provided for their human dignity, designing the program to include the tools the wounded would need for their reentry into the mainstream of society—artificial limb banks, professional retraining programs, and loans for establishing small businesses.

For France's youngest war victims, the 800,000 orphans, Cassin saw to it that the nation stepped into the place of the lost parents, and these children were brought up and educated under the special protection of their country.

Cassin was not content with providing aid after the war's end. He wished to honor those sacrifices made in that long and terrible struggle that had promised to be "the war to end war." He organized the International Confederation of Disabled Veterans [Conférence Internationale des Associations des Multilés et d'Anciens Combattants (CIAMAC)] to enable veterans to participate in the creation of an international climate that would sustain peace. From 1925 to 1939 these

disabled men—ally and adversary alike—joined together to fight for peace through increased communication, understanding, and disarmament. They worked together until violence and Fascism enveloped Hitler's Germany, and the invasion of Poland cut off all hope of salvaging peace.

In the Second World War which followed, when France fell before the German onslaught, Cassin was the first civilian to join General de Gaulle's Free French government administered from London. He was appointed Secretary of the Council of Defense which laid the groundwork for the military endeavors of the Free French, and Commissioner for Justice and Public Education in the General's provisional government. He drafted all of the legal texts of his incipient government and conducted difficult negotiations with the British authorities regarding the legal status of the Free French, which culminated in the Churchill-de Gaulle accord.

At the close of the Second World War, the revelation of the murderous depravity unleashed upon an entire ethnic group, a genocide of proportions the world had never before experienced, created urgent motivation to bring about preventive measures against it ever happening again. The United Nations therefore included a Commission on Human Rights in its Charter. Mrs. Eleanor Roosevelt chaired the Commission, and Cassin paid tribute to the patience which she brought to the complex and difficult task. Cassin was vice-chairman of the Committee and it was he who drew up the Declaration.

While the United Nations Charter did mention promoting human rights, the problem facing the Commission was the total lack of any definition of these rights. The vocabulary which would be appropriate in Western cultures for such a definition—freedom, equality, cultural and economic rights—may have starkly different meanings in other cultures. A striking example was offered by Nobel Committee Chairwoman Lionaes in her presentation speech: "We [Europeans] can readily agree on what we mean by 'the woman's legal position in society,'" she said. "But how is it interpreted by the people in those parts of the world where a woman's value is equated with four camels?"

The Commission, composed in the beginning of 18 members of different nationalities and diverse occupations, took two years to formulate the first section of the Declaration of Human Rights, called "Universal Human Rights," in a version which everyone could accept at the UN General Assembly in Paris in 1948. Although this portion of the three-part Charter of Human Rights does not have a juridically obligatory character, Cassin called it "a historical event of the first magnitude . . . the first document of an ethical sort that organized humanity has ever adopted, and precisely at a time when man's power over nature became vastly increased . . . ." Also of first order importance, Cassin said, "is its universality: it applies to all human beings without any discrimination whatever . . . ."

The second and third portions of the Charter Cassin called "difficult" and "time consuming." The first difficulty concerned whether the rights of people to self-determination should be a principle of a political and essentially collective nature; and should be included with rights exercised by the individual, either separately or communally. Cassin attributed its solution to the movement toward decolonization and the libertarian principles which followed the Second World War.

The second difficulty, which included substantive provision on the obligations of the state and their respective measures of application, was debated before the UN General Assembly for 18 years. In part the slow pace was set by the arrival each year of newly independent nations, each one of which had to form an opinion. But that explanation is only partially valid, Cassin said. The most powerful cause was the desire of certain powers to put off for as long as possible the discussion of the—what he called "paradoxically quite modest"—enforcement measures voted by the Commission on Human Rights, which those powers considered encroachments on the sovereignty of the state.

In 1966, the final unanimous vote came, Cassin said, only because on the eve of the International Human Rights Year it would have been inconceivable to have prolonged the filibuster. Moreover, a heavy price had been paid. "The implementation measures . . . especially those of the Covenant concerning civil and political rights, were considerably weakened," he said.

Is there reason to be satisfied? Cassin considered the question in his Nobel lecture. He answered that the Charter provides the vehicle for safeguarding human rights, however tragically far the reality of today seems from the goal. But he observed that "ultimately, of course, the organizing of peace . . . presupposes tremendous efforts to modify through education some longstanding mental attitudes, to work toward limitation of armaments, to manifest solidarity with the hungry . . . ."

He warned, "Emotional factors and especially the sense of justice must not be left to those who pervert them to the service of hate and destruction . . . ."

"The time has come," Cassin said in conclusion, "to proclaim that, for the establishment of peace and human dignity, each of us must work and fight to the last." These words well summarize René Cassin's long and illustrious life.

Biography

René Samuel Cassin was born on October 5, 1887, in Bayonne in Southern France, son of Henri Cassin, a merchant, and his wife, Gabrielle Dreyfus Cassin. His promising legal career started in Paris following a doctorate degree in juridical, economic, and political sciences. It was interrupted by the First World War when he was mobilized into the infantry.

During the war, he sustained a wound which modified his life, hampering him physically but greatly enriching him spiritually. His experience led him to use his considerable talents in behalf of the wounded of that long and terrible conflict. He saw first to compensatory aid, and from there to the aid they needed in order to reenter the mainstream of life: from artificial limbs to career counseling and training. Moreover, under his direction France assumed responsibility for the security and education of 800,000 war orphans.

Cassin established, with fellow veterans, the International Confederation of Disabled Veterans [Conférence Internationale des Associations des Mutilés et d'Anciens Combattants (CIAMAC)], an organization whose purpose was to unite soldiers from all sides, ally and adversary together, in cooperative work toward a permanent peace. CIAMAC was sustained from 1925 until Hitler's Germany invaded Poland and began the irreversible events leading to the Second World War.

With the fall of France in the early days of that war, Cassin joined de Gaulle in the Free France government administered from London, acting as Commissioner for Justice and Education. With the liberation of France he became president of the Council of the National School of Administration [Conseil de l'École Nationale d'Administration] (1945), and 15 years later he served as president of the French National Overseas Center of Advanced Studies [Centre National des Hautes-Études de la France d'Outremer]. Also after the war, Cassin became vice-president of the Council of State, France's administrative high court (1944-60), and later head of the Constitutional Council (1960-70).

Cassin was vice-chairman, with Mrs. Eleanor Roosevelt as chairwoman, of the Commission for Human Rights in the United Nations (1946-53), and from that time on he alternated as vice-chairman or chairman until 1959. During this period, he was writing and engineering the passage of the Declaration of Human Rights, a procedure that spanned a total of 18 years and ultimately disappointed Cassin, and many others, for its lack of implementation and funding for enforcement. On five different occassions from 1946 to 1968 he served as French delegate to the Assembly of the United Nations. He was one of the founders of the United Nations Educational, Scientific, and Cultural Organization (UNESCO).

Cassin has left a rich heritage in the judiciaries of France and Europe: he served as president of the Court of Arbitration at The Hague from 1950 to 1960, and as a member of the International Institute of Human Rights in Strasbourg (1959-65) and its president (1965-68), during which time he joined the American Jewish Committee in the sponsorship of a conference which was ultimately to influence the Helsinki Declaration of 1975.

He received numerous honors and awards, and held honorary D.C.L. degrees from Oxford, Mainz, Jerusalem, and Brandeis.

Besides the *Declaration of the Rights of Man*, his publications include *Law on Contracts, Inheritance and Family, International Law and Relations, Domicile, Status of Companies in France, The Council of State, The League of Nations, The United Nations*, and *Human Rights*.

René Cassin married Simone Yzomard in 1917. She died in 1969. In 1975 he married Ghislaine Bru, whom he had met in the Free French headquarters in London in the Second World War.

He died on February 20, 1976.

See also: Articles: *International Bill of Human Rights*

Bibliography ───────────────

International Labour Review 1969 Tribute to René Cassin, Nobel Peace Prize winner. 99(2)

RUTH C. REYNOLDS

International Labour Organization (ILO)
(1969)

In his will, Alfred Nobel stated that the Peace Prize was to be awarded to the person who had done the most to promote fraternity among nations. Mrs. Aase Lionaes, Chairwoman of the Nobel Committee, said it was with this consideration in mind that the 1969 Peace Prize was awarded to the International Labour Organization (ILO). "It is the international activity of ILO through 50 years that in my opinion makes it a worthy Peace Prize winner," she said.

In his Nobel lecture, David Morse, Director-General of ILO, traced the history of that international development, ILO was conceived within the Versailles Peace Treaty ending the First World War. That war had acted as a powerful leveler between the classes. The working classes had fought and suffered side by side with the upper classes; and consequently, at the war's end, trade unions demanded that workers should participate in the discussions of the peace treaty. Moreover, the architects of the Versailles Treaty had before them the example of the Russian Revolution, and they realized that the treaty should accommodate not only peace among nations, but peace between classes as well.

The Peace Conference established an international committee which included delegates not only from governments, but also from employers and from employees. Called "tripartism," this was the most daring and the most valuable innovation of the ILO constitution. "Universal and lasting peace can be established only if it is based upon social justice," declared the preamble to the ILO's constitution.

The preceding decades had brought profound economic and social change in Europe; industrialization in particular had led to an unprecedented growth of the economic power of European nations and to fierce competition between them, a competition ultimately contributing to the outbreak of war. Similarly, industrialization had led to the emergence of a large industrial working class which was often in open conflict with the established order. Alfred Nobel himself warned in 1892 of the dangers of an impending social revolution, of a "new tyranny . . . lurking in the shadows," and of its threat to world peace; Frédéric Passy, winner of the first Nobel Peace Prize in 1901, stressed the need for governments to ensure international stability through social reforms if international peace was to be preserved.

Therefore the peace movement was becoming inextricably linked with a movement for international action to promote improved conditions of labor. ILO was the product of currents of reformist and socialist thought and action in the nineteenth and early twentieth centuries in Europe, and it mirrors within its internal structure an accommodation to these changes. The demands of the workers for effective international action have often conflicted with their governments' views, which saw ILO as an instrument for strengthening the stability of the sovereign nation-state. "In spite of the political calamities, failures and disappointments of the past half century, ILO has patiently, undramatically, but not unsuccessfully, worked to build an *infrastructure of peace*." Morse declared. "It has provided the world with a meeting ground, an instrument for cooperation and for dialogue among very different interests, at times when men were more disposed to settle their differences by force than by talk . . . ."

"If the ILO had done nothing more than offer the world a forum for tripartite discussion, it would have already rendered a great service to the cause of peace," Morse told his award ceremony audience. At the time of its inception, the idea of tripartism was hardly known even at national levels, and its implications have been far reaching. "It resulted in trade unions and organizations of employers acquiring a position at home which they would not otherwise have had. It gave the world a new approach to the resolution of social conflict, an approach based on dialogue . . . ."

"Its tripartite structure has also enabled it to broaden the scope of cooperation between countries. The ILO is still the only world-wide organization where international cooperation is the business not only of diplomats and government representatives, but also of the representatives of employers and workers. It thus provides opportunities for contacts and for greater understanding within the three groups . . . it is only in the ILO that free enterprise employers meet regularly with managers of state enterprises in Socialist countries," Morse explained.

The second great principle of ILO is its universality. This organization has struggled towards a goal of universal membership in the belief—stated in the preamble to its constitution—that "the failure of any nation to adopt humane conditions of labour is an obstacle in the way of other nations which desire to improve conditions in their countries." In 1944, in Philadelphia, a declaration was adopted that "poverty anywhere constitutes a danger to prosperity every-

where."

It would be fair to question whether this is idealism beyond hope of implementation. Four months before the announcement of the award of the Peace Prize, ILO celebrated its fiftieth anniversary, and upon that occasion a conservative US journal, *Business Week* (June 1969) devoted a major article to the question, "Should US business support the ILO?" The conclusion reached was that there were many reasons for a positive answer; that ILO is not run as a lobby for labor interests, even though it deals with labor topics, but "speaks with several voices—government, worker and employer." The author found it regrettable that most US business ignores ILO. Director-General Morse is convinced that searching out causes will ultimately contribute to wiser action. Therefore, he has supported the Institute for Labor Studies set up in Geneva in 1960. It receives a third of its funds from ILO. Presently it is coordinating a vast research program on worker participation in industry.

Another ILO operation is the Center for Advanced Technical and Vocational Training. It tailors its instructions to the level of sophistication in the country involved.

ILO has made major contributions to international law, proving that moral persuasion and moral pressure can be effective instruments to secure the observance of the rule of law at the international level. It also offers technical assistance to developing countries. "Many developing countries are so weak, politically and economically, and so lacking in social cohesion and stability," Morse observed in his Nobel lecture, "they could offer little resistance to subversion or aggression by an ambitious outside power. To provide these countries with the resources, the technical and managerial know-how, and the institutional and administrative framework which are essential for viable nationhood in the modern world . . . seems to me an essential aspect of the problem of peace-building in the modern world. And it is for this reason that the ILO gives top priority in its work today to the strengthening of developing nations."

Morse enumerated many of the unresolved problems facing ILO: an uneven distribution of their help so that rural areas lag behind in assistance. "We shall encourage the use of labour-intensive techniques of agricultural and industrial production wherever it is economically feasible to do so," he said. There remains the plight of those desperately poor who live outside a closed circle of affluence; the racial or religious minorities, the migrant workers, those in slum areas, elderly people. Morse observed that the ILO must address problems of discrimination; it must work for greater freedom, for greater participation of workers in decisions affecting their welfare. "The task," he said, "is far from finished . . . but there has been a growing recognition of the need for a truly world-wide solidarity in the fight against poverty and injustice with the aim of building a more peaceful world . . . ."

"The ILO has given the world the concept of the industrial dialogue," Morse said. "In the years to come it must seek to broaden the scope, and increase the substance of that dialogue . . . it will continue to seek to promote social evolution by peaceful means, to identify emerging social needs and problems and threats to social peace . . . ." He pledged to devote the ILO to defusing what Nobel Laureate Frédéric Passy (1901) had warned were "dangerous explosives in the hidden depths of the community," making possible the building of a truly peaceful world order based on social justice.

Beneath the foundation stone in the ILO's office in Geneva lies a document on which is written: "*Si vis pacem, cole justitiam*"—if you desire peace, cultivate justice.

History

The International Labour Organization (ILO) was created in 1919 by Part XIII of the Versailles Peace Treaty ending the First World War. It grew out of nineteenth- and twentieth-century labor and social movements which created widespread demands for social justice. In 1946, after the demise of the League of Nations, the ILO became the first specialized agency associated with the United Nations. The original membership of 45 countries in 1919 had grown to 150 by May 1983.

ILO's tripartite policy of giving equitable voice to representatives of workers and employers and government is unique among world organizations. The annual International Labour Conference, the ILO deliberative body, is composed of four representatives from each member country: two government delegates, one worker and one employer delegate, all working independently.

The ILO has three major tasks: first, the adoption of international labor standards, called "Conventions and Recommendations," which contain guidelines on child labor, protection of women workers, hours of work, rest and holidays, labor inspection, vocational guidance and training, social security protection, housing, occupational safety, and protection of migrant workers. They also cover basic human rights, such as freedom of association, collective bargaining, and the abolition of forced labor and of discrimination in employment.

Second, technical cooperation to assist developing nations. More than half of ILO's resources are devoted to such programs. ILO's ultimate goal is a World Employment Program, designed to help countries provide employment and training opportunities to growing populations.

Third, standard setting and technical cooperation are backed by extensive research, training, education, and publications programs. The ILO is a major source of publications and documentation on labor and social matters.

The ILO's Directors-General read as follows: Albert Thomas (1919-32) of France; Harold B. Butler (1932-38) of the United Kingdom; John G. Winant (1938-41) of the United States; Edward J. Phelan (1941-48) of Ireland; David A. Morse (1948-70) of the United States; Wilfred Jenks (1970-) of the United Kingdom Francis Blanchard (174-89) of France; Michel Hansenne (1989-99) of Belgium; and Juan Somavia (1999-) of Chile.

Bibliography

Business Week 1969 Should U.S. business support the ILO? June 14

Lucal J 1969 The Church and the ILO. *America* 120 (May 31)

RUTH C. REYNOLDS

Norman Borlaug
(1970)

The Nobel Peace Prize for 1970 was awarded to the agronomist Norman Ernest Borlaug because, the Nobel Committee said, "more than any other single person of his age, he has helped to provide bread for a hungry world. We have made this choice in the hope that providing bread will also give the world peace."

Borlaug began his crusade against famine as a geneticist and plant pathologist with the Rockefeller Foundation at a research station in Campo Atizapan, Mexico, where he began a momentous series of cross-breeding experiments that developed strains of wheat which increased the yields in Mexico sixfold since his start there in 1944. "I am impatient and do not accept the need for slow change and evolution to improve the agriculture and food production of the emerging countries," he once wrote. "I advocate instead a 'yield-kick, or a yield blast-off.' There is no time to be lost considering the magnitude of the world food and population problem." During the many years he has worked in Mexico he has collaborated with scientists from other countries, adapting wheat to the particular needs of the region in which it is grown. In India, for example, where he introduced the stocky wheat better able to support the rapid growth and heavier yields of grain, the annual yield soared from 12 million tons in 1965 to 21 tons in 1970. West Pakistan (now Pakistan) also planted the strain, and in five years also nearly doubled its yield.

Although Borlaug is a scientist with an M.S. and Ph.D. in plant pathology, he prefers field work to academic life. The hunger that afflicts a major share of the human family stimulated his ingenuity, and as director of the Rockefeller Foundation's wheat breeding program he set out in the 1950s to develop a dwarf wheat that could perform well in the varied conditions to be found in Mexico. He amassed germ plasm from Japan, the United States, Australia, and Columbia, and then began growing two alternate crops of wheat each year at sites with contrasting climatic and environmental conditions. The combination of the widely chosen ancestry of his seeds and the varying "laboratory" fields in which they were developed resulted in a dwarf wheat with wide adaptability to differing conditions. Borlaug pioneered in this work in geographic adaptability of cereals; before this, most cereal varieties grew well only under conditions similar to those under which they were first bred.

As a result of his innovative measures Borlaug became known as the "father of the Green Revolution." In his Nobel lecture Borlaug introduced some qualifications to be considered within that popular term. "Perhaps the term 'green revolution,' as commonly used, is too premature, too optimistic, or too broad in scope," he said. "Too often it seems to convey the impression of a general revolution in yields per hectare and in total production of all crops throughout vast areas comprising many countries . . . ."

"These implications both oversimplify and distort the facts. The only crops which have been appreciably affected up to the present time are wheat, rice and maize. Yields of other important cereals, such as sorghums, millets, and barley, have been only slightly affected; nor has there been any appreciable increase in yield or production of the pulse or legume crops which are essential in the diets of cereal-consuming populations."

Borlaug cautioned that there are no miracles in agricultural production, no elixir to cure all the accumulated ills of a stagnant, traditional agriculture. The importation of new seeds and new technology to developing countries must be backed by a crop-production campaign strategy wherein the government's economic policies would be tailored to assure the farmer a fair price for grain, and to guarantee that the fertilizers, insecticides, weedkillers, and machinery needed would be available. Traditional methods of threshing grain with bullocks, followed by winnowing, must be replaced by thousands of small threshing machines to accommodate the greatly increased harvest. Borlaug also cautioned against inadequate planning wherein some farmers, able to use the new seeds, would increase their net incomes up to fourfold, while those unable to use the new seeds for lack of water, or lack of credit to buy the equipment necessary to use the new techniques, would have to market their small yields in an economy adjusted to sharp increases in total harvests. The "Green Revolution" must be accompanied by equivalent and political breakthroughs. There must be, for instance, effective ways of distributing the additional food to vast underprivileged masses who have little or no purchasing power.

Borlaug emphasized that world leaders needed to tackle the problem of population control. The new wheats and the high-yielding rices being developed, together with continuing research toward increased protein contents, can only buy time. If corresponding means for stabilizing world populations are not developed at the same time, Borlaug warned that the "Green Revolution" would achieve only a "temporary success in man's war against hunger and deprivation, a breathing space in which to deal with the 'population monster,' and the subsequent environmental and social ills that too often lead to conflict between men and between nations."

"And yet I am optimistic for the future of mankind," Borlaug said in closing his lecture, "for in all biological populations there are innate devices to adjust population growth to the carrying capacity of the environment. Undoubtedly, some such device exists in man, but so far it has not asserted itself to bring into balance population growth and the carrying capacity of the environment on a worldwide scale. It would be disastrous for the species to continue to increase our human numbers madly until such devices take over . . . ."

Borlaug continued: "Since man is potentially a rational being, however, I am confident that within the next two decades he will recognize the self-destructive course he steers along the road of irresponsible population growth and will adjust the growth rate to levels which will permit a decent standard of living for all mankind ... he may still see Isaiah's prophesies come true: 'and the desert shall rejoice, and blossom as the rose .... And the parched ground shall become a pool, and the thirsty land springs of water ....'" (Isaiah 35: 1,7).

Biography

Norman Ernest Borlaug was born in Cresco, Iowa, on March 25, 1914. Educated in Iowa primary and secondary schools, he attended the University of Minnesota where he took a B.S. in 1937, an M.S. in 1939 and a Ph.D. in 1942. He originally studied forestry, and went on to work for the US Forestry Service at stations in Massachusetts and Idaho. But it was as an agriculturist, using the tools of genetics and plant pathology, that he became a pioneer in the increased production of cereal crops over the world.

Following his masters degree and doctorate in plant pathology, Borlaug served as microbiologist on the staff of the duPont de Nemours Foundation, where he was in charge of research on industrial and agricultural bactericides, fungicides, and preservatives. In 1944 he accepted an appointment as geneticist and plant pathologist for the Cooperative Wheat Research and Production Program, a joint undertaking of the Rockefeller Foundation and the Mexican Government. Twenty years later Borlaug was awarded an honorary doctoral degree for the impressive results he achieved in improving wheat production, especially in the developing countries. In 1959, he became Assistant Director of the Rockefeller Foundation and Director of the Inter-American Wheat Research and Production Program, and in 1964 Director of the Wheat Program of the International Center for Maize and Wheat Improvement Center.

His success in Mexico paved the way for him to implement his practical humanitarian vision. Known by this time as the architect of the "Green Revolution," Borlaug arranged to put the new cereal strains into extensive production to help feed the world's hungry people. From Mexico, Borlaug went to other countries with large underfed populations to help them improve the yield of their food crops. At the invitation of the Food and Agriculture Organization he went to Pakistan in 1959, where he persuaded the authorities not only to import the new variety of wheat seeds, but to adopt appropriate technology in its use.

Borlaug is also concerned with the problems of population explosion, the control of which is essential no matter what the food supply. He sees the "Green Revolution" as a means for buying time until essential sociopolitical problems of equitable food distribution are resolved and the population brought to numbers commensurate with the support capacities of the Earth.

Borlaug has won recognition and awards from all over the world: he was a foreign member of the Royal Swedish Academy of Agriculture and Forestry (1971), and of the Indian Natural Science Academy (1973); an honorary member of the Acad. Nacional de Agronomia y Veterinaria de Argentina, and of the N.I. Vavilovi Acad. (USSR); an Honorary Fellow of the Indian Society of Genetics and Plant Breeding (1968); an Honorary D.Sc. (Punjab Agric. Univ., 1969; Royal Norwegian Agricultural College, 1970; Michigan State University, 1971; University of Florida, 1973; and others). He was given the Medal of Freedom in 1977 and holds numerous Mexican awards.

Borlaug married Margaret G. Gibson in 1937. They have a son and a daughter.

Bibliography

Brown L 1970 Nobel Peace Prize: Developer of high-yield wheat receives award. *Science* 170 (October 30)

RUTH C. REYNOLDS

Willy Brandt
(1971)

The Nobel Peace Prize for 1971 was awarded to Willy Brandt, then Chancellor of the Federal Republic of Germany, in recognition of the "reconciliatory hand he extended across the old enemy frontiers." If Brandt's gesture toward peace is accepted, the Nobel Committee said that "Willy Brandt will live in our history as the great German chancellor of peace and reconciliation."

Brandt is often thought of as a Berliner, but he became a Berliner only after the Second World War. He was born Herbert Ernst Karl Frahm in the Lubeck workers' district of St. Lorenz. A poverty-ridden childhood instilled in him a deeply ingrained reverence for human dignity and social justice. He was greatly influenced by his grandfather, an ardent Social Democrat.

At 13 he was granted a scholarship to high school, where his talent for journalism quickly surfaced.

While still in his teens he was writing articles for the local Social Democratic paper using the name "Willy Brandt."

In the 1930s, with the ominous rise of the Nazi Party, the young journalist was known as a member of a group openly hostile to the Nazis. When Hitler came to power Frahm escaped to Norway using his assumed name "Willy Brandt." There he learned Norwegian and began to write for trade-union magazines, keeping in touch with the socialist underground in Germany. When the Germans invaded Norway he again fled, this time to Sweden. "I was a two-fold immigrant: a German who had fled to Norway, and a Norwegian who had escaped to Sweden," Brandt recalls.

After the war he was assigned to cover the *Nuremberg Trials for Scandinavian Social Democratic Party newspapers.* In 1946 the Norwegian Foreign Minister asked Brandt to join the country's diplomatic service, and sent him to Berlin as press attaché with the rank of major attached to the Norwegian military mission. He found Berlin covered with deep craters and mountains of rubble, its people hungry, suffering from the cold, despairing. In 1947 he made an important decision: he relinquished the personal and material privileges he enjoyed with a Norwegian diplomatic passport and applied for renaturalization.

He began to work first for a free Berlin because he was convinced that the defeat of Berlin carried in it the germ of a defeat for any hope of peace in Europe. He regarded Berlin as a microcosm of the East-West problem. Willy Brandt was destined to become its mayor.

The Nobel Committee commented on his leadership: "As Mayor of Berlin, at a time when the city was menaced by political pressures which eventually crystallized in the form of the Berlin Wall of 1961, Willy Brandt was, in critical situations, proof of a moderation and a courage, often a despairing courage, which saved Berlin from the risks of an immense catastrophe."

Brandt shared with Chancellor Adenauer the conviction that the next step was to "talk to the Russians," taking care to preserve and nourish the Federal Republic's ties to the Western bloc. The building of the Berlin Wall in August 1961 was a powerful factor in persuading Brandt of the urgent need to press for a policy of reconciliation. Under international law the Wall was illegal. Brandt saw that as Mayor he would have to walk a delicate path between legal claim and brute force. But he had become convinced that an approach must be tried, no matter what the risks. His policy of reconciliation,

Ostpolitik, with the German Democratic Republic, the Soviet Union, Poland, and other members of the Soviet bloc led to an agreement on the renunciation of force between Bonn and Moscow. Brandt asserted that peace was needed not just in the sense of freeing a situation from conflict, but also as a prerequisite for the cooperative effort that must be made for solving problems. "It is not enough to pronounce peace-loving intentions, we must also actively endeavor to organize peace," he said. He had faith that peace is self-reinforcing; that where people work together, helping one another, trust will develop with time.

Brandt discussed the events of 1961 and 1962 in his Nobel lecture: "As Mayor of Berlin, I experienced how critical situations influence our thinking. I knew, though, that steadfastness serves the cause of peace." Recalling the Berlin Wall, with its "absurd division of what had remained intact of the whole organism of a metropolis," he said that passionate protests were justified and necessary, but they did not alter the situation. The Wall remained; people had to learn to live with it. He pursued every opportunity to open up fences, to create paths for people to cross borders *legally.*

In 1966 Brandt became Foreign Minister in Kurt Kiesinger's coalition government. He announced the policy of unequivocal safeguarding of peace as the common denominator to all actions. "Everyone must ask himself what specific contribution he should make," he said, and he made this the cornerstone of procedures in the Federal Republic of Germany.

Brandt's critics called his Ostpolitik "naive" and "risky," but Brandt declared his experience with coexistence had not vindicated these apprehensions. "Realistic self-confidence need not fear contact with the political and ideological antagonist; the uncertainty of the present time must not be permitted to make us uncertain too. What was the point," he asked, "of getting in touch with the other side without being prepared to speak? Speaking surely also means negotiating and being open to conciliation, not unilateral concessions. An active peace policy will remain for a long time to come the test of our intellectual and material vitality."

In 1969 Brandt became Chancellor in a new coalition between the Social Democrats and Liberals. Convinced that a strong Western Europe was necessary before confrontation could successfully be turned into collaboration with Eastern Europe, one of his first official acts was to persuade France to begin talks with the United Kingdom on expanding the European Common Market, and he encouraged other nations to join.

In his policy of détente with the communist bloc countries of Eastern Europe and with the Soviet Union, Brandt was always prepared to accept new relationships and new understandings provided his communist negotiators did not force him into violating good relationships with the North Atlantic Treaty Organization (NATO) and the West. He exercised great patience in his efforts to improve relations with the government of the German Democratic Republic. "Short steps are better than no steps at all," he said.

Chancellor Brandt argued persistently for a sense of proportion, resolution, and endurance, holding them to be essential to the transition from classical power politics to the businesslike peace policy that his government sought. Actively practicing a peace-oriented policy means a change, he stressed, from the imposition of one-sided views to the balancing of differing interests.

There are strong forces in opposition to the organization of peace, Brandt warned. Like freedom, peace is no original state which existed from the start; we shall have to make it, he asserted. "To achieve this, we shall have to know more about the origin of conflicts . . . learning is in our world the true credible alternative to force."

Willy Brandt closed his Nobel lecture with some observations about the contemporary human condition: "Today we know how rich and at the same time how limited Man is in his possibilities. We know him in his aggression and in his brotherliness. We know that he is capable of applying his inventions for his own good, but also of using them to destroy himself . . . . I believe in active compassion and therefore in Man's responsibility. And I believe in the absolute necessity of peace . . . . Under the threat of mankind's self-destruction, co-existence has become a question of the very existence of man. Co-existence becomes not one of several acceptable possibilities, but the only chance of survival . . . . May all those who possess the power to wage war have the mastery of reason to maintain peace."

Biography

Born Herbert Ernst Karl Frahm on December 13, 1913, in Lubeck, son of Martha Frahm, Willy Brandt was educated through high school in Lubeck. He began a distinguished career as a journalist at an early age, writing for the Social Democratic paper under the name "Willy Brandt" while still in Lubeck. He continued writing in Norway, to which he escaped upon the coming of Hitler to power in Germany

in 1933. He participated in German and Norwegian resistance movements during the Second World War. At the close of the war he served in Berlin as Norwegian Press Attaché. He decided upon renaturalization, keeping the name Willy Brandt. He rose swiftly within the Social Democratic Party becoming Secretary to the Executive Committee, 1948-49, member of the Executive Committee, 1950-63, Deputy Chairman of the SPD, 1954-58, and Chairman in 1958. He became Mayor of Berlin in 1957, serving until 1966. He was a member of the Federal Parliament (Bundestag), 1949-57, and again from 1969; and in 1966 he was appointed Minister of Foreign Affairs and Vice-Chancellor. He was elected Chancellor in 1969 and served until 1974. He was President of the Socialist International, 1976, a member of the European Parliament from 1979 to 1983, and Chairman of the Committee on Development Issues, which produced the influential Brandt Reports, 1977-79. The reports of the commission, to which Brandt's name was attached, were published as: *North-South: A Programme for Survival*, 1980 and *Common Crisis: Co-operation for World Recovery*, 1983. He has been awarded honorary degrees from Pennsylvania University (1959), Maryland University (1960), Harvard University (1963), Oxford University (Hon. DCL, 1969) and Leeds University (1982). He was given the Reinhold Niebuhr Award (1972), the Aspen Institute for Humanistic Studies Prize (1973), and the B'nai Brith Gold Medal (1981). A prolific writer, his publications include: *Krigen i Norge* (1945), *Ernst Reuter* (with R. Lowenthal, 1957), *Von Bonn nach Berlin* (1957), *My Road to Berlin* (1960), *The Ordeal of Co-Existence* (1963), *Begegnung mit Kennedy* (1964), *A Peace Policy for Europe* (1968), *Peace and Politics, 1960-1975* (1978), *Links und Frei* (1982).

He married Rut Hansen in 1948; they divorced in 1980. He married Brigitte Seebacher in 1983. He was the father of three sons and one daughter.

Willy Brandt died in 1992.

See also: Articles: *Ostpolitik; North-South Conflict*

Bibliography ────────────────────────────

Brandt W 1972 Let me speak of peace policy in our time. Nobel lecture delivered at Oslo, December 11, 1971. *Vital Speeches* 38(7)

Nation 1972 The two Germanys: Lurching toward confrontation. 214(15)

The New Republic 1971 Hectoring Herr Brandt. 164(4)

Wechsberg J A 1974 *The New Yorker* January 14, 1974

RUTH C. REYNOLDS

Prize Not Awarded
(1972)

Henry A. Kissinger
(1973)

The 1973 Nobel Peace Prize went to Le Duc Tho and Henry Kissinger, who had been working for nearly four years toward negotiating a ceasefire in Vietnam. The award proved controversial. Le Duc Tho refused the prize, objecting that peace in Vietnam had still not been completely achieved. Two of the five members of the Peace Prize Committee resigned in protest. Ripples of concern surrounded the choice of Henry Kissinger because his announcement "peace is at hand," made just before the US November elections, was followed in the next month by heavy US bombing in Vietnam. Ceasefire was achieved, however, on January 23.

The Nobel Committee made its award in recognition of the sustained efforts of Kissinger and Le Duc Tho to find a common policy favorable to establishing a way forward to peace. "No one," the Committee acknowledged, "could know whether this road would be followed; but they had lit a torch on the long and difficult road to peace among men." They had been, the Committee said, responsible politicians at the center of events, seeking the use of negotiation rather than war, intent on finding solutions to controversies rather than military victory.

This principle has been central in Henry Kissinger's philosophy as scholar and statesman. In his doctoral thesis he examined the protracted period of peace in Europe following 1814. While many historians explain these 100 years without war in terms of a military balance of power wherein no country was sufficiently strong to seek domination, Kissinger stressed the international order that existed in that period. Within an agreed set of rules, states dealt with their stresses on set principles of behavior. Although there were political systems which differed widely, as there are now, with the Great Powers swayed by conflicting interests, they respected the principles and rules through which they could prevent their differing systems and interests leading to war.

The circumstances in which Le Duc Tho and Henry Kissinger sought to negotiate were in opposite circumstances, during the pressures created by an ongoing, long, costly war. Meeting in secret for over three years, the diplomats found a formula to exchange war prisoners and to end the domestically unpopular involvement of US troops without the appearance of the United States abandoning an ally.

It is in recognition of these efforts of Henry Kissinger and Le Duc Tho to lead the contesting nations toward peace through increased understanding and in the hope of the Committee that the award might act as an effective spur toward renewed and conclusive negotiations that the Nobel award for peace was made.

Kissinger was born in Germany in 1923. His family fled from Nazi Germany in 1938, so it was as an adolescent that the young Kissinger arrived in the United States. Naturalized as a citizen in 1943, he began a three-year service in the US Army Counter-Intelligence Corps. From 1946 to 1949 he was a captain in the Military Intelligence Service.

Kissinger quickly distinguished himself as a student and attended Harvard on a series of scholarships. This was the beginning of a long and distinguished career at Harvard, where he taught in the Department of Government and at the Center for International Affairs. During the next 15 years he served in many posts, often simultaneously: he was Associate Director of the Center, Study Director of Nuclear Weapons and Foreign Policy at the Council of Foreign Relations, Director of the Special Studies Project for the Rockefeller Fund, Director of the Harvard International Seminar, and Director of the Harvard Defense Studies Program.

In 1968, Kissinger accepted an appointment as adviser to the President on national security affairs. As chief foreign policy adviser to President Nixon he initiated the Strategic Arms Limitation Talks (SALT) in 1969.

Kissinger prepared the way for President Nixon's visit to the People's Republic of China in 1972 and the opening of diplomatic relationships with that country through a number of unpublicized trips. He accompanied President Nixon to Moscow in 1972, an occasion that created a marked improvement in Soviet-US relations. By this time he was engaged in the intensive, protracted one-to-one negotiations with Le Duc Tho which culminated in a ceasefire in early 1973. In 1973, he became Secretary of State following the resignation of William P. Rodgers. He played a major role in Nixon's policy of disengaging US troops and replacing them by South Vietnamese. He gave diplomatic assistance in the resumption of diplomatic relations between the United States and Egypt, making a whirlwind tour of the capitals of Middle East countries and entering into consultation with the Soviet leader, Brezhnev. In February 1974, he announced from Cairo the resumption of diplomatic relations between the United States and Egypt, which had been severed for six years, and the reopening of the Suez Canal.

Secretary Kissinger has often been called a "realist." In his acceptance message to the Nobel Committee, Kissinger addressed this attitude: "To the realist, peace represents a stable arrangement of power; to the idealist, a goal so preeminent that it conceals the difficulty of finding the means to its achievement. But in this age of thermonuclear technology, neither view can assure man's preservation. Instead, peace, the ideal, must be practised. A sense of responsibility and accommodation must guide the behavior of all nations. Some common notion of justice can and must be found, for failure to do so will bring only more 'just' wars."

Secretary Kissinger's schedule as conciliator was unremitting. But his heavy schedule did not preclude a fine sense of the delicacy of his mission. In his acceptance speech as Nobel Laureate, Kissinger remarked, "Our experience has taught us to regard peace as a delicate, ever-fleeting condition, its roots too shallow to bear the strain of social and political discontent. We tend to accept the lessons of that experience and work toward those solutions that at best relieve specific sources of strain, lest our neglect allow war to overtake peace."

Bernt Ingvaldsen, Vice-President of the Committee, said it was interesting to follow Kissinger's development from doctoral dissertation to the long and patient negotiation leading to the ceasefire in Vietnam. "The views he has evolved testify to a mind free from prejudice, an analytical ability to learn the lessons of history, and constructive imagination."

Biography

Henry Alfred Kissinger was born in Furth, Germany, on May 27, 1923. He emigrated to the United States with his family in flight from Nazi Germany in 1938. He was naturalized as a citizen in 1943, and entered the US Army

Counter-Intelligence Corps where he served as captain from 1946 to 1949. He earned his B.A. *summa cum laude* from Harvard, followed by an M.A. in 1950 and a Ph.D. in 1954. He taught at Harvard in the Department of Government and at the Center for International Affairs. He was Associate Director of the Center, 1957 to 1960: Study Director of Nuclear Weapons and Foreign Policy at the Council of Foreign Relations, 1955 to 1956; Director of the Special Studies Project for the Rockefeller Fund, 1956 to 1958; and Director of the Harvard International Seminar, 1951 to 1971.

Kissinger has served as consultant to a wide variety of officials and agencies: the Department of State, the US Arms Control and Disarmament Agency, Rand Corporation, National Security Council, Weapons Systems Evaluation Group of the Joint Chiefs of Staff, Operations Coordinating Board, and the Director of the Psychological Strategy Board and Operations Research Office. A Guggenheim Fellow, he also received the 1958 Woodrow Wilson Prize for the best book in the fields of government, politics, and international affairs. In 1973 he received the American Institute for Public Service Award, the International Platform Association Theodore Roosevelt Award, the Veterans of Foreign Wars Dwight D. Eisenhower Distinguished Service Medal, and the Hope Award for International Understanding.

While assistant to the President for National Security Affairs, Kissinger negotiated arrangements for President Nixon's trips to both the People's Republic of China and the Soviet Union. He accompanied the President on these trips, which proved important occasions, resulting in improvement in US relations with both countries. In 1972, he entered into negotiations with Le Duc Tho, seeking to achieve peace in Vietnam, and this resulted in a ceasefire in 1973. A visit to Moscow to see the Soviet leader, Brezhnev, followed by a tour of seven Middle East capitals, led to the signing of a ceasefire between Egypt and Israel. In 1974 full-scale diplomatic relations were resumed between the United States and Egypt after six years, and the Suez Canal was reopened. Kissinger remained as Secretary of State under President Ford until the 1977 elections. Since that time, following Ford's election defeat, Kissinger has been Professor of Diplomacy in Georgetown University, since 1977; Counselor to the Center for Strategic and International Studies, Georgetown University, since 1977; Contributing Analyst for ABC news, since 1983; and Senior Fellow, Aspen Institute, since 1977. In 1983, he became Chairman of the National Bipartisan Committee on Central America.

Kissinger's other honors include the American Institute for Public Service Award, 1973, American Legion Distinguished Service Medal, 1974, Wateler Peace Prize, 1974, Presidential Medal of Freedom, 1977, among many other awards and prizes. His publications include: *Nuclear*

Weapons and Foreign Policy (1956); *A World Restored: Castlereagh, Metternich and the Restoration of Peace 1812-22* (1957); *The Necessity for Choice: Prospects of American Foreign Policy* (1961); *The Troubled Partnership: A Reappraisal of the Atlantic Alliance* (1965); *American Foreign Policy* (3 essays) (1969); *White House Years* (1979); *For the Record* (1981); *Years of Upheaval* (1982); *International House* (1984); and numerous articles on us foreign policy, international affairs, and diplomatic history.

Henry Kissinger married Nancy Maginnes in 1974. He has a son and a daughter, Elizabeth and David, from a former marriage.

RUTH C. REYNOLDS

Le Duc Tho
(1973)

The decision to award the 1973 Nobel Peace Prize to the two negotiators, Henry Kissinger and Le Duc Tho, who had been working for nearly four years toward achieving a ceasefire in Vietnam proved a controversial one. One of the two winners, Le Duc Tho, refused the prize with the objection that peace in Vietnam eluded them still. Two out of the five members of the Peace Prize Committee resigned in protest. Controversy raged around the choice of Henry Kissinger when his announcement "peace is at hand," made just prior to the us November elections, was followed in December by heavy us bombing in Vietnam. Ceasefire eventually came about on January 23 of the following year.

The Nobel Committee explained that their decision was based on the persistent efforts made by Kissinger and Le Duc Tho to find a promising course of action likely to lead the way to peace. "No one," Mrs. Aase Lionaes, Chairwoman of the Committee, acknowledged, "could know whether this road would be followed; but they had lit a torch on the long and difficult road to peace among men."

The Nobel Committee was under no illusion that peace had been attained. But Mrs. Lionaes called attention to precedents for their decision under such circumstances. Ralph Bunche had received the prize for his contribution in negotiating a ceasefire between Israel and the Arab states. Later, that ceasefire had been superseded by open war in the Middle East. Still, the principle behind Bunche's award and, likewise, the award offered Secretary Kissinger and Le Duc Tho remained intact: they were responsible politicians at the heart of the search for a negotiated peace, rather than military victory seeking to resolve bitterly divisive issues through discussion, not war.

It is in recognition of the efforts of Henry Kissinger and Le Duc Tho to start the nations of today toward peace through increased understanding and negotiation that the Nobel award for peace was made.

Biography

Le Duc Tho was born in what is now Vietnam in 1912. As a teenager, he joined an anti-French revolutionary youth movement, and by the age of 17 he was a member of Indochina's Communist Party.

Reports differ on whether Le Duc Tho, who had been frequently incarcerated by the colonial government during his youth, spent all of the Second World War in prison, or whether he escaped and spent some of that time with Ho Chi Minh in China.

Following the war, he went south to participate in the successful war of independence from the French. He returned to North Vietnam and became a member of the Politburo and Secretary of the Vietnam Workers' Party. He was a chief negotiator in seeking a ceasefire from the military conflict and ultimately to create peace in Vietnam. He signed the ceasefire without the satisfaction of feeling that true peace had been obtained in that country. On that basis he refused the offered Nobel Peace Prize.

RUTH C. REYNOLDS

Sean Mac Bride
(1974)

Sean MacBride, winner with Eisaku Sato of the 1974 Nobel Peace Prize, has devoted much of his life to the advancement of human rights. With endless skill and devotion, this Peace Prize Laureate has been prominent in the introduction of human rights legislation and in its implementation in countries the world over.

MacBride had addressed problems of peace and human rights as journalist, lawyer, and distinguished member of the Irish government. In his youth he participated in Ireland's struggle for independence, and it proved a lasting influence. He gave up a career as a journalist to study law, a profession which better equipped him for taking up battle against the injustices he observed around him.

For sometime he worked in the Irish government, entering the Dáil Éireann (Irish National Assembly) in 1947 and remaining for 11 years. During the period 1948-51 he served as Ireland's Foreign Minister. The Council of Europe was then drafting the European Convention on Human Rights with the view to securing worldwide protection for human rights, and MacBride played a dominant role in guiding this convention to a successful conclusion. This proved to be the beginning of a battle against the twin forces of violence and injustice which he was to wage over much of the world, acting sometimes in the capacity of public servant, often as a private citizen.

From 1961 to 1974, as a fearless and vigorous leader of Amnesty International, he brought that organization from infancy to a position of respect and efficacy throughout the world community. Sometimes he combined the role of leader and field worker, his areas of activity ranging over Africa, Asia, and America. He fought injustice in many forms, exposing persecution and torture, seeking the release of prisoners incarcerated without trial or defense.

MacBride has emphasized the importance of extending and enforcing the legislative obligations to protect human rights. He was active as Secretary-General within the International Commission of Jurists during many of the years when he was also working for Amnesty International. In the Commission of Jurists a number of leading jurists from various countries worked to issue valuable publications and to operate in cooperation with the United Nations.

During this time, in September 1967, he participated in a Nobel symposium in Oslo. There he launched the idea of establishing a convention among the nations of East Europe for the protection of fundamental freedoms. He hoped that through regional agreements it would be possible to bring about a network of progress. He also worked in behalf of the UN's Declaration of Human Rights. It should, he felt, become an effective instrument through the establishment of a universal Human Rights Court with authority to act in behalf of individuals needing its protection. MacBride is of the opinion that no state

can claim absolute national sovereignty where universally accepted principles of justice are concerned.

MacBride possesses an abiding faith in the power of the individual to participate in the cause of justice. Much of the work of Amnesty International is accomplished by volunteers. During the UN's Human Rights Year in 1968 he took the initiative in setting up a joint committee for the various nongovernmental organizations working for justice. MacBride himself was pressed into command, and he applied his skill as a practical administrator to impressive effect.

In accord with his philosophy of meeting a problem by actively working toward solutions, MacBride has toiled within the International Peace Bureau (IPB), holding various positions of trust within that organization, to seek preventative measures against the greatest perpetrator of injustice and suffering of all, modern warfare.

At the time of the Peace Prize award MacBride was facing a new and demanding task as the UN's High Commissioner for Namibia. It is no surprise that such a man, steeped in the problems of injustice as practiced by the individual, by the nation, and by clusters of nations, should be an eloquent orator on the subject. He opened his Nobel lecture somberly: "It is nearly with a feeling of despair that I come to your beautiful country ... despair partly because we are living in a world where war, violence, brutality and ever increasing armament dominate the thinking of humanity; but more so because humanity itself gives the appearance of having become numbed or terrified by its own impotence in the face of disaster."

MacBride observed that this threat of nuclear catastrophe and the growing menace against human rights have a common denominator. Both reflect a disintegration of ethics and morality. "The stupendous scientific and material revolution has changed practically every factor in our ecology and society," he asserted. "Perhaps as a result, or coincidental with it, there has taken place a near collapse of public and private morality in practically every sector of human relationships. The previously existing standards of public and private morality may have left a lot to be desired, but at least they existed ... now they have ceased to be either accepted or observed."

"It is a rule of international law that weapons and methods of warfare which do not discriminate between combatants and civilians should never be used .... The bombing of hospitals and civilian targets was outlawed. All these principles and standards have suddenly vanished .... The use of the most cruel, terrible and indiscriminate weapon of all time is not even outlawed .... One frightening aspect of this particular breakdown in our public standards of morality has been the comparative silence of many of the established guardians of humanitarian law .... Governments go to war directly or by proxy without declaring war. In these undeclared wars, civilians— men, women and children—are bombed and massacred indiscriminately; chemical agents are used to destroy humans, animals and crops. Prisoners are not only ill-treated, but are tortured systematically in a manner worse than at any barbaric period of history .... Secret services are used to assassinate political opponents or to provoke internal dissension in another country or to procure the overthrow of a democratically elected government."

MacBride further said that in earlier wars soldiers fought out of a belief in the defense of family and nation. "But in a war using hydrogen bombs, everything man might propose to defend will perish with him." MacBride defined the overriding obligation of the atomic age: "Peace has to be the DESPERATE IMPERATIVE of humanity," he declared.

MacBride drew his Nobel lecture to a close with the encouraging observation that the technology of the last 30 years may have brought the means which could enable us to protect ourselves, with mass media and higher standards of literacy and education. When we use these tools, we can attain a much greater degree of influence for public opinion in the world than it has ever enjoyed in the past.

He reminded his audience that it was US and world public opinion which forced the United States to withdraw from Vietnam. It was the first time ever that a country at war had been stopped in its tracks by public opinion. MacBride said also (perhaps optimistically) that the same thing was happening in the Soviet Union in regard to human rights and the right to intellectual freedom.

Cautioning that great vigilance will be needed to keep the press and mass media from control by governments or financial interests, MacBride encouraged the nongovernmental sector to use the media constructively. He stressed the importance of voluntary organizations. "In recent years the non-governmental organizations have been playing an increasingly important role. They are virtually the only independent voices that are heard and that can alert public opinion. They are the only bodies possessing the necessary independence and initiative to restore some faith and idealism in our world."

He encouraged women to seek more prominent roles. "I have found that women have a much better understanding of the imperatives of peace and are much less easily 'taken in' by the specious argu-

ments of experts or diplomats," he observed.

Sean MacBride ended his lecture with a clarion call to the private citizen: "If disarmament can be achieved it will be due to the untiring selfless work of the non-governmental sector," he said. "It is more urgent than ever before. The signpost just ahead of us is 'Oblivion.' The march on this road can be stopped," MacBride urged, "if public opinion uses the power it now has."

Biography

Sean MacBride was born on January 26, 1904, in Paris, son of Major John MacBride and Maud Gonne MacBride; and was educated in Paris and subsequently at university in Dublin. He took an active part in Irish independence as a young man, suffering imprisonment several times. In 1926 he married Catalina Buford; their daughter, Anna, was born in 1927. MacBride worked as a journalist for many years before being called to the bar in 1937. He founded the Republican Party (Clann na Poblacon) in 1946; and was elected to the Irish Parliament (Dáil Éireann) in 1947, retaining his seat for the next 11 years.

MacBride held numerous posts both within the Irish government and with outside organizations: while a member of the Irish Parliament he was Minister for External Affairs 1948-51, Vice-President of the Organization for European Economic Cooperation 1948-51, and President of the Committee of Ministers of Council of Europe in 1950. He became Secretary-General of the International Commission of Jurists in 1963, and Consultant to the Pontifical Commission Justice and Peace (Iustitia et Pax). He chaired three organizations: the Amnesty International Executive, the Special Committee of the International Non-Governmental Organizations on Human Rights, and the Executive International Peace Bureau. He was president of this organization at the time of his Peace Prize award.

Also current to the time of his award, MacBride was Vice-Chairman of the Congress of World Peace Forces (Moscow, 1973) and Vice-President of the Continuing Committee of the World Federation of United Nations Associations (WFUNA).

He was elected by the General Assembly of the United Nations in 1973 to the post of United Nations Commissioner of Namibia with the rank of Assistant Secretary-General of the United Nations, a position he was also holding at the time of the award.

MacBride has been accorded many honors: elected to the International Gaelic Hall of Fame in 1974; Man of the Year, Irish United Societies, 1975; Lenin International Prize for Peace, 1977; American Medal of Justice, 1978; International Institute of Human Rights Medal, 1978; LLD College of St. Thomas, Minnesota, 1975, Guelph University of Canada, 1978; Trinity College, Dublin, 1978, University of Cape Coast, 1978; and D.Litt. Bradford University, 1977.

His publications include: *Civil Liberty* (pamphlet, 1948); *Our People—Our Money* (1951).

Sean MacBride died in 1988.

See also: *Amnesty International* (*1977*)

Bibliography ────────────

Time 1974 What price glory? 104 (October 21)

RUTH C. REYNOLDS

Eisaku Sato
(1974)

Alfred Nobel expressed a hope that dynamite would bring about the permanent cessation of war "a great deal more rapidly than peace congresses would ever succeed in doing." Fifty years later the creators of the atomic bomb likewise believed the unparalleled power of the bomb would force assurance of no future military use of atomic energy. The two recipients of the 1974 Nobel Peace Prize, Sean MacBride and Eisaku Sato, bear witness, each in contrasting ways, to the disillusion of these expectations. Eisaku Sato had experienced nuclear warfare practiced against his country and had seen the specter of planetary annihilation which it introduced to the planet.

In awarding the Peace Prize for 1974 to Eisaku Sato, the Nobel Committee wished to emphasize the important role the Japanese people had played in promoting close and friendly cooperation with other nations under his leadership as Prime Minister. The Committee took note of Sato's development and implementation of the doctrine that Japan shall never own, produce, or acquire nuclear arms. It is important, the Committee said, that under his leadership Japan signed a pact on the nonproliferation of nuclear arms in February 1970. The Committee observed the heartening precedent Prime Minister Sato had provided for sustained, successful use of dialogue and negotiation on the part of a leader of a major power.

Sato became Prime Minister of Japan in 1962, following 14 years in the House of Representatives and various governmental posts of responsibility. In his Nobel lecture Sato told his audience, "It is only natural that for any statesman at the helm of any government, the question of his country's security should be a concern of the utmost importance."

"Upon assuming the reins of government, I adopted, always conscious of the importance of the role of the United Nations, a policy of following a formula of collective security based on the Charter of the United Nations for the maintenance of my country's security."

Reminding his audience that in the nuclear age the common task confronting all countries is to find the means to survive, Sato said that as Prime Minister he had established the doctrine that Japan will not manufacture nuclear weapons, possess them, or bring them into the country. Also under Sato's administration, the Japanese government supported and signed the nuclear Non-Proliferation Treaty.

Sato, convinced of the possibility of peaceful negotiation between two democratic countries with sound economies, sought the return of the Pacific islands of Ogasawara and Okinawa from the United States. He hoped thereby to relax tensions in Asia, where many of the world's divided, unstable countries exist. His ultimate goal was global in scope: the creation of conditions amenable to world peace. His specific task proved complex. He recalled that the negotiations were not easy, but he finally saw the realization of his goal. The territories were returned through diplomatic negotiations. This accomplishment stands as a rare event in world history.

Sato recited to his Nobel audience a phrase which had long been a favorite saying of his; "Here I stand and there stand you: but we remain friends." Thus he encapsulated the philosophy within which he sought to develop a good neighbor policy in Asia. When challenged by difficulties, he said that he always conducted himself with the utmost sincerity and remained always open to dialogue.

The normalization of relations with Korea testified to the extent of his success in stabilizing an insecure area of Asia. Against a background of hostility, and despite the division within Korea, the spirit of mutual cooperation and the realistic advantage to be found in friendship between close neighbors brought about the highly desirable Treaty on Basic Relations between Japan and the Republic of Korea.

Sato described to his Nobel audience three non-nuclear principles which express the determination of the Japanese people to achieve peace: "First, we need the creation of international safety standards. Research and development in the peaceful use of nuclear energy should be carried on under common worldwide regulations that take the environment into account. Next, an international agreement on the exchange and allocation of nuclear fuel will have to be concluded . . . it would be most desirable to establish a system where, under the terms of an agreement concluded for the exchange and allocation of nuclear fuel, such fuels would be placed under the control of an international agency." Lastly, Sato recommended international cooperation in research and development on nuclear fission, deploring the inadequate progress made toward the peaceful uses of atomic energy. He felt it was clear that narrow-minded nationalism was hampering progress in the peaceful utilization of atomic energy.

"All peoples should be united in positive efforts to make peace a reality and to strengthen the foundations on which that peace rests so as to secure for all humanity progress and a better life," Sato concluded. "For my part, I shall devote myself to increasing still my people's capacity to contribute to the well-being of the international community, and to obtaining the world's understanding for such efforts."

Biography

Eisaku Sato was born on March 27, 1901, in Tabuse, Yam-

aguchi Prefecture, Japan. Educated in German jurisprudence at Tokyo Imperial University (now Tokyo University), he passed the senior civil service examinations and joined the Ministry of Railways. In 1948 he first entered the political world as Chief Cabinet Secretary of the second Yosida Cabinet, an appointed post. The next year he was elected to the House of Representatives, following which he held many government and party posts: Chairman of the Policy Affairs Research, member of the Council of the Liberal Party, Secretary-General of the Liberal Party, Minister of Postal Services and Telecommunications, concurrently Minister of Construction and Minister of State in charge of Hokkaido Development, Chairman of the Executive Council of the Liberal Democratic Party, Minister of Finance, Minister of International Trade and Industry, Minister of State in Charge of Science and Technology, Minister of State in Charge of the 18th Olympic Games. In 1964 he became President of the Liberal Democratic Party and Prime Minister, a post he held until June 1972.

Eisaku Sako married Hiroko Sato in 1926. They had two sons, Ryutaro and Shinji.

Eisaku Sato died on June 3, 1975.

Bibliography

Time 1974 What price glory? 104 (October 21)

RUTH C. REYNOLDS

Andrei Sakharov
(1975)

The Nobel Peace Prize for 1975 was awarded to Andrei Dimitriyevich Sakharov for his fearless personal commitment in upholding the fundamental principles for peace between men. "Uncompromisingly and with unflagging strength, Sakharov has fought against the abuse of power and all forms of violation of human dignity, and he has fought no less courageously for the idea of government based on the role of law," Mrs. Aase Lionaes told the award ceremony audience. "In this way, in a particularly effective manner and under highly difficult conditions, he has enhanced respect for the values that rally all true peace lovers."

Something of these difficult conditions were reflected in the Soviet Union's refusal to allow Sakharov to attend the ceremony on the grounds that he had possession of secret military information, although he had done no research since his fall from

grace in 1968.

Andrei Sakharov's evolution from a pinnacle position in the Soviet scientific community as "Father of the Soviet hydrogen bomb" to a Nobel Laureate, and "fearless combatant for peace among men," is a story of an unfolding social conscience. "I had money . . . title, and everything which my work entitled me to have. But I had a very tragic feeling," Sakharov said of his years as an atomic scientist working on development of nuclear arms. Though the work of his group also included harnessing nuclear power for peaceful purposes in industry, Sakharov said that the tragedy which befell Hiroshima and Nagasaki distressed him "both as an atomic physicist and simply as a man of the Planet Earth."

In his book, *Sakharov Speaks*, he describes his changing way of thinking: "Beginning in 1957 (not without the influence of statements on this subject made throughout the world by such people as Albert Schweitzer, Linus Pauling, and others), I felt myself responsible for the problem of radioactive contamination from nuclear explosions." He was frank with the authorities about his convictions, hoping to generate a free and open exchange of opinion. In this he met with disappointment, although Sakharov believes that his views did influence the Soviet decision to join with the United States in an agreement in 1963 on a ban on nuclear testing.

Between 1953 and 1962, much of what happened was connected with the development of nuclear weapons and with the preparations for and realization of the nuclear experiments, he said. "At the same time I was becoming ever more conscious of the moral problems inherent in this work. In and after 1964, when I began to concern myself with the biological issues, and particularly from 1967 onwards, the extent of the problems over which I felt uneasy increased to such a point that in 1968 I felt a compelling urge to make my views public." That year he wrote his famous essay, *Progress, Peaceful Coexistence, and Intellectual Freedom*, based on the belief that socialism and capitalism would eventually converge, and that a workable world government could become a reality. His growing fear of nuclear war motivated his writing this early essay, and he wrote it from a global point of view, appealing to responsible citizens worldwide. It was published abroad in 1968.

At the time, as a socialist, Sakharov was optimistic about the progress within his own country both toward lessening restrictions upon the citizens within its borders, and increased Soviet cooperation internationally. But he had misjudged the period of relative liberalism which he thought had arrived in the Soviet Union, and looking back he came to assess the context within which he wrote it as one of isolation in a highly privileged scientific milieu, without contact with the community outside. That same year Soviet tanks rolled into Czechoslovakia amidst a new wave of repression in the Soviet Union. Sakharov's security clearance was revoked and he was dismissed from his research position and assigned to the Physics Institute of the Academy of Scientists.

As Sakharov's life changed, his outlook expanded. Along with his long-time concern with global problems, he now confronted personal and human ones. His intimate contact with the daily life of the ordinary Soviet citizen propelled him into a commitment for an intense struggle in their behalf, a commitment which he openly indicated in letters to the authorities demanding reforms.

"From 1970 onwards," Sakharov said, "the defence of human rights and the defence of the victims of political trials became all-important to me." He founded the "Committee for Human Rights" that year, forming a committee with friends and fellow scientists. They labored to achieve the following aims while attempting to work within the framework of the law: the abolition of secret trials, a new press law ensuring that people would have full information, reforms in the prison system, the amnesty of political prisoners, the abolition of the death penalty, open frontiers, and a ban on the use of psychiatric institutes for political ends.

Sakharov's ideas on the conditions necessary for peace and détente have found an echo in the "Agreement on Security and Cooperation" in Europe. Signed in Helsinki on August 1, 1975, by 35 different nations, it was an endorsement of the leading states of the world that human rights are an essential factor in détente between nations. Sakharov's Nobel lecture, read by his wife, Elena Bonner Sakharov, opened with the declaration, "Peace, progress, human rights"—these three goals are insolubly linked to one another: it is impossible to achieve one of these goals if the other two are ignored. This is the dominant idea that provides the main theme of my lecture."

"I am convinced that international confidence, mutual understanding, disarmament, and international security are inconceivable without an open society with freedom of information, freedom of conscience, the right to publish, and the right to travel and choose the country in which one wishes to live."

"I am likewise convinced that freedom of conscience, together with other civil rights, provides the basis for scientific progress and constitutes a guarantee that scientific advances will not be used to despoil mankind, providing the basis for economic and social progress."

Sakharov strongly recommended against any attempt to reduce the tempo of scientific and technological progress. "In actual fact all important aspects of progress are closely interwoven; not one of them can be dispensed without a risk of destroying the entire setup of our civilization. Progress is indivisible," he warned.

He pleaded for a proportional and simultaneous military deescalation for all countries, with attention to finding some solution to the economic and social problems involved.

Sakharov took the rare opportunity afforded to him through his Nobel lecture to speak of the repressions in the Soviet Union, thus opening a window upon that area of information so restricted to the Western world. He honored by name many Soviet compatriots who had suffered prison, banishment, and other deprivations as punishment for following their conscience, and begged to share his Nobel honors with them, and with the many who yet remain unnamed.

Sakharov addressed the problem of disarmament, defining it as one of the central problems of our present age. "It is imperative," he said, "to promote confidence between nations, and carry out measures of control with the aid of international inspection groups. This is only possible if détente is extended to the ideological sphere, and it presupposes greater social openness."

He concluded his lecture with some prerequisites he deemed essential for peace: "We need reform, not revolution. We need a pliant, pluralist, tolerant community, which selectively and tentatively can bring about a free, undogmatic use of the experiences of all social systems. What is détente? What is rapprochement? We are concerned not with words, but with a willingness to create a better and more friendly society, a better world order."

No Peace Prize Laureate has re-created so closely the dynamics behind the original decision by Alfred Nobel to create a prize for peace as has Sakharov. Nobel's invention of dynamite led Nobel to an acute awareness of the development in weaponry he had made possible, and he thought much about the consequences for humanity, ultimately giving of effort and money toward the prevention of its use. Sakharov, inventor of the hydrogen bomb, likewise became haunted by what his discovery might mean to humanity, and he, too, has made all the efforts within his power toward prevention of its use. His was a singularly appropriate award.

Biography

Andrei Dimitriyevich Sakharov was born in Moscow in 1921. He studied physics at Moscow State University, and attracted considerable attention at an early age with the publication of a number of scientific papers. In 1945, Sakharov joined the P. N. Lebedev Physics Institute in Moscow, where he worked with Igor Tamm, the specialist on quantum mechanics and subsequent winner (in 1958) of the Nobel Prize for Physics. Under Tamm's guidance,

Sakharov obtained his doctorate in physical and mathematical sciences in 1947—a formidable achievement at such an early age in the Soviet Union.

During the years 1948-56, Sakharov was engaged almost exclusively in nuclear research as a member of a team of scientists engaged in the development of nuclear arms. A virtual press blackout was imposed on these activities; but such was the extent of his achievements that in 1953 Sakharov became the youngest scientist ever to be elected to the prestigious Soviet Academy of Sciences. He became a member of the American Academy of Sciences in 1945, of the National Academy of Sciences in 1972, and a Foreign Associate of the Academie des Sciences in 1981. In 1968, however, a significant change occurred in his status and way of life. In that year he published his famous essay on *Progress, Peaceful Coexistence, and Intellectual Freedom*; and these statements presaged the role he was later to play as a critic of his society. In addition to the Nobel Peace Prize, he has received the following honors: the Eleanor Roosevelt Peace Award, 1973, Cino del Duca Prize, 1974, Reinhold Niebuhr Prize, Chicago University, 1974, Fritt Ord Prize, 1980. Married to Elena Bonner, they have one son and one daughter. In addition to scientific works, his publications are: *Progress, Peaceful Coexistence, and Intellectual Freedom* (1968), *Sakharov Speaks* (1974), *My Country and the World* (1975), and *Alarm and Hope* (1979).

Bibliography

Sakharov A D 1968 *Progress, Peaceful Coexistence, and Intellectual Freedom*. Norton, New York

Sakharov A D 1975a *My Country and the World*. Knopf, New York

Sakharov A D 1975b The need for an open world. *Bull. At. Sci.* 31(9)

Sakharov A D 1978 *Alarm and Hope*. Knopf, New York

Science 1975 Letter to Izvestiya. 190 (December 19)

Snapley D 1975 Sakharov: Scientists welcome award of Nobel Peace Prize. *Science* 190 (October 24)

York H F 1981 Sakharov and the nuclear test ban. *Bull. At. Sci.* 37(9)

RUTH C. REYNOLDS

Mairead Corrigan and Betty Williams

(1976)

Two women shared the Nobel Peace Prize for 1976. Given retroactively in 1977, the Prize honored Betty Williams and Mairead Corrigan, co-founders of the Northern Ireland Peace Movement, who, the Nobel

Committee said, "have shown us what ordinary people can do to promote the cause of peace . . . . They never heeded the difficulty of their task, they merely tackled it because they were so convinced that this was precisely what was needed." The Committee expressed admiration that these two women, without talk of "ingenious theories, of shrewd diplomacy or pompous declarations," unleashed in their war-torn country a fervent desire for peace lying latent in thousands of hearts. Out of this grew a peace movement, and, the Committee concluded, "with poignant simplicity and confidence they have accepted responsibility for what they started."

It was a campaign born in a moment of carnage on a street in Belfast. In August 1976 a British soldier shot the driver of an Irish Republican Army (IRA) get-away car. The driver, Danny Lennon, was killed instantly, and the out-of-control vehicle slammed into a mother and her three small children. The children died instantly, their mother was gravely injured. Violent death has become familiar in Northern Ireland, a community long-divided by hatred and sectarian bitterness. In 1969 a student-led civil rights movement sparked the simmering hostility into violence. The Provisional wing of the IRA, committed to an armed struggle for a united, Catholic Ireland, and the Ulster Defence Association (UDA), implacable opponents of the IRA in their commitment to a separate Protestant Ulster, engaged in such violent exchanges that in desperation the British government stepped in and imposed direct rule from London backed up by martial law. Yet senseless, sudden death continued: some 1,700 people were killed in the following seven years, and the citizens seemed too numbed to protest at the horror permeating their lives.

Betty Williams witnessed the horrific accident in August 1976 and the deaths of the three young children, and in that moment she was overwhelmed with a passionate determination to end the bloodshed. Galvanized into action, she went from door to door begging her neighbors to join her in demonstrating for an end to the violence. Her appeal touched a spontaneous, emotional response, and 200 people rallied around her. One of the first to join her was Mairead Corrigan, aunt of the dead children.

In that first week the two women, with Ciaran McKeown, a journalist, founded the "Movement of the Peace People." One week later 10,000 people—Protestants and Catholics—marched the streets of Belfast. To the cries of "treason" and "traitor" hurled at them by agitators from both sides, they replied, "We condemn all violence whether it is from the UDA, the IRA, or the British Army."

The two women acknowledged that they were facing a long-range and complex task. Betty Williams described the nature of the tenacious Irish conflict in an interview: "Most wars are wars of insanity. But ours is doubly insane, because we're fighting over something they call 'faith': Catholic and Protestant. We live on an absolutely beautiful land, and we cultivate it with our blood" (*Christian Century* 1977).

Though Ireland has long been locked into the warring factions Betty Williams describes, and though reason would declare that the use of arms could never bring about a lasting peace, no-one had seemed capable of suggesting a viable alternative. The "two women of peace from Ulster" challenged this deadlock. "We know that this insane and immoral imbalance of priorities cannot be changed overnight; we also know that it will not be changed without the greatest struggle," they conceded.

In her Nobel lecture Mrs. Williams called for "an incessant struggle to get the human race to stop wasting its vast resources on arms, and start investing in the people who must live out their lives on the planet we share, east and west, north and south. And that struggle must be all the greater because it has to be an unarmed, nonviolent struggle, and requires more courage and more persistence than the courage to squeeze triggers or press murderous buttons. Men must not only end war, they must begin to have the courage not to even prepare for war."

"We have to think, and think hard, but if we do not have compassion before we even start thinking, then we are quite likely to start fighting over theories," Mrs. Williams said, "We are divided on the surface of this planet by physical barriers, emotional barriers, ideological barriers, barriers of prejudice and hatreds of every kind . . . yet the whole human family can be united by compassion." She said that now the moment in history has come when, for very survival, compassion and understanding must be given "pride of place over the vainglorious adventures that lead to war."

The Nobel Committee acknowledged the perilous challenge facing the two women, "But," the Committee said, "one incontrovertible fact remains: they took the first courageous step along the road to peace. They did so in the name of humanity and love of their neighbour: someone had to start forgiving."

"We admire Betty Williams and Mairead Corrigan for tackling so fearlessly the perilous task of leading the way into no-man's land, in the cause of peace and reconciliation . . . a courageous, unselfish act that proved an inspiration to thousands, that lit a light in the darkness, and that gave fresh hope to people who believed that all hope was gone."

Biography

Mairead Corrigan was born in January, 1944, in Belfast, one of eight children of Mr. and Mrs. Andrew Corrigan. Educated at St. Vincent's Primary School, Belfast, and at Miss Gordon's Commercial College, she worked from the age of 16 in various positions as a shorthand typist. She volunteered in Catholic Organizations establishing clubs for physically handicapped children and for teenagers, and she worked in preschool play groups. She was also a visitor to internees in Long Kesh Prison. On August 10, 1976 her sister's three children were crushed by a runaway car driven by an IRA man who had been shot by British soldiers on the streets of Belfast. A week later, as the outcome of a spontaneous and emotional response, she co-founded the Community of Peace People with Mr. Ciaran McKeown and Mrs. Betty Williams. She had been prominent in the Peace Movement since that time, and was Chairman of the Peace People Organisation, 1980-81. She has been awarded the Carl Von Ossietzky Medal for Courage from the Berlin section of the International League of Human Rights, an Honorary Doctor of Law from Yale University, and the Norwegian People Peace Prize, 1976. In September 1981, Mairead Corrigan married Mr. Jackie Maguire, her former brother-in-law. Mr. Maguire's wife, Ann, Miss Corrigan's sister, committed suicide in 1980.

Betty Williams was born in May, 1943, in Belfast to Mr. and Mrs. Smyth. She was educated at St. Teresa's Primary School in Belfast and St. Dominic's Grammar School and worked as an office receptionist. She married Mr. Ralph Williams on June 14, 1961, and they had a son, Paul, and a daughter, Deborah. In August 1976, following the tragic death of a neighbor's three small children, crushed on the streets of Belfast by a car driven by an IRA member who had been shot by British troops, Betty Williams co-founded the Northern Ireland Peace Movement. She has received the Carl Von Ossietzky Medal for Courage from the Berlin section of the International League of Human Rights, an Honorary Doctor of Law from Yale University, and the Norwegian People Peace Prize, 1976. In February 1980, after falling out with her co-founders, Betty Williams resigned from the executive committee and ceased to be associated with the Peace Movement. In October 1982, she married Mr. Jim Perkins in Florida.

Bibliography

Christian Century 1977 Good news from Norway. 94(34)

Keerdoja E 1978 Ulster's women of peace. *Newsweek* 91

Kennedy R S. Klotz-Chamberlin P 1977 Northern Ireland's 'guerrillas of peace': An interview with Betty Williams and Nancy McDonnell. *Christian Century* 94(25)

Time 1977 Two Peace Prizes from Oslo. 110(17)

Willenson K, Collings A 1977 Two women of Ulster. *Newsweek* 90

RUTH C. REYNOLDS

Amnesty International
(1977)

Amnesty International received the 1977 Nobel Peace Prize, in an award ceremony shared with the initiators of the Northern Ireland Peace Movement, Mairead Corrigan and Betty Williams, who were receiving the 1976 Peace Prize retroactively. With these awards the Nobel Committee expressed its conviction that peace is more than merely abstinence from war; it also embodies such basic human rights as freedom of thought, freedom of conscience, and freedom of religion or faith.

In his acceptance speech for Amnesty International, Mumtaz Soysal expressed gratification with this recognition that a just society is a precondition to a peaceful world. The awareness of this must not grow dim. "Each violation," Soysal explained, "can set in motion a trend toward the debasement of human dignity. From individuals to groups, from groups to nations, from nations to groups of nations, in chain reaction a pattern is set of violence and repression . . . . This must never be allowed to start and the place to stop it is at the level of the individual . . . . Therefore, the protection of the rights of the individual to think freely, to express himself freely, to associate freely with others and to disseminate his thoughts is essential to the preservation of world peace."

These freedoms are interlocked with the economic and social conditions necessary to make them possible. Therefore the aim of economic and social development is to work always towards the ultimate end that individuals are made more free, more able to express and fulfill themselves, more able to contribute to humanity. Soysal explained that where there are communities composed of individuals who are free in this fullest sense there is less likelihood of exploitation of the weaker by the strong. This applies whether for a social class, or a nation, or a group of nations. Therefore promotion of human rights in the fullest possible sense is directly related to the preservation of lasting peace.

The world community stands at a tragic distance from this picture. Information obtained by Amnesty International shows that human rights are violated in all parts of the world, in all major regions, and in all political or ideological blocs.

> By the beginning of 1985, there were 3,430 Amnesty International groups in 55 countries—almost 200 more groups than the year before. There were over 500,000 members, supporters and subscribers with sections in 45 countries.
>
> A total of 4,668 prisoners were adopted as prisoners of conscience or were being investigated as possible prisoners of conscience. During 1984, 1,665 new cases were taken up and 1,516 prisoners released.
>
> Amnesty International issued 319 urgent action appeals on behalf of individuals or groups of prisoners in 67 countries. Of these, 104 were prompted by reports of torture, 22 were made on medical grounds, 67 were issued because of legal concerns, 57 related to extrajudicial executions or "disappearances" and 58 were on behalf of people under sentence of death. (*Amnesty International Report* 1985 p. 359)

Hopeful situations where there have been substantial releases of political prisoners are more than outweighed by deteriorating situations in other parts of the world. In Latin America some countries' security forces have been used as instruments for political murder. Government-sanctioned torture is still practiced. The list of crimes deemed punishable by the death penalty is growing, and the rate of execution is high, especially in Africa and Asia. Long-term banishments are secretively imposed without the basic right of trial. In some instances the laws and court procedures make a mockery of justice.

A great many people have been seized with a sense of horror that is paralyzing, the Nobel Committee noted, but Amnesty International, far from shrinking into the impotence of discouragement, has stepped up its efforts to ensure that governments in all countries should feel morally obligated to abide by the United Nations Universal Declaration on Human Rights.

Amnesty International had its inception in 1960 in a compartment of a train in London, where a British lawyer, Peter Benenson, happened to read an account of two Portuguese students who were being sentenced to long internment in prison for making critical remarks of Salazar's regime. At that moment Benenson decided he would try to do something for the two young men. Gathering together some friends, he organized a letter-writing campaign. What they began so modestly on that day developed into a movement that is renowned today for its worldwide befriending of prisoners. Its early years of rapid growth were administrated under the skillful leadership of 1974 Peace Prize Laureate Sean MacBride.

Called "the conscience of the world" by many, Amnesty International works for the release of prisoners who are incarcerated for their opinions and have made no use of violence or incited others to do so. These it calls "prisoners of conscience."

In behalf of all prisoners anywhere, Amnesty International works for basic rights: that they be accorded fair trial, openly and with legal defense, and if convicted, that prisoners be guaranteed humane treatment. As violence escalates over the world, Amnesty works rigorously to expose torture or cruel, inhumane treatment, to the end that public opinion and censure can be brought to bear against such practices.

An important tool which Amnesty International has guarded carefully since its inception is its own meticulous neutrality. It is committed to political and geographic impartiality. Nor will it accept donations which could compromise its freedom of activity. This absolute neutrality is the sine qua non if it is to maintain credibility.

The people in Amnesty work within groups. Relatively small groups "adopt" prisoners from a country other than their own. With the help of the head office in London these groups trace, help, and seek to secure the release of prisoners of conscience. Wherever possible the adopting group develops a close relationship with the prisoners they seek to help. They write the prisoners letters. They help their families. They seek ways to boost morale, so the forgotten and banished can shed their fear that no-one cares. They expose prisoners' plight in any way possible. The groups organize letter writing, flooding government officials with mail. They demonstrate and use any form of media exposure open to them in behalf of the prisoners. Often release has resulted simply because they have become a nuisance in a situation which has been operating under the cloak of secrecy. The avalanche of mail bombarding officials at all levels can create an untenable annoyance to a government.

Amnesty International never claims responsibility for winning a prisoner's release. As Secretary-General Martin Ennals explained, "No government likes to be told they have done something under duress."

It is clear, the Nobel Committee noted, that the organization's future will depend to a large extent upon its audience with fair-minded people worldwide. At the Belgrade Conference held to negotiate a follow-up on promises made in the Helsinki Agreements to promote human rights, a number of nations maintained that for one country to call attention to a violation of human rights in another country constitutes interference in the internal affairs of that country. Chairwoman Lionaes, speaking for the Nobel Committee, refused to believe that a ruse of this nature would be countenanced by international opinion, holding that human rights recognize no national boundaries.

What have been the results of Amnesty International's activity? At the time of the award, of some 16,000 prisoners aided since 1961, 10,600 had been released. Other factors may well have contributed to these results, but it is a fair reflection on the scope of Amnesty's work. However, statistics cannot adequately measure what hope might mean to an inmate sunk in the depths of despair. No accounting can establish the weight of impact that the defense of human dignity against torture, violence, and degradations has upon the cause of peace in this world.

"This work to protect human dignity," the Committee said in awarding Amnesty international the Peace Prize, "is not a sacrifice we make for others: it is important that all of us should understand that in this age we must act accordingly in recognition of the earnest appeal contained in Aleksandr Solzhenitsyn's words:

> You're defending yourself—
> Your future is at stake."

History

Amnesty International was founded by a London lawyer,

Peter Benenson, in 1961. Sean MacBride, Nobel Peace Prize Laureate of 1974, was its Chairman from 1961 to 1975, leading it from its simple start as a letter-writing campaign on behalf of two unfairly imprisoned students in Portugal to a world-renowned organization working against many aspects of injustice. Amnesty International works for the release of prisoners jailed because of political or religious beliefs, and in behalf of the basic rights and humane treatment of all prisoners everywhere. It also opposes capital punishment.

Their method is exposure of the prisoners' plight through flooding members of governments and influential citizens with mail, and through use of any media open to them. The governments often react to the annoyance thus created by releasing the prisoners. At the time of the Amnesty International Nobel Peace Prize award in 1977, out of 16,000 prisoners in whose behalf they had worked over 10,000 had been released. By the beginning of 1985 there were 3,430 Amnesty International groups in 55 countries. It had over 500,000 members, supporters, and subscribers, sections in 45 countries, and 21 languages were spoken (*Amnesty International Report* 1985 p. 359).

Bibliography ───────────────

Amnesty International Report 1985 Amnesty International Publications, London
Christian Century 1977 Good news from Norway. 94 (October 26)
Christian Century 1984 Events and people: Rights abuses continue. 101 (November 14)
Newsweek 1977 The world's conscience. 90 (October 24)
Stempf T 1984 Getting away with murder. *America* 151 (October 24)
Time 1977 Two Peace Prizes from Oslo. 110 (October 24)

RUTH C. REYNOLDS

Menachem Begin
(1978)

The 1978 Nobel Peace Prize was awarded to Prime Minister Menachem Begin of Israel and President Anwar al-Sadat of Egypt in recognition of the foundation they laid for future peace by opening negotiations between their one-time enemy countries and preparing a pathway toward nonviolent solutions in the Middle East.

The Nobel Committee pronounced their award to be without precedent in many ways: "Never has the

Nobel Committee considered it apposite to award the Peace Prize to statesmen from the troubled and sadly devastated Middle East," Chairwoman Lionaes declared. "Never has the Prize been closely associated with agreements such as the two Camp David agreements. Never has the Peace Prize expressed a greater or more audacious hope—a hope of peace for the people of Egypt, for the people of Israel, and for all the peoples of the strife-torn and war-ravaged

Middle East."

Israel and Egypt lie in the cradle of civilization, inheritors of a turbulent history. Juxtapositioned between the birthplaces of Islam, Judaism, and Christianity, their soil is regarded by followers of each religion as a divinely established birthright. The cultures of the Middle East are diverse, and differing economic interests often clash. Its countries are ravaged by schisms, prey to foreign domination and wars.

Menachem Begin was born in a country also fraught with tensions. In 1913 his birthplace, Poland, was in the grip of unparalleled anti-Semitism. The persecution he witnessed early in life crystallized Begin's determination to see the restoration of the ancient Jewish homeland. Both of his parents and his only brother were killed in the Nazi Holocaust.

Begin's youthful years were turbulent. Twice he was imprisoned: first during his law school years, when he took part in a demonstration for the right of persecuted Jews to emigrate to Palestine; and again in Lithuania, where the Soviets intercepted his family's flight to Palestine and he was sentenced to eight years of forced labor in a Siberian prison camp.

The German attack on the Soviet Union provided the circumstances for Begin's release. He was pressed into service in a new Polish army that the Soviets hoped to deploy in the struggle against Nazism, and was posted to Transjordan, and from there, in 1942, he made his way to Palestine. There he again found Jews denied the means of escape from the threat of extermination at the hands of the Nazis—this time through restrictions on immigration imposed by Great Britain. Begin demanded an open door for Jewish refugees, throwing his energy into opposing the devastating restrictions. His subsequent leadership of the Irgun, an underground combatant organization calling for the independence of Palestine as a Jewish state, brought him a reputation as a terrorist and a price of £30,000 on his head. Commanding a small but well-disciplined force that numbered never more than 2,000 activists, Begin planned and directed a guerrilla campaign against the British that has become what *Current Biography* (1977) termed "something of a classic in the annals of wars of liberation."

In 1948 the State of Israel was founded with the help of the United Nations, and Begin with his former Irgun associates created the Herut ("Freedom") political party, which was radically opposed to the Israeli Labour Party, Mapai, led by Ben Gurion. The creation of this new state exacerbated the long-standing conflict between the Jews and the Arabs, and

four wars have since been fought between them. It was against this background of resentment and hostility that Begin, as newly elected Prime Minister of Israel, accepted Sadat's diplomatic overture and invited the charismatic leader of Israel's ancient "enemy" country to speak before the Israeli Knesset (Parliament).

Years of bitter hostility between the two countries with only brief intervals of truce now stood challenged by the two new leaders who dared to propose a visionary program to establish a permanent peace. Begin described the philosophy that had led him to that momentous occasion: "If through your efforts and sacrifices you win liberty, and with it the prospect for peace, then work for peace because there is no mission in life more sacred."

In his pursuit of that dream, Begin recalled, "We went any place, we looked for any avenue, we made any effort to bring about negotiations between Israel and its neighbors, negotiations without which peace remains an abstract desire . . . in peace, the Middle East will become invigorated and transformed."

With his invitation to Sadat, Begin made a promise: "You will be received with respect and cordiality." And indeed he was. "We knew and learned that we have differences of opinion," Begin recalled. "But whenever we remember those days of Jerusalem we say, always, that they were shining, beautiful days of friendliness and understanding."

The two leaders forged a mutual pledge: "No more war. No more bloodshed. We shall negotiate and reach agreement." Their daring leadership provided the way to the historic agreements at Camp David.

"Admittedly, there were difficult times," Begin told his Nobel award ceremony audience. "Let nobody forget that we are dealing with a conflict of more than sixty years with its manifold tragedies. These we must put behind us in order to establish friendship and make peace the beauty of our lives."

"The President of the United States, Mr. Jimmy Carter, unforgettably invested unsparing effort, untiring energy and great devotion in the peace-making process . . . . If, because of all these efforts, President Sadat and I have been awarded the Nobel Peace Prize, let me from this rostrum again congratulate him."

Nobel Chairwoman Lionaes also recognized Henry Kissinger's role in bringing about the Camp David meetings. "We recall his energetic attempts to get the belligerent parties in the so-called Yom Kippur War to come together in a peace conference in Geneva," she told the Nobel audience. The conference resulted in agreement between Egypt and Israel on a number of important points, and provided the basis for the meeting at Camp David.

Begin summarized their achievement there. "Despite all the differences, we found solutions for problems, agreed on issues, and the Framework for Peace was signed. The path leading to peace was paved."

The Nobel Committee acknowledged that "time-consuming negotiations" on the Israeli-occupied territories of the West Bank, Gaza, and the Golan Heights remained for the future. Their award at this time was based upon recognition that Sadat and Begin had played key roles in creating a vigorous quest for peace between two former enemies.

The Committee commended their long-sustained efforts: "Both men were born in a century marked by global wars and gigantic revolutions, both of them have been active in the mainstream of history ... from their earliest years both identified with the fate of their countries, both have fought and suffered in prison and in labor camp, for the sovereignty of their native land and for the freedom of man."

"Their lives have crossed in an act of peace that may well usher in a new era, a future of material renewal and peace, not only for their two respective countries, but for the entire Middle East."

In his Nobel lecture Prime Minister Begin expanded this vision: "Perhaps the very capability for total destruction of our little planet—achieved for the first time in the annals of mankind—will one day, God willing, become the origin, the cause and the prime mover for the elimination of all instruments of destruction from the face of the earth. And ultimate peace, prayed for and yearned for by previous generations, will become the portion of all nations."

Biography

Menachem Begin was born in the Polish city of Brest-Litovsk (which later became part of the former Soviet Union), son of Wolf Begin and Hassia Kossovsky Begin. Educated at the gymnasium in Brest-Litovsk, he went on to study law at the University of Warsaw, taking a Master of Jurisprudence degree in 1935. As a student, Begin was co-founder of the Jewish Student Defense Unit; and in 1929 had joined Birit Trumpeldor (or BCTK), a militant youth organization associated with the Revisionist wing of the World Zionist Organization. After graduating, he served first as General Secretary of the Czechoslovakian branch (1936-38) before becoming commander of the Polish Betar in 1939. When the Soviet Union annexed Lithuania, his Betar role stamped him as "unreliable" to the communist

regime and he was arrested and sentenced to eight years as a slave laborer in the Arctic wasteland.

After the German attack on the Soviet Union, Begin was released to serve in the new Polish army that the Soviets hoped to deploy in the struggle against Nazism, and was posted to Transjordan. From there, he made his way into Palestine where he became commander of the Irgun Zvai Leumi (National Fighting Organization associated with the Revisionist faction). His opposition to the British refusal to an open door for all escapees from Hitler's Europe and immediate political independence for a Jewish state won him a price of £ 30,000 on his head.

Commanding a small but well-disciplined force that never numbered more than 2,000 activists, Begin planned and directed a guerrilla campaign against the British. He gained a reputation for ruthlessness and was condemned as a terrorist by the British.

When the State of Israel became a reality in 1948, Begin founded a new political party, Herut, in opposition to Ben Gurion. As Chairman of Herut he won a seat in the Israeli Knesset (Parliament) in the first election and was an active member thereafter. In 1977 he became the sixth Prime Minister of Israel. Declaring that the main goal of his government was peace, he called for direct talks with the heads of Egypt, Jordan, and Syria, and expressed hope for strengthened ties with the United States, France, and the Soviet Union. One of his first official actions was to authorize the granting of asylum to 66 Vietnamese refugees picked up at sea by an Israeli ship.

Begin was reelected Prime Minister in national elections in 1981, and remained in office until his retirement in 1983.

Menachem Begin married Aliza Arnold in Poland in 1939 and they have one son, Benyamin, two daughters, Hassia and Leah, and several grandchildren. Begin is the author of an autobiography, *HaMered* (1950), *Be-Leilot Levanim* (1953), *White Nights* (1957), describing his wartime experiences in Europe, and *The Revolt* (1964), which has been read worldwide in many languages, and numerous articles.

See also: Articles: *Camp David Accords*

Bibliography

Deming A, Martin D C, DeFrank T M 1978 A timely award? *Newsweek* 92 (November 6)
Feld B T 1978 Norwegian prophecy or a gamble for peace? *Bull. Atomic Sci.* 34(10)
O'Hare J A 1978 Of many things. *America* 139(15): inside cover *Time* 1978 Alone in Oslo. 112 (December 18)

RUTH C. REYNOLDS

Anwar al-Sadat
(1978)

The 1978 Nobel Peace Prize was shared by Anwar al-Sadat, President of Egypt, and Menachem Begin, Prime Minister of Israel, in recognition of their creation of two frame agreements on peace, one in the Middle East and one between Egypt and Israel.

The Nobel Committee said that three precedents were established in the history of the Nobel Peace Prize by these two choices. Never before had the Prize gone to statesmen from the Middle East, never before had the prize honored agreements such as the two reached at Camp David, and never before, the Committee stated, "has the Peace Prize expressed a greater or more audacious hope—a hope of peace for the people of Egypt, for the people of Israel, and for all the peoples of the strife-torn and war-ravaged Middle East."

The history of the Middle East covers 6,000 years, during which the juxtaposition of diverse cultures, civilizations, and religions has given rise to many longlasting tensions. Islam, Judaism, and Christianity all revere its soil as the birthplace of their belief. The economic interests of the Middle East, positioned as it is at the junction of Asia, Europe, and Africa, have long been entangled, making for a history of continuous foreign invasions.

Such is the legacy which influenced Anwar Sadat early in life. His country's struggle for freedom from British subjugation dominated Sadat's aspirations during his youth. He entered a military career with the dream of throwing off the British yoke, and he was destined to play a vital part in achieving that dream.

Sadat began life in humble circumstances. Born on December 25, 1918, he was one of 13 children in a devout and loving Moslem family, and grew up in a small village in the Nile Delta. He paid high tribute to the childhood he spent there: "Everything I experienced in Mit Abul-Kum made me happy." His boyhood feeling of oneness with nature and closeness with family created a sense of balance between himself, the soil, and his family which brought a sense of inner harmony important to Sadat all his life. "I first felt that inner peace in my village where I still have my roots, deep in the soil of the Nile Valley," he said. "But I really found this peace in Cell 54, a bare damp room in Cairo Central Prison where I spent 18 months for revolutionary activity. I was in solitary, where I could not read or write or listen to the radio . . . . Suffering builds up a human being and gives

him self-knowledge."

Along with his school friend, Gamal Adbel Nasser, Sadat became an army officer, and together they formed a secret group of officers in 1939 devoted to freeing Egypt from foreign domination. Hoping to weaken Britain's hold on his country by cooperating with her enemy during the Second World War, Sadat attempted collusion with the Germans. The attempt proved ill-fated, and for this activity he was stripped of his officer's rank and imprisoned in 1942.

Reinstated in the army in 1950, Sadat played a supporting role to his friend Nasser in the Egyptian revolution which led to the overthrow of King Farouk. During the 18 years of Nasser's presidency which followed, Sadat became intimately acquainted with his country's problems through service in a wide range of posts: as cabinet minister, Secretary-General of the Islamic Conference, Speaker of the National Assembly, editor of the government newspaper, and finally, in 1969, Vice-President.

Sadat was the only member of the original revolutionary officers' group not purged by the suspicious dictator-president. He enjoyed the confidence of Nasser and understood well how the revolution had fallen sadly short of establishing democratic practices. When he became President in September 1970 following Nasser's fatal heart attack, Sadat devoted his energies to addressing this failure.

Sadat's sudden "October war" against Israel in 1975 he described in his autobiography, *In Search of Identity*, as a "paradoxical necessary prelude to any kind of lasting peace in the Middle East . . . . It was for us in Egypt a historic transformation from despair to hope, from complete lack of self-confidence to the regaining of confidence. After the ceasefire we initiated an ambitious program of building and reconstruction . . . constant military preparation had plunged our economy to below zero . . . . Despite these obstacles, we succeeded in restoring our economic path form total isolation to an open-door policy."

"And since that time we have worked wholeheartedly for peace," he said. It was after that struggle, when lasting peace seemed elusive to all efforts, that Sadat sent a message to Prime Minister Begin of Israel expressing interest in coming to address the Israeli Knesset (Parliament). When Begin responded with an invitation immediately, President Sadat startled the world, his fellow countrymen included, by his unprecedented trip to Jerusalem in 1977. "I made that trip because I was convinced that we owe it to this generation and the generations to come not to leave a stone unturned in our pursuit of peace," he said.

Nobel Committee Chairwoman Lionaes commented on that remarkable event: "During the thirty preceding years the peoples of the Middle East have on four separate occasions been the victims of warfare, and there seemed no prospect of peace. President Sadat's great contribution to peace was that he had the sufficient courage and foresight to break away from this vicious circle."

"His decision to accept Prime Minister Menachem Begin's invitation of November 17th, 1977, to attend a meeting of the Israeli parliament on November 19th was an act of great courage, both from a personal and from a political point of view. This was a dramatic break with the past and a courageous step forward into a new age."

With this forward step, Sadat and Begin created a diplomatic climate conducive to their meeting at Camp David in September 1978. There, two major peace documents were created: "A Framework for Peace in the Middle East," and the "Framework for the Conclusion of a Peace Treaty Between Egypt and Israel," which established broad areas of compromise and made arrangements for difficult areas of conflict to be negotiated in the future.

Chairwoman Lionaes referred to an important third personage in the Camp David setting. "The master-builder responsible for the bridge that had to be built between Egypt and Israel in order that these two one-time enemy nations should have any opportunity of coming together ... was the President of the United States, Jimmy Carter." Sadat concurred, opening his Nobel lecture saying "Recognition is due to a man of the highest integrity, President Jimmy Carter, whose signal efforts to overcome obstacles in the way of peace deserves our keenest appreciation."

The Committee, although admitting that difficult problems dealing with the Israeli-occupied territories of the West Bank, Gaza, and the Golan Heights had been left for future negotiations, gave high praise to the effort made and the progress achieved: "Meanwhile, the world must be allowed to share in the happiness of the people of Egypt and Israel, that, for the first time since the re-establishment of the state of Israel in 1948, an agreement has successfully been reached which, on a long term basis, provides a genuine opportunity for peace in an area over which the shadow of war had hovered for so long."

Had President Sadat been allowed to pursue his goal, the future for establishment of permanent peace

between Egypt and Israel would seem promising in the hands of a leader who could say during his historic first appearance before the Israeli Knesset: "Any life lost in war is the life of a human being, irrespective of whether it is an Arab or an Israeli."

"The wife who becomes widowed is a human being, entitled to live in a happy family, Arab or Israeli."

"Innocent children, deprived of paternal care and sympathy are all our children, whether they live on Arab or Israeli soil, and we owe them the responsibility of providing them with a happy present and a bright future."

"For the sake of all this, for the sake of protecting the lives of all our sons and brothers; for our societies to produce in security and confidence; for the development of man, his well-being and his right to share in an honourable life; for our responsibility toward the coming generations, this is our conception of peace which I repeat today . . . ."

Biography

Anwar al-Sadat was born on December 25, 1918, in Talah Monufiya, a village in the Nile Delta. One of 13 children in a devout Moslem family, he attended a local religious primary school and a secondary school in Cairo. As a student in Abbassia Military Academy in 1936 he met Gamal Abdel Nasser. After graduation in 1938, Sadat and Nasser formed the Free Officers Committee, a group intent on liberating Egypt from foreign control.

Sadat's attempt to overthrow the British yoke by conspiring with the Germans in 1942 resulted in his imprisonment. Escaping in 1944, he again incurred imprisonment after a series of attacks against pro-British officials. Released from prison, he worked once more with Nasser in the Free Officers Committee, ultimately deposing Farouk in the Egyptian revolution to bring Nasser to the presidency. As a trusted friend, Sadat worked in various posts under Nasser's authoritarian rule: editor of the government paper, *Al Jumhuriya* and *Al Tahrir* (1955-61); Chairman of the Afro-Asian Solidarity Council (1961); member of the Presidential Council (1962-64). In 1964-66 and 1969-70 he served as Vice-President, which placed him in the role of successor to the presidency upon the death of Nasser in 1970. As President, Sadat liberalized the government within Egypt and worked for an Arab Socialist Union in his foreign policy, a policy which was dominated by the desire to lay down roots for lasting peace.

Anwar al-Sadat was assassinated on October 6, 1981, by members of a violent fundamentalist Moslem sect. His death was mourned by his devoted family, by his countrymen, and by people the world over who valued his role in bilateral negotiations between Egypt and Israel designed to bring a peaceful solution to age-old conflicts in the Middle East.

See also:Articles: *Camp David Accords*

Bibliography ———————————————

Deming A, Martin D C, DeFrank T M 1978 A timely award?

Newsweek 92 (November 6)

Feld B T 1978 Norwegian prophecy or a gamble for peace? *Bull. Atomic Sci.* 34(December)

Sadat A 1978 *In search of identity.* Harper and Row, New York

Time 1978 Alone in Oslo. 112 (December 18)

RUTH C. REYNOLDS

Mother Teresa
(1979)

Mother Teresa of Calcutta received the Nobel Peace Prize for 1979. Over the years the Nobel Committee for the Peace Prize has rewarded diverse virtues. The nominees range from the idealist, who visualizes the creation of a world where war has become obsolete, to the pragmatist, who finds a workable alternative to presently threatening conflicts. Other choices have honored those who have addressed the abuses and deprivations which errant humanity imposes upon itself. With Mother Teresa we saw the pure in heart recognized. Her message transcended nationalities and creeds; her spirit soars across common frailties and speaks to an innate commonality in the human species. She daily ministered through recognition of the potential for fundamental good in humanity without which the hope of peace would falter for us all. Seeing Christ in every human being, making each individual sacred, she told us that every service each of us can offer to the other becomes a means of experiencing God in all of us.

Mother Teresa was born Agnes Gonxha Bojaxhiu, daughter of Albanian parents in Skopje, in what was the former Yugoslavia, on August 27, 1910. By the time she was 12 she knew she wanted to become a nun, and at 18 she took her first vows in an Irish order, the Sisters of Loretto, in which she taught for 20 years in a fashionable school for the daughters of prosperous families of Calcutta. Within this sheltered environment she sensed deeply the suffering and poverty of the destitute nearby, and the poor ultimately became her calling.

In 1948 Mother Teresa received permission to leave her teaching order and she answered the call of the "poorest of the poor," working without funds and starting with an open-air school for homeless children. Two years later she was granted permission to start a new religious order, the Society of the Missionaries of Charities, with canonical sanction. She took Indian citizenship.

Testimony to the success of Mother Teresa's work on the one hand is the picture familiar over much of the world of a beloved nun dressed in a coarse white sari ministering in the streets of India to the sick and dying, child and adult alike; and on the other hand statistics tell of the impressive growth of her order to 158 branches, with 1,800 nuns and 12,000 co-workers including lay doctors and brethren trained in the healing arts. But even on such a scale, achievement itself does not account for the decision made by the Nobel Committee.

Chairman John Sanness said that while the Committee took note of the success of Mother Teresa's Missionaries of Charity, still their admirable record has been but one out of many others also meriting respect. The ingredient within Mother Teresa's success which was decisive for the Committee is the spirit which has permeated her work, he said. "This has been Mother Teresa's fundamental contribution to the Order she has created and run. This it is that explains both why so many people would flock to join the Order, and the interest and respect she has encountered throughout the world. This springs," he stressed, "from Mother Teresa's own fundamental attitude to life and her very special personality."

"The hallmark of her work has been respect for the individual and the individual's worth and dignity. The loneliest and the most wretched, the abandoned lepers, the destitute and the dying, have been received by her and her Sisters with warm compassion, devoid of condescension, and based on the reverence for Christ in man."

"Better than anyone else she has managed to put into practice the recognized fact that gifts given *de haut en bas*, where the recipient has a feeling of onesided and humiliating dependence on the giver, may prove so hurtful to the recipient's dignity as a human being that it may well breed bitterness and animosity . . . ." He said that Mother Teresa teaches that the person who, in the accepted sense, is the recipient is also the giver. And it is the recipient who gives the most. This principle underlies all that she does.

In her Nobel lecture Mother Teresa described powerfully and poignantly her respect and admiration for those she serves: "The poor people are very great people. They can teach us so many beautiful things." She told of a woman whom she picked up from the streets "in a most terrible condition." Mother Teresa ministered to her with all that my love can do. I put her in bed, and there was such a beautiful smile on her face. She took hold of my hand, as she said only: 'Thank you' and she died.

"I could not help but examine my conscience before her, and I asked what would I say if I was in her place. And my answer was very simple. I would have tried to draw a little attention to myself, I would have said I am hungry, that I am cold, that I am dying . . . but she gave me her grateful love. And she died with a smile on her face."

She described the transcendent purity she witnessed in a man whom the Order picked up from the drain half-eaten with worms and brought to the home: "He said 'I have lived like an animal in the street, but I am going to die like an angel, loved and cared for.' And it was so wonderful to see the greatness of that man who could speak like that, who could die like that without blaming anybody, without cursing anybody, without comparing anything. 'Like an angel'—this is the greatness of our people," Mother Teresa told the award audience. "We may be doing social work in the eyes of the people, but we are really contemplatives of the world," she said.

Violence had no place in Mother Teresa's view of the world. And the violence she found cruelest of all is that which is practiced against the smallest and most helpless of victims, the unborn child. She pronounced abortion to be "the greatest destroyer of peace today because it is a direct war, a direct killing— direct murder by the mother herself." Mother Teresa offered concrete alternatives. For those unwanted children who are already conceived, her Order offers adoption. "We will find that child a home," promised this woman who called being unwanted the cruelest disease that can scourge the life of a human being. The Order also teaches natural family planning to the people of the street.

Mother Teresa closed her Nobel address with instructions to her audience, each one, to remember "God loves me, and I have an opportunity to love others as He loves me, not in big things, but in small things with great love." Then, she promised, "you become a burning light in the world of peace."

An Indian journalist wrote recently that "the Sisters with their serene ways, their saris, their knowledge of local languages . . . have come to symbolize not only the best in Christian charity, but also the best in Indian culture and civilization, from Buddha to Gandhi, the great saints, the seers, the great lovers of humanity with boundless compassion and consideration . . . what Shakespeare called the 'quality of mercy.'"

"Mother Teresa's most astonishing and bewildering characteristic was her lack of any sense of indignation," reported an interviewer from the London *Observer* (Polly Toynbee, October 3, 1971). "Mother Teresa reminded one sharply that in the teachings of Christ there is no rage and indignation, no burning desire to change the horrifying injustices of a society that allows such poverty; like it or not, there is only the injunction to love and turn the other cheek." Regarding socially militant Catholic dissidents, such as the Berrigan brothers, she told Toynbee: "If they feel this is the way they must serve Him, that is between them and God . . . . I am called to help the individual, to love each poor person, not to deal with institutions."

Chairman Sanness said Mother Teresa's view of the dignity of humankind has built a bridge across the gulf that exists between the rich nations and the poor nations. "Politics have never been her concern, but economic, social and political work with these same aims are in complete harmony with her own life's work."

Sanness quoted the President of the World Bank, Robert McNamara, whose words describe those of Mother Teresa's qualities being honored in the decision of the Committee: "Mother Teresa deserves Nobel's Peace Prize because she promotes peace in the most fundamental manner, by her confirmation of the inviolability of human dignity."

Biography

Mother Teresa was born in Skopje in what was the former Yugoslavia on August 27, 1910. She was born Agnes Gonxha Bojaxhiu, one of three children of an Albanian peasant family. By the age of 12 she knew she had a calling, and at 18 she left home to join the Sisters of Loretto, an Irish order with a mission in Calcutta; and trained at Loretto institutions in Dublin and in Darjeeling. After 20 years of teaching wealthy children at St. Mary's High School in Calcutta, she responded to "a call within a call" and left her order to minister to the "poorest of the poor." In 1948, after three months of intensive medical training under the American Medical Missionary Sisters in Patna, she established the Missionaries of Charity, in order to work among and minister to the inhabitants of the Calcutta slums. Her first school was in the open air, but her work swiftly attracted both financial donations and volunteer workers—many of whom came to dedicate their lives to the work of the Missionaries of Charity. By 1979 the Order had grown to nearly 200 branches in 24 countries throughout the world. In 1952 the Order opened the Nirmal Hriday, a home for dying destitutes. In 1957 the missionaries began special treatment for lepers, including the opening of a colony for lepers in 1964 in West Bengal. In 1969 the International Association of Co-Workers of Mother Teresa was affiliated to the Missionaries of Charity. Following this, Missionaries of Charity houses were opened in Jordan, in the East End of London and New York City's Harlem. Through the Missionaries of Charity, Mother Teresa had established more than 50 schools, orphanages, and homes for the poor in India and in other countries.

Mother Teresa had been accorded the following honors: the Pope John XXIII Peace Prize (1971); Templeton Foundation Prize (1973); Bharat Ratna (Star of India) (1980); Hon. DD, Cambridge (1977); Hon. OBE (1978); Hon. Dr., Med., Catholic University of Sacred Heart, Rome (1981), Catholic University of Louvain (1982); Hon. Citize 1 of Assisi (1982); Hon. OM (1983); and Presidential Medal of Freedom (1985). She was the author of a book, *Gift for God* (1975).

Mother Teresa died in Calcutta, India in 1997.

Bibliography

Kearney V S 1972 Of many things. *America* 127(December); inside cover
Muggeridge M 1971 *Something Beautiful for God: Mother Teresa of Calcutta*. Collins, London

RUTH C. REYNOLDS

Adolfo Pérez Esquivel
(1980)

The 1980 Nobel Peace Prize was awarded to Adolfo Pérez Esquivel, a devout Argentine Roman Catholic layman and human rights activist, in recognition of his efforts in behalf of peace and justice throughout Latin America. "He is an untiring and consistent champion of the principle of non-violence in the struggle for social and political liberty," the Nobel Committee said. "He has lit a light in the dark, a light which, in the opinion of our Committee, should never be allowed to be extinguished."

Pérez Esquivel's intense commitment to the cause of human rights and nonviolent methods was fueled by the wave of terror that swept over many countries in Latin America, including his own country, Argentina. For Pérez Esquivel, nonviolence involves much more than passively accepting the world as it is. For him it is a strategy in a struggle to change the world, using means that will not stifle the good intentions and the results one aims to achieve.

After graduating from the National School of Fine Arts of Buenos Aires and La Pija in 1956, Pérez Esquivel pursued a successful and politically detached career as a sculptor and Professor of Art for the next 15 years. His sculptures are to be seen in various public places in Argentina. In 1974 he relinquished his teaching post at the Manuel Belgrano National School of Fine Arts in Buenos Aires in order to devote all his time and energy to the work of coordinating the activities of the various nonviolent elements in Latin America under the organization Servico Paz y Justicia (Service for Peace and Justice). Pérez Esquivel served as its secretary-general. On their behalf, he travelled tirelessly throughout Central and Latin America. During a trip to Brazil in 1975 he was briefly jailed; and he was arrested again in Ecuador the following year. In 1976 he initiated an international campaign aimed at persuading the United Nations to establish a Human Rights Commission, and in this connection a document was drawn up recording breaches of human rights in Latin America. "Unjust structures must be changed," Pérez Esquivel declared. He also called for the trial or release of the 6,000 *desaparecidos*, Argentinians who have disappeared during the past years of dictatorial rule, many of whom are now assumed dead. Among these were many people unacquainted with the ways of terrorists, including journalists who not only knew too much of the regime's contraventions of human rights, but who were anxious to publish what they knew.

In the midst of this frightening repression, Pérez Esquivel remained unflinchingly true to his principles of open, nonviolent protest. He paid a price for his public denunciations of Argentine government atrocities. In 1977 when he went to a police station to renew his passport following a trip to visit European human rights activists, he was arrested. Without legal charge, or even an interrogation, the regime held him for 14 months and tortured him in ways that he refuses to discuss in detail. He said that constant prayer and the performance of yoga exercises whenever possible helped him to resist the attempt to break his morale. "When you experience this extreme situation of being between life and death, you try to understand what Christ said on the cross: 'Father, forgive them, for they don't know what they are doing,'" Esquivel recalls. "But I thought that, yes, these people *did* know what they were doing . . . . What I discovered little by little was that what the torturers did not know was that they were persons, and that we were persons. They had lost their identities."

His harrowing experience did not distract Pérez Esquivel from the larger picture of deprivation and tragedy that go hand-in-hand with poverty. "You cannot talk solely of human rights in terms of torture and imprisonment and killing," he said. "True, this is the gravest aspect. But we must also look at the case of the peasant who has no land and is dying of hunger." Pérez Esquivel believes that poverty is the cause of most of Latin America's problems because poverty breeds violence which leads to repression. In turn, repression causes more poverty. Servico Paz y Justicia seeks to break this cycle by helping peasants get land and by supporting workers in their fight for better conditions.

Pérez Esquivel likewise champions the use of nonviolence in relations between nations. He has, for instance, warned of the danger of an escalation of the territorial conflict between Argentina and Chile. Commenting on their recurring border problems, he said that countries which share common historical and cultural roots as do these two must resolve their differences in a manner that is just for both populations. He saw that the people were practically ignorant of what their governments were doing, and along with Msgr. Jaime de Navares and 1976 Nobel Peace Laureate Mairead Corrigan, Servico Paz y Justica set about informing the people and campaigning in support of the papal mediation of the conflict.

Although such activities have political implications, Pérez Esquivel avoids alignment with specific political groups. "For us," he has explained, "the aim of politics should be the search for the common good in a society. In this sense, our activity is political. But if we are talking about party politics, that is a different matter . . . we have no political preference. Our work is oriented towards a wider dimension, in all

sectors."

His organization is ecumenical, and no one is excluded on religious grounds. The Church itself has yet to decide upon its own role. Miguel Amador, writing for the *Christian Century* (1980), reported that the hierarchy of Argentina's Roman Catholic Church followed the news about the award by announcing that the Service for Peace and Justice organization was not to be confused with the Pontifical Commission on Justice and Peace and/or the Argentine Commission on Justice and Peace, which is under the Bishops' Conference. Though some Catholic parishes and some Protestant churches are staunch supporters of Servico Paz y Justicia, and though some Roman Catholic bishops have publicly acknowledged and congratulated the Peace and Justice organization, Amador reports that most of them have kept silent. "Equally accomplices in silence," he said, "are the Protestant and Orthodox churches . . . as of this writing, no pronouncements have appeared from any of the major Protestant churches, or from any of the centers of theological study."

Professor Sanness, Nobel Committee Chairman, said that the Christian teaching in which Servico Paz y Justicia is rooted, in spite of the presence of resistance from the orthodoxy, forged new links between the Church and the broad masses of the people. "This means that clergy and laymen must undertake fresh obligations within the community. The Church must not be content merely to carry out its ritual functions—baptism, mass, funerals," he said. "At a minimum, society is expected not to reconcile itself to conditions that make it impossible for men and women to gain respect for their human dignity or to accord this respect to others . . . this is where people like Pérez Esquivel take their place in the social struggle."

Sanness pointed to the differences that exist between the many countries of Latin America, some poorer than Argentina, many with deeper historical sources of friction between sections of their populations, some of them smaller and more helpless. "Nevertheless," he said, "the Committee is of the opinion that Adolfo Pérez Esquivel has a message that is valid for the whole of Latin America . . . ."

"It is our hope that his work will bear fruit in his own country, that it will hearken to his voice and break out from the vicious circle of terror and counter-terror, of anarchy and reaction, setting an example to the whole of Latin America . . . ."

"These fundamental principles are supported by many excellent spokesmen in numerous countries, men who may be better known than Esquivel," he said. "The reason his voice reached all the way from Latin America to the Norwegian Nobel Committee was not because of its strength, but because of its purity and clarity."

Biography

Adolfo Pérez Esquivel was born in Buenos Aires in 1931. Educated as an architect and sculptor, after graduating from the National School of Fine Arts of Buenos Aires and La Pinta in 1956, Pérez Esquivel pursued a nonpolitical career as a sculptor and Professor of Fine Arts for the next 15 years. His sculpture is shown in permanent collections in the Buenos Aires Museum of Modern Art, the Museum of Fine Arts, Cordoba, and the Fine Arts Museum in Rosario. Then, in 1974, he relinquished his teaching post at the Argentine National School of Fine Arts to accept leadership in the work of coordinating the activities of the various nonviolent protest groups in Latin America.

Pérez Esquivel works through the organization Servico Paz y Justicia, an organization dedicated to assisting rural workers to get land and to help trade unions protect rights of workers through, among other ways, legal aid, and he founded their journal, *Paz y Justicia*. As General Coordinator of Servico Paz y Justicia, he travelled extensively throughout Latin America in support of various groups dedicated to the advancement of human rights and to the prin-

ciples of militant nonviolence. In 1977, he was imprisoned without trial or opportunity for defense. While in prison he was denied all legal rights and severely tortured.

After 14 months he was released subject to various restrictions, including a further period of house arrest. Since 1980 he has been allowed to resume his activities, including travel to coordinate international efforts towards human rights. He is cofounder of the Ecumenical Movement for Human Rights of Argentina, and is President of the Permanent Assembly for Human Rights.

Pérez Esquivel has been awarded the Pope John XXIII prize, and membership of the Pax Christi Organization (1977).

He married his wife Amanda in 1956; they have three sons, the oldest of whom, Leonardo, is active in Servico Paz y Justicia.

Bibliography

Amador M 1980 Silent accomplices. *Christian Century* 97(39)

Brecher J, Rohter L 1980 Peace Prize: 'Why him?' *Newsweek* 96 (October 27)

Lundy M 1980 An interview: Adolfo Pérez Esquivel. *America* 143(21)

RUTH C. REYNOLDS

United Nations High Commisioner for Refugees (UNHCR) (1981)

see United Nations High Commisioner for Refugees (UNHCR) (1954, 1981)

Alfonso Garcia Robles (1982)

The 1982 Nobel Peace Prize was awarded to Alva Myrdal and Alfonso Garcia Robles, two diplomats who had labored long and effectively for disarmament. Though both had long been revered within arms control and peace organizations, they were without the worldwide renown associated with many of the previous winners. Garcia Robles and Myrdal had both worked for the UN Disarmament Commission in Geneva. The choice seemed a recognition by the Nobel Committee of the widespread efforts being made for disarmament by diplomats and international civil servants who labor in the background.

The Committee stated, "In today's world the work

to promote peace, disarmament and the brotherhood of mankind is carried on in different ways . . . . There is the patient and meticulous work undertaken in international negotiations on mutual disarmament, and there is also the work of the numerous peace movements with their greater emphasis on influencing the climate of public opinion . . . ."

Alfonso Garcia Robles has spent his life in public service, working with constant emphasis on creating means to solving international relationships without the use of violence. After studying law he joined Mexico's foreign service in 1939. As State Secretary in the Ministry of Foreign Affairs he served as delegate to the 1945 San Francisco Conference which founded the United Nations. He has been the Permanent Representative of Mexico to the Committee on Disarmament in Geneva. As Mexico's Director-General for Europe in the late 1950s he played a central role in the Law of the Sea Conferences.

In 1962, while Ambassador to Brazil, he was introduced to the idea of making Latin America a nuclear free zone. This concept gained an invaluable advocate in Garcia Robles. Following the Cuban crisis of 1962 he persuaded Mexico to start efforts toward the creation of a non-nuclear Latin America. His years of negotiation resulted in 22 nations signing the Treaty of Tlatelolco (1967), which barred nuclear weapons from their territories. As of August 1982, 15 years later, the number of signatory states stood at 25, of which 22 are already parties to the treaty (see Articles: *Nuclear Weapon Free Zones*).

In his Nobel lecture Garcia Robles pointed out that the Latin American nuclear weapon free zone "has the privilege of being the only one in existence which covers densely inhabited territories. Outside it, only in Antarctica, the Outer Space and the sea bed are similar prohibitions in force."

The preamble of the treaty describes its fundamental aims. They are concrete and important: the people of participating countries are spared from squandering their limited resources on nuclear armaments. In offering protection against possible nuclear attacks on their territories, this treaty also makes a significant contribution toward preventing the proliferation of nuclear weapons. It creates a pathway toward general and complete disarmament.

Garcia Robles says that when countries declare their land a nuclear free zone they are making a realistic statement about the destructive power inherent in nuclear arms. He believes they are taking action upon their recognition that nuclear arms are not defensive weapons, but a threat to the human race and to the planet.

Garcia Robles thought it worth noting that the "Final Document" approved by the first special session of the UN General Assembly devoted to disarmament, meeting in May and June of 1978, contained several declaratory statements of striking similarity to the Treaty of Tlatelolco, written 16 years previously. Both strongly urge the containment of nuclear weapons whose existing arsenals "attack the integrity of the human species and ultimately may render the whole earth uninhabitable." Garcia Robles played a central role in the session and was instrumental in the successful adoption of the "Final Document."

He recommended to the Nobel Committee that when awarding the Peace Prize in the future the highest priority be given to the contribution which the candidates, be they individuals or nongovernmental organizations, have made to disarmament. "The time has come," he said, "to seek security not in weapons, but in disarmament."

Garcia Robles's lifetime of work and accomplishment finds eloquent expression in the reasons the Committee gave for their two choices for the 1982 Peace Prize: "Putting across truth about nuclear arms has been, and still is, the prime concern of this year's Peace Prize Winners. They have clearly shown that the work of promoting peace and disarmament must be carried on at several levels . . . . The challenge facing peace workers is not to be found in a single universal question-and-answer, but in peaceful solutions to a host of conflicts, and in the exertion to achieve peace on many different levels."

"They know—better than most people—what it means to make intense efforts to find constructive proposals . . . they know how vital it is that negotiations on disarmament should be conducted on the basis of down-to-earth realism and on the assumption of give-and-take between the great powers."

Bernard Feld, of the *Bulletin of Atomic Scientists*, endorsed the choices of Myrdal and Garcia Robles for the Peace Prize award in an editorial (December 1982) which places into global context the unique contribution made by these two disarmament negotiators: "Between them the winners represent the vast but usually silent and unrepresented majority of humankind, whose stake in avoiding a nuclear war between the major industrial powers is as great as that of the direct protagonists."

"Never has the urgency been greater for the nuclear giants to recognize that, whatever their political and ideological differences, they have an overriding mutual interest in defusing their nuclear confrontation. But given the self-righteous arrogance of many of our leaders, it is necessary to propel them toward the negotiating table by overwhelming pressures, not only from within their own countries but from the rest of the world as well."

"For their part in raising the level of understanding of and the pressure for action on nuclear disarmament and peaceful accommodation, Alva R. Myrdal and Alfonso Garcia Robles have more than earned their award. By giving the prize to them, the Nobel Peace Prize Committee has not only honored the recipients and their cause: it has gone a long way toward vindicating its own mission as well."

Biography

Alfonso Garcia Robles was born in Zamora in Mexico in 1911. After studying law he entered his country's foreign service in 1939, where he held the following posts: Ambassador to Brazil, 1962-64, State Secretary in the Ministry of Foreign Affairs, 1974-70, Mexico's permanent representative in the United Nations, 1971-75, and Foreign Minister, 1975-76. Since 1977 he has been the Permanent Representative of Mexico to the Committee on Disarmament in Geneva. Garcia Robles played a crucial role in launching and implementing the agreement on a nuclear free zone in Latin America, culminating in the signing of the Tlatelolco Agreement in 1967. The effect of the agreement was to make Latin America the world's largest inhabited nuclear free zone. At the time of the award, however, some countries which signed had yet to implement it (Brazil, Argentina). He is currently Chairman of the UN's Disarmament Committee. His main priority, to which much of his work is directed, is to establish a world disarmament campaign.

He married Juana Maria Szyszlo in 1950. They have two sons.

Bibliography

Feld B T 1982 Nobel Peace Prize. *Bull. At. Sci.* 38 (December)
Newsweek 1982 A disarming Peace Prize. 100 (October 25)
Time 1982 Two disarming choices. 120 (October 25)

RUTH C. REYNOLDS

Alva Myrdal
(1982)

In its choices of Alva Myrdal and Alfonso Garcia Robles, the two winners of the 1982 Peace Prize, the Nobel Committee gave recognition and support to the peace movements which have been proliferating worldwide, all working in various ways to awaken public awareness of the suicidal nature of nuclear weapons. Both winners criticized the governments of the United States and the Soviet Union for escalating the arms race ever closer to Einstein's warning of "unparalleled catastrophe." Both had devoted their lives to seeking ways to promote effective protest.

The Chairman of the Nobel Committee, Egil Aarvik, observed that while humankind at large seems loath to face the threats of nuclear weapons, the first requirement for solutions to political problems is the moral courage to look these problems in the face. "It is such a temptation to shut one's eyes," he said. "It is as though the process of comprehension were obstructed. At some point we recoil, lacking the courage to know what we actually know. The truth . . . is so horrifying that it numbs our ability to comprehend it."

Alva Myrdal long displayed the courage to confront the truth. When she was asked by the Swedish Foreign Minister to become his special disarmament adviser in 1961 she became an expert on the subject, facing every aspect unflinchingly. She wrote *The Game of Disarmament: How the United States and Russia Run the Arms Race*, in which she provides a study of the two Superpowers and their rivalry in producing weapons which presently endanger the world, supported by expenditures ruinous to the world economy, draining resources from health, education, and housing and many other social programs worldwide (see Articles: *Disarmament and Development*).

Myrdal cautioned that peace movements cannot address overly ambitious goals like leading the way to eternal peace, or solving all disputes among nations. The economic and political roots of the conflicts are too strong, she said, and therefore immediate goals must be more modest. We must aim at preventing what, in the present situation, is the greatest threat to the very survival of humankind—the threat of nuclear weapons.

She was especially gratified that the award had gone to citizens representing two nations which are both denuclearized and nonallied. "The mass media call attention to this all too seldom, being one-sidedly concerned with the rivalry between the two superpower blocks," she said. "There are, after all, so many other countries in the world and most have refused to serve as hostages to the superpowers."

Myrdal spoke of the efforts of their two countries to refute objectively attempts by the nuclear weapon powers to conceal or give false explanation of actual facts. "We must exert ourselves to break through the wall of silence which, unfortunately, the great powers have erected to ward off the small powers' influence in the international debate," she warned.

She persuaded her government to underwrite the seismological Hagfors station. This station monitors independently and systematically even the smallest subterranean nuclear tests, using the most modern equipment, and publishes the results internationally, unhampered by any political considerations.

Under Myrdal's influence the Swedish government was persuaded to cover the costs of the Stockholm International Peace Research Institute. A vital purpose of these two organizations is to establish an international network for open verification of nuclear test explosions. The smaller nations can thereby exert more influence on disarmament negotiations than they have previously done.

Myrdal saw a strong correlation between collective military violence and personal violence. She was convinced that the militarization permeating society was eroding basic ethical values. The exercise of force by various nations plays an ominous role in maintaining what Myrdal called the "weaponry and violence cult of our age." She asserted that the mass media exacerbated the problems of violence, affecting not only the countries in which the media were created, but also the Third World countries to which much of the media were imported.

Bernard Feld, writing for the *Bulletin of Atomic Scientists* (1982) endorsed the choices of Myrdal and Garcia Robles for the Peace Prize in an editorial which succinctly summarized their unique contributions: "Between them the winners represent the vast but usually silent and unrepresented majority of humankind, whose stake in avoiding a nuclear war between the major industrial powers is as great as that of the direct protagonists."

"Never has the urgency been greater for the nuclear giants to recognize that, whatever their political and ideological differences, they have an overriding mutual interest in defusing their nuclear confrontation. But given the self-righteous arrogance of many of our leaders, it is necessary to propel them toward the negotiating table by overwhelming pressures, not only from within their own countries, but from the rest of the world as well."

"For their part in raising the level of understanding of and the pressure for action on nuclear disarmament and peaceful accommodation, Alva R. Myrdal and Alfonso Garcia Robles have more than earned their award. By giving the prize to them, the Nobel Peace Prize Committee has not only honored the recipients and their cause: it has gone a long way toward vindicating its own mission as well."

Biography

Alva Myrdal was born in Uppsala in 1902. She graduated from university in 1924 and married Gunnar Myrdal the same year. The couple have made major contributions in the field of social welfare separately and together. In 1974, Gunnar Myrdal won the Nobel Prize in Economics.

In 1943 Mrs. Myrdal was appointed to the Government Commission on International Post-War Aid and Reconstruction. In 1949 she headed the UN's section on welfare policy. In 1955 she was appointed Swedish ambassador to India. In 1962 she served as Sweden's representative to the Geneva disarmament conference. That same year she became a Social Democrat member of Parliament, and in 1967, a member of the Cabinet. Her many articles and books have brought much insight and influence to the current disarmament debate. She won the Federal Republic of Germany's Peace Prize in 1970, the Albert Einstein Peace Prize in 1981, and the People's Peace Prize (awarded by political and pacifist organization in Norway) in the same year.

Alva Myrdal died on February 2, 1986.

Bibliography

Feld B 1982 Noble Peace Prize. *Bull. At. Sci.* 38 (December)
Newsweek 1982 A disarming Peace prize. 100 (October 25)
Time 1982 Two disarming choices. 120 (October 25)

RUTH C. REYNOLDS

Lech Walesa

(1983)

The Nobel Committee awarded the Peace Prize for 1983 to Lech Walesa of Poland in recognition of his continuing struggle, in the face of very powerful opposition, for the recognition of basic human rights. Though Walesa's struggle essentially centered on the right of Polish workers to establish their own trade unions, his campaigning, carried out at great personal sacrifice, engaged the attention and the support of people far beyond his own country. In making this award, the Nobel Committee said that Walesa's defense of workers' rights in Poland was something more than a domestic Polish issue. Walesa's contribution is of essential importance in the historical campaign to establish the freedom of organization as a universal human right. "This workers' movement, known as 'Solidarity' has come," the Committee said, "to represent the determination to resolve conflicts and obliterate disagreement through peaceful negotiation, where all involved meet with a mutual respect for one another's integrity."

Lech Walesa would agree: he insists the struggle must be nonviolent. "We can effectively oppose violence only if we ourselves do not resort to it," he has said. He, too, sees the struggle in a global context: "The civil and human rights sought by Solidarity are the ideals not just of Polish workers, but of people everywhere," he said. "In many parts of the world the people are searching for a solution that would link the two basic values: peace and justice. The two are like bread and salt for mankind." The Committee Chairman, Egil Aarvik, called this ideal "A burning torch which Walesa has lifted unarmed . . . . The word, the spirit and the thought of freedom and human rights were his weapons."

Looking back upon the genesis of Solidarity, the first sign of the free trade union forming on the Baltic Coast came quietly, unobserved by most of the outside world. In January 1979 an underground bimonthly, *The Worker of the Coast*, edited by Walesa, signaled the embryonic stirring of a new movement among the Polish workers. It was followed in July by a charter of workers' rights. With Walesa as one of the signatories, the charter asked for an end to censorship, an eight-hour day, improved job safety conditions, higher wages, and the legalization of the right to strike. Its most important statement presented the basic concept in Solidarity: "Strikes are useful short-term weapons, but free and independent trade unions are necessary to ensure that the gains won through a strike are not later lost. Only they will give us an equal footing in negotiations, a power the authorities cannot ignore."

In his award lecture (read in Oslo by his wife, Danuta Walesa, because Walesa feared that if he attended the award ceremony himself he would not be allowed back into Poland), Walesa traced the charter's precedents, going back to his boyhood: "I belong to the generation of workers who, born in the villages and hamlets of rural Poland, had the opportunity to acquire education and find employment in industry, becoming in the course conscious of their rights and the importance of society."

"These were the years of awakening aspirations of workers and peasants, but also years of many wrongs, degradation and lost illusions," he said. During these years periodic workers' protests were brutally suppressed. In 1956 the desperate struggle in Poznan for bread and freedom was forcefully put down by the authorities. Among the victims was a 13-year-old boy. A similar response was met in 1970 during protest demonstrations in the Gdansk Ship-

yard, and again in 1976 during the strike of workers at Ursus and Radom. Walesa (who at this time was fired for his participation in the labor movement) not only was convinced of the justness of the working people's demands and aspirations, but also became persuaded of the urgent need for their solidarity.

In the following years Walesa lived inconspicuously, providing for his family as best he could despite successive job losses and jailings resulting from his labor activities. Meanwhile, a deteriorating economy in Poland placed new deprivations upon its citizens. Poland overextended itself in an effort to modernize industry, running up high international debts. Also, in an attempt to right the balance of trade and build up buying power with the West, it increased its export of goods, including meat products, which consequently exacerbated food shortages at home.

In July 1980 the Polish government doubled meat prices. Scattered work stoppages followed. On August 14 the Lenin Shipyard was seized by strikers. Among their demands was the reinstatement of three dismissed workers, including Walesa. Scaling the fence, Walesa joined the workers and became the leader of the strike. It was a leap destined to carry his movement far beyond the shipyards into the pages of history. Walesa declared that the settlement of that strike, the Gdansk Agreement, "stands out as a great charter of the rights of the working people which nothing can ever destroy . . . it shall remain the model and the only method to follow, the only one that gives a chance of finding a middle course between the use of force and a hopeless struggle," he said.

"Our firm conviction that ours is a just cause, and that we must find a peaceful way to attain our goals gave us the strength and the awareness of the limits beyond which we must not go . . . . Solidarity as a trade union movement did not reach for power, nor did it turn against the established constitutional order," Walesa declared. It was a shared cause among Poland's workers. "Lying at the root of the social agreements of 1980 are the courage, sense of responsibility, and the solidarity of the working people," Walesa said. He further reflected, "I think it marked also the road to be taken by the authorities if they think of a state governed in cooperation and participation of all citizens."

Even allowing for the considerable tact exercised by Walesa it is obvious that the Solidarity campaign would greatly alarm the rulers of the Soviet bloc because Solidarity stood as an implicit contradiction of the Communist Party's claim to be the sole legitimate representative of the working class. Walesa was careful not to make this contradiction explicit, and steered a course designed to satisfy Polish workers without provoking Soviet intervention. He seemed to know instinctively just how far he could go in challenging the authorities without inviting disaster.

But his caution and tact were not shared by all members of the movement. Less pragmatic workers called for a referendum on Poland's communist government and the country's alliance with the Soviet Union. The authorities imposed martial law, Solidarity was outlawed, and Walesa interned for 11 months.

In June 1981, on the invitation of the Polish government, Pope John Paul II paid a papal visit to Poland during which he met with both the Polish Prime Minister, General Jaruzelski, and Walesa. The Pope spoke repeatedly of the need for national reconciliation and for responsible dialogue, asserting that "the working people in Poland—and everywhere—have this right because the working man is not a mere tool of production, but the subject which throughout the process of production takes precedence over capital."

At the time the Peace Prize was awarded to Walesa, Solidarity had become a forbidden organization. Walesa, reinstated at the shipyards in Gdansk, remains guardedly optimistic. Asked if he thought Solidarity could work within the government's Patriotic Front for National Rebirth, Walesa replied, "They are Poles like myself and probably know what the words honor and dignity mean. I don't want to isolate myself in anger. I will search for all possible solutions" (*Newsweek*, June 20, 1983).

Chairman Aarvik observed at the award ceremony, "Walesa cannot be presented as a victor at the end of a struggle full of sacrifice. His chosen course was not as short and easy as that. And it could seem that the goals he set himself are just as distant still."

"But is Lech Walesa really silent today? Is he completely without victory? Has his cause suffered defeat? Many are of the opinion that his voice has never been stronger nor reached further than it does now. The electrician from Gdansk, the carpenter's son from the Vistula Valley has managed to lift the banner of freedom and humanity so high that the whole world can once again see it . . . the future will recognise his name among those who contributed to humanity's legacy of freedom."

Biography

One of eight children of Boleslaw and Feliksa Walesa, Lech Walesa was born on September 29, 1943, in Popowo during the German occupation of Poland in the Second World War. He was educated in primary and technical schools. As an electrician he began work in the Lenin Shipyard in Gdansk in 1966. He married Danuta Walesa in 1969; they have four sons and three daughters.

In 1970 during the circumstances which led to Gomulka's replacement by Gievak as Party Secretary, Walesa was a member of a 27-strong action committee at the Lenin yards. As a result of his activities as shop steward, he was dismissed in 1976 and thereafter relied on temporary jobs to earn a living. When in the summer of 1980 there were further disturbances among shipyard workers, Walesa was helped into a protest meeting and seized the leadership by proposing that the workers occupy the shipyard. He subsequently became Chairman of the National Co-ordinating Committee of the Independent Autonomous Trade Union (known as Solidarity). The activites of Walesa, a devout Catholic, were supported by the Catholic Church, and in January 1981 he was received by Pope John Paul II—a fellow Pole—in Rome.

When General Jaruzelski became Prime Minister in February 1981 the relationship between Solidarity and the authorities worsened, and in December 1981 martial law was declared. The leadership of Solidarity was arrested, including Walesa, and he was interned for 11 months. He was released in November 1982 and was reinstated at the Lenin Shipyards in Gdansk.

Walesa became the President of Poland after the peaceful revolution of 1989.

Walesa has received numerous honorary awards and recognitions, including: Dr. honoris causa, Alliance College (1981), Providence College (1981), University of Columbia (1981), Catholic University (1981), MacMurray college (1982), Harvard University (1983), St. Denis University, Paris (1982). He was named "Man of the Year," by: *Financial Times* (1980), *The Observer* (1980), *Die Welt, Die Zeit* (1981), *L'Express* (1981), and *Le Soir* (1981). He was awarded the Freedom Medal, Philadelphia, Medal of Merit, Congress of Polish Community in USA (1981), Free World Prize, Norway (1982), Social Justice Award (1983), among other honors and prizes.

Bibliography

O'Hare J A 1983 Of many things. *America* 148 (January 1-8)

Singer D 1983 Honor the man—and the movement. *Nation* 237(13)

Stanglin D 1983a Walesa: We will keep trying. An interview with Walesa. *Newsweek* 101 (June 20)

Stanglin D 1983b Walesa on his struggle. *Newsweek* 102 (October 17)

Willey F, Stanglin D 1983 Poland's man of peace. *Newsweek* 102 (October 17)

RUTH C. REYNOLDS.

Desmond Tutu
(1984)

The 1984 Nobel Peace Prize was awarded to South Africa's Bishop Desmond Tutu. "He is representative of the best in us all," the Nobel Committee said, and its hope was that the award would direct attention to his role as a unifying leader in the campaign to solve South Africa's apartheid problem by peaceful means. In a situation that courts violence and disaster it is all the more remarkable, Chairman Aarvik commented, that a peaceful alternative exists. It rests in large part on the shoulders of Bishop Tutu, whose campaign is waged with the weapons of the spirit and reason: truth, freedom, and justice. The Committee sees Bishop Tutu as a hope for the future, for the country's white minority as well as the black majority. "Desmond Tutu is an exponent of the only form for conflict solving which is worthy of civilized nations," the Committee declared.

In his Nobel lecture Bishop Tutu described the precarious balance between peaceful and violent resolution that exists in South Africa: "Our people are rapidly despairing of a peaceful resolution in South Africa. Those of us who still speak 'peace' and 'reconciliation' belong to a rapidly diminishing minority."

The struggle for democracy and justice has touched Tutu's life in many decisive ways. Growing up in Johannesburg, he learned sympathy for the weak and the underprivileged. Here too he met the man who probably exercised the strongest influence on his formative years, Father Trevor Huddleston, then serving as parish priest in the black slum of Sophiatown. The son of a teacher at a Methodist school, Tutu also taught at mission schools. In 1957 the government took over these institutions, installing a system of Bantu (black) education so inferior that he felt compelled to resign.

Tutu judged that he could best help his people through the church. "It just occurred to me," he has said, "that, if the church would have me, the profession of priest would be a good way of helping my people." He studied in theological colleges in South Africa and London, and was ordained in 1962. For several years he worked for the World Council of Churches' Theological Education Fund, and in 1976 he was elected Anglican Bishop of Lesotho. It was in 1978 that his appointment as the first black to direct the South African Council of Churches plunged him into a leadership role opposing apartheid. With 18 member denominations and 13 million members, of whom 80 percent are black, the South African Council of Churches (SACC) is one of the most eloquent and important voices of opposition to apartheid. Indeed, the Nobel Committee included the South African Council of Churches in the "gesture of support" it hoped to make with the Peace Prize award.

Bishop Tutu has been a fearless and dynamic leader of this council. Courageously he has opposed injustice, and is frequently found at the front of processions demonstrating against the government and its policies. He has maintained that in a situation such as exists in South Africa the church has to be political. "Not party political," he stipulates, "but morally political." His goal of a democratic and just society without racial segregation would seem reasonable throughout much of the world. But he struggles in the reality of a social order which has deported three million human beings from their homes, stripping them of personal possessions, and transporting them to an empty veld with just a tent and a sack of maize as their means of survival.

Bishop Tutu described their plight before the award audience. In pursuance of apartheid's ideological racist dream, hundreds of thousands of families have been dumped in the Bantustan homeland resettlement camps. "I say 'dumped' advisedly;" Bishop Tutu explained, "only things or rubbish is dumped, not human beings. Apartheid has, however, ensured that God's children, just because they are black, should be treated as if they were things, and not as of infinite value created in the image of God." These dumping grounds, designated by the South African government as "tribal homelands," are far from where work and food can be procured easily. Children starve, suffering from the often irreversible consequences of malnutrition. This happens to them not accidentally, the Bishop declared, but by deliberate government policy.

He told of the tragic flight of many of the fathers to the towns, where they labor 11 months of the year separated from their families in a desperate effort to send back support. This, he said, is just a part of the cost of apartheid in human suffering. Apartheid is upheld by a complex mesh of draconian laws: security legislation which permits the indefinite detention of persons without access to family, doctor, or lawyer. Some are held in solitary confinement; some die mysteriously in detention. Laws which uphold the forced population removals, the Bantu education system which educates children for serfdom, the migratory labor system—all are part of a repressive and unjust system. "We see before us a land bereft of much justice, and therefore without peace and security," Bishop Tutu said. "Unrest is endemic, and will remain an unchanging feature of the South African scene until apartheid, the root cause of it all, is finally dismantled . . . ."

"I have spoken extensively about South Africa," he said, "first because it is the land I know best, but because it is also a microcosm of the world and an example of what is to be found in other lands in differing degree. Where there is injustice, invariably peace becomes a casualty . . . . Because there is global insecurity, nations are engaged in a mad arms race, spending billions of dollars wastefully on instruments of destruction when millions are starving."

He does not confine his observations on ethics for those at home. To the US business community he said recently, "What we have to say to those who invest in South Africa is that your investment is a moral as well as an economic issue . . . . This is our last peaceful chance. My fears are the fears of many that we could very well have a blood bath. It is for everyone to speak out—business, bishops, everybody."

Tutu has said that the only true hope for a peaceful solution would come through holding a national convention of the real leaders, black and white. But the whites will do this only under pressure. "It is up to the international community to exert pressure on the South African government," he said, "especially economic pressure . . . . This is our last chance for change because if that doesn't happen . . . it seems the bloodbath will be inevitable." Here Tutu is echoing a request for sanctions made 25 years ago by Zulu Chief Albert Lutuli, recipient of the 1960 Nobel Peace Prize.

No one can remain impartial in a situation of injustice and oppression, Tutu asserts. "To be impartial and not to take sides is indeed to have taken sides already. It is to have sided with the status quo." He urges the international community to disinvest from South Africa. International economic pressure against the regime "is the only alternative to violence," he declared.

Bishop Tutu calls himself only a part of a mass movement of South African blacks seeking fundamental change. He graciously shared his award with his compatriots. He addressed the crowd that welcomed him in Johannesburg after the announcement of his prize: "This award is for you, your mothers who sit at railway stations trying to eke out an existence selling potatoes, selling mealies . . . . This award is for you, the three-and-a-half-million of our people

who have been uprooted and dumped as if you were rubbish . . . . It is for you who, down through the ages, have said that you seek to change this evil system peacefully; for you who have marched against the pass laws peacefully and who, unarmed, have been shot, mown down, and killed. With this award, the world is saying it recognized that you have been peace-loving to a fault."

Chairman Aarvik also honored the black South Africans' patient and courageous seeking out of nonviolent solutions. The award should be seen as "a renewed recognition of the courage and heroism shown by black South Africans in their . . . peaceful . . . struggle against apartheid," he said. It was the Committee's decision "in recognition . . . that it is this alternative vision which must succeed, that the South African Bishop, Desmond Tutu, has been selected as this year's Prize Laureate."

Biography

Desmond Mpilo Tutu was born on October 7, 1931, in Klerksdorp, Transvaal. His parents were Zachariah Tutu, a teacher in a Methodist school, and Aletta Tutu. After graduation from Johannesburg Bantu High School he earned a teacher's diploma at Pretoria Bantu Normal College (1953) and a B.A. at the University of South Africa (1954). He immediately took a teaching position at Johannesburg Bantu High School, where he stayed for one year. In 1955 he began teaching at Munsieville High School in Krugersdorp, and married Leah Nomalizo; they have four children, Trevor Thamsanqa, Theresa Thandeka, Naomi Nontombi, and Mpho Andrea. In 1958 the government installed a Bantu education system abhorrent to Tutu because of its inferiority, and he left teaching. He entered St. Peters Theological College, Rosettenville, Johannesburg, for Ordination Training and earned a Licentiate in Theology in 1960. He was ordained as Priest in 1961. From 1962 to 1965 he was part-time curate at St. Alban's, Golder's Green, London, obtaining his B.D. (honors) in 1965, and his Master's in Theology, both from King's College, London, in 1966. He was part-time curate at St. Mary's Bletchingley, Surrey, 1965-66.

Between 1967 and 1969, he served on the Staff of the Federal Theological Seminary, Alice, Cape, and as Chaplain at the University of Fort Hare. From 1970 to 1972, he served as lecturer in the Department of Theology, University of Botswana, Lesotho and Swaziland, Roma, Lesotho. Between 1972 and 1975 he was Associate Director of the Theological Education Fund of the World Council of Churches based in Bromley, Kent, where he served as honorary curate of St. Augustine's, Grove Park. In 1975 he was made Dean of Johannesburg; in 1976, Bishop of Lesotho.

In 1978 he was appointed General Secretary of the South African Council of Churches. In 1985 he was appointed Bishop of Johannesburg.

Bishop Tutu has earned many awards and honorary degrees: he was elected Fellow of King's College, London (1978), awarded an Honorary Doctorate of Divinity from the General Theological Seminary, USA (1978), an Honorary Doctorate of Civil Law from Kent University, England (1978), and an Honorary Doctorate of Laws from Harvard, USA (1979). He received the Prix d'Athene (Onassis Foundation) in 1980, an Honorary Doctorate of Theology from Ruhr University, Bochum (1981), an Honorary Doctorate of Sacred Theology, Columbia University (1982). He was designated a member of the International Social Prospects Academy (1983), and given the Family of Man Gold Medal Award (1983). In 1984 he received an Honorary Doctorate of Law from Claremont Graduate School, and an Honorary Doctorate of Sacred Theology from Dickinson College, the Martin Luther King, Jr. Humanitarian Award of Annual Black American Heroes and Heroines Day, an Honorary Doctorate of Divinity from Aberdeen University, Scotland, and Doctor of Human Letters,

Howard University, United States. His publications include *Crying in the Wilderness* (1982), *Hope and Suffering* (1983), and various articles and reviews.

Bibliography ————————————————

America 1984 Prophets of South Africa
Canine C, Underwood A 1984 A parable—and a Peace Prize. *Newsweek* 104 (October 29)
Commonweal 1984 Gifts seen and heard. 101(21)
Howell L 1984 Antiapartheid Bishop awarded Peace Prize. *Christian Century* November 14
New York Times 1984 Bishop Tutu given Nobel Prize in Oslo ceremony. December 11
Pohl K I 1985 The ethics of disinvestment. *Christian Century* 102(31)
Progressive 1984 The Bishop's message. 48(12)
Tutu D 1983 *Hope and Suffering*. Eerdmans, Grand Rapids, Michigan

RUTH C. REYNOLDS

International Physicians for Prevention of Nuclear War (IPPNW) (1985)

The Nobel Peace Prize for 1985 was awarded to the International Physicians for Prevention of Nuclear War (IPPNW). The Nobel Committee stated in its announcement that the IPPNW had "performed a considerable service to mankind by spreading authoritative information and by creating an awareness of the catastrophic consequences of atomic warfare." The award was made just prior to the first summit meeting to be held between the United States and the Soviet Union since Ronald Reagan became US President. In this long interval, tensions had heightened and the arms race had accelerated between the two countries, bringing closer the possibility of a nuclear disaster. Nobel Chairman Egil Aarvik linked the choice of the Committee to these upcoming talks: "If this award has any message, it is for the two superpowers to come up with results," he said.

The Committee's decision voices a conviction that nuclear war presents an overall threat to the Earth's peoples, and that ideologically opposed nations must work together to prevent such a disaster despite all disagreements, large and small, between them. The IPPNW is founded on this single, overriding premise. Its co-presidents, American cardiologist Bernard Lown of Harvard's School of Public Health and

Soviet cardiologist Eugene Chazov of the National Cardiological Research Center in Moscow, emphasized this in their message to the 1985 IPPNW Congress: "Combating the nuclear threat has been our total and exclusive preoccupation," they said. They attributed their success largely to an insistent avoidance of association with problems that have embittered relations between the Superpowers, resisting being sidetracked to other issues for any reason.

This organization comes from a distinguished and responsible lineage. In 1961 a group of physicians in Cambridge, Massachusetts, became concerned over the health effects of atmospheric testing of nuclear weapons and alarmed over the growing US confidence in a fallacious civil defense program. They felt these things to be an increasing hazard to the health of their community, and ultimately a threat to the peoples of the Earth. They founded Physicians for Social Responsibility (PSR), whose purpose was twofold: to create an education program, acquainting themselves as physicians with the problems of nuclear age, and to seek preventive measures against the major health hazard therein.

In 1973, a quite different event took place. The problem of sudden death from cardiovascular causes brought together physicians from the East and West to participate in collaborative studies on this health problem. In the resulting series of visits and exchanges of information between US and Soviet physicians, two of the participating cardiologists, Lown and Chazov, began to see the possibility of similar cooperation in facing a potentially far greater health problem—the threat to all life lying within a possible nuclear disaster. Their mutual concern led to a Geneva meeting in December 1980 between three Soviet and three US physicians. There they generated a set of resolutions that became the basis for the founding of IPPNW: they would restrict their focus to preventing nuclear war, and to this end they would involve both Eastern and Western bloc nations and seek to circulate the same factual information about nuclear war throughout the world. Acknowledging that many things divided them politically and ideologically, they agreed not to allow these issues to become divisive. Thus IPPNW provides a model for international cooperation, finding common ground and issuing prescriptions that transcend political and cultural boundaries. Since that day in late 1980, IPPNW has gained a membership of 135,000 physicians in 41 countries. With a large supportive lay membership, they have helped penetrate the fog of psychic denial, persuading millions of people, for the first time, to confront the "unthinkable" reality of nuclear war. They have convinced a large public that there can be no useful medical response to the horrors of blast, fire, and radiation that would come in its wake.

The physicians also deplore the long-term effects on health and welfare imposed by the arms race itself: "Its cost is not only the vast sums being diverted to armaments in a world where tens of thousands of human beings die each day of treatable diseases. The cost is also in the great psychological damage that is occurring, particularly to young people and children who fear they will have no future."

How is one to explain the growing awareness of the unprecedented danger which exists side by side with a persistant refusal to resist that danger? How can one explain that, notwithstanding the education of millions about the consequences of nuclear war, we are still addicted to a nuclear fix?

Chazov and Lown offer an answer and suggest a solution. One fundamental reason for such a calamitous impasse, they say, relates to the fostering of the image of an all-powerful and unscrupulous adversary. In thousands of years of human history the fixed response has been to gather rocks, muskets, and napalm, and now it is to increase nuclear arsenals. To reverse this behavior pattern it is not enough to make apocalyptic predictions, however well-founded, however persuasively put. The enemy stereotypes must be dissipated.

IPPNW has fostered opportunities for a free-flowing dialogue between physicians of the two contending power blocs. One of the main planks of their program has been to eradicate "image of the enemy" stereotyping by promoting closer personal contacts between representatives of the two nations and by better education about each other's countries.

In 1985 IPPNW expanded its platform to include support toward a substantial shift of funding from the nuclear arms race to the health needs of developing countries, especially those of children. Lown and Chazov explained: "We need to set examples and venture imaginatively to harness medical talent East and West for resolution of global health problems. Leading world experts from the USA, USSR and the World Health Organization will detail a program for immunizing children in the Third World against six diseases that claim more than 4 million lives annually and cripple as many."

"We physicians do not accept the inevitability of nuclear conflict," Dr. Lown and Chazov asserted at the close of the 1985 IPPNW Congress. "We reject subverting technology for genocidal weapons rather than employing the fruits of science for improving the quality of life. We meet here because of our abiding faith in human reason and because we hold dear the concept that what humanity creates, humanity can control . . . . Let us pledge—as physicians and world citizens—to work tirelessly toward eradicating the greatest public health threat of all time."

IPPNW embodies the professional tradition of physicians' organizing themselves in favor of life. The great nineteenth-century physician and scientist Rudolf Virchow foresaw that this tradition must embrace societal responsibility: "Should medicine ever fulfill its great ends, it must enter into the larger political and social life of our time, it must indicate the barriers which obstruct the normal completion of the life cycle and remove them. Should this ever come to pass, medicine, whatever it may then be, will become the common good of all." IPPNW has indeed proven Virchow's vision prophetic.

Biography

In December 1980 three US and three Soviet physicians met in Geneva to found the International Physicians for the Prevention of Nuclear War (IPPNW). The three US physicians were members of the Physicians for Social Responsibility

(PSR), an activist group organized in 1961 to educate themselves, their fellow physicians, and their patients about the hazards to health and life itself posed by the nuclear testing being done at that time, and to educate the public about the fallacy of civil defense as a means of preserving life in the event of nuclear warfare. PSR remains the US affiliate of IPPNW.

The IPPNW quickly gained worldwide support. Within months of its inception, doctors from 11 countries attended IPPNW's first annual meeting. At the time of the 1985 annual meeting the membership had grown to 135,000 with 41 countries represented. Its co-presidents are Bernard Lown, a cardiologist from Harvard's School of Public Health, and Eugene Chazov, a cardiologist from the National Cardiological Research Center in Moscow.

IPPNW has been a one-issue organization, seeking only to prevent nuclear war. In 1985, however, an adjunctive plan was adopted wherein IPPNW cooperates with the World Health Organization in the immunization of children in the Third World against six diseases that claim more than four million lives annually and cripple an equal number.

See also: Articles: *Nuclear Winter*

Bibliography ⸻

Abrams H L 1984 Medical resources after nuclear war. *J. Am. Med. Assoc.* 252(5)

Boyer P 1985 Physicians confront the apocalypse—The American medical profession and the threat of nuclear war. *J. Am. Med. Assoc.* 254(5)

Bruwer A 1985 The nuclear weapons freeze and a cancer metaphor—A physician's view. *J. Am. Med. Assoc.* 254(5)

Cassel C K, Jameton A 1982 Medical responsibility and thermonuclear war: An analysis of medical responsibility. *Annals of Internal Med.* 97

Chalmers T C, Lown B, Chazov E 1984 Physicians should contribute to preventing nuclear war (Letter). *J. Am. Med. Assoc.* 252(5)

Day B, Waitzkin H 1985 The medical profession and nuclear war—A social history. *J. Am. Med. Assoc.* 254(5)

Bulletin of Atomic Scientists 1985 Nobel for physicians. 41(11): 2

Gunby P 1980 Sudden death brings East and West together. *J. Am. Med. Assoc.* 243(3)

Hiatt H H 1984 The final epidemic—Prescriptions for prevention. *J. Am. Med. Assoc.* 252(5)

Jennet C, Starr M 1985 A prescription for peace. *Newsweek* October 21

Liebow A A 1965 Encounter with disaster: A medical diary on Hiroshima. *Yale J. Biol. Med.* 38

Lifton R J 1985 Hiroshima and ourselves. *J. Am. Med. Assoc.* 254(5)

Litwin M S 1985 Physician's group seeks nuclear arms ban. *J. Am. Med. Assoc.* 254(5)

Lown B, Chazov E 1985 Cooperation not confrontation: The imperative of a nuclear age. *J. Am. Med. Assoc.* 254(5)

Lundberg G D 1983 Hiroshima. *J. Am. Med. Assoc.* 250(5)

Lundberg G D 1985 Prescriptions for peace in a nuclear age. *J. Am. Med. Assoc.* 254(5)

Southgate M T The shadow of Hiroshima: Two diaries. *J. Am. Med. Assoc.* 252(5)

Ziparyn T, Goldsmith M F 1985 Physicians' antinuclear war group expanding to include child health. *J. Am. Med. Assoc.* 254(5)

RUTH C. REYNOLDS

Elie Wiesel
(1986)

The 1986 Nobel Peace Prize was awarded to Elie Wiesel, an author and historian, who has authored 25 books on the Nazi genocide of European Jewry. The prize was awarded to Wiesel by the Nobel Committee in recognition of his ceaseless efforts to chronicle the injustices and the atrocities of the holocaust in the past and to speak out against the present sufferings of humanity. In awarding him the prize, on October 14, 1986, the Norwegian Nobel Committee cited him as "one of the most important spiritual leaders and guides" in an age characterized by "violence, repression, and racism," and that it would be able to permit him to "speak louder" and "reach more people" for the causes that have driven him throughout his adult life. "I dedicate [the prize] to my fellow survivors and their children," Wiesel told a news conference. "The honor is not mine alone." Shortly afterward, he visited the Soviet Union, where he met with old friends and appealed to the authorities in behalf of Jews wishing to emigrate.

Wiesel, who is said to have been the first to use the term "holocaust" to describe the killing of some 6 million Jews by the Nazis, has also spoken out for the civil rights of such groups as South Africa's black population, the "boat people" of Indochina, the Miskito Indians of Nicaragua, Argentine political prisoners, and Soviet Jewry. He received the ultimate recognition for his commitment to human dignity when he was awarded this prize in 1986.

Wiesel's ambition to become a writer is rooted in the Hasidic storyteller tradition of his childhood, and when he was about twelve, he wrote a book of commentaries on the Bible. In the months following the liberation of Buchenwald, he became convinced that the purpose of his survival was "to give testimony, to bear witness." Nevertheless, he made a vow to remain silent for ten years. "I didn't want to use the wrong words," he explained to John S. Friedman, as quoted in Paris Review (Spring 1984). "I was afraid that words might betray it. I waited."

Wiesel's self-imposed silence came to an end in 1954 after he interviewed Francois Mauriac, the French Roman Catholic writer and Nobel laureate, for *Yedioth Ahronot*. Acknowledging Christian responsibility for the holocaust, Mauriac urged Wiesel to relate his death-camp experiences. Two years later, Wiesel published his first book in Yiddish, the language of his childhood, in Buenos Aires under the title *Un di Velt Hot Geshvign* (And the World Has Remained Silent). Unsuccessful in his efforts to have the 800-page manuscript published in France, Wiesel condensed his memoir to 127 pages and translated it into French. It appeared in 1958 as *La Nuit*, with a foreword by Mauriac, who had arranged for its publication by Editions de Minuit. The book is dedicated to the memory of Wiesel's parents and his sister Tzipora, who died in the concentration camps. Translated into English by Stella Rodway, it was published in the United States, after several rejections, under the title *Night* (Hill & Wang, 1960). "The holocaust was not something people wanted to know about in those days," Wiesel remembered in a *Time* magazine interview (March 18, 1985). "The diary of Anne Frank was about as far as anyone wanted to venture into the dark."

After this first book Elie Wiesel became a prolific writer chronicling the holocaust and the aftermath. In 1960, he wrote *L'Aube*, translated in 1961 as *Dawn*. Some of Wiesel's other works include: *The Accident, The Town Beyond the Wall, The Gates of the Forest, A Beggar in Jerusalem, The Jews of Silence: A Personal Report on Soviet Jewry, The Madness of God, The Trial of God, The Testament, Legends of Our Time and A Jew Today*.

The need to remember and to testify has been the driving force behind Wiesel's literary career, and his writings on the holocaust have been a major factor in increasing public awareness of the near total destruction of European Jewry. Yet Wiesel remains troubled by the "trivialization" in film and literature of the holocaust experience, an event he believes to be unique in human history. Because to him, silence broken by ill-advised words is worse than silence itself, he imposed that vow of silence upon himself at the end of World War II.

The significance that critics have attached to Wiesel's work can be seen in the scores of literary awards that he has received over the years Among them are the Prix Rivarol (1963), the Prix Medicis (1968), the Eleanor Roosevelt Award (1972), the Martin Luther King Medallion (1973), the Frank and Ethel Cohen Award (1973), the Jewish Book Council Literary Award (1965, 1973), the Prix Livre-Inter (1980), the Prix des Bibliothequaires (1981), and the Grand Prix de la Litterature de la ville de Paris (1983).

Elie Wiesel is a person who is a living example of how one can turn hopelessness into victory. Wiesel says that only one enemy is worse than despair: indifference. "In every area of human creativity indifference is the enemy; indifference of evil is worse than evil, because it is also sterile." "There may be times when we are powerless to prevent injustice, but there must never be a time when we fail to protest.

Before Wiesel received the Nobel Peace Prize, he had wanted to meet with Mikhail Gorbachev. He has criticized Moscow's reluctance to allow more Soviet Jews to emigrate, and had asked to meet with Gorbachev to plead their case. Gorbachev sent an emissary who delivered the message of apology for not having been able to meet with Wiesel and wished to meet him as soon as possible. As chairman of the US Holocaust Memorial Council, Wiesel went to the former Soviet Union officially to seek Soviet participation in a conference on non-Jewish victims of Nazism. His efforts to solicit cooperation from the Soviets did not bear much fruit, however, until the dissolution of the Union.

Lately, when the US government released a report that Switzerland knowingly accepted Nazi gold and provided currency and weapons in return, though it was officially neutral during the war, Wiesel came out and spoke. He claimed that the aging holocaust survivors should receive the roughly $70 million in Nazi gold that has been stored since World War II in New York and London. "All this money should go to those survivors who need help, wherever they are," Wiesel said.

Biography

Eliezer Wiesel was born to Shlome and Sarah Wiesel on

September 30, 1928 in the town of Sighet in northern Transylvania, near the Ukrainian border. In 1940 Romania, under German pressure, ceded the area to Hungary, but it was returned to Romania in 1945 by the Soviet Union. Wiesel's father, a shopkeeper, instilled in his only son humanist values and encouraged him to learn modern Hebrew and its literature.

Childhood, a recurrent theme in his work, ended for Elie Wiesel in the spring of 1944 when the Nazis ordered the deportation of Sighet's 15,000 Jews. He and his family were transported to Auschwitz concentration camp in Poland, where his mother and his youngest sister, Tzipora, died in the gas chambers. Separated from his two older sisters, Hilda and Batya, he did not learn of their survival until after the war. In 1945 Elie Wiesel and his father were sent to Buchenwald concentration camp in Germany. There, Shlomo Wiesel died from starvation and dysentery.

After liberation of Buchenwald on April 11, 1945 by the United States Third Army, he was placed on a train bound for Belgium with some 400 other orphans. En route, the train was diverted to France at the intervention of General Charles de Gaulle. Settling first in Normandy under the care of a Jewish children's aid organization, the Oeuvres du Secours aux Enfants, he later moved to Paris, where from 1948 to 1951 he studied literature, philosophy, and psychology at the Sorbonne while earning his living as a choir director, teacher of Hebrew and the Bible, translator, and summer camp counselor. Under the tutelage of Gustav Wahl, Wiesel had mastered the French language.

While attending the Sorbonne, Wiesel became a journalist, and in 1948 he traveled to Israel to cover the newly founded state's struggle for survival for the French newspaper *L'Arche*. On a trip to India in 1952 as the Paris correspondent for the Tel Aviv daily *Yedioth Ahronot*, he acquired a working knowledge of English. In 1956, while reporting on the United Nations in New York City for the same Israeli newspaper, he was struck by a taxicab in Times Square. Confined to a wheelchair for almost a year, he was persuaded by an American immigration official to apply for United States citizenship after unsuccessful efforts to have his French travel documents extended.

Elie Wiesel was married on the eve of Passover, 1969 to Marion Erster Rose, who has a daughter, Jennifer Rose, from her previous marriage. With their teenaged son, Shlomo Elisha, they make their home in New York City. Wiesel, a United States citizen since 1963, was distinguished professor of Judaic studies at the City University of New York from 1972 to 1976. He commutes regularly to Boston, where he has served since 1976 as Andrew Mellon Professor in the Humanities at Boston University.

Bibliography

New York Times 1986
New York Times 1986
Paris Rev 1984 Spring
Brown R Mc 1983 *Elie Wiesel: Messenger to All Humanity*
Cargas H J 1976 *In Conversation With Elie Wiesel*
Fine E S 1982 *Legacy of Night: the Literary Universe of Elie Wiesel*
National World 1997 "Wiesel: gold to survivors." http://www.thonline.com/th/news/051097/National/75899.htm
Stern E N 1982 *Elie Wiesel: Witness for Life*
The Nobel Foundation 1997 "Elie Wiesel." http://nobelsdsc.edu/laureates/peace-1986-1-bio.html

PEDRO B. BERNALDEZ

Oscar Arias Sanchez
(1987)

President Oscar Arias of Costa Rica, whose efforts to end years of armed conflict in Central America have stirred new hope in the region was awarded the 1987 Nobel Peace Prize. Arias was the driving force behind a peace agreement signed August 7, 1987 by five Central American presidents. Arias, the principal author of the accord, is widely credited with persuading Costa Rica's feuding neighbors to take a united stand for peace. For Arias, the award was another milestone in a search for a negotiated peace in Central America that few thought would advance as far as it has.

Oscar Arias Sanchez, president of Costa Rica since 1986, has assumed the role of peacemaker in strife-torn Central America in his determination to prevent his country—known as the "Switzerland" or "Denmark" of the Americas—from being used as a battleground in the conflict between neighboring Nicaragua's Marxist Sandinista government and the United States-supported Contra rebels seeking to overthrow it. Educated in the United States and Great Britain, Arias served with distinction as Costa Rica's minister of planning from 1972 to 1977 and as general secretary of the moderately socialist National Liberation party from 1979 to 1984. As president he has tried to maintain Costa Rica's neutrality, political stability, high cultural level, and relative prosperity, despite serious economic problems. With reference to his country's relationship with the United States, which has contributed more economic assistance per capita to Costa Rica than to any other country except Israel, Arias has said: "I value nothing more than friendship—friendship between people, friendship between nations. Friendship implies loyalty, but loyalty is not synonymous with servitude or unconditionality." The Costa Rican president's efforts to end the strife in Central America earned him the Nobel Peace Prize in October 1987.

Although critical of the Sandinista regime of Nicaragua because of its authoritarianism and its restrictions on civil liberties at home, as well as indications that it was fomenting unrest in Costa Rica through the domestic Communist organization, Arias resisted right-wing pressure to adopt a militant anti-Sandinista stand, and he consistently supported efforts to resolve Central American hostilities through negotiations.

In the elections of February 2, 1986, in which 1,185,222 Costa Ricans—about 80 percent of the eligible voters—went to the polls, Arias emerged as the victor, with 620,315 votes, or 52.3 percent of the total, while Calderon, his opponent, received 542,434 votes, or 45.8 percent. In his victory speech, Arias expressed satisfaction that the people had "chosen bread" over rifles, and he warned the approximately 3,000 Nicaraguan Contras on Costa Rican soil that he would not allow them to abuse the nation's hospitality or to put its sovereignty at risk.

Sworn in on May 8, 1986 for a four-year term as Costa Rica's forty-seventh and youngest president, Arias declared in his inaugural address: "We will keep Costa Rica out of the armed conflicts of Central America and we will endeavor through diplomatic and political means to prevent Central American brothers from killing each other." Referring to Costa Rica as an oasis of peace and freedom, Arias extolled the virtues of democracy and emphasized the need for Latin American economic recovery and the preservation of Costa Rica's neutrality to the assembled dignitaries, who included United States Vice-President George Bush and ten Latin American heads of state. He pledged to support the so-called Contadora peace treaty, sponsored by Colombia, Panama, Mexico, and Venezuela, which would require democratic elections, demilitarization, and internal reconciliation for all of Central America.

On May 24 and 25, 1986, Arias met with the presidents of Guatemala, El Salvador, Honduras, and Nicaragua in a Central American summit conference at Esquipulas, Guatemala to discuss the proposed Contadora peace accord for the region. In their final declaration, the five leaders recognized the need for the Contadora pact to be signed eventually but admitted that fundamental differences on key points remained to be resolved, notably in regard to arms control and limitations on international military maneuvers in the region, and Nicaragua's refusal to sign the pact as long as the United States continued to fund the Contra rebels. At Arias' request, a phrase that described the five signatories as "freely elected by the will of their respective peoples," which he felt did not apply to Nicaraguan President Daniel Ortega Saavedra, was omitted from the final draft. The declaration called for continued dialogue to enhance democracy and pluralism in Central America, to promote regional cooperation for social and economic development, and to establish means for the resolution of differences without outside interference. The leaders also agreed to initiate a Central American parliament.

On the economic front, Arias instituted measures to stimulate the infusion of money from abroad, including a "tax holiday" for foreign investors and the establishment of a free-trade zone near San Jose, but the national economy continued to be vulnerable. Although Arias resumed making interest payments on the country's foreign debt, which had been suspended by Monge, the expenditures of some $250 million a year—about 30 percent of export earnings—exceeded what Costa Rica could expect in new grants and loans from abroad.

Despite his strong criticism of Nicaragua's Sandinista government, Arias has vigorously opposed United States funding of the Contra rebels, contending that the money could be put to better use in promoting the survival of liberal democracy in Central America by peaceful means. "The more you give to the Contras, the more [Nicaraguan President] Ortega gets from the Soviets," he has said, as quoted by Stephen Kinzer in the *New York Times* (September 16, 1986). His program of "stability with growth and social justice" would, in his view, be impossible to achieve if there was no peace.

As a means of safeguarding his country's neutrality, Arias has moved decisively against Contra activities in Costa Rica. During the summer and early fall of 1986 the Arias government arrested several Contra activists and dismissed government officials who permitted a secret Contra hospital to operate on Costa Rican soil. "We're going to throw them out no matter who they are if we catch them helping the Contras," Arias has asserted. In September 1986,

Costa Rican civil guards occupied a secret 6,520-foot airstrip near the Nicaraguan border that was being used for Contra supply flights. It had been built under the supervision of associates of former White House aide Lieutenant Colonel Oliver North, who was later dismissed in connection with the Iran-Contra scandals. When in November 1986 Contra leaders met in San Jose to discuss future plans, Arias denied visas to two of their top men, Adolfo Calero and Enrique Bermudez, whom he considered military rather than political figures.

At a meeting on February 15, 1987 with the presidents of Honduras, Guatemala, and El Salvador, Arias put forth his proposals for a new regional peace plan for Central America, based on the Contadora proposals but broader in scope. The ten-point plan, described by Arias as a "risk for peace," called for immediate cease-fires in all guerilla wars in the region—in Guatemala and El Salvador as well as in Nicaragua. All outside military aid to rebel groups would be suspended; there would be a general amnesty; and negotiations between conflicting parties would be initiated. This would be followed by free elections in the region, guarantees for improved human and civil rights, and a general reduction in military forces. In Arias' view, the plan would put the Sandinistas to a test. "If we arrive at an agreement and Nicaragua does not fulfill the obligations . . . ," he told John Moody in an interview for *Time* (June 29, 1987), "then it will put an end to this ambiguity which has permitted the Sandinistas to receive the support of both democratic and totalitarian governments." Democratic Senator Christopher Dodd of Connecticut, who was present at the initial meeting, termed Arias' proposals "an important first step for the Central Americans to get out of the bleachers and into the playing field in order to begin solving their own problems," and Flora Lewis noted in her *New York Times* column (May 27,1987) that "the beauty of the Arias plan is that it will clarify the issues so badly muddled by shifting United States policy statements and covert actions."

At first, the Arias plan received wide support, in Latin America, the United States, and Western Europe, and even the PUSC opposition in Costa Rica endorsed it. Nicaraguan President Ortega, after an initial negative reaction, also indicated that he was receptive to it. On March 12, 1987, the United States senate, in a nonbinding resolution sponsored by Democratic Senator Terry Sanford of North Carolina, endorsed the Arias plan by a vote of ninety-seven to one, although Republican spokesmen warned that their support of a negotiated settlement should not be interpreted as abandonment of Reagan administration policies.

Eventually, however, the Arias plan became subject to increasing criticism. On June 17, 1987, Arias was invited to the White House in Washington, D.C. to consult with President Ronald Reagan and other officials in a sixty-five minute meeting that was later described by Costa Rican sources as "sharp, tense, and blunt." Reagan reportedly found a number of "loopholes" in the plan and maintained that it made undue concessions to the Sandinistas. The plan also caused concern in El Salvador, whose president, Jose Napoleon Duarte, feared that the agreement would force his government to make concessions to imprisoned leftist rebels. Meanwhile, Sandinista spokesmen accused the United States of trying to isolate Nicaragua and to sabotage the possibility of a negotiated settlement. Discussions of the Arias plan at a summit meeting originally scheduled for June 25, 1987 were postponed.

Finally, on August 7, 1987, after some prodding by the Costa Rican president, the five Central American heads of state, meeting in Guatemala City, signed a regional peace plan essentially based on the Arias proposals and scheduled to go into effect on November 7, 1987. At the same time they shunted aside a plan presented three days earlier by President Reagan and Jim Wright, the speaker of the House of Representatives, that placed greater demands on the Sandinistas, imposed a shorter deadline than was provided for under the Arias plan, and left the door open for renewed United States aid to the Contras. Although the Arias plan left some questions unresolved, it was widely hailed as a breakthrough toward peace, and even President Reagan welcomed what he called "this commitment to peace and democracy by the five Central American presidents."

On September 20, 1987, Arias embarked on an eight-day visit to the United States to promote his peace plan, consult with President Reagan and other United States officials, and address Congress and the UN General Assembly. He made no reference to a proposal by Reagan to ask Congress for $270 million in new aid to the Contras but urged his American hosts to "give peace a chance."

Arias received appropriate recognition for his peace efforts when on October 13, 1987, the Norwegian Nobel committee named him the winner of the Nobel Peace Prize, citing his "outstanding contribution to the possible return of stability and peace to a region long torn by strife and civil war." Although the award was widely hailed, it was seen as a setback for the Reagan administration, whose continued efforts to aid the Contras appeared then to be doomed.

Biography

The scion of one of Costa Rica's most prosperous coffee-producing families, Oscar Arias Sanchez was born in Heredia, near San Jose, the Costa Rican capital on September 13, 1941, to Juan Rafael Arias Trejos and his wife, the former Lilian Sanchez. His paternal grandfather, Juan Rafael Arias Bonilla, was a prominent legislator and government minister, and his grandfather on his mother's side, Julio Sanchez Lepiz, the founder of the family's coffee-growing enterprise, also served in the national legislative assembly.

After studying in the United States, he read law and economics at the University of Costa Rica in the capital, San Jose. As a student he engaged actively in the work of the National Liberation Party. He is the author of a number of books and articles on political and historical subjects. He studied Law and Economics at the University of Costa Rica. His thesis, "Pressure Groups in Costa Rica" earned him the 1971 National Essay Prize. In 1974, he received a doctoral degree in Political Science at the University of Essex, England with a thesis on the subject of "Who rules Costa Rica?". After serving as Professor of Political Science at the University of Costa Rica, Dr. Arias was appointed Costa Rican Minister of Planning and Economic Policy. He won a seat in Congress in 1978 and was elected Secretary-General of the National Liberation Party in 1981. In 1986, Oscar Arias was elected President of Costa Rica. Dr. Arias assumed office at a time of great regional discord. The fall of the Somoza dictatorship in 1979 and the introduction of the Sandinista regime in Nicaragua had already been a source of contention in Central America. The ideological and military interference of the superpowers, still entrenched in the Cold War, threatened to broaden this conflict in both scope and definition. Such intervention heightened the state of civil war that had by then claimed more than one hundred thousand lives in Guatemala. It aggravated internal unrest in El Salvador and Nicaragua, as well as border tensions between Nicaragua and its neighboring states: Honduras and Costa Rica. Despite the previous presidential administration's decision not to become embroiled in the growing conflict, Costa Rica's involvement seemed almost unavoidable. In the face of these threats, Arias intensified his efforts to promote peace. Even before assuming the presidency, Arias traveled throughout Central and South America to personally invite the Latin American heads of state to visit Costa Rica for his presidential inauguration. On the day he took office, the presidents of nine Latin American countries met in San Jose. At this meeting Arias called for a continental alliance for the defense of democracy and liberty. He affirmed the principles that all Central Americans were entitled to the same liberties and social and economic guarantees of democracy, that each nation had the right to select, through free and fair elect-

ions, the type of government that could best meet the needs and interests of its people, and that neither armies nor totalitarian regimes were entitled to make this decision. At that moment Costa Rica, led by Oscar Arias, assumed an active role in the search for democracy and peace for the countries of the region. In 1987, President Arias drafted a peace plan to end the regional crisis. Widely recognized as the Arias Peace Plan, his initiative culminated in the signing of the Esquipulas II Accords or the 'Procedure to Establish a Firm and Lasting Peace' in Central America by all the Central American presidents on August 7, 1987. In that same year he was awarded the Nobel Peace Prize.

In 1988, Arias used the monetary award from the Nobel Peace Prize to establish the Arias Foundation for Peace and Human Progress. Under the auspices of the Foundation, three programs were established: The Center for Human Progress to promote equal opportunities for women in all sectors of Central American society; the Center for Philanthropy to foster change-oriented philanthropy in Latin America; and the Center for Peace and Reconciliation to work for demilitarization and conflict resolution in the developing world. From these same headquarters, Dr. Arias has continued his pursuit of global peace and human security.

Dr. Arias has received honorary doctorates from universities such as Harvard, Washington, Illinois, Oviedo, Franklin and Marshall, and Southern Connecticut; the colleges of Dartmouth, Ithaca, and Quinnipiac; and several other prestigious educational institutions.

He has also received numerous prizes, among them the Jackson Ralston Prize, the Prince of Asturias Award, the Martin Luther King Jr. Peace Award, the Albert Schweitzer Humanitarian Award, the Liberty Medal of Philadelphia, and the Americas Award.

Oscar Arias participates actively in several international organizations. He is the president of the International Press Service (IPS), and serves on the board of Directors of the Stockholm International Peace Research Institute (SIPRI), the International Center for Human Rights and Democratic Development (ICHRDD), and the Institute for International Studies at Stanford. Dr. Arias also serves on the Board for the Inter-Action Council, the International Negotiation Network of the Carter Center, and Transparency International. In addition, he is part of the Commission on Global Governance and an active member of the Inter-American Dialogue, and the Society for International Development.

While Oscar Arias is best known for his international efforts, he is also lauded for his capable management of the Costa Rican economy during his presidential term. Arias believed in minimal government intervention and bureaucracy as a means to a prosperous economy. Under his leadership, Costa Rica's economy thrived and served as a model for neighboring countries. During his term of office, Costa Rica maintained its stronghold as the richest country in the region, with the healthiest economy and highest standard of living. The gross national product increased by an average of 5% during his term in office, and the unemployment rate of 3.4% was the lowest in the hemisphere. This superior economic growth was balanced by a strong social welfare program which included, among other projects, an initiative to provide housing to the poor.

Dr. Arias was a visible president, frequently venturing out in public on his own to listen to the concerns of the citizenry. Since the conclusion of his term in office in 1990, he has continued to be 'a man of the people' promoting such innovative ideas as human security, global governance and human development. By bringing 'human' concerns to the forefront of the international agenda, he provides a link between the impoverished South and the developed North, between the more politically stable West and a conflict-ridden East. To the people of the industrialized countries, he carries a sincere message of solidarity and partnership, "to counter the growing threats faced by nations today and to initiate an era of peace and prosperity for all humankind."

Oscar Arias Sanchez was married in 1973 to Margarita Penon Gongora, a biochemist who graduated from Vassar College in the United States. Their children are Silvia Eugenia and Oscar Felipe. Described in the *Nation* as "a man of intelligence and enormous pride," Arias has, according to James LeMoyne in the *New York Times*,

"some of the reserve and intellectual independence" that is reflected in his British academic training. His published works include *Democracia, Independencia y Sociedad Latinoamericana* (1977), *Los Caminos para el Desarrollo de Costa Rica* (1977), and *Nuevos Rumbos para el Desarrollo Costarricense* (1980), as well as diverse articles in periodicals and scholarly journals.

Bibliography

38th Street Homepage 1998 "Oscar Arias Sanchez." http://ftp.milwaukee.k12.wi.us/schoolas/38th/OscarArias.html

Commonwealth 1986 May 9)

Current Biography Yearbook 1987. "Arias Sanchez, Oscar."

Nation 1986 December 20

Newsweek 1987 October 26

New York Times 1986 February 4

Nobel Foundation 1987 "Oscar Arias Sanchez: Nobel Peace Prize 1987." http://nobel.sdsc.edu/laureates/peace-1987-1-bio.html

Peacejam 1998 "A Nobel Laureate to Study: Oscar Arias." http://www.peacejam.org:8001/peacejam/html.oscaru1c3.html

Time 1987 October 26

PEDRO B. BERNALDEZ

United Nations Peacekeeping Forces
(1988)

The 1988 Nobel Peace Prize was awarded to the United Nations Peacekeeping Forces (UNPF), the fourth UN organ to be awarded the Prize. The Office of the High Commissioner for Refugees garnered the Prize in 1981 and 1954, and the United Nations Children's Fund got it in 1965.

In awarding the Prize, Egil Aarvik, chairman of the Committee stressed that the UN Peacekeeping Forces have done a "decisive contribution" to peace around the world "under extremely difficult conditions." Then UN Secretary-General Javier Perez de Cuellar informed the General Assembly, "The award is a tribute to the idealism of all who have served this organization and in particular to the valor and sacrifice of those who have contributed, and continue to contribute to our peacekeeping operations."

United Nations peacekeepers, wearing distinctive UN blue helmets or berets, have been dispatched by the Security Council to help implement peace agreements, monitor ceasefires, patrol demilitarized zones,

create buffer zones between opposing forces, and put fighting on hold while negotiators seek peaceful solutions to disputes. For a fact, the UN possesses no armed forces, thus, for each peacekeeping mission, Member States volunteer troops and equipment, for which compensation is provided from a special peacekeeping budget. The $390,000 cash prize received by the organization for having been awarded the Nobel Peace Prize was thought to be used to help support the forces.

The UN Peacekeeping Forces may only be employed when parties to a conflict accept their presence. Moreover, they may also be used by the warring parties to avoid having a conflict escalate and also to call off an on-going struggle. The forces are under the leadership command of the Security Council which invokes the principle of collective security enshrined in the United Nations Charter. Control of peacekeeping operations belongs to the Secretary-General and his secretariat.

Two kinds of peacekeeping operations may be distinguished. Unarmed observer groups are allowed to have their presence in the conflict area but not to carry weapons. Lightly-armed military forces are only allowed to employ their weapons for self-defence. The observer groups are concerned with information-gathering work, about actual conditions prevailing in the area. The military forces can perform more extended tasks such as keeping the parties to a conflict apart and maintaining order in the area.

Since 1945, there have been 48 United Nations peacekeeping operations. There are currently 16 operations underway. In fact, thirty four peacekeeping operations were created by the Security Council in the period between 1988, when the Nobel Peace Prize was awarded, and February 1998.

UN interventions are in particular demand in the Middle East, both as regards observer groups and military forces. First UN troops went to the Middle East in 1948. The maiden effort in peacekeeping, established in June 1948, has been the United Nations Truce Supervision Organization in Jerusalem. With headquarters on the Hill of Evil Counsel, the UNTSO's unarmed military observers supervised the first truce between the New Israeli state and the Arab nations after the first Arab-Israeli war. Expanding its mandate from unarmed observation to armed peacekeeping, the United Nations Interim Force in Lebanon was fielded. There have been four other peacekeeping missions in the Middle East. The UN Disengagement Observer Force has been stationed on the strategic Golan Heights between Israel and Syrian troops since 1974. The UN Iran-Iraq Military Observer Group was formed in August 1988 and lasted till February 1991. UNIMOG was intended to observe the ceasefire between the warring Persian Gulf states, monitor their withdrawal of troops to the international border and help implement an exchange of prisoners.

UN officials have singled out UNDOF for being the most successful mission in the region. The peacekeeping troops of UNDOF moved unto the Golan Heights in June 1974 to be a part of the disengagement process between Israel and Syria in the aftermath of the Yum Kippur War in 1973. On the other hand, the UNIFIL is said to have been the least successful. Until 1988, when the Prize was awarded, 5,800 troops have been shot, shelled, kidnapped and held hostages, simply ignored and disparaged by the warring parties. After having been dispatched to Lebanon in March 1978 after Israeli forces thrust into the South, UNIFIL was constrained to deploy fully by Israelis, and Israeli troops even swept across UNIFIL positions in their march north to Beirut. Con-

sequently, relations between UNIFIL and Israeli forces have often been strained. Having been the most extensive UN operation in the Middle East, UNIFIL has been tasked with supervising Israeli withdrawal, maintaining conditions of peace and security, and helping the Lebanese government re-establish its authority.

Beyond the Middle East operations, the United Nations played an important role during the struggles that erupted when the Belgian colony of the Congo achieved independence in 1960. When anarchy and chaos swept the area, a UN force comprising 20,000 troops was set up to help the Congolese government maintain peace and order. It ended up being engaged in bringing a raging civil war to an end and preventing the province of Katanga from seceding. It was while carrying out the UN mission in Congo that Secretary-General Dag Hammarskjold was killed in an air crash.

Since 1949, the animosities characterizing India-Pakistan relations have brought tensions to world security. UN Peacekeeping Forces were deployed and monitored ceasefires. Peacekeeping operations have eased tensions and prevented military escalation along ceasefire line in Kashmir. In 1965-66, peacekeepers have monitored breaches in the ceasefire that helped facilitate the Tashkent agreements which led to complete withdrawal of Indian and Pakistani troops in 1966.

In West New Guinea, peacekeepers assured peaceful transfer of power in 1962-63. UN officers successfully implemented all provisions for the peaceful transfer of power by assuring peaceful negotiations between the Netherlands and Indonesia throughout the transition process. The United Nations Peacekeeping Operations (UN-PKO) maintained order and improved economic, health and education services in West New Guinea.

The UN-PKO in Suez Canal, Sinai, helped in silencing weapons and keeping the peace in 1973-79. The operations achieved ceasefire and facilitated separation and withdrawal of troops. They also monitored borders and carried out inspection through checkpoints along buffer zones. The troops also provided communication, delivered humanitarian aid, and helped exchange prisoners while maintaining ceasefire during operation.

In Afghanistan and Pakistan the UN Peacekeeping Forces monitored troop withdrawals during the period 1988-90. UN Secretary-General's good offices led to the negotiation of the Geneva Accords. Soviet withdrawal was successfully completed with UN monitoring and outposts were established to assure withdrawal. Violations of the Geneva Accords were also investigated to the extent possible and some refugees were returned.

Namibia was created as a free country in 1989-90 with the UN-PKO achieving ceasefire and peaceful withdrawal of South African troops. Thereafter, elections were held, demobilization of South African forces were effected and prisoners were released. Moreover, the UN-PKO assisted in repealing repressive legislations and in creating a new and independent government in Namibia.

Another successful story of UN Peacekeeping was done in Mozambique through the "shift from bullets to ballots" during the period 1992-95. The peacekeeping forces were able to organize free and fair elections, monitored withdrawal of Zimbabwean and Malawian troops, and conducted investigations of ceasefire violations. The troops also demobilized over 80,000 troops and secured transportation corridors. They demobilized over 80,000 troops and secured transportation corridors, facilitated the return of 1.5 million refugees, delivered humanitarian aid and provided technical assistance. Also, the officers monitored and verified ceasefire, demobilized forces, and destroyed weapons while providing security to transportation corridors. The operations were able to coordinate and monitor humanitarian assistance, provided technical assistance, and monitored elections.

In Cambodia, a rebirth of the nation was assisted in 1992-93. Peacekeepers of the UN conducted peaceful, free and fair elections, helped establish a new constitution and government, investigated ceasefire violations, destroyed weapon caches and demined major roads. Likewise, they monitored human rights violations while providing human rights training for military police and judicial personnel. Limited disarmament was achieved and humanitarian relief was provided along with the repatriation of 370,000 Cambodian refugees.

Considered as a resounding success of the UN in the post-Cold War era, peacekeepers were able to deter violence in the Iraq-Kuwait hostilities. Peace officers were likewise able to monitor withdrawal of Iraqi armed forces from Kuwait and they monitored Kyawr 'Abd-Allah waterway and the borders at patrol bases in the demilitarized zone. The officers also provided technical assistance to the United Nations Iraq-Kuwait Boundary Demarcation Commission and assisted relocation of Iraqi citizens from Kuwait to Iraq.

For the period 1991-April 1995, UN-PKO personnel held in ending the civil war in El Salvador and held free and fair elections. A peace accord was successfully implemented ending 12 years of bloody civil war. The peacekeepers were able to disarm combatants and created conditions for free and fair elections. They also monitored human rights abuses while dismantling existing security forces and beginning the creation of a civilian police force. The PKO provided buffer, police and humanitarian observer force to implement peace accord and monitor elections. The troops helped in maintaining public order pending the creation of a national civilian police.

Although some missions, such as in Somalia and Bosnia, exceeded the capacity of the United Nations, often the UN has succeeded in dramatically reducing violence, saving lives, and securing diplomatic solutions to conflict. Each peace operation has a mandate and typical mandates are to supervise ceasefires and troops withdrawals, observe elections, deliver humanitarian aid, and monitor human rights violations.

For half a century, the United Nations peacekeeping missions have helped assure a more stable world, enhance emerging democracies, protect human rights, end conflicts, and prevent the spread of war. When the Nobel Peace Prize was given to the UN Peacekeeping Forces in 1988, Martin Vadset, UNTSO chief of staff at that time reacted, "This is a welcome and very strong encouragement to all those men and women who serve . . . . I am particularly happy to see this happen in 1988, when I believe that the United Nations has been revitalized and has been more active than in years."

With the Cold War over, the challenges to the United Nations peacekeeping operations have also changed. In keeping with such demands the United Nations is adjusting its peacekeeping activities. For the maintenance of world peace the peacekeeping forces of the United Nations is here to stay.

History

The United Nations Peacekeeping Forces have been employed to maintain or re-establish peace in an area of armed conflict. The UN may engage in conflicts between states as well as struggles within states. Since 1945, there have been 48 United Nations peacekeeping operations. There are currently 16 under way. During the last ten years, 34 peacekeeping operations were created by the United Nations.

Traditionally, peacekeepers supervise cease-fires and observe the movements of the opposing forces in an attempt to bring calm to an area and facilitate a negotiated settlement to disputes. Peacekeepers seldom have the capability to enforce the terms of a ceasefire or agreement. The peacekeepers main powers are the moral authority of the UN

United Nations Peacekeeping Operations (1947 to 1998)

Mission Title	Location	Duration
UNSCOB United Nations Special Committee on the Balkans	Greece	October 1947 to January 1952
UNTSO United Nations Truce Supervision Organization	Middle East	June 1948 to date
UNMOGIP United Nations Military Observer Group in India and Pakistan	State of Jammu and Kashmir (India and Pakistan)	January 1949 to date
UNEF I United Nations Emergency Force I	Sinai Peninsula	November 1956 to June 1967
UNOGIL United Nations Observation Group in Lebanon	Lebanon	June 1958 to December 1958
ONUC United Nations Operation in the Congo	Zaire	July 1960 to June 1964
UNSF United Nations Security Force in West New Guinea (West Irian)	West Irian	October 1962 to April 1963
UNYOM United Nations Yemen Observation Mission	Border between Yemen and Saudi Arabia	July 1963 to September 1964
UNFICYP United Nations Peace-Keeping Force in Cyprus	Cyprus	March 1964 to date
DOMREP Mission of the Representative of the Secretary- General in the Dominican Republic	Dominican Republic	May 1965 to October 1966
UNIPOM United Nations India-Pakistan Observation Mission	India and Pakistan	September 1965 to March 1966
UNEF II United Nations Emergency Force II	Sinai Peninsula	October 1973 to July 1979
UNDOF United Nations Disengagement Observer Force	Golan Heights	June 1974 to date
UNIFIL United Nations Interim Force in Lebanon	Southern Lebanon	March 1978 to date
UNGOMAP United Nations Good Offices Mission in Afghanistan and Pakistan	Afghanistan and Pakistan	May 1988 to March 1990
UNIIMOG United Nations Iran-Iraq Military Observer Group	Border Between Iran and Iraq	August 1988 to February 1991
UNAVEM I United Nations Angola Verification Mission I	Angola	January 1989 to June 1991
UNTAG United Nations Transition Assistance Group in Namibia	Namibia	April 1989 to March 1990
ONUCA United Nations Oberver Group in Central America	Costa Rica, El Salvador, Guatemala, Honduras, Nicaragua	November 1989 to January 1992

UNIKOM United Nations Iraq-Kuwait Observation Mission	Border between Iraq and Kuwait	April 1991 to date
UNAVEM II United Nations Angola Verification Mission II	Angola	June 1991 to February 1995
ONUSAL United Nations Observer Mission in El Salvador	El Salvador	July 1991 to April 1995
MINURSO Unied Nations Mission for the Referendum in Western Sahara	Western Sahara	September 1991 to date
UNAMIC United Nations Advance Mission in Cambodia	Cambodia	October 1991 to March 1992
UNPROFOR United Nations Protection Force	Former Yugoslavia	March 1992 to December 1995
UNTAC United Nations Transitional Authority in Cambodia	Cambodia	March 1992 to September 1993
UNOSOM United Nations Operation in Somalia	Somalia	April 1992 to March 1993
UNUMOZ United Nations Operation in Mozambique	Mozambique	December 1992 to December 1994
UNOSOM II United Nations Operation in Somalia II	Somalia	May 1993 to March 1995
UNOMOR Unied Nations Observer Mission Uganda-Rwanda	Border between Uganda and Rwanda	June 1993 to September 1994
UNOMIG United Nations Oberver Mission in Georgia	Georgia and Abkhasia	August 1993 to date
UNOMIL United Nations Observer Mission in Liberia	Liberia	September 1993 to September 1997
UNMIH United Nations Mission in Haiti	Haiti	September 1993 to June 1996
UNAMIR United Nations Assistance Mission to Rwanda	Rwanda	October 1993 to March 1996
UNASOG United Nations Aouzou Strip Observer Group	Aouzou-Strip	May 1994 to June 1994
UNMOT United Nations Mission of Observers in Tajikistan	Tajikistan	December 1994 to date
UNAVEM III United Nations Angola Verification Mission III	Angola	February 1995 to June 1997
UNCRO United Nations Confidence Restoration Operation in Croatia	Croatia	March 1995 to January 1996
UNPREDEP United Nations Preventive Deployment Force	Former Yugoslavia Republic of Macedonia	March 1995 to date
UNMIBH United Nations Mission in Bosnia and Herzegovina	Bosnia and Herzegovina	December 1995 to date

UNTAES United Nations Transitional Administration for Eastern Slavonia, Baranja and Western Dirmium	Eastern Slavonia	January 1996 to January 1998
UNMOP United Nations Mission of Observers in Prevlaka	Prevlaka Peninsula (Croatia)	January 1996 to date
UNSMIH United Nations Support Mission in Haiti	Haiti	June 1996 to July 1997
MINUGUA United Nations Verification Mission in Guatemala	Guatemala	February 1997 to May 1997
MONUA United Nations Observer Mission in Angola	Angola	July 1997 to date
UNTMIH United Nations Transition Mission in Haiti	Haiti	August 1997 to November 1997
MIPONUH United Nations Civilian Police Mission in Haiti	Haiti	December 1997 to date
MINURCA United Nations Mission in the Central African Republic	Central African Republic	April 1998 to date

Source: Comprehensive List of UN Peacekeeping Operations http://www.fib.ethz.ch/ fib/pko/allops1. html

and the legitimacy awarded by the support of the international community. The success of a peacekeeping mission depends on the cooperation of the parties in conflict. A peacekeeping mandate does not include imposing a solution on unwilling parties.

In retrospect, peacekeeping forces have been dispatched to a number of missions, places and on certain dates (see above table).

Latter-day peacekeeping operations of the United Nations have changed in mission goals and activities. Especially guided by *Agenda of Peace*, written by former Secretary-General Boutros Boutros-Ghali, peacekeeping operations have recently been seen to be more closely related to peacebuilding, thus, they have included measures to enhance confidence, to reform combatants into civilians of the society, and to restore the fabric of war-torn societies so as to prevent the recurrence of conflicts.

After ending the Cold War, the United Nations has launched more peacekeeping operations than in its previous 45 years, which included the deployment of some 70,000 troops, military observers and civilian personnel. These operations include notably the United Nations Angola Verification Mission III, the United Nations Observer Mission in El Salvador, the United Nations Observer Operation in Mozambique, the United Nations Observer Mission in Somalia, the United Nations Protection Force in the republics of former Yugoslavia, and the United Nations Transitional Authority in Cambodia.

As the 21st Century promises a no-more-peaceful world,

surely the United Nations Peacekeeping Forces will continue to serve but with a continuously changing character as the demands and needs of the world community also change.

Bibliography

Curtius M 1988 "First UN Troops Went to Mideast in '48" *The Boston Globe*, September 30. http://www.boston.com/globe/search/stories/nobel/1988/19881.html

Diehl P F 1993 *International Peacekeeping*. The Johns Hopkins University Press, Baltimore, Maryland, USA

Kaplan F 1988 "UN Peacekeepers Win Nobel Prize" http://www.boston.com/globe/search/stories/nobel/1988/19881.html

Nobel Prize Internet Archive 1988 "The United Nations Peacekeeping Forces". http://nobel.sdsc.edu/laureates/peace-1988-1-bio.html

United Nations 1995 *United Nations Peacekeeping: Information Notes*. United Nations-DPI, New York, USA

United Nations-Department of Public Information 1998 "UN Peacekeeping: Some Questions and Answers." http://www.un.org/News/factspeacefct.html

United Nations in Canada 1998 "The UN and Peacekeeping." http://www.unac.org/unfaq.peacekee.html

United Nations 1998 "Comprehensive List of UN Peacekeeping Operations." http://www.fib.ethz.ch/fib/pko/allops1.html

PEDRO B. BERNALDEZ

Dalai Lama
(1989)

The Nobel Peace Prize for 1989 was awarded to the Dalai Lama. The Norwegian Nobel Committee awarding the prize to the fourteenth Dalai Lama, said: "The committee wants to emphasize the fact that the Dalai Lama in his struggle for the liberation of Tibet consistently has opposed the use of violence. He has instead advocated peaceful solutions based upon tolerance and mutual respect in order to preserve the historical and cultural heritage of his people."

His Holiness, accepting the Nobel Peace Prize, remarked: "The prize reaffirms our conviction that with truth, courage, and determination as our weapons, Tibet will be liberated. Our struggle must remain non violent and free of hatred."

The Nobel Peace Prize awarded to the Dalai Lama confers international recognition, not only on the spiritual and political leader of the Tibetan people, but also on the values and ideals that he represents.

The Dalai Lama was born on the fifth day of the fifth month of the Wood Hog Year of the sixteenth cycle of the Tibetan calendar, or June 6, 1935, in the village of Taktser. Known by the name of Lhamo, he was the next-to-youngest of five children born to Chokyong Tsering and Sonam Isomo, a peasant couple of Tibetan stock. When the Lamaist hierarchy concluded that he was the Dalai Lama, prolonged negotiations began with the prerevolutionary Chinese governor of the region, who demanded large sums of money. Finally an agreement was reached; the Dalai Lama was escorted to the holy city of Lhasa; and on February 22, 1940 he was formally installed on the Lion Throne. There started his difficult and tumultuous life as the spiritual leader of a small nation under the shadow of a giant power state.

Few persons in the twentieth century have been forced to undergo such a wrenching passage from an ancient world to the modern one as the fourteenth Dalai Lama of Tibet. Enthroned in 1940, at the age of four, as the most recent incarnation of a line of Dalai Lamas who have served as the spiritual and temporal heads of the Tibetan theocracy since the seventeenth century, he was thrust prematurely into the role of a true political leader in 1950, when Communist China invaded and occupied his country. Throughout most of the 1950's he performed a delicate balancing-act, trying to appease the Chinese while preserving as much autonomy as possible for Tibet. But after a nationalist rebellion was crushed by the Chinese in 1959, the Dalai Lama was forced to flee to India, where he has lived ever since. During his more than twenty years of exile, he has tried to maintain the world's interest in the cause of Tibet's independence, and at the same time has performed the complicated duties incumbent on a revered leader of one of the major branches of Buddhism.

In the process, the Dalai Lama has had to come to terms with the ideologies, technologies, and diplomacy of the secular Western world, from which Tibet had remained in almost complete isolation throughout its history. He has traveled widely in Asia and Europe and in 1979 made his first visit to the United States, touring the country for seven weeks. The author of several works on Buddhist theology and practice, he has written an autobiography *My Land and My People* (McGraw-Hill, 1962), that has been well received in the West.

In recent years, the Dalai Lama has patiently negotiated with the Chinese over the terms of his return to Tibet, which has at times seemed imminent, but he has repeatedly announced that he will not return until matters improve for his countrymen. "My people are suffering terribly for want of basic things like food, shelter, and the freedom to move about," he told a reporter for *Newsweek* (September 17, 1979). "The problem is not religion, ideology, or racism by the Chinese, but the fact that they treat us as inferiors . . . . I will not return until the people themselves say they are satisfied with their society."

Considering Tibet a part of its territory, China has at times exercised a vague suzerainty there, but in 1912 the thirteenth Dalai Lama declared his country fully independent and expelled Chinese residents. In 1949, with Mao Tse-Tung's armies victorious, the Chinese again began to harass Tibet, and in October 1950 the Communist armies poured over the border. Pledging to "free three million Tibetans from imperialist aggression," the Chinese crushed the primitive Tibetan forces and advanced rapidly on Lhasa. Acting on the advice of the state oracle, and yielding to heavy pressure from his advisers and the populace, the Dalai Lama agreed to be named king with full powers on November 17, though he was only fifteen. At the end of December he left Lhasa for Yatung on the border with India, in case he should need to escape into exile. A Tibetan delegation was dispatched to Peking, where they were bullied into signing a treaty, the Seventeen Point Agreement, which provided that Tibet would "return" as a province to "the big family of the Motherland—the People's Republic of China." China would have full control over foreign policy and military affairs; in return, the Chinese agreed to respect Tibet's political and religious systems, and not to impose "reforms" the Tibetans did not want.

The Dalai Lama was horrified by the Seventeen Point Agreement, which he alleged was illegally affixed with a Seal of Tibet forged in China, but felt that the only way to deal with the overwhelmingly powerful Chinese was by cooperation and persuasion. In August 1951 he returned to Lhasa and for the next eight years pursued the painful course of trying to resist steady Chinese encroachment without angering the Chinese so severely that they would simply obliterate traditional Tibetan society. In 1954, he traveled to Peking, where he met with Mao several times. He also struck up an acquaintance with Chou En-Lai and toured widely in China. The Chinese appointed him to several largely ceremonial political posts, including Honorary Chairman of the Chinese Buddhist Association (1953-59); delegate to the National People's Congress (1954-59); and Chairman of the Preparatory Committee for the Autonomous Region of Tibet (1955-59).

The Dalai Lama settled in for long years of exile, determined to do his best to keep the Tibetan issue from fading in the world's memory. At first his efforts were hampered by the Indian government's reluctance to let him travel abroad for fear of offending the Chinese. Largely confined to Dharamsala, he worked to maintain unity among Tibetan exile groups, to encourage the preservation of traditional Tibetan culture and religion, and to help provide for the flood of refugees—numbering some 80,000 by 1970—that poured in from Tibet. Since 1960, His Holiness has resided in Dharamsala, a small town in north India, the seat of the Tibetan Government-in-exile.

With the reestablishment of the Tibetan Government in India, the Dalai Lama saw that his immediate and urgent task was to preserve Tibetan culture. He founded 53 agricultural settlements for the refugees to live on. As an economic base developed, he oversaw the creation of an autonomous Tibetan school system (there are over 80 Tibetan schools in India and Nepal today) to raise refugee children with full knowledge of their language, history, religion and culture. He inaugurated several cultural institutes to preserve Tibet's arts and sciences and helped reestablish more than 200 monasteries to keep alive the vast corpus of Buddhist teaching, the essence of the Tibetan spirit.

He studied Western disciplines, including lan-

guages; journalists always found him intensely curious about scientific developments and world affairs. And he continued to perform all the duties of the Dalai Lama, maintaining the patient, pacific posture that Buddhism extols. In an interview with Ved Mehta for the *New Yorker* (July 26, 1969) he remarked that "In Buddhism, you should not mind those who make you angry. You should love those people who irritate you, because they are your gurus." Surprisingly, he also admitted to Mehta that the Chinese had introduced many good reforms in Tibet.

In 1967, the Dalai Lama was allowed to leave India for a visit to Japan; in 1973 he embarked on a six-week tour of Europe, including a meeting with the Pope. He issued a call in 1977 for an internationally observed plebiscite to determine if Tibetans wanted to continue under Chinese rule, but the Chinese showed no inclination to pursue the idea. By the late 1970's, with more moderate leadership having replaced the so-called "Gang of Four," there were many indications that the Chinese were reconsidering their attempts to transform Tibetan society and were searching for ways to accommodate the traditionalists, including the Dalai Lama. Early in 1979 the Chinese reopened the Jhoe Khang, the holiest temple of Tibetan Buddhism, repairing the severe damage done by Red Guards during the Cultural Revolution; several monasteries were reopened also; and, most significantly, the Chinese publicly invited the Dalai Lama to return, but not as a political or religious leader.

The Dalai Lama responded to those overtures reservedly, content to wait until the moment and the terms for his return were propitious. In the meantime he embarked on a new round of travels that may have been calculated to win more international backing for his position. For example in June 1979 he attended the fifth annual Asian Buddhist Conference for Peace, held in Ulan Bator, Mongolia. En route, he passed through Moscow, where he was publicly received by Soviet officials. And in 1979, after eight years of appeals, he was given a visa to visit the United States, apparently because the more conciliatory Chinese attitude made the State Department less fearful of irritating them.

The Dalai Lama was invited to the United States for a seven-week tour as a private citizen whose official contacts were to be kept to a minimum. Even his request to see the Johnson Space Center at Houston—a long-cherished dream—was turned down, apparently because such a visit might be viewed as a political endorsement. The tour therefore focused on religious matters. The Dalai Lama arrived in New York on September 3, and on September 5 was honored at an ecumenical service at St. Patrick's Cathedral hosted by Terence Cardinal Cooke. During his tour, he visited Tibetan and American Buddhist centers in New York, New Jersey, and other states; spoke at fifteen universities including Harvard, Georgetown, Wisconsin, Michigan, and UCLA; and lectured on spirituality at Constitution Hall in Washington, D.C. But his trip also had inevitable political undercurrents: the Dalai Lama had a private and unofficial meeting with members of the Senate Foreign Relations Committee, was the guest of honor at a reception attended by over one hundred Congressmen, and spoke before the Los Angeles World Affairs Council, a foreign policy forum. When he was asked about his view of the Tibetan political situation, his replies were careful but firm.

Although delicate political maneuverings between the Dalai Lama and the Chinese continued through 1980 and 1981, they failed to bring about a reconciliation or even a visit. At the same time that the Dalai Lama was in the United States, a five-man delegation, including one of his brothers, traveled to Tibet, the first visit by his representatives since 1959. A second fact-finding group toured Tibet in mid-1980, but its members were expelled when they set off a spontaneous demonstration in Lhasa in August. The Dalai Lama's sister and another of his brothers also visited at different times in 1980.

In the meantime, the Chinese continued their policy of liberalization, relaxing their economic restrictions on Tibetans and replacing Chinese officials with native Tibetans in the ruling Revolutionary Committee. Because by late 1980 the prospect for a visit by the Dalai Lama in the near future seemed to have faded once again, he resumed his strenuous schedule of world travels. In the autumn he had an audience with Pope Paul II in Rome, and also visited Canada, Japan and Hawaii. In the summer of 1981, he returned to the United States for a number of weeks, lecturing in the Midwest and at the Lamaist monastery in Washington, New Jersey, and delivering a lecture series at the Harvard Divinity School.

In 1963, His Holiness promulgated a democratic constitution, based on Buddhist principles and the Universal Declaration of Human Rights, as a model for a future free Tibet. Since then, the Dalai Lama has been the most vigorous advocate for the refugee's own democratic experiment, while consistently reaffirming his desire not to hold political office once Tibet regains its independence. The Dalai Lama continues to present new initiatives to resolve the Tibetan issue. At the Congressional Human Rights Caucus in 1987, he proposed a Five-Point Peace Plan as a first step toward resolving the future status of Tibet. This plan called for the designation of Tibet as a zone of non-violence, an end to the massive transfer of Chinese into Tibet, restoration of fundamental human rights and democratic freedoms, and the abandonment of China's use of Tibet for nuclear weapons production and the dumping of nuclear waste, as well as urging "earnest negotiations" on the future of Tibet.

The Dalai Lama continued what he viewed as the most realistic effort to create a self-governing democratic Tibet. His proposal, made in Strasbourg in 1988, included the accommodation of China's own interests while preserving the Tibetan peoples' ultimate authority in forming their government. However, the Dalai Lama faced a "closed and negative attitude" from the Chinese leadership in response to his efforts, causing him to declare the Strasbourg Proposal as no longer binding in 1991.

The Dalai Lama has met with several major heads of state as well as other senior political, religious, cultural and business leaders to speak on his belief in the oneness of the human family and the need for each individual to develop a sense of universal responsibility. In October, 1989, during a dialogue with eight rabbis and scholars from the United States in Dharamsala, His Holiness remarked: "When we became refugees, we knew our struggle would not be easy; it would take a long time, generations. Very often we would refer to the Jewish people, how they kept their identity and faith despite such hardship and so much suffering. And, when external conditions were ripe they were ready to rebuild their nation. So you see, there are many things to learn from our Jewish brothers and sisters." His talks in other forums focused on the commonality of faiths and the need for unity among different religions: "I always believe that it is much better to have a variety of religions, a variety of philosophies, rather than one single religion or philosophy. This is necessary because of the different mental dispositions of each human being. Each religion has certain unique ideas or techniques, and learning about them can only enrich one's own faith."

The Dalai Lama has received numerous honorary doctorates from Universities worldwide. In 1989, he received The Nobel Peace Prize in Oslo, Norway. The Norwegian Nobel Committee emphasized the Dalai Lama's consistent opposition of the use of violence in Tibet's struggle for freedom and remarked that, "The Dalai Lama has developed his philosophy of peace from a great reverence for all things living and upon the concept of universal responsibility embracing all mankind as well as nature ... [he] has come forward with constructive and forward-looking proposals for the solution of international conflicts, human rights issues and global environmental problems." Despite his great achievements, the Dalai Lama remains modest, often saying "I am just a simple Buddhist monk — no more, no less."

Biography

His Holiness the 14th the Dalai Lama Tenzin Gyatso, is the head of state and spiritual leader of the Tibetan people. He was born Lhamo Dhondrub on 6 July 1935, in a small village called Taktser in northeastern Tibet. Born to a peasant family, His Holiness was recognized at the age of two, in accordance with Tibetan tradition, as the reincarnation of his predecessor the 13th Dalai Lama, and thus an incarnation Avalokitesvara, the Buddha of Compassion.

The Dalai Lamas are the manifestations of the Bodhisattva (Buddha) of Compassion, who chose to reincarnate to serve the people. Lhamo Dhondrub was, as Dalai Lama, renamed Jetsun Jamphel Ngawang Lobsang Yeshe Tenzin Gyatso—Holy Lord, Gentle Glory, Compassionate, Defender of the Faith, Ocean of Wisdom. Tibetans normally refer to His Holiness as Yeshe Norbu, the Wishfulfilling Gem or simply Kundun—The Presence. The enthronement ceremony took place on February 22, 1940 in Lhasa, the capital of Tibet.

He began his education at the age of six and completed the Geshe Lharampa Degree (Doctorate of Buddhist Philosophy) when he was 25 in 1959. At 24, he took the preliminary examinations at each of the three monastic universities: Drepung, Sera and Ganden. The final examination was conducted in the Jokhang, Lhasa during the annual Monlam Festival of Prayer, held in the first month of every year Tibetan calendar.

On November 17, 1950, His Holiness was called upon to assume full political power (head of the State and Government) after some 80,000 People's Liberation Army soldiers invaded Tibet. In 1954, he went to Beijing to talk peace with Mao Tse-tung and other Chinese leaders, including Chou En-lai and Deng Xiaoping. In 1956, while visiting India to attend the 2500th Buddha Jayanti Anniversary, he had a series of meetings with Prime Minister Nehru and Premier Chou about deteriorating conditions in Tibet.

His efforts to bring about a peaceful solution to Sino-Tibetan conflict were thwarted by Bejing's ruthless policy in Eastern Tibet, which ignited a popular uprising and resistance. This resistance movement spread to other parts of the country. On 10 March 1959 the capital of Tibet, Lhasa, exploded with the largest demonstration in Tibetan history,

calling on China to leave Tibet and reaffirming Tibet's independence. The Tibetan National Uprising was brutally crushed by the Chinese army. His Holiness escaped to India where he was given political asylum. Some 80,000 Tibetan refugees followed His Holiness into exile. Today, there are more than 120,000 Tibetan in exile. Since 1960, he has resided in Dharamsala, India, known as "Little Lhasa," the seat of the Tibetan Government-in-exile.

In the early years of exile, His Holiness appealed to the United Nations on the question of Tibet, resulting in three resolutions adopted by the General Assembly in 1959, 1961, and 1965, calling on China to respect the human rights of Tibetans and their desire for self-determination. With the newly constituted Tibetan Government-in-exile, His Holiness saw that his immediate and urgent task was to save both the Tibetan exiles and their culture alike. Tibetan refugees were rehabilitated in agricultural settlements. Economic development was promoted and the creation of a Tibetan educational system was established to raise refugee children with full knowledge of their language, history, religion and culture. The Tibetan Institute of Performing Arts was established in 1959, while the Central Institute of Higher Tibetan Studies became a university for Tibetans in India. Over 200 monasteries have been re-established to preserve the vast corpus of Tibetan Buddhist teachings, the essence of the Tibetan way of life.

In 1963, His Holiness promulgated a democratic constitution, based on Buddhist principles and the Universal Declaration of Human Rights as a model for a future free Tibet. Today, members of the Tibetan parliament are elected directly by the people. The members of the Tibetan Cabinet are elected by the parliament, making the Cabinet answerable to the Parliament. His Holiness has continuously emphasized the need to further democratize the Tibetan administration and has publicly declared that once Tibet regains her independence he will not hold political office.

In Washington, D.C., at the Congressional Human Rights Caucus in 1987, he proposed a Five-Point Peace Plan as a first step toward resolving the future status of Tibet. This plan calls for the designation of Tibet as a zone of peace, an end to the massive transfer of ethnic Chinese into Tibet, restoration of fundamental human rights and democratic freedoms, and the abandonment of China's use of Tibet for nuclear weapons production and the dumping of nuclear waste, as well as urging "earnest negotiations" on the future of Tibet.

In Strasbourg, France, on 15 June 1988, he elaborated the Five-Point Peace Plan and proposed the creation of a self-governing democratic Tibet, "in association with the People's Republic of China." On 2 September 1991, the Tibetan Government-in-exile declared the Strasbourg Proposal invalid because of the closed and negative attitude of the present Chinese leadership towards the ideas expressed in the proposal. On 9 October 1991, during an address at Yale University in the United States, His Holiness said that he wanted to visit Tibet to personally assess the political situation. He said, "I am extremely anxious that, in this explosive situation, violence may break out. I want to do what I can to prevent this . . . . My visit would be a new opportunity to promote understanding and create a basis for a negotiated solution."

Since 1967, His Holiness initiated a series of journeys which have taken him to some 46 nations. In autumn of 1991, he visited the Baltic States at the invitation of Lithuanian President Vytautas Landsbergis of Lithuania and became the first foreign leader to address the Lithuanian Parliament. His Holiness met with the late Pope Paul VI at the Vatican in 1973. At a press conference in Rome in 1980, he outlined his hopes for the meeting with John Paul II: "We live in a period of great crisis, a period of troubling world developments. It is not possible to find peace in the soul without security and harmony between peoples. For this reason, I look forward with faith and hope to my meeting with the Holy Father; to an exchange of ideas and feelings, and to his suggestions, so as to open the door to a progressive pacification between peoples." His Holiness met Pope John Paul II at the Vatican in 1980, 1982, 1986, 1988 and 1990. In 1981, His Holiness talked with Archbishop of Canterbury, Dr. Robert Runcie, and with other leaders of the Anglican Church in London. He also met with leaders of the Roman Catholic and Jewish communities and spoke at an interfaith service held in his honor by the World Congress of Faiths: "I always believe that it is much better to have a variety of religions, a variety of philosophies, rather than one single religion or philosophy. This is necessary because of the different mental dispositions of each human being. Each religion has certain unique ideas or techniques, and learning about them can only enrich one's own faith."

Since his first visit to the West in the early 1973, a number of western universities and institutions have conferred Peace Awards and honorary Doctorate Degrees in recognition of His Holiness' distinguished writings in Buddhist philosophy and for his leadership in the solution of international conflicts, human rights issues and global environmental problems.

In presenting the Raoul Wallenberg Congressional Human Rights Award in 1989, U.S. Congressman Tom Lantos said, "His Holiness the Dalai Lama's courageous struggle has distinguished him as a leading proponent of human rights and world peace. His ongoing efforts to end the suffering of the Tibetan people through peaceful negotiations and reconciliation have required enormous courage and sacrifice."

The Norwegian Nobel Committee's decision to award the 1989 Peace Prize to His Holiness the Dalai Lama won worldwide praise and applause, with exception of China. The Committees citation read, "The Committee wants to emphasize the fact that the Dalai Lama in his struggle for the liberation of Tibet consistently has opposed the use of violence. He has instead advocated peaceful solutions based upon tolerance and mutual respect in order to preserve the historical and cultural heritage of his people."

On 10 December 1989, His Holiness accepted the prize on the behalf of oppressed people everywhere and all those who struggle for freedom and work for world peace and the people of Tibet. In his remarks he said, "The prize reaffirms our conviction that with truth, courage and determination as our weapons, Tibet will be liberated. Our struggle must remain nonviolent and free of hatred."

He also had a message of encouragement for the student-led democracy movement in China. "In China the popular movement for democracy was crushed by brutal force in June this year. But I do not believe the demonstrations were in vain, because the spirit of freedom was rekindled among the Chinese people and China cannot escape the impact of this spirit of freedom sweeping in many parts of the world. The brave students and their supporters showed the Chinese leadership and the world the human face of that great nations."

His Holiness often says, "I am just a simple Buddhist monk—no more, no less." His Holiness follows the life of Buddhist monk. Living in a small cottage in Dharamsala, he rises at 4 A.M. to mediate, pursues an ongoing schedule of administrative meetings, private audiences and religious teachings and ceremonies. He concludes each day with further prayer before retiring.

Now, when at his home, a bungalow high in a mountainside in Upper Dharamsala, he rises at four in the morning, prays and meditates for several hours daily, takes only two meals, the second at noon, and spends the rest of his time in meetings, listening to radio broadcasts from all over the world, or pursuing his hobbies, which include gardening and tinkering with machines.

Bibliography ─────────────────────────

Barber N 1969 *From the Land of the Lost Continent.*
Museum of Tolerance 1996 "His Holiness the Dalai Lama: recipient of the 1996 Peace Award." http://www.wiesenthal.com/itn/lama.html
New York 1979 September 3
People 1979 September 10
Reader's Digest 1970 February
The Government of Tibet in Exile 1990 "1989 Nobel Peace Prize Citation." http://www.tibet.com/DL/nobel.html
The Nobel Peace Prize Internet Archive 1989 "Dalai Lama:1989 Nobel Peace Prize Laureate." http://nobel-prizes.com/nobel/peace.1989.html
Washington Post 1979 September 10

PEDRO B. BERNALDEZ

Mikhail Gorbachev
(1990)

The 1990 Nobel Peace Prize was awarded to Mikhail Gorbachev for his dramatic policy initiatives which had transformed the Soviet Union and reshaped the world.

On March 11, 1985, when he was selected as general secretary of the Communist Party of the Soviet Union, Mikhail Sergeyevich Gorbachev became one of the two most powerful men on Earth. His power lasted a mere six years though, and his attempts to reform and rescue an ailing government came too late to save it from extinction. Ironically, history will remember Gorbachev as the last president of the U.S.S.R.—the man who presided over the liquidation of the Soviet Union.

Gorbachev came from a peasant family, graduated from law school and joined the Communist Party at age 21. He did well as a party functionary and gradually moved up through the ranks. As leader of the Stavrapol Krai, a popular resort for many high Soviet officials, Gorbachev was noticed by party leaders and elevated to the party's Central Committee in 1971. He studied agriculture, and when the post of agricultural secretary was vacated in 1978, Gorbachev was selected to fill it. His work in that office eventually led to full membership in the powerful Politburo in 1980.

Gorbachev was nearly unknown in the West until 1982, when, upon the death of Leonid I. Brezhnev, his name was thrust forward as a possible successor. Yuri V. Andropov was chosen for the job, but died 15 months later. Gorbachev was again a major contender, but the Politburo this time chose Konstantin Chernenko. Upon Chernenko's death in 1985, Gorbachev finally was selected to lead the Soviet Union.

The youngest Soviet leader since Joseph Stalin succeeded Lenin in 1924, Gorbachev served for twenty-two years as a party official in the southern district of Stavropol before his appointment as agriculture secretary on the Central Committee of the Communist party in 1978, and he soon became part of the Kremlin's inner circle. Since his election, he had continued the program of economic and social reform begun by his mentor, Yuri Andropov, and while maintaining a tough stance toward the United States, he had indicated a desire to pursue a course of peaceful coexistence in the spirit of the detente of the 1970s.

On foreign policy issues, Western observers had predicted that Gorbachev would be less innovative because of the collective nature of Kremlin policy-making and his relative lack of experience in that area. Yet he demonstrated what Hedrick Smith of the *New York Times* called a "knack for diplomatic theater" by announcing in 1985 that the Soviet Union would observe a six-month moratorium on development of its SS-20 medium-range nuclear missiles. Critics pointed out that the Soviet Union had virtually completed the deployment anyway and was already testing a new version of the missile. Nevertheless, Gorbachev's political showmanship reinforced the perception that he would be a formidable diplomatic adversary.

A major point in Gorbachev's foreign policy and defense views was his opposition to the proposed Strategic Defense Initiative, or "Star Wars" plan, of the United States, which he regarded as a dangerous militarization of space. He accused the Americans of violating the guidelines for the Geneva arms talks by refusing to negotiate simultaneously on the space program and on strategic and medium-range nuclear weaponry. In view of the Soviet Union's failure to block deployment of the Pershing II and cruise missiles in Western Europe in 1983, Gorbachev's emphasis on the Star Wars plan has been seen by Western observers as an effort to drive a wedge between the United States and its NATO allies, many of whom are uneasy about the American space initiative.

Although Gorbachev has denounced the United States as "the forward edge of the war menace to mankind," he has also referred to superpower confrontation as "an anomaly," and at Moscow trade talks in May 1985 he told United States Secretary of Commerce Malcolm Baldrige that it was "high time to defrost the potential for Soviet-American cooperation." Many analysts believe that Gorbachev's domestic problems were too pressing for him to take any assertive action that might threaten the current uneasy state of detente.

Gorbachev had announced his resolve to cement ties with other Communist countries, especially China. His statement in his inaugural speech that he intended to "expand cooperation with socialist state" and to "enhance the role and influence of socialism in world affairs" was seen by Western observers as an assertion of continued Soviet dominance within the Communist bloc. In May he signed two economic agreements with visiting Indian Prime Minister Rajiv

Gandhi and discussed with him, among other matters, the possible threat to India and the USSR posed by Pakistani aid to Afghan rebels fighting Soviet-backed troops. He has indicated willingness to accept a political settlement with the Afghan rebels, and a possible rapprochement with Israel, with which the Soviet Union had broken relations in 1967.

In June 1985, rejecting a draft economic five-year plan, Gorbachev called for less emphasis on construction of new factories and more on improving the quality of consumer products. He demanded the retooling and renovation of existing industrial plants, elimination of waste and incompetence, and more efficient use of state supervision of the economy, and he strongly criticized some of the holdover officials from the Brezhnev era for having allowed the economy to stagnate during the 1970s.

As a prelude to summit talks between Gorbachev and President Ronald Reagan scheduled to be held in November 1985 at Geneva, Gorbachev announced a unilateral five-month moratorium on Soviet nuclear tests effective August 6, 1985 and offered to extend the freeze on testing if the United States were to take similar action. But American officials contended that the Soviet Union had already completed its 1985 testing program and that the move was in effect a Soviet propaganda ploy. The Reagan administration also dismissed Gorbachev's endorsement, in September, of a plan for a Central European zone free of chemical weapons because such a ban could not be easily verified.

Experts on Soviet affairs had warned against confusing Gorbachev's more open style with a more liberal political philosophy. He had been described, like his mentor, Andropov, as an "intellectual authoritarian." Although he had indicated an unusual willingness to consult public opinion and a more relaxed attitude toward censorship, Gorbachev was not expected to be especially tolerant to dissidents. As Andrei Gromyko said of Gorbachev in his nomination speech, "Comrades, this man has a nice smile, but he's got iron teeth."

Nevertheless, analysts also noted the absence of evidence in Gorbachev's career of the "killer instinct" often found in Soviet leaders. They pointed out that he rose through the ranks as a result of his own ability and the help of powerful patrons, rather than by means of military prowess or bloody purges. Too young to experience personally the full impact of Stalinism or of World War II, he came of age in an era of expanding Soviet power. As a result, he had a self-confidence and freedom from paranoia noticeably lacking in the old guard. In any case, many

observers agree that after a long period of uncertain leadership, the Soviet Union had a strong, effective, charismatic man at his helm.

Gorbachev's leadership style proved to be a significant departure from that of past Soviet leaders. He lacked the menacing, often brutish appearance of the older men. A child of the post-war generation, Gorbachev was charming, personable and intelligent. He enjoyed public appearances, and was seen frequently on television talking to Soviet citizens. He was an eloquent speaker, with or without a prepared speech.

During Brezhnev's 18-year rule, the USSR had become a society resistant to reform and innovation. The Soviet bureaucracy defied attempts to challenge central economic controls and reduce the gargantuan government bureaucracy. The tenure and privileges of the cadres were unassailable. The Communist Party had become a permanent ruling class, with virtually a lifetime tenure in office, high salaries, special health care, private homes, access to imported consumer goods, quality vacation resorts and elite schools for their children. Intellectual and artistic life continued to be suffocated by Communist dogma. Economic growth had slowed, and technology lagged far behind the West and Japan.

To cope with deteriorating conditions, Gorbachev instituted policies of "glasnost," or openness, intended to liberalize Soviet political life, and "perestroika," or restructuring, intended to revitalize the economy. Political life was democratized somewhat, but the economy did not improve. An unintended result of this relaxed authority was the outbreak of ethnic conflicts and separatist movements.

The U.S.S.R. was on an irreversible downward spiral, and analysts say little could have been done to forestall its disintegration. Gorbachev made moves to share power with the Soviet republics, but the actions brought an attempt by hard-liners to depose him in a coup.

Supported by Boris Yeltsin and other reformers, he resigned from the Communist Party. Gorbachev's further attempts to share power with the republics were to no avail. On December 8, 1991, Russia, Belarus and Ukraine agreed to form the Commonwealth of Independent States. Only one of the former Soviet republics chose not to join. Russia expropriated the U.S.S.R.'s ministries and properties, and Gorbachev was out of a job. He resigned on December 25, 1991. In 1993, Gorbachev became head of the newly-formed environmental organization International Green Cross.

Boston Globe's staff writer, H.D.S. Greenway wrote complimenting Gorbachev as follows:

The aspirations of Mikhail Gorbachev, who wanted to reform his country but keep it intact, have gone for naught. Will he be remembered as a transitional figure who was, ultimately, unable to either comprehend or control the forces that had been loosened—alongside Alexander Kerensky who took over from the Czar only to lose to the Bolsheviks? It may seem so to him now. A sense of failure and regret came through his Christmas Day abdication speech—especially in his sorrow over his people ''ceasing to be citizens of a great power.'' Certainly, if man in the street interviews can be believed, the former Soviet peoples consider him a failure. History will be kinder. The Nobel prize he received for ending the Cold War was well deserved. Every man, woman and child in this country should be eternally grateful. His statue should stand in the center of every east European capital; for it was Gorbachev who allowed them their independence. The same is true for the newly independent countries further east and in Central Asia. No Russian has done more to free his people from bondage since Alexander II who freed the serfs.

Maybe he did cling to power too long, and maybe he put too much faith in communism and its ability to reform. But his place in history has been assured.

Biography

A native of the fertile agricultural area of southern Russia, just north of the Caucasus mountains, Mikhail Sergeyevich Gorbachev was born on March 2, 1931 into a family of peasants in the village of Privolnoye, in the Krasnogvardeisky district of Stavropol territory, where he was educated in local schools. Although he was only eleven when the Germans occupied Stavropol during World War II, the experience left a deep impression on him. From 1946 to 1950, he worked summers at a machine and tractor station as an assistant combine harvester operator in the grain fields of the collective farms of his home area.

In 1955, he was graduated from the Faculty of Law of Moscow State Univesity. In 1967 Gorbachev graduated externally from the faculty of economy of the Stavropol Agricultural Institute majoring in agronomical economy.

In 1970, he was elected to the USSR Supreme Soviet. From 1971 till 1991 Gorbachev was a member of the Communist Party Central Committee. From November, 1978 Gorbachev was a Central Committee secretary in charge of agriculture. In 1978 Gorbachev moved to Moscow for permanent residence. In 1979-1980 he was a candidate to the Polit Bureau of the Communist Party Central Committee.

From October 1980 till August 1991, he was a member of the Polit Bureau of the Communist Party Central Committee. On March 11, 1985 Gorbachev was elected as the General Secretary of the Communist Party Central Committee at the extraordinary Session of the Central Committee.

A member of the Presidium of the USSR Supreme Soviet (1985-1988). In 1985-1988 Gorbachev radically changed the course of the Soviet foreign policy. At the XXVII Congress of the Communist Party (February-March,1986) he unveiled the Soviet program of nuclear-free world to the 2000. From October, 1988 Gorbachev was a chairman of the Presidium of the Supreme Soviet. From May 1989 till March 1990 he was chairman of the USSR Supreme Soviet.

Gorbachev was elected as the President at the third Congress of People's Deputies, held in March 1990, Deputy of the 8-11th USSR Supreme Soviet, and Deputy of the 10-11-th Russian Federation Supreme Soviet. On August 19, 1991 Gorbachev's companions-in-arms attempted to carry out a coup d'etat.

On August 21, 1991 Gorbachev returned to Moscow after the coup d'etat failed due to the Russian authorities' efforts. Since that time practically all Gorbachev's decisions were coordinated with the Russian President Boris Yeltsin who did significantly in quelling the coup. At the end of August Gorbachev resigned from the post of General Secretary of the Communist Party Central Committee. On December 25, 1991, speaking on T.V., he resigned from the post of the Soviet President "for principal considerations".

On December 25, 1991 Gorbachev also signed a decree on transferring control over the strategic nuclear weapons to the Russian President Boris Yeltsin.

Since June 1993 Gorbachev has been the President of the "Green Cross International".

Mikhail Gorbachev's wife, Raisa Maksimovna Gorbacheva, whom he met when they were both university students, was then an unusual asset for a Soviet leader. The attractive, poised, and stylish Mrs. Gorbachev holds a doctor of philosophy degree and teaches Marxist-Leninist theory at Moscow State University. The Gorbachevs are said to have two children, although only one, their daughter Irina, who is a physician and mother of their granddaughter Oksana, has appeared in public with them. The couple have an apartment near the Kremlin and a lakeside dacha outside Moscow. Gorbachev enjoys hiking and listening to classical music, and he has read widely in world literature. He and his wife regularly attend the ballet and the theatre, and they have taken motoring vacations in Italy and France.

Some of the books Gorbachev has written include: *Perestroika and Soviet-American Relations; A Road to the Future: The United Nations Speech; The Challenges of our Time: Disarmament and Social Progress; For a Nuclear Free World: A Time for Peace; The August Coup: the Truth and the Lessons; The Coming Century of Peace: For a Peaceful Future of Europe and of all Mankind; For the Sake of Preserving Human Civilization; Gorbachev: Mandate for Peace; An Opportunity that Must be Seized; Perestroika: New Thinking for Our Country and the World; A Power Factor in World Politics; Restructuring: A Vital*

Concern of the People: Reykjavik: Results and Lessons; The Search for a New Beginning: Developing a New Civilization, and Time for Peace.

Bibliography

Buston T 1985 *Gorbachev*
CNN *Newsmaker Profiles* 1998 "Mikhail Gorbachev: Former Soviet President." http:// cnn.com/resources/ newsmakers/world/ europe/gorbachev.html
Greenway HDS 1991 "Gorbachev's Legacy." *The Boston Globe* http://www.boston.com/globe
Keller B "Gorbachev's Prize." *New York Times Current Events*
Edition. http://proquest.umi.com
London Observer 1984 November 11
Myers L 1990 "World Leaders: Gorbachev richly deserves prize." *Chicago Tribune.* http://proquest.umi.com
National News Service 1998 "Gorbachev Mikhail Sergeevich." http://www.nns.ru/e-elcts/e-persons.gorbach.html
Newsweek 1985 March 25
New York Times 1985 June 17
Shanker T "Gorbachev wins Nobel Prize for Peace Efforts." http://proquest.umi.com
Time 1985 March 25

PEDRO B. BERNALDEZ

Aung San Suu Kyi
(1991)

The 1991 Nobel Peace Prize was awarded to Aung San Suu Kyi, an advocate of human rights in Burma, for insisting on nonviolence in Burma's struggle for democracy. She was not able to accept the prize in person because she was under house arrest and could not leave the country. In her place her oldest son Alexander Aris accepted the prize.

The son of the Burmese prodemocracy activist, referring to the Nobel Peace Prize, called it a reminder of the struggle for human rights in Burma and elsewhere. Alexander Aris, Suu Kyi's husband also said, "She would say this prize belongs not to her, but to all those men, women, and children who, even as I speak, continue to sacrifice their well-being, their freedom and their lives in pursuit of a democratic Burma."

Aung San Suu Kyi could not accept the $1 million prize in person because Burma's military junta said it would not allow her to return if she left the country. Suu Kyi was then detained at her home in Rangoon, and her family had not seen her for two years.

Aung San Suu Kyi was born near the end of World War II in Rangoon to Aung San, a military general and political figure considered the founder of modern Burma. Long a part of the British Empire, Burma aimed to gain independence from colonial rule when Aung San allied with the Japanese for help during the early years of World War II. Her father then switched alliances back with the British when the tides of war turned against Japan. At the war's end Aung San ruled a newly-independent Burma, but was killed by a political assassin in 1947. Later, when Suu Kyi was seven, she watched her brother drown before her, a tragedy she once termed more impact-ing than her father's murder, since she had grown up so close to her brother.

Suu Kyi's mother was part Buddhist, but also part Christian, and in 1961 was named ambassador to India. Sent first to Burma's convent schools for her education, Suu Kyi continued her schooling in India's parochial system while the family was living in New Delhi. Upon graduation she was accepted to St. Hugh's College at Oxford University, where she met her future husband, Michael Aris, an Asian studies scholar. Their romance blossomed through the university years and after graduation, when Suu Kyi worked for the United Nations in New York. The two were wed in a Buddhist ceremony in 1972.

As an adult, Suu Kyi only returned to Burma for short visits to her mother. The assassination of her father, explained Bradley in *Vogue*, "left a political vacuum that was eventually filled by General Ne Win, a military dictator who ruled the country for 26 years through a combination of terror and bizarre form of socialism, jailing opponents and becoming a major target of Amnesty International." Ne Win, who took power in 1962, was usually referred to as "The Old Man." He instituted what he called "The Burmese Way of Socialism," eventually making the country's per capita income one of the lowest in the world, spent most of Burma's material and mineral resources on financing large standing army, and alienated Burma politically from the rest of the world. In 1987 the United Nations granted less developed status to the country that had once been the most prosperous in the region.

Eventually Ne Win also alienated himself, growing increasingly superstitious in his old age and living as a virtual recluse. After he restructured the Burmese currency unit in 1987 and caused massive devaluation and the virtual eradication of the savings of many, a grassroots revolt began. Students, Buddhist monks, and ordinary citizens alike began calling for the restoration of democracy; concurrently, political repression increased. In the midst of this, Suu Kyi's mother suffered a stroke, and in the spring of 1988 Suu Kyi flew immediately to Burma to be at her mother's side. Meanwhile, the death count of protesters at the hands of Ne Win's forces was growing, and some thought the dictator was about to flee the country, especially after turning over his authority to a military committee known as the State Law and Order Restoration Council, or SLORC. The opposition movement soon drafted Suu Kyi, and with virtually one important speech she became its de facto leader.

"When Suu Kyi stepped up to the podium, the half-million listeners were astonished that she looked and spoke exactly like her famous father," wrote Bradley of that moment. "After her ten-minute speech . . . most felt that the nation's political vacuum had been filled." Her growing popularity also made her a target, however, and Suu Kyi was followed by the military and sometimes harassed. In a speech made in the summer of 1989, Suu Kyi—now tagged as Burma's next leader as head of its National League for Democracy (NLD)—asserted, "Ne Win is the one who caused this nation to suffer," *Vanity Fair* journalist Edward Klein quoted her as saying. "Ne Win is the one who lowered the prestige of the armed forces and officials from the State Law and Order Restoration Council, I call you all to be loyal to the state. Be loyal to the people. You don't have to be loyal to Ne Win." Soon after, the dissident was confined to her Rangoon house; she was free to leave, but only if she left the country.

"I got used to it immediately," Suu Kyi told *New York Times Magazine* writer Claudia Dreifus about being confined under military guard to her own house for six years. "I decided, well, I've been placed under house arrest and I need to enjoy it as much as I can. It had better be as useful as possible. I managed to do a lot of things I thought useful—meditating, reading, exercising, sewing curtains for the house." For time, supporting herself became a problem. "Sometimes I didn't even have enough money to eat," she told Klein. "I became so weak from malnourishment that my hair fell out, and I couldn't get out of bed. I was afraid that I had damaged my heart."

To survive, Suu Kyi sold her parent's furniture—but later found out her captors had given her the money but placed the goods in storage—and tried not to worry about the teenaged Alexander and Kim back home with their father in England. "I learned not to think about my sons and my husband, not to let my thoughts dwell on them," she said. "It wouldn't help them or me." Eventually Aris compiled a book of essays about Suu Kyi entitled *Freedom from Fear*, and money from its proceeds was deposited into a Rangoon bank. Suu Kyi's maid withdrew from it to buy food and supplies. When Aris began using the British diplomatic pouch to send his wife items, SLORC seized upon this as a way to undermine her still-buoyant popular support among the Burmese. "In an effort to smear Suu Kyi's reputation, the government publicized the gifts in the newspaper, complete with photos of the offending lipstick and Jane Fonda exercise book."

Burma—renamed Myanmar during the political turmoils of the late 1980s and early 1990s—held general elections in 1990, and Suu Kyi and her NLD party won by a landslide; SLORC nullified the results. In 1991 the Nobel Peace Prize committee awarded her its prestigious honor, bringing both the woman and her plight enormous international publicity. "She instantly became the darling of every human-rights group in the Western world, as well as of the Clinton administration's State Department," noted Klein. The stand-off between Suu Kyi and SLORC continued. They asserted she was not really under house arrest, since she was free to leave—if she left Myanmar. She refused. When queried about the image of a lone woman up against a consortium of armed generals who perhaps did not regard her seriously because of her gender, she said: "I don't think they dismiss me. I think they pretend to dismiss me. But I don't think it's because I'm a woman. It's just because I represent a strong opposition to what they want to do . . . . I think they do not like anyone who stands up to them."

The military government said on April 25, 1992 that it will allow the family of a detained opposition leader, Aung San Suu Kyi, to visit her and announced it had freed a former prime minister and 11 other political prisoners.

The announcement on state radio came one day after the ruling military junta said political detainees who pose no threat to state security would soon be freed.

One US scholar questioned the sincerity of the junta's actions, saying it could be making conciliatory gestures merely to placate criticism of its human rights record.

Burma has effectively been under martial law since September 1988, when a military coup ousted a one month old civilian government. The coup came after almost a year of unrest.

Aung San Suu Kyi was under house arrest for about six years for allegedly "endangering the state." On July 1995, she was released by the Junta apparently due to pressure from international entities and as a move to show some openness which was important to Myanmar's international stature at the time. Nonetheless, Aung San Suu Kyi and her followers have continued to hold rally meetings along University Avenue in front of her house.

On June 7, the generals again banned criticisms of the government and threatened the members of the National League for Democracy with up to 20 years in jail if they defied the junta's dictate. Despite the meeting which continued as usual no arrests were made.

Because the SLORC has invested so much in its Visit Myanmar 1996 program, the SLORC has been doing a balancing act in order not to displease the international community and kind of appease some of its ASEAN neighbors which have been criticizing the heavy-handed approach of the SLORC despite the solid support the Association is giving to Myanmar. SLORC's heavy-handedness in dealing with Suu Kyi's democracy campaign may be embarrassing, "but everyone in ASEAN agrees that talk is the only way to bring about change." Myanmar's membership into the ASEAN finally came in 1997. ASEAN officials believed they can "expedite reform by engaging Myanmar."

On the other hand, however, expecting radical reform in Myanmar may be hard to do. It seems that the generals do not really feel concerned. "We cut ourselves off from the world for 26 years, said an SLORC official." "Myanmar can survive on its own."

Meanwhile, Aung San Suu Kyi remains as the only viable symbol or figure of Burma's democratization. Appealing to the international community's understanding and cooperation, Suu Kyi addressed the Free Burma campaign based in Canada and United States "We want Burma to be free and prosperous. We are not anti-business, but we oppose investment in Burma today because our real malady is not economic but political. What we are really suffering from is not lack of investment or infrastructure but misgovernance. Until we have a system that guarantees rule of law and basic democratic institutions, no amount of aid or investment will benefit our people. Profits from business enterprises will merely go towards enriching a small already privileged elite."

Democracy movement in Burma is in need of support inside and outside. Aung San Suu Kyi provides

the leadership. There is support in Burma itself as well as from outside. Geopolitics can also help. The United Nations has condemned the repressive regime in Burma. Perhaps, the international community can do more.

Biography

Aung San Suu Kyi, one of the world's most famous political prisoners, was born in 1945 in Rangoon, Burma. Her father was the military general and political leader Aung San, who is regarded as the founder of modern Burma. With the outbreak of World War II, he allied Burma with the Japanese to gain his country's independence from Britain. Later, when the tide of the war changed, he switched sides and allied himself with the British. General Aung San was assassinated in 1947. Aung San Suu Kyi's mother was a diplomat who was named ambassador to India in 1961.

Suu Kyi received her primary schooling in Burma and continued her education in New Delhi. Upon graduation she was accepted at Oxford, where she received her degree in the early 1960s. After graduation she worked for the United Nations in New York. Suu Kyi married British scholar Michael Aris, a professor of Tibetan studies, in 1972 despite strong Burmese objections to interracial marriages. She stayed at Oxford for several years pursuing an advanced degree and had two children. Suu Kyi studied Japanese so she could conduct research for a biography of her father. In 1985 she won a fellowship to the University of Kyoto to study her father's wartime ties to Japan.

Suu Kyi had spent most of her adult life outside of Burma, only making short trips to her homeland to visit her mother. The turning point in her life came in 1988. The assassination of her father had left a political vacuum filled by General Ne Win, a military dictator who used terrorism to rule the country for 26 years. He closed Burma off from the world and, through his bizarre brand of socialism, drove the once prosperous country into poverty. Popular discontent and agitation for democracy brought further political repression.

The dictator Ne Win turned over his power to a military junta known as the State Law and Order Restoration Council, or SLORC. At that time, Suu Kyi's mother fell ill and Suu Kyi returned to Burma to care for her. She also planned to open libraries in her father's name. Instead, she was thrust into a political role by the tumultuous current of modern Burmese politics.

On August 8, 1988, the famous 8-8-88 mass uprising erupted in Rangoon and spread to the entire country, drawing millions of people to protest against the BSPP government. In August 26, Aung Sun Suu Kyi addressed a half-million mass rally in front of the famous Shwedagon Pagoda in Rangoon and called for a democratic government. Following September 18 the military reestablished its power and the State Law and Order Restoration Council was formed. The military crushed the pro-democracy killing hundreds of people.

On September 24, 1988 the National League for Democracy "NLD) was formed with Suu Kyi as general secretary. Daw Khin Kuyi, Suu Kyi's mother fell ill and died. The funeral procession drew a huge crowd of supporters which turned into a peaceful protest against military rule. From July 1988 to October 1989, as leader of the NLD, Suu Kyi delivered over a hundred public addresses during extensive campaign tours to Rangoon, Pegu, Magwe, Sagaing, Mandalay, etc. On April 5,1989, Suu Kyi confronted an army unit ordered to aim their rifles at her while campaigning in the Irrawaddy Delta. An army major intervened and prevented her assassination.

To ensure her silence, the junta confined Suu Kyi under military guard to her Rangoon home. Since July 1989, she was put under house arrest for six years, cut off from her family and so poor that she became weak from hunger. Burma held elections in 1990 and Suu Kyi and her NLD party won by a landslide. Still, SLORC refused to relinquish power.

To improve the country's economy, the junta launched a campaign to lure international investment and aid. But the international community withheld investment and criticized the junta for human-rights violations. The stalemate between Suu Kyi and the junta lasted until 1995, when SLORC denied she was under house arrest and stated that she could leave Burma any time she wished. That summer, Aung San Suu Kyi stepped out of her home. But she refused to leave.

Since then, she has continued her role as opposition leader, holding meetings and making public appearances and speeches. SLORC has continued to suppress the democracy movement, restricting freedom of speech of NLD party members and activists. In December 1995 Burma (called Myanmar by the junta) was condemned by the U.N. General Assembly for human rights violations.

Suu Kyi has written a few books on freedom and Asian countries which include: *Let's Visit Burma; Let's Visit Nepal; Aung San: Leaders of Asia Series; Aung San of Burma; Burma and India; and Freedom from Fear.*

She is married to Michael Aris and has two sons.

Bibliography

Boston Globe 1992 "Burma eases dissident's isolation." April 26

Boston Globe 1991 "Peace Prize winner's son picks up Nobel." December 11

Bookscom 1998 "Books by Aung San Suu Kyi." http://melville. books.com/scripts

CNN: Newsmaker Profiles 1998 "Aung San Suu Kyi: Burmese Opposition Leader." http://cnn.com/resources/ newsmakers/ world/ asia/kyi.html

"Daw Aung San Suu Kyi: Brief Biography and Background." http://theodore-sturgeon.mit.edu:8001/peacejam/aung-bio.html

New York Times Magazine 1996 January 7

Vanity Fair 1995 October 6

Vogue 1995 (October)

PEDRO B. BERNALDEZ

Rigoberta Menchu Tum
(1992)

The 1992 Nobel Peace Prize was awarded to Rigoberta Menchu, a courageous and charismatic Quiche Indian woman who has risen above her meager beginnings and sufferings to advocate a peaceful, nonconfrontational end to Guatemala's 30-year-old civil war. She became the first indigenous and the youngest person ever to receive this distinction.

She is internationally known for her work in the promotion of the defense of human rights, peace and Indigenous People's rights. For Rigoberta Menchu Tum, this Nobel Peace Prize acknowledges the struggles of Indigenous Peoples. It is also a symbolic recognition of the victims of repression, racism, and poverty as well as an homage to indigenous women.

Perhaps one of the Norwegian Nobel Committee's most controversial honorees, Menchu who lacked a formal education and who did not learn to speak Spanish until she was 20, became an eloquent spokeswoman for indigenous peoples and the victims of oppression. In its announcement, the committee said, "Rigoberta Menchu grew up in poverty, in a family that has undergone the most brutal suppression and persecution. In her social and political work, she has always borne in mind that the long-term objective of the struggle is peace. Today [she] stands out as a vivid symbol of peace and reconciliation across ethnic, cultural and social dividing lines, in her own country, on the American continent, and in the world." Guatemalan officials were stunned by the award, having considered Menchu and her followers leftist guerrillas. While she had neither backed nor denounced rebels in her country, the committee concluded, after an investigation of her career, that peace was indeed her goal.

"She saw people from her village die around her," testified Michael Delaney, Central American program coordinator of Oxfam America. "Members of her family were tortured and killed in brutal ways. To come out of that working for peace, instead of being embittered, is very striking," he further claimed. "The natural path for a person like her would be to identify with the indigenous people's struggles and ignore the poor non-indigenous and mestizo people. She's unusual in her ability to relate to a wide range of people without seeming to be threatening them. She has become an unusually effective advocate for reconciliation among Guatemala's many ethnic groups."

In the 1970s, her father, Vincente Menchu, began to organize the Committee of Peasant Unity, a group protesting the unequal patterns of land ownership in Guatemala, where 2 percent of the population owns about 65 percent of the land fit for crop planting, and violations of human rights of indigenous peoples.

But Rigoberta Menchu was not directly involved in the work until after her mother, father and brother were killed in separate tragic circumstances in 1980 and 1981.

Her father was burned to death by the Guatemalan army and she carried him out of the Spanish embassy where he had been protesting for better wages for farm workers. He was so badly burned that she could hardly recognize him. Her brother was tortured and burned by the military, and her mother, Juana, was kidnapped, raped and mutilated.

According to her 1983 book, *I, Rigoberta Menchu*, she found her mother's body after Juana's ear had been cut off and she had been left to be consumed by maggots, vultures and dogs.

After the killings, Menchu's two sisters joined Guatemalan guerilla forces and she fled across the border into the Mexican state of Chiapas, where she found refuge in the home of a Catholic bishop.

She was psychologically weakened after seeing most of her family wiped out. It took a lot of time for her to recuperate. But it was their deaths that caused her to become politicized. She felt she was the only one left alive from her family who could do something to stop all the madness.

Working mainly through the Committee of Peasant Unity, Menchu began speaking throughout the Americas and at the United Nations on behalf of indige-

nous peoples and other victims of government repression.

As Menchu became increasingly involved in putting pressure on her government, she was invited to lecture in the United States and Europe by others critical of the situation in Guatemala. However, this was not enough to bring the country's plight to the world stage. Menchu said of Guatemala's problems: "[They seem] insignificant in the lives of other people. I mean, they are amazed when they hear that 46,000 people have disappeared in Guatemala. They say, 'How horrible,' and they are very impressed. But it does not go beyond that."

Guatemalan authorities responded by calling her a communist and accusing her of being linked to the guerilla movement. They made several attempts on her life and the lives of her companions.

What made her an effective advocate for those who oppose oligarchic control of the country is that her speeches are not that elaborate, but go right to the heart of the matter. She looks at issues in a way that touches the everyday life of common people.

Menchu campaigned successfully for designating 1993 as the International Year for Indigenous Populations. She planned to use her $1.2 million Nobel Prize money to campaign for peace in her country and for Indian rights throughout the hemisphere, by establishing a foundation in her father's name to defend the rights of indigenous peoples. "The only thing I wish for is freedom for Indians wherever they are. As the end of the 20th century approaches, we hope that our continent will be pluralistic."

Biography

Rigoberta Menchu, a Guatemalan activist for the rights of the indigenous people and a winner of Nobel Peace Prize, was born in 1959 in a small Guatemalan village of Chimel located in the northern highlands. Her family was Quiche Indian and very poor. The small plot of land that the family owned did not produce enough to feed everyone. Like their neighbors, who were in the same predicament, they traveled to the coast to work as laborers on large coffee or cotton plantations, working up to fifteen hours a day for eight months a year.

Life on a plantation was harsh. People lived in crowded sheds with no clean water or toilets. Children had to start working at an early age or else they were not fed. Rigoberta started working on the plantation at the age of eight. She did not have an opportunity to attend school. Two of her brothers died on the plantation, one as a result of poisoning from pesticides sprayed on coffee plants and another from malnutrition.

In her youth she worked in the fields and later in the city as a domestic employee. She lived in the midst of the injustice, misery, and discrimination suffered by the Indigenous peoples of Guatemala. Various members of her family were tortured and assassinated by the repressive armed forces.

Native Indians in Guatemala had no rights of citizenship, which were restricted to people of Spanish descent and were, therefore, vulnerable to abuses by those in power. When the military-led government and the wealthy plantation owners started taking Indian-occupied lands by force, Rigoberta's father, Vicente, became a leader in the peasant movement opposing this action. He began a series of petitions and then, protests, to secure these lands for the indigenous people who had been living on them until now. He was arrested and imprisoned many times for his activities. In 1979, Rigoberta's sixteen-year-old brother, Petrocinio, was kidnapped by soldiers, tortured and burned alive while his family watched. In 1980, Vicente, along with thirty-eight other Indian leaders, died in a fire at the Spanish embassy, while protesting violations of Indian human rights abuses. Rigoberta's mother, also a leader in her community and a healer, was kidnapped, raped, tortured and killed the following year.

Persecuted, Rigoberta Menchu was exiled to Mexico in 1980. While in Mexico, she dictated her autobiography, *I . . . Rigoberta Menchu* (1984), telling the world not only her own story, but also about the lives of her fellow Indians. Her book and the campaign she led for social justice brought international attention to this conflict between indigenous Indians and the military government of Guatemala.

Self-educated, she has shown herself to be a natural leader of great intelligence. She became an active political worker in labor, campesino and human rights groups as well as in the defense and promotion of the rights and values of Indigenous peoples.

In 1992, Rigoberta Menchu was awarded the Nobel Peace Prize. She used the $1.2 million cash prize to set up a foundation in her father's name to continue the fight for human rights of the indigenous people. Due to her effort, the United Nations declared 1993 the International Year for Indigenous Populations.

Bibliography ─────────────────────

Abrams I 1998 "Heroines of Peace: the nine Nobel women." http://www.nobel.se/essays/heroines/index.html

Bois D 1995 "Rigoberta Menchu." http:/www.netsrq.com/~dbois/menchu.html

Boston Globe 1992 "Nobel Prize winner called charismatic in Guatemala effort." October

Fundacion Rigoberta Menchu Tum 1998 "Rigoberta Menchu Tum: Nobel peace prize laureate

The Nobel Prize Internet Archive 1992 "Rigoberta Menchu Tum: 1992 Nobel Prize in Peace." http://nobelprizes.com/nobel/peace/nobel1992a.html

PEDRO B. BERNALDEZ

Nelson Mandela
(1993)

The Nobel Committee awarded the 1993 Nobel Peace Prize to Nelson Mandela, the leader of the African National Congress for his ceaseless efforts to end apartheid.

In August 1962 Nelson Mandela, who not long before had emerged as a leading member of the African National Congress (ANC), South Africa's oldest civil rights organization, was arrested on charges of inciting workers to strike and leaving the country without valid travel documents. When he appeared in court for a formal remand, which was attended by a number of white attorneys who knew him personally, Mandela had a revelation of sorts. He sensed that on some level the spectators knew that he had committed no crime and that he was simply, in his words, "an ordinary man being punished for his beliefs." "In a way I had never quite comprehended before," Mandela wrote in his autobiography *Long Walk to Free-*

dom (1994), "I realized the role I could play in court and the possibilities before me as a defendant. I was the symbol of justice in the court of the oppressor, the representative of the great ideals of freedom, fairness, and democracy in a society that dishonored those virtues. I realized then and there that I could carry on the fight even within the fortress of the enemy."

Mandela went to do just that, not only in the 1962 trial and in the famous Rivonia Trial of 1963-64, in which he was convicted of treason and sentenced to life in prison, but also throughout the twenty-seven years of his incarceration. Mandela has continued to fight for the creation of a truly democratic society in South Africa since his dramatic release from prison in 1990, as the guiding force in the ANC's negotiations with the white-minority government to end apartheid and to replace it with a multiracial government of national unity. Yet as far as Mandela is concerned, the challenge of transforming South Africa into a nonracial society has only begun. "I have walked that long road to freedom . . . ," Mandela wrote in his autobiography. "But I can rest only for a moment, for with freedom comes responsibility, and I dare not linger, for my long walk is not yet ended."

Mandela's mature ideas about leadership, especially his belief in the importance of leading by consensus, were inspired by the example set by the regent, as Mandela revealed in his autobiography: "I always remember the regent's axiom: A leader, he said, is like a shepherd. He stays behind the flock, letting the most nimble go out ahead, whereupon the others follow, not realizing that all along they are being directed from behind."

After much thought, Mandela found that he had the greatest affinity for ideas promoted by the ANC, whose principal goal was the liberation of black South Africans from the shackles of racism. "I had no epiphany, no singular revelation, no moment of truth, but a steady accumulation of a thousand slights, a thousand indignities, a thousand unremembered moments, produced in me an anger, a rebelliousness, a desire to fight the system that imprisoned my people," Mandela wrote in his memoir. "There was no particular day on which I said, 'From henceforth I will devote myself to the liberation of my people'; instead, I simply found myself doing so, and could not do otherwise."

Mandela joined the ANC in 1944, and shortly after that he and others helped establish the ANC Youth League, which eventually came to dominate the ANC and whose aims were nothing less than "the overthrow of the white supremacy and the establishment of a truly democratic form of government," as Mandela has described them. Those goals became more elusive than ever after the National Party came to power in 1948: in the following years the Nationalists passed a series of sweeping laws that transformed from custom into law the system of racial segregation known as apartheid. In addition to requiring each of South Africa's racial groups to live in separate, designated areas, the law prohibited marriage between people of different races, mandated that all South Africans be registered according to their race, and outlawed the Communist Party in terms so broad that almost anyone could be considered a member.

In response to the new measures, the ANC leadership felt compelled to rethink its strategy to protest the oppression of black South Africans. That rethinking ultimately prompted the ANC to demand, in a let-

ter to the prime minister in 1952, that the government repeal the discriminatory laws. When the demand was rebuffed, as expected, the ANC launched the Campaign for the Defiance of Unjust Laws, which Mandela helped organize. Those involved in the campaign committed such nonviolent—and, according to the new laws, illegal—acts as entering proscribed areas without permission, using "whites only" facilities, including toilets and railway station entrances, and taking part in strikes. Because of his role in the campaign, Mandela, along with many others, was found guilty of "statutory communism," despite the fact that he did not even belong to the party. As a punishment, he was "banned," which meant that he was prohibited from attending rallies or other gatherings (even nonpolitical ones) for several months. Mandela was later banned again, and as a result he did not return to the public eye until 1955.

On December 5, 1956 Mandela was among 156 resistance leaders charged with high treason—specifically, committing acts aimed at toppling the government and replacing it with a Communist regime— an offense punishable by death. In the trial, which did not begin until 1959, the government was unable to show that Mandela or the ANC had plotted any sort of violent revolution, and on March 29, 1961 he and his comrades were acquitted. As might be imagined, Mandela was pleased with the verdict, though he regarded it not "as a vindication of the legal system or evidence that a black man could get a fair trial in a white man's court," as he wrote in *Long Walk to Freedom*, but rather as "a result of a superior defense team and the fair-mindedness of the panel of these particular judges." His circumspection proved to be well founded, for not long after his acquittal a warrant for his arrest was issued, the ANC having been banned by the government in 1960. In the following months Mandela thus lived as a fugitive, posing on many occasions as a chauffeur, cook, or gardener.

Throughout his years of involvement with the ANC, Mandela was committed to fighting to end apartheid through nonviolent means. By the early 1960s, however, he along with other ANC leaders began to question the effectiveness of this approach, for increasingly the government was responding to the ANC's actions with violence. One of the more infamous instances in which the government resorted to violence occurred in the town of Sharpville in 1960, when sixty-nine protesters were killed by police. Whether or not to launch an armed struggle subsequently became the subject of heated debate, especially at an ANC meeting in June 1961. For his part, Mandela, having become convinced that "it was wrong and immoral to subject [his] people to armed attacks by the state without offering them some kind of alternative, "argued that the ANC had no choice but to take up an armed struggle against the state. Notwithstanding his lack of military experience, Mandela was given the task of organizing an armed wing of the ANC, Umkhonto we Sizwe (Spear of the Nation), whose mission was to organize acts of sabotage against the state with the aim of overthrowing the white-minority government. Mandela now had more reason than ever to be mindful of his movements around the country. His uncanny luck and success in evading capture earned him the nickname "the Black Pimpernel," after the Scarlet Pimpernel, the title character of a book by Emmuska Orezy who eludes capture during the French Revolution.

Mandela's underground existence came to an end on August 5, 1962, when he was arrested on charges of inciting workers to strike and leaving the country without proper papers. Instead, he argued that the state had no jurisdiction over his activities since its laws had been made by a government in which he had no representation, and that it was merely his natural desire to live as a free man in a state that denied him freedom that had put him on the wrong side of the law. "There comes a time," he declared to the court at the trial's conclusion, "as it came in my life, when a man is denied the right to live a normal life, when he can only live the life of an outlaw because the government has so decreed to use the law to impose a state of outlawry upon him." On November 7, 1962 he was sentenced to five years in prison with no chance of parole.

Eight months later South African authorities raided the ANC's headquarters at a farm in Rivonia and seized documents outlining the organization's plans to wage guerrilla warfare in South Africa. That discovery enabled the state to try Mandela, along with several other top ANC officials, on new and more serious charges. The Rivonia Trial, as it became known, ended with the defendants being convicted for treason. Although their crime was punishable by death—an outcome that Mandela fully expected—the court sentenced them to life in prison, with no chance of parole, on June 12, 1964. The trial was the subject of considerable media attention around the world, and appeals for clemency were received in South Africa from abroad. An editorial writer for the *New York Times* predicted that history would judge that "the ultimate guilty party is the government in power—and that is already the verdict of world opinion."

For the next eighteen years Mandela was confined to the maximum-security prison on Robben Island,

off South Africa's coast. His first cell there was seven feet square, with a single light bulb and a mat on the floor for sleeping. He had the right to receive only one brief letter and one visitor every six months. But in spite of the harsh conditions, Mandela was determined not to surrender to despair. Indeed, he has said he never seriously considered the possibility that he would not one day walk on South African soil as a free man.

Mandela's release from prison, on February 11, 1990, was one of the most dramatic news events of the year. A few months later Mandela embarked on a world tour, making stops in major cities throughout North America and Europe, where he was welcomed as a hero and a world leader. In Great Britain he met with Prime Minister Margaret Thatcher. In the United States he addressed a joint session of Congress and met with President George Bush. After his meeting with Bush, the two men held a press conference on the White House lawn.

The task of establishing a truly democratic, nonracial government in South Africa fell to the multi-party Convention for a Democratic South Africa, which began in December 1991. The negotiations that ensued, led by Mandela and de Klerk, were by no means without conflict and were broken off at various points. A major hurdle was crossed on September 26, 1992, when Mandela and de Klerk signed the Record of Understanding, which formalized their agreement that a single, freely elected constitutional assembly would both serve as the transitional legislature and draft a new constitution. Another milestone was reached on June 3, 1993, when it was agreed that the first elections open to all South African citizens would be held on April 27, 1994. For his efforts to bring South Africa to that point, Mandela was awarded the 1993 Nobel Peace Prize. Mandela accepted the Nobel Peace Prize as an accolade to all people who have worked for peace and stood against racism. It was as much an award to his person as it was to the ANC and all South Africa's people. In particular, he regards it as a tribute to the people of Norway who stood against apartheid while many in the world were silent.

Nelson Mandela's greatest pleasure, his most private moment, is watching the sun set with the music of Handel or Tchaikovsky playing. Having been locked up in his cell during daylight hours, deprived of music, both these simple pleasures were denied him for decades. With his fellow prisoners, concerts were organized when possible, particularly at Christmas time, where they would sing. Nelson Mandela finds music very uplifting, and takes a keen interest not only in European classical music but also in

African choral music and the many talents in South African music. But one voice stands out above all— that of Paul Robeson, whom he describes as "our hero". The years in jail reinforced habits that were already entrenched: the disciplined eating regime of an athlete began in the 1940s, as did the early morning exercise. Still today Nelson Mandela is up by 4.30 AM, irrespective of how late he has worked the previous evening. By 5 AM he has begun his exercise routine that lasts at least an hour. Breakfast is by 6.30, when the days newspapers are read. The day's work has begun.

With a standard working day of at least 12 hours, time management is critical and Nelson Mandela is extremely impatient with unpunctuality, regarding it as insulting to those one is dealing with. When speaking of the extensive traveling he had undertaken since his release from prison, Nelson Mandela says: "I was helped when preparing for my release by the biography of Pandit Nehru, who wrote of what happens when you leave jail. My daughter Zinzi says that she grew up without a father, who, when he returned, became a father of the nation. This has placed a great responsibility on my shoulders. And wherever I travel, I immediately begin to miss the familiar—the mine dumps, the color and smell that is uniquely South African, and, above all, the people. I do not like to be away for any length of time. For me, there is no place like home."

Nelson Mandela is very much in his home but he is considered the number one freeman of the world— the most popular man throughout the world over. He almost gave his life to eradicate the most inhuman policy ever created by man—apartheid. He stands as the world's symbol of freedom. He travels a lot to other countries to inspire democracy—and freedom-fighters. He is the best inspiration so far for those who value peace, freedom and democracy.

Biography

Nelson Mandela was born Rolihlahla Dalibhunga Mandela on July 18, 1918 in the village of Mvezo, in the Transkei, a region on South Africa's southeastern coast. His father, Gadla Henry Mphakanyiswa, was the chief of Mvezo and a member of the royal house of the Thembu tribe, and his mother, Nosekeni Fanny Mandela, was one of his father's four wives. Following his father's death, when he was nine, Mandela came under the guardianship of Jongintaba Dalindyebo, the powerful regent of the Thembu people, who groomed him for tribal duties as counselor to the chief and whom he came to admire greatly.

Mandela developed a strong admiration for his guardian,

but also was largely influenced by his attendance at Methodist elementary and secondary schools, where he remembers being taught to identify with British interests and adopt the role of a culturally inferior African. At 21, he entered the University College of Fort Hare in Alice.

Mandela fled an arranged marriage and in 1941 went to Johannesburg, where he got a job as a clerk in the office of a liberal Jewish law firm. At that time he also enrolled in a correspondence course at the University of South Africa and received a B.A. degree from that institution. In 1943, he entered the University of the Witwatersrand to work toward a law degree.

In 1944, Mandela joined the African National Congress and embraced its philosophy and platform of the liberation of black South Africans from racism. He and his associates established the ANC Youth League, which soon eclipsed the parent organization in its demands for the overthrow of white supremacy and the establishment of a democratic government.

In 1948, an event occurred which was to change Mandela's life and the course of South African history. The National Party, dominated by Afrikaners, came into power and passed laws establishing a system of racial segregation known as apartheid. These laws required each of the country's racial groups to live separately and register with the government according to their race. The laws also prohibited interracial marriage and outlawed the Communist Party. The government defined Communist Party membership and communistic activities so broadly that it could arrest people indiscriminately, branding them as Communist Party members.

In 1952, the ANC sent a letter to the prime minister demanding the repeal of the discriminatory laws. The government refused, and the ANC began a campaign of non-violent resistance called the Campaign for the Defiance of Unjust Laws. Mandela helped organize the campaign, which included strikes and the use of "whites only" toilets and building entrances. Mandela was arrested, charged with being a communist, and banned from attending rallies and public gatherings for several months. He was then banned a second time. That year Mandela set up the first law practice in South Africa run by blacks, but because of the court ban on his public appearances, he was not active in the movement.

In 1956, Mandela was charged with high treason— allegedly for communist activity intended to subvert the regime—but was acquitted in 1961 due to lack of evidence. In 1960, the government banned the ANC, and Mandela lived a secret life, working at odd jobs and evading arrest. The ANC assigned Mandela the task of organizing an armed wing to carry out sabotage and overthrow the white government.

In 1962, Mandela was sentenced to five years in prison. While in prison, the government seized ANC documents, implicating Mandela in ANC plans to wage guerrilla warfare. The court sentenced him to life in prison on a charge of treason in June 1964. Mandela spent the next 18 years confined to the maximum-security prison on Robben Island, off the coast of South Africa. In 1980 the Johannesburg *Sunday Post* launched a campaign to free Mandela, encouraging readers to sign a petition that he be released. In the 1980s there was a growing movement among blacks to bring about the end of apartheid, and a growing sympathy for their cause abroad. In 1985 President P.W. Botha offered to free Mandela if he agreed to disavow violence. Mandela refused.

In an attempt to find a compromise between the government and the ANC, Mandela had secret discussions from prison with the minister of justice in 1987 and 1988. In 1989 Botha was replaced as president by F.W. de Klerk, who overturned many apartheid laws, released a number of black leaders and lifted the ban on the ANC. He released Mandela from prison on February 2, 1990.

Mandela went on a world tour and was welcomed by government leaders and enthusiastic crowds of admirers. In 1993 Mandela and de Klerk were awarded the Nobel Peace Prize. On April 27, 1994, in the first elections open to all South African citizens, Mandela was elected president.

From his marriage to Evelyn Mase, a nurse, which lasted from 1944 until 1956, Nelson Mandela has three children. In 1958 he married Nomzamo Winnie Madikizela, then a young social worker. The couple had two daughters in the four years they lived together before Mandela's imprisonment. Winnie Mandela became her husband's principal supporter and spokesperson during his years in prison, and she ultimately developed a political power base of her own. Her reputation was later marred by charges of criminal behavior. Following Mandela's release the couple became estranged, and they separated in April 1992. In July 1998, on his 80th birthday, he married the widow of the former president of Mozambique.

In addition to the Nobel Prize, over the years Mandela has received numerous honors and awards. He won the Bruno Kreisky Prize for Human Rights in 1982, and he was named an Honorary Citizen of Rome in 1983. He received the Sakharov Prize in 1988 and the Gaddaff Human Rights Prize in 1989 and shared the Houphouet Prize in 1991. He has received a great number of honorary doctorates, including a joint honorary degree from thirty-eight traditionally black American universities, which he received in 1990 during a ceremony at Morehouse College, in Atlanta.

Bibliography

Benson M 1986 *Nelson Mandela: The Man and the Movement.*
CNN: Newsmaker Profiles 1998 Nelson Mandela: South African President." http://cnn.com/resources/newsmakers/world/Africa/mandela.html
Mandela N 1994 *Long Walk to Freedom.*
Nelson Mandela Biography 1998. http://www/anc.org.za/people/mandela.html

PEDRO B. BERNALDEZ

Frederik Willem de Klerk
(1993)

The Nobel Peace Prize for 1993 was jointly awarded to Nelson R. Mandela and Frederik Willem de Klerk of South Africa "for their work for the peaceful termination of the apartheid regime and for laying the foundations for a new democratic South Africa," stressed the Norwegian Nobel Committee. The Committee further elucidated that "Ethnic disparities cause the bitterest conflicts. South Africa has been the symbol of racially-conditioned suppression. Mandela's and de Klerk's constructive policy of peace and reconciliation also points the way to the peaceful resolution of similar deep-rooted conflicts elsewhere in the world." The two South African leaders were complimented by the Committee by further stressing that "From their different points of departure, Mandeland de Klerk have reached agreement on the principles for a transition to a new political order based on the tenet of one man-one vote. While looking ahead to South African reconciliation instead of back at the deep wounds of the past, they have shown personal integrity and great political courage.

"Five years ago, people would have seriously questioned the sanity of anyone who predicted that Mr. Mandela and I would be joint recipients of the 1993 Nobel Peace Prize," de Klerk said in his Nobel lecture. "We are political opponents. We disagree strongly on key issues and we will soon fight a strenuous election campaign against one another. But we will do so, I believe, in the frame of mind and within the framework of peace that has already been established."

In presenting the award, chairman of the Nobel Committee, Francis Sejersted said, "The danger of setback exists." However, the award served as an encouragement and the laureates deserved indeed the honor for "a brilliant contribution to peace."

Several years after receiving the prize and during a speaking engagement in Seattle, USA, de Klerk reminisced "The dramatic reforms that I initiated would not have been possible without trust and willingness to change. If we do not adapt, we run the risk of being swept aside and left bobbing in the waves of history."

Like any South African of his class, race, and time, de Klerk knew blacks only as servants when he was young. But he said that seeing them rise above servitude did not seem strange. "It was never difficult," he stressed. "At all times, I believed in what I was doing. And it was not haphazardly done. On our knees before God, we decided to make the fundamental change . . . . We believed we must do it and we are humbly proud. The changes were necessary because we could not build the future on injustice."

Frederik Willem de Klerk was born in Johannesburg on March 18, 1936. He is the son of Senator Jan de Klerk, a leading politician, who became minister in the South African government. His brother Willem is a liberal newspaperman and one of the founders of the Democratic Party.

Frederik de Klerk was a youth when apartheid became the law of South Africa, instituted by what became the iron-fisted 40-year rule of the National Party. In the early years, his father Jan quit his job as a history teacher to work for the party's aim of racial separation. As a college student, de Klerk supported the concept of apartheid.

F.W. de Klerk graduated with a law degree from Potchefstroom University in 1958 and then practiced law in Vereeniging in the Transvaal. De Klerk was offered a professorship of administrative law at Potchefstroom in 1972 but he declined the post because he had been elected to Parliament as National Party member for Vereeniging at the time.

As a member of parliament from Vereeniging in the Transvaal from 1972 to 1989, de Klerk was respected for his negotiating skills and his pragmatic approach. He rose quickly in the party. In six years, he was appointed to the cabinet as minister of posts and telecommunications. He has held a variety of posts in the cabinet in both the Vorster and Botha governments. In 1984 he was made minister of home affairs and national education and in 1985 he became chairman of the Ministers' Council in the House of Assembly. Critics say that in his stint in the cabinet he never showed any indication that he would reform the apartheid system some day. His idea of a "new South Africa," seemed to have been rooted in his concept of "group rights." By group rights, de Klerk spoke of the legislation that defined "where people of

specific color may live, worship, attend school, swim, etc." De Klerk said in 1986 in an address to the Parliament: "Each group has its own community life, its own residential areas, own schools, own institutions and systems within which the group can maintain its own character and handle its own interests." But this line of thought would soon change.

In the last years of the 1980s through early 1990s, it was evident that South Africa, like most of the world was ready for change. Given the restlessness of the majority of South Africans who had been oppressed by the draconian laws of the apartheid regime, a revolution was inevitable. Sentiment and insurgency grew; South Africa teetered on the brink of full-scale conflict, becoming more and more isolated in the international community until finally it became clear apartheid was not going to work. The underlying message seemed to be that change happened not so much because it was right, but because it was the right time. As the former Soviet Union crumbled and the Berlin wall fell and P.W. Botha stepped aside after suffering a stroke, de Klerk saw his opportunity.

It was de Klerk who engineered the 1989 coup that toppled former South African President P. W. Botha, a hardline conservative. Botha had been an ardent defender of apartheid, the legally sanctioned system of racial discrimination, especially against blacks. De Klerk was widely expected to permit minor reforms in race relations, while protecting the fundamental institution of apartheid. One by one, under his leadership, the strictures of apartheid were repealed and on February 2, 1990 de Klerk announced the steps towards freeing South Africa from the shackles of despotism. Under de Klerk's direction, the South African government lifted its ban on the African National Congress, the party which had been standing put against the apartheid regime. Soon after, de Klerk released the black nationalist leader Nelson Mandela who had been languishing in prison for long 27 years. The reforms de Klerk introduced did not end there since laws mandating the separation of races were repealed. Blacks were granted rights to vote and hold office. Earlier, he had opened whites-only beaches and whites-only neighborhoods to blacks and overseen the first national election allowing the 26 million black majority to vote. He had freed hundreds of anti-apartheid prisoners and had allowed black protest marches to spill through city streets and had wrought so many other sweeping changes with tremendously significant effects on the lives of the South Africans. In 1994, the country's first elections produced a president in Mandela.

Working closely with Mandela and others, de Klerk also helped negotiate the principles of a new constitution.

It seemed in early 1990s that de Klerk was adapting. Even then, he had not given up his belief that the apartheid was necessary. "We had a 70 percent population of blacks who had wanted the same rights we had. " He had strongly believed in the necessity of racial segregation.

Having been defeated in the presidential election, de Klerk became one of the two deputy presidents under Mandela's government of National Unity that assumed power in 1994. But he was essentially powerless, and he pulled the Nationals out of the government to develop into a legitimate opposition party in time for the scheduled presidential elections in 1999. The National Party failed to improve its standing significantly and moderates began leaving.

In August 1997, de Klerk announced he would be leaving the National Party. "I know the time has come for me to go," he announced to the astonishment of many among his colleagues. De Klerk's resignation plunged his party into chaos. Explaining his decision, de Klerk, who had been a member of the National Party for 25 years and its leaders for eight years, said he wanted to give his replacement time to prepare for the 1999 elections. De Klerk's stature has been diminished by his refusal to acknowledge responsibility to the Truth and Reconciliation Commission for appalling activities of government death squads during the apartheid years.

He planned to write his autobiography and to contemplate more on what he had done so far for his country. "It is crucially important that the events of our recent history should be placed in their correct perspective." It was his role in the unfolding of that history that many will not easily forget the man who dismantled apartheid. Tom Lodge, head of the political studies department at Witwatersrand University said, "When historians remember de Klerk, it will be as the man who actually began the process of democratization in South Africa . . . . He is South Africa's Gorbachev."

A few years ago, de Klerk had been heard to have said, "I would like to be remembered positively as one of the leaders who at the right time did the right things. It must be recognized that South Africa is a far better place today than it was just a few years ago because of de Klerk's vision and courage. But he has paid a heavy price for his break with the past. Rightwing whites consider him a traitor, and most blacks view him as a political relic.

De Klerk has to go but "he shouldn't go very far," comments Dewayne Wickham of *Denver Post*. "As an elder statesman, de Klerk can play a vital role in south Africa's still evolving democracy. He is well-regarded by moderate whites and respected by most black politicians. From his soon-to-be-assumed position above the political fray, he can help keep South Africa's multiracial democracy on course."

Biography

Frederik Willem de Klerk was born in Johannesburg on March 18, 1936. He is the son of Senator Jan de Klerk, a leading politician, who became minister in the South African government. His brother Willem is a liberal newspaperman and one of the founders of the Democratic Party.

Frederik de Klerk was a youth when apartheid became the law of South Africa, instituted by what became the iron-fisted 40-year rule of the National Party. In the early years, his father Jan quit his job as a history teacher to work for the party's aim of racial separation. As a college student, de Klerk supported the concept of apartheid.

F.W. de Klerk graduated with a law degree from Potchefstroom University in 1958 and then practiced law in Vereeniging in the Transvaal. De Klerk was offered a professorship of administrative law at Potchefstroom in 1972 but he declined the post because he had been elected to Parliament as National Party member for Vereeniging at the time.

De Klerk gave us his law practice in 1972 to take up a seat in parliament left vacant by a newly appointed ambassador. He was elected in each succeeding election. In 1982 he became National Party leader in the Transvaal when then-party leader Andries Treurnicht resigned over the National Party policy of power sharing.

In 1978, F.W. de Klerk was appointed Minister of Posts and Telecommunications and Social Welfare and Pensions by Prime Minister Vorster. Under Prime Minister P.W. Botha, he held a succession of ministerial posts, including Posts and Telecommunications and Sports and Recreation (1978-1979), Mines, Energy and Environmental Planning (1979-1980), Mineral and Energy Affairs (1980-1982), Internal Affairs (1982-1985), and National Education and Planning (1984-1989). In 1985, he became chairman of the Minister's Council in the House of Assembly. On December 1, 1986, he became the leader of the House of Assembly.

As Minister of National Education, F.W. de Klerk was a supporter of segregated universities, and as a leader of the National Party in Transvaal, he was not known to advocate reform. In February 1989, de Klerk was elected leader of the National Party and in September 1989 he was elected State President. In his first speech after assuming the party leadership he called for a nonracist South Africa and for negotiations about the country's future.

At this juncture, de Klerk set the political stage for the transition of South Africa from a nation in which for four decades the races were separated by law and force and for centuries the white minority ruled the black majority to one in which equality and democracy became the new order of the day. He lifted the ban on the ANC and released Nelson Mandela. He brought apartheid to an end and opened the way for the drafting of a new constitution for the country based on the principle of one person, one vote. He said that apartheid failed "because of demographic and economic realities. And I feel as much liberated by the changes as blacks do. We were liberated from the mistakes of the past."

Leading the National Party in the 1994 elections, de Klerk was defeated by Mandela in the presidential race. In August 1997, de Klerk resigned from the National Party and decided to leave politics for good. He sought to write about his life and South Africa.

In April 1969, de Klerk married his college sweetheart, Marike Willemse. They had two sons and a daughter. De Klerk divorced his wife in February 1998.

Bibliography

Associated Press 1993 "S. Africa Rivals Accept Nobel: Mandela, de Klerk Lauded in Oslo." *The Boston Globe.* http://www.boston. globe/search/stories/nobel/1993

Ramirez M "De KLerk Rode Waves of History." *The Seattle Times.* http://www.seattletimes.com/extra/browse/ html197/klrk

The Nobel Prize Internet Archive 1996 "The Nobel Prize for 1993." http://www.nobel.se/laureates/peace-1993-press.html

The News Tribune September 1997 "De Klerk: His Place in History Assured." http://proquest.umi.com/

Seattle Post October 1997 "Africa's Man of Change Reflects on What He Did." http://proquest.umi.com/

The Fresno Bee August 1997 "South Africa's De Klerk retires as leader of the National Party." http://proquest.umi.com

The Sun August 1997 "De Klerk resigns as party chief." http://proquest.umi.com/

Wickham D. August 1997 "De Klerk deserves a place in history," *Denver Post.* http://proquest.umi.com/

PEDRO B. BERNALDEZ

Shimon Peres
(1994)

For his efforts to forge a lasting peace in the Middle East, Peres, together with the PLO chairman Yasser Arafat, and the Israeli prime minister, Yitzhak Rabin, was awarded the 1994 Nobel Prize for Peace.

Shimon Peres who has been a dominant figure in Israeli politics for the past two decades, has dedicated his life both to maintaining his country's national security and to upholding the ideals of its democratic socialist founders. An activist even as a youth, during the 1950s Peres served as minister of defense under Israel's first prime minister, David Ben-Gurion, a position in which he distinguished himself by developing Israel's weapons and defense industries. By the early 1970s he, along with Yitzhak Rabin, Menachem Begin, Yitzhak Shamir, and other members of the younger generation of Israeli statesmen, was at the forefront of politics, serving in several cabinet positions, and in 1977 he was named chairman of the Labor Party, a position that automatically made him the party's candidate for prime minister. Although he failed to lead Labor to a clear-cut victory in any of the elections held during his fifteen-year-long tenure as party leader, in 1984 Labor and Likud entered into a power-sharing arrangement according to which

Peres served as prime minister from 1984 until 1986. In 1992, after Peres lost the party chairmanship to his long-time rival Yitzhak Rabin, Labor recaptured a majority of seats in the Knesset, the Israeli parliament, and Peres was named foreign minister.

Although at one time he was considered hawkish on defense issues, Peres has long been committed to a peaceful, negotiated settlement of Israel's long-standing conflict with its Arab neighbors and Palestinian population, and during the late 1980s he formulated a plan for implementing Israeli withdrawal from the West Bank and the Gaza Strip, territories occupied by Israel since the Six-Day War, in 1967, and for granting limited self-rule to the Palestinians. Most significant, he played a key role in the negotiations that led to the historic peace accord endorsed by Israel and the PLO in September 1993.

In early 1952, after returning to Israel, Peres was appointed deputy director-general of the ministry of defense, and several months later he was promoted to director-general. During his seven years in that position, Peres was responsible for developing Israel's government-owned weapons industry. He devoted special attention to nuclear research and weapons procurement, and, in the process, he became known for both his formidable negotiating skills and his conviction that Israel's survival depended on its technological development. One of his most notable accomplishments in that post was his success in forging a relationship between Israel and France at a time when Israel had few dependable allies. Israel's friendship with France, which supplied the newly independent country with much-needed weapons, was crucial to its success in capturing the Sinai Peninsula from Egypt in 1956. France remained Israel's principal supplier of arms for the next two decades. Equally significant, Peres conducted secret negotiations with West Germany on Israel's behalf in 1957, despite the fact that at that time diplomatic relations between the two countries did not exist. According to the *Toronto Globe & Mail* (September 13, 1986), the German-Israeli relationship proved to be important to Israel during the Six-Day War, by which time France had greatly reduced its commitment to Israel's defense. As a result of these achievements, Peres was regarded as a member of the "Young Mapai," a group that consisted of influential members of the younger generation of Israeli politicians.

Peres entered a new phase of his career in 1959, when he ran for and was elected to a seat in the Knesset, as a member of the Mapai Party. The party itself continued its domination of Israeli politics, with the result that Ben-Gurion remained prime minister. Ben-Gurion chose as his deputy minister of defense Peres, who held the position until 1965. One of the more notable events of his tenure was his visit to the United States in 1962, when Peres helped persuade the Kennedy administration to sell Israel its Hawk antiaircraft missile system. The purchase marked the beginning of a new phase in Israel's relationship with the United States, which after 1967 became Israel's main supplier of arms.

By the mid-1960s a rift had developed between David Ben-Gurion and several other key Israeli politicians, including Levi Eshkol, who became prime minister following Ben-Gurion's resignation from that post in 1963. Two years later the conflict between Ben-Gurion and Eshkol came to a head, with Eshkol declaring that Ben-Gurion supporters had no place in the government. As a result, Ben-Gurion resigned from the Mapai Party and formed one of his own-Rafi, or the Worker's List Party. He was joined by a number of his supporters, including Shimon Peres, who became the newly formed party's secretary general. Within a few years, though, it became clear that Rafi was unlikely to win wide-

spread popular support, and in 1968 it merged with other pro-labor groups to form the Israel Labor Party, of which Peres became deputy secretary general.

In 1969 Peres was reelected to the Knesset and was appointed to the cabinet of the new prime minister, Golda Meir. Over the following four years, he held a variety of cabinet portfolios, including immigration absorption, transport and communications, and information; he also served as minister without portfolio with responsibility for economic development in the occupied territories.

Although he lacked a portfolio, Peres remained active on the foreign-policy front during the late 1970s, and in the process he succeeded in cultivating an image as a statesman. Traveling frequently outside Israel, he met with Egyptian president Anwar Sadat and leaders of both communist and non communist nations. In 1978 he supported the Camp David agreement, which Begin worked out with Sadat. Whereas Peres had long been regarded as a hawk on defense issues, when compared to the members of the Likud he was decidedly dovish, for he was markedly more open to the idea of reaching a negotiated settlement with Israel's Arab neighbors and its Palestinian population. Peres also worked hard to breathe new life into the party so as to increase its appeal among the Israeli electorate.

The resignation of Menachem Begin in 1983 provided Labor with an opportunity to recapture its control of the government, and in fact Peres succeeded in leading Labor to a narrow victory over Likud, with Labor winning forty-four seats in the Knesset and Likud taking forty-one. Nevertheless, Peres was unable to form a government, with the result that the two parties came up with a novel power-sharing arrangement: they agreed to form a National Unity government, in which cabinet posts would be evenly divided between them and the leader of each would serve half a term as prime minister. Under this arrangement, Peres served as prime minister of Israel from 1984 until 1986.

According to many political observers, Peres was an unusually effective prime minister. His greatest achievement was his deft handling of the economic crisis in which Israel was mired. "We have to turn first of all to ourselves, control our standard of living, reduce our expenses, and make Israel self-reliant from an economic point of view," he declared soon after taking office, as quoted in *Time* (October 1, 1984). In addition to devaluing the shekel, he cut government spending, persuaded Israel's dominant labor federation to cut real wages, and convinced employers to freeze prices. The net result of these initiatives was that inflation dropped from an annual rate of about 445 percent in 1984 to 25 percent two years later. "Israel's success in halting inflation, with virtually no increase in unemployment, is almost unprecedented," Stanley Fischer, an economic professor at the Massachusetts Institute of Technology, said. "Argentina and Brazil both tried to do it at the same time as Israel, with nowhere near the same results."

Another of Peres's achievements as prime minister was his success in coordinating Israel's withdrawal from Lebanon, which the country had invaded in 1982. Its continued presence there was unpopular not only within the international community but also among Israelis. Peres also developed important diplomatic relationships. For instance, he made an official visit to Morocco, where he met with King Hassan II, an event that made him the first Israeli prime minister to be invited to an Arab country other than Egypt. He also met with President Hosni Mubarak of Egypt.

The principal disappointment of Peres's term as prime minister, according to most observers, was his failure to make any significant progress in the effort to resolve the Arab-Israeli conflict. A major stumbling block to any resolution of the conflict, though, was that Labor and Likud were fundamentally divided on how to negotiate a peace settlement. While Peres and other members of the Labor Party were willing to consider the possibility of turning over to Jordan the administration of the occupied territories in return for guarantees of Israel's security, Likud was adamantly opposed to relinquishing territory.

Despite the near impossibility of the two parties' seeing eye to eye on the issue, Peres received the most criticism for the government's failure to advance the peace process. "When it comes to changing the reality, Peres did nothing—for that you need courage," a left-wing member of parliament complained to Thomas Friedman. "I told him many times: 'With the present language of politics—the language of Golda Meir and Menachem Begin—you did the best you could. But you added nothing of your own-like recognizing the Palestinian's right to self-determination.' Peres did nothing to moderate the basic Israeli attitudes toward the West Bank or the Palestinian problems." Notwithstanding this failure, when Peres turned over the prime ministership to Yitzhak Shamir in October 1986 according to the previously agreed upon power-sharing arrangement, he ended what Abraham Rabinovich, writing in the *Toronto Globe & Mail* (September 13, 1986), called "one of the most successful terms of office ever served by an

Israeli prime minister." Also according to the two parties' agreement, Peres at the same time became vice-premier and foreign minister.

In the campaign that preceded the 1988 elections, Peres and the Labor Party adopted a strategy that many observers considered to be risky: the party promised to resolve the conflict with the Palestinians—which had worsened considerably since late 1987, when the *intifada*, or uprising, erupted in the occupied territories—by trading land for peace. While the Israeli electorate was anxious to conclude a negotiated settlement with the Palestinians, in the end it was persuaded by Likud's argument that a dovish Labor-led government could not be trusted to protect Israel's security interests, and Likud scored a razor-thin victory over Labor, winning forty Knesset seats to Labor's thirty-nine. The outcome of the election left the two parties with little choice but to form another coalition government, though unlike the arrangement devised in 1984, Yitzhak Shamir was to serve as prime minister for the full four-year term. Peres, in addition to remaining leader of the opposition, served as vice-premier and finance minister.

By the early 1990s Israeli public opinion in regard to the Palestinian problem had changed dramatically. With the *intifada* continuing unabated, Israelis were growing increasingly dissatisfied with Likud's apparent unwillingness to advance the peace process. Moreover, the 1991 Persian Gulf war changed the geopolitics of the region in such a way that the United States had begun to exert considerable pressure on Israel to make peace with its Arab neighbors and the Palestinians. "We had reached one of those rare critical junctures," Peres wrote in *The New Middle East* (1993), "that enable discerning statesmen to make a quantum leap in their thinking and perhaps turn the tide of history." Although officially out of power, during this period Peres took part in a series of high-level meeting with PLO officials, meetings that were conducted in secrecy because all contacts between Israelis and members of the PLO was prohibited by Israeli law.

Meanwhile, in 1992, the Labor Party elected Yitzhak Rabin as its new chairman, marking the end of Peres's fifteen-year-long leadership of the party. Rabin had emerged as a more attractive candidate for prime minister than Peres at least partly because of his reputation as a military hero: under his leadership, it was widely thought, Israel's national security would not be jeopardized. Following Rabin's election as prime minister in June of that year, Peres was named foreign minister.

According to an article in the *National Review*

(March 7, 1994) that chronicled the secret PLO-Israeli negotiations that were conducted in the early 1990s, Peres spent the months following the 1992 election taking part in high-level discussions with the PLO. Then, in Oslo in the summer of 1993, an agreement between the two parties was reached, though it was not made public at the time. According to Mark Perry, in August 1993 Peres secretly held an eight-hour telephone conversation with Yasir Arafat, and he later met with PLO officials to initial a "Declaration of Principles on Interim Self-Government Arrangements." This agreement was formally endorsed by both Israel and the PLO on September 13, 1993, on an occasion of state in Washington, D.C. Peres has provided his own account of the peace process in his book *The New Middle East* (1993), which he wrote with the Israeli political scientist Arye Naor and which one critic described as a "textbook lesson in how a small nation negotiates in the changed world after the Cold War, when even larger nations have given up some of their sovereignty."

Biography

Shimon Peres was born on August 16, 1923, in a small village in what was then Poland and is now Belarus. His parents, Yitzhak and Sarah Persky, were nonreligious Jews who embraced Zionist ideals, and according to one source Shimon was involved in the Zionist youth movement in Poland. In 1931 his father immigrated to Palestine, and two years later the rest of his family joined him. On settling in Palestine, Peres attended the Balfour primary school in Tel Aviv, where he was an average student. As he grew older he flourished in his studies, becoming an accomplished writer, rhetorician, and speaker. He also continued his involvement in Zionist youth organizations, including Hano'ar Ha'oved (Working Youth). He received a scholarship to the Ben Shemen Agricultural School, where he was sent by Hano'ar Ha'oved to continue his education and to acquire the agricultural skills so highly valued by Palestinian Jewish Settlers. Peres also found time to read poetry and study the works of Karl Marx.

In 1947, Peres was conscripted into the Haganah Defense Forces and assigned responsibility for manpower and arms purchases, continuing this post during the early part of Israel's War of Independence. A year later, Peres was appointed head of Israel's navy and at the war's end assumed the position of Director of the Defense Ministry's procurement delegation in the United States. In 1953, at the age of 29, Peres was appointed by Prime Minister David Ben-Gurion to the post of Director General of the Defense Ministry, a position he held until 1959. During that period he established Israel's electronic aircraft industry and was responsible for Israel's nuclear program.

In 1959, Peres was elected to Israel's parliament, the Knesset, and has remained a member ever since. From that year, and until 1965, he served as Deputy Defense Minister. In 1965, together with David Ben-Gurion, he left the Mapai Labor Party and became Secretary General of Rafi (Israel Workers List). In 1968, he initiated bringing Rafi back to Mapai to form the Israel Labor Party.

The following year, he was appointed Immigrant Absorption Minister and during 1970-74 served as Minister of Transportation and Communications. In 1974, after a period as Information Minister, Peres was appointed Defense Minister, a position he held until 1977.

Prior to the elections in 1977, which placed the Labor Party in opposition, Peres was elected Chairman of the Labor Party, a post he held until 1992. During that period he was elected Vice President of the Socialist International.

Upon the establishment of a National Unity Government, in September 1984, Peres served as Prime Minister and between 1986-88 as Deputy Prime Minister and Foreign Minister. From November 1988 until the dissolution of the National Unity Government in 1990, he served as Deputy Prime Minister and Finance Minister. In July 1992, after the election of the new Labor Government, Peres was appointed Foreign Minister. In 1994, he was awarded the Nobel Peace Prize along with Prime Minister Yitzhak Rabin and PLO Chairman Yasser Arafat.

On November 5, 1995, following the assassination of Prime Minister Yitzhak Rabin, Peres was appointed acting Prime Minister and on November 22, 1995, after being approved by the Knesset, he was sworn in as Prime Minister and Defense Minister. He served in these two posts until the May 1996 elections.

Shimon Peres has authored ten books including *The Next Step* (1965); *David's Sling* (1970); *Entebbe Diary* (1991); *The New Middle East* (1993) and *Battling for Peace* (1995).

Shimon Peres has been married to the former Sonia Gelman since May 1, 1945. They have a daughter, Zvia, two sons, Jonathan and Nechemia, and numerous grandchildren. In addition to the Nobel Prize, Peres has received a number of awards, including the French Legion of Honor.

Bibliography

Golan M 1989 *The Road to Peace: A Biography of Shimon Peres.*

Israel Labor Party 1998 "Shimon Peres—Chairman Israel Labor Party." http://www.internet.net.il/~avoda/peres.html

New York Times 1993 September

The Jewish Student Online Research Center 1998 "Shimon Peres." http://www.us-israel.org/jsource/biography/peres.html

The Nobel Peace Prize Internet Archive 1994 "Shimon Peres: 1994 Nobel Peace Prize Laureate." http://nobelprizes. com.nobel/peace/1994b.html

Toronto Globe & Mail 1986 September

PEDRO B. BERNALDEZ

Yitzhak Rabin
(1994)

Yitzhak Rabin, the prime minister of Israel who was assassinated on November 4, 1995 at age 73, was a soldier turned politician, statesman, and peacemaker. "He led his country into uncharted territory to make peace with Palestinians and put an end to the wars and bloodshed and terrorism that had plagued his country since its founding."

One year before he was assassinated, as he stood to accept the Nobel Peace Prize, Prime Minister Yitzhak Rabin spoke of the terrible burden of the military leader and a life amidst war. He said in his acceptance speech: "At an age when most youngsters are struggling to unravel the secrets of mathematics and the mysteries of the bible: at an age when first love blooms, at the tender age of sixteen, I was handed a rifle so that I could defend myself."

"Together with the joy of victory and the grief of bereavement, I shall always remember the moment just after taking decisions: the hush as senior officers or cabinet ministers slowly rise from their seats; the sight of their receding backs; the sound of the closing door; and then the silence, in which I remain alone."

Throughout his lifetime, Yitzhak Rabin did not shrink from the awful silence of leadership, the weight of responsibility, or the challenge of history. Now silence has engulfed this warrior turned peacemaker forever. His deep voice has been stilled by an assassin determined to end Rabin's final heroic campaign: peace with the Palestinians. In his last moments, Rabin was anything but silent, anything but alone.

Addressing a peace rally in Tel Aviv, Rabin was surrounded by tens of thousands of Jews who shared his vision of a new Middle East. Shimon Peres, his colleague for more than 40 years, said that Rabin never seemed happier. In the joy of the moment, Rabin, the quiet soldier, joined the crowd in "The Song of Peace." After he finished, Rabin folded the lyrics neatly and placed them in his breast pocket. As he left the stage and approached his car, Yigal Amir, a 25-year-old law student at Bar-Ilan University, shot the prime minister with bullets altered to increase their power. Rabin was pronounced dead an hour later. The blood from his wound stained the lyrics of

"The Song of Peace."

Rabin was born in Jerusalem on March 1, 1922. His father, Nehemiah, who came from a poor family in Ukraine, escaped from Czarist Russia and went to Palestine by way of Chicago and St. Louis. In Palestine, he became a trade union organizer in the labor movement of David Ben-Gurion. His mother, Rosa Cohen, born to a well-to-do family in Gomel, Russia, was active in politics and became the dominant influence on the young man. With his parents often away for long periods of time, Rabin remembered that he became a "withdrawn, bashful child." He wrote in his memoirs: "I did not show my feelings or share them with others." It was a trait he carried with him all his life. He was 7 when Arabs began attacking Jewish settlements. Later, during the 1936 Arab riots and general strike, he was at the Khadouri school, where he was trained in the use of arms by Yigal Allo, who was later to become his commander and mentor.

Five years later, during World War II, Moshe Dayan, then a young commander in the Haganah, invited Rabin to join the Palmach. As part of the British invasion of Greater Syria which was in the hands of the Axis powers, Rabin was sent across the border. He was the youngest in his unit, and it was his job to climb up telephone poles to cut the wires so the Vichy French forces could not call up reinforcements.

In June 1945, just after the end of the war in Europe, Rabin commanded a daring raid to liberate about 200 illegal Jewish immigrants held by the British in a camp at Athlit, on the Mediterranean just south of Haifa. Rabin was arrested by the British and interned for six months in a camp in Gaza. Soon after he was released, the British turned the problem of Palestine over to the United Nations, which, in 1947, voted for a partition into a Jewish and an Arab state.

The Arabs attacked, and, as hostilities intensified between the Jews and the Arabs, Allon, then the commander of the Palmach, appointed Rabin his deputy. During the 1948 Israeli war of independence, Rabin commanded the Har-El Brigade, a makeshift unit that failed to take Jerusalem for Israel but kept open the crucial supply lines between Jerusalem and the sea. In 1953, having finally committed himself to a career in the army, Rabin went to England to study at the British Staff College at Camberly. Back home, he went on to hold a series of high posts in the Israeli army, mainly involving manpower training, and was named chief-of-staff in 1964.

During the War of Independence, Rabin fought British and Arabs alike. While the nation was celebrating the Declaration of Independence, Rabin was leading a military operation to secure the road to Jerusalem. It was Rabin, the commander-in-chief of Israel's armed forces in 1967, who had led the lightning strike that captured broad swaths of Arab territories. Rabin's most illustrious moment as a military leader came in 1967 when he was responsible for the lightning victory of the Six-Day War. The war transformed Israel from a struggling, vulnerable outpost to a regional power. Israelis enjoyed a new, well-deserved sense of self-confidence. Jews in the Diaspora were infused with a deep feeling of pride. By conquering the Sinai, the Gaza Strip, the West Bank and the Golan Heights, Israel gained a strategic depth that it had never before enjoyed.

But along with this territorial windfall came the problem of hundreds of thousands of conquered Palestinians. The West Bank would grow to become a nationalist symbol for Palestinians and Israelis alike—and a hotbed of activism. Rabin's greatest victory would ultimately become the source of his demise.

In 1968, Rabin was appointed ambassador to the United States, where he became known as an effective advocate for Israel and a master at procuring American Phantom jets and other sophisticated material. In his five years as ambassador he developed a close relationship with Henry A. Kissinger, President Nixon's national security advisor and later his secretary of state. Kissinger called on him for intelligence about troop movements in the Middle East and even consulted him on Vietnam. On one occasion, he said Rabin was the only general who was able to forecast precisely where the forces of North Vietnam would strike.

Shortly after he returned to Israel in 1973, Rabin entered national politics for the first time. Then, on Yom Kippur, while the country was in the middle of an election campaign, Syria and Egypt launched a surprise attack. The country's leaders—Prime Minister Golda Meir and her minister of defense, Dayan—were held responsible for the country's lack of preparedness in that October war, but the Labor Party won enough votes to form a new government. Rabin

won in his first attempt at election and was given the post of minister of labor.

Within a month of forming her Cabinet, Meir resigned and the party turned to Rabin, who was out of power at the time of the war and therefore untainted by the heavy casualties. Rabin won a narrow majority in the party vote and in 1974, became Israel's fifth prime minister, and, at 52, its youngest. "the time has come," he said, "for the sons of the founders of the state to take over their role." During his term as prime minister, Rabin faced down terrorists who hijacked an Air France plane en route from Tel Aviv to Paris. At first, he was seen as vacillating and weak because he waited several days before dispatching an assault group to Entebbe, Uganda, where the plane and almost 100 Israeli citizens were being held hostage. When he finally approved a military operation, and when the daring raid succeeded, he was hailed as a hero.

Rabin's first term as premier was a period of national healing, punctuated by disengagement from the armies of Syria and Egypt, and the extraordinary rescue mission in Entebbe in 1976. The government fell in 1977 after it sponsored a military ceremony which offended religious members of the governing coalition. But Rabin would not lead his party in the next election: he resigned as head of Labor when it was revealed that his wife had maintained an American bank account in violation of Israeli law.

Led by Rabin rival Shimon Peres, the Labor Party suffered its first defeat in 1977. For the next seven years, Knesset Member Rabin joined his party in the opposition, a spectator to the historic peace accord with Egypt and the invasion of Lebanon. Rabin marvelled at Prime Minister Menachem Begin's success in striking a deal with Egypt, remarking to a reporter, "If this had happened while I was prime minister of a Labor government, there would have been blood spilled on the streets." The nation once again turned to the former general in 1984 when morale in the country was sapped by the war in Lebanon. Named defense minister in a Likud-Labor national unity government, Rabin brought home the bulk of Israeli troops and established a security zone north of the border.

With Lebanon under control, Rabin next faced the Palestinian uprising. The intifada posed a new and difficult challenge for the seasoned soldier because he confronted civilians, not an army. It was reported that Rabin ordered soldiers to "break the bones" of the Palestinians, instead of shooting to kill. While his policy was anathema to many observers, it earned him the respect of the Israeli public. The intifada also began to convince Rabin that Israel had to deal with the Palestinians' national aspirations, not just their hostility.

While Rabin's reputation grew, that of Labor Party leader Shimon Peres faded after successive defeats at the polls. In 1992 Rabin staged his final comeback, wrestling the Labor chairmanship from Peres and leading his party back to power. Rabin returned to the premiership at an historic turning point. The fall of the Soviet Union eliminated the most important supporter of Israel's enemies and sent hundreds of thousands of new immigrants to Israel. Buoyed by billions of dollars in US loan guarantees, Rabin presided over a period of security and economic expansion.

With the Palestinians substantially weakened, the Rabin government, at the initiation of Foreign Minister Peres, began a dialogue with the PLO that would culminate with the signing of the Israel-Palestinian Declaration of Principles at the White House in September 1993. "This signing of the Israeli-Palestinian Declaration of Principles here today is not so easy, neither for myself as a soldier in Israel's wars, nor for the people of Israel, nor for the Jewish people in the Diaspora who are watching us now with great hope mixed with apprehension," Rabin said.

"Let me say to you, the Palestinians, we are destined to live together on the same soil in the same land . . . . We who have fought against you, the Palestinians, we say to you today in a loud and clear voice, enough of blood and tears, enough . . . . We wish to open a new chapter in the sad book of our lives together—a chapter of mutual recognition, of good neighborliness, of mutual respect, of understanding. We hope to embark on a new era in the history of the Middle East."

In an unusual ceremony on the South Lawn of the White House, one that few had ever expected to see in their lifetimes, Rabin came face-to-face with the man who had been reviled for decades by the Israelis as the mastermind behind one attack after another on their men, women and children. "The time for peace has come," Rabin declared. "We, the soldiers who have returned from battles stained with blood, we who have seen our relatives and friends killed before our eyes, . . . we who have come from a land where parents bury their children, we who have fought against you, the Palestinians—we say today in a loud and clear voice: Enough of blood and tears. Enough." He said "Israel was not seeking revenge. It was seeking peace."

The tragedy was that some of Rabin's own people were seeking revenge. As Rabin came closer and closer to achieving his goal of peace, a wide schism opened within the Israeli populace. The bitterness of those opposed to the peace ended with Rabin's assassination. Rabin became the soldier who paid the ultimate price to make peace. The decision to come to terms with the Palestinians meant more than making peace with a mortal enemy.

For their part, the Palestinians were ready to deal. With the end of the Cold War and the collapse of the former Soviet Union, the PLO was deprived of diplomatic, financial, and military support. At the same time, the PLO was reeling from the loss of contributions from wealthy Arab states that were angered by Arafat's support of Iraq during the 1991 Persian Gulf War.

Just as the conquest of the West Bank let loose a wave of nationalism, the prospect of returning the territories unleashed a crescendo of protest from the mainstream right and its extremist fringe. Terrorist killings and suicide bombings by radical Arab groups opposed to the agreement increased Israelis' sense of insecurity and fueled the fires of right-wing rage.

The massacre of 29 Arab worshipers at the Tomb of the Patriarchs in Hebron by a Jewish settler, Baruch Goldstein, prompted a crackdown on Jewish militant groups but did not soften the rhetoric of opponents of the peace accord. Posters depicting Rabin in the crosshairs of a rifle sight, as a Nazi, an Arab terrorist and a traitor were plastered around the country. New settlements were created in the territories without the consent of the government. Protesters shut down traffic on main arteries. An effigy of Rabin was dressed in a Nazi at one Jerusalem rally attended by Likud leader Benjamin Netanyahu. At the same time, law enforcement authorities were accused of manhandling protesters and Rabin himself was criticized for harshly denouncing his opponents.

But it was a relaxed Rabin who greeted a pro-peace rally on the night of November 4.

"I was a military man for 27 years," he said. "I fought so long as there was no chance for peace. I believe that there is now a chance for peace, a great chance. We must take advantage of it . . . ."

"By coming here today," he told his supporters, "you demonstrated together with many others who did not come, that the people truly desire peace and oppose violence. Violence erodes the basis of Israeli democracy. It must be condemned and isolated. This is not the way of the State of Israel. In a democracy there can be differences, but the final decision will be taken in democratic elections . . . ."

Later, the gun of an assassin silenced his words.

Biography

Yitzhak Rabin was born in Jerusalem on March 1, 1922. His father, Nehemiah, who came from a poor family in Ukraine, escaped from czarist Russia and went to Palestine by way of Chicago and St. Louis. His mother, Rosa Cohen, born to a well-to-do family in Gomel, Russia, was active in politics and became the dominant influence on him as a young man. With his parents often away for long periods of time, Rabin had said that he became a "withdrawn, bashful child." He wrote in his memoirs: "I did not show my feelings or share them with others." It was a trait he carried with him all his life.

Rabin was 7 when Arabs begain attacking Jewish settlements. Later, during the 1936 Arab riots and general strike, he was at the Khadouri school, where he was trained in the use of arms by Yigal Allo, who was later to become his commander and mentor. Five years later, during World War II, Moshe Dayan, then a young commander in the Haganah, invited Rabin to join the Palmach. As part of the British invasion of Greater Syria which was in the hands of the Axis powers, Rabin was sent across the border. He was the youngest in his unit, and it was his job to climb up telephone poles to cut the wires so the Vichy French forces could not call up reinforcements.

In June 1945, just after the end of the war in Europe, Rabin commanded a daring raid to liberate about 200 illegal Jewish immigrants held by the British in a camp at Athlit, on the Mediterranean just south of Haifa. Rabin was arrested by the British and interned for six months in a camp in Gaza. Soon after he was released, the British turned the problem of Palestine over to the United Nations, which, in 1947, voted for a partition into a Jewish and an Arab state.

The Arabs attacked, and, as hostilities intensified between the Jews and the Arabs, Allon, then the commander of the Palmach, appointed Rabin his deputy. During the 1948 Israeli war of independence, Rabin commanded the Har-El Brigade, a makeshift unit that failed to take Jerusalem for Israel but kept open the crucial supply lines between Jerusalem and the sea.

In the middle of the war, on August 23, 1948, Rabin married Leah Schlossberg, who had joined the Palmach and served in his battalion. They had two children, a son, Yuval, and a daughter, Dalia, and three grandchildren. All survive him.

In 1953, having finally committed himself to a career in the army, Rabin went to England to study at the British Staff College at Camberly. Back home, he went on to hold a series of high posts in the Israeli army, mainly involving manpower training, and was named chief-of-staff in 1964. He became Israel's top expert on military matters. With his formidable memory he could recite budgets, the history of

each unit, the name of each officer, where a unit was posted, and where it would be posted. As he rose through the ranks, he became known as the man who knew more than the generals. Eventually, he became a lieutenant general.

The army that fought the six-day war in 1967 was essentially Rabin's army. Shab'tai Teveth, professor of history at Tel Aviv University, said: "It was the army he trained, planned, built, and armed in his three years as chief of staff." But, he added: "There his glory ends." His "glory" ended when, on the eve of the fighting, Rabin had a nervous collapse. A story was circulated that he had nicotine poisoning, but, according to Zeev Schiff, the military editor of the newspaper *Haaretz*, it was a breakdown.

After having retired from the army on January 1,1968, Rabin was appointed ambassador to the United States. During his years as ambassador in Washington, he promoted and consolidated the ties between the two countries.

In the spring of 1973, Rabin returned to Israel and became active in the Labour Party. He was elected Member of the Knesset in December 1973 and when Golda Meir formed her government in April 1974, was appointed Minister of Labour. On June 2, 1974, the Knesset expressed confidence in a new government headed by Prime Minister Yitzhak Rabin.

During Rabin's premiership, the government placed special emphasis on strengthening the economy, solving social problems and reinforcing the IDF. With American mediation, disengagement agreements were signed with Egypt and Syria (1974), followed by an interim agreement with Egypt in 1975. Later in 1975, the first Memorandum of Understanding was signed between the governments of Israel and the United States.

In June 1976, Rabin's government issued the order for Operation Entebbe liberating the hijacked Air France passengers. Following the May 1997 elections, and until the formation of the National Unity Government in September 1984, Rabin served as a Knesset Member of the Labour Party in opposition and was a member of the Foreign Affairs and Defense Committee.

In the National Unity Governments (1984-1990), Rabin served as Minister of Defense. In January 1985, he presented the proposal for the withdrawal of IDF forces from Lebanon and the establishment of a security zone to guarantee peace to the settlements along Israel's northern border.

Yitzhak Rabin was elected chairman of the Israel Labour Party in its first nationwide primaries conducted in February 1992 and led the party to victory in the June 1992 Knesset elections. In July 1992, Rabin formed Israel's 25th government and became its 11th Prime Minister and Minister of Defense, and acting Minister of Religious Affairs and Labour and Social Affairs.

On September 13,1993, Rabin, Arafat and Peres came

together in Washington and signed the first Israel-PLO framework for autonomy in West Bank, Gaza. Later, Rabin, Peres and Arafat shared the 1994 Nobel Peace Prize.

Rabin's biographical book, *Service Notebook*, was published in 1979 and was translated into English and French. His book on Lebanon, written after *"Operation: Peace for Galilee"* was published in 1983.

Yitzhak Rabin was assassinated On November 4, 1995.

Bibliography —————————————————

Austin American Statesman 1995 "The Life of Yitzhak Rabin." http://proquest.umi.com/

Berger M "In Memory of Yitzhak Rabin: His Life." http://k2.scl.cwru.edu/~jdp/

CNN "Assassination and funeral of Yitzak Rabin." http://www.cnn.com/WORLD

Goller H "2 Leaders made pact for peace: Peres-Rabin Relationship matured into friendship." *Sun Sentinel* http://proquest.umi.com/

Israel Ministry of Foreign Affairs "PM Rabin—Nobel Prize for Peace." http://www.israel.org/peace/rabinnob.html

Israel Ministry of Foreign Affairs "Remarks by Prime Minister Yitzhak Rabin on Receiving the Nobel Prize for Peace. http://www.israel.org/peace/rabinnob.html

Laub K 1995 "Pragmatic Rabin shaped by life as military leader," *Austin American Statesman*. http://proquest.umi.com/

Rubin J 1995 "A Hero Falls." *Jewish Monthly* Online http://bnaibrith.org/ijm/ articles/rabin/index.html

The Boston Globe 1994 ". . . And Peace" http://www.boston.com/globe

The Fresno Bee 1995 "Chronology of Rabin's Life." http://proquest/umi.com/

The Nobel Peace Prize Internet Archive 1994 "Yitzak Rabin Winner of the Nobel Prize in Peace." wysiwyg://93/ http://nobelprizes.com/nobel/peace/1994c.html

Wall Street Journal 1995 "Rabin's historical vision of peace." http://proquest.umi.com/

"Yitzak Rabin: Biography." http://www.nobel.se/laureates/peace-1994-3bio.html

PEDRO B. BERNALDEZ

Yasser Arafat

(1994)

Together with Shimon Peres and Yitshak Rabin, Yasser Arafat was awarded the Nobel Peace Prize in 1994 "for their efforts to create peace in the Middle East." For several decades, the conflict between Israel and its neighboring states, and between Israelis and Palestinians, has been among the most irreconcilable and menacing in international politics. "By concluding the Oslo Accords and subsequently following them Arafat, Peres, and Rabin have made substantial contributions to a historic process through which peace and cooperation can replace war and hate," noted the press release by the Norwegian Nobel Committee.

Controversy surrounded the Nobel Committee's decision to award the 1994 Peace Prize and criticism did not only focus on the choice of Arafat, whose organization's primary aim was once been Israel's destruction, but also at Rabin and Peres, who has led offensives against Israel's neighbors.

Palestinian-Arab politician and nationalist leader Yasser Arafat was born Mohammed Abdel-Raouf Arafat al Qudwa al-Hussein in Cairo, Egypt, on August 24, 1929, son of a successful merchant. His mother died when he was 4, and he went to live with an uncle in Jerusalem, a city that was a British pro-

tectorate. It was during those years that Arafat was first exposed to the clash between Arabs and Jews, including many who immigrated to build a Jewish homeland in Palestine.

When Arafat went to college in Cairo, he undertook a study of Jewish life there, associating with Jews and reading the works of Zionists such as Theodor Herzl. By 1946 he had become a Palestinian nationalist and was already procuring weapons in Egypt to be smuggled into Palestine in the Arab cause.

When the first of five Arab-Israeli wars broke out in 1948, some reports say Arafat slipped into Palestine to fight the Jews. He later claimed his compatriots were disarmed and turned back by other Arabs who did not want the help of Palestinian irregulars. After the Jews won the war, Palestinians suffered another humiliation when the three-quarters of a million Palestinian Arabs were left stateless.

After the war, Arafat studied civil engineering at the University of Cairo. He headed the Palestinian Students League and, by the time he graduated, was committed to forming a group that would free Palestine from Israeli occupation. In 1958, he left Egypt to Kuwait where he worked as an engineer and met with Khalil Al Wazeer (Abu Jihad). In Kuwait he discussed the idea of establishing Fatah the Palestinian National Liberation Movement. In the mid-1950s, Arafat and several Palestinian Arab associates formed a movement which became known as Fatah, an organization dedicated to reclaiming Palestine for the Palestinians. This and other groups eventually operated under an umbrella organization, the Palestine Liberation Organization, formed in 1964. Running Fatah became Arafat's full-time occupation, and by 1965 the organization was launching guerrilla raids and terrorist attacks into Israel. Arafat stayed in Jerusalem until 1967, then he left for Jordan. He was said to have returned secretly to Palestine three times after then.

Israel again emerged victorious in the Six-Day War of 1967, and captured the Golan Heights from Syria, the West Bank from Jordan and the Gaza Strip from Egypt. The war widened the Israeli-Palestinian conflict to include other Arabs. In 1968 Arafat and the Fatah got international publicity when they inflicted a significant defeat on Israeli troops who entered Jordan. Arafat led Al-Karamah battle in 1968 with his Palestinian colleagues in Fatah where the Palestinian resistance won the battle against the Israelis. The PLO's activities increasingly troubled Jordan's King Hussein however, and in 1971 he forced the Palestinians to leave Jordan after a civil war. In the aftermath of the September war in 1969 in Jordan, Arafat moved to Lebanon and remained there until 1982 when Beirut was under siege of three months by the Israeli army who failed to conquer the PLO. They set up bases in Lebanon and continued to carry out raids against Israel from there.

In 1972, Arafat was vilified because of an alleged involvement with the Arab terrorist Black September group that massacred Israeli athletes at the Munich Olympics. "Yasser Arafat came before the UN General Assembly with an olive branch and a gun." The symbolic juxtaposition of peace and violence defined Arafat political life. In 1974, Arafat addressed the United Nations in New York. The sympathetic world body voted to give the PLO observer status at the United Nations and said the Palestinians had a right to self-determination. That year Arafat appeared to be willing to depart from his desire to destroy Israel and instead reach a political settlement with the Israelis.

The bleakest period for Arafat and the PLO came in June 1982 when, provoked by terrorist raids, Israel launched an all-out counterattack, destroying the PLO headquarters in Beirut and forcing the PLO out of Lebanon. Arafat re-established PLO headquarters in Tunisia. Soon however, world attention was drawn away from the PLO toward rioting by Palestinians in the West Bank and their plight in the Israeli-occupied territories. The PLO supported the West Bank Palestinians, and the international sympathy they aroused thrust the PLO back into prominence.

Arafat originally sought to establish a secular Palestinian state and was widely recognized as president for the Palestinian people. After the Palestinians in the Israeli-occupied territories launched an uprising—Intifada, in December 1987, Arafat persuaded the PLO to declare in November 1988 an independent Palestinian state, renounced terrorism, and accepted United Nations resolution 242 and Israel's right to exist.

In the Algiers Declaration of November 1988 the PLO proclaimed an independent Palestinian state on the West Bank and the Gaza Strip and raised the prospect of recognizing Israel's right to exist. This was largely based on a 1947 UN proposal to divide Palestine into separate Jewish and Arab states, a cornerstone of Arafat's peace plan. Further, Arafat declared before the United Nations that the PLO renounced terrorism once and for all, and supported the right of all parties to live in peace—Israel included. Named President of the Palestinian government in exile in 1989, Arafat faced opposition from hardliners and Syrian-backed Palestinians within the PLO. His peace proposals were accepted later by Israel. The United States declared itself ready to negotiate, and by the year's end some 70 countries had recognized the PLO. This diplomatic victory was undermined when Arafat backed Iraq in the Persian Gulf War. Hussein's 1990 invasion of Kuwait split the Arab world into pro-and anti-Iraq camps.

Although long deemed a "terrorist organization" by Israel, the PLO recognized Israel in 1990. Arafat's peace proposals were accepted later by Israel. In 1993 Arafat exchanged letters of PLO-Israel recognition with former Israeli Prime Minister Yitzhak Rabin after secret talks in Oslo which led to what is known as Oslo Agreement about Palestinian self-rule in West Bank and Gaza Strip under the Palestinian National Authority (PNA) In 1993, Arafat and Yitzhak Rabin forged a peace agreement, which provided for the gradual withdrawal of Israeli troops from the Gaza Strip and West Bank. The Palestinian Authority—the Palestinian governing body in the occupied territories—was created under the 1993 peace agreement. The Palestinian Authority's legislative body, the 88-seat Palestinian Council, was elected in January 1996, and Arafat won a landslide victory as its president.

Rabin and Arafat shared a Nobel Peace Prize in 1994 for their achievement in bringing peace.

Arafat has been criticized by Israel and others for a lack of control over extremist Palestinians such as Hamas. Arafat has vowed to crack down, and repeatedly has expressed sorrow over Hamas' terrorist acts, but remains the champion of Palestinian rights and their quest for a homeland. Referring to the necessity to pursue the quest for peace, Arafat, in his acceptance speech upon receiving the Nobel Peace Prize, stated: "As long as we have decided to coexist and live in peace, then we should coexist on a solid basis that can last through all time and that is acceptable to the future generations. In this context, full withdrawal from the West Bank and the Gaza Strip requires deep discussions about the settlements that cut through geographic and political unity, prevent free movement between the areas of the West Bank and the Strip, and create hotbeds of tension that conflict with the spirit of peace, which we want to be free of anything that spoils its purity."

Arafat was grim and shaken when he learned of the assassination of Yitzhak Rabin with whom he shared the Nobel Peace Prize, along with Shimon Peres. He was thinking of the peace process and said, "I hope that . . . the Israelis and the Palestinians have the ability to overcome the tragedy against the peace process." Later, in a sign of renewed momentum in the peace process, Arafat and Shimon Peres sat down for talks in Washington on April 30,1996. The Israelis and the Palestinians were due to sign a final peace agreement a week later. On June 4,1996, in his first extended public comments after Israeli elections, Arafat warned against any attempt to reverse the course of Middle East peace process. "The peace process has begun. And the peace train must reach the terminal because the forces for peace in the world will not allow the hands of the clock to be turned back to the times of calamity." In effect, Arafat was saying that the commitments Israel has made to the Palestinians must be honored.

On January 19,1997, greeted by more than 60,000 jubilant Palestinians, Yasser Arafat arrived in Hebron Sunday to celebrate the Palestinian takeover of the city after three decades of Israeli occupation. For Arafat, it was his first visit in more than 30 years to Hebron, the last West Bank city to come under Palestinian rule. Arafat was asked if he trusted the new Israeli Prime Minister Benjamin Netanyahu. "Now we can say that we are friends and that we are partners in the peace process," he said.

In a conversation with a group of Americans in Tunis, Arafat was asked about his place in history: "I hope my people will say I found a home for them; a place in which to live and be buried," Arafat replied. "Imagine the difficulty I faced finding a burial place for the Palestinian representing Kuwait at the United Nations. It took eleven days to find a suitable location. In the end I found a graveyard in one of the churches on the green line between East and West Beirut. We buried him while under fire."

Biography

Yasser Arafat was born Mohammed Yasser Abdul-raju Qudwa Al-Husseini on August 24,1929 in Cairo, Egypt. He lived in both Cairo and Jerusalem during his childhood while escorting his father who was a very rich merchant. His mother died when he was 4, and his father sent him to live with a married uncle in Jerusalem. As a teenager in the 1940s, Arafat became involved in the Palestinian cause. Before the Arabs were defeated by Israel in 1948, Arafat was a leader in the Palestinian effort to smuggle arms into the territory.

After the war, Arafat studied civil engineering at the University of Cairo. He headed the Palestinian Students League and, by the time he graduated, was committed to forming a group that would free Palestine from Israeli occupation. In 1956 he founded Al Fatah, an underground terrorist organization. At first Al Fatah was ignored by larger Arab nations such as Egypt, Syria, and Jordan, which had formed their own group—the Palestine Liberation Organization.

It was not until the 1967 Arab-Israeli War, when the Arabs lost the Gaza Strip, Golan Heights and West Bank, that Arab nations turned to Arafat. In 1968 he became the leader of the PLO. For two decades the PLO launched bloody attacks on Israel, and Arafat gained a reputation as a ruthless terrorist. But by 1988, he told the United Nations that the PLO would recognize Israel as a sovereign state,

Arafat had warmed to diplomacy. Then in 1993, the unthinkable happened. The terrorist leader, who had rarely been seen without his signature ghutra and scruffy beard, met with his avowed enemies. The secret peace talks in Norway led to the Oslo Peace Accords with Israeli Prime Minister Yitzak Rabin. The agreement granted limited Palestinian self-rule and earned Arafat, Rabin and Israeli Foreign Minister Shimon Peres the 1994 Nobel Peace Prize. In January 1996 Arafat was elected the first president of the Palestinian Council governing the West Bank and Gaza Strip.

Bibliography

Beres L R 1997 "Commentary: Oslo Four Years Later: "Peace", Arson and the Burning of Israel." http://www.

btzedek.co.il/comm49.htm

Brittanica Book of the Year 1995 "The Year in Review: People of 1994."

Crane D. 1997 "Netanyahu, Arafat agree to new talks on Mideast peace," *Toronto Star*. http://proquest.umi.com/

CNN Newsmaker Profiles 1998 "Yasser Arafat: Palestinian Leader." http://cnn.com. resources/ newswsmakers/world/ middle.east/arafat.html

CNN Interactive 1996 "Peres, Arafat Meet in Washington." Israel Ministry of Foreign Affairs 1994 Remarks by PLO

Chairman Yasser Arafat on Receiving the Nobel Peace Prize. http://www.israel.org./peace/plonobel.html

Nobel Peace Prize Internet Archive 1994 "Yasser Arafat: 1994 Nobel Prize in Peace." http://nobelprizes.com/nobel/ peace/1994a.html

Newsmakers 1989 "Arafat."

Palestinian National Authority 1998 "The President." http:// www.pna. org/ mininfo/who/president.htm

PEDRO B. BERNALDEZ

Pugwash Conferences on Science and World Affairs
(1995)

On July 9,1957, eleven scientists issued in London a resolution, to wit: "In view of the fact that in any future world war nuclear weapons will certainly be employed, and that such weapons threaten the continued existence of mankind, we urge the Governments to realize, and to acknowledge publicly, that their purpose cannot be furthered by a world war, and we urge them, consequently to find peaceful means for the settlement of all matters of dispute between them." This resolution capped the so-called "Russell-Einstein Manifesto," which, in effect, formed the basis for the establishment of an antinuclear war and weapons movement, the Pugwash Conferences. This Manifesto "solidified into an institution" after Josef Rotblat, one of the signatories, organized a meeting of scientists and others in 1957 at the summer home of an industrialist named Cyrus Eaton in Pugwash, Nova Scotia.

The Pugwash Conferences embarked to wage the battle of keeping the world free from nuclear weapons in the heat of the Cold War—and beyond. For even after the superpower competition for nuclear superpower supremacy had ended, other nuclear powers continued their quest for nuclear might. Thus, in the wake of the nuclear detonations by France and China in 1995, the Nobel Peace Prize was granted to Josef Rotblat and to the Pugwash Conferences on Science and World Affairs. "One of the reasons for the Prize is a sort of protest against testing of nuclear weapons and nuclear arms in general, intimated Francis Sejersted, chairman of the Prize committee. In awarding the Prize, therefore, the Nobel Committee claimed it wanted to send a message of protest to France and China over the nuclear weapons tests they recently conducted despite widespread international opposition. Rotblat said he considered the French and Chinese testing programs "as an outrage." He further

asserted "the French testing program had put nuclear weapons back in the public eye after they had become less of an issue with the end of the Cold War."

Officially, the Norwegian Nobel Committee announced that it has decided to award the 1995 Nobel Peace Prize to the Pugwash Conferences on Science and World Affairs along with its founder, Josef Rotblat, "for their efforts to diminish the part played by nuclear arms in international politics and in the longer run to eliminate such arms." The awarding of the rites took place 40 years since the issuing of the Russell-Einstein Manifesto.

The Conferences are based on the recongnition of the responsibility of scientists for their inventions and they have underlined the catastrophic consequences of the use of the new weapons. Likewise, they have brought together scientists and decision-makers to collaborate across political divides on constructive proposals for reducing the nuclear threat.

The purpose of the Pugwash Conferences is to bring together, from around the world, influential scholars and public figures concerned with reducing the danger of armed conflict and seeking cooperative solutions for global problems. Meeting in private as individual rather than as representatives of governments or institutions, Pugwash participants exchange views and explore alternative approaches to arms control and tension reduction "with a combination of candor, continuity, and flexibility seldom attained in official discussions and negotiations'. But due to the stature and reputation which participants hold in their home countries," insights from Pugwash discussions tend to penetrate quickly to the appropriate levels of official policy-making.

The Pugwash conferences have a loose organizational structure with Josef Rotblat, President of Pugwash and the titular head of the organization and the

Secretary General having the overall executive responsibility. There are over thirty National Pugwash Groups organized independently and approximately twelve Student/Young Pugwash Groups.

Since 1957, in by-invitation-only meetings, Pugwash organizers have brought together famous scientists and scholars dedicated to nuclear disarmament and other topics. With the conference participants attending as private individuals, the conferences have been credited with wielding substantial behind-the-scenes influence on global anti-weapon and peace treaties of the past 40 years. Over the years, the mix of Pugwashites has evolved with the changing social and scientific climate. "In the very beginning it was essentially all physicists," recalled Pugwash secretary general Francesco Calogero, "(n)owadays it has expanded to scientists from all disciplines.

It must be recalled that the Conferences were founded in Nova Scotia and are based in London. They have worked behind the scenes to get scientists and policymakers to "take responsibility for the inventions and their policies." The Nobel Peace Prize citation noted the group's "desire to see all nuclear arms destroyed and, ultimately, in a vision of other solutions to international "disputes than war." "The Conferences . . . have underline the catastrophic consequences of the new weapons," the citation said. "They have brought together scientists and decision-makers to collaborate across political divides on constructive proposals for reducing the nuclear threat."

The Conferences are founded in the desire to see all nuclear arms destroyed and ultimately in a vision of other solutions to international disputes to war. The 1995 Pugwash conference in Hiroshima declared that the opportunity had come of approaching those goals. Although there had been no official connection to the Pugwash Conferences, experts claim that the organization has played an influential role in some of the world's most famous anti-weapons conventions. Having provided avenues for discussion among scholars from the East and the West, it is believed that his dialogue had helped lay the foundation for such agreements as the Partial Test Ban Treaty of 1963, the Non-Proliferation Treaty of 1968, and the Biological Weapons Convention of 1972.

In the almost forty years since the first conference, there have been more than 200 Pugwash sponsored meetings attended by nearly 10,000 participants. Pugwash members convene under very different global circumstances from surrounding the meeting of the first twenty-two conferees in Nova Scotia. The end of the Cold War is said to have "affected Pugwash in a unique channel of communication between the intellectual communities of many cultural-ideological persuasions. Now there are much more opportunities for contact. In a sense this puts a challenge to us because, whereas, in the past it was just enough to have a dialogue, now just having a dialogue is no longer an achievement in itself," Francesco Calogero expounded.

Moreover, although nuclear disarmament remains Pugwash's main concern, the subjects tackled at annual conferences and workshops have branched out in a number of directions. "The range of issues and topics has expanded greatly, particularly with the considerable interest that people have in environmental issues and in some of the problems of developing countries," observed United States Pugwash Committee co-chairman Judith Reppy. "The future that we have to be concerned with is the problem of the developing world—the disparity of income, the hunger—all of the discoveries that arise from poverty" claimed former Pugwash secretary general Martin Kaplan.

In accepting the Nobel Peace Prize in 1995 for the organization, John Hildren, then chairman of the Pugwash Council, concluded his Nobel lecture:

Clearly, then, the work of Pugwash—and of the other nongovernmental organizations that labored through the Cold War years to build up peaceful cooperation and build down military confrontation—is far from done. The agenda of dangers still to be overcome is hardly less daunting than the one faced by the founders of the Pugwash Conferences in the Cold War gloom of the 1960s. But the world did finally escape the Cold War and with a bit of luck, a bit of wisdom, and a lot of work it may escape the remaining dangers, too.

History

The Pugwash Conferences on Science and World Affairs, co-winner of the 1995 Nobel Peace Prize, with Josef Rotblat, its founder, trace their origins to the Russell-Einstein Manifesto which was issued by eleven scientists in July 9, 1957 in London. The Conferences are based on the recognition of the responsibility of scientists for their inventions. They are founded in the desire to seek all nuclear arms destroyed and, ultimately, in a vision of other solutions to international disputes than war.

The signatories of the Manifesto—Max Born, Perry W. Bridgman, Albert Einstein, Leopold Infled, Frederic Joliot-Curie, Herman J. Muller, Linus Pauling, Cecil F. Powell, Josef Rotblat, Bertrand Russell, and Hideki Yukawa—stressed that "(in) view of the fact that in any future world war nuclear weapons will certainly be employed, and that such weapons threaten the continued existence of mankind, we urge the governments of the world to realize, and to acknowledge publicly, that their purposes can not be furthered by a world war, and we urge them, consequently, to find peaceful means for the settlement of all members of disputes between them."

The Pugwash Conferences take their name from the tiny Canadian village of Pugwash, Nova Scotia, where the first such meeting was held. Pugwash was the site of the summer retreat owned by US industrialist Cyrus Eaton, who sponsored the conference. Pugwash means shallow waters in the language of the Micmac Indians of Canada's Atlantic provinces. The 1957 meeting was attended by 22 eminent scientists—seven from the USA, three each from the former Soviet Union and Japan, two each from the United Kingdom and Canada and one each from Australia, Austria, China, France, and Poland.

Even before the first Pugwash conference, Josef Rotblat, co-winner of the Nobel Peace Prize, is said to have already taken a personal stand against nuclear weapons. In 1944, he walked out on his research at the Manhattan Project laboratory in Los Alamos, New Mexico. "When it became evident, toward the end of 1944, that the Germans had abandoned their bomb project, the whole purpose of my being in Los Alamos ceased to be, and I asked for permission to leave and to return to Britain," wrote Rotblat in 1985. It had been rumored also that someone has told Rotblat that the nuclear weapons of the United States had been targeted on the former Soviet Union rather than Germany.

Subsequently, through his work as co-founder of the Atomic Scientists Association and in developing the "Atom Train," a traveling exhibition on the benefits and danger of nuclear energy, he met Bertrand Russell. This affiliation led to the drafting of the Manifesto and, eventually, to the Pugwash Conferences. Science historians and nuclear-age analysts maintain that the Conferences have played an influential role in some of the world's most famous anti-weapons conventions. Through unofficial channels, "the Pugwash Conferences kept the lines of communication open among scholars on both sides of the Iron Curtain." Since the first meeting in Pugwash, Nova Scotia there evolved both continuing series of meetings at locations all over the world (with a growing number and greater diversity of participants) and a rather decentralized organizational structure to coordinate and finance the activities. By the end of 1995, there had been over 210 Pugwash Conferences, Symposia, and workshops, with a total attendance of some 10,000 individuals.

In restrospect, the first half of Pugwash four-decade history coincided with some of the most frigid years of the Cold War, marked by the Berlin Crisis, the Cuban Missile Crisis, the invasion of Czechoslovakia, and the Vietnam War. In this period of strained official relations and few unofficial channels, the fora and lines of communication provided by Pugwash played useful background roles in helping lay the groundwork for the Partial Test Ban Treaty of 1963, the Non-Proliferation Treaty of 1968, the Anti-Ballistic Missile Treaty of 1972, the Biological Weapons Convention of 1972, and the Chemical Weapons Convention of 1993. Pugwash meetings have continued till the present to play an important role in bringing together key analysts and policy advisers for sustained, in-depth discussions of the crucial arms-control issues. Pugwash has also extended its concerns to include problems of development and the environment.

Starting in January 1980, Pugwash's series of Workshops on nuclear forces provided an off-the-record forum where not only military and civilian analysts but also some members of the official negotiations teams compared notes and sought solutions to obstacles in the official negotiations. The Pugwash chemical and biological warfare workshops (22 of them since 1974) have similarly engaged technical experts from the negotiating term, as well as academic and industry experts; this series led in early 1987 to the first visit of Western chemical weapons specialists to an Eastern European chemical complex, and Pugwash contacts were also instrumental in setting up the first access by a U.S. expert to the medical records associated with the disputed 1979 antharx outbreak in Sverdlosk. The Pugwash study group on conventional forces, which originated in the European Security Working Group of the 1982 Pugwash Conference in Warsaw, held in meetings and played a pioneering role in developing concepts for restructuring conventional forces and doctrines into modes less suited for attack, and gaining credibility for these concepts all over the world.

In recognition of their modest but significant achievements, Pugwash Conferences have received international awards: Olympia Prize, Onassis Foundation, 1987; Feltrinelli Prize, Academia Nazionale dei Lincei; Einstein Gold Medal, UNESCO, 1989; and the Nobel Peace Prize, 1995.

Bibliography

Associated Press 1995 "Pugwash Conferences wins 1995 peace prize." http.://www.nanado.net/newsroom/ntn/world/101395/world 152t.html

Broad J M "Champion or meddler, he sees his cause as noble," *Union Tribune*. http://proquest.umi.com/

Kreeger K Y "Nobel Peace Prize Signals New Beginning for Pugwash." http://www.the-scientist.library.upenn.edu/yr1996/jan/pugwash_960108.html

Nobel Prize Award 1995 "The Nobel Prize-Oct.13,1995." http://www.qmw.ac.uk./pugwash/nobel/nobel.html

Pugwash Conferences on Science and World Affairs Internet Archive "A Brief Description." http://www.pugwash.org/archive/description. htm

Reuter Information Service "Text of the 1995 Nobel Peace Prize citation." http://www.nando.net/newsroom/ntn/world/ 101395/ world 152t_side1.html

The Norwegian Nobel Committee Press Release 1995 "The

Nobel Peace Prize for 1995. http://www.nobel.se/laureates/peace-1995press. html

PEDRO B. BERNALDEZ

Joseph Rotblat
(1995)

Prof, Sir Joseph Rotblat is emeritus professor of physics at the University of London, former Secretary-General (1957-73) and emeritus President (1988-1997) of the Pugwash Conferences on Science and World Affairs, and a recipient of the 1995 Nobel Prize for Peace.

Rotblat was born on November 4, 1908 in Warsaw, now Poland and is a British citizen since 1946. He was born and grew up in the same street in Warsaw as one of the best scientists of this century, Marie Curie, and followed her footstep having worked at the Radiological Laboratory of Scientific Society of Warsaw for some time.

Rotblat studied Physics at the Free University of Warsaw and graduated with MA in 1932. He received a Doctor of Physics degree at the University of Warsaw in 1939, a PhD degree at the University of Liverpool in 1950, and a Doctor of Science degree at the University of London in 1953. He also received numerous honorary doctor of science degrees and honors from various academic societies as well as governments. He received the Einstein Peace Prize in 1992 and shared the 1995 Nobel Prize for Peace with the Pugwash Conferences on Science and World Affairs in recognition of his devotion to world peace. Rotblat became the knight Commander of the Order of St. Michael and St. George (KCMG) in 1998.

During the Second World War he lost his family in the Holocaust and himself fled Hitler's Germany and settled in England. Rotblat believed that Germans were about to develop the atom bomb. He was convinced that the only way to stop Hitler from using it was to develop it before them. He began to work on the atom bomb already in 1939 at the laboratory at the University of Liverpool and from 1942 continued his work at Los Alamos after joining the Manhattan Project of the US government. The bomb was not to be used against Germany but to deter Hitler from using it. When it became clear for such weapon and was the only scientist to resign from the Manhattan Project. For this decision Rotblat had to leave the US and was barred from entering it for nearly twenty years. For unknown reasons all his personal belongings including his research findings disappeared in the US on the way to England.

After returning to England he continued his work at the University of Liverpool until 1949. He then moved to London and completely changed the direction of his research and devoted his researches to the study of the chemistry of radioactive substances and the medical applications of these substances. He was a professor of physics at the University of London until his retirement in 1976. During this time he worked as the chief physicist at the St. Bartholomew's Hospital Medical College. Although Rotblat left the bomb project, he was devastated when the bomb was dropped on Hiroshima and nagasaki in 1945. In 1972 while he was visiting Japan he knelt down in Hiroshima and apologized to japanese for his part in developing the atom bomb.

At the height of the Cold War, Rotblat succeeded in convincing Bertrand Russell and other prominent scientist to alert the danger of a nuclear war. In 1955 Albert Einstein, Russell, Rotblat and 8 other prominent scientists including Frederic Joliot-Curie and linus Pauling issued in london a manifesto, known as the Russell-Einstein Manifesto, called on scientists to assemble in conference and adopt a resolution to urge the governments of the world to find peaceful means for the settlement of all matters of dispute between them. The manifesto laid the foundation for the first Conference in 1957 in the remote village of Pugwash in Canada's Nova Scotia province. Over forty years since then they have brought together scientists and decision-makers to collaborate across political divides on constructive proposals for reducing the nuclear threat.

Rotblat personally guided the activities of the Pugwash from the very beginning and was the main pillar of the Movement. In fact, without his personal conviction and devotion there would have been no Pugwash conferences. He developed the Pugwash into a highly influential but unique, international, nongovernmental forum for the development and exchange of ideas about reducing armaments and building security around the world in the last forty years. He was Secretary-General from 1957 to 1973 and president from 1988 to 1997 of the Pugwash. He not only organized all the conferences and workshops, but also edited the newsletters and proceedings of the Pugwash. In 1997 at the age of 89 he decided to retire from leadership of the Pugwash, but he is still active as usual.

Rotblat has devoted the greater part of his long life to the struggle to eliminate nuclear weapons which he once anticipated to develop. His high standing as a scientist and peace advocate earned him much respect among scientists and leaders around the world. He has achieved much more than bringing scientists and influential people together through the world-renowned Pugwash in order to reduce the danger of nuclear holocaust, and contributed much in ending the Cold War between East and West. He played vital roles in solving many urgent problems and in sustaining peace and averting crisis in many conflict ridden regions. Rotblat is not only the champion of peace but one of the great thinkers and humanists of this century. His vision of a nuclear-weapon-free-world is no longer a mere fallacy or an illusion but a possibility. His contribution to understanding the danger of nuclear Holocaust is having far reaching impact on decision makers and scientists. He is a man of boundless energy and vision.

Rotblat is a fellow of the Royal Society of London and a foreign member of the Academy of Sciences of the US, Russia, Poland, Ukraine and other countries. Rotblat was decorated with the highest honor of his native Poland in 1998. He is not only known for his activities through the Pugwash, but also widely recognized for his research work in the field of nuclear medicine. Besides devoting himself fully to the Pugwash, he has published more than 400 scientific papers including 20 books in the field of nuclear physics, medical physics and radiation biology, radiation hazards and the consequences of nuclear war, nuclear power and proliferation of nuclear weapons, arms control and disarmament, and on the Pugwash movement and the social responsibility of scientists.

Biography

The fifth of seven children, Joseph Rotblat was born into a Jewish family in Warsaw, Poland, on November 4, 1908. His father, Zygmunt Rotblat, prospered as a shipper of paper until World War I, when his business failed and the family plunged into poverty. "It came to the stage of literally hunger, starvation . . . ," Joseph Rotblat recalled to Susan Landau for the *Bulletin of Atomic Scientists* (January/Feb-

ruary 1996). "One had to fight for one's survival." To get by, the family sold vodka that they distilled illegally at home. Zygmunt Rotblat's business never recovered, and after the war, Joseph Rotblat became an electrician. He worked outside, laying cable in Warsaw streets—a painfully difficult task in freezing weather. Determined to make a better life for himself, he enrolled at the University of Warsaw as a night student, and in 1932 he earned a master's degree in physics. While studying for his Ph.D., he began working at the Radiation Laboratory of Warsaw under the physicist Ludwik Wertenstein. In reminiscing about Rotblat to Susan Landau, a coworker of his at the laboratory said, "There is hardly a man I know more devoted to science. Highly honest, a very good friend. He had high solidarity with all of his colleagues."

Among the professional posts he has held are the following: research fellow of radiological laboratory of Scientific Society of Warsaw (1933-39); Assistant Director of Atomic Physics Institute of Free University of Poland (1937-39); Oliver Lodge Fellow (1939); research on atom bomb at the University of Liverpool and in Los Alamos (1939-44); Senior lecturer at the Department of Physics, Liverpool University (1945-49); Professor of Physics in the University of London at St. Bartholomew's Hospital Medical College (1950-76); and Chief Physicist at St, Bartholomew's Hospital.

Likewise he has had occupied other appointments as follow: chairman, Photographic Emulsion Panel of the UK Nuclear Physics Committee (1945-50); chairman, Cyclotron Panel of the UK Nuclear Physics Committee (1946-50); co-founder of Atomic Scientists Association (1946-59); organized the Atom Train exhibition for the education on the peaceful and military applications of nuclear energy (1947-50); signatory of the Russell-Einstein Manifesto: chaired press conference (1955); secretary-general of the Pugwash Conferences on Science and World Affairs (1957-63); editor-in-chief of *Physics in Medicine and Biology* (1960-72); co-founder and member of governing board of the Stockholm International Peace Research Institute (1966-71); co-founder of UK Panel on Gamma and Electron Irradiation (1966); president, Hospital Physicists' Association (1969-70); president, British Institute of Radiology (1971-71); President, International Science Forum (1972-75); Member, Advisory Committee on Medical Research, World Health Organization (1972-75); Treasurer. St. Bartholomew's Hospital Medical College (1974-76); Vice Dean, Faculty of Science, University of London (1974-76); Montague Visiting Professor of International Relations, University of Edinburgh (1975-76); Governor, Voluntary Hospital of St. Bartholomew in London (1977); visiting professor of Physics, University of Penang, Malaysia (1977-78); Chairman of the British Pugwash Group (1978-88); member of the Management Group of

World Health Organization (1984-90; and president, Pugwash Conferences on Science and World Affairs (1988-present).

Rotblat at 87 acts like a man half his age. He works in London and shares a dwelling there with one of his sisters-in-law. He has written, co-written, or edited nearly two dozen books, and from 1960 to 1972 he edited the journal *Physics in Medicine and Biology*. He has received many awards in addition to the Nobel Peace Prize, among them the 1983 Bertrand Russell Society Award and the 1992 Albert Einstein Peace Prize.

See also: *Pugwash Movement; Pugwash Conferences on Science and World Affairs*

Bibliography —————————————

Bruce M, Milne T (eds.) 1999 The Force of Reason: Eliminating Nuclear Weapons and Ending War. Macmillan, London

Moore M 1997 forty Years of Pugwash, The Bulletin of Atomic Scientists, Volume 53, Number 6, p. 40-45

Pugwash Council 1997 Pugwash Newsletters November 1997. Pugwash Office, London

Rotblat J 1972 Scientists in the Quest for Peace. MIT Press, Cambridge, Massachusetts

Rotblat J, Steinberger J, Udgaonkar B (eds.) 1993 A Nuclear-Weapon-Free World: Desirable? Feasible? Westview Press, Colorado

PEDRO B. BERNALDEZ; MARK BYUNG-MOON SUH

Jose Ramos-Horta
(1996)

The Norwegian Nobel Committee granted the Nobel Peace Prize for 1996 to Jose Ramos-Horta, together with Carlos Filipe Ximenes Belo "for their work towards a just and peaceful solution to the conflict in East Timor." The citation further explained " Ramos-Horta has been the leading international spokesman for East Timor's cause since 1975. Recently he has made a significant contribution through the reconciliation talks and by working out a peace plan." Stressing the reason for awarding the Peace Prize to the two, the Committee expressed that it wanted "to honor their sustained and self-sacrificing contributions for a small but oppressed people . . . and hopes that this award will spur efforts to find a diplomatic solution to the conflict in East Timor based on the people's rights to self-determination."

Jose Ramos-Horta was born on December 26, 1949, in Dili-East Timor, from a Timorese mother and Portuguese father who had been exiled to East Timor by the Salazar dictatorship. He was educated in a Catholic mission in the isolated village of Soibada, later chosen by the Fretilin as headquarters after the Indonesian invasion. Of his eleven brothers and sisters, four were killed by the Indonesian military.

He was actively involved in the development of political awareness in East Timor which caused him to be banned from his homeland for two years in 1970-1971 and sent to Mozambique for subversive allegations against the Portuguese regime—a family tradition. His grandfather too had suffered exile, from Portugal to Azores, then Cape Verde, Guinea Bissau and finally East Timor.

A moderating influence in the emerging Timorese nationalism, he was then mandated by the pro-independence parties to represent East Timor abroad. He left the island three days before the Indonesian troops invaded. In December 1975, he arrived in New York to address the UN Security Council and urged them to take action in the face of the Indonesian military onslaught which resulted in over 200,000 East Timorese deaths between 1976 and 1981. In 1975, Indonesia invaded and occupied the former Portuguese colony of some 800,000 people whose largely Catholic population has been systematically oppressed since then. According to the Nobel Committee, it has been estimated that one-third of the population of East Timor lost their lives due to starvation, epidemics, war and terror.

Jose Ramos-Horta was the permanent representative of the Fretilin to the UN for the ensuing ten years, and tells of his experience as a diplomat in *Funu: the Unfinished Saga of East Timor*. He is Special Representative of the National Council Of Maubere Resistance (CNRM), the umbrella organization of pro-independence movements and activists inside and outside East Timor; and Personal Representative of Xanana Gusmao, leader of the resistance in prison since 1992.

Jose Ramos-Horta has spent the last 22 years denouncing the invasion and annexation of his homeland by Indonesia, and defending the rights of the East Timorese people to self-determination. He has presented the case of East Timor and pleaded for the respect of human rights where they are violated. He has spoken before the UN Security Council, the Fourth Committee of the UN General Assembly, the UN Special Committee on Decolonization, the UN Commission on Human Rights, the Council on Foreign Relations, and the European Parliament. Ramos-Horta is now the Special Representative of the National Council of Maubere Resistance (CNRM), an umbrella organization of pro-independence movements and activists inside and outside East Timor; as well as Personal Representative of imprisoned resistance leader, Xanana Gusmao.

In 1992, he formally presented the CNRM's three-stage plan before the European Parliament. The plan calls for a phased resolution to the conflict, involving withdrawal of Indonesian troops, release of political prisoners, respect for human rights and the stationing of UN agencies in East Timor. The final phase of the plan calls for a period of autonomy followed by a UN-supervised referendum through which the East Timorese people could choose between independence, integration into Indonesia or free association with Portugal.

In October 1994, he headed a delegation of pro-independence East Timorese who met publicly with Indonesia's Foreign Minister, Ali Alatas as part of an on-going dialogue under UN auspices. This was the first public meeting between an Indonesian Foreign Minister and external leaders of East Timor since Indonesia invaded. He also participated in the UN sponsored talks which brought together East Timorese from both inside and outside the country in Austria in 1995 and 1996.

In 1997, before Ramos-Horta came to Norway to receive the Prize, he intimated his ideas to *News of Norway*. "The lack of awareness and information is the worst enemy for democracy," Ramos-Horta claimed. "The prize will make an enormous difference for the East Timor cause. In the long run I am totally convinced that the prize will have an impact on the democratic process in my country," he continued.

Mr. Ramos-Horta thought then that pressure should be directed at Indonesia by the European Union, the United States, and the UN to make Indonesia withdraw its troops. The Nobel Committee called for a diplomatic solution to the conflict in East Timor based on the people's right to self-determination. In this light, Ramos-Horta hoped Norway at one point might be invited to Indonesia to play somewhat the same type of mediator role that it played in the Middle East in 1993. Portugal should also play a central role. Ramos-Horta has been in Norway several times, first in 1976 to inform Norwegian parliamentarians about the situation in his home country. He visited

again in 1993 to receive the Rafto Prize, a human rights award conferred in Bergen.

On February 7, 1997 Ramos-Horta was in Adelaide, Australia where he spoke to large audience on his recurring plea for Australia's support to the East Timor cause. He was greeted by a long and hearty standing ovation by an emotional crowd. For sure, most of the crowd was undoubtedly aware of the history of Indonesia's invasion of Timor. The Australian government since 1975 came under criticism for their involvement with the Indonesian regime. Successive Australian governments have done little to change Indonesian minds about Timor and "have provided military assistance to the Indonesian army which has continued to kill numerous Timorese," Darren Jones of the University of Adelaide, asserted.

Ramos-Horta intimated that he has been pessimistic about the Australian government's attitude and he did not see any will or imagination in the government to go against two decades of an entrenched policy. But there had been positive actions by the Australian government such as discreetly raising the issue to the Indonesian government for a few times and acting directly to alleviate poverty inside East Timor. Australia has made reasonably positive contribution through AusAid in East Timor. Aside from official actions, "the involvement of Australian non-government organizations and the public at large in the solidarity movement," is seen by Ramos-Horta as helping the East Timor case in a very significant way.

On the other hand, Ramos-Horta claimed that New Zealand has been willing to play a role, "making a discrete but significant shift that shows some courage and it has not come about only after the Nobel Prize announcement. New Zealand no longer holds the view that the annexation of East Timor is irreversible. He further revealed "the foreign minister of New Zealand, Don McKinnon, met with the United Nations Secretary General . . . and East Timor was high on his list of topics for discussion with Kofi Annan . . . ."

Although Ramos-Horta finds most of the international community's complacent acceptance of the invasion "morally despicable," he praises the few steps the US and others have taken to resolve the situation. The Clinton administration has banned the sale of small weapons and riot-control equipment to Indonesia, voted in favor of a UN resolution supporting East Timor in 1993, and repeatedly raised human rights issues with Indonesia. "These are very good things, although there is much more the US can do," he says. In fact, Ramos-Horta is confident the US now has the power to single-handedly end the years of repression and bring about a negotiated settlement. "The key here is for President Clinton himself to feel personally motivated either out of moral conviction or political expediency," he says, noting that large contributions from Indonesians may have kept Clinton from meeting him and the bishop.

"It could take another three to five years, but I'm hopeful it will be resolved," Ramos-Horta says of the lingering problem of East Timor. With the removal of Suharto from power, it remains to be seen whether the East Timor case, which Ramos-Horta unceasingly champions, will take a new twist.

Biography

Jose Ramos-Horta was born on December 26, 1949 in Dili, East Timor. His grandfather was a Portuguese, who had been exiled to Portuguese African colonies thence to East Timor. His father was a Portuguese naval gunner, who was also exiled to East Timor in 1936. His mother is a Timorese, who is currently living in Sydney. There were eleven children in his family but four were killed by the Indonesian military. Like most East Timorese, he is Catholic by religion.

He attended primary school at the Catholic Mission School, Soibada, East Timor and secondary school at the Liceu Dr Machado, Dili, East Timor. He studied International Law at The Hague Academy of International Law in 1983 and trained in Human Rights Law at the International Institute of Human Rights in Strasbourg, France. He also attended post-graduate courses in American Foreign Policy at the Columbia University, New York and in 1984, he completed an MA in Peace Studies at Antioch University, Ohio.

From 1949 to 1970, East Timor was his domicile and stayed in 1970 to 1971 in Mozambique having been exiled from East Timor. During the period 1972 to 1975 he was again in East Timor, occasionally traveling overseas. From 1976 to 1990, he was in the United States and from 1990 to the present, his residence is in Sydney and Lisbon.

He can be said not short of career experiences. He had been employed as a journalist in East Timor from 1969 to 1974. He helped establish a new East Timorese political party, Fretilin in 1974 to 1975. In September to December 1975, he held the post of Minister of External Relations and Information of the first Provisional government of East Timor, prior to the Indonesian invasion. From 1976 to 1985 he was a permanent representative of Fretilin to United Nations in New York from 1986 to date he serves as Special Representative of the National Council of Maubere Resistance (CNRM) overseas. During the period 1987 to 1988 he served as Public Affairs and Media Director of the Mozambique embassy in Washington.

Ramos-Horta presented the CNRM three stage plan to the European Parliament, and Council of Foreign Affairs, New York, in 1992. In 1996 he received the Nobel Peace Prize in Oslo together with Bishop Belo. In pursuit of his mission on behalf of the people of East Timor, he has spoken to and addressed the UN Security Council, Fourth Committee of the UN General Assembly, UN Special Committee on Decolonization, UN Commission on Human Rights, Council on Foreign Relations, New York, and the European Parliament.

He speaks Tetun (first language), Portugese, French, English, and Spanish. Among his literary works, he counts: *Funu: The Unfinished Saga of East Timor, Timor: Amanha em Dili,* and *Dom Quixote, Towards a Peaceful Solution in East Timor,* a booklet of four speeches and numerous articles.

Among his other honors and awards are the: a) fellowship, International Relations, St. Anthony's College, Oxford; b) Doctorate (honoris causa), Pontifical University of Brazil, Campinas; c) Doctorate (Honoris Causa), Antioch University, Ohio; d) Professor Thorolf Rafto Human Rights Prize, 1993 (Norway); e) Gleitzman Foundation Award, 1995 (USA); Unrepresented Nations and Peoples Organization (UNPO) Award, 1996 (Holland); and the Order of Freedom, 1996 (Lisbon), a high level Portuguese government award .

He was once married to Anna Pessoa, an East Timorese judge in Mozambique and he has an only son who was born in 1977 now lives in Mozambique.

Bibliography

Beecher C 1996 "Nobel prizes inspires East Timor activists," *Badger Herald.* http://www.badgerherald.com.news/fall 96

Community Aid Abroad 1997 "East Timor—Path to Peace," *Horizons.* http://www.caa.org.au/horizons/h20/horta.html

International Platform of Jurists for East Timor 1996 "The Nobel Peace Prize for 1996." http://www.antenna.nl/~ipjet/peace/html

News of Norway 1996 "A Peace Laureate's Christmas Wish." http://www.norway.org/dec96/horta.html

Nordic Newsletter of Asian Studies 1996 "The Nobel Peace Prize 1996 and its Implications." http://nias.ku.dk/Nytt/Regional/SoutheastAsia/Articles/timornobel.html

The Nobel Prize Internet Archive 1996 "Jose Ramos-Horta: Winner of the 1996 Nobel Prize in Peace." http://nobel-prizes. com/ Nobel/peace.1996b.html

The Nobel Foundation 1996 "The Nobel Prize in Peace 1996." http://www.nobel.se/announcement-96/peace96.html

WUFI 1998 Dr. Jose Ramos-Horta Profile. http://www.wufie.org.tw/hortapro.html

PEDRO B. BERNALDEZ

Carlos Felipe Ximenes Belo
(1996)

The Norwegian Nobel Committee awarded the Nobel Peace Prize for 1996 jointly to Carlos Felipe Ximenes Belo and Jose Ramos-Horta "for their work towards a just and peaceful solution to the conflict in East Timor."

Committee Chairman Francis Sejersted said that Carlos Belo, bishop of East Timor, "has been the foremost representative of the People of East Timor." The Committee further said that "at the risk of his own life, he has tried to protect his people from infringements by those in power. In his efforts to create a just settlement based on his people's right to self-determination, he has been a constant spokesman for non-violence and dialogue with the Indonesian authorities."

In awarding the 1996 Nobel Peace Prize to Belo and Ramos-Horta, the Norwegian Nobel Committee wanted "to honor their sustained and self-sacrificing contributions for a small but oppressed people." The Nobel Committee also hoped that this award would "spur efforts to find a diplomatic solution to the conflict in East Timor based on the people's right to self-determination."

Sejersted admiringly said of Bishop Belo, "[He] has become much more than a mediator: this man of peace has also become a rallying point for his sorely tried people, a representative of their hope for a better future."

Bishop Belo is the Apostolic Administrator of the diocese of Dili. As the leader of the Catholic Church in East Timor, he must not only administer the needs of the rapidly growing congregations, but live the daily reality of being the center of an international territorial dispute. The Vatican's direct administration of the East Timorese Church reflects the unresolved conflict over East Timorese sovereignty. Therefore, while Bishop Belo must live with all the political machinery of the Indonesian State, and carry an Indonesian passport, his diocese is separate from the Indonesian church.

He constantly travels to the towns and villages of East Timor to hear and respond to the needs of his people. He stresses the importance of the Church having a presence to give strength and protection to people who have suffered greatly over the years.

Like all other Timorese, he lives with the constant presence of the Indonesian military forces that continue to dominate the life and landscape of East Timor. He hears the cries of restless, young people

and old, who are denied the freedom to develop and express their humanity. He speaks out for those who have no voice. His message to their brothers and sisters in Australia is one of peace, justice and reconciliation. He speaks of the need to look forward, to prepare leaders for the future, "who can live and love in justice and peace, who can be a sign of peace amongst their people."

The Bishop advocates nonviolent self-determination for East Timor. By the sheer force of his personality and position, Belo has limited the influence of more militant resisters to Indonesia rule. Often times, the Indonesian government has even solicited Belo's support to help negotiate an end to street riots in Dili and other cities of East Timor.

The history of East Timor consists of a 450-year rule by the Portuguese. After the dictator of Lisbon was overthrown in 1974, the new government wanted to withdraw from the colony. Subsequently, three political parties began to compete for control of the territory, so the Portuguese retreated to a northern island. In 1975, the Indonesian military descended on East Timor to quell the warfare. In 1976 Indonesia "officially" incorporated the territory although sporadic fightings continued until the 1980s. Allegations by critics number the victims of military battles against guerillas to about 200,000. It is claimed that "Indonesia has done more in ten years than the Portuguese in 400 years."

In 1973, about 93 percent of the population was illiterate. But East Timorese claim economic exploitation by military officials is rampant in the area.

Talking about the progress of the peace process in East Timor, Belo said that to make progress in making the East Timorese "become human beings" it is essential "to have dialogue between all parties concerned. In particular all shades of Timorese opinion, and all those individual Timorese whose leadership abilities are recognized by the people, should be involved in any discussion concerning our national future. If justice is to be true then the truth must be heard, as it is perceived and experienced, from all sides. This should include a consultation of the people of East Timor."

Belo claimed that there had, of course, been dialogues of this sort in the past "but it is evident from the social unrest" that the East Timorese suffer in their country "that dissatisfaction with their conclusions persists." For the East Timorese, a happy future would require a testing of public opinion. Sadly, Belo claims that the heavy military presence in East Timor, "far from contributing to peaceful conclusion, is militating against it." He demands therefore that for a fruitful dialogue, "a prerequisite is the reduction, or complete withdrawal, of the armed forces. He called on those concerned: "Stop the violence, stop the oppression, stop the bloodshed! There is no true justice when the innocent still suffer, and when the violators of human dignity do so with seeming impunity."

Biography

Carlos Felipe Ximenes Belo was born in Wailakama, a village in Vemasse, Bacau on February 3, 1948, the fifth child of Domingo Vaz Felipe and Ermelinda Baptista's six children. His father, a school teacher, died when he was two years old. His family had a background of farming and in his childhood, the young Belo developed skills in shepherding water buffaloes in Keikeli, the village of his ancestors.

Belo was sent to missionary school and later graduated from Seminario de Nossa Senorha de Fatima in Dare in 1973. He then left for Portugal and studied at the Novisat Salesian in Lisbon. After a brief return to East Timor in 1974 where he taught at the Salesian College at Fatumaca, he returned to Portugal and studied philosophy at the Instituto Superior de Estudos Teologicos de Lisboa for two years and then another three years at the Universidade Catolica Portuguesa. He then went on to Rome, where he studied Pastoral Theology at the Universita Pontifica Salesiana. In March 1981 he returned to East Timor as Director of Fatumaca College, which is located in the district of Bacau, 130 km east of Dili. Two years later, the Pope appointed him Apostolic Administrator of the Diocese of Dili, which covers the whole of East Timor.

When he was consecrated a bishop, it was a major event, attended by numerous government and church officials and some 30,000 Timorese Catholics. The ceremony was broadcast nationally on Indonesian television. As a leader of the Catholic Church in East Timor, he pushed ahead with programs, to increase the Church's institutional resources, including new schools, seminaries and churches.

Bibliography

Berfield S, Lveard K 1996 "A Nobel Cause," *Asiaweek* October 25

Belo C F X 1996 *The Nobel Lecture*

CAFOD 1996 "A Time for Justice." http://www.tasc.ac.uk/cc/briefing/9706/970613.html

Jakarta Monthly 1992 We want to be free, (August)

Letter to Javier Perez de Cuellar, 1989

Melgreen D 1996 "East Timor's Bishop Belo arrives for Nobel Peace ceremony," Associated Press. http://www.n-jcenter.com/reprise/nobel/nob1209a.html

PEDRO B. BERNALDEZ

Jody Williams
(1997)

The Norwegian Nobel Committee has decided to jointly award the Nobel Peace Prize for 1997 to the International Campaign to Ban Landmines (ICBL) and to the campaign's coordinator Jody Williams for their work for the banning and clearing of anti-personnel mines.

There are at present probably over one hundred million anti-personnel mines scattered over large areas on several continents. Such mines maim and kill indiscriminately and are a major threat to the civilian populations and to the social and economic development of the many countries affected.

The ICBL and Jody Williams started a process which in the space of a few years changed a ban on anti-personnel mines from a vision to a feasible reality. The Convention which will be signed in Ottawa in December 1997 is to a considerable extent a result of their important work.

There are already over 1,000 organizations, large and small, affiliated to the ICBL, making up a network through which it has been possible to express and mediate a broad wave of popular commitment in an unprecedented way. With the governments of several small and medium-sized countries taking the issue up and taking steps to deal with it, this work has grown into a convincing example of an effective policy for peace.

The Norwegian Nobel Committee wishes to express the hope that the Ottawa process will win even wider support. As a model for similar processes in the future, it could prove of decisive importance to the international effort for disarmament and peace.

Williams and the ICBL shared the $1million peace prize for six years of campaigning that resulted in 122 countries signing a treaty banning land mines.

It has been a stunning success for a movement that

began with a sense of desperation. Activists who had worked with land mine victims grew so frustrated at the carnage that they decided to push for the seemingly impossible: a total ban on the devices.

With Williams organizing the effort, the ICBL grew into a global movement backed by more than 1,000 organizations and millions of people, including Princess Diana.

"This campaign was born out of the humanitarian work of the mine-clearer and those putting limbs back on victims," Williams said at the prize ceremony in City Hall, abandoning her prepared text because she said she wanted to speak from the heart.

An estimated 100 million land mines are buried worldwide, killing or maiming an estimated 26,000 people a year. About 80 percent of the victims are civilians.

When Williams arrived for the ceremony, about 2,000 Norwegian children were waiting outside, singing for her and holding candles, flags and banners.

The Nobel prizes were endowed by Alfred Nobel, a Swede who hoped his invention, dynamite, would prove so powerful that it made war impossible. He watched in horror as it was incorporated in weapons and created a peace prize in hopes of preventing war.

"It is a paradox that what we find inside landmines is Nobel's brilliant invention, dynamite," said Francis Sejersted, chairman of the five-man prize committee.

After accepting her medal and diploma, Williams said much remains to be done, such as persuading 40 countries to ratify the treaty to make it binding and convincing holdouts—including the United States, Russia and China—to join.

At treaty negotiations in Oslo in September, the campaign pushed 89 countries to draft a pact calling for immediate elimination of the weapons. The United States walked out of the talks after it could not muster support for watering down the treaty.

The ICBL has been praised by numerous governments and U.N. agencies for being the driving force in the spectacular success of the movement to ban antipersonnel mines. Begun by just a handful of NGOs less than six years ago, the ICBL has played a key role in educating the world about the landmines crisis, and convincing governments to take urgent actions to eliminate the weapon.

The ICBL has also worked in close partnership with the International Committee of the Red Cross and pro-ban governments such as Canada, Austria, Mexico, Belgium, South Africa, and Norway. "The prize is also a recognition that the ban movement represents a new way of conducting international diplomacy, in which middle and smaller powers take the lead in responding to and working with civil society to address urgent humanitarian needs," said Williams.

"In many ways our work has just begun," said Williams. The ICBL has drafted an action plan for promoting the rapid entry into force of the treaty, as well as universalization and monitoring of the treaty, and for expanding programs for mine clearance and victim assistance. "This campaign will not go away. Some might see this as a threat, others a promise. But the ICBL has committed itself to the total eradication of this weapon and to assistance to those who must live with this lethal contamination. When the weapon is completely eradicated, our work might be done."

Biography

Jody Williams is the daughter of a Vermont county judge and a mother who oversees housing projects. She came of age not in Kabul or Luanda or any other of a number of cities where the trauma of war would have given impetus to her quest to eradicate the legacies of the battlefield. Rather, Jody Williams spent much of her life in the serene, clapboard-church-dotted hamlet of Putney, Vermont, USA.

She shared the $1 million award attached to the Nobel Peace Prize for 1997 with her six-year-old coalition, the International Campaign to Ban Landmines (ICBL), which has helped persuade nearly 100 governments to support a treaty to end the production, sale and stockpiling of land mines and to clean up existing minefields around the world. The explosive devices, which can cost as little as $3 apiece and are strewn haphazardly in places like Angola, Cambodia and Bosnia, are responsible for killing or brutally maiming some 26,000 people a year.

Her political biography is easier to follow after Brattleboro High School. She went to the University of Vermont in 1968, rushed the Tri-Delta a sorority during her first year, lost interest during her third, and moved to an off-campus apartment. She has said that "She took part in UVM antiwar demonstrations but was never a leader." After graduating as a French and Spanish major in 1972, she went to Mexico to tutor in English and immerse herself in Spanish. She came back appalled by the chasm between the Mexican upper and lower classes. In 1975 she enrolled in the Master of Arts in Teaching program at SIT in Brattleboro, graduated in 1976, and moved to Washington for graduate work in international studies at the Johns Hopkins center there. After her stint at the Johns Hopkins School of Advanced International Studies, she began her career as an activist, protesting US policy in Central America in the early 1980s. Eventually she became the associate director of the Los Angeles-based humanitarian relief organization Medical Aid to El Salvador.

While the land-mine issue may seem far removed from the lives of many Americans, the urgency of Williams' work is quite clear to a victim like Marianne Holtz of Boise, Idaho, who lost her legs and half her face to the explosives while working with refugees in Zaire. "As a weapon of war, the land mine is inexcusable," says Holtz. "It kills women and children. It kills people long after any battle is over. There is absolutely no argument for it that is valid." Jody Williams is dedicated to ensuring that everyone comes around to that way of thinking.

She has not, however, persuaded the U.S. to disown the mines. Prior to receiving the Nobel Peace Prize, Williams had harsh words for President Clinton, who has refused to sign the treaty until it makes an exception for US land-mine use along the uneasy border between North and South Korea, where 37,000 American soldiers are stationed, and for the use of antipersonnel mines in conjunction with anti-tank mines. Said Williams: "I think it's tragic that President Clinton does not want to be on the side of humanity." And she found it odd that he had not yet called to congratulate her. "I think if the President can call the winner of the Super Bowl, he should call the Nobel Peace Prize winner." If he does call, she knows what she'll say: "What's your problem?"

The Nobel Peace Prize laureate has said partnership between campaign groups and governments creates a new type of superpower. Ms Williams said the real prize for her and the International Campaign to Ban Landmines, which received the award with her, was the Ottawa treaty. "Together we have given the world the possibility of one day living on a truly mine-free planet," she said in her acceptance speech in Oslo, Norway.

She added: "It is amazing. It is historic. It proves that civil society and governments do not have to see themselves as adversaries. It demonstrates that small and middle powers can work together with civil society and address humanitarian concerns with breathtaking speed."

While expressing some reservations about the Ottawa treaty, she said her aim then was to get 40 countries to ratify it in order to make it binding under international law. She said: "Landmines distinguish themselves because once they have been sown, once the soldier walks away from the weapon, the landmine cannot tell the difference between a soldier or a civilian, a woman, a child, a grandmother going out to collect firewood to make the family meal.

Ms Williams said before the Nobel ceremony she remains hopeful of getting the United States to sign up. "It's difficult for the United States but they will feel the pressure to do the right thing. We don't want them as the enemy," Ms Williams, who is an American, said. "Sooner or later they will come on board," she added.

But even as the White House reaffirmed its "rock-solid" position against participation in the accord, Williams was heartened by the news that the once recalcitrant Russia would support the international land-mine ban. The treaty, to be signed in Ottawa in December, will go into effect after 40 nations have ratified it.

What is remarkable about Williams' effort is the speed with which she and her organization have accomplished their mission. Williams was hired by the Vietnam Veterans of America Foundation in 1991 to form an anti-landmine coalition. "When we began, we were just three people sitting in a room," she said. "It was Utopia." The numbers grew quickly. The fruits of her labor resulted in the ICBL, an alliance of more than 1,000 anti-landmine groups. Early on, a participant predicted that it would take at least 30 years for a landmine ban to be enacted.

Williams' cause received heightened attention when it found an impassioned advocate in the late Diana, Princess of Wales. Williams, who never met the princess, was taken aback during a landmine conference in Oslo, Norway, when reporters asked if her campaign would suffer a setback because of Diana's death. She thought the question "a bit shallow."

Bibliography

BBC News 1997 "Landmine campaigner gets peace prize." http://news.bbc.co.uk/hi/english/world/newsid.38000/39 427.stm

Campaign Updates 1997 The Nobel Peace Prize for 1997. October 10

Chicago Tribune 1998 Landmine campaigner accepts Nobel Peace Prize.

Time 1997 "Kudos for a Crusader." http://www.pathfinder. com/time/magazin. . .7/971020/nation.kudos

PEDRO B. BERNALDEZ

International Campaign to Ban Landmines (ICBL) (1997)

The International Campaign to Ban Landmines (ICBL) is a united coalition committed to the goal of the total elimination of antipersonnel landmines. On December 10, 1997, the ICBL and its American co-ordinator, Ms Jody Williams, received the Nobel Peace Prize from the Norwegian Nobel Committee. Ms Williams claimed that "the prize is a recognition of the fact that NGOs have worked in close cooperation with governments for the first time on arms control issue, with the United Nations, with the International Committee of the Red Cross." In awarding the prize, the Nobel Committee wished to express the hope that the Ottawa process will win even wider support. "As a model for similar processes in the future, it could prove of decisive importance to the international effort for disarmament and peace."

The widespread deployment of anti-personnel mines, mainly in developing countries, is a massive human tragedy. Anti-personnel mines are mass-produced, generally inexpensive weapons designed to wound or kill people. Small and lightweight, they are usually detonated when their victims step on them. They have been employed in numerous conflicts throughout the world, and their effects linger long after.

Worldwide, there are more than 250 models of landmines, built by 48 countries. Mines have been placed at bridges, waterways, power installations, rail lines, ports, airports, irrigation systems, and in fields, forests, villages, and cities. The mere presence of mines can bring widespread chaos to an agrarian economy.

Every day, adults and children in 69 countries know that every step they take can bring death or injury from one of an estimated 100 million anti-personnel mines now in the ground. On average, landmines claim 500 new victims each week. Since 1975, there have been more than one million casualties, the majority civilians. There are some 250,000 landmine amputees worldwide. Because anti-personnel mines are so cheap, accessible and easy to use, they are the weapon of choice for combatants in the world's poorest countries. The countries most affected by landmines are Angola, Ethiopia, Eritrea, Mozambique, Somalia, Sudan, Afghanistan, Cambodia, Bosnia and Iraq. There are many ways in which the presence of mines is a serious constraint on development. Many hectares of productive land, particularly in border areas, are completely unsafe and have been abandoned. In areas where farming and herding do continue, casualties lead to disruptions in food supply, causing malnutrition and famine.

Transport and communications are interrupted, undermining trade and commerce and preventing delivery of essential supplies. This in turn creates shortages and local inflation. Soil and water contamination caused by landmines is growing. Weather patterns, such as floods and desertification, cause mines to shift and relocate, adding to the burden of uncertainty.

The toll in human lives has a direct impact, not only in personal and family or community loss, but also in the loss to the country's labor market and economic productivity. Reconciliation and a return to normalcy are extremely difficult in these conditions, and in many locales, recovery and long-term development are nearly impossible.

The landmines problem has assumed a sense of urgency and importance in the post-Cold War world for a number of reasons: a) because of the sheer numbers of mines laid: roughly 67 million of the world's uncleared landmines are estimated to have been deployed in only the last fifteen years; b) because of increasing evidence of the impact of landmines on civilians. Handicap International estimates that, since 1975, landmines have killed or injured more than one million people, the majority—some 80 per cent—civilians. Civilian impact is the primary reason behind the birth of the International Campaign To Ban Landmines. It was quickly recognized that: "you can't just put limbs on people: it's only part of the answer. You have to address the root of the problem. The root cause in almost every instance is the landmine; because the problem is widespread." Uncleared landmines pose a varying problem for some sixty countries in five continents: only Antarctica and Australasia are completely free of them. Most uncleared mines lie in Africa and Asia but the fastest growing region for deployment is now considered to be Central and Eastern Europe, particularly in the republics of the former Yugoslavia. The continuing incidence and seriousness of internal conflicts has assumed international dimensions so far as supply of conventional weapons to conflicts are concerned and for an expanded UN role; and because there is now recognition that the problem of uncleared landmines will not be solved by mine clearance alone because of the scale of the problem. The problems are of a lack of finances and technology, and the fact that more mines are currently being laid than are cleared. For example, in 1993 the international community allocated US$70 million to clear roughly 100,000 mines, while between two and five million more mines were laid.

Over the past few years, a loose-jointed network of nongovernmental organizations and individual activists from around the world has propelled a movement to eliminate landmines. It has gained the support of more than half the countries of the world, and it is now putting pressure on the recalcitrant remainder to join in the effort to abolish those indiscriminate weapons. The effectiveness of this activist campaigns confirms that the information age is altering the nature of social conflict. Organizations that get networked across borders are increasingly able to maneuver large governments. A "global civil society" is emerging and its often self-appointed activists are gaining impressive abilities to use information operations to influence states and corporations.

The campaign to ban landmines is but one of the social "netwars" that civil society networks increasingly are waging against state that persist in emphasizing the traditional power politics. In the latest show of solidarity and unity of purpose, the Ottawa process has been launched by the campaigners which had earned the cooperation of governments. This shows the civilian power of non-governmental organizations to penetrate the policymaking arena which traditionally is the purview of states.

Representatives from 150 governments came together in Ottawa from December 2 to 4, 1997 to participate in The Treaty Signing Conference and Mine Action Forum. The governments were joined by representatives of hundreds of non-governmental organizations (NGOs) and international agencies that, collectively, form the backbone of the campaign for a global ban on anti-personnel mines. During the Conference, a total of 122 governments signed the "Convention on the Prohibition of the Use, Stockpiling, Production and Transfer of Anti-Personnel Mines and on their Destruction". It was in recognition of the vital role they played in this process that the 1997 Nobel Peace Prize was awarded to the International Campaign to Ban Landmines and its co-ordinator Jody Williams.

The Convention on the Prohibition of the Use, Stockpiling, Production and Transfer of Anti-Personnel Mines and on their Destruction is a strong document which bans all anti-personnel mines, with no exceptions or loopholes. Signatory states have committed themselves to: ban the use, stockpiling, production and transfer of anti-personnel mines; destroy existing stockpiles within four years of the treaty coming into force; clear minefields within 10 years, unless they can justify an extension; and co-operate with a compliance regime.

Three countries (Canada, Ireland and Mauritius) ratified the Convention during the Conference, Turkmenistan and the Holy See did so in early 1998, and many more are expected to do so in the near future. The Convention becomes binding in international law six months after the 40th state deposits its instrument of ratification with the Secretary General of the United Nations. 124 states have now signed the Convention, which will remain open for signature in New York.

The Treaty is the first disarmament instrument to ban a widely used weapon of war. It grew from con-

cept to reality in less than 14 months as a coalition of like-minded states, international agencies, and NGOs worked to achieve a legally binding international convention to ban anti-personnel mines.

The Convention establishes a new international norm against these weapons which has already influenced several countries which did not sign the treaty in December, to take steps in line with the treaty's goals. For example, several non-signatories have implemented unilateral moratoriums on the use, stockpiling, production and/or transfer of landmines, and others have made substantial commitments to mine action in the coming years.

A central component of the December 1997 conference was the Mine Action Forum. Recognizing that signing the treaty would not by itself resolve the global humanitarian crisis caused by the millions of mines already in the ground, the Ottawa Conference had as one of its objectives the initiation of a process by which the momentum of the Ottawa Process could be built upon and utilized to ensure that the commitments entailed in the Treaty are met fully, and as quickly as possible. The Mine Action Forum consisted of round-table meetings of experts from governments, NGOs, academia and the international development sector, as well as foreign and defence policy experts. It served as the launching pad for Ottawa Process II, an initiative to build international commitment to expand mine clearance and assistance to victims, to encourage all states to sign the Convention, and to urge all signatories to ratify as quickly as possible so that the Convention becomes binding in international law. The main product of The Mine Action Forum was a document entitled "An Agenda for Mine Action". This document will serve as a "road map" for Ottawa Process II, which lists, among other things, the initiatives to be taken by governments, NGOs and international agencies to help end the anti-personnel mine crisis. The purpose of this document is to maintain the momentum that has built up over the past 18 months, and to keep a coordinated international focus on this important issue.

The Nobel Peace Prize for the ICBL was received by Tun Channareth, a double amputee activist. She said in her acceptance speech " Some people call me a 'landmine victim.' So I am. I carry in my body the injury caused by landmines. Forty thousand people look like me. Many, many more have lost arms or eyes or one leg. Many too carry pieces of sharpnel . . . . Others carry the emotional scars, the memory of loved ones killed, the sense of being useless, no good maimed . . . . We beg the world to stop making mines. We beg the world to give money for de-mining and development so that we can rebuild our lives, our communities, our villages and our countries again!"

History

Seeing first-hand the devastating effects of anti-personnel mines, in the late 1980s surgeons from the International Committee of the Red Cross (ICRC) as well as NGO field workers began to alert the world to this unfolding crisis. Studies of the impacts of AP mines were published in the early 1990s which documented the severity of the situation, and the NGO community issued the first call for a ban on AP mines. By the time that negotiations were underway to amend and strengthen Protocol II of the 1980 UN Convention on Certain Conventional Weapons (CCW), (which deals with landmines) the AP mine issue had begun to impact politically. During the CCW talks, a small group of countries met in Geneva in 1996 to discuss, with the ICRC and the International Campaign to Ban Landmines (ICBL), a coalition of some 350 NGOs, what other action could be taken to reduce the devastating humanitarian consequences of AP mines. It was here that it was decided to move toward a total ban on anti-personnel mines.

In October 1996, following extensive consultations with NGOs, pro-ban states and other states, Canada hosted the first meeting of governments, international organizations and NGOs to discuss a strategy for banning landmines. At the conclusion of the Ottawa Conference, Canada's Minister of Foreign Affairs challenged the global community to return to Ottawa before the end of 1997 to sign an agreement to that effect.

A series of global, regional and sub-regional meetings organized by Canada and its partners employed intensive traditional state diplomacy as well as NGO public advocacy to pressure governments to consider the AP mine issue. Despite considerable opposition from many powerful states, the mounting political will to see a ban began to bear results. One hundred eleven states attended the first formal negotiations on the ban convention in Vienna in February 1997. In June 1997, representatives from 155 countries and more than 100 NGOs met in Brussels to review progress made since Ottawa. In signing the Brussels Declaration, 97 countries declared their support for a treaty to ban anti-personnel mines, for negotiations to be held in Oslo in September, and for a signing ceremony in Ottawa before the end of 1997. Over 100 states gathered in Oslo from September 1 to 18 to negotiate the final text of the treaty, which was opened for signature in December 1997 in Ottawa.

Participants representing the 150 governments came to Ottawa on December 2 to 4, 1997. The governments were joined by representatives of hundreds of nongovernmental organizations and international agencies. A total of 122 governments signed the "Convention on the Prohibitions of the Use, Stockpiling, Production and Transfer of Anti-Personnel Mines and on their Destruction."

On February 20 to 22, the ICBL held its general meeting in Frankfurt, Germany with 70 participants from 40 countries. The ICBL opened the conference with a demonstration at the Rhein Main Air Base to demand that the United States remove its antipersonnel landmines that are stockpiled in Germany, other NATO states and Japan. The ICBL agreed upon its priorities for 1998 in its three main areas of work. With regard to a ban, a top priority is the achievement in 1998 of the forty ratifications of the Ottawa Treaty necessary for it to become binding international law. It will work to universalize the treaty, with, among other initiatives, a regional conference in Hungary in March and a conference in Russia in May. It will explore a role for its members in monitoring the treaty.

The ICBL agreed that a priority for 1998 is to strengthen the advocacy work of the other two key pillars of the campaign-victim assistance and humanitarian mine clearance. In order to provide for comprehensive programs of assistance to mine survivors, the newly formed working group called for a commitment of three billion dollars over ten years. The six key points elaborated by the new demining working group are designed as guidelines for the ICBL in briefing governments and the public as to the priorities of the campaign with regard to humanitarian mine clearance.

The ICBL discussed all aspects of its current structure and reached a number of decisions. The ten existing members of the steering committee, now renamed the coordination committee, were reconfirmed, and six new members were asked to join: Association to Aid Refugees, Japan; Colombian Campaign Against Landmines; Inter-African Union of Human Rights; Landmine Survivors Network; Lutheran World Federation; and, Norwegian People's Aid. Working groups on each of the three main areas of work were established (ban, humanitarian demining, victim assistance) as well as a fourth working group on Legal and Moral Responsibility, in order to demonstrate the importance of this area of work in the campaign. The working group on nonstate actors will continue to develop its plan to involve these nonstate groups in the ban.

Jody Williams, co-recipient of the 1997 Nobel Peace Prize with the ICBL, relinquished her role as the coordinator. Stating that it values and honors the important position that Jody Williams holds in the eyes of the world as a symbol of our work to overcome landmines, the ICBL asked her to accept a new position as ICBL International Ambassador and to participate in the Coordinating Committee. She accepted. Rae McGrath, who delivered the Nobel Lecture for the ICBL, and Tun Channereth, who accepted the Peace Prize for the ICBL, also accepted roles as International Ambassadors. It was decided to form a new coordinating team to succeed Jody Williams.

Liz Bernstein, based in Mozambique, agreed to become the first member of the team. Handicap International will provide financial and human resources to assist the coordinating team. The General Meeting agreed that to best utilize the Nobel Peace Prize funds it would establish an account in trust for the ICBL. The intention of the Campaign is to draw on the interest of the account to advance the campaigning goals of a ban and increased resources for humanitarian demining and victim assistance. The members claimed they will use the trust to attract additional support for the ICBL to ensure its continued work until it has achieved the goal of the total elimination of antipersonnel landmines. The Campaign will launch an appeal to donors to build on the Nobel funds.

Bibliography ———————————————

Department of Foreign Affairs and International Trade of Canada 1998 "Safe Lane: The Ottawa Process and Canada's Position." http://www.mines.gc.ca/ottbck-e.html

Boston Globe 1998 "The Real Story About the International Campaign to Ban Landmines." http://proquest.umi.com/

Nobel Peace Prize Internet Archive 1997 "The Nobel Peace Prize for 1997: ICBL and Jody Williams." http://nobel. se. announcement-97/peace97.html

PR Newswire 1998 "Nobel Laureate Jody Williams in Vienna: New Initiative to Aid Victims of Anti-Personnel Mines." http://proquest.umi.com/

The Oregonian 1998 "Group Names Anti-mine 'Ambassadors.'" http://proquest.umi.com/

Vietnam Veterans of America Foundation 1998 "Campaign Updates" http://www.vvaf.org/landmine/us/updates/ events/news2_24.html

Yankee 1998 "You can never live down the Nobel Prize." http://proquest.umi.com/

PEDRO B. BERNALDEZ

David Trimble
(1998)

Two political rivals with the common goal of ending decades of religious-inspired violence in Northern Ireland were awarded the Nobel Peace Prize for 1998. The award was shared by John Hume, a Catholic, and David Trimble, a Protestant. In announcing the Prize in Oslo, the Norwegian Nobel Committee cited efforts by Hume and Trimble in bringing about a peace agreement signed last April 1998 aimed at "settling the national religious and social conflict in Northern Ireland that has cost over 3,500 people their lives."

David Trimble, 54, is the leader of the Ulster Unionist party. The name Ulster is often used synonymously with Northern Ireland. The name unionists refers to proBritish Protestants in Northern Ireland who wish to remain part of the United Kingdom. It was the second time the Nobel committee sought to encourage peace in Northern Ireland. The 1976 prize went to Betty Williams and Mairead Corrigan of Northern Ireland for their peace efforts in founding the International Peace People group, which later fizzled. "We did hope it would have more of an effect than it did," said Sejersted. But he said that illustrated what a long and complicated process seeking peace in Northern Ireland has been. Sejersted said the committee knows that there is a risk of setbacks and renewed violence even after the Belfast peace accords were signed in April 1998.

David Trimble was born in 1944 and educated at Queen's University, Belfast; he went on to become a barrister and lecturer in the university's law faculty, rising to senior lecturer and assistant dean of faculty. He became politically active when the troubles began in the late 1960s. He was a key member of the Ulster Unionist Council. When Unionism fragmented in the mid1970s he went with the Vanguard Unionist Party, of whom he became deputy leader. But by 1978 he was back in the Ulster Unionist fold and in 1990 won the Upper Bann seat under its banner. When veteran Sir James Molyneaux decided to resign as party leader in 1995 Mr. Trimble was, to many, the surprise choice as the new chief. There was very little support for him from his parliamentary colleagues, but the party rank and file clearly thought differently. In part the success was explained by his high-profile role during a stand-off in Rumcee between members of the Protestant Orange and local Catholic residents. His election was also an indication that rank and file unionists were unhappy with the government's visions of the future for Northern Ireland set out in the so-called Framework Documents, and wanted to see firm leadership at the top of their party.

Earlier, he had shown a hardline streak by standing firmly in support of Orangemen at Drumcree. It concerned some of the old guard but showed the kind of backbone the younger members wanted. He has rarely had time to rest since. He was thrown into the machinations which led to the London-Dublin agreement which set up the multiparty talks process in June 1996. For nearly a year he was able to bend the faltering Conservative Government to his will. The support of his 11 MPs in the House of Commons was essential to John Major. He lost that power when Tony Blair became Prime Minister, with his huge majority, but the sway remained because of the need to have Unionists agree to the political deal being attempted.

A veteran of Northern Ireland politics, Mr. Trimble was involved in the hardline Vanguard Party led by William Craig in the early 1970s. In 1978 he entered mainstream unionism and joined the Ulster Unionist Party, and in 1990 he was elected as MP for Upper Bann. Soon after he was elected party leader, Mr. Trimble showed he was prepared to upset some of the unionist rank and file by meeting with the main party leaders in the Irish Republic. A former lecturer in law at Queen's University, he needed all his negotiating skills for the multi-party talks which concluded with the Good Friday Agreement. He gave his backing to the deal despite the opposition of more than half his parliamentary colleagues, but later won support for his approach from the party rank and file.

Mr. Trimble is an example of why Unionists consider themselves British and insist they will remain so. His ancestors arrived in Ulster from Northumberland 300 years ago. Three centuries later he, and thousands like him, still look to Britain not Dublin for their lead. It is an established culture that no political changes will alter.

Biography

David Trimble was born in Bangor, Country Down, Northern Ireland on October 15,1944 to a couple of humble beginnings. He attended Bangor Grammar School. His father was a junior civil servant and his mother came from a family whose building business failed. That he ascended to leadership of the Ulster Unionists was something unexpected since he is not of the Anglo-Irish "squirearchy" that for generations has controlled unionism in Northern Ireland.

He studied at the Queen's University in Belfast and went on to become barrister and lecturer in the university's law faculty, rising to senior lecturer and assistant dean of faculty. In 1975 he joined the Northern Ireland Constitutional Convention and during the period 1985 to 1990 he was Chairman of the Lagan Valley Unionist Association and Chairman of the Ulster Society. He became the leader of the Ulster Unionist Party in 1995 and a Member for Upper Bann.

He leap-frogged over several others to the top of the party after refusing to support John Major's government in a parliamentary vote on European Union fishing policy. It was his way of underlining his opposition to giving any significant power to a cross-border council that might be formed with the Irish republic.

Bibliography

CNN Interactive 1998 "David Trimble, N. Irish Protestant Peacemaker." http:/www.cnn.com/WORLD/europe/9810/16/RB000452.reut.html

CNN Interactive 1998 "Peace Prize humbles N. Ireland's Hume and Trimble." http://www.cnn.com/WORLD/europe/9810/16/nobel.peace.prize.03/

Focus 1998 "Profile - David Trimble." http://news.bbc.co.uk/hi/english/event, . .n_ireland/ focus/newsid_96000/96787.stm

Norwegian Nobel Institute 1998 "Nobel Peace Prize 1998." http://www.nobel.se/announcement-98/peace98.html

Resoftlinks News 1998 "Nobel Peace Prize to Trimble and Hume." http://news.resoftlinks. com/981016/peacenobel.shtml

Ulster Unionist Party 1998 "Mr David Trimble." http://www.uup.org/text/who/dt-.html

PEDRO B. BERNALDEZ

John Hume
(1998)

The Norwegian Nobel Committee awarded the Nobel Peace Prize for 1998 to John Hume and David Trimble "for their efforts to find a peaceful solution to the conflict in Northern Ireland." John Hume, a Catholic, said that the decision to honor him and Protestant David Trimble meant international approval of their efforts to end three decades of religious-inspired violence in the British province. Speaking to reporters in his home city of Londonderry, Northern Ireland, Hume said "I see this award as a very powerful endorsement of the peace process ... because it underlines massive international goodwill towards it." In announcing the award in Oslo, the Norwegian Nobel Committee cited the men's efforts in bringing about a peace agreement signed last April that aimed at settling; the national religious and social conflict in Northern Ireland that has cost over 3,500 people their lives. The Committee stressed that "John Hume has throughout been the clearest and most consistent of Northern Ireland's political leaders in his work for a peaceful solution."

John Hume championed the cause of peace during the darkest days of Northern Ireland's guerrilla war. His Londonderry home looks out on the Bogside, a Catholic zone which was wrecked by bombs and bullets as republican gunmen and British troops waged a war that seemed without end. But his eyes have been fixed on the dream of a new society in which old enemies would shed sweat, not blood, in shaping a new political and economic landscape.

Hume, 61, is a Catholic nationalist who held out against the poison of violence. His heroes are his father, who told him to steer clear of politics, and Martin Luther King, whose crusade for black American civil rights was built on nonviolence.

The Northern Ireland peace deal—the "Good Friday Agreement"—of April 1998 was a personal triumph for Hume. It was the culmination of a lonely and often reviled quest to bring Northern Ireland the stability that had eluded it since the island was partitioned in 1922.

Hume, leader of the moderate Social Democratic and Labour Party (SDLP), is credited with kickstarting the peace negotiations by secretly meeting Gerry Adams, leader of the guerrilla Irish Republican Army's (IRA) political wing, Sinn Fein, and drafting a plan to end the Northern Ireland conflict.

This prompted the British and Irish governments to draw up the Downing Street Declaration of December 1993, which said Britain would not oppose Irish reunification if a majority of people in Northern Ireland wanted it. This in turn led to a 17-month ceasefire by the outlawed IRA in its war against British rule, starting in August 1994. Hume helped secure a reinstatement of the ceasefire in July 1997.

In September 1997, Hume put aside personal ambition when he decided not to run for the Irish presidency, but to concentrate on the peace process. In 1994, he was nominated for the Nobel Peace Prize.

Despite his father's advice not to be in politics, he did enter politics. He joined the 1968 civil rights movement and fought against anti-Catholic discrimination in everything from housing to education. Two years later, he co-founded the SDLP, which coupled his social democracy leanings with the Catholic minority's wish to reunite the island.

His insistence on reunification based on reconcilia-

tion between the Protestant and Catholic communities and his rejection of violence earned him enemies among hardline republicans in the early days of the province's "Troubles." In the hothouse climate of Northern Irish politics, even his fiercest critics acknowledge his commitment to peace and laud his efforts to secure finance from the European Union to improve living standards for Protestants and Catholics alike.

Hume won powerful allies in the U.S. and a succession of American Presidents and Irish-American politicians have regarded him as an honest broker. In 1985, Hume bravely agreed to a secret meeting with the IRA to try to end its policy of violence. The meeting, aborted after five minutes when Hume refused to let it be videotaped, was condemned by Protestant Unionist leaders and the British government.

He won a seat in the Northern Ireland parliament in 1969 as an independent. He was Minister of Commerce in a powersharing executive which took office in 1973 but collapsed a year later. A fluent French speaker, he says the European Union, and the member states that buried hatred in the cause of peace, are a model for Northern Ireland.

In 1979, he was elected to the European and British Parliaments. In 1983, he helped to launch a forum of nationalist politicians seeking a new political structure to respect both Protestant and Catholic traditions.

Biography

Born on January 18,1937, John Hume finished college in the Irish Republic and became a teacher. His father was instrumental in Hume's early interest in human existence. He was inspired by his father as he combined frontline political leadership with a conviction that jobs and food on the family table are the bedrock of a just and peaceful society.

His father was unemployed for much of his life and John, the eldest of five children, sold newspapers to make ends meet. "I've forgotten more about poverty than most people will ever learn," he said of his childhood.

Despite his father's advice, he did enter politics. He joined the 1968 civil rights movement and fought against anti-Catholic discrimination in everything from housing to education. Two years later, he co-founded the SDLP, which coupled his social democracy leanings with the Catholic minority's wish to reunite the island. In 1973, he was elected to the Northern Ireland National Assembly; he served as Minister of Commerce in 1974 and was elected to the Northern Ireland Convention in 1975. In the first direct elections of 1979, he was elected to the European Parliament. Since 1979, he has served on the Committee for Regional Planning of the EP.

John Hume was subsequently elected to Westminster in 1983 and was a member of New Ireland Forum 1983 and 1984. In 1986 he was co-leader of the International Observer Delegation to monitor Philippine elections.

He founded Derry-Boston Ventures, and Boston-Ireland Ventures as a part of a strategy to win new inward investment, marketing opportunities and trade/industry partnerships. Emphasis on improving employment levels in his constituency is paying dividends with several important investment, government decentralization and job-creation initiatives. He has been a member of the Forum for Peace and Reconciliation convened following ceasefires in 1994. He was nominated for the Nobel Peace Prize in 1994 and was finally awarded in 1998.

Hume, married with five children, is said to have suffered from poor health recently, partly caused by overfatigue.

Bibliography

CNN Interactive 1998 "John Hume, Northern Irish crusader for peace." http://www.cnn.com/WORLD/europe/9810/16/RB000530.reut.html

Nando.net 1998 "Former newsboy Hume's dream of peace comes true." http://search.nando.net/newsroom/ntn/top/052498/topstory_6539_S7_body.html

Nobel Prize Internet Archive 1998 "1998 Nobel Peace Prize Laureate." http://nobelprizes.com/nobel/peace/1998a.html

Resoftlinks News 1998 "Nobel Peace Prize to Trimble and Hume." http://news.resoftlinks.com/981016/peacenobel.html

PEDRO B. BERNALDEZ

THE NOBEL PRIZES

First awarded in 1901, the Nobel Prizes were established through a bequest of $ 9.2 million from Alfred Bernhard Nobel (1833-96), a Swedish chemical engineer and the inventor of dynamite and other explosives, and by a gift from the Bank of Sweden. Nobel's will directed that the interest from the fund be divided annually among people who have made significant discoveries or inventions in the fields of chemistry, physics, and physiology or medicine, as well as to that author who has "produced in the field of literature the most outstanding work of an idealistic tendency," and to that individual or group that has "done the most or the best work for fraternity between nations, for the abolition or reduction of standing armies and for the holding and promotion of peace congresses." In 1968, the 300th anniversary of the Bank of Sweden, an additional prize for outstanding work in the economic sciences was established; it was first granted the following year.

Today, all of the prizes are funded with the help of the Bank of Sweden. Final decisions are made for physics, chemistry, and economics by the Royal Swedish Academy of Sciences, Stockholm; for physiology or medicine by the Nobel Assembly at the Karolinska Institute, Stockholm; for literature by the Swedish Academy, Stockholm; and for peace by the Norwegian Nobel Committee, Oslo.

The prizes are formally awarded annually on December 10, the anniversary of Nobel's death but are announced earlier in the fall. The peace prize is presented in Oslo and other awards are given in Stockholm, by the king of Sweden. The amount of each prize varies according to the interest from the fund. Each 1995 award was $1 million, up from $489,000 in 1989 and $ 362,500 in 1987. Each prize includes a gold medal, diploma, and a gift of money which is awarded at a formal ceremony. There were no prizes awarded from 1940 to 1942.

An expansion of the appendix of the revised version includes a list and brief descriptions of the Nobel Prize awardees in the fields of chemistry, physics, medicine and literature. For a discussion on the history and development of the Prize, readers may refer to the relevant article in Volume III.

The Nobel Prizes

NOBEL PRIZES
IN PHYSIOLOGY OR MEDICINE

1901 Emil A. von Behring (Germany) Marburg Univ. "for his work on serum therapy, especially its application against diphtheria, by which he has opened a new road in the domain of medical science and thereby placed in the hands of the physician a victorious weapon against illness and deaths."

1902 Sir Ronald Ross (UK) University College "for his work on malaria, by which he has shown how it enters the organism and thereby has laid the foundation for successful research on this disease and methods of combating it."

1903 Niels R. Finsen (Denmark) Finsen Medical Light Institute "in recognition of his contribution to the treatment of diseases, especially lupus vulgaris, with concentrated light radiation, whereby he has opened a new avenue for medical science."

1904 Ivan P. Pavlov (Russia) Military Medical Academy "in recognition of his work on the physiology of digestion, through which knowledge on vital aspects of the subject has been transformed and enlarged."

1905 Robert Koch (Germany) Institute for Infectious Diseases "for his investigations and discoveries in relation to tuberculosis."

1906 Camillo Golgi (Italy) Pavia Univ., and **Santiago Ramon Y Cajal** (Spain) Madrid Univ. "in recognition of their work on the structure of the nervous system."

1907 Charles L.A. Laveran (France) Institut Pasteur "in recognition of his work on the role played by protozoa in causing diseases."

1908 Il'ya I. Mečnikov (Russia) Institut Pasteur (Paris), and **Paul Ehrilich** (Germany) Goettingen Univ. and Royal Institute for Experimental Therapy "in recognition of their work on immunity."

1909 Emil T. Kocher (Switzerland) Berne Univ. "for his work on the physiology, pathology, and surgery of the thyroid gland."

1910 Albrecht Kossel (Germany) Heidelberg Univ. "in recognition of the contributions to our knowledge of cell chemistry made through his work on proteins, including the nucleic substances."

1911 Allvar Gullstrand (Sweden) Uppsala Univ. "for his work on the dioptrics of the eye."

1912 Alexis Carrel (France) Rockefeller Institute for Medical Research (New York) "in recognition of his work on vascular suture and the transplantation of blood-vessels and organs."

1913 Charles R. Richet (France) Sorbonne Univ. "in recognition of his work on anaphylaxis."

1914 Robert Bárány (Austria) Vienna Univ. "for his work on the physiology and pathology of the vestibular apparatus."

1915-18 Prize Not Awarded.

1919 Jules Bordet (Belgium) Brussels Univ. "for his discoveries relating to immunity."

1920 Schack A.S. Krough (Denmark) Copenhagen Univ. "for his discovery of the capillary motor regulating mechanism."

1921 Prize Not Awarded.

1922 Sir Archibald V. Hill (UK) London Univ. "for his discovery relating to the production of heat in the muscle"; **Otto F. Meyerhof** (Germany) Kiel Univ. "for his discovery of the fixed relationship between the consumption of oxygen and the metabolism of lactic acid in the muscle."

1923 Sir Frederick G. Banting (Canada) Toronto Univ., and **John J.R. Macleod** (Canada) Toronto Univ. "for the discovery of insulin."

1924 Willem Einthoven (Netherlands) Leyden Univ. "for his discovery of the mechanism of the electrocardiogram."

1925 Prize Not Awarded.

1926 Johannes A.G. Fibiger (Denmark) Copenhagen Univ. "for his discovery of the Spiroptera carcinoma."

1927 Julius Wagner-Jauregg (Austria) Vienna Univ. "for his discovery of the therapeutic value of malaria inoculation in the treatment of dementia paralytica."

1928 Charles J.H. Nicolle (France) Institut Pasteur "for his work on typhus."

1929 Christian Eijkman (Netherlands) Utrecht Univ. "for his discovery of the antineuritic vitamin"; **Sir Frederick G. Hopkins** (UK) Cambridge Univ. "for his discovery of the growth-stimulating vitamins."

1930 Karl Landsteiner (Austria) Rockefeller Inst. for Medical Research (New York) "for his discovery of human blood groups."

1931 Otto H. Warburg (Germany) Kaiser-Wilhelm-Institut (now Max-Planck-Institut) "for his discovery of the nature and mode of action of the respiratory enzyme."

1932 Sir Charles S. Sherrington (UK) Oxford Univ., and **Lord Edgar D. Adrian** (UK) Cambridge Univ. "for their discoveries regarding the functions of neurons."

1933 Thomas H. Morgan (US) California Institute of Technology "for his discoveries concerning the role played by the chromosome in heredity."

1934 George H. Whipple (US) Rochester Univ., **George R. Minot** (US) Harvard Univ., and **William P. Murphy** (US) Harvard Univ. "for their discoveries concerning liver therapy in cases of anaemia."

1935 Hans Spemann (Germany) Univ. of Freiburg im Breisgau "for his discovery of the organizer effect in embryonic development."

1936 Sir Henry H. Dale (UK) National Institute for Medical Research, and **Otto Loewi** (Austria) Graz Univ. "for their discoveries relating to chemical transmission of nerve impulses."

1937 Albert Szent-Györgyi von Nagyrapolt (Hungary) Szeged Univ. "for his discoveries in connection with the biological combustion processes, with special reference to vitamin C and the catalysis of fumaric acid."

1938 Corneille J.F. Heymans (Belgium) Ghent Univ. "for the discovery of the role played by the sinus and aortic mechanisms in the regulation of respiration."

1939 Gerhard Domagk (Germany) Munster Univ. "for the discovery of the antibacterial effects of prontosil."

1940-42 Prize Not Awarded.

1943 Henrik C.P. Dam (Denmark) Polytechnic Institute "for his discovery of vitamin K"; **Edward A. Doisy** (US) St. Louis Univ. "for his discovery of the chemical nature of vitamin K."

1944 Joseph Erlanger (US) Washington Univ., and **Herbert S. Gasser** (US) Rockefeller Institute for Medical Research "for their discoveries relating to the highly differentiated functions of single nerve fibres."

1945 Sir Alexander Fleming (UK) London Univ., **Sir Ernst B. Chain** (UK) Oxford Univ., and **Lord Howard W. Florey** (UK) Oxford Univ. "for the discovery of penicillin and its curative effect in various infectious diseases."

1946 Hermann J. Muller (US) Indiana Univ. "for the discovery of the production of mutations by means of X-ray irradiation."

1947 Carl F. Cori (US) Washington Univ., and his wife **Gerty T. Cori** (US) Washington Univ. "for their discovery of the course of the catalytic conversion of glycogen"; **Bernardo A. Houssay** (Argentina) Institute for Biology and Experimental Medicine "for his discovery of the part played by the hormone of the anterior pituitary lobe in the metabolism of sugar."

1948 Paul H. Müller (Switzerland) Laboratory of the J.R. Geigy Dye-Factory Co. "for his discovery of the high efficiency of DDT as a contact poison against several arthropods."

1949 Walter R. Hess (Switzerland) Zurich Univ. "for his discovery of the functional organization of the interbrain as a coordinator of the activities of the internal organs; **Antonio Caetano de Abreu F.E. Moniz** (Portugall) Univ. of Lisbon "for his discovery of the therapeutic value of leucotomy in certain psychoses."

1950 Edward C. Kendall (US) Mayo Clinic **Tadeus Reichstein** (Switzerland) Basel Univ. and **Philip S. Hench** (US) Mayo Clinic "for their discoveries relating to the hormones of the adrenal cortex, their structure, and biological effects."

1951 Max Theiler (Union of South Africa) Laboratories Division of Medicine and Public Health Rockefeller Foundation (New York) "for his discoveries concerning yellow fever and how to combat it."

1952 Selman A. Waksman (US) Rutgers Univ. "for his discovery of streptomycin, the first antibiotic effective against tuberculosis."

1953 Sir Hans A. Krebs (UK) Sheffield Univ. "for his discovery of the citric acid cycle"; **Fritz A. Lipmann** (US) Harvard Medical School and Massachusetts General Hospital "for his discovery of coenzyme A and its importance for intermediary metabolism."

1954 John F. Enders (US) Harvard Medical School and Research Division of Infectious Diseases, Children's Medical Center; **Thomas H. Weller** (US) Research Division of Infectious Diseases, Children's Medical Center and **Frederick C. Robbins** (US) Western Reserve Univ. "for their discovery of the ability of poliomyelitis viruses to grow in cultures of various types of tissue."

1955 Axel H.T. Theorell (Sweden) Nobel Medical Institute "for his discoveries concerning the nature and mode of action of oxidation enzymes."

1956 Andre F. Coumand (US) Cardio-Pulmonary Laboratory, Columbia Univ. Division, Bellevue Hospital; **Werner Forssmann** (Germany) Mainz Univ. and Bad Kreuznach; and **Dickinson W. Richards** (US) Columbia Univ. "for their discoveries concerning heart catheterization and pathological changes in the circulatory system."

1957 Daniel Bovet (Italy) Chief Institute of Public Health "for his discoveries relating to synthetic compounds that inhibit the action of certain body substances, and especially their action on the vascular system and the skeletal muscles."

1958 George W. Beadle (US) California Institute of Technology, and **Edward L. Tatum** (US) Rockefeller Institute for Medical Research "for their discovery that genes act by regulating definite chemical events"; **Joshua Lederberg** (US) Wisconsin Univ. "for his discoveries concerning genetic recombination and the organization of the genetic material of bacteria."

1959 Severo Ochoa (US) New York Univ., College of Medicine, and **Arthur Kornberg** (US) Stanford Univ. "for their discovery of the mechanisms in the biological synthesis of ribonucleic acid and deoxyribonucleic acid."

1960 Sir Frank M. Burnet (Australia) Walter and Eliza Hall Institute for Medical Research, and **Sir Peter B. Medawar** (UK) University College "for discovery of acquired immunological tolerance."

1961 Georg von Békésy (US) Harvard Univ. "for his discoveries of the physical mechanism of stimulation within the cochlea."

1962 Francis H.C. Crick (UK) Institute of Molecular Biology, **James D. Watson** (US) Harvard Univ., and **Maurice H.F. Wilkins** (UK) University of London "for their discoveries concerning the molecular structure of nuclear acids and its significance for information transfer in living material."

1963 Sir John C. Eccles (Australia) Australian National Univ., **Sir Alan L. Hodgkin** (UK) Cambridge Univ., and **Sir Andrew F. Huxley** (UK) University of London "for their discoveries concerning the ionic mechanisms involved in excitation and inhibition in the peripheral and central portions of the nerve cell membrane."

1964 Konrad Bloch (US) Harvard Univ., and **Feodor Lynen** (Germany) Max-Planck-Institut fur Zellchemie "for their discoveries concerning the mechanism and regulation of the cholesterol and fatty acid metabolism."

1965 François Jacob (France) Institut Pasteur, **André Lwoff** (France) Institut Pasteur, and **Jacques Monod** (France) Institut Pasteur "for their discoveries concerning genetic control of enzyme and virus synthesis."

1966 Peyton Rous (US) Rockefeller Univ. "for his discovery of tumor-inducing viruses"; **Charles B. Huggins** (US) Ben May Laboratory for Cancer Research, Univ. of Chicago "for his discoveries concerning hormonal treatment of prostatic cancer."

1967 Ragnar Granit (Sweden) Karolinska Institutet, **Haldan K. Hartline** (US) The Rockefeller Univ., and **George Wald** (US) Harvard Univ. "for their discoveries concerning the primary physiological and chemical visual processes in the eye."

1968 Robert W. Holley (US) Cornell Univ., **Har G. Khorana** (US) Univ. of Wisconsin, and **Marshall W. Nirenberg** (US) National Institutes of Health "for their interpretation of the genetic code and its functions in protein synthesis."

1969 Max Delbrück (US) California Institute of Technology, **Alfred D. Hershey** (US) Carnegie Institution of Washington, and **Salvador E. Luria** (US) MIT "for their discoveries concerning the replication mechanism and the genetic structure of viruses."

1970 Sir Bernard Katz (UK) University College, **Ulf von Euler** (Sweden) Karolinska Institutet, and **Julius Axelrod** (US) National Institutes of Health "for their discoveries concerning the humoral transmittors in the nerve terminals and the mechanism for their storage, release, and inactivation."

1971 Earl W. Sutherland, Jr. (US) Vanderbilt Univ. "for his discoveries concerning the mechanisms of the action of hormones."

1972 Gerald M. Edelman (US) Rockefeller Univ., and **Rodney R. Porter** (UK) Oxford Univ. "for their discoveries concerning the chemical structure of antibodies."

1973 Karl von Frisch (W. Germany) Zoologisches Institut der Universitat Munchen; **Konrad Lorenz** (Austria) Osterreichische Akademie der Wissenschaften, Institut fur vergleichende Verhaltensforschung; and **Nikolaas Tinbergen** (UK) Dept. of Zoology, University Museum "for their discoveries concerning organization and elicitation of individual and social behavior patterns."

1974 Albert Claude (Belgium) Université Catholique de Louvain, **Christian de Duve** (Belgium) Rockefeller Univ. (New York), and **George E. Palade** (US) Yale Univ. School of Medicine "for their discoveries concerning the structural and functional organization of the cell."

1975 David Baltimore (US) MIT, **Renato Dulbecco** (US) Imperial Cancer Research Fund Laboratory (London), and **Howard M. Temin** (US) Univ. of Wisconsin "for their discoveries concerning the interaction between tumour viruses and the genetic material of the cell."

1976 Baruch S. Blumberg (US) The Institute for Cancer Research, and **D. Carleton Gajdusek** (US) National Institutes of Health "for their discoveries concerning new mechanisms for the origin and dissemination of infectious diseases."

1977 Roger Guillemin (US) The Salk Institute, and **Andrew V. Shally** (US) Veterans Administration Hospital, New Orleans "for their discoveries concerning the peptide hormone production of the brain"; **Rosalyn Yalow** (US) Veterans Administration Hospital, Bronx "for the development of radioimmunoassays of peptide hormones."

1978 Werner Arber (Switzerland) Biozentrum der Universitat, **Daniel Nathans** (US) Johns Hopkins Univ. School of Medicine, and **Hamilton O. Smith** (US) Johns Hopkins Univ. School of Medicine "for the discovery of restriction enzymes and their application to problems of molecular genetics."

1979 Alan M. Cormack (US) Tufts Univ., and **Sir Godfrey N. Hounsfield** (UK) "for the development of computer-assisted tomography."

1980 Baruj Benacerraf (US) Harvard Medical School; **Jean Dausset** (France) Université de Paris, Laboratoire Immuno-Hemetologie; and **George D. Snell** (US) Jackson Laboratory "for their discoveries concerning genetically determined structures on the cell surface that regulate immunological reactions."

1981 Roger W. Sperry (US) California Institute of Technology "for his discoveries concerning the functional specialization of the cerebral hemispheres"; **David H. Hubel** (US) Harvard Medical School, and **Torsten N. Wiesel** (Sweden) Harvard Medical

School "for their discoveries concerning information processing in the visual system."

1982 Sune K. Bergström (Sweden) Karolinska Institutet, **Bengt I. Samuelsson** (Sweden) Karolinska Institutet, and **Sir John R. Vane** (UK) The Wellcome Research Laboratories "for their discoveries concerning prostaglandins and related biologically active substances."

1983 Barbara McClintock (US) Cold Spring Harbor Laboratory "for her discovery of mobile genetic elements."

1984 Niels K. Jerne (Denmark) Basel Institute for Immunology (Basel, Switzerland), **Georges J.F. Köhler** (W. Germany) Basel Institute for Immunology, and **César Milstein** (UK and Argentina) Medical Research Council Laboratory of Molecular Biology (Cambridge) "for theories concerning the specificity in development and control of the immune system and the discovery of the principle for production of monoclonal antibodies."

1985 Michael S. Brown (US) Univ. of Texas Health Science Center at Dallas, and **Joseph L. Goldstein** (US) Univ. of Texas Health Science Center at Dallas "for their discoveries concerning the regulation of cholesterol metabolism."

1986 Stanley Cohen (US) Vanderbilt Univ. School of Medicine, and **Rita Levi-Montalcini** (Italy and US) Institute of Cell Biology of the C.N.R. (Rome) "for their discoveries of growth factors."

1987 Susumu Tonegawa (US) MIT "for discovery of the genetic principle for generation of antibody diversity."

1988 Sir James W. Black (United Kingdom) King's College Hospital Medical School, **Gertrude B. Elion** (US) Wellcome Research Laboratories, and **George H. Hitchings** (US) Wellcome Research Laboratories "for their discoveries of Important Principles for Drug Treatment."

1989 J. Michael Bishop and Harold E. Varmus (US) Univ. of California School of Medicine, San Francisco "for their discovery of 'The Cellular Origin of Retroviral Oncogenes.'"

1990 Joseph E. Murray (US) Brigham and Women's Hospital, Boston, who performed the first kidney transplant (1954), and **E. Donnall Thomas** (US), Fred Hutchinson Cancer Research Center, Seattle, who performed the first successful bone marrow transplant between two people who were not twins (1970).

1991 Erwin Neher (Germany) Max-Planck Institute for Biophysical Chemistry, Göttingen, and **Bert Sakmann** (Germany) Max-Planck Institute for Medical Research, Heidelberg, for developing a technique that allows detection of "incredibly small electrical currents that pass through an ion channel."

1992 Edmond H. Fischer (US) and **Edwin G. Krebs** (US), both of the Univ. of Washington, for a discovery in the 1950s of a regulatory mechanism in almost all human cells linked to some cancers, to the rejection of transplanted organs, and many other processes.

1993 Richard J. Roberts (UK) New England Bio Labs, and **Phillip A. Sharp** (US) MIT, for their discovery in the 1970s that the composition of genes is of several segments, which led to gene splicing and to a better understanding of hereditary diseases and cancer.

1994 Alfred G. Gilman (US), Univ. of Texas Southwestern Medical Center, and **Martin Rodbell** (US), National Institute of Environmental Health Sciences, for their discovery of natural substances known as G-proteins and for showing how they help cells respond to external stimuli like light and odors.

1995 Edward B. Lewis (US) California Institute of Technology, **Eric F. Wieschaus** (US) Princeton Univ., and **Christiane Nüsslein-Volhard** (Germany) Max-Planck Institute in Tübingen, for their discovery of how genes control structural development of the body, helping to explain the causes of birth defects in humans.

1996 Peter C. Doherty (Australia) St. Jude's Medical Center in Memphis, **Rolf M. Zinkernagel** (Switzerland) Univ. of Zurich "for their discoveries concerning the Specificity of the Cell Mediated Immune Defence."

1997 Stanley B. Prusiner (US) Dep. of Neurology, Univ. of California, School of Medicine "for his discovery of Prios—a new biological principle of infection."

1998 Robert F. Furchgott (US) SUNY Health Science Center, **Louis J. Ignarro** (US) UCLA School of Medicine, **Ferid Murad** (US) University of Texas Medical School at Houston "for their discovery concerning nitric oxide as a signalling molecule in the cardiovascular system."

NOBEL PRIZES IN ECONOMIC SCIENCES

1969 Ragnar Frisch (Norway) Oslo Univ., and **Jan Tinbergen** (Netherlands) The Netherlands School of Economics "for having developed and applied dynamic models for the analysis of economic processes."

1970 Paul A. Samuelson (US) MIT "for the scientific work through which he has developed static and dynamic economic theory and actively contributed to raising the level of analysis in economic science."

1971 Simon Kuznets (US) Harvard Univ. "for his empirically founded interpretation of economic growth which has led to new and deepened insight into the economic and social structure and process of development."

1972 Sir John R. Hicks (UK) All Souls College, and **Kenneth J. Arrow** (US) Harvard Univ. "for their pioneering contributions to general economic equilibrium theory and welfare theory."

1973 Wassily Leontief (US) Harvard Univ. "for the development of the input-output method and for its application to important economic problems."

1974 Gunnar Myrdal (Sweden), **Friedrich A. von Hayek** (UK) "for their pioneering work in the theory of money and economic fluctuations and for their penetrating analysis of the interdependence of economic, social and institutional phenomena."

1975 Leonid V. Kantorovich (USSR) Academy of Sciences, and **Tjalling C. Koopmans** (US) Yale Univ. "for their contributions to the theory of optimum allocation of resources."

1976 Milton Friedman (US) Univ. of Chicago "for his achievements in the fields of consumption analysis, monetary history and theory, and for his demonstration of the complexity of stabilization policy."

1977 Bertil Ohlin (Sweden) Stockholm School of Economics, and **James E. Meade** (UK) Cambridge Univ. "for their pathbreaking contribution to the theory of international trade and international capital movements."

1978 Herbert A. Simon (US) Carnegie-Mellon Univ. "for his pioneering research into the decision-making process within economic organizations."

1979 Theodore W. Schultz (US) Univ. of Chicago, and **Sir Arthur Lewis** (UK) Princeton Univ. "for their pioneering research into economic development research with particular consideration of the problems of developing countries."

1980 Lawrence R. Klein (US) Univ. of Pennsylvania "for the creation of economic models and their application to the analysis of economic fluctuations and economic policies."

1981 James Tobin (US) Yale Univ. "for his analysis of financial markets and their relations to expenditure decisions, employment production, and prices."

1982 George J. Stigler (US) Univ. of Chicago "for his seminal studies of industrial structures, functioning of markets, and causes and effects of public regulation."

1983 Gerard Debreu (US) University of California, Berkeley, "for having incorporated new analytical methods into economic theory and for his rigorous reformulation of the theory of general equilibrium."

1984 Sir Richard Stone (UK) Cambridge Univ. "for having made fundamental contributions to the development of systems national accounts and hence greatly improve [*sic*] the basis for empirical economic analysis.

1985 Franco Modigliani (US) MIT "for his pioneering analyses of saving and of financial markets."

1986 James M. Buchanan, Jr. (US) Center for Study of Public Choice "for his development of the contractual and constitutional bases for the theory of economic and political decision-making."

1987 Robert M. Solow (US) MIT "for his contributions to the theory of economic growth."

1988 Maurice Allais (France) Centre d'analys économique "for his pioneering contribution to the theory of markets and efficient utilization of resources."

1989 Trygve Haavelmo (Norway) Univ. of Oslo "for his clarification of the probability theory foundations of econometrics and his analyses of simultaneous economic structures."

1990 Harry M. Markowitz (US) Baruch College of City Univ. of New York, for his Portfolio Theory **William F. Sharpe** (US) Stanford Univ., for Capital Asset Pricing Model; and **Merton M. Mill** (US) Univ. of Chicago, for his work on the Miller-Modigliani Theory. Together, their works revolutionized the financial/business industries.

1991 Ronald H. Coase (UK) Univ. of Chicago Law School, for his work on the role of firms in the economy, and the social cost industry.

1992 Gary S. Becker (US), Univ. of Chicago, for "having extended the domain of economic theory to aspects of human behavior…" including crime, family life, and racial bias. His book on education *Human Capital* (1964), was cited by the Academy as his "most noteworthy contribution."

1993 Robert W. Fogel (US), Univ. of Chicago and **Douglass C. North** (US), Washington Univ. both economic historians, for "applying economic theory and quarantine methods to historic puzzles." Fogel's work on slavery as an efficiency economic system (*Time on the Cross*) caused great controversy.

1994 John F. Nash (US) Princeton Univ., **John C. Harsanyi** (US, b. Hungary) Univ. of California Berkeley, and **Reinhard Selten** (Germany) Univ. of Bonn, for their separate contributions to the field of game theory, used to predict how information and competition affect economic outcomes.

1995 Robert E. Lucas, Jr. (US) Univ. of Chicago, "the economist who has had the greatest influence on macroeconomic research since 1970." His work challenged the Keynesian belief that the government is able to fine-tune the economy.

1996 James A. Mirrlees (UK) Univ. of Cambridge, **William Vickrey** (US) Columbia Univ. "for their fundamental contributions to the economic theory of incentives under asymmetric information."

1997 Robert C. Merton (US) Harvard Univ., **Myron S. Scholes** (US) Stanford Univ. "for a new method to determine the value of derivatives."

1998 Amartya Sen (UK, b. India) Trinity College, Cambridge Univ. "for his contribution to welfare economics."

NOBEL PRIZES IN CHEMISTRY

1901 Jacobus H. Van't Hoff (Netherlands) Berlin Univ. (Germany) "in recognition of the extraordinary services he has rendered by the discovery of the laws of chemical dynamics and osmotic pressure in solutions."

1902 Hermann E. Fischer (Germany) Berlin Univ. "in recognition of the extraordinary services he has rendered by his work on sugar and purine syntheses."

1903 Svante A. Arrhenius (Sweden) Stockholm Univ. "in recognition of the extraordinary services he has rendered to the advancement of chemistry by his electrolytic theory of dissociation."

1904 Sir William Ramsay (UK) London Univ. "in recognition of his services in the discovery of the inert gaseous elements in air, and his determination of their place in the periodic system."

1905 Johann F. W. A. von Baeyer (Germany) Munich Univ. "in recognition of his services in the advancement of organic chemistry and the chemical industry, through his work on organic dyes and hydroaromatic compounds."

1906 Henri Moissan (France) Sorbonne Univ. "in recognition of the great services rendered by him in his investigation and isolation of the element fluorine, and for the adoption in the service of science of the electric furnace called after him."

1907 Eduard Buchner (Germany) Agricultural College "for his biochemical researches and his discovery of cell-free fermentation."

1908 Lord Ernest Rutherford (UK) Victoria Univ. "for his investigations into the disintegration of the elements, and the chemistry of radioactive substances."

1909 Wilhelm Ostward (Germany) Leipzig Univ. "in recognition of his work on catalysis, and for his investigations into the fundamental principles governing chemical equilibria and rates of reaction."

1910 Otto Wallach (Germany) Goettingen Univ. "in recognition of his services to organic chemistry and the chemical industry by his pioneer work in the field of alicyclic compounds."

1911 Marie Curie (France) Sorbonne Univ. "in recognition of her services to the advancement of chemistry by the discovery of the elements radium and polonium, by the isolation of radium and the study of the nature and compounds of this remarkable element."

1912 Victor Grignard (France) Nancy Univ. "for the discovery of the so-called Grignard reagent, which in recent years has greatly advanced the progress of organic chemistry"; **Paul Sabatier** (France) Toulouse Univ. "for his method of hydrogenating organic compounds in the presence of finely disintegrated metals whereby the progress of organic chemistry has been greatly advanced in recent years."

1913 Alfred Werner (Switzerland) Zurich Univ. "in recognition of his work on the linkage of atoms in molecules by which he has thrown new light on earlier investigations and opened up new fields of research especially in inorganic chemistry."

1914 Theodore W. Richards (US) Harvard Univ. "in recognition of his accurate determinations of the atomic weight of a large number of chemical elements."

1915 Richard M. Willstätter (Germany) Munich Univ. "for his researches on plant pigments, especially chlorophyll."

1916-17 Prize Not Awarded.

1918 Fritz Haber (Germany) Kaiser-Wilhelm-Institut (now Fritz-Haber-Institut) "for the synthesis of ammonia from its elements."

1919 Prize Not Awarded.

1920 Walther H. Nernst (Germany) Berlin Univ. "in recognition of his work in thermochemistry."

1921 Frederick Soddy (UK) Oxford Univ. "for his contributions to our knowledge of the chemistry of radioactive substances, and his investigations into the origin and nature of isotopes."

1922 Francis W. Aston (UK) Cambridge Univ. "for his discovery, by means of his mass spectrograph, of isotopes in a large number of nonradioactive elements, and for his enunciation of the whole-number rule."

1923 Fritz Pregl (Austria) Graz Univ. "for his invention of the method of microanalysis of organic substances."

1924 Prize Not Awarded.

1925 Richard A. Zsigmondy (Germany) Goettingen Univ. "for his demonstration of the heterogeneous nature of colloid solutions and for the methods he used, which have since become fundamental in modern colloid chemistry."

1926 The (Theodor) Svedberg (Sweden) Uppsala Univ. "for his work on disperse systems."

1927 Heinrich O. Wieland (Germany) Munich Univ. "for his investigations of the constitution of the bile acids and related substances."

1928 Adolf O.R. Windaus (Germany) Goettingen Univ. "for the services rendered through his research into the constitution of the sterols and their connection with the vitamins."

1929 Sir Arthur Harden (UK) London Univ., **Hans K. A. Simon von Euler-Chelpin** (Sweden) Stockholm Univ. "for their investigations on the fermentation of sugar and fermentative enzymes."

1930 Hans Fischer (Germany) Institute of Technology "for his researches into the constitution of haemin and chlorophyll, and especially for his synthesis of haemin."

1931 Carl Bosch (Germany) Heidelberg Univ. and I.G. Farbenindustrie AG, and **Friedrich Bergius** (Germany) Heidelberg Univ. and I.G. Farbenindustrie AG "in recognition of their contributions to the invention and development of chemical high pressure methods."

1932 Irving Langmuir (US) General Electric Co. "for his discoveries and investigations in surface chemistry."

1933 Prize Not Awarded.

1934 Harold C. Urey (US) Columbia Univ. "for his discovery of heavy hydrogen."

1935 Frédéric Joliot (France) Institut du Radium, and his wife **Irène Joliot-Curie** (France) Institut du Radium "in recognition of their synthesis of new radioactive elements."

1936 Petrus (Peter) J.W. Debye (Netherlands) Berlin Univ. and Kaiser-Wilhelm-Institut (now Max-Planck-Institut) für Physik (Berlin-Dahlem) "for his contributions to our knowledge of molecular structure through his investigations on dipole moments and on the diffraction of X-rays and electrons in gases."

1937 Sir Walter N. Haworth (UK) Birmingham Univ. "for his investigations on carbohyddrates and vitamin C"; **Paul Karrer** (Switzerland) Zurich Univ. "for his investigations on carotenoids, flavins, and vitamins A and B-2."

1938 Richard Kuhn (Germany) Heidelberg Univ. and Kaiser-Wilhelm-Institut (now Max-Planck-Institut) für Medizinische Forschung "for his work on carotenoids and vitamins." (Compelled by the authorities of his country to decline the award, but later received diploma and medal.)

1939 Adolf F. J. Butenandt (Germany) Berlin Univ. and Kaiser-Wilhelm-Institut (now Max-Planck-Institut) für Biochemie "for his work on sex hormones." (Compelled by the authorities of his country to decline the award, but later received diploma and medal); **Leopold Ruzicka** (Switzerland) Federal Institute of Technology "for his work on polymethylenes and higher terpenes."

1940-42 Prize Not Awarded.

1943 George de Hevesy (Hungary) Stockholm Univ. (Sweden) "for his work on the use of isotopes as tracers in the study of chemical processes."

1944 Otto Hahn (Germany) Kaiser-Wilhelm-Institut (now Max-Planck-Institut) für Chemie "for his discovery of the fission of heavy nuclei."

1945 Artturi I. Virtanen (Finland) Helsinki Univ. "for his research and inventions in agricultural and nutrition chemistry, especially for his fodder preservation method."

1946 James B. Sumner (US) Cornell Univ. "for his discovery that enzymes can be crystallized"; **John H. Northrop** (US) Rockefeller Institute for Medical Research, and **Wendell M. Stanley** (US) Rockefeller Institute for Medical Research "for their preparation of enzymes and virus proteins in a pure form."

1947 Sir Robert Robinson (UK) Oxford Univ. "for his investigations on plant products of biological importance, especially the alkaloids."

1948 Arne W. K. Tiselius (Sweden) Uppsala Univ. "for his research on electrophoresis and adsorption analysis, especially for his discoveries concerning the complex nature of the serum proteins."

1949 William F. Giauque (US) Univ. of California, Berkeley, "for his contributions in the field of chemical thermodynamics, particularly concerning the behavior of substances at extremely low temperatures."

1950 Otto P. H. Diels (Germany) Kiel Univ., and **Kurt Alder** (Germany) Cologne Univ. "for their discovery and development of the diene synthesis."

1951 Edwin M. McMillan (US) Univ. of California, Berkeley, and **Glenn T. Seaborg** (US) Univ. of California, Berkeley, "for their discoveries in the chemistry of the transuranium elements."

1952 Archer J. P. Martin (UK) National Institute for Medical Research, and **Richard L. M. Synge** (UK) Rowett Research Institute (Scotland) "for their invention of partition chromatography."

1953 Hermann Staudinger (Germany) State Research Institute for Macromolecular Chemistry "for his discoveries in the field of macromolecular chemistry."

1954 Linus C. Pauling (US) California Institute of Technology "for his research into the nature of the chemical bond and its application to the elucidation of the structure of complex substances."

1955 Vincent du Vigneaud (US) Cornell Univ. "for his work on biochemically important sulphur compounds, especially for the first synthesis of a polypeptide hormone."

1956 Sir Cyril N. Hinshelwood (UK) Oxford Univ., and **Nikolay N. Semenov** (USSR) Institute for Chemical Physics of the Academy of Sciences of the USSR "for their researches into the mechanism of chemical reactions."

1957 Lord Alexander R. Todd (UK) Cambridge Univ. "for his work on nucleotides and nucleotide coenzymes."

1958 Frederick Sanger (UK) Cambridge Univ. "for his work on the structure of proteins, especially that of insulin."

1959 Jaroslav Heyrovsky (Czechoslovakia) Polaro-Institute of the Czechoslovak Academy of Science "for his discovery and development of the polarographic methods of analysis."

1960 Willard F. Libby (US) Univ. of California, Los Angeles "for his method to use carbon-14 for age determination in archaeology, geology, geophysics, and other branches of science."

1961 Melvin Calvin (US) Univ. of California, Berkeley, "for his research on the carbon dioxide assimilation in plants."

1962 Max F. Perutz (UK) Laboratory of Molecular Biology, and **Sir John C. Kendrew** (UK) Laboratory of Molecular Biology "for their studies of the structures of globular proteins."

1963 Karl Ziegler (Germany) Max-Planck-Institut for Carbon Research, and **Giulio Natta** (Italy) Institute of Technology "for their descoveries in the field of the chemistry and technology of high polymers."

1964 Dorothy C. Hodgkin (UK) Royal Society, Oxford Univ. "for her determinations by X-ray techniques of the structures of important biochemical substances."

1965 Robert B. Woodward (US) Harvard Univ. "for his outstanding achievements in the art of organic synthesis."

1966 Robert S. Mulliken (US) Univ. of Chicago "for his fundamental work concerning chemical bonds and the electronic structure of molecules by the molecular orbital method."

1967 Manfred Eigen (W. Germany) Max-Planck Institut für Physikalische Chemie, **Ronald G. W. Norrish** (UK) Institute of Physical Chemistry, and **Sir George Porter** (UK) The Royal Institution "for their studies of extremely fast chemical reactions, effected by disturbing the equilibrium by means of very short pulses of energy."

1968 Lars Onsager (US) Yale Univ. "for the discovery of the reciprocal relations bearing his name, which are fundamental for the thermodynamics of irreversible processes."

1969 Sir Derek H. R. Barton (UK) Imperial College of Science and Technology, and **Odd Hassel** (Norway) Kjemisk Institut "for their contributions to the development of the concept of conformation and its application in chemistry."

1970 Luis F. Leloir (Argentina) Institute for Biochemical Research "for his discovery of sugar nucleotides and their role in the biosynthesis of carbohydrates."

1971 Gerhard Herzberg (Canada) National Research Council of Canada "for his contributions to the knowledge of electronic structure and geometry of molecules, particularly free radicals."

1972 Christian B. Anfinsen (US) National Institutes of Health "for his work on ribonuclease, especially concerning the connection between the amino acid sequence and the biologically active conformation"; **Stanford Moore** (US) Rockefeller Univ., and **William H. Stein** (US) Rockefeller Univ. "for their contribution to the understanding of the connection between chemical structure and catalytic activity of the active center of the ribonuclease molecule."

1973 Ernst O. Fischer (W. Germany) Technical Univ. of Munich, and **Sir Geoffrey Wilkinson** (UK) Imperial College "for their pioneering work, performed independently, on the chemistry of the organometallic, so-called sandwich compounds."

1974 Paul J. Flory (US) Stanford Univ. "for his fundamental achievements, both theoretical and experimental, in the physical chemistry of the macromolecules."

1975 Sir John W. Cornforth (Australia and UK) Univ. of Sussex "for his work on the stereochemistry of enzyme-catalyzed reactions"; **Vladimir Prelog** (Switzerland) Eidgenossische Technische Hochschule "for his research into the stereochemistry of organic molecules and reactions."

1976 William N. Lipscomb (US) Harvard Univ. "for his studies on the structure of boranes illuminating problems of chemical bonding."

1977 Ilya Prigogine (Belgium) Université Libre de

Bruxelles, (Univ. of Texas, US) "for his contributions to nonequilibrium thermodynamics, particularly the theory of dissipative structures."

1978 Peter D. Mitchell (UK) Glynn Research Laboratories "for his contribution to the understanding of biological energy transfer through the formulation of the chemiosmotic theory."

1979 Herbert C. Brown (US) Purdue Univ., and **Georg Wittig** (Germany) Univ. of Heidelberg "for their development of the use of boron- and phosphorus-containing compounds, respectively, into important reagents in organic synthesis."

1980 Paul Berg (US) Stanford Univ. "for his fundamental studies of the biochemistry of nucleic acids, with particular regard to recombinant-DNA"; **Walter Gilbert** (US) Biological Laboratories, and **Frederick Sanger** (UK) MRC Laboratory of Molecular Biology "for their contributions concerning the determination of base sequences in nucleic acids."

1981 Kenichi Fukui (Japan) Kyoto Univ., and **Roald Hoffmann** (US) Cornell Univ. "for their theories, developed independently, concerning the course of chemical reactions."

1982 Sir Aaron Klug (UK) MRC Laboratory of Molecular Biology "for his development of crystallographic electron microscopy and his structural elucidation of biologically important nucleic acid-protein complexes."

1983 Henry Taube (US) Stanford Univ. "for his work on the mechanisms of electron transfer reactions, especially in metal complexes."

1984 Robert B. Merrifield (US) Rockefeller; Univ. "for his development of methodology for chemical synthesis on a solid matrix."

1985 Herbert A. Hauptman (US) The Medica Foundation of Buffalo, and **Jerome Karle** (US) US Naval Research Laboratory "for their outstanding achievements in the development of direct methods for the determination of crystal structures."

1986 Dudley R. Herschbach (US) Harvard Univ., **Yuan T. Lee** (US) Univ. of California, Berkeley, and **John C. Polanyi** (Canada) Univ. of Toronto "for their contributions concerning the dynamics of chemical elementary processes."

1987 Donald J. Cram (US) Univ. of California, Los Angeles, **Jean-Marie Lehn** (France) Université Louis Pasteur, and **Charles J. Pedersen** (US) Du Pont Laboratory "for their development and use of molecules with structure-specific interactions of high selectivity."

1988 Johann Deisenhofer (US) Howard Hughes Medical Institute, **Robert Huber** (W. Germany) Max-Planck-Institut für Biochemie, and **Hartmut Michel** (W. Germany) Max-Planck-Institut für Biophysik "for the determination of the three-dimensional structure of a photosynthetic reaction centre."

1989 Sidney Altman (US) Yale Univ, and **Thomas R. Cech** (US) Univ. of Colorado "for their discovery of the catalytic properties of RNA." (They worked independently.)

1990 Elias James Coret (US) Harvard Univ., for developing new ways to synthesize complex molecules ordinarily found in nature, work that has contributed to "the high standard of living and health, and the longevity enjoyed at least in the Western world."

1991 Richard R. Ernst (Switzerland) Eidgenössische Technische Hochschule, Zurich, for his work in refining nuclear magnetic resonance spectroscopy for use in chemical analysis.

1992 Rudolph A. Marcus (US, b. Canada) Cal Tech, for his mathematical explanation of chemical interactions involving the transfer of electrons between molecules.

1993 Kary B. Mullis (US) who worked for Cetus Corp. in the 1970s when he discovered the polymerase chain reaction (PCR) that allowed scientists to make trillions of copies of DNA from the study of plant and animal fossils and in criminal investigations. **Michael Smith** (Canada) Univ. of British Columbia, for developing the technique that alters the code of genetic molecules that will facilitate new medical therapies and plants that resist disease.

1994 George A. Olah (US, b. Hungary) Univ. of Southern California, for his discovery of new ways of breaking apart and rebuilding carbon and hydrogen compounds. He opened a wholly new field of hydrocarbon research, leading to improved fuels based on coal, methane, and petroleum.

1995 F. Sherwood Rowland (US) Univ. of California-Irvine, **Mario Molina** (US) MIT, and **Paul Crutzen** (Netherlands) Max Planck Institute for Chemistry in Mainz, Germany, for their pioneering work in explaining how production and use of refrigerants, plastic foams, aerosol propellants, and other chlorofluorocarbons deplete the ozone layer, thus increasing the risk of skin cancer, cataracts, and damage to human immune systems.

1996 Robert F. Curl, Jr. (US) Rice Univ., Houston, **Sir Harold W. Kroto** (UK) Univ. of Sussex, Brighton, **Richard E. Smalley** (US) "for their discovery of fullerences."

1997 Paul D. Boyer (US) Univ. of California, Los Angeles, **John E. Walker** (UK) Medical Research Council Laboratory of Molecular Biology, Cambridge "for their elucidation of the enzymatic mechanism underlying the synthesis of adenosine triphosphate (ATP); **Jens C. Skou** (Denmark) Aarhus Univ. "for the discovery of an ion-transporting enzyme, Na^+, K^+-ATPase."

1998 Walter Kohn (US, b. Austria) University of California at Santa Barbara "for his development of the density-functional theory"; **John A. Pople** (US, b. UK) Northwestern Univ. "for his development of computational methods in quantum chemistry."

NOBEL PRIZES IN PHYSICS

1901 Wilhelm C. Röntgen (Germany) Munich Univ. "in recognition of the extraordinary services he has rendered by the discovery of the remarkable rays subsequently named after him."

1902 Hendrik A. Lorentz (Netherlands) Leyden Univ., and **Pieter Zeeman** (Netherlands) Amsterdam Univ. "in recognition of the extraordinary service they rendered by their researches into the influence of magnetism upon radiation phenomena."

1903 Antoine H. Becquerel (France) Ecole Polytechnique "in recognition of the extraordinary services he has rendered by his discovery of spontaneous radioactivity"; **Pierre Curie** (French) Municipal School of Industrial Physics and Chemistry, and his wife **Marie Curie** (France [born in Poland]) "in recognition of the extraordinary services they have rendered by their joint researches on the radiation phenomena discovered by Professor Henri Becquerel."

1904 Lord John William Strutt Rayleigh (UK) Royal Institution of UK "for his investigations of the densities of the most important gases and for his discovery of argon in connection with these studies."

1905 Philipp E. A. Lenard (Germany) Kiel Univ. "for his work on cathode rays."

1906 Sir Joseph J. Thomson (UK) Cambridge Univ. "in recognition of the great merits of his theoretical and experimental investigations on the conduction of electricity by gases."

1907 Albert A. Michelson (US) Univ. of Chicago "for his optical precision instruments and the spectroscopic and metrological investigations carried out with their aid."

1908 Gabriel Lippmann (France) Sorbonne Univ. "for his method of reproducing colours photographically based on phenomenon of interference."

1909 Guglielmo Marconi (Italy) Marconi Wireless Telegraph Co., Ltd., and **Carl F. Braun** (Germany) Strasbourg Univ. "in recognition of their contributions to the development of wireless telegraphy."

1910 Johannes D. van der Waals (Netherlands) Amsterdam Univ. "for his work on the equation of state for gases and liquids."

1911 Wilhelm Wien (Germany) Würzburg Univ. "for his discoveries regarding the laws governing the radiation of heat."

1912 Nils G. Dalén (Sweden) Swedish Gas-Accumulator Co. "for his invention of automatic regulators for use in conjunction with gas accumulators for illuminating lighthouses and buoys."

1913 Heike Kamerlingh-Onnes (Netherlands) Leyden Univ. "for his investigations on the properties of matter at low temperatures which led, *inter alia*, to the production of liquid helium."

1914 Max von Laue (Germany) Frankfurt-am-Main Univ. "for his discovery of the diffraction of X-rays by crystals."

1915 Sir William Henry Bragg (UK) London Univ., and his son **Sir William Lawrence Bragg** (UK) Victoria Univ. "for their services in the analysis of crystal structure by means of X-rays."

1916 Prize Not Awarded.

1917 Charles G. Barkla (UK) Edinburgh Univ. "for his discovery of the characteristic Röntgen radiation of the elements."

1918 Max K. E. L. Planck (Germany) Berlin Univ. "in recognition of the services he rendered to the advancement of Physics by his discovery of energy quanta."

1919 Johannes Stark (Germany) Greifswald Univ. "for his discovery of the Doppler effect in canal rays and the splitting of spectral lines in electric fields."

1920 Charles E. Guillaume (Seitzerland) International Bureau of Weights and Measures "in recognition of the service he has rendered to precision measurements in physics by his discovery of anomalies in nickel steel alloys."

1921 Albert Einstein (Germany) Kaiser-Wilhelm-Institut fürk Physik (now Max-Planck-Institut) "for his services to theoretical physics, and especially for his discovery of the law of the photoelectric effect."

1922 Niels Bohr (Denmark) Copenhagen Univ. "for his services in the investigation of the structure of atoms and of the radiation emanating from them."

1923 Robert A. Millikan (US) California Institute of Technology "for his work on the elementary charge of electricity and on the photoelectric effect."

1924 Karl M. G. Siegbahn (Sweden) Uppsala Univ. "for his discoveries and research in the field of X-ray spectroscopy."

1925 James Franck (Germany) Goettingen Univ., and **Gustav Hertz** (Germany) Halle Univ. "for their discovery of the laws of governing the impact of an electron upon an atom."

1926 Jean B. Perrin (France) Sorbonne Univ. "for his work on the discontinuous structure of matter, and especially for his discovery of sedimentation equilibrium."

1927 Arthur H. Compton (US) Univ. of Chicago "for his discovery of the effect named after him"; **Charles T. R. Wilson** (UK) Cambridge Univ. "for his method of making the paths of electrically charged particles visible by condensation of vapour."

1928 Sir Owen W. Richardson (UK) London Univ. "for his work on the thermionic phenomenon and especially for the discovery of the law named after him."

1929 Prince Louis-Victor de Broglie (France) Sorbonne Univ. "for his discovery of the wave nature of electrons."

1930 Sir Chandrasekhara V. Raman (India) Calcutta Univ. "for his work on the scattering of light and for the discovery of the effect named after him."

1931 Prize Not Awarded.

1932 Wemer Heisenberg (Germany) Leipzig Univ. "for the creation of quantum mechanics, the application of which, has, inter alia, led to the discovery of the allotropic forms of hydrogen."

1933 Erwin Schödinger (Austria) Berlin Univ., and **Paul A. M. Dirac** (UK) Cambridge Univ. "for the discovery of new productive forms of atomic theory."

1934 Prize Not Awarded.

1935 Sir James Chadwick (UK) Liverpool Univ. "for his discovery of the neutron."

1936 Victor F. Hess (Austria) Innsbruck Univ. "for his discovery of cosmic radiation"; **Carl D. Anderson** (US) California Institute of Technology "for his discovery of the positron."

1937 Clinton J. Davisson (US) Bell Telephone Laboratories, and **Sir George P. Thomson** (UK) London Univ. "for their experimental discovery of the diffraction of electrons by crystals."

1938 Enrico Fermi (Italy) Rome Univ. "for his demonstrations of the existence of new radioactive elements produced by neutron irradiation and for his related discovery of nuclear reactions brought about by slow neutrons."

1939 Ernest O. Lawrence (US) Univ. of California, Berkeley, "for the invention and development of the cyclotron and for results obtained with it, especially with regard to artificial radioactive elements."

1940-42 Prize Not Awarded.

1943 Otto Stern (US) Carnegie Institute of Technology (now Carnegie Mellon Univ.) "for his contribution to the development of the molecular ray method and his discovery of the magnetic moment of the proton."

1944 Isidor I. Rabi (US) Columbia Univ. "for his resonance method for recording the magnetic properties of atomic nuclei."

1945 Wolfgang Pauli (Austria) Princeton Univ. "for the discovery of the Exclusion Principle, also called the Pauli Principle."

1946 Percy W. Bridman (US) Harvard Univ. "for the invention of an apparatus to produce extremely high pressures, and for the discoveries he made therewith in the field of high-pressure physics."

1947 Sir Edward V. Appleton (UK) Dept. of Scientific and Industrial Research "for his investigations of the physics of the upper atmosphere, especially for the discovery of the so-called Appleton layer."

1948 Lord Patrick M. S. Blackett (UK) Victoria Univ. "for his development of the Wilson cloud chamber method, and his discoveries therewith in the fields of nuclear physics and cosmic radiation."

1949 Hideki Yukawa (Japan) Kyoto Imperial Univ. and Columbia Univ. "for his prediction of the existence of mesons on the basis of theoretical work on nuclear forces."

1950 Cecil F. Powell (UK) Bristol Univ. "for his development of the photographic method of studying nuclear processes and his discoveries regarding mesons made with this method."

1951 Sir John D. Cockcroft (UK) Atomic Energy Research Establishment, and **Ernest T. S. Walton** (Ireland) Dublin Univ. "for their pioneer work on the transmutation of atomic nuclei by artificially accelerated atomic particles."

1952 Felix Bloch (US) Stanford Univ., and **Edward M. Purcell** (US) Harvard Univ. "for their development of new methods for nuclear magnetic precision measurements and discoveries in connection therewith."

1953 Frits (Frederik) Zernike (Netherlands) Groningen Univ. "for his demonstration of the phase contrast method, especially for his invention of the phase contrast microscope."

1954 Max Born (UK) Edinburgh Univ. "for his fundamental research in quantum mechanics, especially for his statistical interpretation of the wave-function"; **Walther Bothe** (Germany) Heidelberg Univ., Max-Planck-Institut "for the coincidence method and his discoveries made therewith."

1955 Willis E. Lamb (US) Stanford Univ. "for his discoveries concerning the fine structure of the hydrogen spectrum"; **Polykarp Kusch** (US) Columbia Univ. "for his precision determination of the magnetic moment of the electron."

1956 William Shockley (US) Semiconductor Laboratory of Beckman Instruments, Inc., **John Bardeen** (US) Univ. of Illinois, and **Walter H. Brattain** (US) Bell Telephone Laboratories "for their researches on semiconductors and their discovery of the transistor effect."

1957 Chen N. Yang (China) Institute for Advanced Study (Princeton, N.J.), and **Tsung-Dao Lee** (China) Columbia Univ. "for their penetrating investigation of the so-called parity laws which has led to important discoveries regarding the elementary particles."

1958 Pavel A. Cherenkov (USSR) Physics Institute of USSR Academy of Sciences, **Il'ja M. Frank** (USSR) Univ. of Moscow and Physics Institute of USSR Academy of Sciences, and **Igor Y. Tamm** (USSR) Univ. of Moscow and Physics Institute of USSR Academy of Sciences "for the discovery and the interpretation of the Cherenkov effect."

1959 Emilio G. Segrè (US) Univ. of California, Berkeley, and **Owen Chamberlain** (US) Univ. of California, Berkeley, "for their discovery of the antiproton."

1960 Donald A. Glaser (US) Univ. of California, Berkeley, "for the invention of the bubble chamber."

1961 Robert Hofstadter (US) Stanford Univ. "for his pioneering studies of eletron scattering in atomic nuclei and for his thereby achieved discoveries concerning the structure of the nucleons"; **Rudolf L. Mössbauer** (Germany) Technische Hochschule (Munich), and California Institute of Technology "for his researches concerning the resonance absorption of gamma radiation and his discovery in this connection of the effect which bears his name."

1962 Lev D. Landau (USSR) Academy of Sciences

"for his pionering theories for condensed matter, especially liquid helium."

1963 Eugene P. Wigner (US) Princeton Univ. "for his contributions to the theory of the atomic nucleus and the elementary particles, particularly through the discovery and application of fundamental symmetry principles"; **Maria Goeppert-Mayer** (US) Univ. of California, La Jolla, and **J. Hans D. Jensen** (Germany) Univ. of Heidelberg "for their discoveries concerning nuclear shell structure."

1964 Charles H. Townes (US) MIT, **Nicolay G. Basov** (USSR) Lebedev Institute for Physics, and **Aleksandre M. Prokhorov** (USSR) Lebedev Institute for Physics "for fundamental work in the field of quantum electronics, which has led to the construction of oscillators and amplifiers based on the maser-laser-principle."

1965 Schin'ichiro Tomonaga (Japan) Tokyo Univ. of Education, **Julian Schwinger** (US) Harvard Univ., and **Richard P. Feynman** (US) California Institute of Technology "for their fundamental work in quantum electrodynamics, with deep-ploughing consequences for the physics of elementary particles."

1966 Alfred Kastler (France) Ecole Normale Supérieure, Université de Paris "for the discovery and development of optical methods for studying hertzian resonances in atoms."

1967 Hans A. Bethe (US) Cornell Univ. "for his contributions to the theory of nuclear reactions, especially his discoveries concerning the energy production in stars."

1968 Luis W. Alvarez (US) Univ. of California, Berkeley, "for his decisive contributions to elementary particle physics, in particular the discovery of a large number of resonance states, made possible through his development of the technique of using hydrogen bubble chamber and data analysis."

1969 Murray Gell-Mann (US) California Institute of Technology "for his contributions and discoveries concerning the classification of elementary particles and their interactions."

1970 Hannes Alfvén (Sweden) Royal Institute of Technology "for fundamental work and discoveries in magneto-hydrodynamics with fruitful applications in different parts of plasma physics"; **Louis Neel**

(France) Univ. of Grenoble "for fundamental work and discoveries concerning antiferromagnetism and ferrimagnetism which have led to important applications in solid-state physics."

1971 Dennis Gabor (UK) Imperial College of Science and Technology "for his invention and development of the holographic method."

1972 John Bardeen (US) Univ. of Illinois, **Leon N. Cooper** (US) Brown Univ., and **Robert J. Schrieffer** (US) Univ. of Pennsylvania "for their jointly developed theory of superconductivity, usually called the BCS-theory."

1973 Leo Esaki (Japan) IBM Thomas J. Watson Research Center (Yorktown Heights, N.Y.), and **Ivar Giaever** (US) General Electric Co. "for their experimental discoveries regarding tunneling phenomena in semiconductors and super-conductors, respectively"; **Brian D. Josephson** (UK) Cambridge Univ. "for his theoretical predictions of the properties of a supercurrent through a tunnel barrier, in particular those phenomena which are generally known as the Josephson effects."

1974 Sir Martin Ryle (UK) Cambridge Univ., and **Antony Hewish** (UK) Cambridge Univ. "for their pioneering research in radio astrophysics: Ryle for his observations and inventions, in particular of the aperture synthesis technique, and Hewish for his decisive role in the discovery of pulsars."

1975 Aage Bohr (Denmark) Niels Bohr Institute, **Ben Mottelson** (Demark) Nordita, and **James Rainwater** (US) Columbia Univ. "for the discovery of the connection between collective motion and particle motion in atomic nuclei and the development of the theory of the structure of the atomic nucleus based on this connection."

1976 Burton Richter (US) Stanford Linear Accelerator Center, and **Samuel C. C. Ting** (US) MIT "for their pioneering work in the discovery of a heavy elementary particle of a new kind."

1977 Philip W. Anderson (US) Bell Laboratories, **Sir Nevill F. Mott** (UK) Cambridge Univ., and **John H. van Vleck** (US) Harvard Univ. "for their fundamental theoretical investigations of the electronic structure of magnetic and disordered systems."

1978 Pyotr L. Kapitsa (USSR) Academy of Sciences

"for his basic inventions and discoveries in the area of low-temperature physics; **Arno A. Penzias** (US) Bell Laboratories, and **Robert W. Wilson** (US) Bell Laboratories "for their discovery of cosmic microwave background radiation."

1979 Sheldon L. Glashow (US) Lyman Laboratory, Harvard Univ., **Abdus Salam** (Pakistan) International Centre for Theoretical Physics (Trieste) and Imperial College of Science and Technology (London), and **Steven Weinberg** (US) Harvard Univ. "for their contributions to the theory of the unified weak and electromagnetic interaction between elementary particles, including, inter alia, the prediction of the weak neutral current."

1980 James W. Cronin (US) Univ. of Chicago, and **Val L. Fitch** (US) Princeton Univ. "for the discovery of violations of fundamental symmetry principles in the decay of neutral K-mesons."

1981 Nicolaas Bloembergen (US) Harvard Univ., and **Arthur L. Schawlow** (US) Stanford Univ. "for their contributions to the development of laser spectroscopy"; **Kai M. Siegbahn** (Sweden) Uppsala Univ. "for his contribution to the development of high-resolution electron spectroscopy."

1982 Kenneth G. Wilson (US) Cornell Univ. "for his theory for critical phenomena in connection with phase transitions."

1983 Subrahmanyan Chandrasekhar (US) Univ. of Chicago "for his theoretical studies of the physical processes of importance to the structure and evolution of the stars"; **William A. Fowler** (US) California Institute of Technology "for his theoretical and experimental studies of the nuclear reactions of importance in the formation of the chemical elements in the universe."

1984 Carlo Rubbia (Italy) CERN, Geneva, and **Simon van der Meer** (Netherlands) CERN, Geneva "for their decisive contributions to the large project, which led to the discovery of the field particles W and A, communicators of weak interaction."

1985 Klaus von Klitzing (W. Germany) Max-Planck-Institut for Solid State Research "for the discovery of the quantized Hall effect."

1986 Ernst Ruska (W. Germany) Fritz-Haber-Institut der Max-Planck-Gesellschaft "for his fundamental work in electron optics, and for the design of the first electron microscope"; **Gerd Binnig** (W. Germany) IBM Zurich Research Laboratory, and **Heinrich Rohrer** (Switzerland) IBM Zurich Research Laboratory "for their design of the scanning tunneling microscope."

1987 Georg J. Bednorz (Switzerland) IBM Zurich Research Laboratory, and **Dr. K. Alexander Müller** (Switzerland) IBM Zurich Research Laboratory "for the discovery of new superconducting materials."

1988 Leon M. Lederman (US) Fermi National Accelerator Laboratory, **Melvin Schwartz** (US) Digital Pathways, Inc., and **Jack Steinberger** (Switzerland) CERN "for the neutrino beam method and the demonstration of the doublet structure of the leptons through the discovery of the muon neutrino."

1989 Norman F. Ramsey (US) Harvard Univ. "for the invention of the separated oscillatory fields method and its use in...atomic clocks." **Hans G. Dehmelt** (US) Univ of Washington, and **Wolfgang Paul**, Univ. of Bonn (W. Germany) "for the development of the ion trap technique." which allows detailed study of subatomic particles.

1990 Richard E. Taylor (Canada) Stanford Univ., **Jerome I. Friedman** (US) MIT, and **Henry W. Kendall** (US) MIT, whose experiments between 1967 and 1973 confirmed the existence of quarks, the fundamental building blocks of matter.

1991 Pierre-Gilles de Gennes (France) Collège de France, Paris, for his discoveries about the ordering of molecules in a variety of substances but especially liquid crystals, where his work has helped in understanding superconductivity.

1992 George Charpak (France, b. Poland) affiliated with CERN, the accelerator complex, where he developed electronic detectors that traced the paths of subatomic particles with lightning speed.

1993 Joseph H. Taylor Jr (US) Princeton Univ., and **Russell A. Hulse** (US) Princeton Plasma Physics Laboratory, for their 1970s discovery of a binary pulsar and their subsequent success in measuring its pulse rate.

1994 Clifford G. Shull (US) MIT, and **Bertram N. Brockhouse** (Canada) McMaster Univ., for their experiments in the 1940s and '50s that exploited the penetrating power of low-energy neutron beams produced by nuclear reactors. Neutron beams are much more powerful than X-rays or other forms of radiation, and are now widely used by scientists to explore the atomic structure of matter.

1995 Martin L. Perl (US) Stanford Univ. Linear Accelerator Center, and **Frederick Reines** (US) Los Alamos National Laboratory, for their separate discoveries of "two of nature's most remarkable subatomic particles." Perl's discovery of the tau in the 1970s and Reines's discovery of the neutrino in the 1950s were watershed events in scientists' understanding of elementary particle physics.

1996 David M. Lee (US) Cornell Univ. Ithaca, **Douglas D. Osheroff** (US) Stanford Univ., **Robert C. Richardson** (US) Cornekk Univ. "for their discovery of superfluidity in helium-3."

1997 Steven Chu (US) Stanford Univ., **Claude Cohen-Tannoudji** (France) Collége de France and Icole Normale Supirieure, Laboratoire de Physique de Icole Normale Supirieure, **William D. Phillips** (US) National Institute of Standards and Technology, Gaithersburg, Maryland "for development of methods to cool and trap atoms with laser light."

1998 Horst L. Stormer (US, b. Germany) Columbia Univ., **Daniel D. Tsui** (US, b. China) Princeton Univ., **Robert B. Laughlin** (US) Stanford Univ. "for discovery of a new form of quantum fluid with fractionally charged excitations."

NOBEL PRIZES FOR LITERATURE

1901 Sully Prudhomme (pen name of René F.A. Prudhomme) (France) "in special recognition of his poetic composition, which gives evidence of lofty idealism, artistic perfection, and a rare combination of the qualities of both heart and intellect."

1902 Christian M. T. Mommsen (Germany) "the greatest living master of the art of historical writing, with special reference to his monumental work, *A History of Rome.*"

1903 Bjornstjerne M. Bjørnson (Norway) "as a tribute to his noble, magnificent, and versatile poetry, which has always been distinguished by both the freshness of its inspiration and the rare purity of its spirit."

1904 Frederic Mistral (France) "in recognition of the fresh orginality and true inspiration of his poetic production, which faithfully reflects the natural scenery and native spirit of his people, and, in addition, his significant work as a Provencal philologist"; **José Echegaray Y Eizaguirre** (Spain) "in recognition of the numerous and brilliant compositions which, in an individual and original manner, have revived the great traditions of the Spanish drama."

1905 Henryk Sienkiewicz (Poland) "because of his outstanding merits as an epic writer."

1906 Giosuè Carducci (Italy) "not only in consideration of his deep learning and critical research, but above all as a tribute to the creative energy, freshness of style, and lyrical force which charachterize his poetic masterpieces."

1907 Rudyard Kipling (UK) "in consideration of the power of observation, originality of imagination, virility of ideas, and remarkable talent for narration which characterize the creations of this world-famous author."

1908 Rudolf C. Eucken (Germany) "in recognition of his earnest search for truth, his penetrating power of thought, his wide range of vision, and the warmth and strength in presentation with which in his numerous works he has vendicated and developed an idealistic philosophy of life."

1909 Selma O. L. Lagerlöf (Sweden) "in appreciation of the lofty idealism, vivid imagination, and spiritual perception that characterize her writings."

1910 Paul J. L. Heyse (Germany) "as a tribute to the consummate artistry, permeated with idealism, which he has demonstrated during his long productive career as lyric poet, dramatist, novelist, and writer of world-renowned short stories."

1911 Count Maurice (Mooris) P. M. B. Maeter-linck (Belgium) "in appreciation of his many-sided literary activities, and especially of his dramatic works, which are distinguished by a wealth of imagination and by a poetic fancy."

1912 Gerhart J. R. Hauptmann (Germany) "primarily in recognition of his fruitful, varied, and outstanding production in the realm of dramatic art."

1913 Rabindranath Tagore (India) "because of his

profoundly sensitive, fresh, and beautiful verse, by which, with consummate skill, he has made his poetic thought, expressed in his own English words, a part of the literature of the West."

1914 Prize Not Awarded.

1915 Romain Rolland (France) "as a tribute to the lofty idealism of his literary production and to the sympathy and love of truth with which he has described different types of human beings."

1916 Carl G. V. von Heidenstam (Sweden) "in recognition of his significance as the leading representative of a new era in our literature."

1917 Karl A. Gjellerup (Denmark) "for his varied and rich poetry, which is inspired by lofty ideals"; **Henrik Pontoppidan** (Denmark) "for his authentic descriptions of presentday life in Denmark."

1918 Prize Not Awarded.

1919 Carl F. G. Spitteler (Switzerland) "in special appreciation of his epic, *Olympian Spring*."

1920 Knut P. Hamsun (Norway) "for his monumental work, *Growth of the Soil*."

1921 Anatole France (Pen name of Jacques A. Thibault) (France) "in recognition of his brilliant literary achievements, characterized as they are by a nobility of style, a profound human sympathy, grace, and a true Gallic temperament."

1922 Jacinto Benavente (Spain) "for the happy manner in which he has continued the illustrious traditions of the Spanish drama."

1923 William B. Yeats (Ireland) "for his always inspired poetry, which in a highly artistic form gives expression to the spirit of a whole nation."

1924 Wladyslaw S. Reymont (pen name of Reyment) (Poland) "for his great national epic, *The Peasants*."

1925 George B. Shaw (UK) "for his work which is marked by both idealism and humanity, its stimulating satire often being infused with a singular poetic beauty."

1926 Grazia Deledda (pen name of Grazia Made-

sani) (Italy) "for her idealistically inspired writings which with plastic clarity picture the life on her native island and with depth and sympathy deal with human problems in general."

1927 Henri Bergson (France) "in recognition of his rich and vitalizing ideas and the brilliant skill with which they have been presented."

1928 Sigrid Undset (Norway) "principally for her powerful descriptions of Northern life during the Middle Ages."

1929 Thomas Mann (Germany) "principally for his great novel *Buddenbrooks,* which has won steadily increased recognition as one of the classic works of contemporary literature."

1930 Sinclair Lewis (US) "for his vigorous and graphic art of description and his ability to create, with wit and humour, new types of characters."

1931 Erik A. Karlfeldt (Sweden) "the poetry of Erik Axel Karlfeldt."

1932 John Galsworthy (UK) "for his distinguished art of narration which takes its highest form in *The Forsythe Saga*."

1933 Ivan A. Bunin (stateless domicile in France) "for the strict artistry with which he has carried on the classical Russian traditions in prose writing."

1934 Luigi Pirandello (Italy) "for his bold and ingenious revival of dramatic and scenic art."

1935 Prize Not Awarded.

1936 Eugene G. O'Nell (US) "for the power, honesty, and deep-felt emotions of his dramatic works, which embody an original concept of tragedy."

1937 Roger Martin du Gard (France) "for the artistic power and truth with which he has depicted human conflict as well as some fundamental aspects of contemporary life in his novel-cycle *Les Thibault*."

1938 Pearl Buck (pen name of Pearl Walsh) (US) "for her rich and truly epic descriptions of peasant life in China and for her biographical masterpieces."

1939 Frans E. Sillanpää (Finland) "for his deep understanding of his country's peasantry and the exquisite art with which he has portrayed their way of life and their relationship with Nature."

1940-43 Prize Not Awarded.

1944 Johannes V. Jensen (Demark) "for the rare strength and fertility of his poetic imagination with which is combined an intellectual curiosity of wide scope and bold, freshly creative style."

1945 Gabriela Mistral (pen name of Lucila Godoy y Alcayaga) (Chile) "for her lyric poetry which, inspired by powerful emotions, has made her name a symbol of the idealistic aspirations of the entire Latin American world."

1946 Hermann Hesse (Switzerland) "for his inspired writings which, while growing in boldness and penetration, exemplify the classical humanitarian ideals and high qualities of style."

1947 André P. G. Gide (France) "for his comprehensive and artistically significant writings, in which human problems and conditions have been presented with a fearless love of truth and keen psychological insight."

1948 Thomas S. Eliot (UK) "for his outstanding, pioneer contribution to presentday poetry."

1949 William Faulkner (US) "for his powerful and artistically unique contribution to the modern American novel."

1950 Earl Bertrand Arthur William (A. W.) Russell (UK) "in recognition of his varied and significant writings in which he champions humanitarian ideals and freedom of thought."

1951 Pär F. Lägerkvist (Sweden) "for the artistic vigour and true independence of mind with which he endeavours in his poetry to find answers to the eternal questions confronting mankind."

1952 François Mauriac (France) "for the deep spiritual insight and the artistic intensity with which he has in his novels penetrated the drama of human life."

1953 Sir Winston L. P. Churchill (UK) "for his mastery of historical and biographical description as well as for brilliant oratory in defending exalted human values."

1954 Ernest M. Hemingway (US) "for his mastery of the art of narrative, most recently demonstrated in *The Old Man and the Sea,* and for the influence that he has exerted on contemporary style."

1955 Halldór K. Laxness (Iceland) "for his vivid epic power which has renewed the great narrative art of Iceland."

1956 Juan R. Jiménez (Spain [domicile in Puerto Rico]) "for his lyrical poetry, which in Spanish language constitutes an example of high spirit and artistical purity."

1957 Albert Camus (France) "for his important literary production, which with clearsighted earnestness illuminates the problems of the human conscience in our times."

1958 Boris L. Pasternak (USSR) "for his important achievement both in contemporary lyrical poetry and in the field of the great Russian epic tradition." (Declined the prize.)

1959 Salvatore Quasimodo (Italy) "for his lyrical poetry, which with classical fire expresses the tragic experience of life in our own times."

1960 Saint-John Perse (pen name of Alexis Léger) (France) "for the soaring flight and the evocative imagery of his poetry which in a visionary fashion reflects the conditions of our time."

1961 Ivo Andrić (Yugoslavia) "for the epic force with which he has traced themes and depicted human destinies drawn from the history of his country."

1962 John Steinbeck (US) "for his realistic and imaginative writings, combining as they do sympathetic humour and keen social perception."

1963 Giorgos Seferis (pen name of Giorgos Seferiades) Greece) "for his eminent lyrical writing, inspired by a deep feeling for the Hellenic world of culture."

1964 Jean-Paul Sartre (France) "for his work which, rich in ideas and filled with the spirit of freedom and the quest for truth, has exerted a far-reaching influence on our age." (Declined the prize.)

1965 Michail A. Solochov (USSR) "for the artistic power and integrity with which, in his epic of the

Don, he has given expression to a historic phase in the life of the Russian people."

1966 Shmuel Y. Agnon (Israel) "for his profoundly characteristic narrative art with motifs from the life of the Jewish people; **Nelly Sachs** (Germany [domiciled in Sweden]) "for her outstanding lyrical and dramatic writing, which interprets Israel's destiny with touching strength."

1967 Miguel A. Asturias (Guatemala) "for his vivid literary achievement, deep-rooted in the national traits and traditions of Indian peoples of Latin America."

1968 Yasunari Kawabata (Japan) "for his narrative mastery, which with great sensibility expresses the essence of the Japanese mind."

1969 Samuel Beckett (Ireland) "for his writing, which—in new forms for the novel and drama—in the destitution of modern man acquires its elevation."

1970 Alexandr I. Solzhjenitsyn (USSR) "for the ethical force with which he has pursued the indispensable traditions of Russian literature."

1971 Pablo Neruda (Chile) "for a poetry that with the action of an elemental force brings alive a continent's destiny and dreams."

1972 Heinrich Böll (W. Germany) "for his writing which through its combination of a broad perspective on his time and a sensitive skill in characterization has contributed to a renewal of German literature."

1973 Patrick White (Australia) "for an epic and psychological narrative art which has introduced a new continent into literature."

1974 Eyvind Johnson (Sweden) "for a narrative art, far-seeing in lands and ages, in the service of freedom"; **Harry Martinson** (Sweden) "for writings that catch the dewdrop and reflect the cosmos."

1975 Eugenio Montale (Italy) "for his distinctive poetry which, with great artistic sensitivity, has interpreted hyman values under the sign of an outlook on life with no illusions."

1976 Saul Bellow (US) "for the human understanding and subtle analysis of contemporary culture that are combined in his work."

1977 Vicente Aleixandre (Spain) "for a creative poetic writing which illuminates man's codition in the cosmos and in present-day society, at the same time representing the great renewal of the traditions of Spanish poetry between the wars."

1978 Isaac B. Singer (US) "for his impassioned narrative art which, with roots in a Polish-Jewish cultural tradition, brings universal human conditions to life."

1979 Odysseus Elytis (pen name of Odysseus Alepoudhelis) (Greece) "for his poetry, which against the background of Greek tradition, depicts with sensuous strength and intellectual clear-sightedness modern man's struggle for freedom and creativeness."

1980 Czeslaw Milosz (US and Poland) "who with uncompromising clear-sightedness voices man's exposed condition in a world of severe conflicts."

1981 Elias Canetti (UK) "for writings marked by a broad outlook, a wealth of ideas, and artistic power."

1982 Gabriel García Marquez (Colombia) "for his novels and short stories, in which the fantastic and the realistic are combined in a richly composed world of imagination, reflecting a continent's life and conflicts."

1983 Sir William Golding (UK) "for his novels which, with the perspicuity of realistic narrative art and the diversity and universality of myth, illuminate the human condition in the world of today."

1984 Jaroslav Seifert (Czechoslovakia) "for his poetry which, endowed with freshness, sensuality, and rich inventiveness, provides a liberating image of the indomitable spirit and versatility of man."

1985 Claude Simon (France) "who in his novel combines the poet's and the painter's creativeness with a deepened awareness of time in the depiction of the human condition.

1986 Wole Soyinka (Nigeria) "who in a wide cultural perspective and with poetic overtones fashions the drama of existence."

1987 Joseph Brodsky (US) "for his all-embracing authorship imbued with clarity of thought and poetic intensity."

1988 Naguib Mahfouz (Egypt) "who, through works rich in nuance—now clear-sightedly realistic, now evocatively ambiguous—has formed an Arabian narrative art that applies to all mankind."

1989 Camilo José Cela (Spain) a novelist whose "rich and inventive prose, which ... forms a challenging vision of man's vulnerability." His most famous work is *The Family of Pascual Duarte* (1942)

1990 Octavio Paz (Mexico) poet and social essayist. Volumes include *The Labyrinth of Solitude* (1950), *Sunstone* (1957), and *Sor Juana: Or, the Traps of Faith* (1990).

1991 Nadine Gordimer (South Africa) for her "involvement on behalf of literature and free speech in a police state where censorship and persecution of books and people exist." Novels include *A Guest of Honour, Burger's Daughter*, and *My Son's Story*.

1992 Derek Walcott (West Indies, B. St. Lucia) poet and playwright whose works evoke the cultural diversity of the Carribean "but through them he speaks to each and every one of us." His recent book-length poem, *Omeros*, won worldwide acclaim.

1993 Toni Morrison (US) whose novels about racial prejudice are "characterized by visionary force and poetic import." Her novels include *Sula, Tar Baby, Song of Solomon*, and the Pulitzer Prize-winning *Beloved*.

1994 Kenzaburo Oe (Japan) best known for his accounts of the atomic bombing of Hiroshima and for a novel in which he comes to grips with a mentally handicapped son. The poetic force of his writing "creates an imagined world where life and myth condense to form a disconcerting picture of the human predicament."

1995 Seamus Heaney (Ireland) poet and essayist, "for works of lyrical beauty and ethical depth, which exalt everyday miracles and the living past." His works include *Station Island, Lightenings viii, Death of a Naturalist*, and *Door Into the Dark*.

1996 Wislawa Szymborska (Poland) "a poet whose work contemplates the oddities of daily life," "for poetry that with ironic precision allows the historical and biological contest to come to light in fragments of human reality."

1997 Dario Fo (Italy) the dramatist and actor "who emulates the jesters of the Middle Ages in scourging authority and upholding the dignity of the downtrodden." His works include *Morte accidentale di un anarchico, Non si paga, non si paga, and Female Parts*.

1998 Jose Saramago (Portugal) Portuguese writer "who with parables sustained by imagination, compassion and irony continually enables us once again to apprehend an elusory reality."

UNITED NATIONS SPECIALIZED AGENCIES

The specialized agencies are defined in Article 57 of the United Nation's Charter as agencies which have been 'established by intergovernmental agreement and having wide international responsibilities, as defined in their basic instruments, in economic, social, cultural, educational, health, and related fields' and which have been 'brought into relationship with the United Nations.' Under Article 63, their activities may be coordinated by ECOSOC. They are separate, autonomous organizations, each with their own membership and institutions. Some are the successors to similar or organizations associated with the former League of Nations, some have earlier origins.

A fitting addition to the appendix is a list of the specialized agencies of the United Nations. Archival materials found in the Internet were used for this expansion job.

United Nations Specialized Agencies

International Labor Organization (ILO)

4Route Des Morillons
1211 Geneva 22
Switzerland
Telephone: (41-22) 799-61-11
Telex: 415647
Facsimile: (41-22) 798-86-85
Director-General: Michel Hansenne, Belgium (1994-99)

The ILO was established in 1919, its Constitution forming a part of the Treaty of Versailles. In 1946, it became a specialized agency of the UN.

Purposes: The objectives of ILO are set out in the preamble to its Constitution and in the 'Philadelphia Declaration' adopted by the General Conference of the Organization in 1944. ILO seeks to improve working and living conditions through the adoption of international labour conventions and recommendations setting minimum standards in such fields as wages, hours of work and conditions of employment, and social security. It also conducts research and technical cooperation activities, including vocational training and management development, with an aim to promote democracy and human rights: alleviate unemployment and poverty; and protect working people.

Structure:
(a) International Labour Conference
(b) Governing Body
(c) International Labour Office.

Conference: The Conference meets each year to debate world labour problems and draw up and adopt international labour conventions and recommendations. Each member is entitled to be represented by four delegates, two of whom should be representatives of the government, while the other two should be representatives of employers' and workers' groups.

The eighty-third session of the General Conference met in Geneva from June 4 to 20, 1996. The eighty-fourth (Maritime) session of the Conference met in Geneva from October 8 to 22, 1996.

Governing Body: This formulates the policies and programmes of the Organization, guides the activities of the various conferences and committees, and reviews the works of ILO. It also has a tripartite structure, being composed of 56 representatives of governments, employers and workers. Each group has both regular (titular) and deputy members.

Of the 28 government representatives, 10 hold non-elective seats representing member states of 'chief industrial importance' and 18 represent members elected by the Conference. The Governing Body itself determines (as occasion requires) which members are of chief industrial importance. The other regular members are elected every three years at the Conference by electoral colleges composed of the government delegates of all members other than the ten, the employers' delegates, and the workers' delegates. (Members elected by the last two groups sit as individuals.) These electoral colleges also meet separately the deputy government, employer and worker representatives. Deputy members have the right to be present at the sittings of the Governing Body and to speak with the permission of the Chair but they may vote only when replacing a titular member.

In 1986, the Conference adopted amendments to the Constitution concerning the membership of the Governing Body. Under the new provisions, the regular membership will be increased to 56 government members and 28 employers' and workers' members respectively. The category of states of 'chief industrial importance' and the government deputy members will disappear. In addition, there will be five employer and five worker deputy members. The amendments will not come into force, however, until accepted by two thirds of Member States, including five of the 10 states of chief industrial importance.

Pending the entry into force of the constitutional amendment, the International Labour Conference adopted an amendment to its Standing-Orders which added 10 deputy seats to the government group, five deputy seats to the employers' group and five deputy seats to the workers' group so that the total number of deputy members would be the same as provided for under the constitutional amendment. This increase will take effect at the next elections for membership of the Governing Body, to be held during the eight, third session of the Conference in June 1996.

Food And Agriculture Organization (FAO)

Viale Delle Terme Di Caracalla
Rome
Italy
Telephone: (39-6) 52251
Telex: 625852 FAO 1/625853 FAO 1/610181 FAO 1
Facsimile: (39-6) 5225-3152
Director-General: Jacques Diouf, Senegal (1994-99) (Elected) by FAO membership at 1993 conference

FAO was established in 1945, when 44 governments indicated their acceptance of the Constitution, as drafted by an interim commission. The functions and assets of the former International Institute of Agriculture in Rome were transferred to the new body.

Purpose: The preamble of the Constitution defines the aim of the members as being 'to promote the common welfare by furthering separate and collective action ... for the purposes of raising levels of nutrition and standards of living of the peoples under their respective jurisdictions; securing improvements in the efficiency of the production and distribution of all food and agricultural products; bettering the condition of rural populations; and thus contributing toward an expanding world economy and ensuring humanity's freedom from hunger'.

By Assembly res. 50/227 the Food and Agriculture Organization of the United Nations and the World Food Programme absorbed the functions of the World Food Council, and consequently the World Food Council was discontinued.

Structure:

(a) Conference

(b) Council

(c) Committees of the Council

(d) Other intergovernmental bodies

(e) Secretariat.

Conference: The Conference, which consists of all members of FAO, meets in regular session every two years to determine the policies of the Organization and approve the budget, and to make recommendations to members and international organizations on any matter pertaining to the purposes of FAO. The twenty-eighth session of the Conference was held in Rome from October 20 to 31, 1995. The twenty-ninth session of the Conference is scheduled to be held in Rome in November 1997.

Council: The Council is the executive organ of the Conference and exercises powers delegated to it by the Conference. It meets at least three times between the biennial Conference sessions. There are 49 Member Nations which are elected by the Conference for three-year terms, with arrangements for staggered expiry of office and one-third of members stepping down each year.

An Independent Chair of the Council is appointed by the Conference for a renewable two-year term. The present Chair is José Ramón López Portillo, Mexico, who was appointed for two years by the Conference at its twenty-eighth session in 1995. The one hundred and tenth session of the Council was held in Rome from November 2 to 3, 1995.

Committees of the Council: To assist its work the Council has three small elected committee concerned with particular aspects of management—the Programme Committee, the Finance Committee and the Committee on Constitutional and Legal Matters.

Programme Committee, November 1995-November 1997:

N RIMOUCHE, *ALGERIA*	
J B SHARPE, *AUSTRALIA*	
R F ANDRIGO, *CANADA*	
A M ABOUL-NAGA, *EGYPT*	
G REDAI, *ETHIOPIA*	
D F R BOMMER, *GERMANY*, CHAIR	

E KITAHARA, *JAPAN*

M M SEGHAYER, *LIBYA*

R VELÁQUEZ-HUERTA, *MEXICO*

M R CASTILLO, *PHILIPPINES*

W R RUDDER, *TRINIDAD AND TOBAGO*

Finance Committee, November 1995-November 1997

IDI GIOVAN BATTISTA, *ARGENTINA*

R DE CLERCQ, *BELGIUM*

C KIEMTORE, *BURKINA FASO*

MS KHAN, *PAKISTAN, CHAIR*

H J MALTED, *PANAMA*

M KADLECIKOVA, *SLOVAKIA*

JA THOMAS, *SOUTH AFRICA*

MS MA HARDY, *SUDAN*

TA FORBORE, *USA*

Committee on Constitutional and Legal Matters, November 1995-November 1997

COSTA RICA	FRANCE	ITALY
CZECH REPUBLIC	IRAQ	TUNISIA
		USA

The Council also has five major committees covering the activities of the Organization, each non-elective and open to all Member Nations:

Committee on Commodity Problems (CCP): The CCP keeps under review international commodity problems affecting productions, trade, consumption and related economic matters, undertakes surveys of the world commodity situation, and reports to the Council on policy issues arising from its deliberations. It has established intergovernmental groups to consider various problems in connection with the following commodities: rice, cocoa, grains, citrus fruits, jute, kenaf and allied fibres, bananas, oilseed, oils and fats, hard fibres, tea, wine and meat. It has also established a Consultative Subcommittee on Surplus Disposals (CSD) which meets regularly in Washington for consultations on the effects on commercial markets of disposals of surplus agricultural products as aid or at concessional prices.

Committee on Fisheries (COFI): COFI reviews the Organizations's work in the field of fisheries, conducts periodic general reviews of international fishery problems and appraises possible solutions thereto, discusses other specific matters relating to fisheries and makes recommendations as appropriate.

Committee on Forestry (COFO): COFO reviews the Organization's work in the field of forestry, conducts periodic general reviews of international forestry problems and appraises possible solutions thereto, discusses other specific matters relating to forestry

and makes recommendations as appropriate.

Committee on Agriculture(COAG): COAG conducts periodic reviews and appraisals, on a selective basis, of agricultural problems, advises the Council on the medium-and long-term programme of work of the Organization in selected fields of agriculture and on its implementation, reviews other specific matters relating to agriculture, and reports to the Council or advises the Director-General as appropriate.

Committee on World Food Security(CFS): This Committee keeps under continuous review the current and prospective demand, supply and stock position of basic foodstuffs and makes periodic evaluations of the adequacy of current and prospective stock levels to meet the requirements of domestic and world markets, including food aid requirements, in the event of serious crop failure. It also reviews steps, taken by governments to implement the International Undertaking on World Food Security and recommends short- or long-term policy measures to remedy difficulties foreseen in assuring adequate cereal supplies for minimum world food security. The CFS also acted as a preparatory committee for the World Food Summit, held in Rome from November 13 to 17, 1996.

Other Intergovernmental Bodies: The FAO has a wide range of other intergovernmental and expert bodies, of both a global and regional nature, dealing with aspects of agriculture, fisheries and food. Some of these, for example, the Commission of Fertilizers, also include the private sector.

FAO/WHO Codex Alimentarius Commission: The Commission was established by the governing bodies of FAO and WHO in 1962 to implement the Joint FAO/WHO Food Standards Programme, to which FAO contributes 83 percent and WHO 17 percent. The Programme's purpose is to protect the health of consumers and ensure fair practices in the food trade by initiating and guiding the preparation, finalization, publication and revision of international food standards and by promoting the coordination of all food standards work undertaken by international organizations. Membership of the Commission is open to members and associate members of FAO and WHO. Current membership is 153.

To date the Commission has adopted some 240 standards, 40 codes of practice and numerous other recommendations and guidelines. These are published together with details of governments' acceptances in the *Codex Alimentarius*. This publication is intended to promote the harmonization of requirements for foods and, in so doing, to facilitate intergovernmental bodies, comprising five regional coordinating committees for Africa, Asia, Europe, Latin America and the Caribbean, North America and the South-West Pacific, eight general subject committees covering food additives and contaminant, pesticide residues, residues of veterinary drugs in foods analysis and sampling, food hygiene, food labelling, general principles, and Food Import and Export Inspection and Certification Systems, and 17 commodity committees covering cocoa products, sugars, fats and oils, processed fruits and vegetables, fruit juices, soups and broths, ices, cereals, pulses and legumes, milk and milk products, fish and fishery products, meat, processed meat and poultry products, meat hygiene, vegetable proteins, foods for special dietary uses, quick frozen foods, natural mineral waters and fresh fruits and vegetables. Code standards, guidelines and other recommendations are relevant to the implementation of the WTO Agreement on the Application of Sanitary and Phytosanitary Measures and the Agreement on Technical Barriers to Trade.

The Commission has an executive committee to advise it on general matters and its work programme. The executive committee consists of the Chair and three Vice-Chairs of the Commission, with six fur-ther members elected by the Commission to represent the geographic regions of Africa, Asia, Europe, Latin America and the Caribbean, North America and the South-West Pacific. The current membership is:

CHAIR
PROFESSOR PAKDEE POTHISIRI, *THAILAND*
VICE-CHAIRS
J A ABALAKA, *NIGERIA*
D GASCOINE, *AUSTRALIA*
S VAN HOOGSTRATEN, *NETHERLANDS*
REGIONAL MEMBERS
AUSTRALIA
BRAZIL
FRANCE
MALAYSIA
NETHERLANDS
NEW ZEALAND
NIGERIA
THAILAND
TUNISIA
USA

The twenty-first session of the Commission was held in Rome from July 3 to 8, 1995. The next session of the Commission will be held in Rome from June 23 to 28, 1997.

UN **Educational, Scientific and Cultural Organisation** (UNESCO)

7 Place De Fontenoy
75352 Paris 07-SP
France
Telephone: (33-1) 4568-1000
Telex: 204461
Facsimile: (33-1) 4567-1690
Director-General: Federico Mayor Zaragoza, Spain (1993-99)

UNESCO was established in 1945 to promote the aims set out in Article 1, para. 3, of the Charter of the United Nations.

Purposes: The purpose of UNESCO, as stated in Article 1 of its Constitution, is 'to contribute to peace and security by promoting collaboration among the nations through education, science and culture in order to further universal respect for justice, for the rule of law, and for the human rights and fundamental freedoms which are affirmed for the peoples of the world, without distinction of race, sex, language or religion, by the Charter of the United Nations'.

Structure:
(a) General Conference
(b) Executive Board
(c) Secretariat

Conference: The General Conference, the Organization's supreme body, meets biennially. Its twenty-ninth session was held in Paris in October-November 1997.

Executive Board: The Executive Board is elected by the General Conference, and it consists of 58 Member States. Each Member State appoints a representative and it may also appoint alternates. In selecting its representative on the Board, the Member State shall endeavor to appoint a person qualified in one or more fields of competence related to UNESCO and with the necessary experience and capacity to fulfill administrative and executive duties of the Board. Members are elected for a four-year term. The Board meets in regular sessions at least four times during a biennium and as a general rule there are at least two regular sessions per year (normally in May and in October). There is a system of electoral grouping whereby each region is allocated a specific number of Board seats. At present these are allocated as follows:

GROUP I	9
GROUP II	7
GROUP III	10
GROUP IV	12
GROUP V	20

Associated Bodies: Paris is also the headquarters for a number of intergovernmental bodies which come under UNESCO auspices, including:

(a) Intergovernmental Council of the International Hydrological Programme (IHP)

(b) Interactional Coordinating Council of the Programme on Man and the Biosphere (MAB)

(c) International Geological Correlation Programme (IGCP)

(d) Intergovernmental Oceanographic Commission (IOC)

(e) Intergovernmental Council for the General Information Programme

(f) Intergovernmental Committee for the Intergovernmental Informatics Programme

(g) Intergovernmental Council of the International Programme for the Development of Communication (IPDC)

(h) Intergovernmental Committee for Physical Education and Sport*

(i) World Heritage Committee

(j) Intergovernmental Committee for Promoting the Return of Cultural Property to its Countries of Origin or its Restitution in the Case of Illicit Appropriation

(k) Intergovernmental Committee of the World Decade for Cultural Development (WDCD)

(l) Intergovernmental Council of the International Programme for the Social Sciences (MOST).

Note: As it was the case for the 1994-95 biennium, the General Conference of UNESCO, at its twenty-eight Session, decided not to convene the Intergovernmental Committee in 1996-97.

International Civil Aviation Organisation (ICAO)

1000 Sherbrooke St. West
Montreal
Canada H3A 2R2
Telephone: (1-514) 285-8221
Telex: 05-24513
Facimile: (1-514) 288-4772
Secretary-General: Dr Philippe Rochat, Switzerland

The Convention on International Civil Aviation, providing for the establishment of ICAO, was signed at Chicago in 1994. The Organization came into existence on April 4, 1947, after 26 states had ratified the Convention.

Purposes: Article 44 of the Convention assigns to ICAO the functions of developing the principles and techniques of international air navigation and fostering the planning and development of international air transport so as to ensure the safe and orderly growth of international civil aviation throughout the world.

Structure:
(a) The Assembly, composed of delegates from Member States

(b) The Council, the executive body of the Organization, which is elected by the ordinary session of the Assembly every three years. The Council elects its own President.

(c) The Air Navigation Commission, Air Transport Committee, Legal Committee, Committee, on Joint Support of Air Navigation Services, Finance Committee, Personnel Committee and the Committee on Unlawful Interference, Technical Cooperation Committee

(d) The Secretariat, headed by the Secretary-General, who appoints the staff and directs its activities.

Assembly: Sovereign body of the Organization, which meets not less than once in three years to review its work and to establish guidelines for its future activities.

Council: The Council is composed of 33 contracting states. In electing the members of the Council, the Assembly gives adequate representation to:

(a) States of chief importance in air transport.

(b) States not otherwise included which make the largest contribution to the provision of facilities for international civil air navigation.

(c) States not otherwise included whose designation will ensure that all major geographical areas of the world air are represented.

Terms of office for the present council members

expire at the elections at the regular Assembly in 1998. The President of the Council is Dr. Asses Kotaite, Lebanon.

World Health Organization (WHO)

20 Avenue Appia
1211 Geneva 27
Switzerland
Telephone: (41-22) 791-21-11
Telex: 415416
Facsimile: (41-22) 791-07-46
Director-General: Dr Hiroshi Nakajima, Japan (1988-98)

The Constitution of WHO was adopted by representatives of 61 states in 1946. The Organization formally came into existence on April 7, 1948 and became a specialized agency on July 10, 1948.

Purposes : Article 1 of the Constitution defines WHO's objective as 'the arraignment by all peoples of the highest possible level of health'. The detailed functions are set out in Article 2.

Structure:

(a) World Health Assembly

(b) Executive Board

(c) Secretariat

(d) Committees, conferences and regional committees.

Assembly: The World Health Assembly is held annually, usually in Geneva. The forty-ninth was held in Geneva, May 20 to 25, 1996.

Executive Board: The Board is composed of 32 persons technically qualified in the field of health and designated by as many Member States. They serve in a personal capacity, and not as government representatives. Member States entitled to designate a person are elected at each regular session of the Assembly for a three-year term, following the sequence 12:10: 10 in each three-year cycle. The Board's Chair is S Ngedup, Bhutan.

World Bank Group

Headquarters: Washington

Telephone: (1-202) 477-1264
Facsimile: (1-202) 477-6391

The World Bank group comprises:

(a) IBRD: International Bank for Reconstruction and

Development

(b) IDA: International Development Association

(c) IFC: International Finance Corporation.

International Bank For Reconstruction And Development (IBRD)

1818 H Street N W
Washington DC 20433
United States of America
President: James D Wolfensohn, USA (1995-2000)

The articles of the IBRD were drawn up in 1944 at the Bretton Woods Conference. Membership of the Bank, which began operation in 1946-47, is restricted to those members of the IMF which ratify the articles of the Bank and accept the terms laid down by it.

Purposes: The IBRD was established to promote the international flow of capital for productive purposes

and to assist in financing the rebuilding of nations devastated by the Second Word War. Lending for productive projects or to finance reform programmes which will lead to economic growth in its less developed member countries is now the Bank's main objective. The Bank is also attempting to increase the proportion of its lending which directly assists the poorest people in the developing countries. As of March 31, 1996, disbursed loans outstanding totalled $ 184 billion.

Capital: The Bank's authorized capital stock was originally $10.0 billion, but general capital increases in 1959, 1980 and 1988 together with a number of selective capital increases raised it to $184 billion as of March 31, 1996. Subscribed share capital amounted to $179.3 billion at that date, of which $10.9 billion was paid-in and $168.3 billion was on call.

The Bank obtains the bulk of its funds from borrowing on international capital markets, in effect using the callable capital as its security. As of March 31, 1996, it had outstanding borrowings totalling $5.7 billion.

Board of Governors: This comprises one governor and one alternate appointed by each member country. The 1996 annual meeting of the Board, in conjunction with the Board of Governors of the IMF, was held from October 1 to 3, in Washington DC.

In addition the Joint Ministerial Committee of the Board of Governors of the Bank and the Fund on the Transfer of Real Resources to Developing Countries (Development Committee) usually meets in April and September. Each member country (or executive group of member countries) represented on the two Boards appoints a member of the Development Committee.

Executive Directors: On May 1, 1996 there were 24 Executive Directors, of whom five are appointed by members having the largest number of shares, the other 19 being elected every two years by the governors of the remaining members.

International Development Association (IDA)

1818 H Street N W
Washington DC 20433
United States of America
President: James D Wolfensohn, USA (1995-2000)

At the annual meeting of the IMF and the IBRD in 1959, proposals were approved for the establishment of a new international lending organization to be called the International Development Association. IDA began operations in 1960.

Purposes: The purpose of IDA is to promote economic development by providing finance to the less developed areas of the world on much more concessionary terms than those of conventional loans. It is designed especially to finance projects or reform programmes in countries which are not able to service loans from the IBRD.

Capital: The initial subscriptions of all members are proportioned to their subscriptions to the capital stock of the IBRD, but under the article of agreement members of IDA are divided into two groups: part I consists of the more economically advanced countries and part II of the less developed nations. A part I country pays its entire subscription in convertible currency all of which may be used for IDA lending. A part II country pays only one-tenth of its subscriptions in convertible currency; the remaining portion is paid in the member's own currency and may not be used without the member's consent.

IDA lending resources have been supplemented since 1960 by a series of replenishments in which part I and an increasing number of part II member countries contribute funds to IDA. The original subscriptions and subsequent contributions to the first 10 replenishments of IDA resources totalled $90.24 billion as of 31 March 1996. Total development credits outstanding at that time amounted to $72.1 billion.

Board of Governors and Executive Directors: The Association is affiliated to the IBRD. Each member country is represented by the same governor and executive director as represent it for the Bank, and IDA also shares the same president, management, and staff as the Bank.

International Finance Corporation (IFC)

1818 H Street NW
Washington DC 20433
United States of America
President: James D Wolfensohn, USA (1995-2000)

The IFC was established in 1956 and became a specialised agency of the UN in 1957. Although affiliated to the IBRD, it is a separate legal entity, and its capital is entirely separate from that of the Bank. It borrows its funds for relending from both the IBRD and private capital markets. An increase in its authorized capital from $650 million to $1.3 billion, approved in 1985, permitted the IFC to expand its operation into more developing member countries, particularly the lower income ones, and into new sectors such as agro-business, energy and minerals. A further $1 billion increase in IFC's capital was approved in 1991. As of March 31, 1996, investments committed totalled $76 billion in 99 countries.

Purposes and Capital: The IFC is empowered to invest in productive private or partly governmental enterprises in association with private investors, and without government guarantee of repayment in cases where sufficient private capital is not available on reasonable terms, and to serve as a clearing house to bring together investment opportunities, private capital, both foreign and domestic, and experienced management. Its special purpose is to promote the growth of the private sector and to assist productive private enterprises in its developing member countries, where such enterprises can advance economic development.

Board of Governors and Executive Directors: The IFC is affiliated to the IBRD. Each member country is represented by the same governor and executive director was represent it for the Bank. IFC also shares the same president, but has its own management and staff.

Associated Organizations: There are also three associated organizations within the World Bank Group:

(a) CGIAR: Consultative Group on International Agriculture Research

(b) ICSID: International Centre for the Settlement of Investment Disputes

(c) MIGA: Multilateral Investment Guarantee Agency.

CGIAR: The World Bank chairs and, with the FAO and UNDP, co-sponsors CGIAR. In the calendar year 1995, approximately $269 million was provided by 41 countries and organizations. This was used to fund the international agricultural research centres and programmes which comprise the CGIAR network. As of March 31, 1996, 52 governments and international foundations and organizations were members of CGIAR.

ICSID: Membership of the Centre is dependent upon the ratification of the 'Convention on the Settlement of Investment Disputes between States and Nationals of Other States' which was opened for signature at Washington on March 18, 1965. The Convention, serviced by the Centre which is based in the Bank, provides a voluntary mechanism for settling disputes between governments and foreign investors. As of March 31, 1996, 139 members had signed the agreement and 126 nations had ratified the Convention.

MIGA: The international Convention establishing this body took effect on April 12, 1988. MIGA's objective is to encourage the flow of productive investments among member countries, in particular to developing countries. On a fee-paying basis MIGA will guarantee eligible investments against losses resulting from non-commercial risk, such as unexpected restrictions on currency transfer, expropriation, contract repudiation by governments and armed conflict. It will also carry out research and promotional activities. As of March 31, 1996, 154 countries had signed the Convention and 139 countries had ratified it.

As of March 31, 1996, 132 countries were members of MIGA, MIGA's subscribed capital had increased to $1.05 billion, and net income, before provisioning, was $15.4 million, Also, MIGA assumed a total of $2.06 bullion in contingent liabilities in respect of its guarantee programme. In addition, guarantee capacity amounting to $220 million has been committed.

International Monetary Fund (IMF)

700 19th Street NW
Washington DC 20431
United States of America
Telephone: (1-202) 623-7000
Facsimile: (1-202) 623-4661
Internet: http://www.int.imf.org
Managing Director: Michel Camdessus, France
(1987-97)

The Articles of Agreement of the International Monetary Fund were drawn up in 1944 at the Bretton Woods Conference. Membership is open to all countries. Ratification of the Articles and acceptance of conditions laid down by the Fund are conditions of membership.

The Article have been amended three times, in 1969, 1978 and 1992. The first amendment provided for the creation and allocation of Special Drawing Rights (SDRs). The second amendment implemented a review of the Fund's responsibilities and operations that was conducted from 1972 to 1976 following the collapse of the fixed exchange rate system. The third amendment empowers the Fund to suspend the voting and certain related rights of a member that fails to fulfill any of the obligations under the Articles, other than obligations with respect to SDRs.

Purposes: The purposes of the Fund are to:

(a) Promote international monetary cooperation through consultation and collaboration

(b) Facilitate the expansion and balanced growth of international trade, and to contribute thereby to the promotion and maintenance of high levels of employment and real income

(c) Promote exchange stability and orderly exchange agreements

(d) Assist in the establishment of a multilateral system of payments and the elimination of foreign exchange restrictions

(e) Assist members through the temporary provision of financial resources to correct maladjustments in their balance of payments.

Quotas and Drawing Facilities: Each member has an assessed quota which is subscribed and determines voting power. Access to use of the Fund's resources is also determined in relation to quota, taking account of the balance of payments need of the member and the strength of the policies it agrees to implement to restore balance of payments viability. The total of members' quotas at April 30, 1996 was SDR 145,319 million (US $210,721 million).

Members may draw from the general resources of the Fund, which are derived from quota subscriptions, under credit tranches (of 25 percent of quota each) or under special facilities such as the Compensatory Financing Facility for temporary export shortfalls. Drawings (or 'purchases') in the upper credit tranches, in other words beyond the first credit tranche, are subject to the terms of a stand-by arrangement agreed with the member. This arrangement specifies the precise economic policy conditions which the member must meet to qualify for each purchase, and the scheduling of purchases. Stand-by arrangements usually cover a 12-24 month period. Purchases made under a stand-by arrangement are required to be repurchased within the two-year period commencing three years after the purchase date.

There is also an Extended Fund Facility under which members with structural maladjustments and experiencing balance of payments difficulties can enter into extended arrangements with the Fund for periods of up to 36 months, and in amounts larger than is possible under the credit tranches. Purchases

under this facility are required to be repurchased in the six-year period commencing four year after the purchase date.

The general resources of the Fund have been supplemented by borrowing from member countries in strong payments positions. These borrowed resources are on-lent to member countries in conjunction with drawings under the credit tranches or the Extended Fund Facility. They are subject to repurchase in the period commencing three and a half years and ending seven years after the date of purchase,

The total of stand-by and extended arrangements in effect at 30 April 1996 was SDR 24.35 billion (US $35.31 billion), of which SDR 10.28 billion (US $14.91 billion) was utilized. The total amount of Fund credit outstanding under all its facilities at 30 April 1996, including drawings made under earlier agreements, was SDR 36.3 billion (US $52.6 billion), of which SDR 34.6 billion (US $49.9 billion) was financed by general resources and SDR 1.8 billion (US $2.7 billion) comprised borrowed resources.

In addition there is the Structural Adjustment Facility of the Special Disbursement Account, under which trust fund reflows are made available for lending, again on concessional terms, to low income developing countries implementing structural adjustment policies.

During 1988, the Fund began lending operation under the Enhanced Structural Adjustment Facility (ESAF), which provides concessional loans to low income developing members that qualify for assistance in order to support programmes to strengthen substantially in a sustainable manner their balance of payments position and to foster growth. Resources committed under ESAF arrangements are provided by the Structural Adjustment Facility of the special Disbursement Account and by the ESAF Trust Loan Account. At April 30, 1996, ESAF arrangements in effect amounted to SDR 6.6 billion (US $9.6 billion) of which SDAR 4.2 billion (US $6.1 billion) was disbursed.

Special Drawing Rights(SDRs): The Fund has created and allocated SDRs to supplement member countries' reserves and thereby improve the liquidity of the international monetary system. Members may use SDRs to acquire currency from other members for use in alleviating balance of payments difficulties, and in a variety of other transactions. Members in strong balance of payments positions may be designated to accept SDRs from other members with a weak balance of payments in exchange for currency.

Allocations of SDRs are made at intervals. A total of 21.4 billion SDRs has been allocated in all. (At 30

April 1996, 1 SDR equalled US $1.45006.) Allocations are made on a pro rate basis to each member in proportion to its quota.

Board of Governors: The Board comprises one governor appointed by each member country—typically a minister of finance or governor of a central bank. An annual meeting of the Board in conjunction with that of the World Bank Group is held each September. In addition the interim committee of the Board meets in April and September with, as its terms of reference, the supervision of the international monetary system, including the operation of the adjustment process and global liquidity. Each member country or group of member countries represented on the Executive Board appoints a member of the Committee.

Executive Board: This is responsible for the daily business of the Fund, including requests for financial assistance, economic consultations with member countries, and the development of Fund policies. It consists of the managing director as Chair and, at present, 24 executive directors. Of these, five are appointed by members having the largest quotas— USA, Germany, Japan, UK and France. Nineteen directors have been elected by the remaining member countries, representing the interests of those that elect them. Elections are held every two years.

Universal Postal Union (UPU)

Weltpoststrasse 4
Case Postale 3000
Berne 15
Switzerland
Telephone: (41-31) 350-31-11
Telex: 912761
Facsimile: (41-31) 350-31-10
Internet: http://ibis.upu.org/
Director-General: Thomas E Leaves (1995-99)

Purposes: The Universal Postal Union (UPU) was established by the Berne Treaty of 1874 and became a specialized agency in 1948. Its current Constitution was adopted by the Universal Postal Congress in Vienna in 1964 and has been amended by subsequent Congresses at Tokyo in 1969, Lausanne in 1974, Hamburg in 1984, Washington DC in 1989, and Seoul in 1994.

Article 1 of the Vienna Constitution 1964 states that the aim of the Union is to 'secure the organization and improvement of the postal services and to promote in this sphere the development of international collaboration and undertake, as far as possible, technical assistance in postal matters requested by member countries'. To this end the countries which have adopted the convention constitute a single postal territory.

Structure: It was agreed at the 1994 Congress in Seoul to institute a new structure for the Union, with effect from 1995:

(a) Universal Postal Congress

(b) Council of Administration

(c) Postal Operations Council

(d) International Bureau, which is the permanent Secretariat of the Union.

Congress: The UPU holds a quintennial congress (plenipotentiary) at which the general legislation, excepting the Constitution, is revised. An extraordinary congress may be held at the request of two-thirds of the members. The twenty-first congress was held in Seoul from 22 August to 14 September 1994. The provisions at present in force are those of the Seoul Congress of 1994, which came into effect on 1 January 1996.

Council of Administration: The Council carries on the work of the Union between congresses, when elections to it are held. Members are chosen on the basis of an equitable geographical distribution and may not hold office for more than two consecutive terms.

The congress increased the number of seats on the Council from 31 to 39 in 1974, and in 1994 to 40 seats, plus one for the representative of the host country of the congress. There are eight seats for Zone 1, Western Hemisphere; five for Zone 2, Eastern Europe and Northern Asia; six for Zone 3, Western Europe; 10 for Zone 4, Southern Asia and Oceania; 11 for Zone 5, Africa.

International Telecommunication Union (ITU)

Place Des Nations
CH-1211
Geneva 20
Telephone: (41-22) 730-51-11
Telex: 421000
Facsimile: (41-22) 733-72-56
Teletext: 22846815100=uit
Secretary-General: Pekka Tarjanne, Finland (1989-99)

The ITU, founded in 1865 as the International Telegraph Union, held its fourteenth Plenipotentiary Conference at Kyoto in 1994. The latest Plenipotentiary Conference was held in the USA in 1998.

Purposes: The purposes of the Union are:

(a) To maintain and extend international cooperation between all Members of the Union for the improvement and rational use of telecommunications of all kinds

(b) To promote and to offer technical assistance to developing countries in the field of telecommunications and also to promote the mobilization of the material and financial resources needed for their implementation

(c) To promote development of technical facilities and their most efficient operation with a view to improving the efficiency of telecommunications services, increasing their usefulness and making them, so far as possible, generally available to the public

(d) To promote the extension of the benefits of the new telecommunications technologies to all the world's inhabitants

(e) To promote the use of telecommunications services to facilitate harmonization of members' actions in the attainment of those ends

(f) To address issues of telecommunications in the global information economy and society, by cooperating with other world and regional intergovernmental organizations and those non-governmental organizations concerned with telecommunications.

Structure: The Union comprises:

(a) Plenipotentiary Conference, which is the supreme organ of the Union

(b) The Council, which acts on behalf of the Plenipotentiary Conference

(c) World conferences on international telecommunications

(d) The Radio communication Sector, including world and regional radio communication conference, radio communication assemblies and the Radio Regulations Board

(e) The Telecommunication Standardization Sector, including world telecommunication standardization conferences

(f) The Telecommunication Development Sector, including world and regional telecommunication development conferences

(g) The General Secretariat.

Conferences: The 1992 Constitution provides that a Plenipotentiary Conference shall be convened every four years. The Council holds one annual meeting. In addition, world conferences on international telecommunications are held at the request of Plenipotentiary Conferences; radio communication conferences are held every two years along with a radio communication assembly; telecommunication standardization conferences are held every four years (an additional conference may be held at the request of one-quarter of the membership, provided a majority of the members agreement); world development conferences are convened every four years. Subject to availability of resources, regional conferences are held in the four-year period between Plenipotentiary Conferences. Exceptionally, within the period between Plenipotentiary Conferences:

(a) The second world radio communication conference may be cancelled together with its associated radio communication assembly; alternatively, either one may be cancelled even if the other is held

(b) An additional telecommunication standardization conference may be convened

(i) By a decision of a Plenipotentiary Conference

(ii) On the recommendation of the previous world conference of the Sector concerned, if approved by the Council

(iii) At the request of at least one-quarter of the members of the Union, which shall individually address their requests to the Secretary-General

(iv) On a proposal of the Council.

The Council: This is composed of members elected

by the Plenipotentiary Conference to serve until the succeeding Conference. Members are eligible for re-elections. Its 1996 session is to be held from 19 to 28 June.

The present members of the Council were elected in 1994 and serve until the next Plenipotentiary Conference (which was scheduled to take place in Minneapolis, USA in 1998).

World Meteorological Organization (WMO)

41 Avenue Giuseppe Motta
Case Postale no. 2300
1211 Geneva 2
Switzerland
Telephone: (41-22) 730-81-11
Telex: 414199 OMM CH
Facsimile: (41-22) 734-23-26
Secretary-General: G Obasi, Nigeria (1985-96)

The WMO, successor to the International Meteorological Organization which was established in 1873, formally came into existence in 1950 and became a specialized agency in 1951.

Membership: 176 Member States and five territories as of April 30, 1996.

Purposes: Article 2 of the WMO Conception, which was signed in Washington in 1947 and came into force on March 23, 1950, defined the Organization's purposes as being to:

(a) Facilitate worldwide cooperation in the establishment of networks of stations for making meteorological observations, as well as hydrological and other geophysical observations related to meteorology, and to promote the establishment and maintenance of centres charged with the provision of meteorological and related services

(b) Promote the establishment and maintenance of systems of rapid exchange of meteorological and related information

(c) Promote standardization of meteorological and related observations and ensure the uniform publication of observations and statistics

(d) Further the application of meteorology to aviation, shipping, water problems, agriculture and other human activities

(e) Promote activities in operational hydrology and further close cooperation between meteorological and hydrological services

(f) Encourage research and training in meteorology and, as appropriate, in related fields and to assist in coordinating the international aspects of such research and training.

Structure:

(a) World Meteorological Congress

(b) Executive Council

(c) Six regional associations (Africa, Asia, South America, North and Central America, South West Pacific, Europe)

(d) Eight technical commissions (atmospheric sciences, aeronautical meteorology, agricultural meteorology, basic systems, hydrology, instruments and methods of observation, marine meteorology, climatology)

(f) Secretariat.

Congress: World Meteorological Congress, the supreme body of the Organization, brings together the delegates of members once every four years. The twelfth Congress was held from May 30 to June 21, 1995. The thirteenth Congress will be held in 1999.

Executive Council: The 36 members are the President and three vice-presidents of the Organization, the six presidents of the regional associations who are ex-officio members, and 26 directors of Member States' national meteorological or hydrometeorological services. Elections to the Council are held at the World Meteorological Congress, except that the regional presidents are elected by their respective associations. Apart from the regional presidents, the members of the Council serve from the end of one Congress to the end of the next. When a vacancy occurs among the 26 elected members between sessions of the Congress, an acting member is designated by the Executive Council.

The twelfth Congress elected new officers and members of the Executive Council. Membership as of 30 April 1996 is as follows:

PRESIDENT
J W ZILLMAN, *AUSTRALIA*

FIRST VICE-PRESIDENT
C E BERRIDGE, *BRITISH CARIBBEAN TERRITORIES*

SECOND VICE-PRESIDENT
N SEN ROY, *INDIA*

THIRD VICE-PRESIDENT
M BAUTISTA, *SPAIN*

Directors of Meteorological or Hydrometeorological Services: The elected members or acting members of the Executive Council are directors of the national Meteorological or Hydrometeorological Services of the following Member States.

ARGENTINA	FRANCE	SAUDI ARABIA
BOTSWANA	GERMANY	SENEGAL
BRAZIL	IRAN	SOUTH AFRICA
BURUNDI	ISRAEL	UK
CANADA	KENYA	UR OF TANZANIA
CHINA	MALAYSIA	USA
COLOMBIA	MEXICO	TWO VACANT SEATS

CZECH REPUBLIC	POLAND
EGYPT	RUSSIAN FEDERATION

Presidents of Regional Associations: The following is a list of the regional presidents showing the year in which they took office:

REGION I, AFRICA:	KALIBA KONARE, *MALI*, 1990
REGION II, ASIA:	Z BATJARGAL, *MONGOLIA*, 1994
REGION III, SOUTH AMERICA:	W CASTRO WREDE, *PARAGUAY*, 1993
REGION IV, NORTH AND CENTRAL AMERICA:	S POLLONAIS, *TRINIDAD AND TOBAGO*, 1994
REGION V, SOUTH WEST PACIFIC	S KARJOTO, *INDONESIA*, 1993
REGION VI, EUROPE:	S STEINHAUSER, *AUSTRIA*, 1994

International Maritime Organization (IMO)*

4 Albert Embankment
London SE1 7SR
England
Telephone: (44-171) 735-76-11
Facsimile: (44-171) 587-32-10
Secretary-General: William A O'neil, Canada (1990)

Note: Prior to May 22, 1982 (the date of entry into force of the amendments to the IMO Convention) the Organization's name was the Inter-Governmental Maritime Consultative Organization (IMCO)
The Convention on the International Maritime Organization (IMO), concluded at Geneva in 1948, came into force in 1953. The first IMO Assembly was convened in London in 1959.

Purposes: The Organization's main objective is to facilitate cooperation among governments on technical matters affecting international shipping, in order to achieve the highest practicable standards of maritime safety and efficiency in navigation. IMO has a special responsibility for safety of life at sea, and for the protection of the marine environment through prevention of pollution of the sea caused by ships and other craft. IMO also deals with legal matters connected with international shipping, with facilitation of international maritime traffic, and is responsible for providing technical assistance in maritime matters to developing countries.

IMO cooperates with other international bodies on shipping matters and coordinates its activities with other specialized agencies of the UN. It is responsible for convening international conferences on shipping matters and for drafting international conventions or agreements on this subject.

Structure:

(a) An Assembly consisting of representatives of all Member States

(b) Council (consisting of 32 members elected by the Assembly)

(c) Maritime Safety Committee (consisting of all Member States)

(d) Legal Committee (consisting of all Member States)

(e) Marine Environment Protection Committee (consisting of all Member States)

(f) Technical Cooperation Committee (consisting of all Member States)

(g) Secretariat

There is also a subsidiary body of the Council, the Facilitation Committee.

Assembly: Assembly sessions are usually held every two years. The nineteenth session was held from 13 to November 24, 1995. The twentieth session was held in November 1997.

Maritime Safety Committee: IMO's technical work is carried out under the direction of this Committee which since 1978 has been open to all Member States. The subjects covered are extremely varied, and for this reason much of the Committee's work is carried out through subsidiary bodies. The main subjects dealt with include the safety of navigation, radio communications, life-saving appliances and arrangements, search and rescue, ship design and equipment, fire protection bulk chemicals, standards of training and watchkeeping, containers and cargoes, and the carriage of dangerous goods.

Legal Committee: This Committee was set up in 1967. Its functions are to consider any legal matters within the scope of the Organization and to submit to the Council drafts of international conventions which it has developed. It was institutionalized in 1982.

Marine Environment Protection Committee: This Committee, set up in 1973, is responsible for coordinating and administering the activites of the Organization concerning the prevention and control of marine pollution. All members of IMO are entitled to take part, together with representatives of non-IMO states which are Parties to treaties in respect of which the Committee exercises functions. Like the Legal Committee, it was institutionalized in 1982.

Facilitation Committee: This Committee is responsible for the facilitation of international maritime traffic. These activities are aimed at reducing the formalities and simplifying the documentation required of ships when entering or leaving ports or other terminals.

Technical Cooperation Committee: This Committee, first set up by the Council in 1972, has the main functions of establishing directives and guidelines for the execution of IMO's comprehensive programme of assistance to developing countries in maritime transport (particularly shipping and ports), of monitoring the programme's progressive development, and of reviewing its results. It was institutionalized in 1985.

All the committees of IMO are open to participation by all member governments on an equal basis.

Consultative Meeting of Contracting Parties to The London Convention: IMO carries out secretariat functions in respect of the Convention on the Prevention of Marine Pollution by Dumping of Wastes and Other Matter, which was adopted in London in 1972 and regulates the disposal into the sea of waste materials generated on land. Consultative meetings are normally held once a year. A special meeting was held in November 1996 to adopt a Protocol to amend the Convention.

World Intellectual Property Organization (WIPO)

34 Chemin Des Colombettes
1211 Geneva 20
Switzerland
Telephone: (41-22) 730-97-11
Telex: 412912
Facsimile: (41-22) 733-54-28
Director-General: Dr Arpad Bogsch, USA (1991-97)

WIPO was established by a convention signed at Stockholm in 1967, which entered into force in 1970. On December 17, 1974, by res. 3346 (XXIX) adopted unanimously by the Assembly, WIPO became the fourteenth specialized agency of the UN.

Purposes: WIPO was established to promote the protection of intellectual property throughout the world through cooperation among states and to ensure administrative cooperation among the unions established to afford protection in the field of intellectual property.
The principal unions so established are those of Paris and Berne.

(a) The principal union, officially the International Union for the Protection of Industrial Property, is composed of States party to a convention concluded at Paris in 1883 and last revised in 1967.

(b) The Berne Union, officially the International Union for the Protection of Literary and Artistic Works, is composed of States Parties to a convention concluded at Berne in 1886 and last revised in 1971.

Structure:

(a) General Assembly

(b) Conference

(c) Coordination Committee

(d) International Bureau

General Assembly: States Members of WTO and of either the Paris Union or the Berne Union may participate in the biennial General Assembly, convened in late September and early October 1997.

Conference: States Members of WIPO whether or not members of any of the unions are entitled to participate in the Conference, which meets at the same time as the General Assembly.

Coordination Committee: The Paris and Berne Unions elect executive committees from among their members. The joint membership of these two committees constitutes the Coordination Committee of WIPO. These three committees meet annually. The 68 members serve for two years each.

International Bureau: The International Bureau is the Secretariat of WIPO and of the Unions it administers. Its permanent staff comprised, on April 1, 1996, 530 persons. The International Bureau is headed by a Director-General.

International Fund For Agricultural Development (IFAD)

Via Del Serafico 107
00142 Rome
Italy
Telephone: (39-6) 54591
Telex: 620330 IFAD
Facsimile: (39-6) 504-3463
Cable Address: Ifad Rome
President: Mr Fawzi Al-Sultan, Kuwait (1993-96) (Elected by Governing-Council)

The establishment of IFAD was among the proposals from the 1974 World Food Conference (res. XIII). In 1976 a conference of plenipotentiaries adopted the 'Agreement Establishing the International Fund for Agricultural Development' and created a preparatory commission for IFAD. The Agreement entered into force on December 11, 1977.

Aims: The aim of IFAD, as set out in the Agreement, is to mobilize additional financial resources from donors to be made available on concessional terms for agricultural development in developing Member States. To this end the Fund shall provide financing primarily for projects and programmes specifically designed to introduce, expand, or improve food production systems, and to strengthen related policies and institutions within the framework of national priorities and strategies, taking into consideration: the need to increase food production in the poorest food deficit countries; the potential for increasing food production in other developing countries, and the importance of improving the nutritional level of the poorest population in developing countries and the conditions of their lives.

Membership: Countries not original members of IFAD may join after approval of their membership by the Governing Council and accession to the IFAD Agreement. The members of IFAD are divided into three categories. Category I members belong to the Organization for Economic Cooperation and Development (OECD); Category II members are, broadly speaking other developing countries. The Fund is financed almost entirely by contributions from Categories I and II.

As of January 25, 1996, IFAD had a total membership of 160 countries—22 in Category I, 12 in Category II and 126 in Category III.

Governing Council: Each member of the Fund is represented on the Governing Council, in which all the powers of the Fund are vested. The Council meets annually. Special sessions may be held by decision of the Council, or as requested by the Executive Board by a two-thirds majority of the votes cast. Reaffirming its unanimous support for IFAD and its mandate to fight hunger and alleviate poverty and noting with great satisfaction IFAD's continued progress in discharging effectively that mandate, the eighteenth session of the Governing Council of IFAD (Rome, 25 to January 27, 1995) approved the Report and Recommendations of the Special Committee set up in 1994 and adopted a resolution containing the amendments to the Agreement Establishing IFAD. This would abolish the three category system of OECD, OPEC and Developing Country member groups, introducing a new voting system. Member countries will have two types of vote—its original membership vote and votes based on the size of contributions. These amendments will enter into force upon the completion of the Fourth Replenishment of the Fund's resources.

Executive Board: The Executive Board is responsible for the conduct of the general operations of the Fund and to this end exercises the powers given to it by the IFAD Agreement and delegated to it by the Council. It has 18 members, six from each category, with alternates (Category I has five alternate members) elected by the Council for a three-year period.

Membership of the Board during 1996 is given as follows (alternates in brackets):

CATEGORY I

DENMARK (FINLAND)
GERMANY (UK)
ITALY (FRANCE)
JAPAN (CANADA)
SWITZERLAND (NETHERLANDS)
USA

CATEGORY II

ALGERIA (LIBYA)
INDONESIA (IRAQ)
KUWAIT (UNITED ARAB EMIRATES)

NIGERIA (GABON)

SAUDI ARABIA (QATAR)

VENEZUELA (IRAN)

CATEGORY III

EGYPT (CÔTE D'IVOIRE)

UR OF TANZANIA (CAMEROON)

BANGLADESH (ROK)

JORDAN (PHILIPPINES)

ARGENTINA (MEXICO)

BRAZIL (PANAMA)

In 1995 the Executive Board held three regular sessions approving 33 projects, which include loans worth a total of approximately US$391.7 million.

This brought the total number of IFAD-supported projects in 105 developing countries to 429 by the end of 1995. At each session, the Board reviewed several important policy and operational matters.

President and Chairman of Executive Board: The President heads the staff of IFAD. Under the control and direction of the Governing Council and the Executive Board, the President conducts the business of the Fund. The President chairs the Executive Board and is legal representative of the Fund. The current President was elected as Executive Head of the Fund during the sixteenth session of the Governing Council held in January 1993.

UN Industrial Development Organization (UNIDO)

Vienna International Centre
Wagramerstrasse 5
PO Box 300
A-1400 Vienna
Telephone: (43-1) 21131-0
Telex: 135612
Facsimile: (43-1) 232146
Internet: http://www.unido.org
Director-General: Mauricio De Maria y Campos, Mexico (1993-97)

UNIDO was founded in 1966 as a result of Assembly res. 21/2152 (1996). In 1985 it became the sixteenth specialized agency of the United Nations, following the adoption of the Lima Declaration and Plan of Action by the Second General Conference in 1975 and agreement on a constitution for UNIDO at a plenipotentiary conference in 1979.

Purposes: UNIDO is dedicated to bringing a better life through industrial development to people in developing countries and countries in transition to market economies. The Organization's services are intended to help these countries overcome their social and economic difficulties and achieve a greater stake in the global market. To support its services, UNIDO has 356 engineers, economists and technology and environmental specialists in Vienna, as well as 110 professional staff in its network of Investment Promotion Service (IPS) offices and field offices.

UNIDO plays a twofold role as a global forum for supporting and promoting industrial development and as a provider of integrated technical cooperation services. Its work focuses on seven priority areas:

(a) Strategies, policies and institution-building for global economic integration

(b) Environment and energy

(c) Small- and medium-scale enterprises: policies, networking and basic technical support

(d) Innovation, productivity and quality for international competitiveness

(e) Industrial information, investment and technology promotion

(f) Rural industrial development

(g) Africa and least developed countries: linking industry and agriculture.

Structure:

(a) General Conference

(b) Industrial Development Board

(c) Programme and Budget Committee.

The General Conference consists of representatives of all members. The Conference holds a regular session every two years, unless it decides otherwise. The sixth session of the General Conference was held in Vienna from December 4 to 8, 1995.

The Industrial Development Board consists of 53 members of the Organization elected by the General Conference, of which 33 are to be from developing countries, 15 from the developed market economy countries and five from the countries in list D of UNIDO's Constitution. Members of the Board hold office from the close of the regular session of the Conference at which they were elected until the close of the regular session of the Conference four years thereafter. The Board meets once a year in the Conference years and twice in the non-Conference years.

The Programme and Budget Committee consists of 27 members of the Organization elected by the General Conference. Members of the Committee hold office from the close of the regular session of the Conference at which they were elected until the close of the regular session of the Conference at which they were elected until the close of the regular session of the Conference two years thereafter.

Other Related Bodies

International Atomic Energy Agency (IAEA)

Vienna International Centre
Wagramerstrasses 5
P O Box 100
A-1400 Vienna
Austria
Telephone: (43-1) 2060-0
Telex: 1-12645
Facsimile: (43-1) 20607
Internet: http://www.iaea.or.at/worldatom
Director-General: Dr Hans Blix, Sweden (Until 1997)

The Statute of the IAEA entered into force in 1957. It is not a specialized agency, but an independent intergovernmental organization under the aegis of the UN.

Purposes: The purpose of the Agency, as defined in its Statute, is 'to seek to accelerate and enlarge the contribution of atomic energy to peace, health and prosperity throughout the world'. It is charged with responsibility for ensuring, as far as it is able, that assistance provided by it, or at its request, or under its supervision or control, is not used in such a way as to further any military purpose. The Agency is specifically authorized to:

(a) Encourage and assist research on atomic energy for peaceful purposes throughout the world

(b) Act as an intermediary in the supply of materials, services, equipment and facilities

(c) Foster the exchange of scientific and technical information

(d) Encourage the exchange and training of scientists and experts

(e) Establish and administer safeguards against the misuse of aid provided by or through the Agency

(f) Establish safety standards.

The Agency has also been allocated the responsibility for drawing up and implementing the safeguards provisions of the Nuclear Non-Proliferation Treaty (NPT) as well as the Treaty of Tlatelolco, the Treaty of Pelindaba (The African Nuclear Weapon Free Zone), and the Treaty of Rarotonga. These safeguards activities are a relatively new concept in international law and form one of the most important aspects of the IAEA's role and functions. The aim of safeguards is to assist states in demonstrating their compliance with international obligations in the interest of preventing the further proliferation of nuclear weapons. There are now over 885 nuclear installations and other locations under IAEA safeguards. This represents approximately 95 percent of the world's nuclear facilities and materials outside the five nuclear weapon states.

The responsibility of the IAEA in the area of nuclear safety has increased as nuclear power programmes have grown and public attention has focused on safety aspects. Although the IAEA is not a regulatory body, its recommendations have been used by many countries as a basis for national standards and rules. The IAEA also has important functions to carry out under international conventions related to emergency response and preparedness in the event of a nuclear accident, namely the Convention on Early Notification of a Nuclear Accident, which entered into force on October 27, 1986 and has 75 parties and 70 signatories, and the Convention on Assistance in the Case of a Nuclear Accident or Radiological Emergency, which entered into force on February 26, 1987 and has 71 parties and 68 signatories.

In 1994 a Diplomatic Conference at the IAEA adopted a Convention on Nuclear Safety. It was opened for signature on September 20, 1994 during the IAEA General Conference. It has 19 parties and 63 signatories. (Twenty-two parties are needed before it enters into force.) Other conventions administered by the IAEA are: the Convention on Physical Protection of Nuclear Material of February 8, 1987 which has 54 parties and 45 signatories and the Vienna Convention on Civil Liability for Nuclear Damage of November 12, 1977 which has 26 parties and 11 signatories and the Joint Protocol relating to the Application of the Vienna Convention and the Paris Convention of 27 April 1992 which has 20 parties and 22 signatories.

In 1995 preparatory work started on an International Convention on the Safe Management of Radioactive Wastes at the IAEA.

The nuclear safety programme also includes activities related to operator qualification and training, and evaluation of training programmes; an Operational Safety Review Team (OSART) programme to review the operational safety of nuclear power plants upon invitation by Member States; work on the management of severe accidents and on emergency response; the man-machine interface; probabilistic safety assessment; and advanced safety technology, as well as a nuclear incident reporting system and an International Nuclear Event Scale System (INES), and ASSET Missions upon invitation to assess safety significant events of nuclear power plants. Great emphasis is put on evaluation and assistance to improve the safe operation of Eastern European reactors.

Structure:

(a) General Conference

(b) Board of Governors

(c) Director-General.

The IAEA Secretariat, which has its headquarters in Vienna, has 2,200 staff members. There are laboratories in Seibersdorf, Austria, and Monaco; safeguards offices in Tokyo, Japan and Toronto, Canada; UN liaison offices in New York and Geneva. In Trieste, Italy, the IAEA participates in an International Centre for Theoretical Physics operated by UNESCO.

General Conference: This meets annually. The thirty-ninth regular session met in Vienna from 18 to 22 September 1995. The fortieth regular session will meet in Vienna from September 16 to 20, 1996.

Board of Governors: In accordance with the amended version of Article VI of the Statute, which came into force in 1973, the Board was enlarged to 34 (formerly 25) members. An amendment of Article VI (AI), agreed on in 1984, had the effect of increasing the Board to 35. Thirteen members are designated each year by the Board itself to serve for one year, and 11 are elected each year by the General Conference to serve for two years. The term of all members commences at the end of a regular session of the General Conference and is completed at the end of the next or second subsequent regular session.

The amended article requires the Board to designate the 10 members most advanced in the technology of atomic energy, including the production of source materials, and the member most advanced in nuclear technology in each of the following areas not represented by these 10: North America, Latin America, Western Europe, Eastern Europe, Africa, the Middle East and South Asia, South East Asia and the Pacific, and the Far East. The amendment has still not been ratified by the required two-thirds of the Agency's membership, but in 1984 it was agreed that the Board would start acting as if it had entered into force.

The members elected by the General Conference comprise representatives from the following areas: five from Latin America, four from Western Europe, three from Eastern Europe, four from Africa, two from the Middle East and South Asia, one from South East Asia and the Pacific, and one from the Far East. In addition, one member is elected from either the Middle East and South Asia, or South East Asia and the Pacific, or the Far East; and one other member from either Africa, or the Middle East and South Asia, or South East Asia and the Pacific.

The Chairman and Vice-Chairmen are:

CHAIRMAN OF THE BOARD (1995-96)

H E MR VAN EBBENHORST TENGBERGEN, *NETHERLANDS*

VICE-CHAIRMEN

J MISÁK, *SLOVAKIA*

I UMAR, *NIGERIA*

International Consultative Group on Food Irradiation (ICGFI)

Joint FAO/IAEA Division of Nuclear Techniques in Food and Agriculture
International Atomic Energy Agency
Wagramerstrasse 5
P O Box 100
A-1400 Vienna
Austria
Telephone: (43-1) 2060, Extension 21638

Facsimile: (43-1) 20607

In 1982, the Directors-General of FAO, IAEA and WHO invited Member States to consider forming a consultative group to focus on international cooperation in food irradiation. It was conceived as an independent body composed of government-designated experts.

Upon receipt of a favourable response from 44 Member States, a meeting in 1983 drafted a Declaration establishing the International Consultative Group on Food Irradiation (ICGFI). ICGFI, composed of experts or other participants designated by each government, was established in 1984 for an initial period of five years. FAO, IAEA and WHO, through the Joint FAO/IAEA Division of Nuclear Techniques in Food and Agriculture based at the IAEA, Vienna, serve as its Secretariat.

The functions of the ICGFI are:

(a) To evaluate global developments in the field of food irradiation

(b) To provide a focal point of advice on the application of food irradiation to Member States and the three Organizations

(c) To furnish information, as required, through the Organizations, to the Joint FAO/IAEA/WHO Expert Committee on the Wholesomeness of Irradiated Food and the Codex Alimentarius Commission.

ICGFI funds and operates its own programmes, focusing on developing policy guidelines related to the safety assurance of the process, legislation, public information, economic feasibility, food safety and international trade.

ICGFI convenes annual meeting to develop technical recommendations and to consider its programme of work and budget. The current mandate of ICGFI will expire in May 1999.

The International Consultative Group on Food Irradiation is currently composed of 45 Member States, more than half of them being from developing countries:

ARGENTINA	EGYPT	PAKISTAN
AUSTRALIA	FRANCE	PERU
BANGLADESH	GERMANY	PHILIPPINES
BELGIUM	GHANA	POLAND
BRAZIL	GREECE	PORTUGAL
BULGARIA	HUNGARY	ROK
CANADA	INDIA	SOUTH AFRICA
CHILE	INDONESIA	SYRIAN AR
CHINA	IRAQ	THAILAND
COSTA RICA	ISRAEL	TURKEY
CÔTE D'IVOIRE	ITALY	UKRAINE
CROATIA	MALAYSIA	USA
CUBA	MEXICO	VIET NAM
CZECH REPUBLIC	NETHERLANDS	YUGOSLAVIA
ECUADOR	NEW ZEALAND	

International Narcotics Control Board (INCB)

Vienna International Centre
Wagramerstrasse 5
P O Box 500
A-1400 Vienna
Austria
Telephone: (43-1) 213450
Telex: 135612
Facsimile: (43-1) 21345-5867
Secretary: Herbert Sohaepe, Germany
(Appointed by the Secretary-General in 1991)

The establishment of the Board is provided for in the Single Convention on Narcotic Drugs of 1961, which entered into force on December 13, 1964. Under ECOSOC res. 1106 (XL) of 1966, the Board took over the functions of the Permanent Central Narcotics Board and the Drug Supervisory Body. Its task is to monitor international and domestic movement of narcotic drugs and psychotropic substances used for medical and scientific needs and promote compliance by governments with the various drug control treaties. It is the Board's responsibility also to supervise international trade in precursors and essential chemicals, to prevent their diversion to illicit channels and to serve as a link between national competent authorities in these matters, in accordance with Article 12 of the United Nations Convention Against Illicit Traffic in Narcotic Drugs and Psychotropic Substances 1988.

ECOSOC, with due regard to the principle of equitable geographical representation, gives consideration to the importance of including on the Board persons possessing a knowledge of the drug situation in the producing, manufacturing and consuming countries. Board members were originally elected for a three-year period. This term was increased to five years by the 1972 Protocol amending the Single Convention on Narcotics Drugs 1961, which also strengthened the INCB's powers and enlarged its membership from 11 to 13. The members, who serve in their personal capacity and do not represent their governments, are elected by ECOSOC as follows: three members with medical, pharmacological or pharmaceutical experience from a list of at least five nominated by the World Health Organization; and 10 members from a list of persons nominated by the members of the UN and by parties to the Single Convention on Narcotic Drugs which are not UN members.

The Single Convention requires the Board to meet at least twice a year. The meetings are held in closed session, but the Board publishes an annual report on its work, supplemented by two detailed technical reports containing data on the lawful movement of narcotic drugs and psychotropic substances required for medical and scientific purposes, as well as an annual publication on the implementation of article 12 of the 1988 Convention. The fifty-ninth session was held in Vienna from October 30 to November 16, 1995, and the sixtieth session from May 13 to 24, 1996, also in Vienna.

International Trade Centre UNCTAD/WTO (ITC)

54-56 Rue De Montbrillant
Geneva
Switzerland
Postal Address: Palais Des Nations
Telephone: (41-22) 730-01-11
Telex: 414 119
Facsimile: (41-22) 733-44-39
Executive Director: J Denis Belisle, Canada (1994-97)

The International Trade Centre UNCTAD/WTO (ITC) is the technical cooperation arm of the World Trade Organization (WTO) and the United Nations Conference on Trade and Development (UNCTAD) for operational and enterprise-oriented aspects of international trade development. It was created in 1964 through a decision of GATT Contracting Parties and in 1968 UNCTAD joined GATT as co-sponsor of ITC. Its legal status was formally confirmed by the General Assembly in 1974 as a 'joint subsidiary organ' of GATT and the UN, the latter acting through UNCTAD. In 1995, ITC's name was changed to International Trade Centre UNCTAD/WTO, in line with the establishment of the World Trade Organization (WTO), as the successor to GATT.

In 1973, ITC was designated as the focal point in the UN system for technical cooperation in trade promotion and in this capacity ITC works with developing countries and economies in transition to set up effective trade promotion programmes to expand exports and improve import operations. It specializes in six key areas:

(a) Product and Market Development: Direct export marketing support to the business community, through advice on product development, product adaptation and international marketing in order to develop and market internationally competitive products and services to expand and diversify exports

(b) Trade Support Services: Creation and enhancement of foreign trade support services for the business community provided by national and regional public and private institutions to ensure enterprises have facilities to export and import effectively

(c) Trade Information: Establishment of sustainable national trade information services and dissemination of information on products, services, markets and functions to enterprises and trade organizations to provide a sound information base for international business decisions and trade promotion programmes

(d) Human Resource Development: Strengthening national institutional capacities for foreign trade training and organization of direct training for enterprises in importing and exporting to enhance the efficiency of foreign trade operations

(e) International Purchasing and Supply Management: Application of cost-effective import systems and practices in enterprises and public trading entities through the strengthening of advisory services provided by national purchasing organizations, both public and private, to optimise foreign exchange resources expended on imports

(f) Needs Assessment and Programme Design for Trade Promotion: Development of effective national and regional trade promotion programmes based on analysis of supply potential and constraints and identification of related technical cooperation requirements, with the objective of reinforcing the link between trade policy and the implementation of trade promotion activities.

In all of these services, ITC gives particular attention to activities with the least developed countries (LDCs).

Technical cooperation projects are carried out in all developing areas and economies in transition at the national, subregional, regional and interregional levels. They are undertaken at the request of governments. Projects are administered from ITC headquarters in Geneva and are implemented by ITC consultants who work in close liaison with local experts and officials. A project may last from a few weeks to several years, depending on the types of activities involved.

Membership: Because of its legal status, ITC does not have a membership of its own. However, its de facto members are the Member States of WTO and of UNCTAD.

Annual Intergovernmental Meeting: ITC's annual intergovernmental meeting is the 'Joint Advisory Group on the International Trade Centre UNCTAD/ WTO,' or the JAG. This meeting, held in Geneva,

reviews ITC's technical cooperation programme over the preceding year and makes recommendations for its future work programme. The JAG is presided over by a Chair elected from among those participating in the opening meeting of the session. Other officials elected for the session are two Vice-Chairs and a Rapporteur. The report of the JAG is reviewed by the Trade and Development Board of UNCTAD and the WTO General Council during their respective sessions following the JAG.

International Union for the Protection of New Varieties of Plants (UPOV)

34 Chemin Des Colombettes
CH-1211 Geneva 20
Switzerland
Telephone: (41-22) 730-91-11
Telex: 412912
Facsimile: (41-22) 733-54-28
Secretary-General: Dr Arpad Bogsch, USA (1996-97)

UPOV was established by a Convention signed in Paris in 1961, which entered into force in 1968, and was revised in 1972, 1978 and 1991. The revised Act of 1978 entered into force in 1981. The revised Act of 1991 has not yet entered into force. UPOV is not a specialized agency, but an independent intergovernmental organization, working in close cooperation with the World Intellectual Property Organization, the Director-General of which is the Secretary-General of UPOV.

Purpose: The purpose of the UPOV Convention is to oblige Member States of the Union to recognize and secure to breeders of new plant varieties an industrial property right (plant breeder's right), to harmonize such rights and to encourage cooperation between Member States in their administration of such rights.

Structure:

(a) The Council which meets annually consists of the representatives of all the Member States

(b) Committees of the Council

To assist its work the Council has three committees—the Consultative Committee (preparing the sessions of the Council), the Administrative and Legal Committee, and the Technical Committee. Several working groups have also been established.

(c) The Secretariat-General, is entitled the 'Office of the Union.'

Membership: The 30 Member States are:

ARGENTINA	GERMANY	PORTUGAL
AUSTRALIA	HUNGARY	SLOVAKIA
AUSTRIA	IRELAND	SOUTH AFRICA
BELGIUM	ISRAEL	SPAIN
CANADA	ITALY	SWEDEN
CHILE	JAPAN	SWITZERLAND
CZECH REPUBLIC	NETHERLANDS	UKRAINE
DENMARK	NEW ZEALAND	UK
FINLAND	NORWAY	USA
FRANCE	POLAND	URUGUAY

World Trade Organization (WTO)

Centre William Rappard
154 Rue De Lausanne
1211 Geneva 21
Switzerland
Telephone: (41-22) 739-51-11
Facsimile: (41-22) 731-42-06
Telex: 41 2324 GATT CH
Telegram: Gatt, Genève
Internet: http://www.unicc.org.wto

Internet Enquiries: webmaster@wto.org
Director General: Renato Ruggiero, Italy (1995-99)

The World Trade Organization (WTO) is the legal and institutional foundation of the multilateral trading system. It provides the principal contractual obligations determining how governments frame and implement trade policy. It is also the platform on which trade relations among countries evolve through collective debate, negotiation and adjudication.

The basic aim of the WTO is to liberalize world trade and to place it on a secure basis, thereby contributing to economic growth and development and to the welfare of the world's people. It seeks to achieve this partly through an agreed set of rules and market access commitments in relation to trade between members and partly through negotiations aimed at further liberalization of trade.

The WTO is the embodiment of the results of the Uruguay Round—the eighth trade round held under GATT auspices—and the successor to the 1947 General Agreement on Tariffs and Trade (GATT). Governments concluded the Uruguay Round negotiations on December 15, 1993 and Ministers signed the Final Act containing the verified results of the Round at Marrakesh, Morocco, on April 15. 1994. The WTO was established on January 1, 1995.

As of May 25, 1996, there are 122 WTO members. Another eight former GATT members are in the process of completing procedures for joining, while a further 29 prospective members are engaged in negotiating their terms of entry.

The essential functions of the WTO are to:

(a) Administer and implement the multilateral and plurilateral trade agreements which together make up the WTO

(b) Act as a forum for multilateral trade negotiations

(c) Seek to resolve trade disputes, and

(d) Examine national trade policies.

The WTO Agreement contains a unified package of agreements to which all members are committed. It contains 29 individual agreements—covering trade in goods, services and intellectual property. Added to these are a number of ministerial declarations and decisions which spell out further obligations and commitments for WTO members. The WTO Agreement includes, as an integral part the 'GATT 1994,' the amended and updated version of GATT 1947. The GATT 1994 continues to provide the key disciplines affecting international trade in goods.

WTO rules extend to goods sectors previously not fully covered by GATT rules, such as trade in agricultural products and textiles and clothing. For agriculture, the rules cover market access conditions, domestic support measures, export subsidy and food safety, plant and animal health regulations. For trade in textiles and clothing, new rules call for a 10-year phase out of the Multifibre Arrangement and a complete integration of this sector into WTO rules.

The WTO Agreement also sets out rules covering areas such as the origin of goods, anti-dumping practices, subsidies and countervailing measures, customs valuation and import licensing. They are accompanied by various mechanisms to ensure transparency, such as notification procedures. For dispute settlement, the WTO procedures are faster and more automatic than under the old GATT system. An Appellate Body has been created to review, if requested to do so, the decisions of dispute settlement panels.

Principles of the WTO: The WTO system is underpinned by certain fundamental principles:

(a) Trade without discrimination: The 'most favoured nation' clause stipulates that each member must grant to all other members treatment as favourable as that which they grant to any other country

(b) Protection through tariffs: Any protection given to domestic industry should be through the use of tariffs, rather than through less transparent means such as quotas and import licensing

(c) The binding of tariffs at levels negotiated among members: Where tariffs have been bound, they can be increased only if compensation is offered by the importing country

(d) National treatment: Imported products must be treated no less favourably than domestic products with respect to internal taxes, regulations and requirements

(e) Consultations on a basis of equality: Any member may invoke the WTO's dispute settlement provisions in cases where it considers its rights have been nullified or impaired by others.

The WTO Secretariat: The WTO Secretariat is located in Geneva. It has approximately 500 staff and is headed by a Director-General and four deputy directors-general. Its responsibilities include the servicing of WTO bodies with respect to negotiations and the implementation of agreements. It has a particular responsibility to provide technical support to developing countries, and especially the least developed countries. WTO economists and statisticians provide trade performance and trade policy analysis, while legal staff assist in the resolution of trade disputes involving the interpretation of WTO rules and precedents. Some of the Secretariat's work is concerned with accession negotiations for new members and providing advice to governments considering membership.

The official languages of the WTO are English,

French and Spanish.

Principal Standing Bodies of the WTO: The following sets out the principal standing bodies and chairpersons of the WTO as of May 25, 1996:

Ministerial Conference (Meets Every Two Years at Ministerial Level): The Ministerial Conference is the highest authority of the WTO. It is composed of all WTO members and is required to meet at least once every two years. It can take decisions on all matters relating to any of the multilateral trade agreements. The first Ministerial Conference was held in Singapore in late 1996.

WTO General Council-W Rossier, Switzerland: The General Council is composed of all WTO members and meets as required. It reports to the Ministerial Conference and acts on its behalf in regard to the day-to-day work of the WTO. The General Council also convenes in two particular forms—as the Dispute Settlement Body, to oversee the dispute settlement procedures, and as the Trade Policy Review Body, to conduct regular reviews of the trade policies of individual WTO members.

Dispute Settlement Body-C Lafer, Brazil: The Dispute Settlement Body (DSB) deals with disputes between WTO members arising from the agreement contained in the Final Act of the Uruguay Round. The DSB has the sole authority to establish panels, adopt panel and appellate reports, monitor the implementation of rulings and recommendations and authorise retaliatory measures in cases of non-implementation of recommendations.

Trade Policy Review Body-A Anderson, Ireland: The Trade Policy Review Body (TPRB) monitors the trade policies and practices of WTO members. Its objective is to increase the transparency and understanding of members' trade measures and policies and the possible effects of those measures on the multilateral trading system. Depending on the importance of the country in terms of world trade, each WTO member is reviewed every two, four or six years.

Council for Trade in Goods-S Narayanan, India: The Council for Trade in Goods oversees the functioning of the Multilateral Trade Agreements on goods trade contained in Annex 1A of the WTO Agreement, including schedules of market access concessions and commitments, the Understandings on the interpretation of various GATT 1994 articles and the Agreements on Agriculture and Textiles and Clothing. It also covers rules for trade in goods, such as subsidies, safeguards and technical barriers to trade.

Council for Trade in Services-L Bautista, Philippines:

The Council for Trade in Services oversees the General Agreement on Trade in Services (GATS) consisting of a framework of general rules and disciplines for trade in services, together with annexes concerning certain individual services sectors and the national schedules of market access commitments made by WTO members.

Council for Trade-Related Aspects of Intellectual Property Rights-W Armstrong, New Zealand: The Council for Trade-Related Aspects of Intellectual Property Rights (TRIPS) monitors the operation of the TRIPS Agreement which contains basic principles, including national treatment and most favoured nation provisions, and addresses protection for different kinds of intellectual property rights such as copyright, trademarks, geographical indications and patents. The Agreement also sets our transition arrangements and enforcement obligations for members.

Committee on Regional Trade Agreements-J Weekes, Canada: The Committee on Regional Trade Agreements, created in 1996, is responsible for the examination of free trade agreements and customs unions notified to the WTO and also provides a forum for discussion of the relationship between regional agreements and the multilateral trading system.

Textiles Monitoring Body-A Szepesi, Hungary: The Textiles Monitoring Body (TMB) supervises the implementation of the Textiles and Clothing Agreement. It also provides, on request, assistance to members in resolving any bilateral differences arising from the Agreement.

Committee on Agriculture-D Tulalamba, Thailand: The Committee on Agriculture oversees the implementation of the Agriculture Agreement. It provides members with a forum for consulting on any matter relating to the implementation of the Agreement's provisions.

Committee on Trade and the Environment-J C Sanchez Arnau, Argentina: The Committee was established in early 1995 to examine the links between trade and environment and to explore issues such as: the relationship between provisions of multilateral environmental agreements and those of the WTO; the sustainable development, environment and trade interface; the impact of environmental measures on market access, in particular for exports of developing countries; trade in domestically prohibited goods; packaging, labelling and recycling requirements and the transparency of trade-related environmental measures. The Committee is to report to the Ministerial Conference in December 1996.

Committee on Trade and Development-N Benjelloun-Touimi, Morocco: The Committee coordinates work on trade and development issues in the WTO and reviews the participation of developing country members in the multilateral system.

Other Standing Bodies of the WTO :

COMMITTEE ON ANTI-DUMPING PRACTICES

COMMITTEE ON SUBSIDIES AND COUNTERVAILING MEASURES

COMMITTEE ON BUDGET, FINANCE AND ADMINISTRATION

COMMITTEE ON CUSTOMS VALUATION

INTERIM COMMITTEE ON GOVERNMENT

PROCUREMENT (WTO COMMITTEE ENTERS INTO FORCE JANUARY 1, 1996)

COMMITTEE ON IMPORT LICENSING

COMMITTEE ON MARKET ACCESS

COMMITTEE ON RULES OF ORIGIN

COMMITTEE ON SAFEGUARDS

COMMITTEE ON SANITARY AND PHYTOSANITARY MEASURES

COMMITTEE ON TARIFF CONCESSIONS

COMMITTEE ON TECHNICAL BARRIERS TO TRADE

COMMITTEE ON TRADE IN FINANCIAL SERVICES

COMMITTEE ON TRADE-RELATED INVESTMENT MEASURES

Plurilateral Trade Agreements: The WTO also oversees the operation of four 'Plurilateral Trade Agreements'—Civil Aircraft, Government Procurement, Dairy and Bovine Meat—membership of which is optional. These agreements are binding only on those members which join them.

GATT/WTO Accessions: The following 29 governments have requested to join the WTO. Their applications are currently being considered by accession working parties.

ALBANIA	KYRGYZSTAN	CHINESE TAIPEI
ALGERIA	LATVIA	THE FORMER YUGOSLAV
ARMENIA	LITHUANIA	REPUBLIC OF MACEDONIA
BELARUS	MONGOLIA	TONGA
BULGARIA	NEPAL	UKRAINE
CAMBODIA	PANAMA	UZBEKISTAN
CHINA	REPUBLIC OF MOLDOVA	VANUATU
CROATIA	RUSSIAN FEDERATION	VIET NAM
ESTONIA	SAUDI ARABIA	
JORDAN	SEYCHELLES	
KAZAKSTAN	SUDAN	

Former GATT Members Which Are Not Yet WTO Members: Under the WTO Agreement, governments which were GATT members but have not yet become WTO members had until the end of 1996 to accept the Agreement and become WTO members. This group includes the following governments:

ANGOLA	GAMBIA	SOLOMON ISLANDS
CHAD	NIGER	ZAIRE
CONGO		

World Tourism Organization (WTO)

Capitán Haya, 42, E-28020
Madrid
Spain
Telephone: (34-1) 571-0628
Telex: 42188, OMT
Facsimile: (34-1) 571-3733
Secretary-General: Antonio Enriquez Savignac, Mexico (1994-1 September 1996)
Secretary-General AD Interim: Francesco Frangialli (1 September 1996-97)

WTO was established in 1975, as an intergovernmental organization, on entry into force of statutes which had been adopted in 1970 at Mexico City. Following a resolution adopted by its first General Assembly in May 1975, WTO established its headquarters in Madrid, Spain in January 1976.

Its non-governmental predecessor had been found-ed in 1925 as the International Congress of Official Tourist Traffic Associations, renamed in 1934 the International Union of Official Tourist Propaganda Organizations (IUOTPO), a name that in 1947 was changed to the International Union of Official Travel Organizations (IUOTO).

WTO is the only intergovernmental organization whose activities cover all aspects of tourism on a worldwide basis.

In res. 2529 XXIV (1969), the UN General Assembly decided that an agreement should be concluded to establish close cooperation with the future World Tourism Organization, recognizing the central role it was to play in the field of world tourism in cooperation with the existing machinery of the United Nations system. Subsequently, in res. 32/156 (1977) the Assembly adopted without vote an agreement on cooperation and relationship between the UN and

WTO. WTO acts as an executing agency for the UNDP and has consultative status with ECOSOC, UNESCO, IMO and ICAO.

The fundamental aim of WTO is to promote and develop tourism with a view to contributing to economic development, international understanding, peace, prosperity and universal respect for, and observance of, human rights and fundamental freedoms for all without distinction as to race, sex, language or religion (article 3 (1) of its Statutes).

Structure:

(a) The General Assembly, the supreme organ of the Organization, meets every two years. It has established six Regional Commissions: for Africa, the Americas, Europe, the Middle East, East Asia and the Pacific, and South Asia

(b) The Executive Council, which meets at least twice a year, has one Member elected on the basis of equitable geographical distribution for every five full members of WTO. One Associate Member selected by the Associate Members of WTO and a representative of the Affiliate Members of WTO participate in the work of the Council, but have no voting rights. Spain, host country of the Organization, also sits on the Council as an ex-officio member. The Council's work is carried out by its subsidiary organs: the Technical Committee for Programme and Coordination (TCPC), the Committee on Budget and Finance (CBF), the

Environment Committee, the Quality Support Committee and the Subcommittee for the Review of Applications for Affiliate Membership

(c) The Affiliate Members, composed of all the affiliate members of the Organization, participates in WTO's activities, makes recommendations to its organs and carries out its own programmes of work in the framework of WTO activities, by means of working parties

(d) Secretariat.

Membership: There are three categories of members:

(a) Full members: (129 Member States)

(b) Associate members, which are territories or groups of territories not responsible for their external relations but whose membership is approved by the state assuming responsibility for their external relations: Aruba, Macau, Netherlands Antilles and Madeira

(c) Affiliate members, both intergovernmental and non-governmental entities, with specialized interests in tourism as well as commercial and non-commercial bodies and associations whose activities are related to the aims of WTO or fall within its competence (over 300 affiliate members).

Permanent Observer status, with the right to speak but without right to vote, was given to the Holy See at the General Assembly in 1979.

INTERNATIONAL PEACE
INSTITUTES
AND ORGANIZATIONS

This section comprises basic information on currently active peace organizations worldwide. A deviation from the first edition was made in terms of classification. In this edition we use the simple classification by country. For each institution we tried our best to provide the most basic information that will be of use to the average reader.

As can be seen from the sample of organizations presented in this section, peace research is still concentrated in the West. But this situation is changing and it is consequently difficult to be fully up-to-date because development is so rapid: on the one hand, the financing of peace research is so often precarious and even long-established institutes have been forced to close or to scale down their work; on the other, new centers are constantly emerging, stimulated by the continuing need for peace research and peace education at all levels.

In updating the entries, a questionnaire was sent to about 200 organizations. A retrieval of 70 percent formed the basis of the revision and expansion job. A final constraint upon the comprehensiveness of this section has been the responsiveness of the organizations themselves—our original "core list" included some institutions and centers which are, regrettably, not represented here because no reply was received to our questionnaire. Another source for new entries is the *World Directory of Peace: Research and Training Institutions*, UNESCO, Social and Human Science Documentation Center 1994.

International Peace Institutes and Organizations

Peace Research Institutes

Argentina

Centro de Investigaciones en Ciencias Sociales [Social Science Research Center]
Defensa 665-5-c 1065 Buenos Aires, Argentina

Telephone: 54-342-9914
Fax: 54-342-9914
Senior Staff: Director: Beba Balve, Investigadora: Beatriz Balve
Date of Establishment: 1966
Purpose: The fundamental purpose of its activities is to promote research by applying conceptualization, theory, method, description, mediation, and empirical inspection with a special emphasis on the Argentinian society.
Type: National, private, non-profit
Brief History: The dominant perspective theory from which the research was implemented emphasized the "Force-power" dimensions. The investigated social facts show the dominant social confrontation according to the periods.

Principal Activities: Research; publications; seminars; research workshops for the training of researchers, conferences; journals and specialized libraries.
Periodicals: *Studies and Theory*
Major Publications:

(a) *Armed Actions—A Possible Exercise*

(b) *The Street Struggle—The Struggle of Classes*

(c) *The '69 Mass' Political Strike*

(d) *From protest to rebellion: The Subversion*

Australia

Conflict Resolution Network
PO Box 1016, Chatswood NSW 2057, Australia

Telephone: 61-2-9412-1584
Fax: 61-2-9413-1148
E-mail: crn@crnhq.org
Senior Staff: Director: Stella Cornelius, Helena Cornelius
Date of Establishment: 1986
Purpose: The CRN's mandates are to research, develop, teach and implement the theory and practice of Conflict Resolution throughout a national and international network, and to concern ourselves with conflicts from personal and family to international and global issues.
Type: National, public, and non-profit
Brief History: Established in 1986 as a program of the peace and Conflict Resolution Program of the United Nations Association of Australia by Stella and Helena Cornelius.

Principal Activities: Dissemination of information; development of new programs in training, mediation, conflict analysis and consultancy, and on issues of special focus such as conflict-resolving media, and unemployment.

Periodicals: Occasional papers

Major Publications:

(a) Cornelius, H., *Gentle Revolution*,

Peace Research Center
Research School of Pacific & Asian Studies
The Australian National University
Canberra ACT 0200, Australia

Telephone: 61-6-249-3908
Fax: 61-6-249-0174
E-mail: peace@coombs.anu.edu.au
Senior Staff: Professor & Head: Ramesh Thakur
Date of Establishment: 1984
Purpose: The Center intends to conduct high quality, policy-relevant research on issues of international peace and security, especially arms control and disarmament.
Type: Public, national, non-profit
Brief History: In existence since 1984, the Peace Research Center is based in Canberra, located in the Research School of Pacific & Asian Studies of The Australian National University. Its funding comes primarily from the Department of Foreign Affairs & Trade of the Government of Australia.
Principal Activities: The Peace Research Center has:

(a) Engaged in research and published articles and monographs,

(b) Acted as a source of consultancy for the Government of Australia,

(c) Published Working Papers and the quarterly journal *Pacific Research*,

(d) Organized seminars, workshops and conferences.

Periodicals: *Pacific Research* (quarterly)
Major Publications:

(a) *Beyond Peace*,

(b) *Peace and Security in the Asia Pacific Region*,

(c) *The Middle East*,

(d) *The Australian Peace Movement*,

(e) *Chemical Weapons and Missile Proliferation*.

Other Information: Professor R. Thakur, Head of the Peace Research Center, is currently completing editorial work on the papers from the ARF Track Two Seminar on Non-Proliferation, held in Jakarta in December 1996. The Peace Research Center organized a Workshop on Nuclear Weapon Free Zones in December 1996 in Canberra.

Strategic & Defense Studies Center
Australian National University
AXT 0200, Australia

Telephone: 61-6-243-8555
Fax: 61-6-248-0816
E-mail: ksmith@coombs.anu.edu.au
Senior Staff: Head: Paul Dibb, Directors of Graduate Studies: Stewart Woodman
Date of Establishment: 1966
Purpose: The Center aspires to be the leading Australian research center on strategic and defense studies; to develop postgraduate research and teaching on Asia-Pacific strategic affairs which will support the priorities of the Research School of Pacific and Asian Studies to

achieve quality in the publication of its research; to provide advice to the Parliament and the private sector; to promote awareness of an informed public debate on strategic and defense issues.
Type: Public, non-profit
Principal Activities: Research into Asia-Pacific strategic security issues; and Australian defense policy
Major Publications:

(a) *Canberra Papers on Strategy and Defense*,

(b) Working Papers.

World Futures Studies Federation (WFSF)
Queensland University of Technology, c/o The Communication Centre, Australia

Telephone: 61-7-3864-2192/61-7-3864-1723
Fax: 61-7-3864-1813
E-mail: t.stevenson@qut.edu.au.
Senior Staff: Secretary General: Cesar Villanueva

Date of Establishment: 1967
Purpose: The Federation aims at:

(a) Serving as a forum for the exchange of information

and opinions, thus, stimulating cooperative research activities in all fields of futures studies,

(b) Planning and holding regional and global futures studies conferences and courses,

(c) Promoting a higher level of futures consciousness in general,

(d) Encouraging the democratization of futures-oriented thinking and acting,

(e) Stimulating the awareness of the urgent need for futures studies in governments and international organizations, as well as other decision making and educational groups and institutions, to resolve problems at local, national, regional and global levels,

(f) Assisting national and global futures research activities.

Type: International

Brief History: WFSF emerged from the ideas and pioneer work of such persons as Igor Bestuzhev-Lada, Bertrand de Jouvenel, Johan Galtung, Robert Jungk, John McHale and others who in the 1960s conceived of the concept of futures studies at the global level.

Principal Activities: WFSF promotes and encourages futures studies, has issued a futures bulletin from the secretariate (1993-1997), organizes world and regional conferences, coordinates futures research, publishes proceedings of conferences and regional meetings.

Periodicals: *Futures Bulletin*, currently published quarterly.

Major Publications:

(a) *Futures Beyond Poverty—Ways and Means Out of the Current Stalemate*,

(b) *The Future of Democracy in the Developing World*,

(c) *Civilizations, Structure & Visions*,

(d) *The Futures of Communication*,

(e) *Prospective of Studies for Policy-Making*.

Austria

Friedenszentrum Burg Schlaining [Austrian Study Center for Peace and Conflict Resolution and European University Center for Peace Studies]
A-7461 Stadtschlaining/Burg, Austria

Telephone: 43-3355-2498
Fax: 43-3355-2662 (ASPR)/43-3355-2381 (EPU)/
  43-3355-2300 (Peace Library)
E-mail: aspr@aspr.ac.at
Senior Staff: President: Gerald Mader
Date of Establishment: ASPR in 1983, EPU in 1987
Purpose: The purpose of the center includes peace promotion; promotion of peaceful conflict resolution; and political and scientific dialogue.
Type: National, private, non-profit
Brief History: The ASPR was founded in a small town in Austria's most eastern province for the purpose of peace research, peace education, and conflict resolution, and also to establish a peace university. EPU was founded in 1987. Both institutes cooperate very closely and form the Friedenszentrum Burg Schlaining.
Principal Activities: Peace research; peace education; conflict resolution, peace politics conferences; seminars; study and training programs; lectures (external activities); publications; research programs; establishment of a peace museum.
Periodicals: *Dialogue, Contributions to the Peace Studies* (2 editions annually), *Peace Forum* (quarterly), *Peace Education Concrete* (1 edition annually,) *Working Papers* (not regular).
Other Information: At present, the ASPR is conducting a five year research program on basic principles of European security and peace policy. In 1995, the ASPR and the EPU were jointly awarded the UNESCO prize for peace Education. In 1996, a UNESCO-Chair for Peace, Human Rights and Democracy was established at the EPU. The ASPR also conducts the International Civilian Peace-keeping and Peace-building Training Program.

Institute of Conflict Research
Lisztstrasse 3 A-1030, Vienna, Austria

Telephone: 43-1-713-16-40   **Fax:** 43-1-713-99-30

E-mail: institute@ikf.ac.at
Senior Staff: Director: Anton Pelinka
Date of Establishment: 1976
Purpose: The main function of the Institute is the study of political, social and individual conflicts on an interdisciplinary basis. The Institute draws up scientific studies as a support to political decision-making. Studies in basic research build the foundation for this field of activities.
Type: National, private, non-profit.
Principal Activities: Conducts studies on:

(a) Democracy in liberal systems (esp. in the EU),

(b) Labour market and social security of national and foreign employees,

(c) Conflicts in the range of public and personal safety,

(d) Gender research,

(e) Research on prejudice (e.g., xenophobia and racism),

(f) Social change, labour market and political conflicts in the new democracies in Central and Eastern Europe,

(g) Ecology and Policies,

(h) Civics and Conflict Training.

Belgium

Center for Peace Research and Strategic Studies (CPRS)
Katholieke Universiteit Leuven
E. Van Evenstraat 2 B Belgium-3000, Leuven, Belgium

Telephone: 32-16-32-32-57/32-16-32-32-41
Fax: 32-16-32-30-88
E-mail: luc.reychler@soc.kuleuven.ac.be
Senior Staff: Professor-Director: Luc Reychler
Date of Establishment: 1982
Purpose: The Center intends to promote the transdisciplinary study of violence and conflict dynamics; to develop more effective ways and means for constructive conflict transformation and peace building.
Type: National, private, non-profit
Brief History: The Center is an offshoot of a seminar "Peace Research" led by V. Werck in 1967. In 1982, it became a research center at the University of Leuven.
Principal Activities: Conducts studies on:

(a) Genocide (Bosnia, Burundi, Rwanda),

(b) Conflict impact assessment system (CIAS),

(c) Field diplomacy,

(d) Violent conflicts as histories of missed opportunities,

(e) Democratization, development and conflict dynamics in Georgia, Rumania, Tunisia and Burundi,

(f) Leadership in conflicts.

Periodicals: Cahiers of the Center of Peace Research and Strategic Studies.
Major Publications:

(a) Bauwens, W., Reychler, L., *The Art of Conflict Prevention*, 1994, Brasseys.

(b) Reychler, L., Moreels, R., *De Agressie Voorbij*, Roularta 1995.

(c) Reychler, L., *Field Diplomacy: A New Paradigm*,

(d) Reychler, L., *Conflict Impact Assessment System* (CIAS),

(e) *Conflicts as Histories of Missed Opportunities* (Bosnia, Rwanda, Burundi),

(f) *Genocide and Conflict Prevention* (Bosnia, Rwanda, Burundi),

(g) *Democratization, Development and Conflict Transformation* (Georgia, Rumania, Tunisia, Burundi),

(h) *Reconciliation and Mediation*,

(i) *Leadership in Peace-building*.

Groupe de Recherche et d'Information sur la Paix et la Sécurité
33, rue Van Hoorde-B-1030 Bruxelles, Belgium

Telephone: 32-2-241-84-20
Fax: 32-2-245-19-33

E-mail: admi@grip.org or bernard.adam@grip.org
Web Site: www.grip.org

Senior Staff: Director: Bernard Adam
Date of Establishment: 1978
Purpose: The GRIP aims to enlighten citizens and politicians in decision-making towards a better international security based on armament reduction and new defense concepts (global security, common and mutual). All activities aim to be useful and helpful in the process of decision-making.
Type: Non-profit
Brief History: The GRIP is an independent research institute founded in Brussels in 1979.
Principal Activities: The GRIP mainly studies the role of Europe in the international security and the issues concerning the defense economy (military budget, arms production and export). The Institute also has different publications (documents and books), conducts conferences, lectures, radio and TV talks.
Periodicals:

(a) *GRIP-Information* (yearly),

(b) *Les Dossiers du GRIP* (monthly).

Major Publication:

(a) Wautelet, M., *Les Cyberconflits*, mars 1998,

(b) Braeckman, C., Cros, M-F., Villers, G. de., François, F., Reyntjens, F., Ryckmans, F., Willame, J-C., *Kabila Prend le Pouvoir*, 1998,

(c) Dumoulin, A., *La France Militaire et l'Afrique*, 1997, 136 pages,

(d) Willame, J-C., *Les Belges au Rwanda. Le Parcours de la honte*, 1997,

(e) *Memento Défense-Désarmement 1997. L'Europe et la Sécurité Internationale*, Ouvrage Collectif, juillet 1997,

(f) *Conflits en Afrique-Analyse des crises et pistes pour une réflexion*, Fondation Roi Baudouin, Medecin Sans Frontieres, 1997.

Institute of Development Policy and Management
University of Antwerp Middelheimlaan
7 B-2020 Antwerp, Belgium

Telephone: 32-3-218-0670
Fax: 32-3-218-0666
E-mail: phina@maze.ruca.ua.ac.be.
Senior Staff: Academic Secretary: Philip Nauwelaerts, Professor: Filip Reyntsjens
Date of Establishment: 1965
Purpose: The Institute aims at training courses in Development Studies and conducting research projects, e.g., Human Rights

Type: Public, national
Brief History: Since 1972, each year, 80 students from 40 different countries have received the Master Degree in Public Administration and Management. From 1998, a new program started.
Principal Activities: Teaching about international economics research projects and projects in the Third World.
Periodicals: CIMDA-*Papers*

Pax Christi International
International Secretariat, rue du Vieux Marche aux Grains 21 B-1000 Brussels, Belgium

Telephone: 32-502-55-50
Fax: 32-502-46-26
Senior Staff: President: G. Danneels, Secretary-General: E. de Jonghe
Date of Establishment: 1945
Purpose: The aim of Pax Christi is not only to disseminate information and documentation but also to sensitize and mobilize the opinion of the religious community and others to peace and justice issues.
Type: Private, non-profit
Brief History: Pax Christi is an international Catholic

peace movement, founded in the aftermath of the Second World War in France by Msgr. Theas to foster postwar reconciliation and peace. During the 1940s and 1950s, Pax Christi centers were established in the Federal Republic of Germany, Belgium, the Netherlands, Austria, and Switzerland. It was Pope Pius who gave the movement its full status as an international Catholic peace movement.

The Papal Encyclical Pacem in Terris (1963) marked a turning point in Church teachings and became the new "Charter" of Pax Christi. Together with the Vatican Council Constitution Gaudium et Spes (1965) these documents made way for a fuller understanding of the whole idea of peace and its intimate links with so many of the problems that the human race is facing today.

Principal Activities: The activities of the movement are focused in the areas of research and study; operations of the Commission on Security and Disarmament, the Commission for East-West Contacts, and the Human Rights Commission; training sessions seminars, and retreats; and youth and summer activities.

Major Publications:

(a) *Advocating for Peace*, 1992,

(b) *Servants of Peace*, 1992,

(c) *Nuclear Ttesting: Hhigh Time to Stop*, 1992,

(d) *Pax Christi on Chemical Weapons*, 1992,

(e) *Do We Live in a More Peaceful World?*, 1992,

(f) *The Policy of Neutrality*, 1992,

(g) *The Role of the UN Security Council*, 1992,

(h) *Pax Christi on Arms Trade*, 1992,

(i) *Refugees, Asylum Seekers, Racism: 1991-1992*, 1992,

(j) *How Can We Abolish the Institution of War?*, 1992,

(k) *Building for Peace*, 1992,

(l) *Evangelisation of Peace Today*, 1992,

(m) *Our Planetary Village. Pax Christi on Ecology and Peace*, 1991-1992, 1992,

(n) *Statutes and By-laws*, 1993,

(o) Wicker, B. (ed.), *Studying War: No More? From Just War to Just Peace*, 1993,

(p) *Enfants Soldats*, 1993,

(q) *Pax Christi et CELAM*, 1993.

Universite de Paix [University of Peace]
Boulevard du Nord 4, 5000 Namur, Belgium

Telephone: 32-81-22-6102
Fax: 32-81-23-1882
E-mail: universite.de.paix@skynet.be
Senior Staff: Secretary-General: F. Bazier
Date of Establishment: 1960
Purpose: A University devoted to education for peace and intercultural education.
Type: Non-profit
Principal Activities: Training; documentation/information; conference-organization; publication; mediation service.

Periodicals: *U.P. Information*, quarterly.

Major Publications:

(a) *Viver ou mourir ensemble*,

(b) *Les Droits des homains*,

(c) *La Communication non-violente*,

(d) Bailly, Y. et al. (eds.), *La Mediation*,

(e) *Jeux cooperatifs pour batir la paix*, vol 1 & 2.

Canada

Canadian Institute of International Affairs
5 Devonshire Place, Toronto, Ontario M5S 2C8, Canada,

Telephone: 1-416-979-1851
Fax: 1-416-979-8575
E-mail: mailbox@ciia.org
Senior Staff: President and CEO: Alan Sullivan, Chairman: Peter White
Date of Establishment: 1928
Purpose: The mission of the Canadian Institute of International Affairs is to promote a broader and deeper understanding of international affairs and of Cana-

da's role in a changing world by providing interested Canadians with a non-partisan, nationwide forum for informed discussion, analysis and debate.
Type: International, private, non-profit
Brief History: The origins of the Canadian Institute of International Affairs (CIIA) go back further than its founding in 1982. Description of its formation usually began with the 1919 Paris Peace conference. (E. D. Greathed, *The Antecedents and Origin of the Canadian*

Institute of International Peace Conference. In 1925, a delegation of six Canadians, under the chairmanship of John Nelson attended a conference in Honolulu at which the Institute of Pacific Relations (IPR) was founded. The Canadian Institute of International Affairs was formally organized on January 30, 1928, in affiliation with the Royal Institute of International Affairs (RIIA) and the Institute of Pacific Relations (IPR).

Principal Activities: The Institute produces 4 publications, operates a library, provides services to membership, do youth outreach and have numerous briefing missions around the world for members of their corporate council. It also hosts an annual foreign policy conference.

Periodicals:

(a) *International Journal* (quarterly),

(b) *Behind the Headlines* (quarterly),

(c) *Contemporary Affairs* (infrequent),

(d) *Canadian Foreign Policy Bibliography* (every 5 years).

The Center for International Studies
University of Toronto
252 Bloor Street, 8th floor, Toronto, ON M5S-1V6, Canada

Telephone: 1-416-923-6641 (EXT: 3350)
Fax: 1-416-926-4738
E-mail: cis.general@utoronto.ca
Web Site: www.utoronto.ca/cis/
Senior Staff: Director: Louis W. Pauly
Date of Establishment: 1975

Purpose: In the context of an institution-wide re-thinking and re-articulation of its scholarly mission, the University identified international studies as one of its top priorities and a principal area for future growth. The move reflected a widespread sense that a rapidly widening set of intellectual and policy concerns demanded cross-disciplinary approaches and that today's students would be ill-equipped for tomorrow's world if their university experience were limited to a narrow set of specialized fields. The emergence of a global economy, the deepening of cross-cultural linkages, the spread of democratic forms of governance, the acceleration of technological change, the rise of new environmental and public health challenges such developments underlined the need to encourage fruitful discussion, solid research, and innovative teaching across traditional borders between departments, faculties, and professional schools.

Brief History: The University of Toronto, Canada's largest university and the leading research institution in the country, has a long tradition of excellence in the field of international studies. In the mid-1970s, an interdisciplinary Center for International Studies emerged out of established teaching and research programs in international relations based at Trinity College. (The University is actually a federation of colleges and universities, some of which pre-date its establishment. Trinity is one of the oldest colleges in the country.) Over time, the mission of the Center broadened considerably. A constituent unit of the University's School of Graduate Studies, its activities drew together scholars, students, visitors, and interested members of various policy communities.

From the late 1980s through the mid-1990s under the distinguished leadership of Professor Leonard Waverman and Dr. Sylvia Ostry, the Center was prominently identified with advanced research in international economic policy. Major studies sponsored by the Center focused on such topics as the rationale for and impact of freer trade in North America, international institution-building in the trade arena, foreign direct investment, the political economy of competition policy, the implications of global financial integration, and the liberalization of telecommunication regimes. Without losing the critical mass of expertise fostered by such work, CIS entered into an exciting new phase of its history in the summer of 1997.

Principal Activities: In addition to teaching, conference organization and publication, the day-to-day work of CIS is organized around several research programs and projects led by University of Toronto faculty, visiting professors, and post-doctoral students in residence. These now encompass: NAFTA and its effects, new directions in international conflict management and negotiation, development studies, the trade-environment-competitiveness policy nexus, China's integration into the global economy, the G-7 and global governance, regional innovation systems, economic and political transformation in Latin America and the Caribbean, and health and global affairs.

Periodicals: Working papers and occasional Newsletters.

Major Publications:

(a) Doremus, P. N., Keller, W. W., Pauly, L. W., Reich

S., *The Myth of the Global Corporation*, Princeton University Press,

(b) Pauly, L. W., *Who Elected the Bankers?: Surveillance and Control in the World Economy*, Princeton University Press, 1997,

(c) Berry, A., *Poverty, Economic Reform, and Income Distribution in Latin America*, Lynne Rienner Publishers, 1998,

(d) Ostry, S., *The Post Cold War Trading System: Who's on First?*, University of Chicago Press, 1997,

(e) Safarian, A. E., Dobson, W. (eds.), *The People Link: Human Resource Linkages Across the Pacific*, University of Toronto Press 1997,

(f) von Furstenberg, G. M. (ed.), *The Banking and Financial Structure in the NAFTA Countries and Chile*, Indiana University, Kluwer Academic Publishers, 1997,

(g) von Furstenberg, G. M. (ed.), *Regulation and Supervision of Financial Institutions in the NAFTA Countries and Beyond*, Indiana University, Kluwer Academic Publishers, 1997,

(h) Waverman, L., Comanor, W. S., Goto, A. (eds.), *Competition Policy in the Global Economy: Modalities for Cooperation*, Routledge Press, 1997,

(i) Warrian, P., *Hard Bargain: Transforming Public Sector Labour-Management Relations*, McGilligan Books, 1996,

(j) Safarian, A. E., *East Asian Capitalism: Diversity and Dynamism*, University of Toronto Press, 1996.

Institute of International Relations
University of British Columbia
C456-1866 Main Mall, Vancouver, BC V6T lZl, Canada

Telephone: 1-604-822-5480
Fax: 1-604-822-5540
E-mail: instir@unixg.ubc.ca
Senior Staff: Director: Brian L. Job, Members: Robert Jackson, Masaru Kohno
Date of Establishment: 1970
Purpose: The Institute aims to facilitate internationally-oriented interdisciplinary research and curricula among the faculty and students of the University of British Columbia and other institutions.
Type: Academic
Brief History: Established in 1970, the Institute of International Relations at the University of British Columbia is one of the longest standing and most active of its kind in Canada. The Institute administers projects and grants, organizes conferences, sponsors seminars and hosts guest lectures, and postdoctoral fellows and visiting scholars. Although the Institute has never offered courses or degree programs, it has long been closely affiliated with the graduate program in Political Science and with the University's undergraduate, interdisciplinary International Relations Program.
Principal Activities: The Institute administers projects and grants, organizes conferences, sponsors seminars and guest lectures. The Institute also hosts postdoctoral fellows and visiting scholars.
Periodicals: In addition to its *Annual Report*, the Institute also periodically publishes conference proceedings and many other publications written by persons associated with the Institute.
Major Publications:

(a) *Global Order: Values and Power in International Politics*,

(b) *Multilateralism: The Relevance of the Concept to Regional Conflict Management*,

(c) *Ideology and Women in North Korea*.

Institut Qubcois Des Haute Sttudes Internationales
[Quebec Graduate Institute of International Studies]
Universit Laval
Bureau 5460, Pavillon Charles-De Koninck, Cite Universitaire, Qubcois G1K 7P4, Canada

Telephone: 418-656-7771
Fax: 418-656-3634
E-mail: hei@hei.ulaval.ca.

Web Site: http://www.ulaval.ca/iqhei
Senior Staff: Director of the Program: Albert Legault, Prof.: Gerard Hervouet, Gordon Mace

Date of Establishment: June 1994

Purpose: The Institute purports to promote and undertake research and graduate studies in international relations particularly in Foreign Policy Analysis, South-East Asia and Juridical Aspects of International Economic Integration.

Type: Public

Brief History: The Institute was created in June 1994 by Laval University. It had integrated the programs of the former Center qubcois de relations internationales and the Master Degree Program in International Relations.

Principal Activities: Graduate studies; research; publications; conferences, seminars, membership.

Periodicals: *International Studies Quarterly, Peacekeeping Bulletin, The Conflicts in the World.*

Major Publications:

(a) *International Studies; La collection: Strategics et militaries,*

(b) *Les Conflicts dans le monde*—The annual report on conflicts around the world.

Peace History Society
Mount Saint Vincent University
Halifax, NS B3M 2J6, Canada

Telephone: 1-902-457-6128

Fax: 1902-443-4727

E-mail: frances.early@msvu.ca

Web Site: www.msvu.ca

Senior Staff: President: Frances Early

Date of Establishment: 1964

Purpose: Professional historical society engaged in collaborative projects on peace, war, and international conflict resolution.

Type: Non-profit

Brief History: The PHS grew out of an ad hoc committee established at the December 1963 meeting of the American Historical Association. In the aftermath of assassination of U.S. President John F. Kennedy and amidst the dimly seen beginning of the Indochina War, a sizable group of historian organized in the realization that little effort had been made in their field to study the causes of Peace. (The original name was Conference on Peace Research in History. The name was changed in 1986 to Council on Peace Research in History, then Peace History Society in 1994.) Subsequently, the PHS became an affiliated society of the AHA and joined the Consortium on Peace Research, Education and Development, the National Coordinating Committee for the Promotion of History, the International Peace Research Association, and the International Congress of Historical Sciences. It has also acquired Non-Governmental Organization status at the United Nations.

Over the years, the PHS has put peace research on the programs of numerous organizations: the AHA, the Organisation of American Historians, the society for Historians of American Foreign Relations, the International Peace Research Association, the Berkshire Conference of Women Historians, and other professional meetings on problems of peace/war research. It has also gathered and distributed papers to members and interested libraries, and has compiled lists of relevant research in progress.

Principal Activities: Research; documentation/information; conference-organization; publication.

Periodicals: *Peace & Change: A Journal of Peace Research*, quarterly.

Major Publications: Since 1972, the PHS has published its own journal, *Peace & Change: A Journal of Peace Research*, which its members receive free of charge. The journal features scholarly and interpretive articles relating to the achievement of a peaceful, just and humane society, as well as news of the PHS and the Consortium on Peace Research, Education and Development.

Peace Research Institute-Dundas
25 Dundana Avenue Dundas, Ontario, L9H 4E5, Canada

Telephone: 1-905-628-2356

Fax: 1-905-628-1830

E-mail: newcombe-prid@freenet.hamilton.on.ca

Senior Staff: Director and Editor: Hanna Newcombe, Betty Truman, Graeme MacQueen

Date of Establishment: 1976

Purpose: To publish journals and books on peace research studies.

Type: International, public, non-profit

Brief History: Successor to Canadian Peace Research Institute, which was established in 1976.

Principal Activities:

(a) Publication of peace research journals and reviews,

(b) Research on U.N. voting by nations,

(c) Prediction of war from military expenditures, (this project ended in 1991 when Alan Newcombe died),

(d) 1976-80 Peace research summer School.

Periodicals:

(a) *Peace Research Abstracts Journal* (Published by Sage),

(b) *Peace Research Reviews.*

Major Publications:

(a) *Nations on Record,*

(b) *Affinities of Nations,*

(c) *Nations in Group.*

Queens Center for International Relations (QCIR)
Queens University
Policy Studies Building, Room 403, Kingston, Ontario, K7L 3N6, Canada

Telephone: 1-613-545-2381
Fax: 1-613-545-6885
E-mail: qcir@qsilver.queensu.ca
Web Site: www.queensu.ca/cir/
Senior Staff: Director: David G. Haglund
Date of Establishment: 1975
Purpose: The Center has been engaged in research, and training on Canadian and International security policy (including foreign and defence policy), European security and transatlantic relations, hemispheric security, and post-Soviet foreign and defense policies. Publications from the Center continue to reflect these research areas. The Center has well established links with the Royal Military College, also in Kingston.
Type: International
Brief History: The Queen's Center for International Relations was established in 1975 as an interdisciplinary research institution with a mandate to conduct research and writing in strategic studies and other aspects of international relations.
Principal Activities: Research; documentation/information; publication.
Major Publications:

(a) Macfarlane, S. N. (ed.), *Regional Security in Central Asia*, 1995,

(b) Klimow, M., *Moral Versus Practical: The Future of U.S. Armed Humanitarian Intervention*, 1996,

(c) Melakopides, C., *Making Peace in Cyprus: Time for a Comprehensive Initiative*, 1996,

(d) Rehbein, R. E., Informing the Blue Helmets: The United States, UN Peace Operations, and the Role of Intelligence, 1996,

(e) Sokolsky, J. J., *The Americanization of Peacekeeping: Implications for Canada*, 1997.

Research Group in International Security (REGIS)
Université de Montréal
Departement de Science Politique
CP 6128, succursale Centre-ville, Montreal, Quebec, H3C 3J7, Canada

Telephone: 1-514-343-6201
Fax: 1-514-343-2360
E-mail: fortmanm@ere.umontreal.ca
Web Site: http://esi24.ESI.UMontreal.CA:80/ ~fortmanm/english/
Senior Staff: Associate Professor and Chair: Hudson Meadwell, Department of Political Science, McGill University; Associate Professor: Mark Brawley, Professeur titulaire, Michel Fortmann, Département de Science Politique, Université de Montréal; Professeur titulaire, Paul Létourneau, Département d'Histoire, Professeur Adjoint: Pierre Martin, Associate Professor; T.V. Paul, Department of Political Science, McGill University
Date of Establishment: 1996
Purpose: The members of REGIS devote a large part of

their activities to leading-edge research in the field of international relations. This work is focussed on both theoretical study as well as applied research. The Group also produces timely analyses exploring current security issues. This research, over the past several years, has resulted in the development of a high level of expertise among members in many fields of international security

Brief History: Created in 1996, REGIS is the product of over ten years of development. In fact, the Military and Strategic Studies Program at the University of Montreal, created in 1986, continues to evolve.

In 1995, the enlargement of this group's activities came about with the creation of the Joint Program between the University of Montreal and McGill University in the area of security studies. It was from this setting that REGIS was formed in order to frame, diversify and integrate the activities of researchers, students and specialists.

Principle Activities: Research, training, publication,

Major Publication:

(a) Orban, E., Fortmann, M., *Le système politique américain, mécanismes et décisions*, (Montréal,

Presses de l'Université de Montréal, 2e ed., 1994),

(b) Fortmann, M., Legault, A. (dir.), *Prolifération et non-prolifération: stratégies et contrôle*. (Québec, Paris: CQRI-FEDN, 1993),

(c) Fortmann, M., Roussel, S. (dir.), "Multilatéralisme et sécurité régionale", numéro spécial de la revue *Études internationales*, vol. 26, no.4 1995, à paraître,

(d) Létourneau, P. (dir.), "L'Allemagne et l'Europe centrale: enjeux stratégiques, politiques, économiques, *numéro spécial de la Revue d'Allemagne et des pays de langue allemande*, 1995,

(e) Boniface, P., Fortmann, M. (dir.), "La prolifération nucléaire", numéro spécial de la revue *Relations internationales et stratégiques*, no. 17, 1995.

Other Information: REGIS is the result of a partnership between the University of Montreal and McGill University. The goal of this partnership is to consolidate the expertise in the field of security studies.

The York Center for International and Security Studies
York University
3 rd floor York Lanes, 4700 Keele Street Toronto, Ontario, M3J 1P3, Canada

Telephone: 1-416-736-5156
Fax: 1-416-736-5752
E-mail: yciss@yorku.ca
Web Site: www.yorku.ca/research/ciss
Senior Staff: Director: David B. Dewitt
Date of Establishment: 1981
Purpose: Research, documentation/information, conference-organization, publication
Type: Non-profit
Brief History: When founded in 1982 as the Research program in Strategic Studies, the Center focused on the dominant issues of nuclear arms control, non-proliferation, Canadian defense policy, and Canada-US relations. By 1986, the Center had evolved into the York Center for International and Strategic Studies (YCISS), and this change was reflected in a considerably enlarged mandate including peace research, international political economy, and conflict management. During the 1996-97 academic year, the Center received approval from York University's Senate to change the name to the York Center for International and Security Studies.
Principal Activities: From its inception, Center faculty

shared an underlying philosophy that encourages innovative theoretical and empirical research in international relations and strategic studies. YCISS fosters scholarly research of interest to academic and policy communities in Canada and abroad. The Center also coordinates and facilitates a variety of scholarly activities including conferences, workshops, lectures, seminars, and research publications.
Periodicals: The Centre has three publication series: Occasional Papers, Working Papers, and a monograph series. Occasional Papers and Working Papers are succinct, informative papers exploring topical themes that reflect work being undertaken at the Center. Working papers generally are reflective of works-in-progress, but both series are designed to stimulate feedback from other experts in the field. In addition to these papers the Center publishes monographs on an occasional basis which are based on research projects, conferences and specialized work by outside experts. These often consist of longer studies or collections of essays edited under the auspices of the Center.

In addition to these series, the Center publishes specialized series in support of ongoing research projects.

In the past this has included the *North Pacific Cooperative Security Dialogue* Series, now completed. Currently the Center has a series on Multilateral Institutions and Global Security. Lastly, jointly with the Institute of International Relations, UBC, the Center administers the Canadian Consortium on Asia Pacific Security. The CANCAPS Papers series is published from YCISS.

Major Publications:

(a) Dosman, E., Deaudelin, J., *Changing Americas: Adjusting the Sights*, 1997,

(b) Krause, K., Williams, M. (eds.), *Critical Security Studies*, 1996,

(c) Beier, J. M., Mataija, S. (eds.), *Cyberspace and Outer Space: Transitional Challenges for Multilateral Verification in the 21st Century*. Proceedings of the Fourteenth Annual Ottawa NACD Verification Symposium, 1997,

(d) Acharya, A., *Southeast Asia: Region, Regionalism, and the Changing World Order*, 1998,

(e) Adelman, H., Gnamo, A. H., Gachuruzi S., *A Framework for Conflict Resolution, Peacebuilding and National Reconciliation in the Great Lakes Region of Africa* (Analytical Report and Recommendations), 1997.

Chile

Universidad De Chile, Instituto De Estudios Internacionales
Casilla 14187, Suc.21, Santiago, Chile

Telephone: 562-274-5377
Fax: 562-274-0155
Senior Staff: Director: M. T. Infanie Caffi
Date of Establishment: 1966
Purpose: The Institute carries out international studies dealing with role of the international organizations, international relations, international humanitarian law, peacekeeping and conflict resolution.
Type: Public, non-profit
Principal Activities: Research; training; conference-organization; publication.
Periodicals: *Estudios Internacionales* (quarterly)

Major Publications:

(a) Davila, A. T., Varas, A., et al., *ReLa Situacion Estrategica Latinoamericana: Crisis Y Oportunidades*, 1992,

(b) Jorge, H., *Anuario de Politics Exteriores Latinoamericanas 1991-1992 Enfrentando los Cambois Globales*, 1993,

(c) Irigoin, J. (ed.), *Derecho Internacional de Los Refugiados*, 1993.

China

The Chinese People's Association for Peace and Disarmament (CPAPD)
15, Wanshou Road, PO Box 188, 100036, Beijing, China

Telephone: 86-10-68271736
Fax: 86-10-68271736
Senior Staff: President: Li Peiyao, Vice-President: Wang Shuxian
Date of Establishment: 1985
Purpose:

(a) The Association aims to promote mutual understanding, friendship and cooperation between the Chinese people and peoples of the world, and

(b) To make joint efforts to safeguard world peace, strive for disarmament, oppose arms race, realize

the complete prohibition and thorough elimination of nuclear weapons and other weapons of mass destruction, prevent a new world war, protect ecological environment, promote economic development, and advance social progress.

Type: National, non-profit NGO
Brief History: Right after the founding of new China, some well-known social celebrities and activists such as Mme. Soong Ching Ling, Mr. Guo Muoruo, Mr. Mao Dun and others sponsored and established the Committee of the Chinese People for Safeguarding World

Peace. From the 1950s to 1960s, together with world people, the Chinese People made unremitting efforts to maintain world peace. During the "Cultural Revolution", the Committee was forced to terminate its work. In the 1980s, it became the common aspiration and sacred mission of the world people including the Chinese people to safeguard peace and promote development. The Chinese people ardently expected the resumption of the work of a mass peace organization. Meanwhile, many international organizations or research institutes for peace and disarmament also hoped to conduct friendly exchanges with their counterparts in China. Under such circumstances, the Chinese People's Association for Peace and Disarmament came into existence.

Principal Activities:

(a) The CPAPD is very active in conducting peace education and giving publicity to peace in China. Contests of paintings, songs, essays, speeches, calligraphy, photography, football games and long-distance races with peace as the theme in various forms have been held; and all kinds of lectures, symposiums, exhibitions and cultural performances have been organized. The CPAPD was awarded the title of PEACE MESSENGER by the UN for its work during the International Year of Peace in 1986. From 1989 onward, the CPAPD together with concerned organizations has conducted a series of activities of the "International Week of Science and Peace" for 8 years running, which have achieved positive effects. In addition, the CPAPD also has done some research on peace, disarmament, security, and others.

(b) In addition, the CPAPD conducts great varieties of exchanges and cooperation with NGOs, research

institutes and personalities standing for peace, arms control and social progress. It also organizes or attends international seminars on issues like peace, arms control, disarmament, security, and environment protection. By now, the CPAPD has established contacts, and undertaken exchanges and cooperation in different forms with many NGO peace organizations, research institutes, universities, and international organizations in about 90 countries. The CPAPD has successfully hosted the 41st Pugwash Annual Conference on Science and World Affairs; the Symposium on Asia-Pacific Security and Disarmament was co-sponsored with the United Nations Institute for Disarmament Research; the workshop entitled "Women and Peace" at the '95 NGO Forum of the Fourth World Conference on Women; and other bilateral and multilateral seminars on regional security, global security, arms control, the role and reform of the UN, and etc., respectively, co-sponsored with the peace department of the University of Bradford, UK, the UK Oxford Research Group (ORG), the United Nations Institute for Disarmament Research, the NOD Global Network, the Korean Association of Area Studies (ROK), the Korean Association of East-Asian Studies (ROK), the Foundation for Research on International Environment, National Development and Security, All-India Peace and Solidarity Organization, and other research institutes.

Periodicals: A quarterly magazine *PEACE* in English.
Major Publications: The CPAPD edits and publishes an English quarterly, *Peace* mailed to readers in over seventy countries, and *Information of Peace Studies*, an irregular publication in Chinese.

Hong Kong Institute of Asia-Pacific Studies
The Chinese University of Hong Kong
Shatin, New Territories, Hong Kong

Telephone: 852-2609-8780
Fax: 852-2603-5215
E-mail: hkiaps@cuhk.edu.hk
Web Site: www.cuhk.edu.hk/hkiaps/object.html
Senior Staff: Director: Yeung Yue-man, Associate Director: Lau Siu-kai
Date of Establishment: 1990
Purpose: To promote and to coordinate inter-disciplinary studies of Hong Kong, Asian countries and their relations with the larger environment of the Asia-Pacific region. It attempts to serve as a bridge between over-

seas scholars of Asia-Pacific studies and the teaching and research staff of the Chinese University of Hong Kong.

Brief History: The Hong Kong Institute of Asia-Pacific Studies (HKIAPS) was established in September 1990 at The Chinese University of Hong Kong.

Principal Activities: Research and publication

Periodicals: Research monograph series and occasional papers.

Major Publications:

(a) Zhao, S., *In Search of Right Place? Chinese Nationalism in the Post-Cold War World*, April 1997,

(b) Potter, P. B., *From Leninist Discipline to Socialist Legalism: Peng Zhen on Law and Political Authority in the PRC*, 1995,

(c) Tong, J., *The 1989 Democracy Movement in China: A Preliminary Spatial Analysis*, 1994.

Colombia

Codecal Corporacion Integral Para el Desarrollo Cultural Y Social
[Codecal Integral Corporation for Cultural & Social Development]
CRA. 38D No. 60-56 Bogot'a, Colombia

Telephone: 57-2225808/3153185/3153186/3153187
Fax: 57-2225807
E-mail: Codecal@colnodo.apc.org.
Senior Staff: Director: P. Jaime Diaz, Assessor: Pedro Baracaldo, Jaime Escobar, Assistant Director: Martha Guaqueta
Date of Establishment: 14 September 1972
Purpose: The Institute covers education for justice and peace from a humanistic and Christian perspective, particularly in non formal setting.
Type: National, private, non-profit
Brief History: Founded in 1972, Codecal has conducted several national and international projects in association with organizations as UNESCO, Org. of American States, University of Western Ontario—Canada, Partners of the Americas, German Caritas, and Interamerican Foundation. Codecal has trained more than 30,000 leaders in several countries and publish 52 titles of materials for community and school work. Codecal has a fruitful exchange with many organizations. In 1997, Codecal celebrated its Silver Jubilee.
Principal Activities: Codecal trains school teachers and community leaders, specially, in subjects such as Peace, Democratic Participation, Human Rights, Environment Education, researches particularly related to education for human rights and peace through history in the Andean countries, and participates in international events as expert or as speaker.

Costa Rica

Facultad Latinoamericana De Ciencias Sociales (FLACSO) [Latin American School of Social Science]
Entre av. 0 y Av. 8 calle No. 39, Del Automercado Los Yoses, 75 metros al Sur
Apdo. Postal No. 5421000 San Jose, Costa Rica

Telephone: 506-253-0082/506-253-9621
Fax: 506-234-6696
E-mail: svillena@cariari.ucr.ac.cr.
Date of Establishment: 1957
Purpose: The Institute pursues research on various objects of Social Science and promotes a wide agenda of national and international scientific meetings, as well as cultural, publishing and advisory activities.
Type: International, public, private, non-profit
Brief History: With the creation of FLACSO over thirty years ago, the Latin America Social Sciences took a vital step in the achievement of one of their basic goals, the establishment of graduate training programs for future generations in such disciplines as Sociology and Political Sciences.

Principal Activities:

(a) Promotes critical research on the social reality of Latin America, through the analysis of concrete social processes,

(b) Train specialists in the social sciences in Latin America through graduate and specialized studies, and provides the theoretical, methodological and technical tools that will allow them to achieve a high level of efficiency,

(c) Disseminates the results of social science research, particularly spirit of service and cooperation, through the various means available and with governmental and institutional assistance,

(d) Offers scientific advice to governments and/or institutions and centers of learning,

(e) Collaborates with national universities and other research and educational organization to promote greater cooperation in the social sciences. FLACSO promotes collaboration and interchange among national, regional and international organizations at governmental and non-governmental levels,

(f) To undertake academic activities relating to the social sciences which lead to development and integration of the Latin American countries.

Major Publications:

(a) Sergio, B., *Integracion entre regiones fronterizas.* Santiago: FLACSO, Taller latinoamericano, año 1, n

4, 1996,

(b) Jorge, C., *La exportacion del modelo economico chileno.* Santiago: FLACSO, Taller Latinoamericano, ano 1, n 7, 1996,

(c) Ricardo, F-D., *Las economias latinoamericana y el financiamiento externo.* Santiago: FLACSO, Taller latinoamericano, ano 1, n 3, 1996,

(d) Roberto, P., *Chile Mercosur: el escenario posterior a la asociacion.* Santiago: FLACSO, Taller latinoamericano, ano 1, n 6, 1996.

Universidad Para La Paz [University for Peace]
Apartado 138 Cuidad Colon, Costa Rica

E-mail: upazcult@sol.racsa.co.cr
Web Site: www.centralplaza.net/upaz/
Senior Staff: Rector: Barahona Riera, Chancellor Emeritus: Robert Muller.
Date of Establishment: 1980
Purpose: The University intends to promote human rights and the consolidation of a culture of peace in Central America, through intensive programs and projects being carried out in Belize, Guatemala, Honduras, El Salvador, Nicaragua, Costa Rica and Panama.
Type: Non-profit
Brief History: The University for Peace, created by the General Assembly of the United Nations on December 5, 1980, is considered to be one of the most outstanding projects proposed on the eve of the third millennium.

In Resolution 35/55, the representatives of the member countries of the United Nations approved an initiative that was presented in 1978 by President Rodrigo Carazo Odio, on behalf of the people and the government of Costa Rica.

As the proposal for the University rapidly gathered momentum, more and more countries joined the list of signatories of the international Agreement on the Uni-

versity for Peace. On May 4, 1982, the government of Costa Rica and the University signed an agreement establishing its headquarters in that country.
Principal Activities: The master's degree programs in International Relations and Cooperation, and in Ecology and Peace are two of the most important programs offered by the University.

Other master's degree programs that were offered successfully in the past or are just getting under way include human resources, cooperation and development, education for peace and the peaceful settlement of disputes, human rights and communications for peace.

The University for Peace has also made major efforts to promote human rights and the consolidation of a culture of peace in Central America, through intensive programs and projects being carried out in Belize, Guatemala, Honduras, El Salvador, Nicaragua, Costa Rica and Panama.

Also, as part of its dissemination program, the University conducts seminars, meetings and international congresses on topics related to the work and mission of the institution.

Czech Republic

Ustav Mezinarodnich Vztahu (UMV) [Institute of International Relations]
Nerudova 3 118 50 Prague 1, Czech Republic

Telephone: 420-2-57-32-09-57
Fax: 420-2-57-32-10-79
E-mail: umv@iir.cz
Senior Staff: Director: Jiri Sedivy, Deputy Director: Kristina Larischova, Chief Researcher: Jan Eichler
Date of Establishment: 1957

Purpose: The Institute aims to carry out research in international relations, with special Concentration on the process of globalization and European integration, Czech foreign and security policy and bilateral relations with neighbours.
Type: National, public, non-profit

Brief History: The predecessor of the Institute of International relations (IIR) was the Institute of International Politics and Economics (IIPE) founded in 1957. It was abolished in1970 and IIR was established in its place. Members of the staff who had been active in 1968 liberation process were dismissed. After 1989, the IIR underwent radical changes. There was a reorientation of the research programme, the activities of the Institute were substantially expanded and personnel changes were made.

Principal Activities: Scientific research; analytical and prognostic activities; publishing and educational activities; library and information services; conferences.

Periodicals:

(a) *Mezinarodni politika* (International Politics), Czech (monthly),

(b) *Mezinarodni vztahy* (International Relations), Czech (quarterly),

(c) *Perspectives - Review of Central European Affairs*, English (biannually).

Major Publications:

(a) Kotyk, V., *Vztahy Centra a Regionu Ruske Federace.* 1998,

(b) Gedlu, M., *Susaharaska Africa, Problemy Demokracie, Nacionalismu a Mezinarodnich Vztahu*, 1998,

(c) *Ceska Zahranicni Politika.* Uvaha o prioritach, 1997,

(d) *Ceska Zahranicni Politika. Ceska Republika v Rade bezpecnosti OSN (1994-95)*, 1997,

(e) *Kooperativni Usporadani Bezpecnosti v Evrope*, 1997,

(f) *Mezinarodni Organizovany Zlocin v Ceske Republice*, 1997,

(g) *The Security Policy of the Czech Republic*, 1997,

(h) *Studie o sudetonemecke otazce*, 1996.

Major Field of Research:

(a) Foreign policy of the Czech Republic,

(b) European and Czech security policy,

(c) The Czech Republic and enlargement of the EU and NATO,

(d) Relations between the Czech Republic and its neighbours.

Denmark

Association for World Education (AWE)
Attn. Michael Aabling, Østbanegade 7 DK-2100 Copenhagen Ø, Denmark

Telephone: 3142-2413
Senior Staff: President: A. R. Nielsen
Date of Establishment: 1970
Purpose: The Association aims:

(a) to promote intercommunication and interaction among individuals and centers of learning that are working to comprehend and to spread awareness of the global aspects of education,

(b) to facilitate the exchange and the transfer of ideas, knowledge, experience, and examples among such individuals and institutions,

(c) to spotlight those innovations in education and in development which strengthen the linkages between the local and the global,

(d) to encourage research and leadership training related to world education,

(e) to foster, through the evolving concept of world education, concern for "coexistence in peace" and for the development of humankind,

(f) to stress the special contribution of a voluntary, nongovernmental organization in working towards the above purposes.

Type: Private, non-profit
Brief History: The Association was chartered in 1970 as the Association of World Colleges and Universities by a small group of individuals coming mainly from post-secondary institutions of learning who felt the need to be in touch with each other as they sought to introduce broader images of the world and its problems into the educational process. An Association, they felt, could help them to learn from each other's experiments, could help in sharing resources, and could aid them in formulating appropriate goals for "world education."

In 1974, the Association was renamed the Association for World Education. By then, the membership had grown and shown its broad interests and commitment to introducing a global orientation into a variety of learning situation.

The philosophy of the Association is one based on the wholeness and integration of life. The Association wishes to promote images of the world and its problems which emphasize the interconnectedness of the local to the global.

The Association recognizes and benefits from the useful work done by other groups in the study and development of curriculum methods and techniques of education at different levels. It hopes, however, to focus on the rigidities, the provincial outlooks, and alienating features of education. In short, the Association is concerned with the promotion of lifelong learning: of education which enhances the "wholeness" of individuals in their local community environments and helps them to see their links with other communities.

The members draw encouragement from the fact that everywhere in the world are found individuals and groups who are taking initiatives to make education better serve the development of "communities on a human scale"—decentralized but with a deep sense of commonality among all such local communities.

As a nongovernmental organization, the Association is represented at the United Nations which has consultative status with UNESCO.

Principal Activities:

(a) Publication of the quarterly journal, conference reports, and other papers,

(b) Planning and participation in regional and world conferences, and working meetings and conferences,

(c) Operation of communications network of learning resources among members,

(d) Attendance of United Nations and UNESCO conference.

Periodicals: *Journal of World Education*

Major Publications: Conference reports

Copenhagen Peace Research Institute (COPRI)
University of Copenhagen
Fredericiagade 18 1310 Copenhagen K, Denmark

Telephone: 45-33326432
Fax: 45-3326554
E-mail: info@copri.dk
Web Site: http://www.COPRI.dk
Senior Staff: Head: Hågan Wiberg
Date of Establishment: 1985
Purpose: The purpose of COPRI is to stimulate debate and research on international key issues related to Peace and Security Studies. The institute does this through research, seminars, publications, news and information.
Type: Non profit
Brief History: The Copenhagen Peace Research Institute (COPRI) was established as an independent institute by the Danish Parliament in 1985 aimed at supporting and strengthening multidisciplinary research on Peace and Security. In 1996, the status of COPRI was made permanent and changed to that of a Government Research Institute under the Ministry of Research and Information Technology. At the same time, COPRI changed its name in English from the previous one, Centre for Peace and Conflict Research, to its present but retained its Danish name, Center for Freds-og Konfliktforskning
Principal Activities: Research; seminars; publications
Current Peace Research:

(a) Causes and origins of war,

(b) Dynamics of conflict and development in countries of the South,

(c) Intra-social and ethnic conflicts (national identities),

(d) Psychological peace research,

(e) Feminist aspects of peace research,

(f) International law and peaceful order (International Organizations), human rights,

(g) Peace education and theory of peace education,

(h) Ethics of peace, non-violence.

Periodicals: *NOD & Conversion* (International Research Newsletter)
Major Publications:

(a) Andersen, E. A., *Privatiseringens konsekvenser for den russiske befolkning i Estland. Perioden 1987-1995 (The Consequences of Privatization for the Russian Population in Estonia: The Period 1987-1995).* Copenhagen: Samfundslitteratur, 1998,

(b) Batchelor P., Willett, S., *Disarmament and Defense Industrial Adjustment in South Africa*, Oxford University Press/SIPRI,

(c) Biermann, W., Martin, V., *UN Peacekeeping in Trouble: Lessons Learned from the Former Yugoslavia: Peacekeepers Views on the Limits and Possibilities of the United Nations in a Civil war-like Conflict.* Aldershot: Ashgate,

(e) Buzan, B., Herring, E., *The Arms Dynamics in World Politics.* Boulder, CO:Lynne Reinner,

(f) Christensen, S-A., Ole, W., (eds.), *DUPIDOK 1996: Dansk udenrigspolitisk dokumentation (Documentation part of Danish Yearbook of Foreign Policy, 1996).* Copenhagen: DUPI (Danish Institute of International Affairs), 1997,

(g) Dahlgren, B., Holm, U., *De vilde siv. Frankrigs forhold til den algeriske uafh?gighedskrig (The Wild Willows. The French Relation to the Algerian War of Independence).* Copenhagen: Gyldendal,

(h) Hansen, L., *Western Villains or Balkan Barbarism? Representations and Responsibility in the Debate over Bosnia.* Copenhagen: Institute of Political Science, University of Copenhagen,

(i) Holm, U., Olsen, G. R., *Vandring mod Europa. Algeriet-Frankrig (Migration towards Europe: Algeria-France).* Copenhagen: Geografforlaget, 1997,

(j) Joenniemi, P., Prawitz, J. (eds.), *Kaliningrad: The European Amber Region.* London: Ashgate,

(k) Joenniemi, P. (ed.), *Neo-Nationalism or Regionality? The Restructuring of Political Space around the Baltic Rim.* Stockholm: NordREFO, 1997,

(l) Malhotra, V. K., Sergounin, A. A., *Theories and Approaches to International Relations.* New Delhi: Anmol Publications, 1997,

(m) Mouritzen, H., *External Danger and Democracy: Old Nordic Lessons and New European Challenges.* Aldershot: Dartmouth, 1997,

(n) Mouritzen, H. (ed.), *Bordering Russia: Theory and Prospects for Europe Baltic Rim.* Aldershot: Ashgate,

(o) Prikulis, J., Wiberg, H. (eds.), *The Baltic States as partners of Baltic Sea Cooperation.* Riga: Centre of Baltic-Nordic History and Political Studies,

(p) Scherrer, C. P. (ed.), *Ethnicity and State at the Horn of Africa I: The Empire strikes back - Far from Oromia?* Moers: IFEK-IRECOR, 1997,

(q) Scherrer, C. P. (ed.), *Ethnicity and State at the Horn of Africa II: Ethiopia, Eritrea and Sudan between Change and Civil War.* Moers: IFEK-IRECOR, 1997,

(r) Scherrer, C. P., *Ethno-Nationalismus im Zeitalter der Globalisierung. Ursachen, Strukturmerkmale und Dynamik ethnisch-nationaler Gewaltkonflikte. Handbuch zu Ethnizit?* 1997.

Finland

Department of Strategic and Defence Studies
National Defence College
PO Box 266, Fin - 00171 (Maurinkatu 1), Helsinki, Finland

Telephone: 358-9-1812-6320
Fax: 358-9-1812-6324
E-mail: strategian.laitos@stratl.mil.fi
Senior Staff: Researcher: Kalevi Ruhala, Aaro Toivonen
Date of Establishment: 1993
Purpose:

(a) To carry out research on security policy, strategy and international cooperation,

(b) To participate in the long term planning of the Finnish National Defence,

(c) To provide training for the officer degree and to instruct officers at the Senior Staff and General

Staff officer courses.

Type: National, public

Brief History: The Department of Strategic and Defence Studies is the successor of the Office for Strategic Studies at the Institute of Military Science, established in 1970 to carry out research and to participate in the planning of security policy and strategy for the Finnish National Defence.

Principal Activities: Training and research in security policy, strategy and international cooperation at the National Defence College.

Periodicals: *Finnish Defence Studies* (English Language Publication of the National Defence College).

Major Publications:

(a) Finnish defence studies,

(b) Strategic research,

(c) Research reports,

(d) Facts on strategy,

(e) Working papers.

Finnish Peace Research Association
c/o Tampere Peace Research Institute
PO Box 307 Fin-33101 Tampere, Finland

Telephone: 358-3-215-6111
Fax: 358-3-223-6620
Date of Establishment: 1971
Purpose: The Association intends to work for a permanent and just peace in the world by promoting scientific peace research.
Type: Public, national, non-profit
Brief History: Finnish Peace Research Association was established in 1971 in Helsinki, Finland as a scientific association to unite Finnish peace researchers, students and other interested people. It has published studies of Finnish and other scholars, arranged seminars and conferences, given statements and supported its members especially in their international contacts.
Principal Activities: The activities include:

(a) Publishing,

(b) Seminars,

(c) International cooperation, and

(d) Working as a pressure group to advance peace research.

The Association offers also a discussion forum for its member and scholars interested in peace conflict research and research on world politics.
Periodicals: *Kosmopolis*, published quarterly in Finnish (articles with English summaries), *Rauhantutkimus Tanaan* (Peace Research Today), published irregularly, in Finnish.

Rauhankasvatus Instituutti [Peace Education Institute]
Nervanderinkaru 10 L 33, PO Box 722, 00101 Helsinki, Finland

Telephone: 358-9-449169/358-400-204332
Fax: 358-9-454-10141
E-mail: peacedu@rauha.org
Senior Staff: President of the Board: Reijo E. Heinonen, Vice-president: Helena Kekkonen
Date of Establishment: 1981
Purpose: The Institute aims to promote cooperation between peace movement, education and research. To insure the teachers, educators and pupils an access to peace education materials and networks both nationally and internationally and to give schools on different levels a possibility to take part in development projects.
Type: National, public, and non-profit
Brief History: The very first aim of the Institute was to create a training form for non-military civic servants, soon it changed to acting as an umbrella organization for the educational cooperation between peace movement and different educational organizations, schools at all levels and research. The Institute has published textbooks, periodicals, reports and other sorts of educational material on peace-education, conflict resolution, human rights education and arranged a wide range of different sorts of courses, workshops, seminars and congresses and dated as a coordinator for both national and international programs.
Principal Activities: The activities include:

(a) Short courses and information programs for pupils and scholars,

(b) Publications, cultural programs, exhibitions, TV and radio programs,

(c) Development programs between Finnish and African schools,

(d) Network building between peace educators and institutes,

(e) Seminars, congresses.

Periodicals: *Rauhankirje* (peaceletter)

Tampere Peace Research Institute (TAPRI)
Akerlundinkatu 3, 4th floor/PO Box 607, FIN 33101 Tampere, Finland

Telephone: 358-3-215-7696
Fax: 358-3-223-6620
E-mail: ytyruu@uta.fi
Web Site: http://www.uta.fi/laitokset/tapri
Senior Staff: Research Director: Jyrki Kakonen, Senior Research Fellows: Tuomo Melasuo, Unto Vesa.
Date of Establishment: 1970
Purpose: TAPRI has the mandate to:

(a) Carry out scientific research aimed at the maintenance of peace and at the peaceful resolution of conflicts,

(b) Publish the results of such research,

(c) Provide expert assistance,

(d) Participate in international cooperation in the field of peace research.

Type: Public, national, non-profit
Brief History: Founded by the Finnish Parliament in 1969, Tampere Peace Research Institute opened in September 1970. Since August 1, 1994, TAPRI is an independent research center within the framework of the University of Tampere, and is financed from its budget.
Principal Activities:

(a) Scientific research,

(b) Expert assistance. Most of the research carried out in the institute has centered around the following major areas: problems of armament, disarmament and security, the Third World, the structure of the international system, relationships between development and disarmament, as well as peace and development research and peace education. In recent years, much of the research has focused on the European political change, on the Baltic region and on the issue of sustainable development and security in the Arctic.

Periodicals:

(a) Research reports,

(b) Occasional papers, and other publications.

Major Publications:

(a) *Review of International Studies,*

(b) *European Security and Cultural Values,*

(c) *Journal of Moral Education, and many others.*

World Futures Studies Federation
President's Office, PO Box 110, FIN-20521 Turku, Finland

Telephone: 358-2-3383-528/3383-530
Fax: 358-2-2330-755
E-mail: malaska@utn.fi.
Senior Staff: Director: Urpo Kivikari, Senior Associate Researcher: Sandberg Birgitta.
Date of Establishment: 1973
Purpose:

(a) The Federation aims to promote futures studies as an academic discipline,

(b) exchange ideas and discuss vision and plans for alternative, long-term perspective of the future,

(c) stimulate awareness of the urgent need for futures studies in governments and international organizations.

Type: International
Brief History: WFST emerged from the ideas and pioneer work of such persons as Igor Bestnzher-Lada, Bertraud de Jeuvenel, Johan Galtung, Robert Vungk etc., who in the 1960's, conceived of the concept of Futures Studies at the global level. The first International Futures Research Conference was held in Oslo, Norway in Sept. 1967.
Principal Activities: The Federation organizes world conferences every two years as well as regional colloquia, seminars and courses. Associates with centers around the world where Futures-oriented studies and activities are going on and issues *Futures Bulletin.*
Periodicals: *Futures Bulletin* (quarterly)
Major Publications:

(a) *Futures Beyond Poverty—Ways and Means out of the Current Stalemate*, selections from the XIV World Conference of WFSF, Nairobi, Kenya, July 25-29, 1995,

(b) *From a Giant to a Gateway in East-West Trade: Finland's Adoption to Radical Changes in Eastern Europe,*

(c) *Transition in Eastern Europe—Dimensions of Transition, Environmental Changes and Implications for Western Managers.*

World Peace Council (WPC)
WPC Liaison Office, Lonnrotinkatu 25A/V SF-00180 Helsinki, Finland

Telephone: 358-693-1044
Fax: 358-693-3703
E-mail: compuserve: 100144, 1501.
Senior Staff: President: A. Sisulu
Date of Establishment: 1950
Purpose: The World Peace Council (WPC) earnestly seeks to fulfill the demand of the slogan: "Peace is everybody's business!" The principles embodied in its Rules and Regulations are:

(a) Prohibition of all weapons of mass destruction and ending of the arms race; abolition of foreign military bases; general, simultaneous and controlled disarmament;

(b) Elimination of all forms of colonialism and racial discrimination;

(c) Respect for the territorial integrity of states;

(d) Noninterference in the internal affairs of nations;

(e) Establishment of mutually beneficial trade and cultural relations based on friendship and mutual respect;

(f) Peaceful coexistence between states with different political systems;

(g) Replacement of the policy of force by that of negotiations for the settlement of differences between nations.

Type: Private, non-profit

Brief History: The foundations of the WPC were laid in Wroclaw, Poland, a city devastated during the Second World War in August 1948. At that time, men and women met in a World Congress of Intellectuals and issued a strong appeal for peace action by all people. Their Appeal brought delegates from 72 countries to the First World Congress of Defenders of Peace, held simultaneously in April 1949 in Paris and in Prague. An international committee was subsequently set up to continue the work done by these assemblies and a presiding body of 12 members was created. By the fall of 1949, national committees were set up in 70 countries, and other congresses conferences and demonstrations were held in all five continents. Picasso's peace dove became the universal symbol of the Congress, and is still a familiar symbol of the movement.

In 1950, the Second Congress of the Movement was held in Warsaw, and here the World Peace Council was born, destined for a future of growing significance. Its first President was Frédéric Joliot-Curie, the world famous French scientist and Nobel Prize laureate, who had been the chairman of the first Congress

Principal Activities: The WPC initiates and supports all efforts for international cooperation with the following aims:

(a) To stop the development of any new US missiles in Europe, to remove those already deployed, and to create conditions for reopening negotiations on the balanced and controlled reduction of nuclear armaments, East and West;

(b) To demand all nuclear powers to pledge, unilaterally or by negotiation, not to be the first to use nuclear weapons;

(c) For an immediate freeze of tests, production, and the stockpiling of nuclear arms;

(d) For the banning of the neutron bomb and of chemical bacteriological weapons;

(e) Against the military use of outer space;

(f) To establish nuclear weapon free zones in the Nordic countries, the Balkans, Central Europe, and other areas;

(g) To end military intervention and aggression, to support the struggle of the peoples for the realization of their national rights and the safeguarding of their independence;

(h) To achieve a just settlement of conflicts on the basis of the UN Charter and the positions of the nonaligned movement and the Organization of African Unity;

(i) To free Africa and the Middle East, the Indian Ocean areas, and the Far East, Latin America, and the Carribean from nuclear weapons and foreign military bases and blocs. Asia, Southwest Asia, and the Mediterranean should be transformed into zones of peace and cooperations;

(j) To support the campaign for the Eastablishment of

a New International Economic Order, with special reference to its links with the problems of the arms build-up and the danger of nuclear war;

(k) To defend human rights and people's rights, and to struggle against racism, racial discrimination, and policies and practices of oppressive regimes.

Periodicals: *Peace Courier*, 12 p.a. (monthly), *New Perspectives* (bi-monthly)

Major Publications: In order to assist the campaigns of the peace and antiwar movements the WPC produces a variety of publications in different languages, as well as booklets, posters, and other smaller items of publicity,

(a) *European Integration: an Introduction*, 1990,

(b) *Session of World Peace Council*. Documents, 1990,

(c) *Assembly of the World Peace Council*, 1993.

France

Centre de Philosophie de la Strategie [Center for Philosophy of Strategy]
20 Rue de Beaune 75007 Paris, France

Telephone: 33-01-42-61-06-81
Senior Staff: President: Jean-Paul Charnay
Date of Establishment: 1972
Type: Private, non-profit
Brief History: Established in 1972 as the Centre D'etudes Et De Recherches Sur Les Strategies Et Les Conflits, Universite de Paris. Sorbonne; it is now the 1993 Centre De Philosophie De La Strategie.

Major Publications:

(a) *Sociologie Religieuse de l'Islam*. Paris, Sindbad, 1987; 2nd ed. *Augmentee, Hachette Pluriel*, 1995,

(b) *La Strategie*, Paris, Presses Universitaires de France, Que Sais-je,1995.

Centre de Relations Internationales et de Strategie
[Center for International Relations and Strategy]
9 Rue Malher, 75181 Paris Cedex 04, France

Telephone: 33-1-44-78-33-65
Fax: 33-1-44-78-33-33
E-mail: Cris@univ.paris1.fr
Senior Staff: Prof: Jean Klein, Prof: Pierre Dabeeies, Senior Researcher: Patrice Buffotot.

Date of Establishment: 1992

Purpose: The Center aims to studies in International Relations; Contributing to the fields of defense and security studies (European defense, disarmament, and conflict studies).

Type: Public, non-profit

Brief History: The CRIS replaced the Institute National Superire d'Etudes de dfense et de dsarmement (INSED), and is the research center associated with the department of politics—section International Relations section of the Sorbonne (Paris I. Pantheon Sorbonne).

Principal Activities: Research on European defense and security; conflict studies; conferences; seminars, etc.

Major Publications:

(a) *Disarmament—Arms Control*,

(b) *European & French Defense*,

(c) *Conflict Resolution—War Studies*.

Centre Interdisciplinaire de Recherche
sur la Paix et d'Etudes Stratégiques (CIRPES)
Maison des Sciences de l'Homme 71 boulevard Raspail 75006 Paris, France

Telephone: 1-42-22-01-07
Fax: 1-42-22-48-21
Senior Staff: President: A. Joxe, Researcher: A. Brigot, J. P. H bert, S. Pallida, A. Santos, J. Sapir

Date of Establishment: 1982
Purpose: CIRPES' general purpose is the furtherance of research on war and peace in the contemporary international systems.

Type: Private, non-profit

Brief History: The Centre was established in 1982 to further research on war and peace in the contemporary international world. Its objective is to develop analytical tools through interdisciplinary methods for the evaluation of the problems of security, evolution of strategic doctrines and disarmament.

Current Peace Research:

(a) Dynamiques politiques et conomiques et évolutions militaires en Russie

(b) Evolution de la pensée stratégique aux Etats-Unis

(c) Les Etats-Unis et la sécurité de l'Europe

(d) Frontiéres de l'Europe

Periodicals: *Paix et Conflits*

Major publications: The Centre publishes in the following areas:

(a) A series of working documents, restricted to members and associated research groups,

(b) A collection of papers with research findings,

(c) New American war-fighting strategy and security in Europe,

(d) The European debate on European security,

(e) The War in Lebanon,

(f) Defense efforts and the Soviet Economy,

(g) Infranuclear deterrence,

(h) Geopolicy and geostrategy: Central America and the Caribbean.

The Club of Rome
34 avenue d'Eylau 75116 Paris, France

Telephone: 33-1-47-04-45-25
Fax: 33-1-47-04-45-23
E-mail: cor.bs@dialup.francenet.fr
Senior Staff: President: Ricardo Diez Hochleitner, Secretary General: Bertrand Schneider
Date of Establishment: 1968
Purpose: To adopt a global perspective, to seek a deeper understanding of interactions within the tangles of contemporary problems, to suggest effective solutions and to take a longer term perspective in studies than governments do.
Brief History: In 1967, worried by the fact that governments were unable to solve their most serious problems or to engage in thinking about the long term, an Italian industrialist, Aurelio Peccei, and a Scots scientist, Alexandre King, decided with other like-minded people and citizens of the world to share their ideas further. Their aim was to tackle problems and future trends at both the local and global levels. They wanted to try to understand what was happening, and then

mobilize thinking people everywhere to take action to build a saner and more sustainable world. Bypassing ideological and political constraints, they appealed directly to the media and public awareness. Thus the overall strategy of the Club of Rome has been to construct its own philosophy gradually around certain beliefs.
Principal Activities: Organizing meetings and symposia to which selected members are invited, frequent contacts with decision makers in both public and private sectors, a communication policy and publications in different languages.

Major Publications:

(a) *The First Global Revolution*, 1991,

(b) *Latin America Facing Contradictions and Hopes*, 1993,

(c) *For a Better World Order, a Message from Kuala Lumpur*, 1993.

Institut du Droit de la Paix et du Dveloppement [Institute of Peace, Rights and Development]
7 Avenue Robert Schuman 06050 Nice Cedex 1, France

Telephone: 33-(0)4-92 15 71 99
E-mail: truong@unice.fr
Senior Staff: Prof. & Dean: Louis Balmond, Professor Maurice Torrelli, Professor: Jacque Basso.
Date of Establishment: 1968
Purpose: The Institute aims to study international rela-

tions in tans of private, and public law in the areas of politics, economy, and strategy.
Type: Public, national, non-profit
Brief History: This Institute was founded by Prof. Rene Jean Dupuy of the College de France in 1968.
Principal Activities: Post-graduate teaching

Periodicals:

(a) *Esface et Ressources Maritimes*,

(b) *Approach—Asia.*

Major Publications:

(a) Manor, J., *Le Processus de paix entre Israel et le monde arabe 1880-1988*, 1989,

(b) Torrelli, M., *Terrorisme et coopération politique europenne: le terrorisme est-il une nouvelle forme de guerre?* 1988,

(c) *Les droits de l'homme: quels droits? quel homme?*, Georges Vedel, Doyen honoraire de la Facult de droit de Paris, Ancien membre du Conseil constitutionnel, novembre 1989.

Germany

Arbeitsgruppe Friedensforschung und Europaische Sicherheitspolitik
[Peace Research and European Security Studies] (AFES)
Alte Bergsteige 47 74821 Mosbach, Germany

Telephone: 49-6261-1-29-12
Fax: 49-6261-1-56-95
Senior Staff: President: H. G. Brauch, Assistant Professor: J. Grin, C. Mesjasz, B. Müller
Date of Establishment: 1983
Purpose: The organization concentrates its research effort on European security and arms control.
Type: Private, non-profit
Brief History: The organization was formed in 1983 to study the effect of destabilizing strategic weapons on European security and arms control.
Principal Activities: The organization conducts research on destabilizing strategic weapon technologies and their impact on European security and arms control focusing on the following topics: ballistic missile defense, antisatellite weapons, theater nuclear and chemical weapons and warfare relating to Europe. Other topics include: French defense policy, Franco-German military cooperation in arms production, the Greek-Turkish conflict and NATO's southern flank confidence-building measures, antisubmarine warfare, and conventional alternative defense postures for Europe.

Organization members conduct lectures and seminars. In 1985 AFES organized two conferences in cooperation with the Landeszentrale für Politische Bildung Baden-Württemberg on the following topics:

(a) Militarization of Outer Space—Technology Programs and Arms Control, and,

(b) From "Star Wars" to the SDI—Implications for Europe.

Current Peace Research:

(a) Armament and disarmament policy,

(b) Non-offensive defence, conversion,

(c) From the East-West conflict to financial cooperation.

Major Publications:

(a) Brauch, H. G., van der Graaf, Grin, J. et al. (eds.), *Controlling the Development and Spread of Military Technology*, 1992,

(b) Grin. J., Smith, W. A., Voronkov, L. (eds.), *Military Technical Innovation and Stability in a Changing World*, 1992,

(c) Møller, B., *Common Security and Non-offensive Defence. A Neorealist Perspective*, 1992,

(d) Meijer, W. K., *Costs of Multinational Verification Organizations in Europe*, 1992,

(e) Brauch, H. G., Neuwirth, G. (eds.), *Confidence and Security Building Measures in Europe: From the Stockholm to the Vienna Document*, 1992,

(f) Brauch, H. G., Neuwirth, G. (eds.), *Confidence and Security Building Measures in Europe II: From Vienna 1990 to Vienna 1992*, 1992,

(g) Brauch, H. G. (ed.), *Controlling Military Research Development and Exports of Dual Use Technologies*, 1992,

(h) Cordier, S. S., *Scandinavia and Finland: Security Policies and Military Capabilities in the 1990s*, 1992,

(i) Brauch, H. G. (ed.), *Confidence-building, Verification and Conversion*, 1993,

(j) Mesjasz, C. (ed.), *Security Challenges after the Cold War*, 1993,

(k) Mesjasz, C. (ed.), *Security and Disarmament in North-East Asia*, 1993,

(l) Brauch, H. G., Kennedy, R. (ed.), *Alternative Conventional Defence Postures in the European Theatre*, 3 vols., 1993,

(m) Marquina, A., Branch, H. G. (ed.), *Confidence Building and Partnership in the Western Mediterranean*, 1994,

(n) Brauch, H. G., *From Chapultepec to Helsinki: CSCE as an Emerging Regional Collective Security System*, 1994.

Arbeitsstelle Friedensforschung Bonn
[The Information Unit Peace Research Bonn]
Beethovenallee 4 D-53173 Bonn, Germany

Telephone: 49-228-35-60-32
Fax: 49-228-35-60-50
Senior Staff: Director: K. H. Koppe
Date of Establishment: 1984
Purpose: The AFB exists to carry out information, consultation, and mediation functions in the field of peace and conflict research on a national and international level.
Type: Non-profit
Brief History: AFB was established in 1984 as an independent institution affiliated to the Peace Research Institute Frankfurt (PRIF)
Principal Activities: The tasks of the AFB include the following:

(a) establishing links with German, foreign, and international peace research organizations,

(b) arranging contacts between representatives of peace research and other disciplines, especially between foreign scientists and peace researchers in the Federal Republic of Germany,

(c) providing information on structure, tasks, and results of peace and conflict research,

(d) providing advice on peace and conflict research problems,

(e) organizing workshops on specific topics among experts representing both scientific and practical aspects (politics, administration, pressure groups, media, etc.) and among scientists themselves,

(f) assistance in publicizing research results (and scientific publications) in Bonn

Periodicals: *AFB-Texte*, irr. (in English and German), *Mitteilungen der Arbeitsstelle Friedensforschung, AFB-Info*, 2 p.a. (in English and German)

Berghof Research Center for Constructive Conflict Management
Altensteinstrabe 48a. D-14195 Berlin, Germany

Telephone: 49-(0)-30-8318090-99
Fax: 49-(6)-30-831-5985
E-mail: n.n@berghof.b.shuttle.de
Senior Staff: Director: Norbert Ropers, Members: Renate Christaller, Petra Haumersen, Frank Liebe, Katrin Maute, Aleksej Nazarenk, Siasnne Rindt, Anja Weiss, Olivwe Wolleh
Date of Establishment: 1993
Purpose: The work of the Berghof Center for Constructive Conflict Management is aimed at identifying constructive procedures and models for dealing with ethnopolitical and socio-cultural conflicts in Europe, and at providing scientific analysis of, and support for, the practical application of such methods. Stress is explicitly laid on the constructive aspect in order firstly to highlight the fact that conflicts are an important and necessary component of social change in all European societies, and that the challenge lies not in containing them, but in dealing with them constructively, and secondly, to emphasize that, within these processes of change, the goal must be to reduce violence and promote social justice.
Type: Private, non-profit

Brief History: The Berghof Research Center was set up by the nonprofit-making Berghof Foundation for Conflict Research, founded in 1971 by Prof. George Zundel. Its Board of Trustees, convened by Prof. Zundel, is chaired by Prof. Dieter Senghaas.

Principal Activities: Most of the Center's work is conducted in the form of action-research projects undertaken in collaboration with individuals and institutions in the field, and with other academic bodies.

Major Publications:

(a) Ropers, N., *Peaceful Intervention: Structures, Processes, and Strategies for the Constructive Regulation of Ethnopolitical Conflicts,*

(b) Liebe, F., *Intercultural Mediation: A Difficult Brokerage. An Empirical-Analytical Attempt to Access the Impact of Cultural Differences.*

Bundesinstitut für Ostwissenschaftliche und Internationale Studien (BIOST)
Federal Institute for Russian, East Europe, and International Studies
Lindenbornstraße 22 50823 Köln, Germany

Telephone: 49-221-5747-110
Fax: 49-221-5747-110
E-mail: biost.koeln@mail.rrz.uni-koeln.de
Web Site: http://www.uni-koeln.de/extern/biost
Senior Staff: Head of department IV: Gerhard Wettig
Date of Establishment: 1961
Purpose: Its purpose is to survey and analyze current political, social, economic, and legal developments in Eastern Europe and especially in the Russian Federation. The Institute deals with international relations, international security, comparative economic systems, and comparative political systems.
Type: Public, national, non-profit
Brief History: At the end of the 1950s, the Federal Government decided to create a research institute that would provide quickly accessible expertise about and academic analysis of recent developments in communist-ruled countries and communist parties. Following this dual orientation, the Federal Institute (Bundesinstitut) has close working relations with the respective desks in various Federal Ministries and political decision-makers and at the same time maintains with the academic world. The Institute began its work in April 1961, after moving to a new building in Köln-Ehrenfeld, the Institute received its present name.

Principal Activities: Policy consulting; publications; conferences.

Major Publications:

(a) *Berichte des Bundesinstitutes* (with English summary),

(b) *Aktulle Analysen des Bundesinstituts,*

(c) *Schriftenreihs des Bundesinstituts,*

(d) *Band 31,*

(e) *Klaus Fritsche* (Hrsg.),

(f) *Rußland und die Dritte Welt,*

(g) *Auf der Suche nach dem verlorenen Imperium?*

(h) *Nomos Verlagsgesellschaft, Baden-Baden 1996, 314 S.*

Deutsche Friedensgesellschaft-Vereinigte Kriegsdienstgegner/Innen (DFG-VK)
Schwanen str.16, 42551 Velbert, Germany

Telephone: 49-2051-4217
Fax: 49-2051-4210
Senior Staff: Stephan Brües
Date of Establishment: 1982 (DFH)/ 1974 (DFG-VK)
Purpose: The organization works against militarism and for non-violent solutions of conflicts work against atomic bombs and nuclear plants, against weapons and military in general and for conscientious objection as a human right.
Type: National, private, non-profit
Brief History: DFG was created in 1892 to fight for peaceful solutions of international conflicts and for United Nations. In the 1920s conscientious objection and antimilitarism were additional topics of the DFG. After World War II there were separations and fusions which resulted in 1974 in founding the DFG-VK (a fusion of DFG and the Union of Conscientious Objectors). First president was the well-known reverend Martin Niemoller.

Principal Activities: Advise for conscientious objectors, non-violent action against militarism, production of weapons, etc. in local groups up to the federal office.

Periodicals: *Zivilcourage* (6 times per year)

Institut für Friedensforschung und Sicherheitspolitik
an des Universitat Hamburg (IFSH)
Falkenstein 1, D-22587 Hamburg, Germany

Telephone: 49-40-866-0770
Fax: 49-40-866-3615
E-mail: ifsh@ttz.uni-hamburg.ed
Senior Staff: Director: Dieter S. Lutz, Deputy Director: Reinhard Mutz, Researcher: Hans Georg Ehrart, Erwin Muller, Gotz neumeck
Date of Establishment: 1971
Purpose: Peace Research
Type: Non-profit
Principal Activities: Research on security and peace issues emphasis on collective security, European security architecture, global governance, Eastern and Central Europe, and OSCE

Periodicals:

(a) *Hamburger Beifruge zur Friedensforschung und Sidierheitspolitik,*

(b) *Hamburger informationen zur Friedensforschung und Sidierheitspolitik,*

(c) *Padagogische informationen zur Friedensforschung und Sidierheitspolitik,*

(d) *Hamberger Vorfrage am Institute fur Friedensforschung und Sidierheitspolitik,*

(e) *IFSH - aktuell.*

Major Publications:

(a) *Demokratie, Sicherheit, Frieden,* (Monograph series, until 5, 1998),

(b) *OSZE- Jahrbuer / OSCE year book* (since 1995),

(c) *Friedensgertachteu* (annually since 1987).

Peace Research Institute Frankfurt (PRIF)
Leimenrode 29, D-60322 Frankfurt/Main, Germany

Telephone: 49-69-95-91-04-0
Fax: 49-69-55-84-81
E-mail: hsfk@em.uni-frankfurt.de
Web Site: http://www.rz.uni-frankfurt.de/hsfk
Senior Staff: Director and Chairman of the Executive Board: Harald Mller, Members of the Executive Board: Lothar Brock, Hans-Joachim Spanger, Christian Buttner.
Date of Establishment: 1970
Purpose: PRIF research interests focus on the possibility of dealing with international conflicts without the application of military force. Through its research publications, PRIF keeps politicians and society at large informed about the kinds of conditions that have to be created and the decisions that have to be taken in order to promote peace as a process of decreasing violence and increasing justice.
Type: Public, national, non-profit
Brief History: The Peace Research Institute Frankfurt (PRIF) was established in 1970 by the government of the German Federal State of Hesse as a foundation under public law. It operates as a research institute from its base in Frankfurt. PRIF was the first—and is still the largest-peace research institute in Germany. PRIF's statutes guarantee its complete freedom of scholarly inquiry. The Institute does not engage in any research on behalf of other bodies.
Principal Activities: During the East-West conflict the Institute conducted researches on promotion of detente and arms control and disarmament. PRIF has now reformulated its research program to problems and issues connected with the political restructuring of Europe and the roles that the OSCE, NATO, WEU and EU can play in it, as well as European foreign relations and many other fields of research.

Periodicals:

(a) *HSFK-Reports,*

(b) *PRIF-Reports,*

(c) *HSFK-StandPunkte/Friedensforschung Aktuell, Friedensgutachten.*

Major Publications:

(a) *Communicators in The Cold War: The Pugwash Conferences, the U.S.-Soviet Study Group and the ABM Treaty. Natural Scientists as Political Actors. Historical Success and Lessons for the Future,*

(b) *Still a Chance for Negotiated Peace: Applying the Lessons of the CSCE with a View to a Conference on Security and Co-operation in the Middle East,*

(c) *Nuclear Disarmament: With What End in View? The International Discourse about Nuclear Arms Control and the Vision of a Nuclear-Weapon-Free World.*

Stiftung Wissenschaft und Politik [Research Institute for International Affairs]
Zeller Weg 27, D-82067 Ebenhausen, Germany

Telephone: 49-8178-70-0
Fax: 49-8178-70-312
E-mail: swp@swp.extern.lrz-muenchen.de
Senior Staff: Head of Administration: Johann Pfannenstiel, Research Coordination/Organization: Michael Paul, Gisa Helms, Helga Schubert
Date of Establishment: 1962
Type: National, private, non-profit
Purpose: SWP aims to give independent academic advice to the German government and parliament to support the Federal Republic's foreign policy planning by interdisciplinary, policy-oriented analyses and conferences. With due regard given to Bundestag members and/or government departments, SWP attempts to use the specific staff members' expertise to scrutinize current and foreseeable developments in the international arena. Most of the research therefore focuses on conceptual approaches to international relations.
Brief History: The Stiftung Wissenschaft und Politik (SWP) is a foundation established in 1962 for the purpose of furthering analytic research into problems of international politics and security. Publicly founded, but politically independent, the SWP today maintains the largest research institute of its kind in Germany.
Principal Activities: The research activities of the SWP seek to combine the requirements of the general research in international affairs with the specific needs and interest of policymakers. Its research planning reflects this dual purpose. The institute develops its own research agenda. Currently the research activities are divided into four broadly defined subject areas:

(a) Western Europe and Transatlantic relations, Eastern affairs, and political developments in the successor states of the Soviet Union,

(b) International Security Policy (defense, arms control, and technological advances),

(c) International Economics (East, West and the Third World) and issues involving technological change,

(d) Development outside Europe and North America (Asia; Near and Middle East, Africa, Latin America) relevant to the other research areas.

Periodicals:

(a) *Internationale Politik und Sicherheit,*

(b) *Aktuelle Materialien zur Internationalen Politik.*

Major Publications:

(a) *Soviet Risk-Taking and Crisis Behavior—A Theoretical and Empirical Analysis,*

(b) *Between Tokyo and Moscow—The History of Uneasy Relationship, 1972 to the 1990s.*

India

Ahimsa Shodh Sanahthan
Gujarat Vidyspith, Ashrm Road, Ahmadabad 380014 Bujarat State, India

Telephone: 91-79-75-10714/75-11110/75-11517
Fax: 91-79-75-42547
E-mail: gvpahd@adl.vsnl.net.in
Senior Staff: Chairman: Ramalal Parikh, Director Coordinator: Sadhana Vora, Devavrat Pathak
Date of Establishment: 1971
Purpose: The association exists to promote a non-violent society as envisaged by Mahatma Gandhi.
Type: National, public-charitable, non-profit
Brief History: Peace Research Center is an offshoot of Bujarat Vidyapith, which was founded by Mahatma Gandhi in 1920, with the object of achieving a society based on truth and non-violence. In October 1969, on the occasion of Gandhi century a seminar on Science, Education and Non-violence was held in the Gujarat Vidyapith in cooperation with UGC, Indian National Commission for UNESCO, Council of Scientific and Industrial Research and Atomic Energy Commission. Eminent personality attended the seminar from within and outside the country felt the need for studies and research on peace, Gujarat Vidyapith, with the initial help of UNESCO and USC should institute it, the Vidyapith had begun this task in November 1971. It has now culminated into the establishment of the institute of studies in quest of non-violence.
Principal Activities: The Center imports inter-disciplinary post-graduate, masters, doctoral and post-doctoral courses and research on peace and New Global Society, Peace Education, Human Rights, Peace Action and Environmental Issues, Disarmament, Ethics in Business, Science and Non-violence and Society, and Gandhian thought.

Memorial lectures, seminars, conferences, and workshops are organized on above subjects and training in peace brigade is being arranged for school teachers.

Periodicals:

(a) *Peace Digest*, Journals, 1 per annum,

(b) STEU, Bulletin of Documentation on Peace Research.

Major Publications:

(a) *Perspective of Peace Research,*

(b) del Vasto, L., *Pilgrimage to Non-violence,*

(c) Galtung, J., *The Struggle for Peace,*

(d) Pathak, D. N., *Intimation of Peaceful Society,*

(e) Unnithan, T. K., *Change Without Violence: Gandhian Theory of Social Change,*

(f) Kothari, L. K., *Man, Medicine and Morality.*

Centre for Studies in Peace and Non-Violence
Sri Venkateswara University
Tirupati 517-502, India

Telephone: 91-8574-24166 (EXT: 343)
Fax: 91-8574-212-11
Senior Staff: Research Assistant: Sudhakara Bandi
Date of Establishment: 1976
Purpose: The aims of the Center focus on:

(a) Conducting studies and action oriented research in Peace & Non-Violence,

(b) Maintaining liaison with research institutions devoted to study of Peace, Non-Violence and themes allied thereto,

(c) Disseminating the existing knowledge in the field of Peace and Non-Violence through public talks and extension lectures,

(d) Providing documentation and library service in the related areas,

(e) Organizing seminars and conferences at state, national and international levels and by publications on themes relevant to Peace & Non-Violence.

Brief History: The Center was instituted by Prof. K. Satchidan Ndamurti, the then vice chancellor, and the Center was inaugurated by Prof. Statish Chandra, the then Vice-Chairman. The university grants commission. The infrastructure facilities are provided by T. T. Devasthanams and State Government. Starting regular courses on Gandhi and Nehru are under consideration. The above mentioned purposes are achieved at the shortest period.

Principal Activities: Conducts studies on:

(a) Peace Research in India,

(b) Disarmament and Development,

(c) Violence in Politics,

(d) The Menace of Terrorism and the way out.

Periodicals: *Studies in Peace and Non-Violence*, Quarterly

Major Publication:

(a) *Non-Alignment,*

(b) *India and World Peace,*

(c) *The Need for Peace and Non-Violence in the Contemporary Scene,*

(d) *Relevance of Gandhi to Modern Times,*

(e) *Human Rights and Development,*

(f) *Perspectives of Peace: A Multi-Dimensional Approach,*

(g) *The Need of Mahatma Gandhi's Ideals to Today's Youth.*

Other Information: To bring awareness among the students at all levels in the areas of Peace and Non-Violence, periodical elocution and essay compositions are arranged and prizes are distributed.

Centre for the Study of Developing Societies
29, Rajpur Road, Delhi-110054, India

Telephone: 91-231190/2942199/2511151
Fax: 2943450

E-mail: sscsds@ren.nic.in
Senior Staff: Director: Sr. Fellow, Ashis Nandy,

Senior Fellow: Dipankar Banerjee, Giri Deshingkar, P. R. Chari

Date of Establishment: 1963

Purpose: The Centre was founded to create a capacity for theoretical and empirical research in social and political process and to understand their implication for human choices. It strives and believes that peace as a part of larger issue to be understood with its linkages in politics of cultures and politics of knowledge, and provide space for studies on violence, ethnicity and diversity and seek through this a theoretical space for politics of alternative human future.

Brief History: The CSDS was founded in 1963 and formally registered in 1967. Its main source of funding is the Indian Council of Social Science Research. Consisting of a Board of Governors, Faculty and Supporting Staff, the Centre is located in Old Delhi, close to the University of Delhi. The Centre's research program has four main foci, democratic politics and its future, politics of cultures and politics of knowledge.

Principal Activities: Research Projects; Ph. D. Programs; Undergraduate Training Programs; Survey Research; Seminars; Workshops.

Periodicals:

(a) *Alternatives*,

(b) *China Report*.

Major Publications:

(a) *Ref. CSDS: An Introduction*.

Gujarat Vidyapith
Ashram Road, Ahmedabad-380014, India

Telephone: 91-79-446148/446349

Fax: 91-79-6569547

E-mail: gujvi@adinet.ernet.in.

Senior Staff: Chancellor: Ramlal Parikh

Date of Establishment: 1920

Purpose: The principal objective of the Vidyapith shall be to prepare works of character, ability, education and conscientiousness necessary for the conduct of the movements connected with the regeneration of the country in accordance with the ideals given by Mahatma Gandhi.

Type: National, non-profit

Brief History: The Gujarat Vidyapith was founded by Mahatma Gandhi, its life-long Chancellor, in the year 1920. It was started as a National Institute of University Education and was the first of its kind established in the wake of the non-cooperation movement. Sardar Vallabhbhai Patel was its Vice-Chancellor from 1935 and, after Gandhi's demise, the Chancellor Dr. Rajendra Parsad remained the Chancellor until the end of his life. Shri Morarji Desai is the Chancellor at present.

Principal Activities: The Peace Research Institute is an inter-disciplinary center for research and studies in Peace and Non-violence, Peace Education and Non-Violence World Order, Alternative Development Strategies, Social Tensions, New Society, World Education etc. It provides an information service.

Periodicals:

(a) *Vidyapith* for research studies,

(b) *Lokjivan* for neo literates.

Major Publications:

(a) *Non-violence in Medical Science*,

(b) *Struggle for Peace*,

(c) *Change Without Violence—Gandhian Theory of Social Change*.

Indian Institute for Peace, Disarmament and Environmental Protection
537, Sakkardara Road, Nagpur 440009, India

Telephone: 91-712-745806

Fax: 91-712-743664

Senior Staff: President: Balkrishna Kurvey

Date of Establishment: 1993

Purpose: Research on peace and environmental protection. Public education and awareness on various aspects of peace, disarmament and environment.

Type: National, public, and non-profit

Brief History: IIPDEP is created in 1993 as a need to research public education and awareness on peace which is lacking in India. The Headquarter of the institute is in Nagpur. It is coordinating with like minded peace and environmental Institutes in India and world.

Principal Activities:

(a) Peace and human rights in developing countries,

(b) Nuclear disarmament in South Africa,

(c) Role of women in peace building and environmental protection in developing countries,

(d) Environment and sustainable development,

(e) Ethic conflict/regional conflict in Indian sub-continent and its peaceful resolution.

Periodicals: *IIPDEP Newsletter* (3 per annum)

Major Publications:

(a) *Peace Education,*

(b) *Human Rights, Pre-requisite for Democracy, Development, Security and Freedom,*

(c) *Nuclear Disarmament: Pros and Cons in South Africa,*

(d) *Environment and Sustainable Development in Developing Countries,*

(e) *The Role of Traditional Culture and Religion in the 21st Century.*

India Peace Center
CK Naidu Road, Civil Lines, Nagpur 44001 Maharashtra, India

Telephone: 91-712-556952
Senior Staff: Director: Hansi De
Date of Establishment: 1988
Purpose: Training; workshops; study camps; documentation/information; conference-organisation and

publication.
Type: Non-profit
Principal Activities: The center carries out research activities on militarism, disarmament, environment, peace and development, justice and human rights.

Institute for Peace Research and Action (IPRA)
81, Gagan Vihar, Delhi 110051, India

Telephone: 91-11-2243036
Fax: 91-11-2422986
Senior Staff: Director: Susheela Bhan
Date of Establishment: 1985
Type: National, public, non-profit
Brief History: The Institute has developed a peace program to bring about awareness of peace issues. Secondly, it has been working towards building structures (of consciousness and of society) conducive to a culture of peace. Thirdly, it has developed a peace research program in support of the awareness program as well as the peace movement.
Principal Activities: IPRA works in the areas of violence against children and women, ethic violence, peace education and health-peace relationship.

Periodicals: *Peace Dialogue* (annually)

Major Publications:

(a) *Terrorism: an Annotated Bibliography*, New Delhi, 1989,

(b) *Child Abuse, an Annotated Bibliography* (in two Volumes), Northern Book Center, 1991,

(c) *Health for Peace*, New Delhi, 1992,

(d) *Criminalization of Politics in India*, Delhi,1995,

(e) *Impact of Ethnic Violence on Youth: A Study of Tribal-non-tribal Violence in Kokkhrajar*, Delhi, 1998.

Institute of Gandhian Thought and Peace Studies (IGTPS)
University of Allahabad, Gandhi Bhawan Allahabad 211002 Uttar Pradesh, India

Telephone: 54900
Senior Staff: Director: J. S. Mathur
Date of Establishment: 1976
Purpose: The Institute is essentially an interdisciplinary advanced center for study and research in Gandhian and peace thought. This covers research on conflict resolution, new world order, nonviolence and social

change, and other allied subjects with particular emphasis on the relevance of Gandhian thought and technique for contemporary society.
Type: Public, non-profit
Brief History: The foundation of the Institute was laid by the Nobel Peace Laureate Mother Teresa in 1976, on the anniversary of Gandhi's birth. The Institute is an

extension of Gandhi Bhawan, University of Allahabad, the foundation of which was laid by Sri Prakasa, the then Governor of Maharashtra State on February 6, 1961.

Principal Activities: Research; training; documentation/information; conference-organization; publication; exhibitions

Periodicals: *Journal of Gandhian Studies*, 4 p.a.

International Association of Educators for World Peace (IAEWP)
216 Laxminagar Nagpur 440.022 Maharashtra, India

Fax: 91-712-524079
Senior Staff: President: S. N. Prasad, Executive Vice-President: C. Mercieca, Secretary-General: J. Schuster
Date of Establishment: 1969
Purpose: The IAEWP is a member of the International Non-Governmental Organization group of the United Nations and UNESCO. Its aims are:

(a) To promote education which stresses the importance of individuals being able to realize their potential development in the family, the local community, the country, and the world family of nations,

(b) To encourage the development of colleges and universities for peace research,

(c) To achieve maximum understanding by fully communicating and clarifying controversial views,

(d) To develop education which helps to form character traits capable of controlling aggression so that peaceful conflict resolution may occur,

(e) To put into practice the University Declaration of Human Rights.

The IAEWP philosophy is "World peace through wisdom."
Type: Public, non-profit
Brief History: The IAEWP was founded in May 1969 for the purpose of advancing the cause of peace through education. Originating from an idea of Charles Mercieca, Professor of Educational Philosophy and Sociology, the Association has grown rapidly and is represented by over 12,000 members in 58 countries covering every area of the world.

A constitution was ratified in March, 1969 and a first founding session was held in Huntsville, Alabama in April of that year. A second founding session was held in Huntsville in December, 1969. A plenary session, the "Oslo Founding Session Meeting" in August, 1970, under the chairmanship of Hans Ulrich Winstef, wrote new by-laws and elected officers.

Four newsletters in five languages have been published throughout the world.

IAEWP World Congresses have been held in Bucharest, Romania in 1974; Varanasi, India in 1978; and Washington, DC in 1982.

(a) The role of peace keeping within the United Nations,

(b) Nationalist movements in global perspective,

(c) The cultural and conceptual framework of peace,

(d) Refugees and international law,

(e) Psychological problems of American veterans,

(f) Aggressive behavior in Chinese society,

(g) The right to wage war: The A9 syllogism,

(h) IAEWP pilot schoot.

A Peace Education Program, a four-year curriculum leading to a B.Ed. degree with a concentration area in Peace Sciences has been developed by the IAEWP National Chapter of Thailand, and will be put into practice as a pilot study in the near future. There is a report of its written program in Peace Progress (1983, Vol. 3, No. 1)

The National High School of Iassy in Romania became a pilot school of the IAEWP, in 1983. As a result, hundreds of teenagers are now given the opportunity to learn how they could live and contribute to the promotion of world peace.

The IAEWP organizes UNESCO seminars and workshops for teaching peace and human rights throughout the United States of America and has planned to extend them throughout the world by the promotion of international understanding through foreign languages.

Principal Activities: Research, documentation/information, conference-organizationa, publication, radio-TV programmes, exhibitions

Current Peace Research:

(a) World peace through education,

(b) Peace education pilot schools project,

(c) Research in Islam and its contribution to the development of human rights and world peace,

(d) Education for democracy through culture,

(e) Education for human rights.

Periodicals: *Peace Education, 1 p.a., Peace Progress*, 1 p.a.

Major Publications:

(a) Mercieca, C., *Social Program and the Survival of Mankind*, 1991,

(b) Pillai, K. S. (ed.), *Relevance of Peace Education*, 1991,

(c) Mercieca, C., *Education for Peace : What it Entails*, 1992,

(d) Mercieca, C., *Disarmament and Development*, 1992,

(e) Prasad, S. N., *Human Rights Education and Peace*, 1991,

(f) Nanubhai, J., *Global Peace and Development*, 1992.

National Women's Welfare Center (NWWC)
Vanitha Bhawan, Ariyancode, Ottasekharamangalam PO, Pin 695 125, Kerala, India

Telephone: 91-471-255209
Senior Staff: S. Lilly Genet, L. Indiradevi, D. Ladamma, S. R. Sheeja
Date of Establishment: 1985
Purpose: World Peace, and disarmament through education, training, publication, meetings, camps, and conferences on eradication of poverty and illiteracy.
Type: International
Brief History: The Center is a women and children development and welfare organization. Established on 24 October 1985. The institute is not affiliated to any political of religious group. The aim of the Center is to provide all round development and progress for other groups.
Principal Activities: Research; training skill develop-

ments; job oriented programs; child welfare schemes; materials production and publicity and others.

Periodicals: Annual reports; conference reports; meetings discussion papers and posters.

Major Publications:

(a) *National Environment Awareness Campaign*, 1993,

(b) *Social Animators Residential Program*,

(c) *Youth Leadership Training Program*,

(d) *World AIDS Day Seminar*, December 1994,

(e) *Adult Education through Peace Activities*,

(f) *Continuing Education for Disarmament.*

Peace and Disarmament Society of Kerala (PADS)
Poozhikunnu, Ottasekharamanagalam PO, Pin 695125 Kerala, South India

Telephone: 91-471-255202
Senior Staff: K. Sivadasanpillai
Date of Establishment: 1985
Purpose: The Society conducts activities related to training, documentation/information, publication, and exhibitions

Type: Public, non-profit
Principal Activities: The Center deals with peace and disarmament research and training programs.
Major Publications: Progress-reports; conference proceedings; charts and booklets.

School of Gandhian Studies and Peace Science
Mahatma Gandhi University
Priyadarsini Hills PO, Kottayam 686 560, Kerala, India

Telephone: 91-481-597954
Fax: 91-481-597494
E-mail: mgu@md2.vsnl.net.in
Senior Staff: Director: Antony K. Chirappanath, M. S.

John, M. P. Mani, R. C. Mathew, Joseph Mukalel.
Date of Establishment: 1983
Purpose: The school carries out peace research including the definition of the concept of peace, education

for peace, peace and development, justice and religion, peace movements, women and peace, international order, conflict, theory and methodology for conflict resolution, mediation, managing communal and ethic conflicts. It also deals with weapons, disarmament, militarism, the arms trade, the conversion of military industries and non-violent defence, extension work for peace.

Type: Public, non-profit

Brief History: School of Gandhian Thought and Development Studies of Mahatma Gandhi University was established on October 2, 1983. The University has got 0.25 million students in its 150 affiliated colleges. The School tries to promote teaching, research and extension work among the students. Fifteen batches of post-graduate students have passed out from this school, and there are about 100 scholars working for Ph.D.

Principal Activities: The main activities of the school can be grouped under three heads:

(a) Teaching, the school has two MA programs and five M.Phil. programs,

(b) Research, there are various types of research

undertaken in the school. They are doctoral research, post-doctoral research, D.Litt. level research and research projects,

(c) Extension activities, the school considers extension activities as the third dimension and an integral part of higher education. Accordingly the extension wing is active taking the University to the villages and the villages to the University.

Periodicals: *Grama Swaraj* (Village Republic) (quarterly journal of Grama Swaraj extension project)

Major Publications:

(a) George, V. C., *The Fourfold End of Human Life*, 1997,

(b) Bernd, P., *A Gandhian Perspective*, 1996,

(c) Mukalel, J. C., *Psychology of Language Learning*, 1998,

(d) Zacharias, T., *Current Topics in Economics, Commerce and Management*, 1998,

(e) Chirappanath, A. K., *Journey in Spirit*, 1994.

Ireland

The Irish Commission for Justice and Peace
169 Booterstown Avenue, Blackrock, Co. Dublin, Ireland

Telephone: 01-288-50-21/288-48-53/288-38-66
Fax: 01-283-41-61
E-mail: icjp@tinet.ie
Senior Staff: Executive Secretary: Jerome Connolly, Research Officer: Pauline Eccles, Education Officer: Mary O'Connor
Date of Establishment: 1970
Purpose: The purpose of the Commission is to help, interpret and implement in an Irish context the Church's teaching on justice, peace, human rights and development in the modern world. It also aims to advise the Bishops' Conference accordingly and to act on its own initiative in fidelity to its mandate from the Conference.
Type: National, private, non-profit
Brief History: The Irish Commission for Justice and Peace since its establishment has worked extensively in the promotion of Human Rights. It played an important role in mediation and conciliation during the Hunger Strikes in Northern Ireland in 1981. ICJP and the Irish Council of Churches established the Joint Peace Program in 1979. This promotes inter-community and cross-border initiatives for mutual understanding, as well as publishing materials for use on an inter-church

basis.
Principal Activities: Main activity focuses on promoting the abolition of the legal status of illegitimacy, abolition of the death penalty, criminal justice. ICJP monitors the implementation by Ireland of the main international human rights treaties, e.g., the UN Covenant on Civil and Political Liberties.

It presented submissions to the All Party Committee for the Reform of the Irish Constitution. In 1996 it challenged the Government which was promoting a referendum on the curtailment of the right to bail in certain cases. ICJP made a submission on the bill dealing with mandatory reporting of Child Sexual Abuse.

In its Peace Education Program ICJP has published resources for the promotion of Peace and Justice education and it advises and supports teachers in the education of Peace and Justice.

ICJP promotes the role of women in development and is a member of the international organization, Women in Development Europe.

Major Publications:

(a) *Yes, You Do Count—A Comprehensive Teaching*

Module on Human Rights,

(b) *Looking at Churches and Worship in Ireland,*

(c) *So Everybody Fights?,*

(d) *Power to Hurt,*

(e) *Power to Heal,*

(f) *More Power to Heal,*

(g) *Choose Life,*

(h) *Towards an Island that Works,*

(i) *Towards Peace and Stability,*

(j) *Living the Kingdom,*

(k) *Burying Our Dead,*

(l) *Remembering Our Past,*

(m) *World Development Note 1, 2, 3, 4, 5,*

(n) *Disarmament and Development—The Vital Links,*

(o) *Making Every Penny Count,*

(p) *A Wealth of Women,*

(q) *The Role of Women,*

(r) *The Effects of Militarization on the Development of Third World Countries,*

(s) *Riding the Tiger.*

Israel

Jaffee Center for Strategic Studies
Tel-Aviv University Ramat-Aviv, Tel-Aviv 69978, Israel

Telephone: 972-3-6409926
Fax: 972-3-6422404
E-mail: Jcss2@post.tav.ac.il
Senior Staff: Researcher: Emily Landau, Head of Center: Zeev Maoz, Researcher: More Haller
Date of Establishment: 1977
Purpose: The objectives of the center are to advance research and contribute to the expansion of knowledge on relevant subjects, and to promote public understanding of, and pluralistic thought on matters of Israel national security and Middle eastern strategic affairs. In so doing, JCSS seeks to address the Israeli public and Israeli's defense and decision making echelons, as well as world Jewry, and decision makers, strategic planners, and the media in the world at large.

The Center relates to the concept of strategy in its broadest meaning, namely the complex of processes involved in the identification, mobilization and application of resources in peace and war, in order to solidify and strengthen national and international security.
Type: Non-profit
Brief History: The Center for Strategic Studies was established in 1977 at the initiative of Tel Aviv University. In 1983 the Center was named the Jaffee Center for Strategic Studies (JCSS) in honor of Mr. and Mrs. Mel Jaffee. Major General (res.) Aharon Yariv, former government minister, member of Knesset, and Director of Military Intelligence, took upon himself, at the University's request, the organization and management of the Center, and headed it until shortly before his death

in 1994. Among the primary supporters of JCSS at its founding were Abba Eban, who served as first chairman of its International Board of Trustees, and the late Joseph H. (Buddy) Strelitz, then President of the American Friends of Tel Aviv University and later Chairman of the International Board of Trustees. Funds for the Center's creation were provided mainly by members of the Jewish communities of the United States, who have been aware of, and sensitive to, the need for such an institution in Israel.
Principal Activities: In fulfilment of its aims, JCSS initiates and conducts research on multiplicity of factors—political, military, economic, psychological, sociocultural, etc.—that involves strategic issues relevant to Israeli national security.

The Center maintains a staff of specialists in the various disciplines related to strategic studies. As projects require, experts from other institutions in Israel and abroad are employed.

Periodicals: *JCSS Bulletin* (bi-annually)

Major Publications:

(a) *The Middle East Military Balance,*

(b) *International Terrorism in 1988,*

(c) *Domestic Sources of Global Change,*

(d) *War in the Gulf: Implications for Israel,*

(e) *Israel's Nuclear Image.*

Other Information: The Center conducts long-term projects and researches which include a computerized data base of all Middle Eastern armies, defense infra-structure, and arms transactions. It provides the foundation with the Center's annual *Middle East Military Balance*, as well as for arms control research and data service.

The Leonard Davis Institute for International Relations
The Hebrew University of Jerusalem
Alfred Davis Building, Mount Scopus, Jerusalem 91950, Israel

Telephone: 972-2-588-2312
Fax: 972-2-582-5534
E-mail: msdavis@pluto.mscc.huji.ac.il
Senior Staff: President of Hebrew University: Hanoch Gutfreund, Dean, Faculty of Social Sciences: Yaakov Metzer, Director: Sasson Sofer, Chairman of the Department of International Relations: Yaacov Bar-Siman-Tov, Representative of the Department of Political Science: Baruch Knei-Paz, Representative of the Department of International Relations: Norman Rose
Date of Establishment: 1972
Purpose: The Institute plans its programs in accordance with three broad aims:

(a) To promote scientific research in the theory of international relations, adopting a broad interdisciplinary perspective aimed at the entire spectrum of the discipline,

(b) To present the universal themes of international politics to the Israeli public, thereby enhancing the national discourse on these matters,

(c) To put our expertise and consulting capability at the service of national institutions conducting the security and foreign affairs of Israel.

Type: International, non-profit
Principal Activities: The Institute has long served as a center where researches from the International Relations, Political Science, and related departments at the Hebrew University, as well as at other Israeli universities and academic centers, can develop and coordinate research programs.

Periodicals:

(a) *Davis News,*

(b) *Davis Papers on Israel's Foreign Policy and International Politics,*

(c) *Dynamics of Dependence,*

(d) *The Illusion of Deterrence: The Roosevelt Presidency and the Origins of the Pacific War.*

Major Publications:

(a) *Bringing Capital Accumulation Back In: Differential Capital Accumulation and Weapondollar/ Petrodollar Coalition,*

(b) *Russia and Iran: A Strategic Partnership?,*

(c) *Peaceful Territorial Change,*

(d) *Pluralistic Security Communities and 'Negative' Peace in the Third World: A Comparison of South America and West Africa.*

Meretz-International Department
Homa O'migdal 2 Tel-Aviv 61201 POB 20177, Israel

Telephone: 972-3-6360181/972-50-284406
Fax: 972-3-5375107/972-8-9436282
E-mail: mpollack@metvosopm.net.il
Senior Staff: International Secretary: Monica Pollack
Date of Establishment: 1977
Purpose: Meretz is a political party in its framework and active in international department as it is involved in spreading information, establishing ties with progressive forces worldwide, cooperating on a regional and international level and carrying on the practical research as well as monitoring workshops and seminars for the advancement of peace.

Brief History: After the merger of 3 political parties (1977), the former Institute and International Department of MAPAM continues its activities within the framework of Meretz, which organizes and participates in activities aimed to further peace in the Middle East, works for Israeli Palestinian coexistence, for a Mediterranean dialogue and for international cooperation.

Principal Activities:

(a) Young leadership projects,

(b) Life counselling,

(c) Arab women's participation in community life,

(d) Conferences, symposiums, publications,

(e) Courses on desert agriculture and agricultural corporativism (for Latin American Organizations).

Periodicals:

(a) *B'Meretz* (Hebrew) (6 times per year),

(b) *Newsletter* (English) (quarterly).

Major Publications:

(a) *Middle East Peace Process,*

(b) *Mediterranean Dialogue and Cooperation,*

(c) *Agricultural Cooperation,*

(d) *Women Participation,*

(e) *Religious Coercion vs. Pluralism.*

Italy

Centro Educazione Alla Pace
University of Napoli
Mostra D'Oltremare Pad, 19, 80125, Napoli, Italy

Telephone: 39-81-7253417
Fax: 39-81-7253449
E-mail: ADRAGO@NA.INFN.IT
Senior Staff: Prof. of History of Physics: Antonino Drago
Date of Establishment: 1980
Purpose: The center strives:

(a) To promote peace education in schools,

(b) To promote analysis on peace education,

(c) To institutionalize education of Italian civil servants,

(d) To promote a national nonviolent defense.

Type: National, non-profit
Brief History: It was created by the collaboration of four University persons in order to introduce Peace Education in academic activities.

Principal Activities:

(a) Promotion of a National Prize on Peace Education (1983-1995),

(b) Production of papers in peace education,

(c) School for civil servants,

(d) Psychological research on children on Mafia.

Major Publications:

(a) *Between Cannons and Engines: The Birth of thermodynamics,* Proc. Int. Conf. Proust, Segovia, 1992,

(b) UNA *Strategia Di Pace: La Difensa Popolaire Nonviolenta,* Fuorithema, Bologna, 1993,

(c) *Peace Education in the Middle of a Paradigm Shift,* Comm. to II EUPRA Conference, Budapest, 1993,

(d) *A Dozen Years of Peace Education in Italy as Embodied in "F. Pagano" Prize,* comm. XV IPRA Conference, Malta, 1994,

(e) *Game Theory and Conflictual Theories in History of Physics,* 5th Nat. Conf. Game Theory, Bergamo, 1995,

(f) *Per* UN *Modello Di Difesa Nonviolento,* Editoria Universitaria, Venezia, 1995,

(g) *"The Role of Science in Intercultural Education. A Criticism of* UNESCO *Sevilla Statement and a New Proposal,"* A.V. Baldassarre (ed.): *Interculturality and Education,* Bari, 1996,

(h) *Peacekeeping and Peacebuilding,* Qualevita, Sulmona, 1997.

Other Information: The Center promoted a National Project of Research on Peace Education which involved groups in Rome, Florence, Bologna, Turin, Bari and Verona (Prof. Butturini, Univ. of Verona, Faculty of letters)

CIPAX-Centor Interconfessionale Per La Pace
Via Peralba 2/A-00141 Roma, Italy

Telephone: 39-06-87181670
Fax: 39-06-87181670
E-mail: cipax@rm.nettuno.it
Senior Staff: Executive Director: Gianni Novelli, President: Fabrizio Trnini
Date of Establishment: 1982
Purpose: The center aspires to increase the participation of religious institutions and people in the modern peace and justice campaigns and promote the commitment of churches to justice, peace, and integrity of creation.
Type: Private, non-profit
Brief History: At the time of Cold War and the great danger of nuclear holocaust the major religious associations and institutions in Italy were absolutely out of the peace movement for the fear of political manipulation. The aim of the Cipax is to increase cooperation and involvement in ecumenical amongst civil and religious forces in the modern issues of "Justice; peace and integrity of creation."

Principal Activities: Pray and work; peace education; nonviolent training; diffusion of book and media resources; international contacts.
Periodicals: *Strumenti di pace*, every two months.

Major Publication:

(a) *Spirituality and Theology of Peace*,

(b) *Peace Education*.

Other Information: The Association is independent from church and political parties and it is supported by voluntary contribution.

Forum Per I Problemi Della Peace E Della Guerra
[Forum on the Problem of Peace and War]
Via Gianpaolo Orsini, 44, 50126 - Florence, Italy

Telephone: 39-55-6800165
Fax: 39-55-6581933
E-mail: forum@comune.fi.it ~ forumcd@tin.it
Senior Staff: President: Rodolfo Ragionieri
Date of Establishment: 1984
Purpose: The Forum focuses on research and exchange of knowledge on problems of peace and war, disarmament, security, and conflict resolution. The forum also aims to promote research works through development of scientific relation with other institutes, conference-organisation, and participation in national and international conferences.
Type: International, public and non-profit
Brief History: FPPW was founded in 1984 as an important non-partisan association, by a group of scholars, mostly teaching at the University of Borenes. Members and auditors of the forum are from a wide variety of people with scientific background, and lend the association a truly interdisciplinary character.
Principal Activities: Research projects; teaching activities; workshops; public debates; seminars, and international conference-organizations.

Periodicals:

(a) *Quadermi Forum* (quarterly),

(b) *The future of the European Union*,

(c) *International Constraints and National Debates in the Israeli-Palestinian Peace Process*,

(d) *Politica ed Economica nell' area Mediterranea*.

Major Publications:

(a) Martini, L. (ed.), *Mare di Guerra, Mare di Religioni*, 1994,

(b) Addis E., Russo, V., Sebesta, L. (eds.), *Donne Soldato*, 1994,

(c) Bozzo L., Catalano, G. (eds.), *Transparenza e Controllo? Il Registro Delle Armi Convenzionali Delle Nazioni Unite*, 1995,

(d) *Controllo o Disordine. Il Futuro Della Proliferazione Nucleare*, 1995.

Instituto Internazionale "Jacques Maritain", Centro Di Studi E Ricerche
Villa Albrizzi-Franchetti 31022 Preganziol Treviso, Italy

Telephone: 39-42-249-0938/0968

Fax: 39-42-249-1176

E-mail: maritian@stellapolare.it
Senior Staff: Director: Antonio Pavan
Date of Establishment: 1974
Purpose: The Center acts as an observatory of the processes of change; a forum for comparing and for intellectual cooperation; a research laboratory in the field of philosophy and the human science pointing to social development and a new culture of man.
Type: International
Brief History: Established in the Veneto in 1981 as a permanent, organized laboratory for the Institute's action in the world, the Center has gradually made its functions and strategies more precise within the Insti-tute.

Principal Activities: Research is the principal goal of the Institute, organized around programs carried out by working groups involved in courses, workshops, seminars, conferences etc.
Periodicals: *Pour une Recherche Personnaliste.*
Major Publications:

(a) *Balcani in fiamme; quale pace etinca? 1995,*

(b) *Globalizzare l' economia, 1995,*

(c) *Cinque parole per la pace, 1997,*

(d) *La democrazia, le religion e la pace, 1998.*

International School on Disarmament and Research on Conflicts (ISODARCO) Department of Physics, University of Rome "Tor vergata", via della Ricerca Scientifica, I-00133 Rome, Italy

Telephone: 39-6-7259-4560/1
Fax: 39-6-2040309
E-mail: schaerf@Roma2.INFN.IT
Senior Staff: President: Carlo Schaerf
Date of Establishment: 1966
Purpose: ISODARCO is an NGO that offers a unique international forum on security problems throughout the world. ISODARCO's purpose is to bring together those with a great variety of experiences and approaches relating to security problems. Their discussions focus on commissioned expert papers.
Type: International, private, non-profit
Brief History: ISODARCO, founded on the initiative of Professors Edoardo Amaldi and Carlo Schaerf, is an international school devoted to the study of the scientific and technical problems of disarmament, arms control and conflict resolution. Since its inception in 1966, ISODARCO has provided an open forum for University professors, students, journalists, military staff, diplomats and other motivated individuals from all over the world.
Principal Activities: The School itself is held during the summer season mainly in Italy and is designed to last approximately 10 days during which formal lec-

tures and specific seminars are provided by invited lecturers. Since 1988 also ten winter schools have been organized and seven seminars abroad: four of them held in Popular China, one in Taipei and one in Jordan.

Major Publications:

(a) Gottestein, K. (ed.), *Aspects of Security Policy in a New Europe*, 1992,

(b) Carlton, D. (ed.), *Controlling the International Transfer of Weaponry and Related Technology*, 1993,

(c) Ingram, P. (ed.), *Rising Tension in the Former Soviet Union and Eastern Europe*, 1995,

(d) Bekker, S. (ed.), *Racism, Xenophobia and Ethnic Conflicts*, 1995.

Other Information: A second dimension of ISODARCO's activity is research. Most recently, ISODARCO has compiled an extensive chronology of acts of political violence in Italy starting from the disruptive year 1969. The results and analysis of this study have recently been published.

Italian Peace Research Institute (IPRI) Centro Studi "Domenico Sereno Regis" Via Garibaldi 13-10122 Torino, Italy

Telephone: 39-11-532824
Fax: 39-11-532824
Senior Staff: President: Giovanni Salio, Research Programs Director: Giuseppe Barbiero, International Library Director: Carla Toscana

Date of Establishment: IPRI 1977/Centro Studi "Domenico Sereno Regis" 1982
Purpose: IPRI is an institute that specifically intends to promote peace research and peace education at the academic level. The Center "Domenico Sereno Regis" has

promoted many qualified publications about peace education in collaboration with other associations.

Type: National, private, non-profit

Brief History: IPRI was founded in Naples in February 1977; the Study Center "Domenico Sereno Regis" was founded in Turin in 1982. Other affiliated offices of IPRI are in Rome, Florence, Bologna, Genoa, Turin and Ivrea.

Principal Activities: Our activities cover a very wide field:

(a) Seminars of formation for educators of conscientious objectors,

(b) An advanced planning of a formation-school for conflicts resolution,

(c) An intensive and continuous work with teachers, students, parents and families in the different orders of school and the realization of a demonstrative laboratory about technologies for energetic saving. All these activities have led to the constitution of a specialized library.

Periodicals: *IPRI Newsletter*

Major Publications:

(a) Salio, G., *Le Guerre del Golfo*, Edizioni Gruppo Abele, 1991,

(b) Salio, G., *Il potere della nonviolenza*, Edizioni Gruppo Abele, 1995,

(c) IPRI, *I movimenti per la pace*, vol. I II III, Edizioni Gruppo Abele, 1986-1989.

Other Information: The IPRI is linked to the IPRA (International Peace Research Association), that counts beyond a thousand of members, above all teachers of the main universities all over the world. The IPRA was recognized by the UN as an INGO with advisory status on the problems of peace and disarmament. It also collaborates actively with the UNESCO in programs of peace education.

Japan

Hiroshima Peace Culture Foundation
1-2 Hakajima-cho, Haka-ku, Hiroshima 730, Japan

Telephone: 81-82-241-5246
Fax: 81-82-242-7452
E-mail: mayorcon@pcf.city.hiroshima.jp
Senior Staff: President: Takashi Hiraoka, Chairman, Board of Directors: Minoru Ohmuta, Executive Director (Secretary General): Yosimichi Hasegama
Date of Establishment: 1976
Purpose: Based on the "Hiroshima" experience and keeping a perspective that encompasses all of humankind, the Foundation informs the world about A-bomb disasters and at the same time works with peace research organizations and related bodies both domestically and overseas to contribute to the promotion of world peace and the advancement of human welfare.
Type: Public, national, non-profit
Brief History: The Hiroshima Peace Culture Foundation was established as a bureau within the Hiroshima City Government (April 1, 1976). Organized as a foundation by Hiroshima City to promote peace based on closer ties with citizens (May 22, 1991). The World Conference of Mayors for Peace through Inter-city Solidarity (secretariat in our foundation) registered as a United Nations Economic and Social Council NGO (Category II), (March 1994). Office transferred to the East Building of the newly constructed Hiroshima Peace Memorial Museum.

Principal Activities:

(a) Presenting A-bomb documentary films and testimonies of A-bomb survivor experiences to students who visit Hiroshima on school excursions,

(b) Lending A-bomb materials and holding A-bomb exhibitions/propagating the Peace Declaration,

(c) Publishing newsletters and peace related literature,

(d) Holding citizen lectures, lecture meetings, and symposiums,

(e) Holding the United Nations Disarmament Week Commemorative Project (soliciting peace drawings and pesters, holding gatherings, etc.),

(f) Constructing the peace data base/conducting Hiroshima studies for United Nations Disarmament Fellows and other overseas visitors,

(g) Holding the United Nations Conference on Disarmament Issue in Hiroshima,

(h) Producing A-bomb survivor testimony videos,

(i) Collecting A-bomb and peace related materials,

(j) Promoting the world peace and inter-city solidarity program.

Periodicals:

(a) Newsletter of the foundation: *Peace Culture*, (Japanese). A4 pages, 8 pg., published 6 times per year beginning 1997-A4 pages, 12 pages, published 4 times per year,

(b) Newsletter of the foundation: *Peace Culture*, (English) A4 pages, 8 pg., published 2 times per year,

(c) Newsletter for the World Conference of Mayors for Peace through Inter-city Solidarity: *Inter-city Solidarity*,

(d) *Newsletter*, (Japanese and English),published 1-2 times per year.

Major Publications:

(a) *Photographic Record Hiroshima* (Japanese and English explanations),

(b) *Photographic Record Hiroshima and Nagasaki* (Japanese and English explanations),

(d) Kosakai, Y., *Hiroshima Peace Reader* (also published in English),

(d) Kotani, T., Maruyama, M., Sakurai, J., Fujii, T., *Peace: Nation, Nuclear Problems, Educations*,

(e) Shoji, M., *Peace Education: A Guide for Parents and Children* (also published in English),

(f) Kuwabara, T., *A Talk on the United Nations*,

(g) Yamada, H., *The History of Armament and Disarmament*,

(h) The Hiroshima Peace Culture Foundation (ed.),

Appeals from the A-bomb Survivors (also published in English),

(i) Matsuo, M., *An Introduction to Peace Studies*,

(j) Ubuki, S., *The History of the Peace Memorial Ceremony*,

(k) Okamoto, M., *Creating Peace Studies-Conception, History, and Issues*,

(l) Iwata, K., *The Soviet Union, Russia, and World Peace*,

(m) Hayashi, T., *The History of Eastern Europe and Ethnic Problems*,

(n) Takeuchi, J., *Development and Poverty: Poverty within Abundance, and Abundance within Poverty*,

(o) Nakatsuji, K., *The World after the Cold War and US-China Relations*,

(p) The Hiroshima Peace Culture Foundation (ed.), *Peace Encyclopedia* (published through Keiso Shobo Publishers),

(q) Kosakai, Y. (ed.), *A-bomb: A City Tells its Story* (English),

(t) Matsumoto, Y., *My Mother Died in Hiroshima* (Japanese and English),

(s) The Hiroshima Peace Culture Foundation (ed.), *Wishing for Peace: Letters Sent to the A-bomb Dome Preservation Campaign*.

Other Information: The foundation was established by the Hiroshima City Government, and is financed by subsidies from the city as well as its own revenue sources. The staff includes personnel dispatched from Hiroshima City as well as those hired exclusively by our foundation.

Institute of International Relations for Advanced Studies on Peace and Development in Asia
Sofia University
7-1 Kioi-cho, Chiyoda-ku, Tokyo 102, Japan

Telephone: 81-3-3238-3561
Fax: 81-3-3238-3592
E-mail: kokusai@hoffman.cc.sophia.ac.jp
Date of Establishment: 1969
Purpose: The purpose of the Institute is to promote the educational and research goals suggested by its name. In keeping with its traditions as a Catholic and international institutions of higher learning, Sofia University, through the IIR, seeks to address the issues raised by the great social, economic, and political transformations taking place within the human community in today's world. The IIR's interdisciplinary staff of social scientists conduct research on a wide range of topics in international and comparative studies and constitute a core staff for Sofia University's post graduate degree programs in international relations and for an undergraduate minor program in international relations. The IIR's activities include publication of a periodical and occasional papers, as well as collaboration on and sponsorship of books, study groups, symposia, and

scholarly exchanges both domestically and internationally.

Type: National, private, non-profit

Brief History: The Institute of International Relations for Advanced Studies on Peace and Development in Asia (IIR) was established at Sofia University.

Principal Activities: Research on:

(a) "Domestic Change and the International System" (1989),

(b) "Japan-U.S.S.R. Relations in the Post-Cold War Era (1989-1992),

(c) "A New International Studies" (1994),

(d) "Japan in International Society and International Relations in Japan" (1995).

Periodicals: *The Journal of International Studies* (semiannual).

Major Publications:

(a) *Towards Surmounting Global Syndromes through the Promotion of Science,*

(b) *International Ramification of German Unification,*

(c) *Bridging State and Society, East and West.*

Peace Research Insitute
Soka University
1-236, Tangi-cho, Hachioji, Tokyo 192, Japan

Telephone: 81-0426-91-5333
Fax: 81-0426-91-9364
E-mail: ki900359@s.soka.ac.jp
Date of Establishment: 1976
Purpose: Based on Soka University's founding spirit "Be the fortress for the Peace of Mankind", the Institute promotes research for non-violent ways of Conflict Resolution, building conditions for peace.
Type: International, private, non-profit
Brief History: The Peace Research Institute of Soka University was established in 1 April 1976, and the opening ceremony was held on 18th June. The first director of the institute was Prof. Mata-ichi Kido. In June 1996, the 20th Anniversary Symposium on "Challenges of Peace Studies of Peace Studies for Cultivating Global citizenship" was held.
Principal Activities: Soka University started an open lecture for peace in 1983, and opened a Liberal Art Lecture for Peace (World Peace and Human Right) in 1987 in order to establish a curriculum for teaching the outline of Peace Studies.

Moreover, the Institute made a curriculum guide of Peace Studies for students who have a great interest in Peace Studies and/or global issues to show some useful classes concerning Peace Studies, International Studies, Global Communications and so on.

Periodicals:

(a) *Soka University Peace Research,*

(b) *Newsletters,*

(c) *Fortress for Peace.*

Major Publications:

(a) *Security Problems and the Role of Japan in the Pacific Basin* (The Report of the Pacific Basin Research Project) 1984,

(b) *Intellectual Challenges for Peaceful Society*, 1986,

(c) *Buddhism and Leadership for Peace*, Conference Proceeding, 1986.

The Sasakawa Peace Foundation
Sasakawa Hall 10F, 3-12-12 Mita Minota-Ku
Tokyo 108-0073, Japan

Telephone: 81-3-3769-2081
Fax: 81-3-3769-2090
E-mail: pr@spt.or.jp
Senior Staff: Tabuchi, A. Iriyama, M. Yokoyama, Chief Program Officer: Y. Wakakama,
Date of Establishment: 1986
Purpose: Promotion of Peace

Type: Private, non-profit
Principal Activities: Research; conference-organization; publication; Current peace researches are:

(a) Reconstruction of the new global order,

(b) SPF initiative for globalization of local communities in Japan,

(c) Human resource development program for the people of Cambodia,

(d) Global environment issues and Japan's contribution.

Periodicals: Bulletin; monographs; progress-report; conference proceedings.

Major Publications:

(a) *A Japan Think Tank: Think Tank of the World,*

(b) *Russia/Far Eastern Economic Yearbook,*

(c) *Vietnam, Laos, Cambodia: the Path of Economic Development.*

Peace Studies Association of Japan (PSAJ)
c/o Institute for Peace Science, Hiroshima University
1-1-89, Higashisendamachi, Nakaku, Hiroshima 730 Japan

Telephone: 81-82-243-9428
Fax: 81-82-245-0585
E-mail: psaj@ipc.hiroshima-u.ac.jp
Senior Staff: President: Hatsuse Ryuhei, Vice-Presidents: Alexander Ronni, Ishi Mayako, Secretary General: Matsuo Masatsugu.
Date of Establishment: 1973
Purpose: The purpose of PSAJ is to focus on conflicts between nations, to carry out scientific research on the causes of any resultant strives and conditions for peace, and to contribute to academic progress in related fields of study.
Brief History: PSAJ had only 72 members when it was founded in 1973. Now with 750 registered individual members and 12 corporate members, it is one of the largest national peace research organizations in the world. PSAJ tries to maintain good relations with all variants of peace researchers around the world, both individual and organizational.
Principal Activities: The Association is engaged in

the following activities:

(a) Two major conferences every year,

(b) Smaller ad hoc meetings,

(c) Coordination of national and foreign academic societies and other related institutions, as well as the promotion of exchange among researchers,

(d) Sponsoring of various activities which are considered to be necessary and appropriate in achieving the purpose of this Association.

Periodicals:

(a) *Annals of PASJ, Peace Studies* (in Japanese),

(b) *Peace Studies Newsletter* (in English),

(c) *PSAJ Newsletter* (in Japanese).

The United Nations University
53-7, Jingumae 5-chome, Shibuya-ku, Tokyo 150, Japan

Telephone: 81-03-3499-2811
Fax: 81-03-3499-2828
E-mail: mbox@hg.umu.edu
Senior Staff: Senior Academic Officer: Jean-Marc Coicaud
Date of Establishment: December 1973 by the United Nations General Assembly (Resolution 3081 XXVIII).
Purpose: The UNU aims to engage in research, postgraduate training and dissemination of knowledge on the pressing global problems of human survival, development and welfare.
Type: International
Brief History: The UNU commenced operations in Tokyo, Japan, in September 1975. For the first ten

years, the University carried out its work from the Headquarters in Tokyo with networks of associated and cooperation institutions located in many countries. In 1985, the UNU's first research and training centre was established, the UNU World Institute for Development Economics Research (UNU/WIDER) in Helsinki, Finland. Subsequently, 7 research and training centres and programs have been established. UNU Institute for New Technologies (UNU/INTECH) in Netherlands, UNU Institute for Natural Resources in Africa (UNU/INRA), UNU International Institute for Software Technology (UNU/IIST) in Macao.
Principal Activities: Research, postgraduate training and dissemination of knowledge on four programs:

(a) Peace and governance,

(b) Development,

(c) Environment,

(d) Science and technology.

Periodicals: UNU/Program for Biotechnology in Latin America and the Caribbean (UNU/BIOLAC), UNU International Leadership Academy (UNU/ILA) in Jordan, the UNU Network on Water, Environment and Health (UNU/INWEH) in Canada, and the UNU Institute of Advanced Studies (UNU/IAS) in Japan.

Korea

The Center for Social Sciences
Seoul National University
San 56-1, Shinrim-dong, Kwanak-ku, Seoul 151-742, Korea

Telephone: 82-2-880-5476
Fax: 82-2-886-0976
E-mail: css@plaza.snu.ac.kr
Senior Staff: Director: Tai-Hwan Kwon, Prof.: Sung-Hwi Lee, Hyun-Chin Lim, Kwang-Ok Kim, Il-Sub Choi
Date of Establishment: 1997
Purpose: The Center aspires to provide systematic scientific reflections and analysis on the Korean society in its tradition as it is about to enter the 21st Century
Type: Non-profit
Brief History: In responding to the necessity to map out the future of social science, Seoul National University (SNU) decided to promote social science studies by strengthening the basic researches and to build a system of studies that will orchestrate different studies in varied fields of social science. Centering around the Institute of Social Science, an official affiliate of the University since 1976, other SNU Social Science College affiliated research institutions such as Institute of World Economy, Institute for Social Development and Policy Research, Institute for Cross Cultural Studies, and Institute of Social Welfare came together to build the Center for Social Sciences at SNU.
Principal Activities:

(a) Theories of Social Sciences: As a comprehensive program in the field of social science, this program focuses on the development of new methodologies and theories of social sciences,

(b) Area Studies: The purpose of this program is to enhance the scientific understanding of various relations and regimes through multidimensional analyses conducted by area specialists,

(c) Policy Researches: This program includes survey research and other related activities which have significance to national and international policy formulation, implementation and evaluation,

(d) North Korean Studies: This program aims not only at promoting the study of the political social and economic situations of North Korea, but also at developing closer relations between South and North Korea,

(e) Conference organization,

(f) Publication.

Periodicals:

(a) *Korean Social Science Review,*

(b) *Korean Journal of Population and Development* (bi-annually),

(c) *Korean Journal of Social Welfare Studies* (bi-annually).

Major Publications:

(a) *Man and Society in Korea's Economic Growth: Sociological Studies,* 1977,

(b) *Reciprocity and Korean Society: An Ethnography of Hasami,* 1984,

(c) *Nuclear Proliferation, World Order and Korea,* 1983,

(d) *Political and Economic Transformations of Korea and Central European Countries,* 1997,

(e) *The Local Political System in Asia,* 1987,

(f) *Korea and Her Neighboring Economies,* 1988,

(g) *Asian Peoples and Their Cultures,* 1986,

(h) *UN Politics and Korean Issues,* 1995,

(i) *Asian Perspectives in Social Science,* 1985.

Center for the Reconstruction of Human Society
Kyung Hee University
1, Hoegi-dong, Dongdaemoon-ku, Seoul 130-701, Korea

Telephone: 82-2-961-0205
Fax: 82-2-966-1804
E-mail: khsd2701@nms.kyunghee.ac.kr
Senior Staff: Director-General: Gong-Young Il, Professor: Byung-Rok Song, Hyung-Sik Yun
Date of Establishment: 1976
Purpose: The center for the Reconstruction of Human Society was founded in 1976, with the ultimate goal of constructing a bright and harmonious human society. The Institute strives for the ideal moral integration of a spiritual and physical realm, and an establishment of common norms and values of humanity for the purpose of building a more beautiful, affluent, rewarding, and civilized welfare society. It hopes to establish permanent peace for the world community.
Type: Public, national, private, non-profit
Brief History: Since its foundation, the Center for the Reconstruction of Human Society, headed by Young Seek Choue, actively researches and publishes works, and holds regular academic symposiums, and a weekly "Thursday Seminar." In 1995, after long and intensive study, the institute published a textbook entitled *World Citizenship* focusing on the various challenges that present society faces and the methods by which we can move forward. The institute also held an international seminar entitled "Democracy and World Citizenship in the 21st Century" on September 1997, as a culmination of three years from 1995 to 1997, of joint international research supported by the Korea Research Foundation.

Principal Activities:

(a) Researches on the reconstruction of human society,

(b) Organizes regular domestic and international seminars,

(c) Cooperates with other related institutes at home and abroad,

(d) Publishes periodicals and books in Korean and in English.

Periodicals: *Oughtopia*
Major Publications:

(a) *21st Century: Its Prospect and Problems*, 1979,

(b) *Oughtopia—Theory and Practice*, 1979,

(c) *Meanings of Human Being*, 1979,

(d) *Can Modern Society Be Humanized?*, 1979,

(e) *Crises and Thoughts of Modern Society*, 1983,

(f) *Research on Chui-Saengsongism and Chon-Seunghwa*, 1984,

(g) *Conversation for the Reconstruction of Human Society*, 1986,

(h) *World Citizenship: A Reader*, 1986,

(i) *Textbook on World Citizenship*, 1986,

(j) *Global Human Family Looking at the 21st Century*, 1987,

(k) *Ideals and Realities of Global Village*, 1988,

(l) *The Age of Integral Civilization*, 1988,

(m) *New World Order: The Post-Ideological World in the 21st Century*, 1992,

(n) *Democracy and New International Order*, 1993,

(o) *The New World Order and the Role of the UN*, 1994,

(p) *World Citizenship*, 1995.

The Graduate Institute of Peace Studies
Kyung Hee University
Jinjob-up, Namyangju-gun, Kyonggi-do 473-860, Korea

Telephone: 82-346-528-7001/20
Fax: 82-346-528-7630
E-mail: iips@gip.Kyunghee.ac.kr
Senior Staff: Rector: Jae-Shik Sohn, Professors: Pyo-Wook Han, Hahn-Been Lee, In-Won Choue, Pedro B. Bernaldez
Date of Establishment: 1984

Purpose: The Graduate Institute of Peace Studies (GIP) was established in 1984 to play an active role in the creation of a more integrated and harmonious human society. The Institute strives to train tomorrow's national and international leaders as able and effective proponents of the cause of peace and mutual understanding.

Although the modern world faces a daunting combination of old and new dilemmas, mankind has never known a more auspicious time to advance the cause of peace, given to recent historical events and technological advancements. In this vein, the Graduate Institute of Peace has designed its curriculum to create the "integral man." Using modern technology tempered with a conscientious appreciation of the individual's responsibility to his fellow companions, GIP steers its students away from narrowly specialized fields that fail to see or take into account the presence and importance of other fields of study, and instead, encourages its students to integrate a wide range of disciplines in order to provide sophisticated three-dimensional answers to the equally sophisticated global problems of today and tomorrow. In recognition of its contribution to global peace education, the GIP was awarded the 1993 UNESCO Prize for Peace Education.

Type: Private, non-profit

Principal Activities: Research; training; documentation/information; publication

Periodicals: *Peace Forum*

Other Information: The Graduate Institute of Peace studies provides an interdisciplinary education for students pursuing post graduate study or careers in academia, politics, or technical fields. The Institute provides an integrated educational approach that enables students to successfully cope with the fluid domestic and international environment.

GIP's academic program consists of two and half years of study in English and internship experience, in which students spend two years of intensive study at the Institute's dormitory located at Kwangnung campus, and another six months as off-campus internship period.

All students admitted to GIP receive a full scholarship covering tuition, school fees, educational materials, room and board.

Courses:

(a) Peace and Security Studies,

(b) Human Welfare,

(c) Public and International Policy,

(d) North East Asian Studies.

Subjects Taught: Peaceful Coexistence, Disarmament, Conflict Resolution, Role of the International Organizations, Nonviolence, War, International Conflict, International Security

Target Group: Non-specialists, nationals and foreign students

Level of course: Regular course

Duration: Two and a half years

Admission requirements: Prospective students must either have a Bachelor's or Master's degree or be in their final year. Moreover, they must have maintained at least a B average of academic records in the final two years as well as pass selective admission procedures (written examination and interviews)

Scholarships available: Yes, contact the Office of Admission of GIP, at Kyung Hee University

Degree/Diploma: M.A. in Political Science; M.A. in Public Administration

Institute for Far Eastern Studies
Kyungnam University
28-42 Samchung-dong, Chongro-ku, Seoul 110-230, Korea

Telephone: 82-2-3700-0700

Fax: 82-2-3700-0707

E-mail: kfes@soback.kornet.nm.kr

Senior Staff: Director: Tae-Hwan Kwak, Managing Director: Suk-Ju Han, Prof.: Su-Hoon Lee, Taik-Young Hamm

Date of Establishment: 1972

Purpose: The primary goals of the Institute are the promotion of world peace and the unification of Korea. IFES attempts to realize these goals through scholarly contributions concerning Northeast Asian and international affairs research. Since its establishment, the Institute has been engaged in the following activities.

Type: Public, non-profit

Principal activities:

(a) Research projects on issues concerning North Korea, the Unification of the Korean Peninsula, and East Asian affairs,

(b) Organizing and sponsoring seminars, workshops, conferences, and lectures by Korean and foreign scholars,

(c) Publication of original and translated works in Korean and foreign languages, and

(d) Providing research and library facilities for scholars and students working in Asian and international affairs.

Periodicals:

(a) *Asian Perspective*, 2 per annum,

(b) *Korea and World Politics*, 2 per annum,

(c) *IFES Newsletter*, quarterly.

Major Publications:

(a) *The US-ROK Alliance*, 1996,

(b) *Culture Development in a New Era and in a Transforming World,* 1994,

(c) *The Changing Order in Northeast Asia and the Korean Peninsula*, 1993,

(d) *Current Issues in Korea-US Relations: Korean-American Dialogue*, 1991,

(e) *Law and Political Authority in South Korea*, 1990,

(f) *The United States and the Defense of the Pacific*, 1989,

(g) *US Defense Posture*, 1989,

(h) *Koreans in North America*, 1988,

(i) *State-Building in the Contemporary Third World*, 1988,

(j) *Alliance Under Tension*, 1988,

(k) *The Strategic Defense Initiative*, 1987,

(l) *The Foreign Relations of North Korea*, 1987.

Other Information: During its 24 years of history, IFES has strived to achieve its goals. It has also expanded the scope of its interests, adopting a more global perspective and incorporating newly developed perspectives, while retaining its original focus on East Asia.

Reflecting the new era of globalization and facilitating the greater promotion of the Institute, along with the more effective gathering and dissemination of information, exchange of scholars, and international cooperation in research projects, the institute is opening a number of branch offices, both, in Korea and abroad.

Annotation: Devoted to the promotion of world peace and Korean unification, the institute carries out research on international security

Courses: Summer Studies Program in Korea

Subjects Taught: Conflict Resolution, Peace and Development, Polemology, International Security

Target Group: Professionals

Level of the Course: Doctorate

Type of the Course: Summer course

Duration: 3 Months

Admission Requirements: Applicants must reside outside Korea, possess a Ph.D or equivalent and teaching or research experience in the social sciences

Course Fees: None

Scholarships: None

Degree/Diploma: None

Institute for Peace Studies
Korea University
5-ga Anam-dong, Sungbuk-ku, Seoul 136-701, Korea

Telephone: 82-2-3290-1644/5
Fax: 82-2-925-3906
Senior Staff: President: Jin-Young Suh
Date of Establishment: 1988
Purpose: This Institute strives to contribute to moving toward a new era of peace and harmony from old age of conflict and confrontation and to real not only independent, peaceful unification of Korea but also world peace and co-prosperity of human society
Type: Public, non-profit
Principal Activities: Research; training; conference

organization; publication; documentation; information, international academic exchanges
Periodicals: *Peace Studies*, Newsletter for peace
Other Information: Conducts interdisciplinary research and studies concerned with international relations and international security as well as education for peace focusing on North-South relations in the Korean peninsular, social conflicts and conflict resolution, international trade and economic cooperation with East Asia.

The Institute for the GCS International
Kyung Hee University
1 Hoegi-dong, Dongdaemoon-ku, Seoul 130-701, Korea

Telephone: 82-2-961-0163
Fax: 82-2-957-2836
E-mail: gcs@nms.kyunghee.ac.kr (or gcskorea@nuri.net)
Senior Staff: Director: Byung-Kon Hwang, Professor: Man-je Choue, Dae-soon Shin, Hwan-ho Lee, Young-Ae Ma
Date of Establishment: 1975
Purpose: The Institute is aimed at providing a theoretical foundation for the Movement for a Brighter Society. Its charter clarifies that we should reaffirm the dignity of humanity and contribute to the restoration of human rights, that we should realize a beautiful, affluent and rewarding society through good-will, co-operation and service, and that we should have love for our country and contribute to international peace with the whole society based on a sense of one family. The international version of the Movement is the GCS Movement (Good-will, Cooperation, and Service),

which is participated in by more than one thousand organizations of large and small size.
Type: Public, non-profit
Principal Activities: Research; training; documentation; conference organization; social movement
Periodicals: *Global Cooperation Society*
Major Publications:

(a) *The Significance of Global Cooperation Society*, 1978,

(b) *The Global Cooperation Society Movement*, 1981,

(c) *Prospects and Suggestions for Humankind of the 21st Century*, 1991,

(d) *The Theory of the Brighter Society Movement*, 1994.

The Institute of East and West Studies
Yonsei University
134 Shinchon-dong, Seodaemoon-ku, Seoul 120-749, Korea

Telephone: 82-2-361-3507
Fax: 82-2-393-9027
E-mail: iews@bubble.yonsei.ac.kr
Senior Staff: President: Myung-Soon Shin
Date of Establishment: 1972
Purpose: The goal of the Institute is to promote area and specific country studies inclusive of indigenous development as well as their cumulative impact on and linkages with Korea. To this end, the Institute places special importance on building of institutional ties with various research institutions and organizations in an effort to facilitate the dissemination of findings relevant to Korea's regional and global role in the 21st century.
Type: Non-Profit
Brief History: To pursue the various academic activities, the Institute comprises of twelve research programs. But in order to better pursue these activities and to stimulate creativity, the research programs have been restructured to form a research center.

Since the inception of the Canada Center in 1990, the Europe Center, North Korea Center, Russia Center, and Southeast Asia Center were created in 1992, followed by SLOC (Sea Lines of Communication), NEADC

(Northeast Asia Development Center) in 1994, and most recently APPCIC (Asia-Pacific Philanthropy Consortium Information Center).

Besides the eight research centers, there are eight regional studies programs as well as three functional programs. Research activities of the above-mentioned centers and programs are directed by faculty members of Yonsei University.
Periodicals:

(a) *Global Economic Review*,

(b) *East and West Studies Series* (bi-annually),

(c) *Korean Journal of Canadian Studies*.

Major Publications:

(a) From the various activities at the Institute, two periodicals and six books were published,

(b) Also, occasional paper series and other publications were published as well. The academic journal, the *Journal of East and West Studies*, is issued, in English, biannually. Also, one issue of *Dongsuh Yon'gu* (East-West Studies) published.

The Institute of International Peace Studies (IIPS)
Kyung Hee University
1, Hoegi-dong, Dongdaemoon-ku, Seoul 130-701, Korea

Telephone: 82-2-961-0201/82-346-60-7005
Fax: 82-2-966-1804
E-mail: iips@gip.Kyunghee.ac.kr
Senior Staff: Chancellor: Young-Seek Choue, Director: Jae-Shik Sohn, Professors: Jong-Chul Park, Pedro B. Bernaldez, Executive Secretary: Suk-Ho Lee, Researcher: Jong-Ok Kim, Hyun-Chul Kim
Date of Establishment: 1979
Purpose: The Institute of International Peace Studies (IIPS), under the aegis of International Association of University Presidents (IAUP) and Kyung Hee University, was founded in 1979. Facing local wars, conflicts, mutual distrust and increasing terror, humankind is replete with challenges to solve these problems in pursuing a more peaceful world in the 21st century. Then, pursing the harmonious global human societies, IIPS would do to:

(a) Establish Peace Studies as a science through the conduct of scholarly research involving systematic interdisciplinary and rational analyses,

(b) Strengthen research activities on peace by collaborating with other institutes for the resolution of local and global conflicts based on the humanistic goals of mankind,

(c) Promote peace education and peace movement for ensuring a more peaceful world in the future.

Type: Non-profit

Background of Foundation: The Members of International Association of University Presidents, assembled in Bangkok from June 7 through 10, 1979, in its biennial meeting, unanimously resolved to inaugurate an IAUP Peace Institute. Kyung Hee University, designated as the location of the institute by the members of IAUP, established the Institute on December 29th of 1979. The Resolution for organizing the Institute was adopted by IAUP as follows: "As part of our efforts for world peace through education specified in the Charter, we, the members of Executive Committee, holding its 1979 meeting in Bangkok from June 7 through 10, have unanimously resolved:

(a) To recognize an Institute for Peace Studies to be established at Kyung Hee University as an affiliated research institute on world peace in the spirit of Global Familism,

(b) To request Kyung Hee University to bear the major financial burden until it becomes financially independent and ask all other member Institutes to support the Institute with all possible means,

(c) To make a request to the Institute to distribute its publications, if possible, to the IAUP member Institutes and submit its triennial report to the Executive Committee."

To accomplish the purposes, the IIPS designs the following programs:

For the promotion of peaceful world and in pursuit of better human life for all mankind, the research activities focus on the following areas:

(a) Peace-making and unification on the Korean peninsula,

(b) Security and peace-promotion on the Northern Asia and Pacific,

(c) International peace embodiment throughout the world, and

(d) Peace education and peace movement.

Principal Activities: Research; training; conference organization; publication
Periodicals: *Peace Studies* (bi-annually), Monograph Series (annually)
Major Publications:

(a) *Modern World Crisis and Peace*, 1982,

(b) *Is World Peace Realizable*, 1983,

(c) *World Peace Through United Nations*, 1984,

(d) *UN: the Past, Present and Future*, 1985,

(e) *World Encyclopedia of Peace*, 1987,

(f) *Search for the Causes of International Conflicts and Ways to Their Solutions*, 1988,

(g) *Peace beyond the East-West Conflict*, 1990,

(h) *Peace in Northeast Asia*, 1994,

(i) *Restoration of Morality and Humanity*, 1995,

(j) *Tolerance, Restoration of Morality and Humanity*, 1996,

(k) *Peace Strategies for Global Community and the Role of the UN in the 21st Century*, 1997.

Korea Institute for National Unification
CPO Box 8232 Seoul 100-682, Korea

Telephone: 82-2-234-9113
Fax: 82-2-238-3291
E-mail: reunitek@hitel.kol.co.kr
Date of Establishment: 1991
Purpose: The Korea Institute for National Unification (KINU) is a Non-profit making organization devoted to studies on issues related to the unification of the Korean peninsula and to supporting the formulation of unification policy options for the Government of the Republic of Korea.
Type: Non-profit
Brief History: Since its inaugural year 1991, the Institute has focused mainly on recruiting strongly motivated and devoted researchers. The Institute currently has 61 full-time researchers, including 45 PhDs in diverse fields. They are engaged in a variety of research projects and activities, including policy round-tables.
Principal Activities:

(a) Examines current, medium-term and long-term issues of unification policy and create an analytical framework for related studies,

(b) Formulates integrated policy options and programs directly relevant to the needs of the nation in the post-unification period as well as in the process of unification,

(c) Provides public forum for the broader discussion of issues critical to the ROK government's unification policy planning process,

(d) Publishes and widely disseminate position papers, policy recommendation, and monograph or book-length studies,

(e) Provides various consulting services for the government and the private sector on North-South Korean relations including economic exchange and cooperation.

Periodicals:

(a) *Korean Journal of National Unification* (English),

(b) *The Korean Journal of Unification Studies* (Korean).

Major Publications:

(a) *A Study on Power Elite of the Kim Jong-il Regime,*

(b) *Ideas for the Establishment of Peace System on the Korean Peninsula,*

(c) *A Study on Bilateral Cooperation in Nuclear Energy between the Two Koreas and Multilateral Cooperation among Different Countries of Northeast Asia.*

Peace Research Institute
Kyungpook National University
1370 Sankyuk-dong, Puk-ku, Taegu 702-701, Korea

Telephone: 82-53-950-6626
Fax: 82-53-950-6887
E-mail: www.@www.kyungpook.ac.kr
Senior Staff: Director: Jae-Ho Eom, Professor: Ji-Han Kang
Date of Establishment: 1974
Purpose and Brief History: This Institute was established on November 1, 1974. The purpose of the Institute is to conduct academic research and surveys on world peace and, particularly as a gradual and primary step toward world peace, on the establishment of peace and the peaceful reunification of Korea.
Type: Public, non-profit
Principal Activities:

(a) Collects research data on status within and outside Korea, particularly those on peace and unification,

(b) Publishes collected papers and other materials on peace and unification,

(c) Sponsors academic symposia, seminars, and other lectures on peace and unification,

(d) Provides research funds and invite Korean and foreign scholars and officials,

(e) Answers the inquiries of the government and other organizations on peace and unification,

(f) Provides co-operation and exchanges valuable data

with other Korean and foreign research organization,

(g) Serves the community in accordance with the Institute objectives, educate and enlighten citizens on national security and the maintenance of peace,

(h) Performs other meaningful academic activities in accordance with the objectives of the Institute in mind.

Periodicals: *Peace Studies*

The World Peace Association—Seoul
The World Peace House, Suite 401 Seokyodong
KPO Box 196 Mapo Seoul 476-530, Korea

Telephone: 82-2-323-5544
Fax: 82-2-323-6464
Senior Staff: President Prof.: Byung-Kyu Kang, Prof.: Kyu-Hen Kim, Ynas-Dal Sun
Date of Establishment: 1960
Principal Activities: Research; training; publication
Current Peace Research: The Nuclear quagmire in the Korean peninsula, Multilateral security arrangement in the Asia-Pacific area
Periodicals: *New State Affairs Studies* (bi-monthly)

Major Publications: *The Denuclearization of the Korean peninsula and its Impact on Northeast Asia security*
Other Information: The Association carries out world peace activities and studies for disarmament, reduction of nuclear weapons and safety control of atomic energy. It is concerned with victims of violence and mistreatment, a world movement for peaceful unification of the Korean peninsula, and environmental protection.

Netherlands

Institute for International Studies
Leiden University
Wassenaarseweg 52 2333 AU Leiden, Netherlands

Telephone: 31-71-5273411
Fax: 31-71-5273619
E-mail: Everts@Rulfsw.Leichenuniv.nl
Senior Staff: Director: Philip Everts, Lecturer: Tom Draisma
Date of Establishment: 1970
Purpose: The Institute strives to promote cooperation in research and teaching on contemporary international problems among the relevant university departments.
Type: Public, national, non-profit
Brief History: Over the years the institute has developed a forum on:

(a) Problems of Foreign Policy, especially the Netherlands,

(b) European Security,

(c) Public Opinion on International Affairs,

(d) Arms Trade and Arms Production.

Principal Activities:

(a) Courses at undergraduate level,

(b) Collective research projects,

(c) Publications of journal on peace studies.

Periodicals: *Transaktie* (quarterly)

Major Publications:

(a) *Between Order and Chaos. The Organization of Security in the New Europe,*

(b) *Dilemmas in the Foreign Policy of the Netherlands.*

International Fellowship of Reconciliation
Spoorstraat 38, 1815 BK Alkmaar, Netherlands

Telephone: 31-72-512-3014
Fax: 31-72-515-1102

E-mail: office@ifor.ccmail.compuserve.com
Web Site: www.gn.apc.org/ifor/

Senior Staff: Program co-ordinator, David Grant
Date of Establishment: 1919
Purpose: The organization deals with non-violence education and training; women peacemakers; youth empowerment and children rights; disarmament and peace teams; and interreligious cooperation.
Type: Public, non-profit.
Principal Activities: Research; training; documentation/information; conference-organisation; publication and networking.
Periodicals: *Reconciliation International* (Journals); bulletins; monographs; progress reports and conference proceedings.

Major Publications:

(a) *Non-violence Training in Africa* (guest-edited by fellowship of Reconciliation Zimbabwe),

(b) *Cross the lines/Francher les liqnes*, newsletter of the IFOR Women's Peacemakers Program,

(c) *Patterns in Reconciliation the third way - reclaiming jesus' nonviolent alternative*,

(d) *Reconciliation International.*

Peace Palace Library
Carnegiepiein 2 NL-2517 KJ The Hague

Telephone: 31-070-3024242
Fax: 31-070-3024166
E-mail: ingrid.kost@ ntfw.ppl.nl
Senior Staff: Deputy Director Librarian: Ingrid, Kost
Date of Establishment: 1913
Purpose: Library to the International Court of Justice
Type: International, non-profit
Brief History: The Peace Palace Library contains important and unique materials about Peace Movement, covering the period from 1899 to 1940, accumulated by Dr. J. C. Ter Meullen, Head Librarian of the Peace

Palace Library from 1924-1952.
Principal Activities: Collection of materials about Peace Movement.
Periodicals:

(a) Acquisitions list (6 monthly),

(b) Bibliography (yearly) for the Hague,

(c) *Academy of International Law.*

Peace Research Centre
Th Van Aquinostraat 1, PO Box 9108 6500 Kk Nijmegen, Netherlands

Telephone: 31-24-3615687
Fax: 31-24-3611839
E-mail: b.bomert@bw.kun.nl
Senior Staff: Head: Bert Bomert, Researcher: Ben Schennink, Leon Wecke
Date of Establishment: 1967
Purpose: The centre deals with:

(a) Scientific research on problems of war and peace,

(b) Teaching of undergraduate courses,

(c) Collection of documents and information on problems concerning war and peace.

Type: Public, national, non-profit
Principal Activities: The centre is a part of the University of Nijmegen, which is engaged with research activities, and undergraduate programs.

Periodicals:

(a) *Cahiers*—Quarterly Monographs, mainly in Dutch,

(b) *Jeerboek Vrede en Veiligheid*—yearbook on peace and security.

Major Publications:

(a) *East-West Relations,*

(b) *European Security,*

(c) *Public Opinion/Enemy Images,*

(d) *Conflict Prevention,*

(e) *UN Interventions.*

Transnational Institute (TNI)
Paulus Potterstraat 20, 1071 DA, Amsterdam, Netherlands

Telephone: 31-020-6626608
Fax: 31-020-6757176
E-mail: tni@worldcom.nl
Senior Staff: Research Director: Mariano Aguirre, Fellows: Dan Smith, Jochen Hippler, Fred Halliday
Date of Establishment: 1973
Purpose: The Institute strives to provide supervision and to promote scientific research in the field of culture, politics and social sciences, and to create and promote international co-operation in the study of and research into solutions for world problems such as: pollution, militarism, social injustice and racism on the one hand and development on the other hand, and furthermore, to perform any operations that are directly or indirectly concerned with international peace issues.
Type: International, public, non-profit
Brief History: Established in 1973 as the Transnational Institute of the Institute for Policy Studies, Washington, TNI became an independent entity in 1995. Coordinated from Amsterdam, TNI is comprised of 22 fellows and 8 advisors, all prominent intellectuals drawn from the USA, Europe (East and West), Asia, Latin America and Africa. In the 1970s, TNI was best known for its work on world hunger and the promotion of a new international economic order. In the 1980s, TNI took up issues to do with nuclear armament, militarism and debt. In the 1990s, the focus is on economic globalization, modern armed conflicts and democratization.
Principal Activities: Research project; book and policy paper publication; seminars; conferences.
Periodicals: *TNIdeas*

Books are published by Pluto Press, London as well as by Intermon Spain and Konkret Verlag, Germany. Most are published in a number of languages.

Major Publications:

(a) *Peace and Security*,

(b) *Democratization*,

(c) *Global Economy*.

New Zealand

Centre for Peace Studies
University of Auckland
Private Bag 92019 Auckland, New Zealand

Telephone: 64-9-373-7599/8364/8575
Fax: 64-9-373-7445
E-mail: r.white@auckland.ac.nz
Senior Staff: Director: Robert White, Deputy Director: John Gribben
Date of Establishment: 1988
Purpose: The center seeks to develop research and teaching activities in the broad area of peace studies; to make information available widely within and outside New Zealand in peace related areas; to develop contacts with similar organizations in our region
Type: Public, non-profit
Principal Activities: The Center has established two series of publications covering its activities; Working Papers covering research and occasional papers, seminars and workshops held by the Center.
Major Publications:

(a) White, R. E., *The Neither Confirm Nor Deny Policy: Obstructive and Obsolete*, 1990,

(b) White, R. E., *Nuclear Free New Zealand: 1984- New Zealand Becomes Nuclear Free*, 1997,

(c) Gribben, J. (ed.), *Arms and Security in the Asia Pacific Region*, 1997.

The Foundation for Peace Studies
29 Princes St, PO Box 4110, Auckland 1, New Zealand

Telephone: 64-9-373-2379
Fax: 64-9-379-3017
E-mail: peace@fps.ak.planet.co.nz
Senior Staff: National Coordinator and Trainer for Cool Schools: Yvonne Duncan, Resource Person: Betty Cole
Date of Establishment: 1975
Purpose: The Foundation exists

(a) To create harmonious relationships among all people at all levels,

(b) To promote non-violent forms of conflict resolution,

(c) To create a more peaceful world through education and research,

(d) To foster understanding and tolerance through increasing awareness and communication,

(e) To create peace through action in all areas, both individual and collective.

Brief History: The Peace Foundation grew out of concern for growing violence in the world. Advice and patronage over the years has been given by Dr. Norman Alcock, U. Thant, Sir Guy Powles, Archbishop Paul Reeves, and many others. In 1975 the Peace Foundation initiated what is now known as the Clinton Roper Peace Lectures. Lecturers have included Prof. Johan Galtung, Dr. Helen Caldicott, Marilyn Waring and Prof. Lloyd Geering. In 1984, the Peace Foundation began the Media Peace Awards, and from 1991 has run the highly successful Cool Schools Peer Mediation Program.

Principal Activities:

(a) Operation of the largest Peace Education Library and Resource Centre in New Zealand,

(b) Training of CS Peer Mediation Program to Primary and Secondary Schools, and Parents groups,

(c) Holding of annual Clinton Roper Peace Lecture Series and Media Peace Awards,

(d) Lobbying government and business groups,

(e) Arranging talks, interviews and debates in schools, universities and the community,

(f) Publishing books such as *A Volcano in My Tummy, Learning Peaceful Relationships* and an Anger Rules poster,

(g) Promoting Peace Studies in schools, tertiary institutes and in the general community.

Periodicals:

(a) *Newsletter*,

(b) *Peace Lectures*—annually.

Major Publications:

(a) *Alternatives to ANZUS* Vol I and II,

(b) *Waging Peace Vol I and II—Surveying Public Attitudes to Peace and Security Issues*,

(c) *Partnership and Peace—Essays on Biculturalism*,

(d) *Learning Peaceful Relationships*,

(e) *Extending Peaceful Relationships*,

(f) *A Volcano in My Tummy—Helping Children to Handle Anger*,

(g) *Cool Schools Peer Mediation Program.*

Other Information: Resource Catalogue and Mail Order Service available internationally.

Operation Peace Through Unity
4 Allison Street, Wanganui, New Zealand

Telephone: 64-6-345-5714
Fax: 64-6-345-5714
E-mail: optu@mailcity.com
Senior Staff: President: Anthony Brooke, CEO: Gita Brooke
Date of Establishment: 1975
Purpose: To educate and network information with a view to raising public awareness on world affairs and the need for individual and corporate responsibility to unite beyond all differences in the work of establishing right human relations in a healthy environment in accordance with the principles outlined in the preamble of the UN Charter.
Type: International, public, and non-profit
Brief History: A charitable trust founded in Sweden, now based in New Zealand. Accredited NGO in association with the United Nation department of public information. Affiliated member of UNA of New Zealand National Council. Patron New Zealand guild of Artist Trust (UNESCO); Patron Rainbow Children Theatre. Co-convenor of New Zealand forum for United Nation renewal, and an active member of CAMDUN.

Principal Activities: Introduced the world Disarmament Campaign to Australia, New Zealand, the Philippines, Hong Kong, India and other places. Antarctica - A World Peace Park project; world travel (10 Years) for peace (using various educational tools and information and statistics). Promoted "Peacechild" musical in New Zealand, and initiated the communities locally.

The institute is actively seeking to create public interest in and debate on the possibility of establishing a United Nations second (peoples) Assembly.

Periodicals: *Many To Many*, quarterly publication (since 1982), presently to 47 countries; Numerous reports (e.g. Rainforest of Sarawak, United Nations Reform etc); occasional pamphlets on special issues.

Norway

Institute for Alternative Development Research
PO Box 870 Sentrum, 0104 Oslo, Norway

Telephone: 47-22-37-73-63
Fax: 47-22-37-73-63
Senior Staff: Director: Amalendu Guha, Researchers: Kullar Harbinger Singh, Yassin Hassan Samatar.
Date of Establishment: 1979
Purpose: The Institute works to effect research and teaching on Alternative Development Models and Theories, Human Rights and Human Development, Immigration and Emigration, Conflict and Peace/ Armament and Disarmament, Natural/ Human/ Economic Ecology, International Relations and Policy Research, North-South/ South-South/ East-West Studies, Women and Youth Studies, Global Social Indicators, Studies on European Economic Community/Union, Norway and the World, etc.
Type: International, private, non-profit
Brief History: The Institute was established on October 29, 1979, by a group of like-minded social scientists and researchers of international origin and with inter and multi-disciplinary outlooks, with a view to affecting both the theoretical and applied social science research on the basis of non-traditional, or, in other words methodology.
Principal Activities: Research
Periodicals: Social and Development Alternative (stopped due to financial difficulties).

Major Publications:

(a) *Development Alternative* 1985,

(b) *LDC Immigrants in Nordic Countries* 1983,

(c) *Conflict and Peace: Theory and Practice* 1985,

(d) *Immigrant Women and Children in Industrial Europe* 1985,

(e) *Fourth World* 1985,

(f) *Immigrant Women in Norway* 1983,

(g) *Global Mal-development* 1985,

(h) *Gandhian Non-Violence* 1996,

(i) *Ecology of Human and Economic Development* 1996,

(j) *Racism in Northern Europe* 1997,

(k) *Indian* (in Germany) 1976,

(l) *Crisis of Development* 1997.

Other Information: Independent and neutral research and teaching activities without any obligation to the state structure and favor.

Institute for Fredsforskning [International Peace Research Institute] (PRIO)
Fuglehauggata 11 N-0260 Oslo 2, Norway

Telephone: 47-22-54-7700
Fax: 47-22-54-7701
E-mail: info@prio.no
Web Site: http://www.prio.no/
Senior Staff: Director: Dan Smith, Project Leader: Graham Dyson
Date of Establishment: 1959
Purpose: The International Peace Research Institute,

Oslo (PRIO) is an international research institute whose purpose is to engage in scholarly research, concerning the conditions necessary for peaceful relations between nations, groups, and individuals. In addition to its main purpose, the Institute seeks to stimulate research cooperation nationally and internationally, direct training and teaching, holds conferences and seminars, and disseminates information based on research carried out by the Institute and in other institutions.

Type: Public, non-profit

Brief History: PRIO is an independent institution with a high degree of autonomy. It was established in 1959 as a section of the Institute for Social Research, a private institution with public financial support. In 1966 PRIO became an autonomous institute. Changes of the Institute statutes in 1970 made the staff meeting its (highest) internal ruling body. The Board has to approve the budget and elections of institute director and deputy institute director. All PRIO staff members have the right to participate in the staff meetings. The research director and the institute director serve for a period of one year, on a rotation basis. Between staff meetings, the research committee and the administrative committee decide on research and administrative matters respectively. The staff meeting also elects the editorial committees of the institute's two quarterly journals.

Principal Activities: PRIO is an interdisciplinary research institute with a high degree of self-management. Many of the staff members come from outside Norway, and the main working language is English. The Institute tries to develop projects that contribute to both theoretical and applied knowledge. Most projects are formulated by the Institute's own staff, but some contract work is also undertaken. the Institute encourages pluralism, openness, and public debate, within a research tradition that is very much aware of social injustice, of conflicts and their resolution, and of humankind's capacity for self-destruction.

Current Peace Research:

(a) International conflicts and governance,

(b) South Asian internal and ethnic conflicts,

(c) Economics of military spending,

(d) Conscientious objection in Norway,

(e) Enemy-images in the Norweigian media,

(f) Regional integration and environmental security in West Africa,

(g) Conversion and the environment,

(h) South Africa's ethnic divisions and alternative approaches,

(i) Threat perception and ethnocentric projections,

(j) The wages of peace,

(k) The peace divided in Norway,

(l) Walls, Geopolitical shifts to modern Europe,

(m) Environment degradation and armed conflict,

(n) Regional integration and environmental security in West Africa.

Periodicals:

(a) *Journal of Peace Research,*

(b) *Security Dialogue.*

Major Publications:

(a) Forland, T. E., *Economic Warfare and Strategic Goods: A Conceptual Framework for Analyzing,* 1991,

(b) Forland, T. E., *Selling Firearms to the Indians: Eisenhower's Export Control Policy 1953-54,* 1991,

(c) Gledistch, N. P., Cappelen, A., Bjerkholt, O., *Guns, Butter and Growth: The Case of Norway,* 1991

(d) Jayaweera N., *Sri Lanka: Towards a Multi-ethnic Democracy?,* 1991

(e) Lodgaard, S., *Environmental Security: World Order and Environmental Conflict Resolution,* 1991,

(f) Logarrd, S., *Vertical and Horizontal Proliferation in the Middle East/Persian Gulf,* 1991,

(g) Lodgaard, S., *Confidence-building Measures: A Critical Appraisal,* 1991,

(h) Hetthe, B. et al., *Northern Europe and the Near Future,* 1991,

(i) Ottosen, R., *The Gulf War with the Media as Hostage,* 1991,

(j) Rupesinghe, K, Rubio, G. (eds.), *The Culture of Violence. Forms of Violence and its Transformation,* 1992,

(k) Ottosen, R., *Enemy Images in Foreign New Coverage. A Survey on Changes in Enemy in Three Norwegian Dalies,* 1993

(l) Tishkov, V., *Ethnicity, Nationalism and Conflict in and after the Soviet Union,* 1997,

(m) Markakis, J., *Resources of Conflict in the Horn of Africa*, 1997,

(n) Smith, D., *He State of War and Peace Atlas*, 1997,

(o) Simonsen, S. G., *Conflict in the OSCE Area*, 1997.

Courses: Peace Research Course, International Summer School
Subjects Taught: Peace research; disarmament; conflict resolution; nonviolence; peace and development; international conflict; international security
Principal Instructors: Mr T. Hoivik
Target Group: Foreign students
Level of Course: Graduate
Type of Course: Summer course
Duration: Six weeks
Working Language: English
Admission Requirements: Completed first degree
Scholarships Available: Yes
Degree/Diploma: 6 graduates credits given

The Philippines

Institute of Peace and Security
Bicol University
PNP Region V. Camp Ola, Legazpi City 4501, The Philippines

Telephone: 63-52-481-4001
Fax: 63-52-481-4000
Senior Staff: President: Emiliano Aberin, Director: Emiliano A. Aberin, Vice President for Academic Affairs: Nella S. Ciocson.
Date of Establishment: 1995
Purpose: Promotion of peace and security through teaching and research on some of the most current issues and problems of contemporary global society; peace processes and activities, violence, peace, human rights, armed conflict and economic and political tensions.
Principal Activities:

(a) Offers Peace and Security Studies Program in the undergraduate and graduate levels,

(b) Designs, revises and upgrades curriculum on peace education in the elementary, secondary and tertiary levels,

(c) Prepares, devices design, and reproduces instructional materials for teaching peace and security studies,

(d) Works coordinatively with government agencies, PVCs and NGOs in the conduct of peace processes and initiatives.

Southern Philippines Center for Peace Studies (SPCPS)
Mindanao State University
Marawi City, The Philippines

Senior Staff: Director: C. A. Umpa, N. T. Madale
Date of Establishment: 1979
Type: Public; non-profit
Principal Activities: Research; training; documentation/information; conference-organization; publication; radio and TV programmes
Geographical Coverage: Southern Philippines
Type of Publication: Bulletin; conference proceedings
Periodicals: *Bulletin of Peace and Development*, 4 p.a.
Annotation: Its objective is to promote education for peace and conflict resolution through peace research, education and action in southern Philippines.
Courses: Introduction to Peace Studies; Reading in Peace Studies
Subjects Taught: Peace research; peaceful coexistence; conflict resolution; nonviolence; peace and development; improvement of Muslim-Christian relations
Target Group: Non-specialists; nationals; social science faculty and students
Level of the Course: Masters; college undergraduate
Type of Course: Regular course
Duration: One semester, three hours/week (for 3 units credit)
Working Languages: English
Admission Requirements: Major in Social Sciences
Course Fees: Yes
Scholarships Available: None
Degree/Diploma: None

Poland

Instytut Stosunkow Miedzynarodowych (ISM) [Institute of International Relations]
Uniwersytet Warszawski
Ul. Krakowskie Przedmieście 3, 00-047 Warsaw, Poland

Telephone: 48-26-21-09
Senior Staff: Director: J. Kukułka
Date of Establishment: 1976
Type: Public
Principal Activities: Conference-organization
Current Peace Research: Peace research, theoretical and empirical issues
Types of publication: Journal; monograph
Periodicals: *Stosunki Międzynarodowe* (International Relations), 2 p.a.

Major Publications:

(a) Kukułka, J. (ed.), *Peace in theory and practice of international relations*, 1990 (in Polish).

Annotation: Carries out research through its three divisions: the International Relations Theory Division, the International Relations History Division and the International Organizations Division. Fields of interest cover the whole scope of international relations including peace issues.

The Polish Peace Research Council
ul. Rajcow 10, 00-220 Warsaw, Poland

Telephone: 48-31-16-85
Fax: 48-635-7840
Senior Staff: Scientific Secretary: I. Wyciechowska, Chairman: H. Kubiak
Date of Establishment: 1987
Parent Organization: International Peace Research Association (IPRA)
Principal Activities: Research; documentation/ information; publication

Current Peace Research: Reason of state and nationalism
Major Publications:

(a) Frontier Regions: Interdependence and Cooperation, 1993 (in Polish).

Annotation: Coordinates research on the problems of peace, weapons, disarmament, conflicts, and seeks to formulate peace proposals.

Polski Instytut Spraw Miedzynarodowych [Polish Institute of International Affairs] (PIIA)
Ul. Warecka la, PO Box 1000, 00-950 Warsaw, Poland

Telephone: 22-26-30-21
Fax: 22-27-47-38
Senior Staff: Director: A. Kaminski, Prof.: W. Góralski
Date of Establishment: 1947
Type: Public; non-profit
Principal Activities: Research; training; documentation/ information; conference-organization; publication

Current Peace Research:

(a) Possibilities of disarmament in Central Europe,

(b) Role of the CSCE process in East-West relations,

(c) Shaping of new structures of European security in the nineties,

(d) International peaceful order and Polish foreign policy,

(e) Problem of German unity and security of Poland and Europe,

(f) The double role of conversion: from planned economy to market economy and from military to civil use: the Polish experience,

(g) Relationship between the economy and defence of Poland in new geopolitical conditions.

Periodicals:

(a) *The PISM Occasional Papers,*

(b) *Sprawy Międzynarodowe*, 12 p.a.,

(c) Zbiór Documentów/Recueil des Documents, 4 p.a.,

(d) Zeszyty Amerykanistyczne,

(e) Zeszyty Niemocoznawcze.

Major Publications:

(a) Michałowski, S., *Economic Security in East-West Relations*, 1990 (in Polish),

(b) Multan, W., *The Principle of Rational Sufficiency of Military Potential Defensive*, 1989 (in Polish),

(c) Perczyński, M., *Global Problems of Economic Security*, 1990 (in Polish),

(d) Kostecki, W., *Collapse of the Soviet Union: International Effects,*

(e) Kostecki, W., *Recent Developments in What used to be the Soviet Union: What does it Mean for Peace?,*

(f) Zukrowska, K., *Determinants of Systematic Changes*, 1990 (in Polish),

(g) Zukrowska, K., *The Double Role of Conversion: From Planned to Market and from Military to Civil Use*, 1992,

(h) Zukrowska, K., *Different Strategies of Systematic Changes in East Central Europe*, 1993.

Annotation: Carries out research on international relations, international law, international politics, peace research, weapons and disarmament, international security, European integration, cooperation and security.

Courses: Séminaire de Doctorat

Subjects Taught: Peaceful coexistence; disarmament; conflict resolution; arms control; role of the international organizations; nonviolence; peace and development; international conflict; international security

Principal Instructors: Prof. W. Multan, Prof. W. Góralski, Prof. J. Prokopczuk, Prof. Dr. L. Pastusiak, Prof. Dr. M. Tomala, Prof. F. Gołembski (Assistant Professor)

Target Group: Professionals; nationals

Level of the Course: Doctorate

Duration: Three years

Working Languages: Polish

Admission Requirements: None

Course Fees: None

Scholarships Available: None

Degree/Diploma: Doctorate in Political Science; Habilitation in Political Science

Russia

Center for Peace Research and Conflict Resolution
2, Vlianov St. Nizhniy Novgorod 603005, Russia

Telephone: 831-2-39-01-88/831-2-39-02-24
Fax: 831-2-65-85-92
E-mail: history@history.nnov.ru
Senior Staff: President: Oleg Kolobov, Director: Alexander Kornilov, Scientific Secretary: Olga Khokhlysheva.
Date of Establishment: 1993
Purpose: The center aims to do research on peace and conflict resolution, to provide the public with information on the importance of peace issues and peace culture, and to educate students on peace studies and problems.
Type: Public, non-profit
Brief History: The Center was established by the special order of the Rector of the Nizhniy Novgorod State University to do peace research and to study conflicts in the former Soviet Union and abroad. The Center has more than 100 foreign addresses at correspondence and held a few international conferences on peace research, established *Nizhniy Novgorod Journal of International Studies*, and launched an experimental training program.
Principal Activities: Research; publication; conference-organization.

Periodicals:

(a) *Nizhniy Norgorod Journals of International Studies,*

(b) *Angelos, Herald of Peace.* Bulletin of the Center.

Major Publications:

(a) Kolobov, O. A., Kornilov, A. A. et al., *Problems of War and Peace in the XX Century*, Nizhniy Novgorod Series of documents on international relations history, 1996-1997,

(b) Khokhlysheva, O., *Real World and Illusion of Peacemaking*, 1996,

(c) *Sword and Plough of David Ben-Gurion*, 1996,

(d) Kolobov, O. et al., *The West: New Dimensions of National and International Security*, 1997.

Institut Evropi, Rossiiskaia Akademiia nauk
[Institute of Europe, Russian Academy of Sciences]
Mohovaya St. 8-3, Moscow 103 873, Russia

Telephone: 7-095-203-7343
Fax: 7-095-200-4298
Senior Staff: Director: V. V. Zhurkin, Deputy Director & Specialist: S. A. Karaganov, Specialist: D. Danilov, N. A. Kovalsky, P. T. Podlesny, K. E. Sorokin, V. V. Zhurkin
Date of Establishment: 1988
Principal Activities: Research; publication
Current Peace Research: Issues of all-European security, cooperation, the limitation, and reduction of armaments in Europe
Periodicals: *Europe*, 12 p.a.

Major Publications:

(a) Baev. P., Karaganov, S., Shein, V., Zhurkin, V., *Tactical Nuclear Weapons in Europe*, 1990,

(b) Zhurkin, V., *Gross Baustelle Europe*, 1991,

(d) Karaganov, S. (ed.), *Security in Future Europe*, 1993,

(d) Kovalsky, N., Nosenko, T., Podlesny, P., *Russia in the Black Sea Region*, 1993,

(e) Karaganov, S., Podlesny, P., et al., *New Geopolitical Situation in Europe and Russian Security Interests*, 1994,

(f) Sorokin, K., *Russia's Security in a Rapidly Changing World*, 1994.

Annotation: Concerned with the European security system, nuclear weapons, arms control, disarmament, geopolitics and environmental security issues.

Institut Mira, Rossiiskaia Akademiia Nauk [Institute Mira, Russian Academy of Sciences]
Ulitsa Profsoiuznaia, 23, 117418 Moscow, Russia

Telephone: 7-095-128-93-89
Fax: 7-095-310-70-27
Cable: Moscow B-418, prim
Senior Staff: Director: A. K. Kislov
Date of Establishment: 1989
Principal Activities: Research; documentation/ information, conference-organization, publication, exhibitions

Periodicals: *Ways Towards Security* (in Russian and English)
Annotation: The main goals of the Institute include scientific research on questions pertaining to peace, disarmament, conversion, international security, peace movements and regional conflict resolution.

Institut Mirovoi Economiki I Mejdunarodnykh Otnoshenii, Rossiiskaia Akademiia Nauk
[Institute of World Economy and International Relations, Russian Academy of Sciences]
Profsoyuznaya 23, 117859 Moscow, Russia

Telephone: 7-095-120-52-36
Telex: 7-095-411687
Senior Staff: Director: V. A. Martynov, Prof.: E. V. Bougrov, Researcher: O. N. Bykov
Date of Establishment: 1956
Type: Public; non-profit
Principal Activities: Research; training; documentation/information; conference-organization; publication
Current Peace Research:

(a) Strategic stability,

(b) Conventional forces reduction and stability in Europe,

(c) Naval arms control,

(d) Non-proliferation of nuclear weapons.

Periodicals:

(a) *Disarmament and Security*, IMEMO Yearbook, 1 p.a.,

(b) *International Yearbook of Politics and Economics*, 1 p.a.,

(c) *World Economy and International Relations*, 12 p.a..

Annotation: Carries out research on disarmament, the limitation of strategic weapons, space arms control, foreign policy and international relations.

Institut Nauchnoi Informatsii Po Obschestvennym Naukam, Rossiiskaia Akademiia Nauk
[Institute of Scientific Information in the Social Sciences, Russian Academy of Sciences]
Ulitsa Krasikova, 28/21, 117418 Moscow, Russia

Telephone: 7-095-128-88-81
Fax: 7-095-420-22-61
Senior Staff: Director: V. A. Vinogradov
Date of Establishment: 1969
Principal Activities: Research; documentation/ information; publication
Current Peace Research:

(a) Conflict resolution,

(b) Non-violence,

(c) Peace coexistence,

(d) Disarmament.

Bulletins: Information Bulletin
Major Publications:

(a) *Social Sciences in the USSR.* Annotated bibliography for 1987-1990.

Annotation: Research deals with problems of creating comprehensive systems of international security, disarmament and the avoidance of regional conflict, the solution of global problems, Russian-American relations, the concept of a common European home, problems of security, the development of cooperation in the Asian- Pacific region and relations of ethnic groups in the Russian Federation.

Institute of Europe
Russian Academy of Sciences
Mohovaja Street, 113 Moscow, Russia

Telephone: 7-095-203-7343/7-095-201-6708
Fax: 7-095-200-4298
E-mail: 2469.g23@g23.relcom.ru
Senior Staff: Director: Vitaly Zhurkin, Deputy Director: Vladimir Shenaev, Sergi Karaganov, Nikolai Shmelev, Eugeni Mironenkov
Date of Establishment: 1988
Purpose: To promote scientific analysis of dramatic changes in Europe, of their prospects and of attempts to define a new security system in Europe and the European cooperation in economic, political and humanitarian spheres.
Type: International
Brief History: During the period 1988-98, the institute became one of the well known scientific organizations in Russia and abroad. The Institute's activities include not only fundamental scientific elaboration for the higher power bodies of the Russian Federation: the Presidential, Parliamentary, Government, Foreign Ministry, etc. The Institute's staff includes many well known scientists, academicians, corresponding members, doctors of science, Ph.D.
Principal Activities: The Institute undertakes interdisciplinary studies of political, economic, military-political, social and other issues related to Europe. Forecasting is one of the top priorities of research. The Institute constantly strives to crown the basis research with practical conclusions and recommendations.
Periodicals: *Reports on Europe*, monthly.
Major Publications:

(a) *Security in Future Europe,*

(b) *Russia and Europe: Experience of Economic Transformations,*

(c) *The Specifics of the Economic Development in Western Europe,*

(d) *The Scientific and Technical Integration of Western Europe,*

(e) *Building a Greater Europe,*

(f) *Tactical Nuclear Weapons in Europe,*

(g) *The European Communities in 1990s,*

(h) *The EC-East European Economic Relations,*

(i) *The Christian Roots of the European Idea,*

(j) *Russia: the Mediterranean and Black Sea Region.*

Institute of Universal History
32a Leninskii Prospect, Moscow 117334, Russia

Telephone: 7-95-938-10-09

Fax: 7-95-938-22-88

E-mail: dima@Lgh1.msk.su

Senior Staff: Vice-Director: Victoria I. Ukolova, Leading Researcher: Nataliya I.Yegorova, Tattana A. Tavlova,

Date of Establishment: 1968

Purpose: The Institute works on study of world history, study of philosophy and methodology of history, historiography; interdisciplinary studies, research, publications, co-ordination and spreading of historical knowledge.

Type: Public, national, non-profit

Brief History: The Institute of History of the Academy of Sciences of the USSR was created in 1936. In 1968, the Institute of History was divided into Institute of Universal History and Institute of history of Russia. At present Institute of Universal History is one of the leading institutions of Russian Academy of Sciences.

Principal Activities: Conducts studies on: world historical process, philosophy and methodology of history, a human being in history, comparative theory and history of civilizations, and history of international conflicts.

Periodicals:

(a) *Novaya i noveishaya istoria* (New and modern history),

(b) *Odyssey, European Almanac.*

Major Publications:

(a) Chubaryan, A. C., *European Idea in History. A View from Moscow.* London, 1994,

(b) Chatfield, C., Ilukhina, R. (eds.), *Mir/Peace: An Anthology of Historic Alternatives to War.* Syracuse Univ. Press, N.Y.-Nauka Press, Moscow, 1994 (in English and in Russian),

(c) Nadzhafov, D. G. (ed.), *XXth Century: Main Problems and Tendencies of International Relations.* Materials of International Conference held in Moscow 21-23 November 1989. Moscow, 1992, Institute of Universal History Press,

(d) Filitov, A., *The German Question: from Dissent to Unity.* Moscow, Mezhdunarodnye Otnoshenia, 1993,

(e) *Long Way of Russian Pacifism. Ideals of International and Inner Peace in Russian History.* Moscow, 1997, Institute of Universal History Press,

(f) Nauka, P. H., *XXth Century. Variety, Contradictions, Integrity.* Moscow, 1996.

Singapore

Institute of Southeast Asian Studies
30 Heng Mui Keng Terrace, Pasir Panjang, Singapore 119614, Singapore

Telephone: 65-778-0955

Fax: 65-778-1735

E-mail: rajan@iseas.edu.sg

Web Site: http://www.iseas,edu.sg/iseas.html

Senior Staff: Director: Chia Siow Yue, Co-ordinator: Joseph Tan

Date of Establishment: 1968

Purpose: The institute aims to nurture a community of scholars interested in the region and to engage in research on the multi-faceted problems of stability and security, economic development and political, cultural and social change.

The objective is not only to stimulate debate within scholarly circles, but also to enhance public awareness of the region and facilitate the search for viable solutions to the varied problems confronting the region.

Brief History: The Institute of South Asian Studies (ISEAS) was established as an autonomous organization in 1968. It is a regional research center for scholars and other specialists concerned with modern Southeast Asia and its wider geostrategic and socio-economic environment.

Slovak Republic

Institute of State and Law
813 64 Bratislava, Klemensova I9, Slovak Republic

Telephone: 421-7-361833

Fax: 421-7-362325

Senior Staff: Doc., DrSc., Scientist: Jan Azud, Stefan Sebesta

Date of Establishment: 1953
Purpose: Research of legal sciences
Type: Public, national, non-profit
Brief History: The institute of State and Law had been established on the basis of the decision of the presidency of Slovak Academy of Sciences in 1953 as the Cabinet of Sciences of Law with a new name Institute of State

and Law. In this form the Institute exists in present time.
Principal Activities: Research; analyses; judgements; theory of state and law; private law; public law
Periodicals: *PRAVNY OBZOR* published 6 times per year
Major Publications: Major research materials such as; constitutional law, administrative law, social law, penal law, international law, commercial law, competition law.

Slovenia

Mirovni Institut, Ljubljana [Peace Institute, Ljubljana]
Hotimirova 19, 61000 Ljubljana, Slovenia

Telephone: 61-159-40-59
Fax: 61-159-40-59
Senior Staff: Director: J. Vlasta, Researcher: S. Gazdić, Programme Director: T. Gregor
Type: Private; non-profit
Principal Activities: Research; documentation/ information; conference-organization; publication

Current Peace Research:

(a) Sociology of the military,

(b) Political extremism and violence against foreigners and other marginals.

Type of Publication: Monograph
Major Publications:

(a) Kuzmanić, T. (eds.), *Yugoslavian War*, 1992,

(b) *A Story for Maci*, 1994.

Annotation: Fields of interest include the sociology of the military, violence and conflict resolution.

South Africa

Centre for Intergroup Studies
University of Cape Town
37 Grotto Road, Rondebosch 7700, South Africa

Cable: ALUMNI CAPETOWN
Telephone: 27-21-650-2503
Fax: 27-21-685-2142
Telex: 5-21439
E-mail: ccr@uctvax.uct.ac.za
Senior Staff: Executive Director: L. Nathan, C. Arendse, Senior Researcher: V. Botha, Senior Researcher: S. Collin, Senior Researcher: J. Honwana
Date of Establishment: 1968
Type: Public; non-profit
Principal Activities: Research; training; documentation/information; conference- organization; publication

Current Peace Research:

(a) Peace and security,

(b) Training project,

(c) Community project for peace and justice,

(d) Mediation/training team.

Periodicals: *Track Two: Constructive Approaches to*

Community and Political Conflict
Major Publications:

(a) Bathan, L., *Beyond Arms and Armed Forces: a New Approach to Security*, 1992,

(b) Nathan, L., *Towards a Conference on Security, Stability, Development and Cooperation in Africa*, 1992,

(c) Nathan, L., Phillips, M., *Cross-Currents: Security Developments in South Africa*, 1991,

(d) Smuts, D., Westcott, S., *The People shall Govern: a South African A to Z of Nonviolent Action*, 1991,

(e) Van der Merwe, H. W., Meyer, G., *Principles and Practice of Mediation and Facilitation in South Africa*, 1993.

Annotation: The Institute seeks to contribute to a just peace by promoting constructive, creative and cooperative approaches to conflict resolution and the reduction of violence.

Center for the Study of Violence and Reconcilation (CSVR)
PO Box 30778, Braamfontein 2017, Johannesburg, South Africa

Telephone: 27-11-403-5650
Fax: 27-11-339-6785
E-mail: csvr@wn.apc.org
Web Site: www.wits.ac.za/csvr
Senior Staff: President: G. Simpson, Education Coordinator: T. Vienings, Criminal Justice Policy Unit **Coordinator:** A. Dissel.
Date of Establishment: 1989
Purpose: Its aim is to research into the reduction of education on and treatment for victims of violence and related issues, provides social and political analyses of current violence and interethnic conflict.
Type: Non-profit, NGO
Principal Activities: Research; training; documentation/information; conference-organisation; publication; radio and TV programs; consulting; trauma counselling; intervention programs; educational programs and drama performance.
Major Publications: The Institute publications are categorized into, arms control, crime, correctional services, death penalty, development, election, gangs, human rights, militarization, and many others.

Spain

Centro De Investigacion Para La Paz (CIP) [The Peace Research Center]
Alcalá, 117-60 derecha, 28009 Madrid, Spain

Telephone: 91-431-0280
Fax: 91-575-9550
Senior Staff: President: A. Martinez Gonzáles-Tablas, Coordinator: M. Aguirre, Specialist: Mr. N. Barceló, Researcher: V. Fisas Armengol, V. Garrido, A. Piris, Mr. J. M. Ruiz, P. Sáez, Economics Coordinator: G. Malgesini, Chairman: A. Martínez González-Tablas
Date of Establishment: 1984
Type: Private; non-profit
Principal Activities: Research; training; documentation/information; conference-organization; publication; exhibitions; peace prize forum
Current Peace Research:

(a) Crisis de seguridad en el Mediterráneo,

(b) Proliferación nuclear en el Magreb,

(c) Reforma y propuestas de actuaction para las Naciones Unidas,

(d) Impacto de las politicas immigratorias y convivencia intercultural en España,

(e) Comercio justo y solidaridad con América Central,

(f) Recursos hidricos en el Mediterráneo,

(g) Repercusiones ambientales de las politicas de transporte en España,

(h) Sostenibilidad y cambios en la economia española,

(i) Presupuestos militares Españoles,

(j) Campos de tiro y la destrucción ecológica,

(k) El Seguimiento del fin de la Guerra Fria y los cambios en la politica de bloques militares,

(l) Educatión para la paz.

Periodicals:

(a) *Ecologia Politica*, 2 p.a.

(b) *Papeles para la Paz*, 4 p.a.

Bulletins: *Infor-Paz*

Major Publications:

(a) Malgesini, G., Aguirre, M. (eds.), *Misiles o Microchips: la Conversión de la Industria Militar en civil*, 1991,

(b) Leger Sivard, R., *El Planeta en la Encrucijada: Gastos Militares, Sociales y Crisis Ecológica*, 1992,

(c) *Anuario del CIP 1992-1993: Retos Del Din de Siglo*, 1993,

(d) *Desarrollo Económico*, 1993,

(e) *Ecología y Seguridad en el Mediterráneo*, 1993,

(f) *La Situactión en el Mundo*, 1993,

(g) Aguirre, M., Matthews, R., *Guerras de Baja Intensidad,*

(h) *El Conflicto-Norte Sur. Guía Didáctica,*

(i) *La Conversión de la Industria Militar en Civil,*

(j) *Defensa 2001,*

(k) *Medidas Para Controlar el Comercio de Armas,*

(l) *La ONU y el Empleo de la Fuerza Armada,*

(m) *Propuesta de Creación de un Fondo Económico de Cooperación Para el Mediterráneo Occidental,*

(n) *Propuestas Para la Reforma de las Naciones Unidas,*

(o) *Propuestas para una Seguridad Integrada en el Mediterráneo.*

Annotation: Carries out research on issues of international politics, international security, environment and economics from the multidisciplinary perspective of peace research. More particularly concerned with Spanish militarism, the crisis security in the Mediterranean, shooting ranges and ecological destruction, the following of the end of the Cold War and the changes in the policies of the military blocs. Promotes social justice, disarmament, environmental protection, democracy and development.

Centre D'estudis Sobre La Pau I El Desarmement
Universitat Autónoma De Barcelona
Edificio B, 08193 Bellaterra/Barcelona, Spain

Telephone: 34-3-581-24-24
Fax: 34-3-581-20-02
Telex: 52040 EDUCI E
Senior Staff: Director: E. Barbe, Researcher: L. Feliu, R. Grasa, L. Lemkov, P. Mir, A. Oliveres, N. Sainz, M. Salomón, E. Sánchez, J. Sánchez, C. Segura
Date of Establishment: 1990
Type: Public
Principal Activities: Research; publication; conference-organization
Current Peace Research:

(a) The Role of Spain in the Mediterranean Region: global challenge and local conflicts,

(b) New dimensions of security (migrations and environment): the relations between Spain and the Maghreb,

(c) Spain and Portugal in EPC,

(d) National interest and integrative politics in transnational parliamentary assemblies: the CSCE Assembly.

Periodicals: *Estudis Internacionals*, 4 p.a.
Major Publications:

(a) Salomón, M., *Les Nacions Unides entre la crisi i*

la consolidació, 1991,

(b) Hurtado, A., *Armes quimiques, biológiques i geofisques*, 1992,

(c) Palou, J., *La Politica exterior xinesa*, 1992,

(d) Barbé, E., *Spanish responses to the security institutions of the new Europe: Mediterranean objectives and European instruments*, 1992,

(e) Sainz, N., *La Conferencia sobre la seguretat i la Cooperació a Europa*, 1993,

(f) Sánchez, J., *El Liban: creació i destrucció d'un estat*, 1993,

(g) Garcia, C., *Catalonia as an international actor: the Latin arch*, 1993,

(h) Mir, P., *Economy and external sector of AMU (Arab Maghreb Union) countries*, 1993,

(i) Grasa, R., *Global security: a Mediterranean approach*, 1994.

Annotation: Carries out research on international conflicts, peace, security and disarmament from the perspectives of international economy and international relations.

Fundacio Jaume Bofill [The Jaume Bofill Foundation]
Carrer Provença 324, Primer, Barcelona 08037, Spain

Telephone: 93-4588-700
Fax: 93-4588-710
Senior Staff: Director: J. Porta, Researcher: V. Fisas, A. Oliveres, M. Ludevid
Date of Establishment: 1969
Type: Private; non-profit

Principal Activities: Research; publication
Current Peace Research: Economical viability of disarmament: the Spanish case

Periodicals:

(a) *Butlletí Informatiu*, 1 p.a.

(b) *Index d'Estudios Socials*, 1 p.a.

Major Publications:

(a) Arbós, X., Castellà, J. M., *La Libertat Individual i els Seus Limits*, 1992,

(b) Ludevid, M., *Les Polítiques Internacionals de*

Resposta al Canvi Global en el Medi Ambient, 1993,

(c) Trilla, C., *Un Nou marc per a la Politica d'habitage*, 1993.

Annotation: Concerned with disarmament, non-offensive defence and the process of European unity.

Gernika Gogoratuz, Peace Research Center
Artekale, 1-1, E-48300 Gernika, Bizkaia, Spain

Telephone: 34-94-6253558
Fax: 34-94-6256765
E-mail: gernikag@sarenet.es
Web Site: www.sarenet.es/gernikag
Senior Staff: Director: J. Gutierrez, Public Relation Officer: Michael Kasper
Date of Establishment: 1987
Purpose: Gernika Gogoratuz backed by scientific reflection wants to contribute to the creation of an emancipatory and just peace in the Basque Country, and Internationally. Gernika Gogoratuz tries to project and spread the culture of peace and reconciliation, and the promise of conflict resolution through the symbol of Gernika.
Type: International, private and non-profit
Brief History: Gernika Gogoratuz was born from a commitment to peace. It has origin in a private initiative, supported by an unanimous decision of the Basque Parliament, to establish a Center for the Study of Peace that could perpetuate the symbol and memory of Gernika and the bombing of the town.

Principal Activities: The organization is structured in four areas:

(a) Reconciliation area, whose task is basically to manage and develop the Gernika network in support of reconciliation processes,

(b) Area of teaching and training in Conflict Resolution and the production of a tool box for transmitting the acquired experience from those activities,

(c) Area concerning the maintenance and care of the symbol of Gernika as a city of Peace and Reconci-

liation,

(d) Intermediary role in the Basque conflict whenever any of the involved parties demands for it.

Periodicals: Working Papers;

(a) Mitchell, C. R., *Conflictos Intratables: Claves de Tratamiento*. July 1997,

(b) Mitchell, C. R., *Intractable Conflicts: Keys to Treatment*. July 1997,

(c) Gernika Gogoratuz, *Petra Kelly-Gernika: Gesto de Reconciliacion*. April 1997.

Major Publication:

(a) Juan, G., *Reconciliación*,

(b) Micael, K., *Gernika y Alemania. Historia de una Reconciliación*, April 1998,

(c) Michael, K., *Gernika und Deutschland. Geschichte einer Versöhnung*,

(d) Paul, L. J., *Construyendo la paz: reconciliación sostenible en sociedades divididas*,

(e) Mary, F., *Más allá de la violencia. Procesos de resolución de conflictos en Irlanda del Norte*, April 1998,

(f) Johan, G., *Resolución, reconstrucción y reconciliación: las interfaces*,

(g) Gogoratuz, G. *Caja de Herramientas- Educación por la paz*, October 1998.

Instituto Espanol de Estudios Estrategicos [Spanish Institute of Startegic Studies]
Mo. Defensa (Digenpol) Paseo de_la Castellana 109-28046 Madrid, Spain

Telephone: 34-91-556-51-07/555-91-77
Senior Staff: Director: Miguel Adonso Baquer, Analysts: Alejandro Cuerda Ortega, Cristobal Gil.

Date of Establishment: 30 April 1970
Purpose: The Institute undertakes studies on politico-military strategic economic and sociological matters

related to national security and defense, with the aim to enhance national conscience on defense issues in public and private institutions and universities. It collaborates with similar institutes and centers both national and foreign alike, and organizes round tables with universities and other institutes and centers.

Type: National, private, non-profit

Brief History: The Spanish Institute for Strategic Studies (IEEE) was established in 1970 as a body of the already existing high center studies on national defense (CESEDEN) as a military institution. Part of the organization of the chief of defense staff from March 1997 has been transferred to the ministry of defense as part of the general directorate for defense policy.

Principal Activities: Research; round tables; seminars; conferences.

Major Publications:

(a) *Cuadernos de Estrategia* [Strategy Papers],

(b) *Casto Militar e Industrializacion* [Military Caste and Industrialization],

(c) *Obtencion de los Medios de Defensa ante el Entorno Cambiante* [Obtaining the Means of Defense before an Internal Change],

(d) *La Politica Exterior y de Seguridad Comun (PESC) de la Union Europea (UE)* [Foreign Policy and Common Security of the European Union],

(e) *La red de carreteras en la peninsula Iberica, conexion con el resto de Europa mediante un sistema integrado de transportes* [The Networks of Roads in the Iberian Peninsula, Connection with the Rest of Europe through a System of Integrated Transformations],

(f) *El derecho de intervencion en los conflictos* [The Right of Intervention During Conflict],

(g) *Dependencias y vulnerabilidades de la economia Espanola: su relacion con la Defensa Nacional* [Dependence and Vulnerability of the Spanish Economy: its Relation with the National Defence],

(h) *La corporacion Europa en las empresas de interes para la defensa* [The European Corporation in the Undertakings of Interest for the Defense],

(i) *Los cascos azuies en el conflicto de la ex Yugoslavia* [The Blue Berets in the Conflict of Former Yugoslavia],

(j) *El sistema nacional de transportes en el escenario Europeo del siglo XXI* [The National System of Transport in the 21st Century Europe]

(k) *El embargo y el bloqueo como formas de actuacion de la comunidad internacional en los conflictos* [Embargo and Blockade as a Form of Action of the International Community During Conflicts],

(l) *La Policia Exterior y la Seguridad Comun (PESC) para Europa en el marco del Tratado de no Proliferacion de Armas Nucleares (TNP)* [Foreign Policy and Common Security for Europe in the Frame of Non-proliferation of Nuclear Arms Treaty].

Instituto Español de Estudios Estratégicos Del Ceseden (IEEE)
Centro Superior de Estudios de la Defensa Nacional Paseo de la Castellana, 61
28071 Madrid, Spain

Telephone: 34-441-71-81

Fax: 34-441-92-98

Senior Staff: Permanent Secretary: Gen. M. A. Baquer, Specialist: Dr. J. Diez, Ambassador C. Fernández-Espeso, Dr. J. I. Martinez

Date of Establishment: 1970

Type: Public, non-profit

Principal Activities: Research; documentation/ information; publication

Current Peace Research:

(a) Strategic studies in Spain,

(b) The air-naval balance in the Mediterranean. Zones of power projection,

(c) North-South dialogue on western Mediterranean issues,

(d) Double-use technologies in defence industries,

(e) Defence costs and economic growth. Approach to the Spanish case,

(f) Sociological contribution to the Spanish society to the national defence,

(g) El Derecho de intervención en los conflictos,

(h) Factorial method for the study of belligerent impulses.

Periodicals: *Cuadernos Estratégicos*, 12 p.a.

Major Publications:

(a) *La Función de las fuerzas armadas ante el panorama international de conflictos,*

(b) *Las Corrientes fundamentalistas en el Magreb y su influencia en la politica de defensa,*

(c) *Factores de la estructura de seguridad europea,*

(d) *Las Fuerzas armadas en los procesos iberoamericanos de cambio democrático (1980-1990),*

(e) *Factores de riesgo en el aréa mediterranea.*

Annotation: Mainly concerned with polemology, weapons, security, strategy and economics of defence.

Paz y Cooperacion
Meléndez Valdés, 68, 4. 28015 Madrid, Spain

Telephone: 34-1-543-52-82
Fax: 34-1-543-52-82
Date of Establishment: 1982
Senior Staff: President: J. Antuña
Type: Private, non-profit
Principal Activities: Documentation/information; publication; exhibitions
Geographical Coverage: Arab States; Latin America
Type of Publication: Journal; monograph
Periodicals: *Premio Escolar Paz y Cooperación,* 1 p.a.
Major Publications:

(a) *Educatión para un futuro solidario,*

(b) *Los refugiados,*

(c) *Año internacional de la familia,*

(d) *Conocerse mejor para un futuro solidario,*

(e) *Los emigrantes. El derecho al trabajo.*

Annotation: Devoted to education for peace and international understanding

Sociedad De Estudios Internacionales (SEI)
Hortaleza 104, piso 2, 28004 Madrid, Spain

Telephone: 34-563-69-15
Senior Staff: Director: F. de Salas López, Specialist: Mr. J. L. Fernandez Florez, J. Lopez Medel, J. López-Solórzano Arquero
Date of Establishment: 1934
Type: Private; non-profit
Principal Activities: Research; training; conference-organization; publication; radio and TV programmes
Current Peace Research:

(a) Disarmament,

(b) NATO.

Major Publications:

(a) Fernandez Florez, J. L., *La Guerra y el derecho,* 1993,

(b) Fernandez Florez, J. L., *La Carta de las Naciones Unidas y la cooperación,* 1994,

(c) de Salas López, F., *La Paz es urgente en la*

Antigua Yugoeslavia.

Annotation: Undertakes research on conflict and war, peace and disarmament, and international security.
Courses: International Studies Programme
Subjects Taught: Disarmament; conflict resolution; role of the international organizations; education for peace
Target Group: Professionals; foreign students
Level of the Course: Postgraduate
Type of Course: Regular course
Duration: From February to July
Working Languages: Spanish
Admission Requirements: Candidates must hold a doctorate and a high level degree from Spanish or foreign universities
Closing date of applications: 15 February
Course Fees: Yes, 70,000 Spanish pesetas
Scholarships Available: 12 scholarships are available each year; apply to Mr. de Salas López, Director
Degree/Diploma: Diploma of High International Studies

Sweden

Den Transnationella Stiftelsen för Freds-och Framtidsforskning (TFF)
[The Transnational Foundation for Peace and Future Research]
Vegagatan 25, S-223 57 Lund, Sweden

Telephone: 46-145909
Fax: 46-144512
Senior Staff: Director: J. Øbrg
Date of Establishment: 1986
Type: Private, non-profit
Principal Activities: Research; documentation/ information; conference-organization; publication; exhibitions; practical conflict-mitigation

Current Peace Research:

(a) Conflict mitigation: theory and in-the-field in former Yugoslavia, the Commonwealth of Independent States and between Japan and Russia,

(b) World images and peace thinking,

(c) European orders of peace and cooperation,

(d) New regions: markets, states, people and democracy,

(e) The Peace of everyday living,

(f) Ghandi's relevance in the contemporary world,

(g) Economy, ecology and ethics,

(h) The UN in the emerging world order,

(i) Demilitarization and sustainable development,

(j) Lund in the world, the world in Lund.

Periodicals: *TFF Newsletter*, 2 p.a.
Major Publications:

(a) Aliboni, R. (ed.), *Southern European Security in the 1990s*, 1991,

(b) Buzan, B. et al., *The European Security Order Recast: Scenarios for the Post-Cold War Era*, 1991,

(c) *After Yugoslavia, What?*, 1991,

(d) *Preventing Violence and War in Kosovo*, 1992,

(e) Øberg, J. (ed.), *Nordic Security in the 1990s. Options in the Changing Europe*, 1992,

(f) *Yugoslavia: a Conflict Management Crisis*, 1993,

(g) *Reconstructing Croatia I: Why Croats and Serbs Fight Each Other*, 1994,

(h) *Reconstructing Croatia II: how Croats, Serbs and the United Nations can Achieve Peace Together*, 1994,

(i) *Build Peace from Below: a Special Study from Western Slovania*, 1994.

Other Information: The Institute works on conflict resolution, peace research and education for peace to improve conflict understanding at all levels and promote alternative collective security and global development based on nonviolence, sustainability and ethics of care. The results are aimed at policy making bodies and individuals and combining innovative thinking and theories with workable, practical solutions.

Department of Peace and Conflict Research
PO Box 514, S-751 20 Uppsala, Sweden

Telephone: 46-18-187652
Fax: 46-18-695102
E-mail: Staffan.Argman@pcr.uu.se
Senior Staff: Professor: Peter Wallensteen
Date of Establishment: 1971
Purpose: To conduct research within the area, and to offer courses for students in peace and conflict studies.
Type: International, public
Brief History: The Department of Peace and Conflict Resolution was established in1971 to conduct research and offer courses in peace and conflict studies. At present some 200-300 students are enrolled every academic year. The training offered includes an undergraduate and a Ph.D. program as well as an advanced program and special seminars.

There is one full professorship-Dag Hammarskjold Chair of Peace and Conflict Research. The first and present holder was appointed in 1985. There are now several associate and assistant professorships, financed on a regular or temporary basis.

Principal Activities: Research is basic to the Department. The teaching offered often reflects recent research. Teaching is also given by Ph.D. candidates and researchers engaged in research projects.

Periodicals:

(a) Reports,

(b) *Journal of Peace Research,*

(c) *Journal of Pacific Affairs.*

Major Publications:

(a) *Neutrality and Foreign Military Sales,*

(b) "Sweden's Search for Military Technology," in Brzoska, M., Lock, P. (eds.), *Restructuring of Arms Production in Western Europe,*

(c) *Arm in Arm: Swedish-Australian Military Trade and Cooperation.*

Institutionen för Freds-OCH Utvecklingsforskning
Göteborgs Universitet [Peace and Development Research Institute] (PADRIGU)
Brogatan, 4, S-413 01 Göteborg, Sweden

Telephone: 46-31-773-1000
Fax: 46-31-773-4910
E-mail: A.Forssell@Padrigu.gu.sc
Senior Staff: Prof: B. Hettne, Lecturer: J. Carlsson, Friberg, H. Lindholm, L. Ohlsson, M. Schulz
Date of Establishment: 1971
Type: Public; non-profit
Principal Activities: Research; training; documentation/information; conference- organization; publication
Current Peace Research:

(a) Development strategies and the nation-state project,

(b) Subnational challenges to the nation state,

(c) Transnational challenges to the nation state,

(d) Conflict resolution in Sweden and Malaysia.

Major Publications:

(a) *Regional Conflicts and Conflict Resolution: Case Studies II,* 1991,

(b) Falkemark, G., Alvstam, C-G., *Geopolitik,* 1991,

(c) Hettne, B., *Etniska konflikter och Internationella Relationer,* 1992,

(d) Karlsson, S., *Freds-och Konfliktunskap: en Introduktion,* 1992,

(e) Ohlsson, L. (ed.), *Regional Case Studies of Water*

Conficts, 1992,

(f) Lindholm, H. (ed.), *Ethnicity and Nationalism: Formation of Identity and Dynamics of Conflict in the 1990s,* 1993.

Annotation: Research focuses on social conflicts, conflict resolution and peace
Courses:

(a) Peace and Development Research (Ph.D.)

(b) Link between Peace Studies and Development Issues (Masters)

Subjects Taught: Peaceful coexistence; disarmament; conflict resolution; role of the international organizations; nonviolence; peace and development; democracy and peace; war; international conflict; international security; regional conflict; terrorism; education for peace; rural communities; economic structures; international development assistance; ethnicity
Principal Instructors: Mr. H. Abrahamsson; Mr. B. Andersson; Mr. J. Carlsson; Prof. B. Hettne; Mr. B. Jørgensen; Dr. S. Karlsson; Ms. H. Lindholm; Mr. L. Ohlsson; Mr. M. Schulz
Target Group: Nationals; foreign students
Level of the Course: Masters; postgraduate
Type of Course: Regular course
Duration: Three semesters or more depending on level
Working Languages: Swedish; English
Admission Requirements: Yes
Degree/Diploma: Ph.D. in Peace and Development Research

Life & Peace Institute
751 70 Uppsala, Sweden

Telephone: 46-18-169500

Fax: 46-18-693059

E-mail: lpi@algonet.se

Senior Staff: Director: Bernt Jonsson, Research Director: Lucia Ann McSpadden, Director/Horn of Africa: Sture Normark, Program Officer/ Horn of Africa: Susanne Thurfjell Lunden.

Date of Establishment: 1985

Purpose: The Institute aims to conduct scientific research, primarily from Christian/ethic perspectives on questions of international conflict and to support the work of the churches in reconciliation, peace and justice.

Type: International, non-profit

Brief History: The Life & Peace Institute was founded in 1985 by the Swedish Ecumenical Council. Originally designated to pursue peace and conflict research it has in parallel—through practical action in conflict areas—developed an action-oriented research.

Principal Activities:

(a) Research on: The Role of Religion in Conflicts and Peace; Human Rights and Economic Justice; Nonviolent Conflict Transformation,

(b) Practical support for grass roots peace-building initiatives in the Horn of Africa region and in the former Yugoslavia,

(c) Documentation of work in two journals, research and conference reports, occasional, conference and working papers.

Periodicals:

(a) *New Routes 4 issues/year,*

(b) *Horn of Africa Bulletin 6 issues/year.*

Major Publications:

(a) *South Africa: Democratization and Transformation,*

(b) *Disarmament, Debt and Development: Seeing the Connection,*

(c) *Keeping the Peace: Exploring Civilian Alternatives in Conflict Resolution,*

(d) *After the Revolution. Democracy in East Central Europe.*

Stockholm International Peace Research Institute (SIPRI)
Frosunda, S-169 70 Solna, Sweden

Telephone: 46-8-655-97-00
Fax: 46-8-655-97-33
E-mail: sipri@sipri.se
Web Site: http://www.sipri.se
Senior Staff: Director: Adam Daniel Rotfeld.
Date of Establishment: 1966
Purpose: The Institute exists in order to conduct scientific research on questions of conflict and co-operation of importance for international peace and security, with the aim of contributing to and understanding of the conditions for peaceful solutions of international conflicts and for a stable peace (2 Statutes of the Stockholm International Peace Research Institute).

Brief History: SIPRI is an independent international institute. It was established in 1966 to commemorate Sweden's 150 years of unbroken peace.
Principal Activities: Research
Major Publication:

(a) Alexander, A., Sergounin, Sergey V. Subbotin, *Russian Arms Transfers to East Asia in the 1990s.* SIPRI Research Report No. 15, Oxford University Press, 1999,

(b) P. J., Towards, *a Regional Security Regime for the*

Middle East: Issues and Options, SIPRI, 1998,

(c) Singh, R. P. (ed.), *Arms Procurement Decision Making: Vol. I, China, India, Israel, Japan, South Korea and Thailand*, Oxford University Press, 1998,

(d) Singh, R. P. (ed.), *Chemical Weapon Destruction in Russia: Political, Legal and Technical Aspects*, SIPRI Chemical & Biological Warfare Studies No. 17, Oxford University Press, 1998,

(e) SIPRI Yearbook 1998: *Armaments, Disarmament and International Security*, Oxford University Press, 1998,

(f) Batchelor, P., Willett, S., *Disarmament and Defence Industrial Adjustment in South Africa*, Oxford University Press, 1998,

(g) Anthony, I. (ed.), *Russia and the Arms Trade*, Oxford University Press, 1998,

(h) Arnett, E. (ed.), *Nuclear Weapons and Arms Control in South Asia after the Test Ban*, SIPRI

Research Report No. 14, Oxford University Press, 1998,

(i) *SIPRI and UNESCO Peace, Security and Conflict Prevention*, SIPRI-UNESCO Handbook, Oxford University Press, 1998,

(j) Stock, T., Lohs K. (ed.), *The Challenge of Old Chemical Munitions and Toxic Armament Wastes*, SIPRI Chemical & Biological Warfare Studies No. 16, Oxford University Press, 1997,

(k) Kiss, Y., *The Defence Industry in East-Central Europe: Restructuring and Conversion*, Oxford University Press, 1997,

(l) SIPRI Yearbook 1997: *Armaments, Disarmament and International Security*, Oxford University Press, 1997,

(m) Gill, B., Mak, J. N. (ed.), *Arms, Transparency and Security in South-East Asia*, SIPRI Research Report No. 13 I, Oxford University Press, 1997,

(n) Zanders, J. P., Eckstein, S., Hart, J., *The Chemical Weapons Convention*, SIPRI Fact Sheet, April 1997,

(o) Arnett, E. (ed.), *Military Capacity and the Risk of War: China, India, Pakistan and Iran*, Oxford University Press, 1997,

(p) Albright, D., Berkhout, F., Walker, W., *Plutonium and Highly Enriched Uranium 1996: World Inventories, Capabilities and Policies*, Oxford University Press, 1997,

(q) Baranovsky, V. (ed.), *Russia and Europe: The Emerging Security Agenda*, Oxford University Press, 1997.

The Transnational Foundation for Peace and Future Research
Vegagatan 25, S-224 57 Lund, Sweden

Telephone: 46-46-145909
Fax: 46-46-144512
E-mail: tff@transnational.org
Web Site: www.transnational.org
Senior Staff: Director: Jan Oberg, Assistant Under-Secretary: Ulf Svensson
Date of Establishment: 1986
Purpose: The foundation aims to contribute to a less violent world and assist the disadvantaged. It is Independent of all special interest groups. It is also:

(a) Multidisciplinary, small, dynamic and public service,

(b) Nordic board, multicultural advisory panel. Meets grant-makers' criteria for professional management with minimum administration,

(c) Networking and teamworking but no permanent research staff,

(d) Does not accept funds derived from activities related to warfare,

(e) Strongly believe that conflict-resolution is a science and an art and that if human beings learn to handle conflict better, violence can be reduced.

Type: Independent non-profit, public

Brief History: The foundation was founded by Christina Spannare and Jan Øberg as an independent not-for-profit public charity in 1986 under Swedish law. Accordingly it can not have tax exempt status but operates in parallel with such organizations abroad. It reports annually to the local government authority for foundations.

TFF works in partnership with The Nuclear Age Peace Foundation in Santa Barbara, California, a non-profit organization with IRS exempt status under 501(c)(3).
Principal Activities: The Foundation involves in Conflict-mitigation, peace research and education to improve conflict understanding at all levels. To promote alternative security and global development based on non-violent politics, economics, sustainability and ethics of care. The results, which aim at decision-makers and citizens alike, combine innovative thinking and theories with workable practical solutions.
Periodicals: *Bulletin of Peace Proposals*
Major Publications:

(a) Joenniemi, A., Øberg, W., Current Research on Peace and Violence 1-2, 1986, Special issue on Nordic security,

(b) TFF Statement # 1, *Confidence-Building and Arms Restraint at Sea*,

(c) TFF Statement # 2, *On Nordic Initiatives at the United Nations Special Session on Disarmament,* 1988,

(d) Galtung, Wiberg, Väyrynen, Øberg, Elworthy. *Disarmament—But How? Swedish Professionals against Nuclear Arms.*

Utrikespolitiska Institutet [The Swedish Institute of International Affairs]
PO Box 1253, 11182 Stockholm, Sweden

Telephone: 46-8-23-40-60
Fax: 46-8-20-10-49
Cable: INTAFFAIRS
Senior Staff: President: Ambassador L. Leifland, Managing Director: R. Lindahl, Researcher: B. Dunér, G. Herolf, L. Jonson, J. Prawitz, G. Sjöstedt, B. Sundelius, M. Winnerstig
Date of Establishment: 1938
Type: Private; non-profit
Principal Activities: Research; documentation/ information; conference-organization; publication
Current Peace Research:

(a) Arms control and security in the strategic North,

(b) West European security cooperation,

(c) Russian security strategies,

(d) Non-military security,

(e) Human rights,

(f) Transatlantic relations,

(g) Environmental regime building and governance.

Periodicals:

(a) *Internationella Studier*, 4 p.a.,

(b) *Research Reports,*

(c) *Världspolitikens Dagsfrågor.*

Major Publications:

(a) *Mapping the Unknown, Yearbook 1992-1993*, 1993.

Other Information: Deals with international relations, international conflict, defence and peace

Switzerland

Association Mondiale pour l'Ecole Instrument de Paix (EIP)
[World Association for the School as an Instrument of Peace]
5-7 rue du Simplon CH-1207 Geneva, Switzerland

Telephone: 268-22-735-24-22
Fax: 268-22-736-48-63
Senior Staff: Secretary General: M. Prindezis, Specialist: M. Bastien, E. Contoz, A. O. Diallo
Date of Establishment: 1967
Type: Private, non-profit
Principal Activities: Research; training; documentation/information; conference-organization; publication; exhibitions
Courses: Session Internationale et de la Paix de Fomation l'Enseignement des Droits de l'Ho-mme pour les Enseignants des Ecole Primaires, Secondaires et Professionnelles,; Session Africaine de Formation à l'Enseignement des Droits de l'Homme
Subjects Taught: Role of the international organizations; peace and development; conflict resolution; human rights

Principal Instructor: Ms M. Prindezis, Mr J. Henaire, Mr Y. Labor, Mr P. Adossama, Ms E. Contoz, Mr J. Tuvilla, Mr M. Kourouma
Target Group: Professionals, foreign students, non-specialists, nationals
Type of Course: Regular course
Duration: One week
Working Language: French, English, Spanish
Admission Requirements: Primary, Secondary or vocational school teachers, head masters of teacher training schools, or professionals involved UNESCO projects and UNESCO National Commissions Associated Schools
Scholarships Available: Yes, contact Ms M. Prindezis, Secretary General, EIP
Degree/Diploma: Attendance Certificate

Forschungsstelle Für Sicherheitspolitik Und Konfliktanalyse
[Center for Security Studies and Conflict Research]
Swiss Federal Institute of Technology, ETH-Zentrum, 8092 Zurich, Switzerland

Telephone: 268-411-632-40-25
Fax: 268-411-363-91-96
Senior Staff: Director: K. R. Spillman, S. Klötzli, S. Libiszewski, C. Lang
Date of Establishment: 1986
Principal Activities: Research; training; consulting
Current Peace Research:

(a) Ecological degradation and conflict,

(b) ENCOP: Environment and conflict project.

Periodicals:

(a) *Bulletin zur schweizerischen Sicherheitspolitik*

(b) *Swiss Security Policy Bulletin*

Major Publications:

(a) Fischer, S. A., *Namibia becomes Independent. The U.S. Contribution to Regional Peace,*

(b) Wisler, D., *La Violence Politique en Suisse et les Mouvements Sociaux* (1969-1990),

(c) Libiszewski, S., *What is an Environmental Conflict?*, 1992,

(d) Klötzli, S., *Sustainable Development: a Disputed Concept*, 1992,

(e) Klötzli, S., *Der Slowakisch-Ungarishe Konflikt um das Staustufen Projekt Gabcíkovo*, 1993,

(f) Klötzli, S. et al., *Umweltzerstörung: Krieg oder Kooperation?* 1993.

Annotation: Researching and teaching in the fields of security policy and conflict analysis including political, economic, social and environmental dimensions.

Graduate Institute of Development Studies
24 rue Rothschild, PO Box 136, 1211 Geneva 21, Switzerland

Telephone: 268-41-22-906-59-40
Fax: 268-41-22-906-59-47
E-mail: duc@uni2a.unige.ch
Web Site: http://www.unige.ch/iued/
Senior Staff: Director: Jean-Luc Maurer
Date of Establishment: 1961
Purpose: The Institute is managed by the "Foundation for Development Studies." Its goal is to promote the training and studies about development problems and to welcome students of developing countries.
Type: Non-profit
Brief History: Created in 1961 by the Geneva State, the "Centre genevois pour la formation des cadres africans" became in 1962 the "Institut d'etudes du developpement" and finally in 1977, after a convention with the Geneva University, the "Institut universitaire d'etudes du developpement" (Graduate Institute of Development Studies).
Principal Activities:

(a) Training program giving a diploma, a research diploma or a doctorate,

(b) Short courses and tailor-made training are also organized,

(c) Researches focused on culture and development, economic development and sectoral or global policies, development and political institutions, development and the environment,

(d) Studies and projects providing services such as management of development cooperation projects or evaluations.

Periodicals:

(a) Horizons IUED,

(b) Nouveauk cahiers de l'IUED,

(c) Annuaire Suisse-Tiers Monda/Jahrbach Schweiz-Dritte welt.

Major Publications:

(a) *Development Rural et Libration Economique en Inde, Le cas de l'Etat d'Orissa,*

(b) *Ninos Jovenes en Situacion De Calle Espacio Y Campo Social,* Ciudad de Cordoba, Argentina.

Institut Universitaire De Hautes Etudes Internationales (IUHEI)
[The Graduate Institute of International Studies]
PO Box 36, 132 rue de Lausanne, CH-1211 Geneva 21, Switzerland

Telephone: 268-22-731-17-30
Fax: 268-22-738-43-06
Cable: INSTONAL GENEVA
Senior Staff: Director: A. Swoboda, Secretary General: J.-C. Frachebourg, Prof.: C. Gasteyger
Date of Establishment: 1927
Type: Private; non-profit
Principal Activities: Research; training; documentation/information; conference- organization; publication
Periodicals: *Relations Internationales*, 4 p.a.

Periodicals:

(a) *Cahiers d'Histoire et de Politique Internationales,*

(b) *Newsletter/Lettre d'Information.*

Major Publications:

(a) Kunsberg, P., *Global Missile Defense in the New Era: SDI in Perspective*, 1992,

(b) Waslekar, S., *Indian and Pakistani Approaches Towards Nuclear Nonproliferation*, 1993,

(c) Scott, D. S., *The Chemical Weapons Convention*, 1993,

(d) Lukic, R., *The Wars in Former Yugoslavia*, 1993,

(e) Chubin, S., *Changing North-South Security Relations*, 1993,

(f) Dreyer, R., *The Changing Southern Africa: the Quest for Independence of Namibia and Peace in Angola*, 1993,

(g) Meiers, F.-J., *From START I to START II: the Future of Strategic Arms Control*, 1993.

Annotation: The Institute is devoted to the advanced study of international relations. Research deals with international security, strategy and arms control, con-temporary history, international cooperation, international organizations, international social history, international law, the law of armed conflicts, and quantitative methods

Courses:

(a) Programme for Strategic and International Security Studies (PSIS),

(b) International Training Course (ITC) in International Security and Arms Control,

(c) Relations Internationales (Licence; DES; Ph.D.; Certificat).

Subjects Taught: International security; disarmament; peace research; peaceful coexistence; conflict resolution; arms control; role of the international organizations; peace and development; war; international conflict
Target Group: Professionals; nationals; foreign students; diplomats and officers
Level of the Course: Bachelors; postgraduate; masters; doctorate
Type of Course: Regular course; short session
Duration: Licence in International Relations: 4 semesters; Diploma of Higher Studies (DES): 4 semesters; Ph.D. in International Relations: 10 semesters (max.); Certificate of International Studies: 3 semesters; ITC: 1 year
Working Languages: French; English
Admission Requirements: Yes, candidatures are examined by an Admission Commission
Closing Date for Applications: April 15
Course Fees: 555 Swiss Francs per semester (for regular students)
Degree/Diploma: Licence en Relations Internationales; DES en Relations Internationales; Ph.D. en Relations Internationales; Certificat en Relations Internationales

Schweizerische Friedensstiftung [Swiss Peace Foundation]
Wasserwerkgasse 7, Postfach 75, CH-3000 Berne 13, Switzerland

Telephone: 268-41-31-311-55-82
Fax: 268-41-31-311-55-83
Senior Staff: President: R. Stähelin, Director: G. Bächler, Specialist: G. Bächler
Date of Establishment: 1988
Type: Non-profit, private
Principal Activities: Research; documentation/ infor-mation; conference-organization; publication
Current Peace Research: Probable present and future conflicts in the international system caused by ecological problems

Major Publications:

(a) Krummenacher, H., Wisler, D., *La Métapolitique*

de Maître du Risque. Vers une Nouvelle Politique de Sécurité en Suisse, 1990,

(b) Bächler, G., Meyer-Schweizer, R., Vogt, W. R., *Das Militär: Konfrontiert mit Akzeptanzproblemen, Legitimationsverlust und Wertewandel*, 1990,

(c) Bächler, G., *Ökologische Sicherheit und Konflikt*, 1990,

(d) Senghaas, D., Bächler, G., *Frieden und Demokratie in Europa*, 1990,

(e) Böge, V., *Proposal for an Analytical Framework to Grasp "Environmental Conflict"*, 1992,

(f) Böge, V., *Bougainville: a "Classical" Environmental Conflict?*, 1992,

(g) Suliman, M., *Civil War in Sudan: the Impact of Environmental Degradation*, 1992,

(h) Bächler, G. (ed.), *Peace and Conflict Research in times of Radical Change*, 1992,

(i) Hafiz, M. A., Islam, N., *Environmental Degradation and Intra/Interstate Conflicts in Bangladesh*, 1993,

(j) Bächler, G., *Conflict and Cooperation in the Light of Global Human/Ecological Transformation*, 1993,

(k) Bächler, G. (ed.), *Environmental Refugees. A Potential of Future Conflicts?*, 1994.

Annotation: Aims at shaping Swiss peace and security policy. Concerned with global environmental problems, North-South relations and regional conflicts.

Women's International League for Peace and Freedom
1, Rue de Varemb CP 28, CH 1211 Geneva 20, Switzerland

Telephone: 268-41-22-733-61-75
Fax: 268-41-22-740-10-63
E-mail: womensleague@gn.apc.org
Senior Staff: Secretary General: Barbara Lochbihler
Date of Establishment: 1915
Purpose: The League aims at bringing together women of different political philosophical tendencies united in their determination to study, made known and help abolish the political, social, economic and psychological causes of war, and to work for a constructive peace.
Type: International
Brief History: On 28 April 1915, a unique group of women met in an international Congress in the Hague, the Netherlands, to protest against the war then raging in Europe, and to suggest ways to end it and prevent war in the future. The organizers of the Congress were prominent women in the International Suffrage Alliance who saw the connection between their struggle for equal rights and the struggle for peace. They rejected the theory that war was inevitable and defied all obstacles to their plan to meet together in wartime. They assembled more than 1,000 women from belligerent and neutral countries to work out principles on the basis of which they believed the war could be stopped and a permanent peace constructed. The Congress established an International Committee of Women for Permanent Peace which four years later became the Women's International League for Peace and Freedom.

Principal Activities:

(a) International meetings and conferences on peace and security issues,

(b) Lobby work at the United Nations,

(c) International programs in the field of disarmament, human right and development,

(d) Fact finding and peace missions to counties in conflict.

Periodicals: *International Peace Update* (bi-monthly)

Major Publications:

(a) *Search For Peace in the Middle East*, WILPFs missions and meetings, policies and action, 1930-96,

(b) *Conversion and Essential Practical Component for Effective Disarmament*, 1996,

(c) *Women and Militarism*, 1994,

(d) *Justice Denied, Human Right and the International Financial Institution*, 1994,

(e) *War and Rape*, 1993,

(f) *Health and Environment Effect of Nuclear Radiation from Weapons Production and Testing*, 1990.

World Association for the School as Instrument for Peace
5, Rue Simplon, CH-1207 Geneva, Switzerland

Telephone: 268-41-22-735-24-22
Fax: 268-41-22-735-06-53
E-mail: cifedhop@mail-box.ch
Senior Staff: Director, Monique Prindezis
Date of Establishment: 1967
Type: Non-profit
Brief History: The International Training Centre on Human Rights and Peace Teaching is a foundation devoted to the furthering of human rights and peace education throughout the world.

The Centre was founded in1984 by the World Association for the School as an Instrument of Peace (EIP), an international non-governmental organization with consultative status to the United Nations, UNESCO, ILO, and the Council of Europe. As EIP's activity in the promotion of human rights and peace increased, they saw the necessity to devote resources specifically to the pedagogical aspects and so created CIFEDHOP with a team of professional instructors and researchers specified in the field.

Principal Activities:

(a) It promotes human rights and peace education, particularly within primary, secondary and vocational schools and teacher training colleges, as well as in continuing education programs for teachers and adults,

(b) Promotes the instruction of trainers on how to teach human rights and Peace,

(c) Undertakes, encourages and supports research on the most effective means of teaching human rights and peace and to disseminate the results as widely as possible,

(d) Remains up-to-date on material, methodologies, and issues concerning human rights and peace education,

(e) Provides help to educators who want to develop human rights education in their country.

Major Publications:

(a) Terminology, a guide to understanding the basic terms and concepts relating to human rights, women's and children's rights,

(b) Selected and commented Bibliography on Human Rights, Peace and Development.

Thailand

Institute of Asian Studies (IAS)
Chulalongkorn University
Prajadhipol-Rambhai Barni Center for Public Affairs 7th Floor, Phayathai Road, Bangkok 10330, Thailand

Telephone: 662-251-5199
Fax: 662-255-1124
Cable: INSTASIA BANGKOK
Senior Staff: Director: W. Sucharithanarugger
Date of Establishment: 1967
Type: Public, non-profit
Principal Activities: Research; documentation/ information; conference-organization; publication

Current Peace Research:

(a) Borderland problems between Thailand and Malaysia,

(b) Burmese student political refugees: the health and mental health effects of trauma and exile.

Periodicals:

(a) *Asia Yearbook*, 1 p.a. (in Thai),

(b) *Asian Review*, 3 p.a. (in Thai), 1 p.a. (in English),

(c) *Asian Studies Information*, 4 p.a.

Major Publications:

(a) Ashley, D. W., *Pol Pot Peasants and Peace: Continuity and Change in Khmer Rouge Political*

Thanking 1985-1991,

(b) Chantavanich, S., *Refugee Flows from Indochinese: Mass Movements and Challenges for the 1990s,*

(c) Chirasopona, R. et al, *Contents of Newspapers in*

ASEAN Countries on the Kampuchean Problems (in Thai).

Annotation: Research body dealing with Asian and ASEAN countries and covering international relations, international cooperation, security problems, women and refugee relief cooperation.

Trinidad and Tobago

Institute of International Relations (IIR)
University of the West Indies
St. Augustine, Trinidad and Tobago

Telephone: 809-662-2002
Fax: 809-663-9685
Cable: STOMATA
Senior Staff: Director: C. D. Parris, Lecturer: A. Francis, A. V. Henry
Date of Establishment: 1966
Type: Public, non-profit
Principal Activities: Research; training; documentation/information; publication
Current Peace Research:

(a) Peace, development and security in the Caribbean,

(b) Ethnicity and its impact on the international system.

Major Publications:

(a) Francis, A., *The Maintenance of Peace and Security in Law and Practice*, 1994,

(b) Parker, J. E., *Cautioning Intervention in Ethnic*

Conflicts: Peoples' Cultural Autonomy, 1994.

Annotation: Conducts research on international security issues and peace and development
Courses: International History and Politics; International Law
Subjects Taught: Conflict resolution; role of the international organizations
Target Group: Nationals
Level of the Course: Postgraduate; masters; doctorate
Type of Course: Regular courses, included in the university curricula
Duration: Postgraduate Diploma: 1 year; Masters: 2 years
Working Languages: English
Admission Requirements: Bachelor's Degree
Closing Date for Applications: 31st March
Course Fees: Yes
Degree/Diploma: Postgraduate Diploma; M.Sc.; Ph.D.

Tunisia

Association des Etuces Internationales (AEI)
BP 156, 1012 Tunis Belvédère, Tunisia

Telephone: 216-1-791-663
Fax: 216-1-796-593
Senior Staff: President: R. Driss
Date of Establishment: 1981
Type: Non-profit
Principal Activities: Research; training; documentation/information; conference-organization; publication
Periodicals: *Etudes Internationales/Dirassat Dawlya*, 4 p.a.
Annotation: Carries out research in international relations.
Courses: Relations Internationales
Subjects Taught: Peace research; peaceful coexis-

tence; disarmament; conflict resolution; role of the international organizations; nonviolence; peace and development
Target Group: Professionals; non-specialists; nationals; foreign students
Level of the Course: Postgraduate; masters; doctorate
Type of Course: Regular course; short session
Duration: 2 years
Working Languages: Arabic; French
Course Fees: No
Scholarships Available: No
Degree/Diploma: Dipiôme de Fin de Cours

Turkey

Institute of Social Science
Gazi Universitesi
Tunus Cad. 35, Yenişehir, Ankara, Turkey

Date of Establishment: 1982
Senior Staff: Director: N. Tenker, Prof.: Y. Inan, R. Yinanç, S. Başeren
Principal Activities: Training
Courses: International Relations Degree Programme
Subjects Taught: Disarmament; conflict resolution; role of the international organizations; democracy and peace; international conflict; international security; regional conflict; terrorism
Principal Instructors: Prof. Dr. Y. Inan, Prof. Dr. R. Yinanç, Prof. Dr. S. Başeren
Target Group: Nationals; foreign students

Level of the Course: Graduate; masters; doctorate
Type of Course: Regular course; evening course
Duration: 2 years
Working Languages: Turkish
Admission Requirements: Yes, undergraduate degree for masters programme; masters degree for doctorate
Closing Date for Applications: End January or end August
Course Fees: Yes, US$ 150 and US$ 600
Scholarships Available: No
Degree/Diploma: Masters, Ph.D., and Diploma in International Relations

Ukraine

Ukrainian Academy of Sciences, Koretsky Institute of State and Law
4 Trjochavjatitelska str, 252001 Kiev 1, Ukraine

Telephone: 7-44-228-51-55
Fax: 7-44-228-54-74
Senior Staff: Director: Iu. S. Shemshuchenko, Researcher: V. N. Denisov
Date of Establishment: 1969
Type: Non-profit
Principal Activities: Research; training; conference-organization; publication
Current Peace Research:

(a) International legal problems of the creation of a world security system,

(b) Ukraine in the world community in a new era,

(c) Ukraine and nuclear disarmament,

(d) Ukraine and the creation of European security on new ground.

Periodicals: *Pravo Ukrayiny* [The Law of Ukraine]

Major Publications:

(a) Denisov, V. N., *The Legal Aspects of Disarmament in a Nuclear Weapon Era*, 1990 (in Russian),

(b) Yevintov, V. E., *International Community and Legal Order*, 1990 (in Russian),

(c) *The Ideas of Peace and Cooperation in Modern International Law*, 1990 (in Russian),

(d) Martynenko, A. P., *The Right of Peoples in Modern International Law*, 1993 (in Russian),

(e) *Ethno-National Development of Ukraine*, 1993 (in Ukrainian),

(f) *The Victims of Repressions*, 1993 (in Russian).

Annotation: The Institute deals with international law, international security, peace, international cooperation, disarmament and rights of peoples

United Kingdom

Centre for Conflict Analysis
University of Kent
Canterbury, Kent, CT2 7NX, UK

Telephone: 44-1227-764000

Fax: 44-1227-827033

E-mail: M.Spice@ukc.ac.uk or N.Cooper@ukc.ac.uk
Senior Staff: Director: A.J.R. Groom, Senior Researcher: Keith Webb, Vivienne, Jabri, Research Director: Mark Hoffman
Date of Establishment: 1965
Purpose: The Centre aspires:

(a) The engagement in the facilitation of internationalized disputes,

(b) The development of conflict theory with particular reference to mediation techniques, especially track two diplomacy and the role of international organizations in mediation and facilitation, both govern-

mental and non-governmental.

Type: International, private, non-profit
Brief History: The Centre for Conflict Analysis is a network of scholars interested in conflict theory and facilitation techniques based in universities in the UK, USA, Australia, South Africa, New Zealand, and Germany. From time to time they form teams to undertake facilitation exercises with top decision-makers in internationalized disputes. Their theoretical publications are undertaken through their home institutions, and facilitation exercises are of a highly confidential nature.

Centre for Conflict Resolution
Department of Peace Studies, University of Bradford
Bradford, West Yorkshire, England BD7 1DP, UK

Telephone: 44-1274-384172
Fax: 44-1274-385240
Web Site: http://www.brad.ac.uk/acad/confres/crchome.htm
Senior Staff: Director: Tom Woodhouse, Program Director: Nick Lewer
Date of Establishment: 1990
Purpose: The Centre for Conflict Resolution (CCR) has emphasized on combining the ideas and experiences of both academics and practitioners as well as the transference of research findings into practical applications. It also focuses on increasing understanding of how the various agencies of the international community can cooperate in order to improve opportunities for effective conflict resolution in situations of major armed conflicts.
Brief History: The Centre for Conflict Resolution, which is based in the Department of Peace Studies, was established in 1990. This was made possible by the generosity of Alec Horsley, a British Quaker and long time supporter of Peace Studies, who provided the funding necessary for the purchase of Horsley House where the CCR is located.
Principal Activities: As part of the Department of Peace Studies, staff teaches on the BA, MA, and Ph.D

Peace Studies courses. These include modules on 'Conflict Resolution in Domestic Society,' 'Conflict Resolution and Peacekeeping Skills,' and 'Peacekeeping and Humanitarian Intervention.' In addition to these, staff and researchers have build up a considerable base of experience and resource materials by tracking and analyzing some of the Worlds conflicts, such as Balkans, Sri Lanka, Somalia and Cyprus conflicts.
Periodicals: *International Peacekeeping News*, (bimonthly).
Major Publications:

(a) *Conflict in Bosnia-Herzegovina: Problem with the Delivery of Humanitarian Aid,*

(b) *Peacemaking, Peacekeeping: European Security and Yugoslav Conflict,*

(c) *In the Middle: Non-Official Mediation in Violent Situations,*

(d) *The Medical Peace Movement: An Evaluation of the Historical and Contemporary Roles of Physicians in Peacemaking Processes, with Specific Reference to the Development of Expertise in Mediation.*

Centre for Defense and International Security Studies (CDISS)
Cartmel College
Lancaster, La1 4YL, Lancaster, UK

Telephone: 44-1524-594254/55
Fax: 44-1524-594258
E-mail: p.elliott@lancaster.ac.uk

Web Site: http://www.cdiss.org
Senior Staff: Director: Martin Edmonds, Deputy Director: David Gates

Date of Establishment: 1990

Purpose: CDISS exists to research, raise awareness and stimulate debate on a wide range of defense and security issues relevant to both the UK and the International Community.

Type: International, public, non-profit

Brief History: The Center for Defense and International Security Studies was established by order of the Lancaster University Senate on August 1, 1990. It is a merger of the two Centres: the Centre for Defense and Security Analysis (1989) and the Centre for the Study of Arms Control and International Security (1978). The resources of the two Centres and the opportunity for synergism that the merger created places CDISS in a strong position to contribute to debates on national and international security issues into the 21st century and to be of practical service to government, industry, the Armed Services, the media and the general public.

Principal Activities: Research as on:

(a) Civil-military relations,

(b) Defense technology,

(c) the UN,

(d) Regional security studies,

(e) Missile threats and responses,

(f) Airpowers,

(g) European security,

(h) Terrorism, and teaching commercial collaboration.

Periodicals: *Defense Analysis* (three times a year)

Major Publications:

(a) *Ballistic Missiles: The Approaching Threat,*

(b) *Cruise Missiles: Precision & Countermeasures,*

(c) *Airpower: the Future?*

(d) *The Devil's Brews I: Chemical and Biological Weapons and their Delivery Systems.*

Centre for Defense Economics
University of York
Alcuin College Heslington, York, YO1 5DD, UK

Telephone: 44-1904-433680

Fax: 44-1904-432300

E-mail: mmcl@york.ac.uk

Senior Staff: Director: Keith Hartley, Deputy Director: Nick Hopper

Date of Establishment: 1990

Purpose: The Centre undertakes research into all aspects of the economics of defense, disarmament, conversion and peace.

Type: Public, non-profit

Brief History: The Centre was created in April 1990 to bring together the University of York's established and expanding research and teaching interests in defense economics. It is a self-contained unit within the Department of Economics and Related Studies (Alcuin College).

Principal Activities: The Centre has a range of activities such as:

(a) Short and long-term research projects,

(b) Commercial research and consultancy,

(c) Lectures and short courses for students, the Armed Forces and industry,

(d) Information, statistical and advisory services,

(e) Bibliographical and literature search services,

(f) Access to national and international networks of scholars and researches,

(g) Facilities for visitors.

Periodicals: *Defense and Peace Economics*

Major Publications:

(a) *The Economics of Offsets: Issues, Policies and Prospects,*

(b) *The Future of the Defense Firm in Europe, North America and East Asia,*

(c) *The Economics of Defense Policy,*

(d) *The Economics of Defense, Disarmament and Peace: an Annotated Bibliography.*

Centre for Defence Studies (CDS), King's College
University of London
Strand, London WC2R 2LS, UK

Telephone: 44-71-873-2338
Fax: 44-71-873-2748
Senior Staff: Executive Director: M. Clarke, Researcher: M. Clarke, C. Smith, S. Willett, J. Gow
Date of Establishment: 1990
Type: Public
Principal Activities: Research; conference- organization; publication

Periodicals:

(a) *Bulletin of Arms Control*, 4 p.a.

(b) *International Security Digest*, 10 p.a.

Major Publications:

(a) Willett, S., *The Gulf Crisis: Economic Implications*, 1991,

(b) Thompson, J. et al., *The Gulf Crisis: Political and Military Implications*, 1991,

(c) Gow, J., *Yugoslav End Games: Civil Strife and Interstate Conflict*, 1991,

(d) Jasani, B., *The Prospects for British and European Space Programmes*, 1991,

(e) Navias, M., *Saddam's Scud War and Ballistic Missile Proliferation*, 1991,

(f) Heuser, B., *Nuclear Weapons and the Future of European Security*, 1991,

(g) Moss, N., *The Politics of Global Warming*, 1991,

(h) Economides, S., *The Balkan Agenda: Security and Nationalism in the New Europe*, 1991,

(i) Wicker, B., *Chemical Weapons: Are British Reservations still Justified?* 1991,

(j) Sims, N. A., *Reinforcing Biological Disarmament: Issues in the 1991 Review*, 1991,

(k) Plant, G. (ed.), *Environmental Protection and the Law of War*, 1992,

(l) Clarke, M. (ed.), *New Perspectives on Security*, 1992,

(m) Gow, J. (ed.), *Iraq, the Conflict and the World Community*, 1992.

Annotation: Fields of research include national defence policy and decision making, European security, democratization and future threats to peace and security, ethnic identity in Eastern Europe and economic security in Britain. Monitoring the progress of arms control, weapons and international security is part of the remit of the Centre.
Courses: Security and Democracy in the New Europe
Subjects Taught: International security; democracy; peace
Target Group: Professionals
Type of Course: Special course run in three separate sessions
Duration: 3 weeks
Working Languages: English
Admission Requirements: Yes. Submission of candidature, 2 letters of recommendation submitted separately, and evidence of English language proficiency

Center for European Studies
University of Essex
Wivenhoe Park, Essex CO4 3SQ, UK

Telephone: 44-1206-87-3418
Fax: 44-1206-87-2724
E-mail: emil@essex.ac.uk or susyd@essex.ac.uk
Web Site: www.essex.ac.uk/centres/european.html
Senior Staff: Director: Emil J. Kirchner
Date of Establishment: 1990
Purpose: The Centre works:

(a) To act as a focus for staff and students of European affairs at Essex University,

(b) To foster regular contacts between members of the University,

(c) To provide a base within the University from which new course options in European studies may be generated, and aims

(d) To establish links with counterparts in Europe and engage in transnational collaboration.

Brief History: The establishment of the Center for European Studies in 1990 was a natural development for the University of Essex which has a number of centers of excellence, a long association with Europe and a faculty whose expertise on Europe is well recognized. One of its main features is its pan-European, inter-disciplinary and Erasmus/Tempus-linked approach.

Principal Activities:

(a) To organize and undertake research into European

affairs and to promote research collaboration between members of different Departments using interdisciplinary and comparative approaches,

(b) To disseminates information about European affairs through organizing conferences and seminars and publishing working papers and books.

Department of Peace Studies
University of Bradford
Richmond Road, Bradford BD7 1DP, UK

Telephone: 44-1274-385235
Fax: 44-1274-385240
E-mail: P.F. Rogers@bradford.ac.uk
Senior Staff: Professor of Peace Studies & Head of Department: Paul Rogers, Professor of International Security: Malcolm Dando, Director of the Centre for Conflict Resolution: Tom Woodhouse
Date of Establishment: 1973
Purpose: The Department aperates

(a) To promote thinking and action on peace issues,

(b) To teach peace studies,

(c) To provide independent, critical research and analysis of peace and related issues,

(d) To be involved with policy development and formation in Britain and overseas,

(e) To aid peace campaigning and policy formation through its publications program, direct support for peace groups and an evolving relationship with the media. Its policy studies have expanded into wider areas of concern as the Department has grown in size.

Type: National
Brief History: It is the only university department in Britain concerned exclusively with the study of peace, and remains the largest university centre of its kind in the world, offering a full program of undergraduate and postgraduate programs. The MA programs have a strong international emphasis, with at least a dozen countries represented each year. The academic staff and research students together form a large research community of over 50 people.
Principal Activities: Research is carried out on conflict resolution, peacekeeping, mediation, control of the arms trade and of nuclear and biological weapons, conflict prevention, the prospects for peaceful social change and the development of civil society. The

Department is a source of advice for a wide range of public bodies and also aids the development of new peace studies centers. Staff maintain close links with government departments and institutions and they also act as consultants and advisers for many NGOs. All this work is seen as an important additional output for policy-orientated research.
Periodicals: *International Peacekeeping News* (bi-monthly)

Major Publications:

(a) Darweish, M., Rigby, A., *Palestinians in Israel: Nationality and Citizenship*, Peace Research Report No. 35, University of Bradford, October 1995,

(b) Pankhurst, D., *A Resolvable Conflict? The Politics of Land in Namibia*, Peace Research Report No. 36, University of Bradford, February 1996,

(c) Smith, M., *On Rocky Foundations: NATO, the UN and Peace Operations on the Post-Cold War Era*, Peace Research Report No. 37, University of Bradford, October 1996,

(d) Broadhead, L. A. (ed.), *Issues in Peace Research 1995-96*, University of Bradford, 1996,

(e) *The Bradford Arms Register Series* (BARS), resulting from the Department's major program on the UN Arms Transfers Register and published by Westview Press.

Other Information: The Department has sought to promote its work since 1980 with policy opinion formers, non-government organizations and the media. It now has a national and international reputation as one of the few academic centers willing and able to provide independent and critical analyses of major peace issues.

Global Security Programme
University of Cambridge
Faculty of Social and Political Sciences, Free School Lane, Cambridge CB2 3RQ, UK

Telephone: 44-223-334509
Fax: 44-223-335065
E-mail: GSP@PHX.CAM.AC.UK
Senior Staff: Director: G. Prins, Deputy Director: C. Albin, Deputy Director & Researcher: C. Albin
Date of Establishment: 1989
Type: Non-profit
Principal Activities: Research; training; publication; conference-organization; radio and TV programmes; public education
Current Peace Research: United Nations project: humanitarian intervention
Periodicals: *GSP Newsletter*, 12 p.a.
Major Publications:

(a) *Worldwide Security: the New World Order*, 1991,

(b) Prins, G., *The United Nations and Peacekeeping in the Post-Cold War World: the Case of Naval Power*, 1991,

(c) Mack, A., Sopiee, N. (eds.), *Maritime Security and Common Security*,

(d) *The Environmental State of the Earth: Are We Secure?*,

(e) *Public Medicine and Global Security: the Challenge and the Opportunities*, 1992,

(f) *Renewable Energy and its Enemies*, 1992,

(g) *The Rio Summit*, 1992,

(h) Ball, D., Horner, D. (eds.), *A New Focus for Security Studies*, 1992,

(i) Hopkinson, G. W., *Changing Options: British Defence and Global Security*, 1992,

(j) Mohammed, N. A. L., *Conflict in Southern Sudan*, 1993,

(k) Prins, G. (ed.), *Threats Without Enemies*, 1993,

(l) Whitman, J., Bartbolomew, I., *Collective Control of UN Peace Support Operations: A Policy Proposal*, 1994.

Annotation: Fields of research include violence and the threat of violence in international relations; ecology and environmental international security; temperate and tropical food security; gender, risk and security; the political theory of globalization; negotiation and conflict resolution in face of threats to international security; social and political aspects of information technology revolution; ethics of collective security.
Courses: Global Security Programme
Subjects Taught: Conflict resolution; role of the international organizations; democracy and peace; international conflict; international security
Principal Instructors: Dr. G. Prins
Target Group: Students; professionals; visiting fellows
Level of the Course: Undergraduate; graduate; post-graduate
Type of Course: Regular courses, included in the B.A. (Hons.) and Ph.D. curricula
Working Languages: English
Scholarships Available: One MacArthur Scholarship available per year for Ph.D. candidates: contact Programme Administrator

Institute of Development Studies (IDS)
University of Sussex
Brighton BN1 9RE, UK

Telephone: 44-1273-606261
Fax: 44-1273-621202
E-mail: ids@sussex.ac.uk
Web Site: http://www.ids.ac.uk/ids
Senior Staff: Director: Keith Bezanson
Date of Establishment: 1996
Purpose: The Institute aims to provide a national Centre for teaching and researching on development.
Type: Non-profit
Brief History: The Institute was established as a national Centre to support the newly created UK over-

seas aid program, IDS has grown to become one of the largest institutes of its kind in Europe. It houses the British Library for Development Studies.
Principal Activities:

(a) Research into various aspects of development,

(b) Postgraduate teaching,

(c) Training program for administrators/ development professionals,

(d) Advisory work,

(e) Development information/Library.

Periodicals:

(a) *IDS Bulletin*,

(b) *IDS Policy Briefings*,

(c) Various Woking Papers/Research Reports.

Major Publications:

(a) *Poverty, Policy and Aid*,

(b) *Evaluating Program Aid*,

(c) *The Potential for Donor Mediation in NGO-State Relations: An Ethiopian Case Study*.

International Trade Union Committee for Peace and Disarmament
1 Woodlands Terrace, Glasgow G3 6DD, UK

Telephone: 41-331-1216
Fax: 41-332-4649
Senior Staff: President: C. Christie
Date of Establishment: 1982
Type: Non-profit
Principal Activities: Research; documentation/information; publication
Current Peace Research: Research/survey on transport of nuclear weapons and materials by land, sea and air
Periodicals:

(a) *Dublin Committee Newsletter*,

(b) *Quarterly Newsletter*

Major Publications:

From Military Confrontation to the Peace Dividend: a Challenge of the Nineties, 1993.

Annotation: The Committee Initiates and organizes international meetings and coordinated actions with the world trade unions movement. The Committee Deals with disarmament and peace and development issues.

National Peace Council (NPC)
88 Islington High st. Lodon N1 8EG, UK

Telephone: 44-71-354-5200
Fax: 44-71-354-0033
E-mail: gn:NPC
Senior Staff: Networking: A. McLeod, Specialist: L. Peck, D. Thompson
Date of Establishment: 1908
Purpose: The Council aims to forge links between member organizations and to act as a clearinghouse for information.
Type: Private, non-profit
Brief History: The National Peace Council was founded in 1908 at an international peace congress in London. One of its first resolution was against the spending of £63 million on war preparations. Through the years of two world wars, the Council opposed militarism, urged cooperation, issued pamphlets, and worked for peace education. Great names associated with the NPC include Leonard Woolf, H. G. Wells, Philop Noel-Baker, Victor Gollancz, and Lord Soper.
Principal Activities: Every month sees the issue of a mailing that is widely recognized as one of the best independent sources of news and comment about the peace movement and related issues. The mailing contains the Newsletter; information on new policies and initiatives; and special briefings on current topics that range from Northern Ireland to the Flaklands and Lebanon; from nuclear disarmament and nuclear power to world development and human rights.

Through representation, the NPC links the British peace movement internationally to other independent, nonaligned organizations. It is a member of the International Peace Bureau and the Special Non-Governmental Organizations Committee on Disarmament in 1978 and 1982. There is close cooperation with the United Nations Association and with the Campaign Against the Arms Trade.

The United World Trust is the NPC's education and research body which has legal charitable status. Set up in 1955, the Trust became known for its annual conferences for diplomats on international issues and for its weekend conferences for trainee teachers.

Current Peace Research:

(a) Building up databases on local and national British peace organizations and organizations concerned with peace work in Northern Ireland,

(b) Consultative process in UK into the creation of a bill of rights for Northern Ireland,

(c) Investigation into treatment of deserters and war

resisters from former Yugoslavia by the UK government.

Major Publications:

Ex-Yugoslavia file by the United World Trust (charitable "arm" of the NPC): Towards Disarmament: The United Nations Second Special Session and Beyond, a handbook for teachers.

Oxford Research Group
32 Warnborough Road, Oxford OX2 6JA, UK

Telephone: 44-865-242-819
Fax: 44-865-794-652
Senior Staff: Director: S. Elworthy, Researcher: I. Davis, H. Miall, Coordinator: T. Voss
Date of Establishment: 1982
Type: Non-profit
Principal Activities: Research; training; documentation/information; conference-organization; publication; radio and TV programmes; consulting
Current Peace Research:

(a) Research towards reducing spending on military research and development,

(b) The defence debate in UK and Germany prior to general elections,

(c) Conflict resolution,

(d) Beliefs of decision-makers,

(e) Co-ordination of foreign policy and mutual security in political Europe,

(f) Converting the defence industry,

(g) Military research and development in Europe,

(h) International arms trade,

(i) New conflicts in Europe,

(j) Proliferation issues,

Periodicals: *Media Bulletin*, 4 p.a.
Major Publications:

(a) Ramsbotham, O., Miall, H., *Beyond Deterrence: Britain, Germany and the New European Security Debate*, 1991,

(b) Miall, H., *The Peacemakers: Peaceful Settlement of Disputes Since 1945*, 1992,

(c) Voss, T., *Converting the Defence Industry: Have We the Political Will?*, 1992,

(d) Miall, H., *New Conflicts in Europe: Prevention and Resolution*, 1992,

(e) Davis, I., *Military Research and Development in Europe: Collaboration Without Control?*, 1992,

(f) Barnaby, F., *The Plutonium Legacy: Nuclear Proliferation out of Control?*, 1993,

(g) Halliwell, P., Lowry, D., *The Emerging Nuclear Nations*, 1993.

Annotation: The Institute carries out research on how and by whom nuclear weapons decisions are made, and studies law decision-making structures and how processes can evolve in the light of changed circumstances, and analysis of current decisions and debates in the field of defence and disarmament
Courses: Training in Research Techniques in Peace
Subjects Taught: Peace research
Target Group: Non-specialists

Pugwash Conferences on Science and World Affairs
Flat A, Museum Mansions, 63A Great Russell St.
London WC1 3BG, UK

Telephone: 44-171-405-6661
Fax: 44-171-831-5651
E-mail: pugwash@qmw.ac.uk
Senior Staff: President: Michael Assyah, Secretary

General: G. Rassfens
Date of Establishment: 1975
Purpose: International association of scientists to discuss problems, which have arisen as a result of the

progress of science and in particular the development of weapons of mass destruction and disarmament problems.
Type: Private, non-profit

Principal Activities: Conference-organization
Periodicals: *Pugwash Newsletter* (quarterly)
Major Publications: Bulletin; monograph; conference proceedings.

The Richardson Institute for Peace Studies
Department of Politics and International Relations, Lancaster University
Lancaster LA1 4YF, UK

Telephone: 44-1524-594290
Fax: 44-1524-594238
E-mail: ri@Lancaster.ac.uk
Web Site: http:// www.lancs.ac.uk/users/richinst/ riweb1.htm
Senior Staff: Director: Hugh Miall, Former Director: Morris Bradley
Date of Establishment: 1965
Purpose: The Institute aims:

(a) To promote understanding of peace and war, peacemaking and peaceful change,

(b) To be a Centre of excellence in peace and conflict research,

(c) To offer opportunities for undergraduate and post-graduate study and research,

(d) To encourage the practical application of its work.

Type: National, private, non-profit
Brief History: The Richardson Institute grew out of the peace research Centre established in Lancaster in 1959, the peace and conflict research program at Lancaster University since 1965, and the London-based Richardson Institute. Previously directed by Paul Smoker and Michael Nicholson, the Institute carries out basic and applied research in peace and conflict studies, inspired by the vision of Lewis Richardson.
Principal Activities: The Institute offers Ph.D. research in peace studies, MA degrees in peace studies and conflict resolution, and a BA in peace studies with international relations. Current research is focused on: conflict prevention, conflict resolution, the psychology of co-operation, Northern Ireland, the Southern Balkans, and training and professionalization of agents of peace.
Periodicals: *Newsletter* (occasional).
Major Publications:

(a) *Conflict Prevention,*

(b) *Conflict Resolution and Peace Processes,*

(c) *Northern Ireland,*

(d) *The Psychology of Cooperation,*

(e) *Training and Professionalization of Peacemakers,*

(f) *Conflict Prevention in the Southern Balkans.*

Royal Institute of International Affairs
Chatham House, 10 st. James's Square, London SW1Y 4 LE, UK

Telephone: 44-171-957-5700
Fax: 44-171-957-5710
Web Site: http://www.riia.org
Senior Staff: Director: Sir. Tim Garden
Date of Establishment: 1920
Purpose: The Institute aims to promote the study and understanding of all aspects of international affairs through lectures, discussions, conferences, research and publications. It is independent of government and owes no allegiance to any political party.
Type: International, non-profit
Brief History: The Institute was set up by former dele-gates to the Paris Peace Conference of 1919, it received its Royal Charter in 1926. Chatham House is historic premises home of three Prime Ministers.
Principal Activities: Research; lectures; discussion groups; conferences publications.
Periodicals:

(a) *World Today* (monthly),

(b) *International Affairs* (quarterly).

Major Publications:

(a) *International Economics,*

(b) *Asia/Pacific,*

(c) *Russia/Eurasia,*

(d) *Middle East,*

(e) *Europe,*

(f) *South Africa Study Group,* (Publications in all areas).

United States

ACCESS
1511 K Street, NW, Suite 643, Washington, DC 20005, USA

Telephone: 1-202-783-6050
Fax: 1-202-783-4767
Senior Staff: Executive Director: M. E. Lord, R. J. Bee
Date of Establishment: 1985
Type: Non-profit
Principal Activities: Documentation; information; publication

Periodicals:

(a) *ACCESS Resource Brief,* 2 p.a.

(b) *ACCESS Security Spectrum,* 4-6 p.a.

Major Publications:

(a) *International Affairs Internship in the Washington DC Area,* 1992,

(b) *The Future of NATO and US Interests,* 1991,

(c) *The ACCESS Guide to the Persian Gulf Crisis,* 1991,

(d) *The Arab-Palestinian-Israel Conflict: US Policy Options,* 1991,

(e) *Change and Challenge in the Former USSR: The End of the Cold War and the Dawn of a New Era,* 1992,

(f) *International Affairs Directory of Organizations: the ACCESS Resource Guide,* 1992,

(g) *US Policy Towards Africa in the Post-Cold War Era,* 1993,

(h) *The ACCESS Guide to Ethnic Conflicts in Europe and the Former Soviet Union,* 1993,

(i) *ACCESS Issue Packet on Africa,* 1993,

(j) *Going to War? Bosnia and Beyond. A Study Circle Discussion Program,* 1993.

Annotation: International information and referral service on international security, peace issues, arms control and cold war history, trade and defence budget, regional conflicts and ethnic conflicts

The Albert Einstein Institution
50 Church Street, Cambridge, MA 02138, USA

Telephone: 1-617-876-0311
Fax: 1-617-876 0837
Senior Staff: President: C. Kruegler, Senior Scholar: G. Sharp, C. Kruegler
Date of Establishment: 1983
Type: Non-profit
Principal Activities: Research; documentation. information; conference-organization; publication; radio and TV programmes; financing; scholarships/grants
Current Peace Research:

(a) Protocol for the assessment of nonviolent direct action (PANDA), program on nonviolent sanctions,

(b) Study of Peace Brigades International and its practice of nonviolent accompaniment,

(c) Study of the rise and decline of US peace action in the 1980s,

(d) Compilation of an encyclopedia of nonviolent action.

Periodicals: *Nonviolent Sanctions,* 4 p.a.

Major Publications:

(a) Sharp, G., *The Role of Power in Nonviolent Struggle,* 1990,

(b) Sharp, G., *Civilian-Based Defense: A Post-Military Weapons System,* 1990,

(c) Parkman, P., *Insurrectionary Civic Strikes in Latin America 1931-1961,* 1990,

(d) Holst, J. J., *Civilian-Based Defense in a New Era*, 1990,

(e) Roberts, A., *Civil Resistance in the East European and Soviet Revolutions*, 1992,

(f) Eglitis, O., *Nonviolent Action in the Liberation of Latvia*, 1993,

(g) Bleiker, R., *Nonviolent Struggle and the Revolution in East Germany*, 1993,

(h) McCarthy, R., Kruegler, C., *Toward Research and Theory Building in the Study of Nonviolent Action*, 1993,

(i) Ackerman, C., Kruegler, C., *Strategic Nonviolent Conflict: The Dynamics of People Power in the 20c.*, 1994.

Annotation: A non-profit making organization advancing the study and use of strategic nonviolence in conflicts throughout the world.

Arms Control Association (ACA)
11 Dupont Circle, NW, Suite 250, Washington, DC 20036-1207, USA

Telephone: 202-797-4626
Senior Staff: Executive Director: S. Keeny
Date of Establishment: 1971
Type: Non-profit
Principal Activities: Research; training; documentation/information; conference- organization; publication

Periodicals: *Arms Control Today*, 12 p.a.
Annotation: Its purpose is to promote understanding of arms control and its contribution to national security. It operates in association with the Carnegie Endowment.

Asia/ Pacific Research Center
200 Encina Hall Stanford, CA 94305-4055, USA

Telephone: 1-415-723-9741
Fax: 1-415-723-4530
Date of Establishment: 1976
Purpose: To create an inter disciplinary research center focused on public policy issues involving the United States and Northeast Asia.
Type: Private—Part of Stanford University
Brief History: The Center was founded in 1976 as the Northeast Asia-United States Forum or International Policy at Stanford University. We changed our name to the Asia/Pacific Research Center in 1990 and expanded our focus to include the rest of Asia.
Principal Activities: A/PRC researches political and

economic issues in Asia and between the United States and Asia.
Periodicals: Publications of research published throughout the year as well as an annual report.

Major Publications:

(a) *The Syndrome of Ever Higher Yen, 1971-1995: American Mercantile Pressure on Japanese Monetary Policy*,

(b) *The China-United States Bilateral Trade Balance: How big is it Really?*,

(c) *Managing US Relations with China.*

The Baker Institute for Peace and Conflict Studies, Juniata College
Huntingdon, Pennsylvania 16652-2119, USA

Telephone: 1-814-643-4310
Fax: 1-814-643-3620
Senior Staff: Director: A. Murray, Prof.: C. Cook Huffman
Date of Establishment: 1986
Type: Private, non-profit
Principal Activities: Research; training; documentation/information; conference-organization; publication; exhibitions

Current Peace Research:

(a) The use of biotechnology for aggressive purposes. Present and future dangers,

(b) Public acceptance of biological weapons,

(c) Critical thinking in peace education in peace education courses.

Major Publications:

(a) *Peace and Conflict Studies as Applied to Liberal Arts.*

Annotation: Major emphasis is given to organized violence and war as an urgent global problem. The Institute offers flexibility to design an interdisciplinary programme suited to the educational and vocational interests of the students. Individualized programmes may be created by combining PACS courses with other areas (i.e., international relations, communication, management, sociology, religion).

Courses: Peace and Conflict Studies Academic Program (PACS)

Subjects Taught: Peace research; disarmament; peaceful coexistence; conflict resolution; role of the international organizations; nonviolence; peace and development; polemology; war; international conflict; international security; psychology and anthropology of war and peace; resource distribution and conflict; empowerment in the nuclear age; Latin American revolutions; the holocaust; international politics; the military and politics in the Third World; international law and organization; rebellion, religion and pacifism

Principal Instructors: Dr. A. Murray (Programme Director)

Target Group: Non-specialists

Level of the Course: Undergraduate

Type of Course: Regular course. Various special opportunities include practical experience on the administrative committee for the PACS programme, making budgetary and curricular decisions and participating in long range planning; field trips to other institutions; simulations including an International Issues Lab allowing students to experience as well as read about certain decision making processes and conflict situations; Internships; and study abroad

Duration: 4 years

Working Languages: English

Course Fees: Yes

Scholarships Available: Yes, 3 scholarships are available (the application process normally includes an essay). Apply to: the Office of Admission, Juniata College

Degree/Diploma: B.A. in Peace and Conflict Studies; B.SC. in Peace and Conflict Studies

---

The Brookings Institution (BI)
1775 Massachusetts Avenue, NW, Washington, DC 20036-2188, USA

Telephone: 202-797-6000
Fax: 202-767-6004
E-mail: EAPUBLIC@BROOK.EDU
Cable: BROOKINST WASHINGTON
Senior Staff: President: B. K. MacLaury; Senior Fellow: F. M. Deng, Senior Research Analyst: T. Lyons, J. E. Nolan, W. B. Quandt, J. D. Steinbruner
Date of Establishment: 1927
Type: Private, non-profit
Principal Activities: Research; publication
Periodicals:

(a) *The Brookings Review,*

(b) *Brookings Papers on Economic Activity*, 2 p.a.,

(c) *Brookings Papers on Economic Activity- Microeconomics*, 1 p.a..

Major Publications:

(a) Deng, F., Zartman, I. W. (eds.), *Conflict Resolution in Africa*, 1991,

(b) Quandt, W., *Peace Process: American Diplomacy and the Arab-Israeli Conflict Since 1967*, 1993,

(c) Deng, F., *Protecting the Dispossessed*, 1993,

(d) Lincoln, E., *Japan's New Global Role*, 1993,

(e) Sadowski, Y., *Scuds or Butter?* 1993,

(f) Kaufmann, W., *Assessing the Base Force*, 1993,

(g) Nolan, J., *Global Engagement: Cooperation and Security in the 21st Century*, 1994.

Annotation: Its peace related activities are carried out through its research programs devoted to foreign policy studies, national security, and arms control.

Carnegie Endowment for International Peace (CEIP)
2400 N Street, NW, Washington, DC 20037-1118, USA

Telephone: 1-202-862-7900
Fax: 1-202-862-2610

Telex: 248329
Senior Staff: L. Fabian

Date of Establishment: 1910
Type: Private, non-profit
Principal Activities: Research; conference-organization; publication
Current Peace Research:

(a) US policy towards Africa,

(b) Major powers and Southeast Asia,

(c) Strategic issues and US alliance relationship,

(d) Arms control and proliferation in the Near East

and Southeast Asia,

(e) American policy in Asia,

(f) NATO-Warsaw Pact relations,

(g) European/American and East-West relations.

Periodicals: *Foreign Policy*, 4 p.a.

Annotation: Conducts research in international relations, arms control, foreign policy and peace negotiations

Center for Applied Conflict Management
Political Science Department, Kent State University
PO Box 5190, Kent, OH 44242-0001, USA

Telephone: 1-330-672-3143
Fax: 1-330-672-3362
E-mail: cacm@Kent.edu
Senior Staff: Director, Assistant Professor: Jennifer Maxwell, Assistant Professor: Patrick Coy, William Schultz, Associate Professor Emeritus: Dennis Carey
Date of Establishment: 1971
Purpose: The mission of the Center for Applied Conflict Management is to conduct research, develop theory, and offer education, training, and public service in the field of conflict management. CACM courses and programs are designed to provide diverse populations with the knowledge and skills necessary to do social, political, and cultural analysis of conflict settings, and to develop and implement intervention and conflict management strategies.
Type: Public
Brief History: Formerly the Center for Peaceful Change, the Center was established in 1971 as a living memorial to the events of May 4, 1970, when State students protesting the Vietnam War were killed and injured by Ohio National Guardsmen.
Principal Activities:

(a) Offering an undergraduate baccalaureate degree in Applied Conflict Management,

(b) Research, theory-building, and publishing in the field of conflict studies,

(c) Training programs for community groups,

(d) Contract services for public and private sector organizations,

(e) Consulting on conflict management processes.

Periodicals: None currently. From the late 1970's to the mid 1980's, the Center for Peaceful Change published *Peace and Change: Journal of Peace Research*.
Major Publications:

(a) *A Revolution of the Heart: Essays on the Catholic Worker,* Temple University Press, 1988, and New Society Publishers, 1992,

(b) Woehrle, L., "Constructing Identity and Oppositional Knowledge: The Framing Practices of Peace Movement Organizations During the Persian Gulf War," *Sociological Spectrum*, Vol. 16, No. 3, 1996,

(c) Kool, V. K. (ed.), "Protective Accompaniment: How Peace Brigades International Secures Political Space and Human Rights Nonviolently," in *Nonviolence: Social and Psychological Issues*, University Press of America, 1993,

(d) "Cooperative Accompaniment and Peace Brigades International in Sri Lanka," in Chatfield, C., Pagnucco, R., Smith, J. (eds.), *Solidarity Beyond the State: The Dynamics of Transnational Social Movements*, Syracuse University Press, 1997,

(e) "Conscription and the Catholic Conscience in World War II," in Klejment, A., Roberts, N. (eds.), *American Catholic Pacifism*, Praeger, 1996,

(f) "Introduction," Coy, P. G. (ed.), *A Revolution of the Heart*, 1988, Gorman, A. O., "Houses of Hospitality: A Pilgrimage into Nonviolence," in Coy, P. G. (ed.), *A Revolution of the Heart*, 1988; 1992.

Center for Defense Information (CDI)
1500 Massachusetts Avenue, NW, Suite 24, Washington, DC 20005, USA

Telephone: 1-202-862-0700
Fax: 1-202-862-0708
Telex: 904059 WSH (CDI)
E-mail: cdi@igc.apc.org
Senior Staff: President: G. R. La Rocque, Director: E. Carroll, Jr., Specialist: G. R. La Rocque, Captain: J. T. Bush, D. M. Smith, P. M. Wood
Date of Establishment: 1972
Type: Non-profit
Principal Activities: Documentation/information; publication; radio and TV programmes
Periodicals: *The Defense Monitor*, 10 p.a.
Major Publications:

(a) *Profiles of Major US Military Contractors and Their Recent Foreign Sales*, 1993,

(b) *Illegal and Covert Arms Transfers*, 1993,

(c) *Offset Agreements and Arms Exports*, 1993,

(d) *The US Arms Trade and Security Assistance Community*, 1993.

Annotation: Its purpose is to support an effective defence while opposing excessive expenditures for weapons and policies that increase the danger of war. It deals with military research and analysis on defence, arms control, nuclear weapons, US foreign policy, conflicts, and conventional arms transfer.

Center for Economic Conversion
222 View St. Mountain View, CA 94041, USA

Telephone: 1-415-968-8798
Fax: 1-415-968-1126
E-mail: cec@igc.org
Web Site: http://www.conversion.org/about2.html
Senior Staff: Executive Dir.: Michael Closson, Associate Dir.: Joan Holtzman
Date of Establishment: 1975
Purpose: To promote and facilitate the transfer of military resources to productive civilian uses and contribute to the process of building a sustainable and equitable peace oriented economy.
Type: National, private, non-profit
Principal Activities: Conversion planning assistance; public policy shaping; education and advocacy; public outreach; resource library and information clearinghouse; directed research
Periodicals: *Positive Alternatives*
Major Publications:

(a) *Changing Course*,

(b) *Defense Conversion in the US: An Unfulfilled Promise*,

(c) *Defense Conversion in Russia*,

(d) *Conversion in Western Europe: The Restructuring of Defense Industries*.

Center for European Studies
Duke University
2212 Campus Drive, Durham, NC 27708-0406, USA

Telephone: 1-919-684-6449
Fax: 1-919-684-8749
E-mail: ces@acpub.duke.edu
Web Site: www.duke.edu/web/european/
Senior Staff: Director: David F. Bell, Geeta Beeharry-Paray
Date of Establishment: 1994
Purpose: The Duke-UNC Center for European Studies seeks to promote programs, courses and research that directly address questions concerning the new Europe. The goal of the Center is to ensure that faculty, students and the larger community have access to the finest scholarship and the most current resources on modern Europe.
Brief History: The Duke-UNC Center has been designated as a comprehensive National Resource Center since 1994. This year the center has also been designated by the European Commission in Brussels as a European Union Center.
Principal Activities: The center currently supports development of innovative courses on Europe; hiring of regular and visiting faculty; organization of conferences, lectures and workshops on issues of contemporary concern; and bringing prominent European leaders and scholars to the area.

Center for European Studies
University of Minnesota
309 Social Science Building, 267 Nineteenth Avenue South, Minneapolis, MN 55455-0499, USA

Telephone: 1-612-625-1557
Fax: 1-612-626-2242
E-mail: cesiis@tc.umn.edu
Web Site: http://cla.umn.edu/europe
Senior Staff: Director: Edward Farmer
Date of Establishment: 1979
Purpose: The Center gives special consideration to projects that involve young scholars and future teachers through travel related to research and language study. CES strives to cultivate working relationships between graduate students and more experienced scholars.
Brief History: The Center for European Studies was

established in 1979 and was funded as a National Resource Center in Western European Studies by the US Department of Education under Title VI of the Higher Education Act of 1965.
Principal Activities: The Center for European Studies supports activities in all disciplines that will develop expertise and scholarship on European culture, economics and society. CES also supports projects, speakers, and courses that anticipate future political and cultural developments in Europe and it frequently sponsors activities with other departments and centers at the University of Minnesota.

Center for Global Peace
American University
4400 Massachusetts Avenue, NW, Washington, DC 20016-8071, USA

Telephone: 1-202-895-1326
Fax: 1-202-966-2561
E-mail: salima@american.edu
Web Site: www.american.edu/academic.depts/acainst/cgp/
Senior Staff: Director: Abdul Aziz Said
Purpose: The Center for Global Peace provides a framework for programs and initiatives that advance the study and understanding of world peace grounded

in a search for a just and sustainable world order. The Center works to embody the invitation in American University's Statement of Common Purpose, "turning ideas into action…and actions into service."
Principal Activities: The Center activities focus on the interdependent global system, identifying common interests and working toward common security. It is also engaged in training, publication, research projects and conference organization.

Center for International Affairs (CFIA)
Harvard University
Faculty of Arts and Sciences, 1737 Cambridge Street, Cambridge, MA 02138, USA

Telephone: 1-617-495-4420
Fax: 1-617-495-8292
Senior Staff: Director: J. S. Nye Jr.
Date of Establishment: 1958
Type: Private, non-profit
Principal Activities: Research; documentation/ information; conference-organization; publication
Periodicals: *Centerpiece*, 4 p.a.
Major Publications:

(a) Downing, B., *Military Revolution and Political Change: Origins of Democracy and Autocracy in Early Modern Europe*, 1991,

(b) Chehabi, H. E., *Iranian Politics and Religious Modernism: The Liberation Movement of Iran Under the Shah and Khomeini,*

(c) Feaver, P., *Civil-Military Relations and the Control of Nuclear Weapons,*

(d) Karp, A., *The Global Politics of Missile Proliferation,*

(e) Wirtz, J. J., *Intelligence Failure in War: The American Military and the Tet Offensive.*

Annotation: The Center conducts research concerning the basic subjects and problems of international relations. The main areas of research can be grouped into three categories: 1) US international relations and foreign policy; 2) regional studies; and 3) global issues including international economics, international institutions, multilateral negotiations, conflict resolution and nonviolent sanctions in conflict and defence.

Center for International and Comparative Studies (CICS)
Northwestern University
618 Garrett Place, Evanston, IL 60208-4135, USA

Telephone: 1-708-467-2770
Fax: 1-708-467-1996
E-mail: jgibson@nwu.edu
Web Site: www.nwu.edu/cics/
Senior Staff: Director: Bruce Cumings, Assistant director: Judith Gibson, Program Assistant: Frances Lowe
Date of Establishment: 1851
Brief History: Northwestern University was established in 1851 to serve the people of the Northwest Territory, an area that now embraces the states of Ohio, Indiana, Illinois, Michigan, Wisconsin, and part of Minnesota. In 1853 the founders purchased a 379-acre tract of land on the shore of Lake Michigan 12 miles north of Chicago. The town that grew up around the University was named Evanston in honor of one of the University's founders, John Evans.

After completing its first building in 1855, Northwestern began classes that fall with 2 faculty members and 10 students. By 1900, the University had grown to include seven undergraduate and graduate schools with 2,700 students and an annual budget of more than $200,000.

Today, Northwestern is one the country's leading private research universities, with an annual budget of more than $840 million and 5,700 employees. Appro-ximately 17,700 full-time and part-time students are enrolled in the University's 12 colleges and schools, which are located on campuses in Evanston and Chicago.

Principal Activities: CICS has a strong mandate to expand its focus beyond the campus, reaching out to the Chicago region and the Midwest. The center's seminars and lecture series are open to the public. Plans are under way to operate a recording studio to tape interviews with prominent speakers for broadcast by local television and radio media. CICS periodically publishes a newsletter distributed throughout the area to people with an interest in international affairs. The center's facilities, including library, media resource room and study lounge, are open to the larger Evanston community as well as to Northwestern students.

CICS collaborates with other Chicago-based organizations dealing with international affairs. The center is represented on the advisory committee of the Chicago Public Schools in Japan Project, which enhances the teaching about in Japan in the Chicago public schools. This project is administered by Education for Global Involvement, an outreach agency which enhances international and multi-cultural education, primarily in the Chicago Public School system. EGI and CICS will administer a new program in 1996-1997, "Agenda on the Pacific Rim: Educating about Japan, Latin America, and the Relationships between Japan and the Americas." CICS coordinates with the Chicago Council on Foreign Relations, the United Nations Association, Loyola University and other Institutions.
Periodicals: CICS Newsletters

Centre for International and Security Studies (CISSM)
University of Maryland
c/o School of Public Affairs, College Park, MD 20742-1811, USA

Telephone: 1-301-405-7610
Fax: 1-301-403-8107
Senior Staff: Director: I. M. Destler, Acting Director & Asst.: I. H. Daalder, Dean: M. Nacht, Prof.: T. Schelling, S. Turner
Date of Establishment: 1987
Type: Non-profit
Principal Activities: Research; training; conference-organization; publication
Current Peace Research:

(a) Managing nuclear proliferation in south Asia,

(b) Women in international security project,

(c) Cooperative security,

(d) Multilateral intervention,

(e) US-Japan relations,

(f) US nuclear weapons policy in a New World Order,

(g) New US-European dialogue.

Major Publications:

(a) Daalder, I. H. et al., *Reversing the Arms Race: The Bush-Gorbachev Initiatives on Nuclear Weapons*, 1991,

(b) Recktenwald, M., *Soviet Third World Policy in a*

Changing Society, 1991,

(c) Heuser, B., *Nuclear Weapons and the Future of European Security*, 1991,

(d) Daalder, I. H., *Cooperative Arms Control: A New Agenda for the Post-Cold War Era*, 1992,

(e) Hawes, J., *Arms Control: A New Style for a New Agenda*, 1993,

(f) Daalder, I. H., Terriff, T. (eds.), *Rethinking the Unthinkable: New Directions for Nuclear Arms Control*, 1993,

(g) Brown, M. E., *The "End" of Nuclear Arms Control*, 1993,

(h) Quester, G. H., *The Multilateral Management of International Security: The Nuclear Proliferation Model*, 1993,

(i) Lumpe, L., *Zero Ballistic Missiles and the Third World*, 1993,

(j) Durch, W. J., *Rethinking Strategic Ballistic Missile Defense*, 1993,

(k) Daalder, I. H., *Stepping Down the Thermonuclear Ladder: How Low Can We Go?* 1993,

(l) Tanner, F., *Arms Control in Times of Conflict: A Contribution to Conflict Management in the Post-Cold War World*, 1993,

(m) Gronlund, L., *From Nuclear Deterrence to Reassurance: The Role of Conflict-Building Measures and Restrictions on Military Development*, 1993,

(n) Hoopes, T., *Whither UN Peacekeeping?* 1994.

Annotation: Research programmes focus on three areas: building cooperative security in the new post-Cold War era with special focus on conflict management and arms control; managing complex interdependence among advanced industrial nations particularly the US, Japan and Europe and reforming the foreign policy process to respond to the new global challenges facing the United States.

Center for International Development and Conflict Management (CIDCM)
University of Maryland at College Park
Mill Building, College Park, MD 20742-4515, USA

Telephone: 1-301-314-7703
Fax: 1-301-314-9256
Senior Staff: Director: E. Kaufman, Senior Fellow: S. Abed, M. Polakoff, N. Gonzales, Researcher: S. B. Bushrui, J. Davies, Prof.: T. Gurr
Date of Establishment: 1981
Type: Non-profit
Principal Activities: Research; training; documentation/information; policy-making; publication; consulting

Current Peace Research:

(a) The Minorities at risk,

(b) The Global event-data system,

(c) The Religion and peace project,

(d) Evolving Palestinian democratization,

(e) Women in conflict resolution,

(f) Partners in conflict in the former Yugoslavia,

(g) Conflict between the individual and the State,

(h) Conflict between and among groups and the State,

(i) Conflict between and among nations and states.

Periodicals: *Nations & Needs: Newsletter*
Major Publications:

(a) Gonzales, N., *Dollar, Dove and Eagle: One Hundred Years of Palestinian Migration to Honduras*, 1992,

(b) *Minorities at Risk: A Global View of Ethnopolitical Conflicts*,

(c) Gonzales, N., *A Tale of Two Villages*, 1993,

(d) Kaufman, E., Abed, S., Rothstein, R. (eds.), *Democracy, Peace and the Israeli-Palestinian Conflict*, 1993.

Annotation: The Center dedicates itself to interdisciplinary research in the areas of international development, theoretical and practical conflict resolution, international conflict and international cooperation. The Center's fields of interest also include intra- and inter-state conflict from micro to macro levels, human rights, democratization and their interactive relationship with peace, ethnic groups, the cultural and religious dimensions of conflict.

Center for International Relations (CIR)
University of California, Los Angeles
11381 bunche Hall, UCLA, 405 Hilgard Avenue, Los Angeles, CA 90024-1486, USA

Telephone: 1-310-825-0604
Fax: 1-310-206-2582
Senior Staff: Acting Director: R. Rosecrance
Date of Establishment: 1975
Principal Activities: Research; training; documentation; information; conference-organization; publication

Periodicals: *Scope*, 4 p.a.
Annotation: Research covers international security, international cooperation, international relations theory, economics and security, and international environmental cooperation.

Center for International Security and Arms Control (CISAC)
Stanford University
320 Galvez Street, Stanford, CA 94305-6165, USA

Telephone: 415-723-9625
Fax: 415-723-0089
Senior Staff: Co-director: D. J. Holloway, M. May, Director of Studies: C. Blacker
Date of Establishment: 1970
Type: Non-profit
Principal Activities: Research; training; documentation/information; conference- organization; publication
Current Peace Research:

(a) Strategic stability,

(b) Defense conversion,

(c) Nuclear weapons proliferation,

(d) Ethno-nationalism and regional conflict.

Major Publications:

(a) Abrams, H. L., *The President has been Shot: Confusion, Disability and the 25th Amendment in the Aftermath of the Assassination Attempt on Ronald Reagan*, 1992,

(b) Bunn, G., *Arms Control by Committee: Managing Negotiations with the Russians*, 1992,

(c) Bernstein, D., Smith, K., *Collaborative Project on Soviet Defence Conversion*, 1992,

(d) Bernstein, D., Perry, W. J., *Defense Conversion: A Strategic Imperative for Russia*, 1992,

(e) Bunn, G., *Does the NPT Require its Non-Nuclear-Weapon Members to Permit Inspection by the IAEA of Nuclear Activities that have not been Reported to the IAEA?*, 1992,

(f) Fainberg, A., *Strengthening IAEA Safeguards: Lessons from Iraq*, 1993,

(g) Harvey, J., Michalowski, S., *Nuclear Weapons Safety and Trident*, 1993,

(h) McFaul, M. (ed.), *Can the Russian Military-Industrial Complex be Privatized?* 1993,

(i) McFaul, M., Bernstein, D., *Industrial Demilitarization, Privatization, Economic Reform and Investment in Russia*, 1993,

(j) Blacker, C. D., *Hostage to Revolution: Gorbachev and Soviet Security Policy*, 1993,

(k) McFaul, M., *The Troubled Birth of Russian Democracy: Parties, Personalities and Programs*, 1993,

(l) Sagan, S. D., *The Limits of Safety: Organizations, Accidents and Nuclear Weapons*, 1993.

Annotation: Research covers international security and arms control including security in the Asian-Pacific region, and Russian security policy and in the new Europe. Focus is on USA-Russian security relations including defence conversion and restructuring; USA-China and USA-Japan security relations; security on the Korean peninsula; the proliferation of advanced weapons technologies and USA technology and science policy.

Center for International Studies
Massachusetts Institute of Technology
MIT CIS, E38-651, 292 Main Street, Cambridge, MA 02139, USA

Telephone: 1-617-253-8093
Fax: 1-617-253-9330
E-mail: lauries@mit.edu
Web Site: http://cis-server.mit.edu/CIS/index.html
Senior Staff: Director: Kenneth A. Oye, Executive Director: Elizabeth Leeds
Date of Establishment: 1951
Purpose: The Institute exists:

(a) To conduct research on international affairs and in comparative studies that will contribute both to basic understanding and to the solution of some of the long-term problems which confront decision-makers,

(b) To contribute to policy debates on international issues and to identify new issues in international affairs that should be placed on the public agenda,

(c) To facilitate research by individual faculty members and to promote interdepartmental, interdisciplinary studies in international affairs and comparative area studies within MIT,

(d) To provide research training opportunities for graduate students and to stimulate undergraduate interest in international and comparative studies,

(e) To make available to the MIT community important points of view on international issues by bringing to the MIT campus informed, intellectually stimulating and influential scholars and public figures,

(f) To forge ties among scholars at MIT and other institutions with international interests, especially scholars abroad,

(g) To promote closer ties between the MIT academic community and business and government.

Brief History: Founded in 1951 with Max F. Millikan as Director, the Center soon established itself as a major research center for the study of political and economic development, international communications, communist studies, and international security. Under the leadership of a distinguished group of economists, including Paul Rosenstein Rodan, Walt W. Rostow, Everett Hagen, Richard Eckaus, and Max Millikan, the Center pioneered in studies of economic growth in developing countries. Ithiel de Sola Pool, Daniel Lerner, Harold Isaacs, Lucian W. Pye, Frederick Frey, and Myron Weiner made important contributions to the study of political development, communications, and behavior. Research on national security was conducted by William Kaufmann, on international organization and foreign policy by Lincoln P. Bloomfield, on international aspects of science and technology by Eugene Skolnikoff, and on international communism by William Griffith and Donald Blackmer. Those mentioned, all of whom became members of the Economics or Political Science Departments at MIT, were joined over the years by research associates from other universities and countries who came to MIT to work on Center projects.

Principal Activities: Security Studies Program is a graduate teaching and research activity in international security studies. Its teaching is closely associated with the Massachusetts Institute of Technology (MIT) Political Science Department and emphasizes strategy, technology, and bureaucratic politics issues. Its research program and the various workshops it organizes are under the auspices of the Center. The program supports the research work of graduate students, faculty, and fellows and sponsors seminars, conferences, and several publication series to bring its teaching and research results to the attention of the MIT community and the wider public.

Periodicals:

(a) *Technology Review,* monthly magazine,

(b) *The Tech*, weekly newspaper,

(c) *Boston Review*, a progressive bimonthly journal of culture and politics.

Major Publication:

(a) Robert, D. B., Sturmer, M. (eds.), *Allies Divided* 1997,

(b) Richard A. F., Newman, R. D., Thayer, B. A., *America's Achilles' Heel*, 1998,

(c) Michael E. B., Coté, Jr., O. R., Lynn-Jones, S. M., Steven, E. (eds.), *America's Strategic Choices Miller,* 1997.

Center for International Studies
University of Southern California
Social Sciences Bldg., Rm.B-1, Los Angeles, CA 90089-0035, USA

Telephone: 1-213-740-4296
Fax: 1-213-742-0281
Senior Staff: Director: J. S. Odell
Date of Establishment: 1985
Principal Activities: Research; training; conference-organization; publication

Periodicals: *International Organization*
Annotation: The Center carries out research on theoretical and policy implications of global changes in international security conditions, including alternative world order institutions and changes in the world international economy.

Center for Nonviolent Communication
3468 Meadowbrook Blvd., Cleveland, OH 44118-3660, USA

Telephone: 1-216-371-1123
Fax: 1-216-371-1703
Senior Staff: Director: M. Rosenberg
Date of Establishment: 1983
Type: Private, non-profit
Principal Activities: Training; documentation/ information; publication
Current Peace Research: Training of Israeli police in the Ashkelon District and follow-up on percentage decrease in complaints of police brutality
Periodicals: *Network News*, 1 p.a.
Major Publications:

(a) *A Model for Nonviolent Communication,*

(b) *Nonviolent Communication Workbook.*

Annotation: Concerned with nonviolence and education for peace
Courses: Nonviolent Communication Seminars
Subjects Taught: Peaceful coexistence; conflict resolution; nonviolence; culture of peace; education for peace
Target Group: Professionals; non-specialists
Level of the Course: Undergraduate; graduate; postgraduate
Type of Course: Regular course; short session
Duration: 1 to 8 days
Working Languages: English
Admission Requirements: No
Course Fees: Based on ability to pay
Scholarships Available: Some help with funding
Degree/Diploma: None

Center for Peace and Conflict Studies (CPCS)
Wayne State University
2320 FAB Detroit, MI 48202, USA

Telephone: 1-313-577-3453
Fax: 1-313-577-8269
E-mail: fpearso@cms.cc.wayne.edu
Senior Staff: Director: Fred Pearson, Director, MADR graduate program: Michaelene Pepera
Date of Establishment: 1965
Purpose: The Center aims to sponsor programs, activities, and publications in areas of scholarship related to peace, war, social justice, arms control, global issues, and conflict resolution.
Type: Public, non-profit
Brief History: The center was founded as part of the University's school of education and graduate studies program. Professor Russell Broadhead was its first director. The center was first under the administrative purview of the Vice-President for Urban Affairs, and

subsequently reported to the provost's office, and then the Dean of Liberal Arts. Now, the college is part of the college of Urban, Labor, and Metropolitan Affairs.
Principal Activities: The Center offers an undergraduate co-major in Peace and Conflict Studies, in addition to our masters of arts in dispute resolution program. Also, the center offers programs, research, training, and program evaluation in conflict resolution and global education. The center also facilitates interracial conflict resolution in local neighborhoods.
Periodicals: Newsletter

Major Publications: Director Fred Pearson's recent publications include:

(a) *International Relations: The Global Condition in the Late Twentieth Century* (Third Edition),

(b) *Arms and Warfare*,

(c) Chasdi, R., *Middle East Terrorism 1968-1993: An Empirical Analysis, of Terrorist Group Type Behavior*,

(d) Pepera, M., Pearson, F., *Representation and Practice as Issues in Teaching Negotiation and Conflict Resolution Issues in the Urban Context*,

(e) Saperstein, A., *Complexity, Chaos, and National Security Policy: Metaphors or Tools?*,

(f) Magraw, D., *Resolving Environmental Conflict: Approaches of the International Joint Commission, the North American Commission on Cooperation, and the World Trade Organization*.

Center for Peaceful Change
Kent State University
Kent, Ohio 44242-0001, USA

Telephone: 1-216-672-3143
Fax: 1-216-672-7991
Senior Staff: Director: D. P. Carey
Date of Establishment: 1971
Type: Public; non-profit
Principal Activities: Research; training; documentation/information; conference-organization; publication; mediation service
Current Peace Research: Conflict resolution curriculum for the State?
Annotation: The Centre's activities focus on the dynamics of change in human systems. Research projects deal with education for peace, conflict resolution, mediation, peaceful coexistence, intergroup relations, behaviour, decision making and systems change.
Courses: B.A. in Peace and Conflict Studies (Major and Minor)

Subjects Taught: Peace research; disarmament; conflict resolution; role of the international organizations; nonviolence; peace and development; mediation
Target Group: Professionals; non-specialists; educators; public policy professionals
Level of the Course: Undergraduate; bachelors
Type of Course: Regular course; short session; summer course; evening course
Duration: Four years to receive a BA major in Peace and Conflict Studies
Working Languages: English
Admission Requirements: Requirements of the State University for the State of Ohio
Course Fees: Yes
Scholarships Available: No
Degree/Diploma: B.A. in Peace and Conflict Studies

Center for Peace Studies
Georgetown University
Washington, DC 20057, USA

Telephone: 1-202-337-1040
Fax: 1-202-337-1040
Senior Staff: Director: R. T. McSorley
Date of Establishment: 1968
Type: Private
Principal Activities: Training; conference-organization; publication
Annotation: Its primary areas of concern are on disarmament, foreign policy, theology of peace, education for peace, nuclear problems, and religion.
Courses: Interdisciplinary Major in Peace Studies; Interdisciplinary Minor in Peace Studies
Subjects Taught: Peaceful coexistence; conflict resolution; nonviolence; justice; polemology; war; interna-

tional conflict; Christian ethics
Principal Instructors: Rev. R. T. McSorley
Level of the Course: Undergraduate
Type of Course: Regular course
Duration: A minimum of 36 credits must be taken in the Major with 12 courses (including 4 required courses and 8 electives). The Minor includes 2 required courses and 4 electives chosen from 35 available courses.
Admission Requirements: Must be accepted into undergraduate program at Georgetown University
Course Fees: Yes
Scholarships Available: Yes
Degree/Diploma: Yes

Center for Peace Studies
University of Akron, Akron Ohio 44325-6234, USA

Telephone: 216-972-7008
Date of Establishment: Director: J. F. Seiberling
Purpose: Education, research, and public service.
Type: Public, non-profit
Brief History: On June 18, 1970, the Board of Trustees at the University of Akron, Akron, Ohio, gave formal approval for the establishment of a Center for Peace Studies after several months of discussion particularly by the then university president, Norman P. Auburn, and history department chairman, Warren F. Kuehl. Following the establishment of the Center, an undergraduate certificate in peace studies was prepared and offered in the spring of 1972. A second certificate program on conflict resolution/management was inaugurated in 1986.
Principal Activities: In addition to the academic offerings of the Center, further educational instruction featuring guest speakers and known authorities has been provided through such special topic courses as international terrorism, outer space, the world in the year 2000, and nuclear war. A Center-sponsored three-day minicourse on "Juman Rights and the Younger Generation" was expanded into a subsequent national conference on the teaching of human rights. Specialized summer workshops for elementary and secondary teachers are conducted to provide instruction and discussion on basic questions about war and peace as they arise in the classroom.

Researchs have taken many forms and these have included The Library of World Peace Studies, a joint project of the Center for Peace Studies and the Clearwater Publishing Company of New York. Begun in the mid-1970s, this library has reproduced, on microfiche, periodicals and out-of-print series on peace and internationalism under the general editorship of Professor Kuehl. Additionally, the Center obtained a Rockefeller Foundation Grant for research and study to develop the first model undergraduate humanities course on human rights to be offered anywhere in the world.

Both peace research and public service efforts by the Center have resulted in the co-direction of audiovisuals available for classroom presentation and adaptable for television broadcast. The Center completed a Biographical Dictionary of Internationalists that led to the formation of a Society for the Study of Internationalism. The membership consists of scholars interested in the study of internationalism. The Center serves, too, as a clearinghouse not only on data for this Society but also on its extensive resource files on peace education and research in many universities and organizations around the world.

The Center also has outreach programs. These have included an annual film series on the problems of war and peace. The Center extends public service by supporting local and national organizations involved in peace work and issues. Finally, the general public, campus student organization, and individual student interns can utilize the resources of the Center, which touch on a spectrum of issues and activities from global hunger, nuclear warfare, national model United Nations simulations, many curriculum materials, and peace-related ideas.

Periodicals: *International Peace Studies Newsletter*
Major Publications: Kueho W. F. (ed.), 1983 Biographical Dictionary of Internationalists, Greenwood Press, Westport, Connecticut
Courses: Certificate in Conflict Management and and Resolution; Certificate in Peace Studies
Subjects Taught: Peaceful coexistence; disarmament; conflict resolution; role of the international organizations; nonviolence; peace and development; war; international conflict; international security; education for peace; democracy and peace; regional conflict
Target Group: Non-specialists, nationals, foreign students
Type of Course: Regular course; summer course
Working Language: English
Admission Requirements: Yes, must be admitted to the University as an undergraduate, graduate of post-baccalaureate student
Course Fees: Yes
Degree/Diploma: Certificate in Peace Studies; Certificate in Conflict Management and Resolution

Center for Russian and East European Studies (CREES)
Stanford University
Encina Hall, Room 200, Stanford, CA 94305-6055, USA

Telephone: 1-415-723-3562
Fax: 1-415-725-2592

Senior Staff: Director: A. Dallin
Date of Establishment: 1966

Type: Non-profit
Principal Activities: Research; training; documentation; information; conference-organization; publication; financial support
Periodicals: *Newsletter*
Annotation: The Center promotes the interdisciplinary study of the history and politics of the Russian Federation and Eastern Europe including the interaction of Russian domestic and foreign policy, and international security and arms control.
Courses: Russian and East European Studies (M.A.; Ph.D.)
Subjects Taught: International relations; international security
Level of the Course: Masters; doctorate
Type of Course: Regular courses, including for the M.A. a minimum of 40 course units in at least 3 academic disciplines
Duration: One year
Admission Requirements: Yes. For the M.A., applicants are expected to have at least 3 years of college-level Russian (or other East European language) or the equivalent, and relevant work at the undergraduate level
Course Fees: Yes
Degree/Diploma: M.A. and Ph.D. in Russian and East European Studies

Center for Science and International Affairs (CSIA)
79 John F. Kennedy Street, Cambridge, MA 02138, USA

Telephone: 1-617-495-1170
Fax: 1-617-502-0440
Date of Establishment: 1973
Senior Staff: Director: W. Clark, Prof: J. Montgomery
Principal Activities: Research; training; conference-organization; publication
Current Peace Research: Pacific basin research project
Periodicals: *International Security*, 4 p.a.
Major Publications:

(a) *Cooperative denuclearization,*

(b) *Soviet nuclear fission.*

Annotation: The Center places special emphasis on the role of science and technology in the analysis of international security affairs. Its research programmes assess methods to achieve arms control and to reduce the likelihood of war.

Center for the Global South
American University
4400 Massachusetts Avenue, NW, Washington, DC 20016, USA

Telephone: 1-202-885-1612
Fax: 1-202-885-1186
E-mail: glsouth@american.edu
Web Site: www.american.edu/academic.depts/acainst/cgs/
Senior Staff: Director: Clovis Maksoud
Date of Establishment: 1992
Purpose: The Center seeks to examine issues related to global inequality, development, environment, human rights, women, population, the changing international legal order and regional cooperation, as well as new roles for the United Nations and other international and regional organizations. The Center acts as a catalyst to promote dialogue about how these issues affect peoples and nations of the global South. The fundamental concern of the Center is to serve a broad public interest in helping assess what role the South can constructively play in the development of a new global order.
Brief History: The Center for the Global South was founded at American University's School of International Service (SIS). Founded and directed by Ambassador Clovis Maksoud, the Center is a multi-dimensional intellectual resource, which examines critical issues affecting the poorer developing countries of the world, increasingly characterized collectively as the South.
Principal Activities: The Center uses a variety of outreach programs to address economic, political, social, and individual development. Through these activities, the Center helps policy-makers, scholars and students understand the complexities of issues facing the global South and assists them in developing policy decisions that will achieve the desired outcomes. The Center works closely with the United Nations and its specialized agencies, other multilateral institutions, non-governmental organizations (NGOs), and universities around the world to maximize the benefit of its outreach programs.
Periodicals:

(a) *Reclaiming Civil Society in the Global South*, Conference Proceedings, March 9, 1995,

(b) *Empowering Women in the Global South: Preparing for Beijing*, Conference Proceedings, April 12-13, 1995,

(c) *Women Preparing for the Next Millennium: Voices from the Global South*, Conference Proceedings, September 9, 1995,

(d) *Beijing: Strategies for Implementation*, Conference Proceedings, November 7, 1995.

Center for War, Peace, and the News Media
New York University
10 Washington Place, New York, NY 10003, USA

Telephone: 1-212-998-7960
Fax: 1-212-995-4143
Telex: 235128 NYU UR
E-mail: cwpnn@acfcluster.nyr.edu
Senior Staff: Director: R. K. Manoff, Specialist: E. Cohen, R. Leavitt, R. K. Manoff, J. Raskin, B. Zellen
Date of Establishment: 1985
Type: Public, non-profit
Principal Activities: Research; training; documentation/information; conference-organization; publication
Current Peace Research:

(a) The Nuclear non-proliferation project,

(b) The European security project,

(c) The Soviet reportage project,

(d) The national security "sourcing project,"

(e) Asia-Pacific security project,

(f) Media and conflict project.

Type of Publication: Bulletin; monograph; progress-report; conference proceedings
Periodicals: *Deadline*, 6 p.a.
Annotation: The Center is concerned with international reporting on military conflict, defence policy, nuclear weapons proliferation, political and other international security issues.

Center of International Studies (CIS)
Princeton University
Bendheim Hall, Princeton, New Jersey 08544, USA

Telephone: 1-609-258-4851
Fax: 1-609-258 3988
Senior Staff: Director: J. Waterbury
Date of Establishment: 1951
Type: private; non-profit
Principal Activities: Research; documentation/information; research promotion; conference-organization; policy-making; publication
Current Peace Research:

(a) Research programme in international security,

(b) World order models project.

Periodicals: *World Politics*, 4 p.a.
Major Publications:
Waterbury, J. (ed.), *Toward New Orders in the Middle East.*
Annotation: Its research interests are focused on international relations and national development. It deals with peace, international law and foreign policy. Places emphasis on the relevance of its research to the development of a viable world order, and on the applicability of the understanding conveyed by basic research to contemporary problems.

Consortium on Peace Research, Education and Development (COPRED)
c/o Institute for Conflict Analysis and Resolution
George Mason University
4103 Chain Bridge Road, Suite 315, Fairfax, Virginia 22030-4444, USA

Telephone: 703-273-4485
Fax: 703-993-1302

E-mail: bwien@gmu.edu
Senior Staff: Executive Director: B. Wien

Date of Establishment: 1971
Type: Private; non-profit
Principal Activities: Research; conference-organization; publication; curricula development
Current Peace Research: Impact of military spending on domestic quality of life (links between development and disarmament)
Periodicals:

(a) *Peace and Change*, 4 p.a.

(b) COPRED *Peace Chronicle*, 6 p.a.

(c) *University Peace Studies Newsletter*, 2 p.a.

Major Publications:

Directory of Peace Studies Programs in the U.S., 1990.

Annotation: Its aim is to provide the link between research, education and action for peace and social justice, and to promote education for peace. Study groups are organized around major problems and issues such as disarmament, human rights, nonviolence, poverty, war, conflict and community building.

Correlates of War Project
Department of Political Science, University of Michigan
Ann Arbor, MI 48109-1045, USA

Telephone: 1-734-763-6590
Fax: 1-734-764-3622
E-mail: jdsinger@j.imap.itd.umich.edu
Web Site: www.umich.edu/~compap/
Senior Staff: Director: J. David Singer
Date of Establishment: 1963
Purpose: The early years of the Correlates of War Project were conceptually oriented with a small band of scholars struggling to define a research strategy and initiate the enormous job of generating a number of new and crucial data sets. Empirical analyses were usually bivariate analyses concerned with the outbreak of war (and major power war in particular), with less attention focused on other forms of conflict. In many ways, these early studies were "brush clearing" exercises and constituted some of the first data-based work on their topics (e.g., the impact of alliance configurations on the incidence of war). Furthermore, the initial research was concentrated on the systemic level and its attributes; the belief was, and still is, that the characteristics of the international system are not only themselves critical in affecting the chances for war between states, but must serve as control variables when examining the effects of state behavior, interstates linkages, and so forth.

Over the history of the COW Project, the research output has evolved in several ways, although the basic thrust of the project has not been substantially altered. The data generation effort has concentrated more on updating existing files than developing new ones. Several exceptions, however, reveal a new direction for the project. The newly developed data sets on militarized disputes and the Behavioral Correlates of War (BCOW) indicate an extension of the original emphasis on war exclusively to a broader focus on all interstate conflicts involving the use or threat of military force.

Type: Public and non-profit
Brief History: The Correlates of War (COW) Project traces its intellectual origins to the pioneering work of Sorokin, Wright, and Richardson. Yet the actual beginnings of the COW Project date to a grant proposal submitted to the Carnegie Corporation in 1963. Under the guidance of J. David Singer and Melvin Small, this grant funded an exploratory study of the conditions associated with the outbreak of war. In the years since those relatively humble origins and modest aims, the COW Project has produced over one hundred and fifty journal articles and book chapters, and a dozen or more books.

Principal Activities: Research; training; publication; occasional radio and TV programs
Major Publications:

(a) Gochman, C., Sabrosky, A. (eds.), *Prisoners of War?: Nation-States in the Modern Era*. Lexington, MA: Lexington Books, 1990,

(b) Singer, J. D., Diehl, P. (eds.), *Measuring the Correlates of War*, Ann Arbor: University of Michigan Press, 1990,

(c) Singer, J. D. (ed.), *Models, Methods, and Progress: A Peace Research Odyssey*. Boulder: Westview Press, 1990.

Council for a Livable World
110 Maryland Avenue, NE Suite 409 Washington, DC 20002, USA

Telephone: 1-202-543-4100
Fax: 1-202-543-6297
E-mail: clw@clw.org
Senior Staff: President: John Isaacs
Date of Establishment: 1962
Purpose: The main purpose of the Council for a Livable World was to warn the public and Congress of the threat of nuclear war and lead the way to rational arms control and nuclear disarmament. The Council's program provides senators with sophisticated technical and scientific information that helps them make intelligent decisions about nuclear arms control, strategic and conventional weapons, the military budget and United Nations peacekeeping. The Council was instrumental in passing the1993 Limited Test Ban Treaty and the1992 nuclear testing moratorium, the Intermediate-Range Nuclear Forces (INF) Treaty, the Conventional Forces in Europe Treaty and the START Treaties, advancing the Chemical Weapons Convention, banning biological weapons production and the Midgetman missile, and limiting MX and B-2 deployment.
Type: National
Brief History: The Council was founded in 1962 by Leo Szilard and other pioneers in nuclear weapons research to combat the menace of nuclear war. The Council later expanded its campaign to include other weapons of mass destruction, both chemical and biological.
Principal Activities: Council for a Livable World operates as a lobby group and a political action committee which endorses and raises funds for candidates for US Senate. The candidates must demonstrate a commitment to a firm arms control agenda. Peace PAC is an affiliate of the Council and supports candidates running for the US House of Representative.
Periodicals:

(a) *Comprehensive Test Ban Treaty*,

(b) *Gridlock—or Bipartisanship: Election Analysis*,

(c) *F-22 Advanced Tactical Fighter*,

(d) *Ballistic Missile Defense*,

(e) *The B-2 Bomber*.

Major Publications:

(a) *U.S. Leadership and the Future of Nuclear Arsenals*,

(b) *Arms Control Briefing Book: Arms Control and Security in the Post-Cold War Era*,

(c) *The U.S. Role in U.N. Peace Operations*,

(d) *U.S. Nuclear Policy for the21st Century*.

Council on Economic Priorities, International Security Program
30 Irving Place, 9th Floor, New York, NY 10003, USA

Telephone: 1-212-420-1133
Fax: 1-212-420-0988
E-mail: CEP@AOL.COM
Senior Staff: Director: Jordana Friedman
Date of Establishment: 1969
Purpose: The Council on Economic Priorities (CEP) is a non-profit public service research organization dedicated to accurate and impartial analysis of the social and environmental records of corporations. Our research is designed to enhance the incentives for superior corporate social and environmental performance and to encourage the transfer of Cold War resources to a productive civilian economy.
Type: International, private, non-profit
Brief History: CEP was founded in 1969 by Alice Tepper Martin to provide factual research for investors on corporate practices.
Principal Activities: The International Security program pursues research and advocacy on global military spending and arms control issues. The Council coordinates the year 2000 campaign to redirect military spending to human development.
Major Publications:

(a) *Environmental Reports*—on the environmental records of corporations,

(b) *Screen Profiles*—information on over 700 publicly held US companies in eight social and environmental research categories,

(c) *Shopping for a Better World*—popular guidebook

providing ratings on 200 companies with 2000 brand products in 17 industries,

(d) *Research Reports*—summaries of findings from

CEP's research divisions which include corporate Social responsibility, International security, the environment, child labor and international sourcing.

Council on Foreign Relations (CFR)
Harold Pratt House, 58 East 68th Street, New York, NY 10021, USA

Telephone: 212-734-0400
Fax: 212-861-1789
Telex: 239852 CFRUR
Cable: COUNFOREL, New York
Senior Staff: Chairman: P. G. Peterson, President: L. H. Gelb
Date of Establishment: 1921
Type: Private; non-profit
Principal Activities: Documentation/information; conference-organization; publication
Current Peace Research:

(a) Evolving strategic balance in Asia,

(b) East-West relations.

Periodicals:

(a) *Foreign Affairs*, 5 p.a.

(b) *The Reader*, 3 p.a.

(c) *Council Briefings*.

Major Publications:
Mandelbaum, M., *The Otherside of the Table: The Soviet Approach to Arms Control*, 1990.
Annotation: The CFR is devoted to promoting improved understanding of international relations and military strategy. It also Carries out research on long-range foreign policy problems.

Council on Peace Research in History (CPRH)
Department of History, Miami University
Oxford, Ohio 45056, USA

Telephone: 1-513-529-5125
Fax: 1-513-529-3841
E-mail: jkimball@miamiu.acs.muohio.du
Senior Staff: Director: J. Kimball
Date of Establishment: 1964
Type: Non-profit

Principal Activities: Research; documentation/ information; conference-organization; publication

Current Peace Research:

(a) Conflict and compromise in history,

(b) Gender, race and ethnicity.

Periodicals: *Peace and Change: a Journal of Peace Research*, 4 p.a.
Periodicals: *CPRH News*

Major Publications:

(a) Small, M., Hoover, W. D. (eds.), *Give Peace a Chance: The Vietnam Antiwar Movement*, 1992,

(b) Chatfield, C., Ilukhina, R. (eds.), *Peace/Mir: Alternatives to War*, 1994.

Annotation: The CPRH is focoused on professional historical society engaged in collaborative projects on peace, war and international conflict

Defense and Arms Control Studies Program (DACS)
Massachusetts Institute of Technology
292 Main Street, Cambridge, MA 02139, USA

Telephone: 1-617-253-5265
Fax: 1-17-258-7858
Senior Staff: Director: H. M. Sapolsky, Prof.: J. Ruina, G. Rathjens, M. Miller, T. Postol, S. Meyer, B. Posen, G. Lewis, C. Kaysen

Date of Establishment: 1974
Principal Activities: Research; training; documentation/information; conference-organization; publication
Current Peace Research:

(a) The Defence and arms control studies program (DACS),

(b) Post Soviet security studies working group.

Periodicals:

(a) *Breakthroughs*

(b) *DACS Facts, Russian Security Studies*

Major Publications:

(a) Choucri, N., North. R. C., Yamakage, S., *The Challenge of Japan before World War II and After*, 1992,

(b) Meyer, S. M., *The Military*, 1992,

(c) Rathgens, G., Miller, M. *Nuclear Proliferation After the Cold War 1992*,

(d) Samuels, R. J., *Reinventing Security: Japan Since Meiji*, 1992,

(e) Bloomfield, L. P., *Policing World Disorder*, 1993,

(f) Posen, P. R., *The Security Dilemma and Ethnic Conflict*, 1993.

Annotation: The DACS focuses on international security, arms control policies, defence and environmental issues, democratization and ethnic conflicts.
Courses:

(a) International Relations: War and Peace;

(b) Defence Politics: Foundation of Security Studies;

(c) Military Forces and Foreign Policy;

(d) Soviet Defence Planning;

(e) Nuclear Weapons and Arms Control: Technology

Subjects Taught: Peaceful coexistence; disarmament; conflict resolution; role of the international organizations; peace and development; democracy and peace; war; international conflict; international security; regional conflict; terrorism
Principal Instructors: Prof. H. M. Sapolsky (Prof., Defence Politics); Prof. G. W. Rathjens (Prof., Nuclear Weapons and Arms Control); Prof. J. P. Ruina (Prof., Nuclear Weapons and Arms Control); Porf. S. M. Meyer (Prof. Soviet Defence Planning); Prof. B. Posen (Prof. Security Studies)
Target Group: Professionals; non-specialists; nationals
Level of the Course: Doctorate; masters
Type of Course: Regular course; summer course
Working Languages: English
Admission Requirements: Yes, for masters and doctorate students admissions are handled through the Dept. of Political Science: prior academic record, graduate record examination, letters of recommendation are necessary.
Closing Date for Applications: Varies
Course Fees: yes, MIT tuition fees: US$19,000 p.a.
Scholarships Available: Yes: contact Jeanne Washington, Political Science Dept., MIT E53-465, Cambridge, MA 02139, USA
Degree/Diploma: M.S. in Political Science; Ph.D. in Political Science

Defense Budget Project
Center on Budget and Policy Priorities
777 N. Capitol Street NE, Suite 710, Washington, DC 20002, USA

Telephone: 1-202-408-1517
Fax: 1-202-408-1526
Senior Staff: Director: A. Krepinevích
Date of Establishment: 1983
Type: Non-profit, private
Current Peace Research: Defense spending trends; military plans and programmes; defense economic adjustment strategies

Major Publications:

(a) Krepinevích, A., *The Bottom-up Review: An Assessment*, 1994,

(b) Kosiak, S., *The FY 1995 Defense Budget*, 1994,

(c) Bitzinger, R., *Adjusting to the Drawdown: The Transition in the Defense Industry*, 1993.

Annotation: The project carries out research on the defence budget, strategic and conventional arms control, NATO burden-sharing, conventional force balance, defence spending and the economy and national security policy choices and their budget implications. The aim is to facilitate public and political discussion and decision making.

Five College Program in Peace and World Security Studies (PAWSS)
c/o Hampshire College
Amherst, MA 01002, USA

Telephone: 1-413-582-5563
Fax: 1-413-549-0707
Senior Staff: Director: M. T. Klare, Assoc. Prof.: A. Bandarage, J. Der Derian, Prof.: N. Crawford, Assoc. Prof.:
Date of Establishment: 1983
Type: Private, non-profit
Parent Organization: The Five College, Inc. (a consortium of Amherst College, Hampshire College, Mount Holyoke College, Smith College, and the University of Massachusetts at Amherst)
Principal Activities: Training; documentation/ information; conference-organization; publication; radio and TV programmes; curriculum development; summer internship programme
Periodicals: *Peace and World Security Report*
Major Publications:

(a) *Guide to Careers and Graduate Education in Peace Studies*, 1990,

(b) Klare, M., Thomas, D. (eds.), *World Security: Challenges for a New Century*, 2nd edition, 1994,

(c) Klare, M. (ed.), *Peace and World Security Studies: A Curriculum Guide*, 6th edition, 1994.

Annotation: Multidisciplinary educational programme designed to stimulate student and faculty interest in critical issues of peace and international security affairs.
Courses:

(a) Concentration in Peace and World Security Studies,

(b) PAWSS Summer Faculty Institute on World Security Affairs; PAWSS Winter Workshop: Principles and Methods of Conflict Resolution.

Subjects Taught: Peace research; peaceful coexistence; disarmament; conflict resolution; role of the international organizations; nonviolence; peace and development; human rights; proliferation and non-proliferation; polemology; war; international conflict; international security; international relations; international law; terrorism; ethnic conflict
Principal Instructors: Prof. M. Klare (Programme Director)
Target Group: Professionals; non-specialists; nationals; foreign students; college and secondary school teachers; college students
Level of the Course: Undergraduate; bachelors
Type of Course: The Institute offers programme comprising many individual courses and workshops, lectures and conferences. It also offers regular courses for college students, short sessions for college teachers and summer internships for students in peace and public policy at governmental agencies and non-profit making organizations.
Duration: Varies
Working Languages: English
Admission Requirements: Yes, for regular courses, students must be enrolled in one of the member institutions
Course Fees: Yes
Scholarships Available: Yes, apply to the student Aid Offices of participating colleges and universities.
Degree/Diploma: None

The Fund for Peace
345 East 46th Street, Suite 712, New York, NY 10017, USA

Telephone: 1-212-661-5900
Fax: 1-212-661-5904
Senior Staff: Chairman: J. Compton, Executive Director: N. K. Solarz;,Director: L. Leatherbee
Date of Establishment: 1957
Type: Private, non-profit
Principal Activities: Research; documentation/ information
Type of Publication: Bulletin; monograph; conference proceedings

Periodicals: *First Principles*
Major Publications: *The Conquest of War: Alternative Strategies for Global Security*
Annotation: It is a multi-project organization dedicated to the elimination of war and the attainment of a just, free and peaceful world. It includes a recent research programme such as Alternative Defence Project, the Resolving Conflict Creatively Programme, and other studies related to conflict resolution, security and international conflict.

Global Studies Program
Bethel College
North Netwon, Kansas 67117, USA

Telephone: 1-316-284-5217
Fax: 1-316-284-5286
Senior Staff: Director: P. McKay
Date of Establishment: 1972
Type: Private, non-profit
Principal Activities: Training; conference-organization
Annotation: The GSP deals with religious-ethical foundations of peacemaking, concepts and methods of peace studies and research, environmental and peace and development issues in the Third World.
Courses: Theory and Practice of Conflict Management; Nonviolence Theory and Practice; Peacemaking and International Conflict; Global Issues in Environment, Human Conflict and Development

Subjects Taught: Peaceful coexistence; disarmament; conflict resolution; role of the international organizations; nonviolence; peace and development; international conflict; international security; regional conflict, culture of peace; education for peace; peace and the environment
Level of the Course: Undergraduate; bachelor's degree
Type of Course: Regular course
Working Languages: English
Admission Requirements: Bethel College admission requirements
Course Fees: Approx. US$ 500 per course
Scholarships Available: No
Degree/Diploma: B.A. and B.SC. in Global Studies (with concentration on Peace Studies)

Graduate School of International Studies (GSIS)
University of Denver
University Park, 2201 South Gaylord Street, Denver, Colorado 80208-0280, USA

Telephone: 1-303-871-2324
Fax: 1-303-871-2456
E-mail: TROWE@DU.edu
Senior Staff: Dean: E. T. Rowe, Prof.:J. R. Adelman, J. Donnelly, A. N. Gilbert, B. B. Hughes, Assoc. Prof.: K. A. Feste, Asst. Prof.: J. Frazer
Date of Establishment: 1964
Type: Private; non-profit
Principal Activities: Research; training; documentation/information; conference- organization; publication

Current Peace Research:

(a) Immigration: policy, ethics, law advocacy,

(b) Negotiations in the Middle East,

(c) Conflict resolution among ethnic communities,

(d) Social movements and human rights,

(e) Human rights and international security.

Periodicals:

(a) *Africa Today*, 4 p.a.

(b) *Africa Rights Monitor*, 4 p.a.,

(c) *Global Justice, University of Denver Bulletin*, 6 p.a.

Major Publications:

(a) Adelman, J., *Symbolic War: Chinese Military*

Diplomacy, 1993,

(b) Donnelly, J., *International Human Rights*, 1993,

(c) Goldfischer, D., *The Best Defense*, 1993,

(d) Hughes, B., *International Futures*, 1993,

(e) Hughes, B., *Continuity and Change in World Politics*, 1994,

(f) Ireland, P., *The Political Challenge of Ethnic Diversity*, 1994,

(g) Ishay, M., *Internationalism and its Betrayal*, 1994.

Annotation: The GSIS concerned with interethnic relations, ethnic conflicts, conflict resolution and multiethnic societies.
Courses: International Conflict Concentration (M.A.; M.A.I.I.C.; M.I.M.; Ph.D.); Peace Research (M.A.; M.I.M.; Ph.D.)
Subjects Taught: a) International Conflict Concentration: domestic instability and revolution; repression and other forms of violence; international conflict and war; the danger of nuclear holocaust; great power intervention; promotion of domestic and international peace and justice; conflict resolution; b) Peace Research: theory; institutional framework of European peace research; cause and range of recent changes; security; strategies; arms control; peace social movements and

their links to parties; older frameworks of international relations as the concept of "Mitteleuropa", small states, neutrality, German reunion/neutralization and regional security systems; new approaches of causes of war and arms transfer. Also: peace and development; democracy and peace; international security; regional conflict; international law; role of the international organizations; decision making in crisis to conflict resolution positions

Target Group: Professionals; non-specialists; nationals; foreign students

Level of the Course: Postgraduate; masters; doctorate

Type of Course: Regular courses, summer courses,

part of the "M.A. in International Studies", the M.A.I.I.C., the M.I.M., and Ph.D. curricula

Duration: M.A.: 2 years; Ph.D.: 3 years

Working Languages: English

Admission Requirements: B.A.

Course Fees: Yes

Scholarships Available: Yes, financial aid ranges from partial tuition assistance to a maximum of US$ 14,000 per year + US$ 3,000. Research assistantships are also available. Please apply to Ms. Semra Koknar, GSIS

Degree/Diploma: M.A. in International Studies; M.A.I.I.C.; M.I.M.; Ph.D.

Henry L. Stimson Center
21 Dupont Circle NW, Fifth Floor, Washington, DC 20036-1109, USA

Telephone: 1-202-223-5956
Fax: 1-202-785-9034
Senior Staff: President: M. Krepon, Chairman & Specialist: B. M. Blechman, Exec. Dir. & Specialist: J. Cirincione, Senior Researcher: W. J. Durch, C. S. Fisher, M. Krepon, A. E. Vaccaro
Date of Establishment: 1989
Type: Non-profit, private
Principal Activities: Research; publication
Current Peace Research:

(a) The United Nations and the US foreign policy,

(b) Training for peacekeeping: alternative means of strengthening current standards,

(c) Implementing the chemical weapons convention,

(d) International center for support of the chemical weapons convention,

(e) Project on confidence-building measures for regional security,

(f) Conventional weapons proliferation: demand side,

(g) Eliminating weapons of mass destruction,

(h) Campaign for the non-proliferation treaty.

Major Publications:

(a) Itty, A., *Argentina-Brazil and India-Pakistan: Stepping Back from the Nuclear Threshold?* 1993,

(b) Fortna, V. P., *Regional Organizations and Peacekeeping*, 1993,

(c) Ghali, M., *The Multinational Forces: Non-UN*

Peacekeeping in the Middle East, 1993,

(d) Smithson, A. E. (ed.), *Administering the Chemical Weapons Convention: Lessons from the IAEA*, 1993,

(e) Arbatov, A. (ed.), *Implications of the START II Treaty for US-Russian Relations*, 1993,

(f) Blechman, B. MM et al., *Key West Revisited: Roles and Missions of the United States Armed forces in the Twenty-First Century*, 1993,

(g) Hensha, J. H., *The Origins of COCOM: Lessons for Contemporary Proliferation Control Regimes*, 1993,

(h) Krepon, M., McCoy, M., Rudolph, M. C. J., *A Handbook of Confidence-Building Measures for Regional Security*, 1993,

(i) Smithson, A. E. (ed.), *The Chemical Weapons Convention Handbook*, 1993,

(j) Blechman, B. M. et al., *The American Military in the Twenty-First Century*, 1993,

(k) Durch, W. J. (ed.), *The Evolution of UN Peacekeeping: Case Studies and Comparative Analysis*, 1993,

(l) Irwin, S. M., *Technology Policy and America's Future*, 1993.

Annotation: The Center's research focuses on the potential of international peacekeeping forces, emphasizing international security, peace, arms control, disarmament, conflict resolution, international conflict, terrorism, peaceful use of atomic energy, weapons and defence policies and strategies.

Hudson Institute
Herman Kahn Center
5395 Emerson Way, PO Box 26-919, Indianapolis, IN 46226-0919, USA

Telephone: 1-317-545-1000
Fax: 1-317-545-9639
Senior Staff: President: L. Lenhowsky, Senior Fellow: M. Helprin, R. W. Judy, W. E. Odom, Specialist: G. A. Keyworth, D. F. Mikheyev, N. Pickett
Date of Establishment: 1961
Type: Private; non-profit
Principal Activities: Research; documentation/ information; conference-organization; publication

Current Peace Research:

(a) The US/Korean naval relations,

(b) International security assistance,

(c) Regional stability study,

(d) AID/Baltics,

(e) Transatlantic security cooperation,

(f) Global food center,

(g) Baltic public policy research,

(h) Taiwan/mainland relations in international arena.

Periodicals: *Hudson Briefing Paper*, *Hudson Country Report*
Major Publications:

(a) ASEAN *in the 1990s: New Challenges, New Directions,*

(b) Odom, W. E., *Trial After Triumph: East Asia After the Cold War*, 1992,

(c) Geipel, G. L. (ed.), *Germany in a New Era*, 1993,

(d) Judy, R. W., *Russia at Risk*, 1993,

(e) Dujarric, R., *Russia and the 'Islamic' Threat*, 1994,

(f) Geipel, G. L., *Expanding NATO: Good for Europe and Good for the U.S.*, 1994.

Annotation: The Center's fields of interest include arms control, military/defense and military/strategic issues, disarmament, peaceful coexistence, national and international security, and international order.

Institute for Defense & Disarmament Studies
675 Massachusetts Avenue, Cambridge, MA 02139, USA

Telephone: 1-617-354-4337
Fax: 1-617-354-1450
E-mail: forsberg@idds.979
Purpose: A nonprofit center for research and education on ways to minimize the risk of war, reduce the burden of military spending, democratic institutions.
Type: International, non-profit
Brief History: After its establishment, the Institute has published two regularly updated reference works:

(a) *The Arms Control Reporter*, a monthly chronology of the positions of all nations in all arms control negotiation, with copies of official documents,

(b) *The IDDS Almanac: World Arms Holdings, Production, and Trade*, a detailed annually updated statistical survey of major weapon inventories, production, and trade by nation and region, annually since 1990 and projected to 2010.

Principal Activities: The Institute distributes large quantities for free of reprints on military spending and the arms trade to college professors for college classes and grassroots groups.

In 1997 IDDS distributed over 15,000 copies to over 200 Universities. The Institute staff members are focusing on two main projects: "Arms and Security" a study of post-Cold War changes in security matters: and "What Drives US Military Spending?" a study of the links between US military spending, forces and security policy. The International Fighter Study has published a first volume, *The Arms Production Dilemma: Contraction and Restraint in the World Combat Aircraft Industry*, published by MIT Press, Nov 1994.

Major Publications:

(a) *IDDS Almanac 1996: World Combat Aircraft Holdings, Production, and Trade,*

(b) *Analysis of US Army RDT&E Funding FY 1980-FY 1995,*

(c) *Analysis of US Air Force RDT&E Funding FY 1980-FY 1996,*

(d) *Arms Control Reporter.*

The Institute for Foreign Policy Analysis, Inc. (IFPA)
675 Massachusetts Avenue, Tenth Floor Cambridge, Massachusetts 02139, USA

Telephone: 1-617-492-2116
Fax: 1-617-492-8242
E-mail: mail@ifpa,org
Additional Branch Address: 1725 DeSales Street, NW, Suite 402, Washington, DC 20036
Telephone: 202-463-7942
Fax: 202-785-2785
E-mail: ifpa@aol.com
Senior Staff: President: Robert L., Jr. Pfaltzgraff, Executive Vice President: Jacquelyn K. Davis, Vice President, Director of Studies: Charles M. Perry, Senior Research Associates: David R. Tanks, Jack A. Kelly, Andrew C. Winner, Michael J. Sweeney
Date of Establishment: 1976
Purpose: The IFPA research agenda is designed to assist senior government policy makers, industry executives, technology developers, and the broader public to assess the implications of the momentous shifts in global affairs that continue to reshape the security landscape. Our programs are based on the realization that decision-makers, whether in government or industry, cannot make adequate choices without the benefit of a strategic perspective. IFPA programs draw together critical interagency and alliance leadership to address, outside the official constraints of the interagency process, national and global problems that are increasingly multifaceted and for which integrative approaches are needed.
Type: National, private, non-profit
Brief History: Since its founding in 1976 as an independent research organization, the Institute for Foreign Policy Analysis (IFPA) has provided a forum for the examination of political-economic, national security, and defense-industrial issues confronting the United States in a rapidly changing world. The Institute's work over the past twenty years has anticipated such issues as: the role of the cruise missile in US defense planning; the importance of space as a new strategic-economic frontier; the debate over strategic modernization and power projection; the need to adapt alliance structures to changes in US- Allied relations; problems of trade and technology transfer and the marketing challenges they create for industry; post-Cold War deterrence planning; priorities for missile defense, and arms control constraints that shaped defense.
Principal Activities: IFPA is an independent, nonpartisan research organization, whose major purposes are to conduct research, publish studies, convene seminars and conferences, strengthen education, and train policy analysts in the fields of foreign policy and national security affairs. The Institute maintains a core staff of specialists. It has offices in Cambridge, Massachusetts, and Washington, DC; draws upon the expertise of scholars, scientists, journalists, members of the business community, and other foreign affairs experts; supports a specialized library of periodicals, books, and information files for the use of scholars, students, and the general public; and awards fellowships and internships to promising graduate students.
Periodicals: *Update*
Major Publications:

Books:

(a) Pfaltzgraff, Jr., R. L., Shultz Jr., R. H. (eds.), *War in the Information Age: New Challenges for U.S. Security Policy,*

(b) Pfaltzgraff Jr., R. L., Shultz Jr., R. H. (eds.), *Ethnic Conflict and Regional Instability: Implications for U.S. Policy and Army Roles and Missions,*

(c) Shultz, R. H., Pfaltzgraff Jr., R. L., Stock, W. B. (eds), *Special Operations Forces: Roles and Missions in the Aftermath of the Cold War.*

Monographs:

(a) Pfaltzgraff Jr., R. L., Keridis, D. (eds.), *Security in Southeastern Europe and the U.S.-Greek Relationship,*

(b) Pfaltzgraff, Jr., R. L. (ed.), *Security Strategy & Missile Defense,*

(c) Davis, J. K., Perry, C. M., Sweeney, M. J., *The Submarine and U.S. National Security Strategy Into the Twenty-First Century.*

Monograph Series	
Special Reports	Occasionally
National Security Papers	Bi-annually
Foreign Policy Reports	Occasionally
Conference Reports	Occasionally

IFPA also publishes a large number of other works for contract work, including analytical reports and detailed studies as well as conference reports. These include:

(a) *Allied-Central European Workshop on Post-Cold War Concepts of Deterrence* (1996),

(b) *Joint Requirements Oversight Council: Planning in a Revolutionary Era* (1996),

(c) *European Issues and Developments* (annually),

(d) *Asia-Pacific Issues and Developments* (annually),

(e) *Security Perspectives & Defense Priorities in the Asia-Pacific* (1995),

(f) *Opportunities & Challenges for Security Cooperation in the Asia-Pacific Region: Summary of a Trans-Pacific Dialogue* (1995),

(g) *Workshop Summary for Next Steps for Cooperative Engagement: PACOM's Multilateral Military Initiatives* (1995),

(h) *UN Transparency in Armaments: A Current & Future Assessment & Future Prospects* (1995),

(i) *Service Manning and Assignments to Fulfill Peacetime Engagement and JTF Requirements: Summary of a High-Level Workshop Discussion* (1995).

Major Fields of Research:

(a) Proliferation issues and the future of missile defense,

(b) European perspectives on security and US policy,

(c) Security policy analysis in Europe, the Middle East, and Pacific rim,

(d) Peacekeeping and conflict management,

(e) prospects for multilateral collaboration,

(f) Linkages between environmental tensions and communitarian conflict,

(g) Post-Cold War academic curricula on nuclear and other weapons of mass destruction issues,

(h) Security in Southeastern Europe and the US-Greek relationship,

(i) Requirements for forward presence and regional security,

(j) Undersea warfare and US national security in the 21st century,

(k) Deterrence planning for the new security environment,

(l) Air power in the 21st century: long-range bombers and aircraft carriers,

(m) US defense policy: issues of military doctrine, force structure, and the revolution in military affairs,

(n) Exploring US missile requirements for 2010: policy and technology challenges,

(o) Asia-Pacific perspectives on security and US policy,

(p) Arms control and U.S. force structure beyond START II.

Future Projects: New strategic dynamics in the Nordic/Baltic region: implications for NATO enlargement, European security, and US relations,

Redefining European security in the post-Cold War world.

Conferences:

(a) International roundtable conferences with the Netherlands Atlantic Commission (250),

(b) US-Allied theater missile defense, nuclear planning, and deterrence issues (35),

(c) Future force structure requirements and priorities (75),

(d) Security in Southeastern Europe and the US-Greek relationship (75),

(e) Annual conference on US security issues (in conjunction with the Fletcher School of Law and Diplomacy, Tufts University, 300),

(f) US relations in the Asia-Pacific area in a changing Security setting (70),

(g) Post-Cold War academic curricula on nuclear and other weapons of mass destruction issues (50),

(h) Seminar on undersea warfare (45),

(i) Seminar on missile defense (40),

(j) Seminar series on the future of the US Army (45).

Institute for International Peace Studies
University of Notre Dame
PO Box 639, Notre Dame, Indiana 46556-0639, USA

Telephone: 1-219-631-6970
Fax: 1-219-631-6973
Telex: 469669 Notre Dame CI
Senior Staff: Director: R. Väyrynen, Director of Grad-

uate Studies: R. C. Johansen, Director of Undergraduate Studies: G. A. Lopez, Prof.: R. V. Väyrynen
Date of Establishment: 1986
Type: Private; non-profit

Principal Activities: Research; training; publication
Current Peace Research:

(a) Empowering international institutions and enforcing peace,

(b) Conflict and conflict theory,

(c) Transnational social movements,

(d) Ethics of peace and development.

Major Publications:

(a) Johansen, R. C., *Military Policies and the State System as Impediments to Democracy*, 1992,

(b) Johansen, R. C., *Japan as a Military Power? Why it's a Bad Idea*, 1993,

(c) Johansen, R. C., *Toward a New Code of International Conduct: War, Peacekeeping, and Global Constitutionalism*, 1993,

(d) Johansen, R. C., *Unilateral Initiatives*, 1993,

(e) Johansen, R. C., Falk, R. A., Kim, S. S., *Global Constitutionalism and World Order*, 1993,

(f) Johansen, R. C., Falk, R. A., Kim, S. S. (eds.), *The Constitutional Foundations of World Peace*, 1993,

(g) Väyrynen, R., *Finland and the European Community: Changing Elite Bargains*, 1993,

(h) Väyrynen, R., *From the Cold War to the New World Order*, 1993,

(i) Väyrynen, R., *The Nature of Conflicts in Future International Relations*, 1993.

Annotation: The Institute conducts peace research using a pragmatic methodology and a multidisciplinary approach. Fields of concern include the definition of conflict theory and of criteria for an international order, the roles of international organizations, governments, and social movements in conflict resolution, social conflicts, cultural, social and religious values, political ideologies, and ethics of peace.

Courses:

(a) Concentration in Peace Studies (CPS);

(b) International Scholars Program;

(c) Master of Arts in Peace Studies

Subjects Taught: Peaceful coexistence; disarmament; conflict resolution; role of the international organizations; nonviolence; peace and development; war; international security; culture of peace; social change for peace and human rights; religious dimensions of peace and justice
Principal Instructors: Dr. R. C. Johansen (Director of Graduate Studies), Dr. G. Lopez (Coordinator CPS)
Target Group: Nationals; foreign students
Level of the Course: Undergraduate; masters
Type of Course: Regular course
Duration: CPS involves five courses (15 hours) of work taken in two or more university departments; the International Scholars Program: one year; M.A. degree: 12 to 18 months
Working Languages: English
Admission Requirements: a) For the CPS: any student of any major who is interested in the themes of peace, violence, justice and human rights. b) International Scholars Program: baccalaureate degree or equivalent; fluency in English; age under 27. c) M.A. degree in Peace Studies: B.A. or B.Sc. equivalent; fluency in English; scores from the Graduate Record Exam; the regular M.A. programme has no age requirement or limitation, however, the international Scholars Program has an age limit of 30
Closing Date for Applications: January 15
Course Fees: US$ 15,690 per academic year
Scholarships Available: Yes, please contact Ms. Rosemarie Green, Admissions Coordinator
Degree/Diploma: M.A. in Peace Studies

Institute for International Studies
Stanford University
Stanford, CA 94305, USA

Telephone: 1-415-725-3490
Fax: 1-415-725-3770
E-mail: hf.mjb@Forsythe.stanford.edu
Web Site: www-iis.stanford.edu/
Senior Staff: Director: Ken-ichi Imai, Executive Director: Ronald B. Herring
Date of Establishment: 1970

Purpose: IIS seeks solutions to real-world, international problems. In order to find solution to international problems the Institute invites experts from a variety of disciplines within the university together with long- and short-term visitors from other academic, government, and corporate institutions to study contemporary policy issues. Research is focused primarily on international security, the global environment, and international political economy.

Major Publications:

(a) Boston, J., Commins, S., *Are There Universal Human Rights?* Experimental unit. (SPICE), Stanford University, 1996,

(b) Boston, J., Commins, S., *Neither a Borrower Nor a Lender Be: Debt and Development in Brazil*, Experimental unit. (SPICE), Stanford University, 1995,

(c) Boston, J., Commins, S., *Pollution Knows No Boundaries*, Experimental unit. (SPICE), Stanford University, 1995,

(d) Bunn, G., *May Nuclear Weapons Be Used to Respond to Chemical Attack by a Non-Nuclear-Weapon Country?" Arms Control Today*, May 1996,

(e) Bunn, G., Rhinelander, J. B., *Extending the NPT: What are the Options?" Arms Control Today*, March 1995,

(f) Call, C. T., *From 'Partisan Cleansing' to Power-Sharing? Lessons for Security from Colombia's National Front*, November 1995.

Annotation: IIS is organized as a federation, composed of a central unit and a series of affiliated centers. These centers such as Asia/Pacific Research Center, or Center for International Security and Arms Control are research-oriented, although they also engage in teaching and outreach. All are housed on the Stanford campus.

Institute for Multi-track Diplomacy (IMTD)
1133 20th St. NW, Suite 321, Washington, DC 20036, USA

Telephone: 1-202-466-4605
Fax: 1-202-466-4607
Senior Staff: Chairman, Ambassador: J. W. McDonald, Executive Director: L. Diamond
Date of Establishment: 1992
Principal Activities: Research; training; publication
Current Peace Research:

(a) Catalysts for change in Cyprus,

(b) Securing peace after Norway: social peacebuilding and identity group needs in Israel and Palestine.

Periodicals: *Peacebuilder*

Major Publications:

Multi-track Diplomacy: A Systems Approach to Peace, 1993.

Annotation: Research and training concentrate on conflict resolution including preventive diplomacy, post-conflict peace-building training and ethnic conflict and regional conflict

Courses: Courses on Conflict Resolution
Subjects Taught: Diplomacy; conflict resolution; ethnic conflict; regional conflict
Target Group: Professionals; nationals
Level of the Course: Short session
Duration: 2-10 days
Working Languages: English
Admission Requirements: None

Institute for Peace and International Security (IPIS)
237 Brattle Street, Cambridge, MA 02138-4645, USA

Telephone: 1-617-547-3338
Fax: 1-617-547-3338
E-mail: CDPIPIS@ARISA.XEROX.COM
Senior Staff: Director: P. F. Walker
Date of Establishment: 1986
Type: Private; non-profit
Principal Activities: Research; training; conference-organization; publication; consulting
Geographical Coverage: North America; Europe; Central America; Middle East
Periodicals: *The Peace Papers*
Major Publications:

(a) *Strategy Workbook,*

(b) *New Directions for NATO: Adopting the Atlantic Alliance to the 1990s,*

(c) *From Protest to Policy: Beyond the Freeze to Common Security.*

Annotation: The Institute is concerned with international security, defence policy and peace and seeks to strengthen analysis and collaborative research in the development of alternative policies

Institute for Peace and Justice (IPJ)
4144 Lindell Blvd 124, St. Louis, MO 63108, USA

Telephone: 1-314-533-4445
Senior Staff: Executive Officer: J. McGinnis, Executive Officer & Specialist: J. McGinnis, K. R. McGinnis
Date of Establishment: 1970
Principal Activities: Research; training; documentation/information; publication
Periodicals: *Parenting for Peace and Justice Network Newsletter*, 6 p.a.
Major Publications:

(a) *Educating for a Just Society*, 1993,

(b) *Educating for Peace and Justice: Religious Dimensions*, 1993,

(c) *Celebrating Racial Diversity*, 1994.

Annotation: Fields of interest include peace, conflict resolution, justice, multiculturalism and education for peace.

Courses:

(a) Educating for Peace and Justice,

(b) Parenting for Peace and Justice.

Subjects Taught: Conflict resolution; nonviolence; racial justice and reconciliation; education for peace
Principal Instructors: Dr. J. McGinnis; Ms K. McGinnis
Target Group: Elementary & secondary school teachers
Type of Course: Summer course
Working Languages: English

Institute for Strategic Studies on Terrorism
Box 1006, Hereford, Texas 79045, USA

Telephone: 1-806-344-2145
Senior Staff: Director: A. E. Gerringer
Date of Establishment: 1982
Type: Private; profit
Principal Activities: Research; training; documentation/information; conference- organization; publication; consulting
Current Peace Research: International terrorism: 2000 and beyond
Annotation: A private professional organization mainly providing research and consultation on terrorism and counter-terrorism, training for law enforcement and military and corporate security
Courses: Terrorism, Anti-Terrorism and Counter-Terrorism

Subjects Taught: Conflict resolution; role of the international organizations; war; international conflict; international security; regional conflict; terrorism
Principal Instructors: Mr. A. E. Gerringer
Target Group: Professionals; non-specialists; nationals; foreign students
Level of the Course: Bachelors; graduate
Type of Course: Regular course
Duration: One week
Working Languages: English
Admission Requirements: Yes
Course Fees: Yes, US$ 350-US$ 500 plus travel expenses
Degree/Diploma: None

Institute for the Study of American Wars (ISAW)
PO Box 25005, Wilmington, DE 19899, USA

Telephone: 1-302-992-9660
Fax: 1-302-764-1512
Senior Staff: President: J. R. Radell
Date of Establishment: 1984
Type: Private; non-profit
Principal Activities: Research; conference-organization; publication
Current Peace Research:

(a) War, its effect on humanity,

(b) The role governments play to prevent war,

(c) Strength of democracy and democracy's military as a deterrent to war,

(d) The role military plays in peace,

(e) Avoiding the battlefield military as crisis manager.

Periodicals:

(a) *Freedom Chronicles,*

(b) *World Leadership Journal.*

Annotation: The Institute carries out research on American wars focusing on World War II, Korea, Vietnam and the Persian Gulf.

Institute for Victims of Trauma, Joint Program on Conflict Resolution
6801 Market Square Drive, McLean, Virginia 22101-2922, USA

Telephone: 1-703-847-8456
Fax: 1-703-847-0470
E-mail: IVT@AOL.COM
Senior Staff: Executive Director: L. F. Dane
Date of Establishment: 1987
Type: Non-profit
Principal Activities: Training; conference-organization; publication
Major Publications:

(a) *Examining the Merits of Conflict Resolution as an*

Academic Discipline: Its Applications to Everyday Real Life Situations in the Middle East,

(b) *Building Tolerance to Diversity: A Preliminary Report of the Third Working Conference, 1994.*

Annotation: The Objective of the program is to encourage the identification of principles of conflict resolution and promote the development of academic programmes of teaching these principles. Fields of interest include trauma, conflict resolution, and reconciliation

Institute of War and Peace Studies
13th Floor International Affairs Building, 420 W. 118th St. New York, NY 10027, USA

Telephone: 1-212-854-4616
Fax: 1-212-864-1686
E-mail: audrey@columbia.edu
Senior Staff: Director: Richard Betts
Date of Establishment: 1951
Purpose: The Institute aims to promote understanding of the "disastrous consequences of war upon man's spiritual, intellectual, and material progress" (D. Eisenhower). Its role is interpreted broadly to include both military and nonmilitary aspects of international relations. Although the Institute does not take positions on policy issues, individual members regularly write on public affairs, lecture, and serve as consultants to government departments and agencies.
Type: Private
Brief History: The Institute of War and Peace Studies was founded in 1951 by Dwight D. Eisenhower during his tenure as president of Columbia University. Under

its first director, William T.R. Fox, the Institute became one of the foremost research centers on international relations.
Principal Activities: Members of the institute teach core political science courses on international politics, security, political economy, and law. Many also publish regularly in *Foreign Affairs* and other scholarly journals as well as serving as consultants, guest lecturers and experts in Congressional testimony.
Major Publications:

(a) *Vietnam's Strategic Predicament,*

(b) *Road Map or False Trial: Evaluating the Precedence of the Ozone Regime as Model and Strategy for Global Climate Change,*

(c) *History Versus Neo-realism: A Second Look.*

Institute of World Affairs (IWA)
375 Twin Lakes Road, Salisbury, Connecticut 06068, USA

Telephone: 1-203-824-5135
Fax: 1-203-824-7884
Senior Staff: Executive Director: B. P. Johnson, Special Project Adviser: I. J. Rikhye, J. Leich, Programs &

Research Assoc.: C. Barnes
Date of Establishment: 1924
Type: Private; non-profit
Principal Activities: Research; training; documenta-

tion/information; conference- organization

Current Peace Research: Training designs for professional development seminars on conflict resolution and negotiation for international diplomats

Periodicals:

(a) *International Reports,*

(b) IWA *International.*

Major Publications:

Hadelen, M. M., *Quest for Peace: Personal and Political.*

Annotation: The IWA aims at providing opportunity for people from around the world to explore topics of contemporary significance and to strengthen international understanding. Special focus on developing conflict resolution approaches and negotiation skills of diplomats.

Institute on Global Conflict and Cooperation (IGCC)
University of California, San Diego
9500 Gilman Drive La Jolla, CA 92093-0518, USA

Telephone: 1-619-534-3352
Fax: 1-619-534-7655
Web Site: http://www-igcc.ucsd.edu/igcc/igccmenu.html
E-mail: ph13@sdcc12.ucsd,edu
Senior Staff: Director: Susan L. Shirk, Research Director: Stephan Haggard, Barbara F. Walter, Director Emeritus: Herbert F. York
Date of Establishment: 1983
Purpose: The Institute on Global Conflict and Cooperation was established to serve two major purposes. By studying the causes of international conflict, the Institute can help to devise options for resolving it through international cooperation. Equally important is IGCC's commitment to educate the next generation of problem solvers and peacemakers through research and teaching activities.
Type: International, public, non-profit
Brief History: IGCC was founded by Dr. Herbert York in 1983 as a multicampus research unit serving the entire University of California (UC) system. Unlike most other university research institutions, IGCC's system wide structure enables it to draw from an enormous pool of talented specialists on virtually any topic. During IGCC's first 5 years (1983-88), research focused largely on averting nuclear war through arms control and confidence building measures between the superpowers. Since then, IGCC has diversified to encompass: regional relations, international environment policy, internal conflict, and proliferation of weapons of mass destruction.
Principal Activities:

(a) IGCC is involved in numerous research project in the aforementioned areas,

(b) Outreach programs like seminars and briefings,

(c) Grants which sponsor research and workshops among colleagues,

(d) Dissertation fellowships to UC doctoral candidates for work in academic disciplines related to IGCC's mission,

(e) Publications that explain research findings and policy recommendations.

Periodicals:

(a) IGCC *Newsletter*—circulated internationally and provides opinions on current issues, and reports ongoing research,

(b) *Policy Briefs*—encourage and inform public debate on critical issues concerning global conflict and cooperation,

(c) *Policy Papers*—include contributions to and summaries from IGCC workshop series and colloquia,

(d) IGCC *Online*—the location of IGCC publications and information on the World Wide Web Major.

Major Publications:

(a) *The China Circle: Economics in the PRC, Taiwan, and Hong Kong,*

(b) *Regional Orders: Building Security in a New World,*

(c) *Developing Nations and the Politics of Global Integration,*

(d) *Environmental Security,*

(e) *Conflict: Fear, Diffusion, and Escalation,*

(f) *Peace, Stability, and Nuclear Weapons.*

Intercommunity Center for Justice and Peace (ICJP)
20 Washington Square North, New York NY 10011, USA

Telephone: 1-212-475-6677
Senior Staff: Executive Director: M. Danaher
Date of Establishment: 1974
Purpose: From its beginnings, the Center identified its goal as the solving of social problems in a way that is consistent with Gospel values. Efforts have been directed toward helping the poor and other victims of injustice by seeking to change the systems that are the cause of poverty and injustice in out world.
Type: Private, non-profit
Brief History: The Intercommunity Center for Justice and Peace began in 1974. After extensive research on existing offices of justice and Peace in Milwaukee, Chicago, Pittsburgh, Boston and Topeks, and after carefully studying the goals and objectives of similar agencies in the New York area, it was concluded that no-one was maximizing the enormous potential for structural change that could be harnessed if religious congregations in the New York area were to unite in their efforts for justice.

Principal Activities: The chief strategy employed by the Center is to coordinate the efforts of the total membership in the greater New York area in pressing for the systemic change needed for effecting greater justice and peace in the world. To accomplish this end, the Center has focused its activities in the following areas: legislative action; human rights; women; corporate responsibility; disarmament; justice and peace education; and alcoholism.

Periodicals: *Focus on Central America* (monthly), *Justice in the Schools* (quarterly newsletter)

International League for Human Rights
432 Park Avenue Souta, Suite 1103, New York, NY 10016, USA

Telephone: 1-212-684-1221
Fax: 1-212-684-1696
E-mail: ilhr@igc.org
Senior Staff: Executive Director: Lightman Marjorie, Program Coordinator: John Maltras, Gertz Ben
Date of Establishment: 1942
Purpose: The League works to bring violations of international human rights to the attention of the world community, and to develop innovative approaches to stress their human rights in the institutions of government and private sphere

Type: International, non-profit
Principal Activities:

(a) Country reports and interventions to the monitoring committees of the UN,

(b) Briefings,

(c) Missions,

(d) Publications.

International Peace Academy
777 United Nations Plaza, New York, NY 10017-3521, USA

Telephone: 1-212-687-4300
Fax: 1-212-983-8246
E-mail: ipa@ipacademy.org
Senior Staff: Senior Fellow: Michael Doyle, Senior Associate: Margaret Vogt
Date of Establishment: 1970
Purpose: International Peace Academy (IPA) is an independent, non-partisan, international institution dedicated to promoting the prevention and settlement of armed conflicts between and within states.
Type: International, non-profit
Brief History: Twenty five years ago, International Peace Academy (IPA) was founded with the mission to promote the prevention and settlement of armed conflicts. The principal inspiration came from UN Secretary-General U Thant, and a truly remarkable woman of our times, Ruth Forbes Young. They were animated by the conviction that such an independent institution, free from official constraints, could make a unique contribution to multilateral peace activities through practical and policy-oriented initiatives.

Principal Activities:

(a) Research programs,

(b) Expansion of Training Program,

(c) Programs for East/Central Europe and Former Soviet Union.

Periodicals:

(a) *International Peacekeeping Journal* (quarterly),

(b) *IPA Initiatives Newsletter* (quarterly).

Major Publications:

(a) *Peacemaking and Peacekeeping for the Next Century,*

(b) *Keeping the Peace: Lessons from the Multidimensional UN Operations in Cambodia and El Salvador.*

Iowa Peace Institute
PO Box 480, Grinnell, IA 50112, USA

Telephone: 1-515-236-4880
Senior Staff: President: R. E. Krill, Director, Conflict Resolution Programs: G. Buntz, Director, Iowa Conflict Resolution Project: W. Reinecke
Date of Establishment: 1986
Type: Non-profit
Principal Activities: Training; documentation/ information; publication; radio and tv programmes
Major Publications:

(a) *Fostering Peace: A Comparison of Conflict Resolution Approaches for Students (K-12),*

(b) *The Mediation Process; Why it Works: A Model Developed by Students,*

(c) *Directory of Iowa Experts in Soviet Affairs.*

Annotation: The Institute carries out research on conflict resolution and the mediation process

Jane Addams Peace Association (JAPA)
777 United Nations Plaza New York NY 10017, USA

Telephone: 1-212-682-8830
Senior Staff: Executive Director: A. Spencer-Linzie
Date of Establishment: 1948
Purpose: The purpose of the JAPA is to promote understanding among the peoples of all nations and races, so that war and strife may be avoided and a lasting peace enjoyed.
Type: Non-profit
Brief History: JAPA was founded in 1948 to sponsor and finance educational programs of the Women's International League for Peace and Freedom. Among the founders of WILPF in 1915 was Jane Addams, the first American woman to win the Nobel Peace Prize (see Nobel Peace Prize Laureates: Jane Addams).
Principal Activities: Conference-organizations; publication
Periodicals: *Building Peace*
Major Publications: The Committee for World Development and World Disarmament has published materials and organized national, regional, and organized national, regional, and local conferences on world disarmament and economic development.

John M. Olin Institute for Strategic Studies
Harvard University
1737 Cambridge Street, Cambridge, MA 02138-3099, USA

Telephone: 1-617-495-4432
Fax: 1-617-495-1384
E-mail: kcarnago@cfia.mhs.harvard.edu
Senior Staff: Director: S. P. Huntington, Senior Researcher Associate: M. C. Desch, Researcher: A. I. Johnston Research Co-director: E. B. Kapstein, Research Director: S. P. Rosen, Co-director: R. Vernon
Date of Establishment: 1989
Principal Activities: Research; conference-organization; publication
Current Peace Research:

(a) Economics and national security programme,

(b) Russian and American post-Cold War visions,

(c) The changing security environment and American national interests,

(d) Asian security.

Major Publications:

(a) Huntington, S., *The Third Wave: Democratization in the Late Twentieth Century*, 1991,

(b) Brown, M. E., *The Flying Blind: The Politics of the U.S. Strategic Bomber Program*, 1992,

(c) Downing, B. M., *The Military Revolution and Political Change*, 1992,

(d) Feaver, P. D., *Guarding the Guardians*, 1992,

(e) Kapstein, E. B., *Global Arms Production*, 1992,

(f) Kapstein, E., *Political Economy of National Security: A Global Perspective*, 1992,

(g) Macdonald, D. J., *Adventures in Chaos*, 1992,

(h) Resen, S., *Winning the Next War*, 1992,

(i) Cogan, C., *The In-Culture of the DO (Directorate of Operations, CIA)*, 1993,

(j) Cogan, C., *Partners in Time: The CIA and Afghanistan since 1979*, 1993,

(k) Desch, M., *When the Third World Matters: Latin America and U.S. Grand Strategy*, 1993,

(l) Huntington, S. P., *American Democracy in Relation to Asia*, 1993,

(m) Huntington, S. P., *The Clash of Civilizations?*, 1993,

(n) Huntington, S. P., *Why International Primacy Matters*, 1993,

(o) Mearsheimer, J., *The Case for a Ukrainian Nuclear Deterrent*, 1993,

(p) Mearsheimer, J., Pape, R., *The Answer: A Three-Way Partition Plan for Bosnia and How the U.S. Can Enforce it*, 1993,

(q) Vernon, R., *Where are the Multinationals Headed?*, 1993,

Annotation: Research deals with security and strategy including security problems confronting the USA and its allies. Current fields of interest cover: the 3 problems for American security stemming from the military-technological revolution, the clash of civilizations, and the increased salience of economic power; security issues in East Asia; and Russian foreign policy and defence policy.

Kansas Institute for Peace and Conflict Resolution
Bethel College
300 E 27th Street, North Newton, KS 67117, USA

Telephone: 1-316-284-5217
Fax: 1-316-284-5286
E-mail: lhawkley@menno.bethelks.edu
Synonymous Name: Kansas Peace Institute
Senior Staff: Director: L. Hawkley
Date of Establishment: 1985
Type: Non-profit
Principal Activities: Training; conference-organization; publication; peace lecture series
Major Publications:
Hawkley, L., Juhnke, J. C. (eds.), *Nonviolent America: History through the Eyes of Peace*.
Annotation: Fields of interest include: peace studies, environmental and justice dimensions of peace, security and ethics, conflict resolution, domestic and international conflicts, international security issues, international organizations, mediation, education for peace, peace movements, and U.S.-Russian relations

Courses: Summer Institute for Teachers
Subjects Taught: Culture of peace; nonviolence: environmental and justice dimensions of peace; economic conversion; mediation; global awareness
Target Group: Non-specialists; general public; college students; area teachers
Level of the Course: Undergraduate
Type of Course: Short session; summer course; evening course
Duration: "Summer Institute for Teachers": one week; "Peace Lecture Series": four evening lectures per year
Working Languages: English
Admission Requirements: No
Course Fees: Yes, US$ 200 (Summer Institute for Teachers)
Scholarships Available: No
Degree/Diploma: No

Lentz Peace Research Laboratory, St. Louis (LPRL, St. Louis)
1538 N. 17th st. A St. Louis MO 63106, USA

Telephone: 314-721-8219
Fax: 314-241-5008
Senior Staff: Director: P. Coy, Research Director: W. Eckhardt
Date of Establishment: 1945
Purpose: The purpose of peace research is to study the causes of war and the conditions necessary for peace. The results of this study indicate so far that violence is caused by personal attitudes and is conditioned by social institutions. It is believed that there is more to learn about making and keeping peace, because the job is being poorly done despite the best of intentions and the tremendous efforts being expended for peace against war. The Peace Research Laboratory seeks to contribute to this work.
Type: Private, non-profit
Brief History: The Peace Research Laboratory is the oldest continuously operating peace research center in the world. It was founded by Theodore F. Lentz in 1945 following the atomic bombing of Hiroshima and Nagasaki. Until Lentz's death in 1976, PRL emphasized the role of attitudes in relation to peace and war. The name of the Laboratory was changed from the the Peace Research Laboratory to the Lentz Peace Research Laboratory in 1986.
Principal Activities: Major activities of the PRL are, first and foremost research on attitudes, events, ideologies, philosophies, theories, and values as these are related to peace and war. It also promotes peace research by presenting papers at professional meetings, churches, civic groups, radio, and television programs. The PRL also publishes research results in books and articles in professional journals. It presents the Lentz International Peace Research Award to outstanding peace researchers and provides partial funding for the Lentz Center for Peace Research in Lancashire, United Kingdom

Periodicals: Peace Research
Major Publications:

(a) *Towards a Science of Peace,*

(b) *Towards a Technology of Peace,*

(c) *Humatriotism,*

(d) *Compassion: Toward a Science of Value,*

(e) *Governments under Fire: Civil Conflict and Imperialism,*

(f) *Compassion Manual,*

(g) *Pioneers of Peace Research,*

(h) *Factors of War/Peace Attitudes,*

(i) *Ideology and Personality in Social Attitudes.*

Mario Einaudi
Center for International Studies (CIS)
Cornell University
Ithaca, New York 14853, USA

Telephone: 1-607-255-2778/1-607-255-6370
E-mail: dl55@cornell.edu
Web Site: www.einaudi.cornell.edu/
Senior Staff: Director: Ron Herring
Date of Establishment: 1961
Purpose:

(a) The Center stands to serve as the umbrella organization for international programs at Cornell University by providing leadership in an environment where scholars from all colleges can meet and work on international subjects,

(b) To assist the university directly and through the colleges in developing and maintaining a balance between the demands of international research, graduate teaching, undergraduate teaching, and faculty development,

(c) To provide advice, funding, and logistical support to international program development,

(d) To enhance the international dimensions of the university's curriculum and to increase faculty competence in international studies,

(e) To report on the development of the international programs at Cornell and to keep the university informed of important issues and changes,

(f) To provide Cornell with information on key national and international trends and the developments in order to retain the university's strength in international studies,

(g) To represent and publicize Cornell's international programs beyond the university,

(h) To oversee the operations of Cornell Abroad and the International Students and Scholars Office.

Brief History: The Mario Einaudi Center for International Studies (The Einaudi Center) was established in 1961 to encourage, coordinate, and support comparative and interdisciplinary research on international subjects. Charged with the responsibility of furthering international and comparative research and teaching-involving efforts in almost every unit of the University, the Einaudi Center has evolved into an administrative focus for over 20 international programs during the past three decades.

Periodicals:

(a) The LASP Newsletters,

(b) Conference proceedings.

Merson Center
Ohio State University
199 West 10th Avenue, Columbus, OH 43201-2399, USA

Telephone: 1-614-292-1681
Fax: 1-614-292-2407
Cable: MERSHCTR
Senior Staff: Director: C. F. Hermann, Specialist: C. F. Alger, R. K. Herrmann, J. R. Kruzel, R. C. Remy
Date of Establishment: 1967
Type: Private; non-profit
Principal Activities: Research; training; documentation/information; conference-organization; publication
Geographical Coverage: Western Europe; Eastern Europe; Middle East; Russian Federation; China; USA; global
Current Peace Research:

(a) The uses of military force in the quest for peace: compatibilities and contradictions,

(b) ethnic identification and national movements,

(c) Geography of inequality and instability in the former Soviet Union.

Type of Publication: Bulletin; monograph; progress-report; conference proceedings; training materials
Bulletins: *Communiqué*, 4 p.a., *Mershon Memo*, 4 p.a.
Major Publications:

(a) Alger, C. F., *The UN in Historical Perspective: What have We Learned about Peacebuilding*, 1991,

(b) Hoyt, P. D., Herrmann, R. K., *Change and Stability in the Middle East: how do we get there from here?*, 1991,

(c) Agüero, F., *The Military and the Limits to Democratization in South America*, 1992,

(d) Casto, R. M., *The Turmoil of Turf: Interprofessional Collaboration in the War Zone*, 1992,

(e) Karns, M., *Maintaining International Peace and Security: UN Peacekeeping and Peacemaking*, 1993,

(f) Herrmann, R. K., *Soviet Behavior in Regional Conflicts: Old Questions, New Strategies, and Important Lessons*, 1992,

(g) Kruzel, J. J., *After the Storm: Perspectives on the Gulf War*, 1992,

(h) Starr, S. F., *Prospects for Stable Democracy in Russia*, 1992,

(i) Sylvan, D. A., Thorson, S. J., *Ontologies, Problem Representation, and the Cuban Missile Crisis*, 1992,

(j) Hogan, M. J., *The End of the Cold War: Its Meaning and Implications*, 1992,

(k) Millett, A. R., *In Many a Strife: General Gerald C. Thomas and the US Marine Corps, 1917-1956*, 1993,

(l) Alger, C. F., *Peacebuilding in the Post-Cold War era*, 1993,

(m) Gunther, R., *Politics, Society and Democracy: The Case of Spain*, 1993,

(n) Krugel, J. J. (ed.), *1993 American Defense Annual*, 1993,

(o) Litterer, J., Saunders, D., Minton, J., *Negotiation: Readings, Exercises and Cases*, 1993,

(p) Zisk, K. M., *Engaging the Enemy: Organization Theory and Soviet Military Innovation 1955-1991*, 1993.

Annotation: The Center explores the critical issues of war and peace through problem oriented research and education. Research is aimed at achieving a better understanding of the role of collective violence and furthering the knowledge of military and non-military means of conflict resolution and strategies for peace in world affairs, the involvement of the U.S. in international organizations and its international relations with the rest of the world. Programme clusters include: International Security and Military Affairs; Citizenship Development for a Global Age; Foreign Policy Analysis and World Politics Program; Global Relations and Peace Studies.

National Institute for Dispute Resolution (NIDR)
1901 L St. NW, Suite 600, Washington, DC 20036, USA

Telephone: 1-202-466-4764

Senior Staff: President: M. Baker, Researcher: T. Fee, Senior Program Assoc.: J. Filner, A. Stern, Program Assoc.: L. Work

Date of Establishment: 1982

Type: Public; non-profit

Principal Activities: Research; training; documentation/information; conference- organization; publication

Current Peace Research:

(a) Public policy dispute resolution,

(b) Survey of the United States' courts,

(c) Private environmental mediation techniques,

(d) Building the collaborative community.

Periodicals:

(a) *Dispute Resolution Forum,*

(b) *NIDR Report.*

Major Publications:

(a) *Dispute Resolution in America,*

(b) Trolldalen, J. M., *International environmental Conflict Resolution: The Role of the United Nations*, 1992,

(c) Bush, R. B., *The Dilemmas of Mediation Practice: A Study of Ethical Dilemmas and Policy Implications*, 1992,

(d) Blaustone, B., *Settle or Sue, What Else Can I do?* 1993,

(e) Dillon, K., *Statewide Offices of Medikation: Experiments in Public Policy*, 1993,

Annotation: Concerned with conflict resolution, arbitration, mediation and negotiation

National Peace Foundation (NPF)
1835 K. Street NW, Suite 610, Washington, DC 20006, USA

Telephone: 1-202-223-1770

Senior Staff: President and Executive Director: S. P. Strickland

Date of Establishment: 1982

Type: Private, non-profit

Principal Activities: Documentation/information; publication

Geographical Coverage: USA

Type of Publication: Journal; bulletin; monograph

Periodicals: *Planning for Peacemaking*

Bulletins: *Peace Reporter*

Annotation: Mainly concerned with conflict resolution and peacemaking.

Nuclear Age Peace Foundation (NAPF)
1187 Coast Village Road, Suite 123, Santa Barbara, CA 93108-2794, USA

Telephone: 1-805-965-3443
Fax: 1-805-568-0466
Senior Staff: President: D. Krieger, Specialist: D. Babst, P. Hashend, D. Hull, F. Kelly, N. Kohn
Type: Public; non-profit
Cooperating Organization: ECOSOC
Principal Activities: Research; training; documentation/information; conference-organization; publication
Geographical Coverage: Global
Current Peace Research:

(a) Nuclear non-proliferation,

(b) Abolition of nuclear weapons,

(c) Development of a permanent International Criminal Court.

Type of Publication: Journal; bulletin; monograph; booklets; audio tapes
Periodicals:

(a) *Global Security Studies,*

(b) *Waging Peace Bulletin*, 4 p.a.

Major Publications:

(a) *A Student's Guide to Global Responsibility: An Internship Project of the Nuclear Age Peace Foundation*, 1993,

(b) *The Nuclear Age: Rights, Responsibilities and Accountability. A Course Outline: An Internship Project of the Foundation*, 1993,

(c) Babst, D., *Do Dictators Use U.S. Arms to Suppress Their Own People?*, 1993,

(d) Babst, D., Deraps, B., Krieger, D., *Building a Peaceful World*, 1993,

(e) Curle, A., *New Challenges for Citizen Peacemaking*, 1993,

(f) Krieger, D., *Individual Accountability for International Crimes*, 1993,

(g) Krieger, D., *North Korea's Challenge to the Global Community*, 1993,

(h) Krieger, D., *Security, Sovereignty and Survival in the Nuclear Age*, 1993,

(i) Krieger, D. (ed.), *The Nuclear Age: A Chronology of Significant Events*, 1993,

(j) Krieger D. (ed.), *Nuclear Age Peace Calendar: Days of Remembrance, Days of Renewal*, 1993,

(k) Krieger, D., Woetzel, R., *A Magna Carta for the Nuclear Age*, 1993,

(l) Rotblat, J., *The Feasability of a Nuclear-Weapon-Free World*, 1993,

(m) Suter, K., *The 1993 Chemical Weapons Convention*, 1993,

(n) Tsuchida, A., *The Nuclear Arming of Japan*, 1994.

Annotation: Its purpose is to develop innovative and action-oriented ideas, to revise the nuclear weapons sale and to find strategies for peace and nonviolent global conflict resolution.
Courses: Designing a Future of World Peace; Global Responsibility
Subjects Taught: Peace research; disarmament; conflict resolution; role of the international organizations; nonviolence; peace and development; democracy and peace; war; international conflict; international security; education for peace
Principal Instructors: Dr. D. Krieger
Target Group: Non-specialists
Level of the Course: Undergraduate; bachelors
Type of Course: Regular course; short session; summer course; evening course
Duration: Varies
Working Languages: English
Admission Requirements: No
Course Fees: Yes
Degree/Diploma: No

Nuclear Control Institute
1000 Connecticut Avenue NW, Suite 704, Washington, DC 20036, USA

Telephone: 202-822-8444
Senior Staff: President: P. Leventhal
Date of Establishment: 1981
Type: Non-profit, private
Principal Activities: Research; documentation/ information

Annotation: The Institute develops studies and strategies for preventing nuclear weapons proliferation, and investigates worldwide commerce in plutonium and the effects of international safeguards and conducts legislative research on current nuclear policies. The vulnerabilities of nuclear weapons to terrorism are also studied.

The Paul H. Nitze School of Advanced International Studies (SAIS)
The Johns Hopkins University
1740 Massachusetts Avenue, NW, Washington, DC 20036, USA

Telephone: 1-202-663-5600
Fax: 1-202-663-5656
Telex: JHUUR 264170
Senior Staff: Dean: G. R. Packard, Prof.: Dr. E. A. Cohen, Asst. Prof.: Dr. M. Coppedge, C. F. Doran, M. Khadduri, Research Prof.: W. L. Kohl, G. Liska, M. Mandelbaum, B. Parrott, S. Serfaty, W. S. Smith, S. J. Stedman, I. W. Zartman
Date of Establishment: 1943
Principal Activities: Training
Courses:

(a) Multilateral Negotiation,

(b) Negotiating Arms Control,

(c) Principles and Practices of Conflict Management,

(d) Seminar in Crisis Simulation

Subjects Taught: International conflict; conflict resolution; security; arms control; diplomacy; decision making; nuclear nonproliferation; strategies
Principal Instructors: Prof. I. W. Zartman (Programme Director)
Target Group: Professionals; nationals; foreign students
Level of the Course: Graduate; masters; doctorate
Type of Course: Regular courses, included in the M.A. Degree in International Relations
Duration: 2 years for the M.A.
Working Languages: English
Admission Requirements: Yes
Closing Date for Applications: 1 February
Course Fees: Yes
Scholarships Available: Yes
Degree/Diploma: M.A. International Relations, subfield "International Law and Institutions and Conflict Management"

Peace Action
1819 H Street NW, Suite 420 Washington, DC 20006, USA

Telephone: 1-202-862-9740
Fax: 1-202-862-9762
E-mail: paprog@igc.apc.org
Senior Staff: Exec. Director: Gordon S. Clark, Program Director: Fran Teplitz, Field Director: Van Gosse
Date of Establishment: 1957
Purpose: Peace Action is the nation's largest grassroots peace organization. Members of the organization come from all walks of life. They work at all kinds of jobs, who are people from every religious faith and every race and ethnic background. What unites the members is their commitment to a peaceful America and a peaceful world.
Type: National, private, non-profit

Brief History: Peace Action is the merger of the Committee for a Sane Nuclear Policy (SANE) and the Nuclear Weapons Freeze Campaign (Freeze). Beginning in 1957, SANE had pressed for an end to the atmospheric testing of nuclear weapons. In the 1980s, the Freeze mobilized millions of citizens against the nuclear arms race and the threat of nuclear war. It changed its name to Peace Action in 1993.
Principal Activities: Peace Action works to abolish nuclear weapons, for a more peaceful economy, for an end to weapons trafficking, and for non-military solutions to international conflicts.
Periodicals: *Peace Action* (quarterly newsletter)

Peace and Justice Studies Program
University of San Francisco
2130 Fulton Street, San Francisco, CA 94117-1080, USA

Telephone: 1-415-666-6349
Fax: 1-415-666-2346
Senior Staff: Director: R. Elias, Researcher: J. Turpin
Date of Establishment: 1989
Principal Activities: Research; training; publication
Periodicals: *Peace Review*, 4 p.a.

Major Publications:

(a) Elias, R., *Victims Still,*

(b) Elias, R., Turpin, J. (eds.), *Rethinking Peace*, 1994,

(c) Turpin, J., *Reinventing the Soviet Self*, 1994,

(d) Turpin, J., Kurtz, L. (eds.), *The Web of Violence: from Interpersonal to Global*, 1994.

Annotation: The Program examines themes of peace and war, human rights and violence, political movements, economic development, and environmental protection from a multidisciplinary perspective, emphasizing the role of critical thinking and social responsibility.

Courses: Peace and Justice Studies
Subjects Taught: Peace; war; human rights; violence; political movements; economic development; environmental protection
Principal Instructors: Mr. R. Elias (Director)
Level of the Course: Undergraduate
Type of Course: Academic
Working Languages: English
Degree/Diploma: Certificate in Peace & Justice Studies

Peace Studies Institute and Program in Conflict Resolution
Manchester College
Box 27 Manchester College N. Manchester Indiana Y6962, USA

Telephone: 1-219-982-5343
Fax: 1-219-982-5043
E-mail: Klbrown@Manchester.edu
Senior Staff: Director: Kenneth Brown, Bretnren Colleges Abroad, Allen, Deeder, Conflict Resolution Prof.: Gray Zimmerman, Political Science Assistant Prof.: Benson Onyeji
Date of Establishment: 1948
Purpose: Undergraduate majors in peace studies:

(a) Interpersonal and intergroup,

(b) International and global,

(c) Religions and philosophical bases.

Type: Private, non-profit
Brief History: The Institute was established in 1948.

It was first in US major and minor degrees in Peace Studies, and founded by Gladdys Muir, Director from 1948-61.
Principal Activities:

(a) B.A. Degrees in Peace Studies,

(b) Concentrations in Global and International Peace,

(c) Religious and philosophical bases of peace,

(d) Interpersonal conflict resolution

Periodicals: Bulletin of the peace studies institute and programs in conflict resolution (annual)

Peace Studies Program
Colgate University
Hamilton, New York 13346-1398, USA

Telephone: 1-315-824-1000
Fax: 1-315-824-1000/292
Senior Staff: Director: N. J. Young
Date of Establishment: 1970
Type: Private, non-profit
Principal Activities: Research; training; documentation/information; conference- organization; publication; study abroad programmes
Current Peace Research:

(a) Transnational peace studies,

(b) Alternative peace orders in Europe,

(c) The Role of a peace movement in Europe.

Periodicals: *Newsletter*
Major Publications:

Campaigns for peace, 1989.
Annotation: Devoted to research on peace movements, the formation and role of the state, media and war, peace studies and education for peace.
Courses:

(a) Introduction to Peace Studies: Violence and Non-violence;

(b) Images of War and Peace in Modern Film, Art and Literature;

(c) Social Movements for Peace and Change;

(d) War, State and Society;

(e) Contemporary Issues in War and Peace

Subjects Taught: Peace research; disarmament; conflict resolution; arms control; violence; nonviolence; peaceful social change; polemology; war; international conflict; war resistance and social movements; military and the state

Principal Instructors: Prof. N. J. Young
Target Group: Nationals
Level of the Course: Undergraduate
Type of Course: Courses include regular course and study group. Peace studies courses are elective but a major or minor concentration in peace studies is possible with a number of required and recommended course

Duration: 4 year degree program, including 1 semester abroad
Working Languages: English
Admission Requirements: Admission procedures of Colgate University in order to receive credit
Course Fees: US$ 9,000 for one semester (4 courses) at Colgate University, including room and board
Scholarships Available: Yes, through the financial Aid Office at Colgate University
Degree/Diploma: B.A. in Peace Studies

Peace Studies Program
Cornell University
130 Uris Hall, Ithaca, New York 14853-7601, USA

Telephone: 1-607-255-6484
Fax: 1-607-254 5000
Senior Staff: Director: J. Reppy, Prof.: J. Borneman, V. Bunce, J. Goldgeier, P. Katzenstein, B. Strauss, Assoc. Director: L. Sheinman
Date of Establishment: 1970
Type: Private, non-profit
Current Peace Research:

(a) Ethnicity and international conflict,

(b) Global environmental change and social justice,

(c) Issues of nuclear proliferation,

(d) Women in the military: the role of technology,

(e) The "Nation" as a form of identity and justice in post-unity Germany,

(f) International cooperation in Eastern Europe after the Cold War,

(g) The Interaction between international organizations and ethnic groups in conflict,

(h) The Prospects for cooperation in the relations between the states of the former Soviet Union,

(i) Ethnicity, ethnic conflict and the role of legal and administrative regimes in channeling and creating particular expressions of cultural difference, similarity and conflict,

(j) Japan and Germany in a changing world,

(k) Sociology of war and peace.

Major Publications:

(a) Crawford, B. (ed.), *Eastern Europe as a De-stabilizing Force on the New Europe*, 1992,

(b) Telhami, S., *The Palestinians and the End of the Cold War*, 1992,

(c) Scheinman, L., *The Role of Multilateral Regimes in Non-Proliferation*, 1992,

(d) Bush, K., *From Bullet Holes to Bird Nests: The Role of NGOs in the Peacebuilding Process*, 1993,

(e) Katzenstein, P., Okawara, N., *Japan's National Security: Structures, Norms and Policy Responses in a Changing World*, 1993,

(f) Kuznetsov, Y., *Defense Industry Downsizing in Shortrun Crisis Management: The Case of the Former Soviet Union and its Implications for the USA Adjustment*, 1993,

(g) Pilat, J., *Technology Deployment and Denial: A Unilateral Approach to Arms Control*, 1993,

(h) Reppy, J., *Planning Courses on Economic Peace and Security*, 1993,

(i) Takahara, T., *US-Japanese Postwar Military Relations: Towards a Security Community via Asymmetrical Integration*, 1993,

(j) Thomas, D., *World Security: Challenges for a New Century*, 1993.

Annotation: It is interdisciplinary programme devoted to problems of war and peace, arms control and disarmament, and more generally, instances of collective violence. Current research deals with ethnic conflicts, environmental change, nuclear proliferation, international security, international relations and the role of the international organizations.
Courses: Peace Studies Courses
Subjects Taught: Peaceful coexistence; disarmament;

arms control; role of the international organizations; conflict resolution; defence; peace and development; war; international conflict; international security; regional conflict; terrorism

Level of the Course: Undergraduate; graduate

Type of Course: Regular courses including seminars and lectures

Working Languages: English

Admission Requirements: Cornell University gradu-ate school admission requirements

Course Fees: Tuition fees: US$ 18,170 per year

Scholarships Available: Yes, contact: Dr. J. Reppy, Director, Peace Studies Program. Students admitted to one of the regular fields at Cornell University who indicate an interest in Peace Studies would be considered for a fellowship if funds available

Degree/Diploma: Ph.D.

Program in Arms Control, Disarmament and International Security (ACDIS)
University of Illinois at Urbana-Champaign
330 Davenport Hall, 607 South Mathews Avenue, Urbana, IL 61801, USA

Telephone: 1-217-333-7086

Fax: 1-217-244-5157

Telex: UI TELCOM URUD

E-mail: acdis@uiuc.edu

Senior Staff: Director: S. P. Cohen, Prof.: S. P. Cohen, R. E. Kanet, E. A. Kolodziej, J. D. Sullivan, Assoc. Prof.: P. F. Diehl,

Date of Establishment: 1978

Type: Public, non-profit

Principal Activities: Research; training; documentation/information; conference-organization; publication

Current Peace Research:

(a) Coping with regional conflict: a guide to theory and practice,

(b) "Brass-tacks": nuclear crisis behaviour in South Asia,

(c) South Asian nuclear proliferation issues,

(d) Ethics of nuclear deterrence,

(e) Hydrodynamic monitoring of underground nuclear explosions,

(f) Japan in the post-Cold War world.

Periodicals: *Swords and Ploughshares*, 4 p.a.

Major Publications:

(a) Lynn, J. A. (ed.), *Feeding Mars: Logistics in Western Warfare from the Middle Ages to the Present*, 1992,

(b) Cohen, S. P. (ed.), *South Asia After the Cold War: International Perspectives*, 1993,

(c) Kolodziej, E. A., Kanet, R. E. (eds.), *Coping with Conflict After the Cold War*, 1994,

(d) *A Guide to Sources in Early Modern European Military in History in Midwestern Research Libraries*, 1991,

(e) Diehl, P. F., *International Peacekeeping*, 1993,

(f) Lepingwell, J. W. R., *A Russian Reversal on SDI*, 1992,

(g) Kumar, C., *Beyond Earth Summit '92: Redefining the International Security Agenda*, 1993,

(h) Mims, E., *Open Skies*, 1993,

(i) Munck, G. L., Kumar, C., *Peaceful Conflict Resolution Through International Intervention: A Comparative Study of Cambodia and El Salvador*, 1993.

Annotation: Research deals with inter- and intra-regional approaches to security policy and arms control; scientific and technological issues relevant to arms control and disarmament, including development, testing and deployment of space weapons; legal, philosophical and cultural issues of peace and international security; causes, onset, conduct and impact of war and the development and influence of militarism throughout history and; regional security and arms control, both nuclear and conventional.

Courses:

(a) War and Peace in Cross-Cultural Perspecitve;

(b) Introduction to Remote Sensing Technology for Verification of Arms Control Agreements;

(c) War, Military Institutions and Society;

(d) The Ethics of Nuclear Deterrence;

(e) International Conflict: Perspectives from the Humanities;

(f) Nuclear Weapons, Nuclear Wars and Arms Control;

(g) Introduction to International Security and Arms Control;

(h) War, Genocide, and Disaster in the 20st Century;

(i) Third Parties in International Security and Conflict

Subjects Taught: Disarmament; conflict resolution; role of the international organizations; nonviolence; peace and development; democracy and peace; war; international conflict; international security; regional conflict; terrorism

Target Group: Professionals; non-specialists; nationals; foreign students

Level of the Course: Undergraduate; bachelors; graduate; postgraduate; masters; doctorate

Type of Course: Regular course

Duration: Undergraduate programme: 4 years; graduate programme: 7 years

Working Languages: English

Admission Requirements: Yes, requirements dependent on the degree granting programme applied to. Undergraduate students contact: Admission and Records, UIUC, 10 Henry Administrating Building, 506 S. Wright Street, Urbana, IL 61801; graduate students contact the major department or the Graduate College, UIUC, 202 Coble Hall, 801 S. Wright Street, Champaign, IL 61820

Closing Date for Applications: Undergraduate applications for Fall admission: 1 October to 31 December of the preceding year; graduate applications for Fall admission, October to December of the preceding year

Course Fees: Yes, actual amount varies, contact University for current tuition and fees schedules

Scholarships Available: Yes, undergraduates to contact: Office of Student Financial Aid, UIUC, Turner Student Services Building, 610 E. John Street, Champaign, IL 61820

The Program on Negotiation
Harvard Law School
Pound Hall 513, Cambridge, MA 02138, USA

Telephone: 1-617-495-1684
Fax: 1-617-495-7818
E-mail: hillis@law.harvard.edu
Web Site: www.law.harvard.edu/Programs/PON/
Senior Staff: Executive Director: Marjorie C. Aaron
Date of Establishment: 1817
Purpose: The curriculum consists of 251 courses and seminars and includes such diverse subject areas as constitutional law, environmental law, criminal law, corporate finance, negotiation, family law, and international and comparative law. A strong clinical program offers students a wide range of fieldwork and simulation courses as well as opportunities to participate in for-credit and extracurricular practice-related activities in one of several Harvard-operated legal services clinics, among them the Hale and Dorr Legal Services Center of Harvard Law School and the Immigration and Refugee Clinic.

Brief History: Founded in 1817, Harvard Law School is the oldest existing law school in the United States. Harvard's first classes in law were held in College House #2, also known as the Weber farmhouse, until Dane Hall was designed for the Law School in 1832. Austin Hall, completed in 1883, replaced Dane Hall as the center of activity and, along with Gannett House (1838) and Hastings Hall (1889), serves as a present-day reminder of the Law School's history of change and growth.

Principal Activities: The School provides comprehensive and enlightened training to prepare its graduates for law practice, for public service at the local, state, federal and international levels, and for law teaching and legal scholarship. Through its faculty, students, and graduates, Harvard Law School seeks to make substantial contributions toward solving complex social and international problems.

Program in Science and Technology for International Security
Massachusetts Institute of Technology
77 Massachusetts Avenue, Cambridge, MA 02139, USA

Telephone: 617-253-3647
Fax: 617-253-4235
Senior Staff: Director: K. Tsipis, Specialist: K. Tsipis

Date of Establishment: 1977
Type: Non-profit
Geographical Coverage: USA

Current Peace Research:

(a) The Future of U.S. national security,

(b) Development aid and security.

Periodicals: *PSTIS Research Report*
Major Publications:

(a) *Common Security Regimes for the Balkans,*

(b) *Annual Review of Military Research and Development,*

(c) *Arms Control Verification.*

Annotation: The Institute carries out research on technical issues of national and international security, nuclear arms control, nuclear weapons systems and

policy. It also investigates the redeployment of defence research and development resources to the civilian sector.
Courses: Technology Transfer for Development
Subjects Taught: Peace and development; international security
Target Group: professionals; non-specialists; nationals
Level of the Course: Undergraduate; masters
Type of Course: Regular course
Duration: One semester
Working Languages: English
Admission Requirements: Yes, admission to MIT
Closing Date for Applications: 1 January
Course Fees: Yes, MIT tuition fees
Scholarships Available: Yes
Degree/Diploma: Yes

Program on the Analysis and Resolution of Conflicts, Maxwell School of Citizenship and Public Affairs (PARC) Syracuse University
712 Ostrom Avenue, Syracuse, NY 13244-4400, USA

Telephone: 1-315-443-2367
Fax: 1-315-443-3818
E-mail: parc@suvm.acu.edu
Date of Establishment: 1985
Senior Staff: Director: L. Kriesberg, Prof.: L. Kriesberg, N. Katz, S. Thorson, M. Provine, Researcher: M. Bonham, S. Wadley
Type: Non-profit
Principal Activities: Research; training; documentation.information; conference- organization; publication
Current Peace Research:

(a) Strategies for resolving inter-communal conflicts in different time factors,

(b) Developing specifications for computer-based early warning system,

(c) Comparative human rights law,

(d) Hindu-Muslim conflicts and religious identities in rural North India,

(e) Cognitive mapping and cognitive factors in international conflicts,

(f) Somalia project.

Periodicals: *PARC Newsletter*

Major Publications:

(a) Kriesburg, L., Thorson, S. (ed.), *Timing the De-escalation of International Conflicts,* 1991,

(b) Kriesburg, L., *The US-USSR and Middle East Cases,* 1992,

(e) Kriesburg, L., *Dilemmas in Nonviolently Settling International Conflicts,* 1991,

(d) Kriesburg, L., *Formal and Quasi-Mediators in International Disputes: An Exploratory Analysis,* 1991,

(f) Thorson, S., Bennett, J., *Reasoning and Intelligibility,* 1991,

(g) Kriesburg, L., Segal, D.R. (ed.), *Social Movements, Conflicts and Change: The Transformation of European Communist Societies,* 1992,

(h) Agnew, J., *The US Position in the World Geopolitical Order at the End of the Cold War,* 1992,

(i) Agnew, J., *The United States and Hegemony in Germany,* 1992,

(j) Arzt, D., Zughaib, K., *Return to the Negotiated Lands: The Likelihood And legality of a Popula-*

tion Transfer Between Israel and a Future Palestinian State, 1992.

Annotation: PARC is an interdisciplinary research and theory-building center, focusing on conflict resolution. Areas of concern include environmental and international conflicts, interpersonal and ethnic conflicts, local and religious conflicts in comparative settings.
Courses: Peace Studies (M.A.; Ph. D.)
Subjects Taught: Peace research; conflict resolution; arms control; role of the international organizations; nonviolence; peace and development; international conflict; international security; regional conflict; social conflict theory
Principal Instructors: Prof. L. Kriesburg, Mr. M. Boroujerdi, Prof. M. Bonham, Prof. S. Thorson
Target Group: Professionals; non-specialists; nationals; foreign students; graduates

Level of the Course: Doctorate; masters; College and Summer Institutes
Type of Course: Regular course; short session; summer course. Part of M.A. (1-2 yrs) and Ph.D. (3-5 yrs) available through social science disciplines and international relations
Duration: Varies
Working Languages: English
Admission Requirements: Varies with degree-granting program related to PARC
Course Fees: Yes
Scholarships Available: Yes, apply to: Syracuse University, Admissions, 210 Tolley Administration Building, Syracuse, N.Y. 13244, USA
Degree/Diploma: Credits for a M.A. or Ph.D. in one of the social science disciplines or an interdisciplinary programme such as international relations or other graduate programme of the University

Rand National Security Research Division (RAND/NSRD)
1700 Main Street, PO Box 2138, Santa Monica, CA 90407-2138, USA

Telephone: 1-310-393-0411
Fax: 1-310-393-4818
Date of Establishment: 1948
Senior Staff: Director: D. C. Gompert, F. Fukuyama, R. Asmus, R. W. Benjamin, NSRD Assoc. Program Director: B. Bennett, C. Keeley, Corporate Research Manager: J. Pollock
Type: Non-profit, private
Principal Activities: Research; training; documentation/information; conference-organization; publication
Current Peace Research:

(a) US/Russian strategic partnership,

(b) Values, modernization and ethnic conflict,

(c) Psychological dimensions of peacekeeping,

(d) Greater Middle East studies center,

(e) Controlling arms transfers in the Middle East,

(f) Confidence building and crisis management measures related to the Arab-Israeli peace process (1922-),

(g) Lessons learned from peace operations,

(h) Multilateral operations: enhancement of non-US capabilities,

(i) Force implications of peace operations,

(j) NATO's mechanisms for peace operations,

(k) Bosnia policy options.

Type of Publication: Bulletin; monograph; progress-report; conference proceedings
Bulletins: *RAND Research Review*
Major Publications:

(a) Davis, L., *Peacekeeping and Peacemaking After the Cold War*, 1993,

(b) Wilson, M, M., *The Day After …; Nuclear Proliferation in the Post-Cold War World*, 1993,

(c) Yager, B., *Fairness: The Scylla and Charybdis of US-Japan Relations*, 1993.

Annotation: RAND/NSRD conducts a wide range of projects on peace and security including ethnic conflicts, culture of peace and peace operations.
Courses: Introduction to National Security Analysis; Systems Analysis for Defense Problems
Subjects Taught: Defence; security; arms control
Target Group: Nationals; foreign students
Level of the Course: Graduate; postgraduate; doctorate
Type of Course: Regular course, part of the RAND Graduate School Programme

St. Louis Center for International Studies
University of Missouri
8001 Natural Bridge Road, St. Louis, MO 63121-4499, USA

Telephone: 1-341-553-5753
Fax: 1-341-553-6757
E-mail: srabaum@umslvma.umsl.edu
Senior Staff: Director: J. N. Glassman, Specialist: R. Baumann, K. Cochrane, Project Coordinator: C. M. Lieber, Assoc. Prof.: J. M. Mushaben, Prof.: J. M. Rochester, Asst. Prof.: K. Thomas
Date of Establishment: 1968
Type: Public
Principal Activities: Research; training; documentation/information; conference- organization; publication
Current Peace Research:

(a) German foreign and security policy,

(b) International military interventions,

(c) Reform of the United Nations,

(d) Teaching about conflict, security and peacemaking.

Periodicals: *Newsletter*
Major Publications:

(a) Rochester, J. M., *The Production and Transmission of Knowledge About International Relations*, 1992,

(b) Rochester, J. M., *Waiting for the Millenium: The United Nations and the Future of World Order*, 1993,

(c) Mushaben, J. M., *Identity without a Hinterland? Continuity and Change in National Consciousness in the German Democratic Republic*, 1949-1989, 1993,

(d) Cochrane, K., *The Best of Teaching about National and International Security and Peacemaking*, 1993,

(e) Rochester, J. M., *The United Nations in a New World Order: Reviving the Theory and Practice of International Organizations*, 1994,

(f) Mushaben, J. M., *Citizenship as Process. The Reconstruction of Post-Wall German Identity*, 1994,

(g) Lieber, C. M., *Making Choices about Conflict, Security and Peacemaking from Personal and Global Perspectives. Educators for Social Responsibility*, 1994,

(h) Baumann, R., *International Military Interventions*, 1946-1988.

Annotation: The Center's research deals with conflict, peace, security and intercultural education. The Center designs and coordinates programmes and courses in East Asian, European and Latin American studies

School of International Service
American University
4400 Massachusetts Ave, NW, Washington, DC 20016-8071, USA

Telephone: 1-202-885-1600
Fax: 1-202-885-2494
E-mail: goodman@american.edu
Web Site: www.american.edu/academic.depts/sis/
Senior Staff: Dean: Louis W. Goodman
Date of Establishment: 1957
Purpose: The School of International Service is dedicated to building a community, which positively and constructively meets the challenges of global complexity and inter-connectedness. The telecommunication revolution has transformed global relations and the impact that this has had on our daily lives. These challenges demand the sustained attention of the world's most capable and dedicated professionals. The School of International Service at American University offers unique opportunities for learning about other peoples for professional careers requiring international and intercultural understanding.

Principal Activities: SIS offers both Ph.D. and Master's programs. The Ph.D. in International Relations program is designed to prepare graduates for careers in university teaching and research. The curriculum combines core offerings in international relations theory, comparative politics and methodology with a structure that allows students considerable flexibility. Major emphasis is placed on research; in addition to the dissertation, students are encouraged to present conference papers, engage in collaborative work with faculty and submit articles to referred journals.

The SIS Master's program, together with the many co-curricular opportunities the School offers, provides key links between theory and practice. The program, with its seven major fields of study, equips graduates with the competence and skills necessary for professional careers in today's increasingly complex and globalize environment.

Periodicals:

(a) *The Journal of Public and International Affairs*, an annual periodical published by students in APSIA,

(b) *SIS Newsletters*, 5 per annual,

(c) *Swords & Ploughshares*, journal,

(d) *The Development NET*, newsletter published by the International Development Program,

(e) *Demokratizatsiya, The Journal of Post-Soviet Democratization*, founded at SIS.

Major Publication:

(a) J. M. Naim, M.,Tulchin, J., Baltimore, G. B., *Lessons from the Venezuelan Experience*, Co-edited with Forman, MD: The Johns Hopkins University Press, 1995,

(b) *Small Nations, Giant Firms*, New York: Holmes & Meier, 1987, published in Spanish as Paises Pequenos, Empresas Gigantes, Mexico City: LIMUSA, 1993,

(c) LeoGrande, W., Forman, J. M., *Political Parties and Democracy in Central America*, Co-edited Boulder, CO: Westview Press, 1992.

Stanley Foundation
216 Sycamore st. Suite 500 Muscatine Iowa 52761, USA

Telephone: 319-264-1500
Senior Staff: President: R. H. Stanley
Date of Establishment: 1956
Purpose: The Foundation works to achieve the goal of a secure peace with freedom and justice by encouraging study, research and discussion on international issues.
Type: Private, non-profit
Brief History: The Stanley Foundation was incorporated in 1956. Foundation activities are financed almost entirely from the earnings and proceeds of stocks donated by Mr. and Mrs. Stanley.
Principal Activities:

(a) Programs, conferences for diplomats, scholars, business leaders and public officials from every continent are conducted by the Foundation each year,

(b) Common Ground, a radio series on world affairs, is aired weekly nationwide,

(c) Educational seminars for US Congressional staff members are convened annually at the United

Nations and in the Washington, DC area,

(d) Project Enrichment, an international education model, has operated in Muscatine, Iowa, schools and community for over a decade,

(e) The Outreach Program supports Midwestern groups that seek information on international issues.

Periodicals: *World Press Review*, 12 p.a. (magazine)
Major Publications:

(a) *Collective Security and the United Nations: An Old Promise in a New Era*, 1991,

(b) *Redefining Arms control in US foreign policy*, 1991,

(c) *Changing Realities in the Horn of Africa: Implications for Africa and US Policy*, 1991,

(d) *US Policy toward a Post-socialist USSR*, 1991.

Thomas J. Watson Jr. Institute for International Studies (WIIS)
Brown University
2 Stimson Avenue, Box 1970, Providence, RI 02912, USA

Telephone: 1-401-863-2809
Fax: 1-401-863-1270

Date of Establishment: 1986
Senior Staff: Acting Director: V. Gregorian, Henry R.

Luce Prof.: T. Biersteker, Senior Research Fellow: J. G. Blight, Specialist: P. T. Hopmann, Senior Advisor: J. Kalicki, Senior Research Assoc.: J. MacKinlay, Research Director: R. Smoke, Assoc. Director & Researcher: T. G. Weis

Type: Private, non-profit

Principal Activities: Research; training; documentation/information; conference- organization; publication

Current Peace Research:

(a) Humanitarianism and war project,

(b) Security for Europe project,

(c) Second generation multinational operations,

(d) RUBK (Russian Foderation, Ukraine, Belarus, Khazakhstan) project,

(e) Carter-Brezhnev project study on US/USSR period of detente.

Major Publications:

(a) Weiss, T. G. (ed.), *Humanitarian Emergencies and Military Help in Africa*, 1990,

(b) Gordenker, L., Weiss, T. G. (eds.), *Soldiers, Peacekeepers and Disasters*, 1991,

(c) Minear, L. et al., *Humanitarianism under Siege: A Critical Review of Operation Lifeline Sudan*, 1991,

(d) Weiss, T. G., Kessler, M. A. (eds.), *Third World Security in the Post-Cold War Era*, 1991,

(e) Kramer, M., *The Czech-Slovak Rupture and European Security*, 1992,

(f) Rueschemeyer, D., Shuber Stephens, E., Stephens, J. D., *Capitalist Development and Democracy*, 1992,

(g) Shenfield, S. D., *Goals and Strategy of Limited Military Intervention in Bosnia and Herzegovina*, 1992,

(h) Weiss, T. G., Blight, J. G. (eds.), *The Suffering Grass: Superpowers and Regional Conflict in Southern Africa and the Caribbean*, 1992,

(i) Weiss, T. G., Chopra, J., *United Nations Peacekeeping: and ACUNS Teaching Text*, 1992,

(j) Coate, R., Forsythe, D., Weiss, T. G., *The United Nations and World Politics: Learning from Change*, 1993,

(k) Jonah, J. O. C., *Differing State Perspectives on the United Nations in the Post-Cold War*, 1993,

(l) Khrushchev, S. N., *Nikita Khrushchev, Crisis, and Missiles*, 1993,

(m) Minear, L., Weiss, T. G., *Humanitarian Action in Times of War: A Handbook for Practitioners*, 1993,

(n) Weiss, T. G., Kessler, M. A. (eds.), *Third World Security in the Post-Cold War Era*, 1991,

(o) Kramer, M., *The Czech-Slovak Rupture and European Security*, 1992,

(p) Rueschemeyer, D., Shuber Stephens, E., Stphens, J. D., *Capitalist Development and Democracy*, 1992,

(q) Shenfield, S. D., *Goals and Strategy of Limited Military Intervention in Bosnia and Herzegovina*, 1992,

(r) Weiss, T. G., Blight, J. G. (eds.), *The Suffering grass: Superpowers and Regional Conflict in Southern Africa and the Caribbean*, 1992,

(s) Weiss, T. G., Chopra, J., *United Nations Peacekeeping: And ACUNS Teaching Text*, 1992,

(t) Coate, R., Forsythe, D., Weiss, T. G., *The United Nations and World Politics: Learning from Change*, 1993,

(u) Jonah, J. O. C., *Differing State Perspectives on the United Nations in the Post-Cold War*, 1993,

(v) Weiss, T. G., Minear, L. (eds.), *Humanitarianism Across Borders: Sustaining Civilians in Times of War*, 1993,

(w) Blum, D., Shenfield, S. D. (eds.), *Russia's Future: Consolidation of Disintegration*, 1994,

(x) Goldscheider, C. (ed.), *Population, Ethnicity and Nation Building*, 1994,

(y) Minear, L., Weiss, T. G., *Qualities of Mercy: War and the Global Humanitarian Community*, 1994.

Annotation: Research on peace includes North-South/East-West relations, regional security, transnational organizations, security studies, world hunger, population, comparative study of development, geographical medicine, primary health care, humanitarianism and war, regional conflict and military strategy.

United States Arms Control and Disarmament Agency (ACDA)
320 21st Street, NW, Washington, DC 20451, USA

Telephone: 1-202-647 2034
Fax: 1-202-647 6721
Senior Staff: Director: J. D. Holum
Date of Establishment: 1961
Type: Public; non-profit
Principal Activities: Research
Periodicals: *Arms Control and Disarmament Agree-*

ments; *Arms Control Report*; *Documents on Disarmament*; *World Military Expenditure and Arms Transfers*
Annotation: The Agency sponsors research projects conducted by private research organizations in the fields of international relations, arms control, disarmament and military strategy.

United Research Centers on Organized Crime in Eurasia
Center for the Study of Transnational Crime and Corruption
American University
SPA, Tenley Campus, Dunblane Hall, Washington, DC 20016, USA

Telephone: 1-202-895-4916/1-202-895-4918
Fax: 1-202-895-4964
E-mail: lshelle@american.edu or vbrovkin@american.edu
Web Site: www.american.edu/academic.depts/acainst/transcrime/
Senior Staff: Director: Louise Shelley
Date of Establishment: 1997
Purpose: United Research Centers on Organized Crime in Eurasia is a project at the Center for the Study of Transnational Crime at the School of Public Affairs at American University in Washington, DC.

The Center aims to comprehend the nature of organized crime in Russia, contribute to the process of democratization, and building the rule of law society.

The Project brings together Russian and American scholars at various Universities and Law faculties in a joint endeavor to analyze, study, and develop strategies for fighting Organized Crime—one of the main impediments to the strengthening of democratic institutions.

It also facilitates interactions between scholarly community, non-government organizations, legislative and executive branches of government, law enforcement agencies and the public at large on Organized Crime problems.
Brief History: The Center was founded in 1997 by a grant from the Department of Justice of the United States government.

Principal Activities:

(a) Conduct original research on Organized Crime and Corruption,

(b) Develop curricula at Law Faculties on OC-related courses,

(c) Contribute to raising public awareness about the OC threat to democracy and the rule of law society,

(d) Prepare legislative advice to local and central government on OC-related legislation,

(e) Create a library and a database on OC by region,

(f) Communicate with print and media on OC in specific regions,

(g) Conduct seminars, conferences and international symposia on OC and corruption,

(h) Facilitate dissemination in Russia of information on legislation and OC problems in other countries,

(i) Publish research results, OC surveys by region and conference materials in the scholarly literature in Russia and the US.

Periodicals: *Journal of International Affairs*, quarterly

United States Institute of Peace (USIP)
1550 M Street, NW, Suite 700, Washington, DC 20005-1708, USA

Telephone: 1-202-457-1700
Fax: 1-202-429-6063
Senior Staff: Acting President: C. E. Nelson

Date of Establishment: 1984
Type: Public, non-profit
Principal Activities: Research; training; documenta-

tion/information; conference-organization; publication; financing; sponsoring of the Jennings Randolph Fellowship Program
Geographical Coverage: Global
Current Peace Research:

(a) Study on the causes of peace and war,

(b) Strengthening the UN Charter System and the international law,

(c) East-West relations after "glasnost" and "perestroika".

University Center for International Studies
University of Pittsburgh, 4 Forbes Quadrangle, Pittsburgh, PA 15260, USA

Telephone: 1-412-648-7374
Fax: 1-412-648-4672
E-mail: ucis+@pitt.edu
Web Site: www.ucis.pitt.edu/
Senior Staff: Directors: Burkart Holzner, Patricia Stranahan, and Billie Dewalt,
Date of Establishment: 1968
Purpose: The Center aims to establish Pitt's leadership role in the advancement of global dimensions in the arts, sciences, and professions. The center builds global partnerships that showcase the University's and the region's strengths as an international resource and competitor. The center employs education, research, and public service to provide others' access to its vast network of international resources, concerns and ties. UCIS's critical responsibilities include:

(a) Knowledge-building within multi-national frameworks,

(b) Activities in the international arena on behalf of the University,

(c) Knowledge transfer to and from the Pittsburgh region and the Commonwealth of Pennsylvania Partnership-building and fundraising for the University's globally focused initiatives.

Brief History: Established in 1968, UCIS has worked for 30 years to establish Pitt's leadership role in the advancement of global dimensions in the arts, sciences, and professions. Most notable, Pitt remains one of a handful of universities nationwide that has earned the award of five National Resource Centers.
Principal Activities: The center's work encompasses education, research, and public service and draws on vast and historic international resources, concerns, and ties. The University Center for International Studies (UCIS) cultivates, supports, and coordinates international activities campus-wide at the University of Pittsburgh.
Periodicals: *UCIS Update* (quarterly)

World Conference on Religion and Peace (WCRP)
777 UN Plaza, Suita 9A, New York NY 10017, USA

Telephone: 1-212-687-2163
Fax: 1-212-983-0566
E-mail: info@wcrp.org
Senior Staff: Secretary, WCRP/Netherlands: Hans van Willenswaard, WCRP/Europe: Johann Lahnemann, Gunther Gebhardt, Secretary General, WCRP/Int: William Vendley
Date of Establishment: 1970
Purpose: WCRP is dedicated to promoting cooperation among the world's religions for peace, engaging in vigorous peace promoting initiatives throughout the world in cooperation with religious, development, and UN agencies.
Type: International, private, non-profit
Principal Activities:

(a) International Standing Commission on Religion and Peace Education,

(b) International Standing Commission on Religion and the Child,

(c) International Standing Commission on Religion and Conflict Transformation,

(d) International Standing Commission on Religion and Development.

Periodicals: *Religions for Peace* (newsletter 3 x per year).

World Federalist Movement
777 UN Plaza New York NY 10017, USA

Telephone: 1-212-599-1320
Fax: 1-212-599-1332
E-mail: wfm@igc.agc.org
Senior Staff: Exec. Director: William R. Pace, Exec. Officer: Lydia Swart.
Date of Establishment: 1947
Purpose: Promote peace through strengthening UN international law.
Type: International
Principal Activities: Conducts programs on:

(a) UN reform,

(b) Democratization of the UN,

(c) Hague appeal for Peace 1999,

(d) Coalition for an International Criminal Court.

Periodicals: *World Federalist News*
Major Publications: *Uniting the Peoples and Nations: Readings in World Federalism.*
Other Information: Member organizations in 20 countries.

World Jurist Association of the World Peace through Law Center (WPTLC)
Suite 202 1000 Connecticut Avenue NW, Washington, DC 20036, USA

Telephone: 202-466-54286/440456
Fax: 202-452-8540
Senior Staff: Executive Vice-President: M. M Henneberry
Date of Establishment: 1963
Purpose: The Center is the first worldwide venture to combine the efforts of judges, lawyers, law professors, and others throughout the world into an effective cooperative endeavor to mold a future legal order for humankind that will foster peace by helping to strengthen the world's legal system, both its law rules and its legal institutions and by evaluating world law and developing a new international legal machinery to provide for the peaceful settlement of disputes between nations under the rule of law. Its ultimate goal is the achievement of a worldwide system of law strong enough to replace force as the controlling factor in the fate of humanity. The Center is a nonpolitical and non-profit institution.
Type: Private, non-profit
Brief History: The Center was founded in 1957, origi-

nally as a Special Committee of the American Bar Association. In that year, Charles S. Rhyne became the President of the ABA. In 1963, the Special Committee within the ABA was given a status independent of, but closely associated with the ABA, and it became a worldwide organization. At a meeting held June 28-July 6, 1963 in Athens, Greece, sponsored by the ABA, the World Peace Through Law Center was established with Charles S. Rhyne as World President.
Principal Activities: Sections within the Center have been organized on human rights, and law and computer technology. The Center organizes biennial conferences, held in major international cities, on preselected themes relating to international law.
Periodicals: *The World Jurist 6 p.a., Law Technology 4 p.a*
Major Publications: The Center publishes conference materials, research reports, draft treaties, and other technical papers which have direct bearing on its areas of concern.

World Order Models Project
475 Riverside Drive, Suite 246 New York, NY 10115, USA

Telephone: 1-212-870-2391
Fax: 1-212-8790-2392
E-mail: womp@igc.org
Senior Staff: President: Saul Mendlovitz, Executive Director: John Fousek
Date of Establishment: 1968
Purpose: World Order Models Project is a global network of scholars, activists and distinguished political

figures involved in research, education, dialogue and action aimed at promoting a just world order. Since its inception, WOMP has worked to stimulate efforts to comprehend and solve the major problems confronting the people of the planet.
Type: International
Brief History: In 1968, WOMP was created under the auspices of the World Law Fund. Its major thrust was

to produce materials for use in academic environments throughout the globe. WOMP has since begun to emphasize a more normative approach, specifically the extent to which transnational changes are taking place in the world system and how these may relate to the overall guest for a just world order.

Principal Activities:

(a) Basic research, publications, education,

(b) The limitation and Abolition of International Arms (LAIA) project,

(c) The world court project, the Global Civilization Project, the UN study group,

(d) Transnational Academic Program.

Periodicals: *Alternatives: Social Transformation and*

Humane Governance in association with the Centre for the study of Developing societies (Delhi) and the ICU Peace Research Institute (Tokyo), Quarterly.

Major Publications:

(a) *On Humane Governance: Toward a New Global Politics (The World Order Models Project Report of the Global Civilization Initiative),*

(b) *Preferred Future for the United Nations,*

(c) *Arms Control Today,*

(d) *Social Alternatives,*

(e) *Toward a Theory of War Prevention,*

(f) *International Law,*

(g) *Disarmament and Economic Development.*

Worldwatch Institute
1776 Massachusetts Ave, NW Washington, DC 20036, USA

Telephone: 1-202-452-1999
Fax: 1-202-296-7365
E-mail: Worldwatch@worldwatch.org
Senior Staff: Senior Researcher: Michael Renner
Date of Establishment: 1974
Purpose: The Institute's program is to collect, evaluate, and disseminate information, research, and policy advice about emerging environmental and environmentally related issues, such as climate change, energy efficiency, population growth, food production, and water resources.
Type: Private, non-profit
Brief History: Worldwatch Institute, founded in 1974, is an independent, public policy research institute dedicated to fostering an environmentally sustainable society.
Principal Activities: The Institute's program is to collect, evaluate, and disseminate information, research, and policy advice about emerging environmental and environmentally related issues, such as climate change, energy efficiency, population growth, food production, and water resources. Within this broad program, program elements include research briefs, the Worldwatch database disk, and communications.

Periodicals:

(a) *State of the World,*

(b) *Vital Signs,*

(c) *World Watch Magazine,*

(d) *The Worldwatch Papers,*

(e) *The Environmental Alert Series,*

Major Publications:

(a) *Tough Choices: Facing the Challenges of Food Security,*

(b) *Last Oasis: Facing Water Scarcity,*

(c) *Full House: Reassessing the Earth's Population Carrying Capacity,*

(d) *How Much is Enough? The Consumer Society and the Future of the Earth,*

(e) *Who Will Feed China? Wake-up Call for A Small Planet.*

World without War Council
1730 Martin Luther King Jr. Way, Berkeley, CA 94109, USA

Telephone: 1-510-845-1992
Fax: 1-510-845-5721
E-mail: wwwc@sirius.com

Senior Staff: President: Robert Pickus
Date of Establishment: 1958 (under different name: Acts for Peace)

Purpose: The World Without War Council challenges Peace organization stereotype even as it seeks feasible alternatives to the Pentagon's. Its focus is on the multiple arenas in which nongovernmental organizations seek to shape American purposes in world affairs. It is also a thought center, challenging both pacifists' and conventional realists' prescriptions for America, and initiating and planing center for an American public effort for peace more sound in its analysis, prescription and strategy of work.

Type: Non-profit

Brief History: The Council began its work in Northern California in 1958, when twelve national peace organizations cooperated in establishing Acts for Peace. The project, founded by Robert Pickus, developed in 1961 into Turn Toward Peace (TTP), a cooperative national effort of some 60 peace and liberal internationalist organizations. In 1969, TTP split between those who opposed "America's war" in Vietnam and those who sought an end to the killing by Hanoi as well. The latter group formed WWWC, whose strategy of work shifted from a focus on the peace movement to an engagement with the whole spectrum of organizations interested in America's role in world affairs and the nonviolent resolution of group conflict. The Council's goal became wiser, richer, more effective in American and World Affairs field in which WWWC sought to build support for alternatives to war in mass political conflict and in the defense of democratic values.

Principal Activities:

(a) Americans and World Affairs Fellows Training Program,

(b) Governance in World Politics—a program for creating "standards" and "initiatives" for governance,

(c) The Common Good Program's Immigrants and Citizenship: Choices for America,

(d) The Organizational Map Project to link the world affairs field,

(e) Work in pre-collegiate education, with conscientious objectors, connecting Department of State to non-governmental organizations.

Periodicals: *Democratic Values*

Major Publications:

(a) *World Affairs Organizations in Northern California: A Guide to the Field* (1995),

(b) *Neither Victims Nor Executioners* (republication of Camus' essay with preface by Robert Pickus, 1972),

(c) *All Men are Brothers* (republication of Gandhi's book),

(d) *World Peace Through World Law* (republication of Clark and Sohn's book),

(e) *War Peace Film Guide*,

(f) *Christian Pacifism in History*,

(g) *War and Peace in Literature*,

(h) *To End War*.

Yale Center for International and Area Studies
Yale University
PO Box 208206, New Haven, CT 06520-8206, USA

Telephone: 1-203-432-3410
Fax: 1-203-432-9383
E-mail: peg.limbacher@yale.edu
Web Site: www.yale.edu/ycias/
Senior Staff: Director: Gustav Ranis
Purpose: The Yale Center for International and Area Studies seeks to understand the world outside the borders of the United States, and America's role in the world, an integral part of the liberal education and professional training to which Yale University is dedicated. YCIAS is the University's principal agency for inspiring, nurturing and coordinating teaching, research and public service on international affairs and societies and cultures around the world, in both organizational

and intellectual terms.
Principal Activities: The Yale Center for International and Area Studies supports and provides advanced training and scholarly research; undergraduate education; enrichment of the Yale community; and links between Yale and the international security community as well as the larger public.
Major Publications:

(a) Ku, C., Weiss, T. G. (eds.), *Toward Understanding Global Governance: The International Law and International Relations Toolbox*, Reports and Papers 1998 No. 2,

(b) *1997 Membership Directory, Reports and Papers*

1998 No. 1, by the ACUNS Secretariat,

(c) *Diez Años Después de Esquipulas: Mirando Hacia el Futuro, Ten Years After Esquipulas: Looking Toward the Future*, Reportes y Ensayos 1997 No. 4/Reports and Papers 1997 No. 4, by H.E. Dr. Oscar Arias Sanchez,

(d) Sutterlin, J. S., *The Imperative of Idealism*, Reports and Papers 1997 No. 3,

(e) Jolly, R., *Human Development: The World After Copenhagen*, Reports and Papers 1997 No. 2,

(f) Puchala, D. J., *The Ethics of Globalism*, Reports and Papers 1995 No. 3.

Uruguay

Asociacion Sudamericana De Estudios Geopoliticos E Internationales (ASEGI)
Casilla de Correo 5006, Montevideo 11200, Uruguay

Telephone: 598-2-692953
Fax: 598-2-961923
Telex: P. Booth 901
Senior Staff: Director: B. Quagliotti de Bellis, Specialist: P. Boggio Marzet, J. Fernández Atijamibia, R. González, Director & Specialist: B. Quagliotti de Bellis
Date of Establishment: 1979
Type: Private; non-profit
Principal Activities: Research; training; documentation/information; conference-organization; publication
Current Peace Research:

(a) Border conflicts between Latin American countries,

(b) Defence cooperation in the South Atlantic,

(c) The Economic and military importance of Antarctica,

(d) Cooperación e integración en América Latina,

(e) Integración económica en el Cono Sur latinoamericano,

(f) Vias navegables en el Cono Sur. Hidrovías,

(g) Acuerdos pesqueros en el Atlántico Sur.

Periodicals: *Geosur*, 6 p.a.
Major Publications:

(a) *El Caso Cubano*,

(b) *Desarrollo y Desarme en América Latina*,

(c) *Nueva Política de Derechos Humanos en Paraguay*,

(d) *Política Social en el Chile Democrático*.

Annotation: Participates in various research projects in the field of geopolitics, international security, defence cooperation and conflict resolution in Lation America
Courses: Course on Peace and Disarmament
Subjects Taught: Peaceful coexistence; disarmament; conflict resolution; role of the international organizations; peace and development; democracy and peace; international security; terrorism
Target Group: Professionals; non-specialists; nationals
Level of the Course: Undergraduate; postgraduate
Type of Course: Regular course; short session; evening course
Duration: 6 hours during 6 weeks; 2 semesters p.a. (Feb.-June, July-November)
Working Languages: Spanish
Admission Requirements: None
Closing Date for Applications: One month before beginning of course
Course Fees: 350 dollars per semester (in 1994)
Scholarships Available: None
Degree/Diploma: Certificate of Attendance

Vatican City

Pontifical Council for Justice and Peace
Palazzo S. Calisto 00120 Vatican City

Telephone: 39-6-68-89-7191
Fax: 39-6-68-80-7205
E-mail: pcjustpax@justpeace.va
Senior Staff: Secretary: Msgr. Diarmuid Martin.

Date of Establishment: 1967
Purpose: The Council aims to carry out action-directed studies that are fitted into a pastoral evangelizing perspective; to be at the service of the Church's mem-

bers and institutions, enabling them to translate into concrete commitments, valid as Christian witness, the Commission's recommendations and advice; to encourage progress and renewal while seeing the fundamental guideline and the guarantee of effectiveness in the Church's supreme authority; and to perform this work in an ecumenical perspective.

Type: International, non-profit

Brief History: The Second Vatican Council had proposed the creation of a body of the universal Church whose role would be "to stimulate the Catholic Community to foster progress in needy regions and social justice on international scene". It was in reply to this request that Pope Paul VI established the Pontifical Commission "Justitia et Pax" by a Motu Proprio on 6 January 1967.

Principal Activities: The primary work of the Pontifical Council is to engage in action-oriented studies based on both the papal and episcopal social teaching of the Church. Through them, the pontifical Council also contributes to the development of this teaching in the fields of Justice, Peace and Human Rights.

Periodicals: *JUSTPAX* (in English, French and Spanish is in preparation)

Major Publications:

(a) *Peace and Disarmament. Documents of the World Council of Churches and the Roman Catholic Church,*

(b) *Ways of Peace. Papal Massages for the World Days of Peace,*

(c) *Assisi: World Day of Prayer for Peace,*

(d) *The Holy see at the Service of Peace,*

(e) *Human Rights and the Church. Historical and Theological Reflections,*

(f) *World Development and Economic Institutions.*

Venezuela

Centro de Estudios del Desarrollo [Center for Development Studies]-cendes-de la Universidad Central de Venezuela
Ed. FUNDAVAC, Av. Neveri, Colinas de Bello Monte, Caracas 1041, Venezuela
Apartado 47.604, Caracas 1041 A, Venezuela

Telephone: 58-2-753-34-75/58-2-753-30-89/58-2-753-36-99

Fax: 58-2-751-26-91/58-2-753-35-20

E-mail: cendes@conicit.ve

Senior Staff: Senior Research Fellow: Luis Gomez C., Lourdes Yero, Junior Research Fellow: Francisco Javier Velasco, Director: Heinz R., Sonntag

Date of Establishment: 1961

Purpose: The center aims:

(a) To accomplish research on the problems of development in a national, regional and international perspective,

(b) To maintain training activities (graduate studies) in the fields of national, regional and international development and of public policies and planning,

(c) To serve as consultants to governmental institutions, no governmental organizations, public enterprises and international agencies.

Type: Public, national, non-profit

Brief History: After its establishment, CENDES did basic and applied research on development problems on the base of an interdisciplinary approach. During the sixties, the main projects dealt with the perspective of sociopolitical change in Latin America and Venezuela, the agrarian reforms in different countries of the region, urban development in Latin America and Venezuela and "development styles". During the seventies, important projects on the sociohistorical process of Venezuela and Latin America and Venezuela and on the position and the role of the countries of this region within the world-system were carried out. The Center's training activities became more and more diversified. Since 1980 it has even a PhD Program in Development Studies.

Principal Activities: For CENDES, Development Studies are an important part of peace research, perhaps today (after the end of the "Cold War") the most relevant one.

Periodicals: *CUADERNOS DEL CENDES*, institutional review, published three times a year; *CENDES BOLETIN*, institutional newsletter, published monthly.

Major Publications:

(a) Coleccion-Homenaje a los exdirectores del CENDES:
Colleccion Jorge Ahumada
Colleccion Jose Agustin Silva Michelena
Colleccion Luis Lander

(b) Subcomision Estudios de Postgrado
Serie Mencion Publicacion
Serie Aportes a la Docencia

Instituto Venezolano De Estudios Sociales Y Políticos (INVESP)
[Venezuelan Institute of Social and Political Studies]
Apdo 80948, Zona 1080, Caracas, Venezuela

Telephone: 58-2-6615196
Fax: 58-2-6621655
Senior Staff: Director: A. Serbin, Senior Researcher: A. Dilisio, Academic Coordinator: F. Jacome
Date of Establishment: 1986
Type: Private; non-profit
Principal Activities: Research; documentation/ information; conference-organization; publication
Current Peace Research:

(a) Peace, cooperation and integration in the Caribbean,

(b) Threat perceptions and ethnocentrism in Latin America and the Caribbean,

(c) Environmental security and regional cooperation in Latin America and the Caribbean,

(d) Global changes and hemispheric security,

(e) Towards a culture of peace in Latin America.

Type of Publication: Journal; bulletin; monograph; conference proceedings
Periodicals:

(a) *Cuadernos del INVESP*

(b) *Carta del INVESP*, 2 p.a. (newsletter)

(c) *Papeles del INVESP*, 8 p.a.

Major Publications:

(a) VVAA, *La Nueva Agenda de Segurided en el Caribe*, 1994.

Annotation: Carries out research in the fields of disarmament, environmental and international security, international cooperation and culture of peace.

Universidad Simón Bolívar, Postgrado En Ciencia Política
Edf. Físico y Electrónica I, Apartado Postal 89000, Caracas 1080, Venezuela

Telephone: 2-906 3611
Fax: 2-93 77 20
E-mail: CPCP@USB.VE
Cable: UNIBOLIVAR
Senior Staff: Coordinator: M. Haluani, Coordinator & Research: M. Haluani, Researcher: K. Nweihid, A. Romero
Date of Establishment: 1977
Principal Activities: Research; training; documentation/information; conference-organization
Current Peace Research: Structures of security issues in the Middle East
Subjects Taught: Political science; disarmament; role of the international organizations; democracy and peace; international conflict; international security; regional conflict; terrorism
Principal Instructors: Dr. M. Haluani, Dr. A. Romero,

Dr. K. Nweihid
Target Group: Professionals; non-specialists; nationals; foreign students
Level of the Course: Postgraduate; masters
Type of Course: Regular course
Duration: 3 years; 2 years for completion of a minimum of 36 obligatory credits and 1 year for writing, presenting and defending the thesis
Working Languages: Spanish; English
Admission Requirements: Yes. Undergraduate degree; average/above average grades
Course Fees: Admission fee is 300 Bolivares; each credit is 2000 bolivares; graduate fee is 2200 Bolivares
Scholarships Available: Yes, apply to Dr. M. Haluani, Coordinator, Postgrado in Ciencia Politica
Degree/Diploma: Postgrado en Ciencia Politica

Yugoslavia

Institute of International Politics and Economic (IIPE)
PO Box 750. 11000 Belgrade, 25, Makedonska Str., Yugoslavia

Telephone: 381-11-3225-611
Fax: 381-11-322-4013
E-mail: impp@eunet.yu
Senior Staff: Director: Predrag Simi, Researcher: Konstantin Obradovi, Vid, Vukasovi, Zlatko Isakovi, Zoran Stanojevi, Alek Andar, Fati
Date of Establishment: 1947
Purpose: To study international relations, international law, world economy and social, economic and political developments in individual countries of the world.
Type: National, non-profit
Brief History: Institute of International Politics and Economics (IIPE) was founded in 1947 by the decision of the government of the Federal People's Republic of Yugoslavia. From a small group of researchers who since early 1948 laid foundations of the Yugoslav science on international relations, the Institute has gradually turned into the largest scientific institution of this kind in the country. With broad research and educational activity, and with the largest library in the country in the field of international relations and a small publishing house, the Institute has established regular or occasional contacts with over 200 research institutions and universities.

Principal Activities: Research in the field of international relations, international law, world economy, and social, economic and political developments in individual countries of the world, international contacts with other institutions of this kind, organization of domestic and international conferences, round tables and seminars, library and documentation activity, publishing activity.

Periodicals: *INTERNATIONAL PROBLEMS* (quarterly in Serbian and English)

Major Publications:

(a) *Yugoslav Crisis and the World,*

(b) *International Law and the Changed Yugoslavia,*

(c) *The Migration of Scientists and Professionals,*

(d) *Social Democracy in Europe Today,*

(e) *The Charter of Economic Rights and Duties of States-Ten Years of Implementation,*

(f) *American and Yugoslav Views on the 1990's.*